REASON
AND
PRACTICE

REASON
AND
PRACTICE
·
A MODERN
INTRODUCTION
TO PHILOSOPHY
·
Kai Nielsen
UNIVERSITY OF CALGARY

HARPER & ROW, PUBLISHERS
NEW YORK / EVANSTON / SAN FRANCISCO / LONDON

to Elisabeth

CONTENTS

v

PREFACE

The center of attention in this book is on those primary problems of philosophy which are of general human interest. In struggling with them, I not only state each one and critically examine what others have said, I also argue out my own philosophical convictions concerning these matters. While I try to argue firmly, I also attempt to convey that these matters are controversial and that my own arguments are but the views of one philosophy professor among many. (This is obvious but in certain contexts the obvious can be forgotten.) It is a source of comfort to me to know that the teachers who will use this book will most certainly inspect my arguments with a critical eye and make the errors evident to those students who have not uncovered them on their own. But it is important, I believe, both pedagogically and humanly, that writers of introductory problems-texts and teachers of such courses take a stand on these central and absorbing philosophical issues. Students should see actual thinking and philosophical argument going on, and not simply characterizations of what others have thought; they should see an honest effort being made to either solve or dissolve these philosophical problems and perplexities that in one form or another touch us all.

Reason and Practice contains a crucial feature that to my knowledge is not found in any other problems-text. There is an intermittent but continuing commentary on the nature of philosophy. Both Michael Scriven in his *Primary Philosophy* and James W. Cornman and Keith Lehrer in their *Philosophical Problems and Arguments* have written excellent introductory texts that carefully argue out philosophical points of view in the manner I have just commended, but they have said little about what Dewey might have called 'the office and function of philosophy'. Yet, given as perplexing and in someways as alien a subject as philosophy, and given the present cultural climate and the transformations of the subject in the last two centuries, this is surely something with which a reflective student will want to concern himself. It is natural to ask, Why get entangled in philosophy in the first place? To answer this question in anything like a satisfactory way is extremely difficult, for among other reasons 'What is philosophy?' is itself a distressingly complex philosophical question. Yet, we want answers here and we need them as well.

Aware of students' expectations concerning philosophy, all too aware of my own ambivalences concerning what can and should be accomplished in philosophy, and aware of how much this question is shied away from by philosophers, I have tried to come to grips with it. In the first chapter I discuss it in a preliminary way, but in various places in the book, where renewed commentary grows naturally out of the specific material at hand, I return to this central topic. My thrust here is to try to give (1) a sense of the range and the limitations of philosophical endeavors, (2) some sense of the conflicts about the nature of philosophy, and (3) some indication of how I think they are to be resolved.

There is another unique feature of the book that ought to be explained. The level of difficulty gradually increases as the book progresses, and the student's familiarity with and training in philosophical argument develops. The first two parts are the most elementary, parts three and four are somewhat more advanced, while sections on the mind/body problem and on meaning and metaphysics are much more complex. (The one exception to this is the second chapter on the ontological argument. That chapter may be skipped, but my experience in teaching has been that there will be students who will get caught up by the ontological argument. For them this chapter is essential.)

A central strategy of this book also dictates this movement to greater philosophical complexity. I try to establish that a resolute attempt to answer what I call the primary problems of philosophy leads to a consideration of questions of meaning and to questions of philosophical methodology. It is an underlying strategy of the book to show this, but arguments for such claims are unavoidably complex if they are at all adequate. The last part of the book is in part taken up with these questions and thus there is no escaping philosophical arguments that in the nature of the case are somewhat demanding. An instructor or reader may of course stop before this discussion, but the reader who wishes to probe more deeply into the rationale underlying the key arguments utilized in discussing God, freedom, and morality should not neglect this discussion. Chapter 35 as a back-up and additional support for Chapter 34 is particularly central, but it is also the most difficult chapter of the book. While the arguments and discussions stand on their own, there are some references there and elsewhere to the contemporary literature which provide the reader both with sources beyond the confines of my book for further pursuit and with additional materials to utilize in a critical inspection of my own arguments.

My book is self-contained and can be profitably studied without reference to any of the literature referred to, but ideally I envisage it being used in conjunction with an anthology or with other primary sources. I have provided at the end of each section bibliographical references, and there are a number of excellent anthologies available that can be used in conjunction with *Reason and Practice*. See, for example, William P. Alston and Richard B. Brandt (eds.), *The Problems of Philosophy*, (Boston: Allyn and Bacon, 1967); Paul Edwards and Arthur Pap (eds.), *A Modern Introduction to Philosophy*, (New York: The Free Press, 1965); Joseph Margolis (ed.), *An Introduction to Philosophical Inquiry*, (New York: Random House, 1970); or Frank A. Tillman, Bernard Berofsky, and John O'Connor (eds.), *Introductory Philosophy*, 2nd ed. (New York: Harper & Row, 1971).

Everyone in philosophy works out of a tradition and with certain preconceptions. Mine are—not unsurprisingly—analytical and informalist, although I remain somewhat of a maverick. Some readers have thought that this tradition blinkers me in my treatment of existentialism. I have, of course, tried to avoid that, but I may not have succeeded and I cannot rightly claim to bring to this tendency in philosophy the same comparatively detailed knowledge I have of contemporary analytical philosophy. And, Nietzsche and Kierkegaard apart, it is indeed true that I have little patience with the existentialist manner of philosophizing. Perhaps it shows. Be that as it may, I have thought it worthwhile to discuss certain aspects of existentialism, because it seems to me that in the questions existentialists ask, as distinct from their manner of asking and answering them, they are bringing to the fore unique and crucial considerations and are providing an important perspective that very much needs serious study in philosophy. But bear in mind that this is not a book on the history of philosophy but an examination of certain central problems of philosophy; my discussion of existentialist thinkers has been against that background. And if I have been unwittingly unfair to them, I have provided the references and bibliographical aids for the student and teacher to spot that unfairness.

Reason and Practice grew out of my Sunrise Semester lectures of 1966–1967 and from a course I have given over a number of years, first at Amherst College, then at Harpur College, and finally at New York University. I owe more than I can tell to my students, who by criticism and questioning have made this a much better book than it would otherwise have been. For searching criticism of earlier versions of my manuscript, I owe much to my wife Elisabeth, and to Professors Sidney Gendin, Robert Hoffman, Michael Kuttnauer, Eleanor Kuykendall, Charles Reid, and Mr. John Shafer. I am confident errors remain, and sometimes I have persisted in what one or another of my readers has taken to be a wrong-headed course, but without their criticisms my errors would have been much more numerous than they are.

Finally, I would like to thank Pat Myers, William Bean, Dierk Freytag, Kurt Neureither, Mary Lou Mosher, Lynette Ford, Peter Haynes, Brian Monrad, Mark Portnoy, Béla Szabados, Shepard Saslow, Thomas Wood, and Riley Wallihan for helping me in various ways; and Miss Pamela Long for typing the first part and Frau Gertrude Stauffer for so perfectly typing the last half in a language which she only imperfectly remembered from her English lessons in school.

Kai Nielsen

1

WHAT IS
PHILOSOPHY?

In this chapter I want to do three things. First, I want to say something about what philosophy is. Secondly, I want to say something about why philosophy is worth bothering with. And finally, I want to say something about the respective roles of the historian, philosopher, sage, and artist.

Let me warn you that much of what I say in this chapter needs qualification, is controversial, and is in one way or another superficial. But we must make a start somewhere. It is tempting to follow the example of many philosophers and simply leap into the middle and begin with some live philosophical issue and show by example and practice what philosophy is and how it is relevant to life. After this introductory chapter, this is exactly what I shall do. But now, with some misgivings, I want to try to give a general picture of what is involved in getting "hooked on" philosophy and something of what might legitimately be expected of philosophy. If my generalizations seem opaque or unenlightening, bear with me; they will become clearer in light of the philosophical issues and problems to be wrestled with in the following chapters.

I

What is philosophy, and why should it be so difficult to say what it is? Don't philosophers know what they are doing? Don't philosophy professors know their jobs? The hesitation here should make you suspicious, especially when you hear that 'What is philosophy?' is itself a central problem in philosophy. After all, 'What is physics?', 'What is botany?', and 'What is history?' are not problems *in* physics, botany, and history respectively. Textbooks on these subjects usually give definitions or descriptions of the subject matter in the first few pages—characterizations that do not seem essentially wrong to other people in the field. Not so with philosophy! Some philosophers have even contended that 'What is philosophy?' is the most fundamental philosophical problem.

Definitions and characterizations of philosophy differ radically. Some philosophers find the definitions offered by other philosophers to be totally wrong or near gibberish. Maritain, Carnap, Ortega y Gasset, and Heidegger are all philosophers with international reputations, yet each characterizes philosophy very differently from the next, and to me and many others they all seem badly mistaken. What are we to make of an activity in which there is a chronic dispute over what it is all about? Why should philosophy be such a Tower of Babel? Perhaps, as some philosophers have said, philosophy is a batch of conceptual confusions that one should avoid or treat therapeutically in the most effective way (if one has already been unfortunate enough to catch the disease). If this is so, all philosophy books should be antiphilosophy books.

Yet throughout history man has persistently grappled with certain questions; his tools have been the heterogeneous activities covered by the term 'philosophy'.[1] Given this historical fact, one would have to have very good grounds indeed for saying the problems of philosophy were *all* pseudoproblems—symptoms of a conceptual malaise. And this very claim itself would have to be made out on philosophical grounds or at least given some very careful justification. So while it is reasonable to remain skeptical and suspicious about philosophy, it is not reasonable to dismiss it so readily as a putative discipline specializing in conceptual confusion.

Let us look at 'What is philosophy?' This is, as I have remarked, a philosophical question itself. That is to say, it engenders dispute, an admittedly philosophical dispute, among philosophers. But why couldn't someone standing outside of philosophy—say, a specialist in the history of ideas—simply observe the various activities that philosophers engage in and regard as philosophical, note what common properties they have, and then build a philosophically neutral definition or characterization of philosophy on those common features? Surely this is not an impossibility for a philosophically trained, diligent historian. But this assumes what might not be the case: that there are some properties common to and peculiar to everything that has normally been called 'philosophy'. Perhaps such historians could only conclude that philosophy is X or Y or Z or V. But even if they did find some common features in virtue of which they could say that philosophy is so and so, this would still not be sufficient for the philosopher with *his* problem: 'What is philosophy?'

Why not? Well, note that philosophers have often been well aware of certain general characterizations of their discipline, and yet they have gone out of their way to say either that this is not what philosophy is or that such characterizations actually obscure the "true goals" of philosophy. The great innovators in philosophy—Socrates, Descartes, Hume,

Kant, Marx, Husserl, Dewey, Wittgenstein, for example—have thought the old philosophical foundations were in shambles and have sought to conceive of philosophy in a radically new way.

I know perfectly well that Carnap regards philosophy as the logic of the sciences and that Heidegger regards it as "the correspondence to the Being of being"; but I regard both such conceptions as radically inadequate because (1) Carnap's is wildly one-sided and Heidegger's approximates gibberish, and (2) they do not get at what I take to be the heart of the matter—what is really fundamental in philosophy. But the historicist in me and the historicist in you should ask: Is what Nielsen takes to be fundamental really fundamental? Is what Nielsen regards as gibberish really gibberish? Perhaps my own reaction simply gives voice to one culturally and historically circumscribed conception of what philosophy is. How, one is tempted to ask, could it be anything else? But if it couldn't be anything more, then why accept it?

This brings out the fact that when a philosopher says what philosophy is, he is normally concerned at least to say what *good* philosophy is, or what 'good technique' in philosophy is, or what the 'true ends' of philosophy should be. If he knows the history of his subject at all, he knows that philosophy has been very many things—that philosophers have long fought over its very characterization. Mindful of this, he will try to give a characterization that reflects what he as a philosopher tries to do and wants his fellow philosophers to do. Moreover, he may also be concerned, as I am, to characterize philosophy so that "consumers" of philosophy may have a clearer idea of what they may *legitimately* expect from philosophy and what they may find there that is of value.

II

I am far from being an eclectic, but I do not believe that philosophy is simply one thing—for example, the logic of science or the study of reality as such. I think that a good bit of what passes as philosophy is a waste of time; even that some of the things philosophers say are, to put it crudely, a lot of hot air. However, I do not think there is only one adequate characterization of philosophy, and I do not think philosophy should be limited or constrained in one direction. I think of myself primarily as what is nowadays called an 'analytic philosopher' or 'linguistic philosopher', but I do not think for one moment that philosophy is, or should be exclusively, what is now called conceptual analysis.[2] In short, I think Mill and Nietzsche, Feuerbach and Kierkegaard, Marx and Hägerström, Dewey and Collingwood were all profound philosophers who had things of great importance to say, although what they did was often very different from what I am going to call 'conceptual analysis'. I would say that more traditional philosophers—Aristotle and Aquinas, Scotus and Descartes, Leibnitz and Kant—have typically and characteristically done what is now called conceptual analysis. But it should be borne in mind that there are various types of conceptual analysis and that philosophy has not been and should not be limited only to conceptual analysis.

I will, however, argue that it is with conceptual analysis that philosophy should start, and with conceptual analysis that students should start in philosophy. I am going to offer what is admittedly a partisan characterization of philosophy. *Philosophy is an analytical study of concepts.* (I do not say that philosophy is *only* an analytical study of concepts.) This is not only a partisan slogan, it also needs explaining. What is an analytical study of concepts? I shall rely initially on the reader having some understanding of the terms 'analytical' and 'concept', and begin my examination of what is involved in that slogan by working with an example.

Jews, Christians, and Moslems must believe that God is omnipotent, perfectly good, and all-knowing. And if they are reflective or even observant beings, they note that there is evil in the world. But given such beliefs, a conceptual problem arises for them. How can there be evil, or at least how can there be so much evil, if their God actually exists? If God is omnipotent He could prevent evil if He so desired. And if God is perfectly good He would want to prevent evil if He could. Therefore, if God exists and is both omnipotent and perfectly good, it follows that there is a being who not only *could* prevent evil, but also would desire to do so. But then how can there be so many evils in the world? Or, how could there be such a God, since there are these evils in the world? I do not say this is *only* a conceptual puzzle—it may also be a test of faith—but it *is* a conceptual problem and the kind of problem that philosophy, as an analytical study of concepts, endeavors to examine.

Philosophers try to determine whether it is possible to assert consistently both that there is evil in the world, and that there exists an all-good, all-knowing, all-powerful being. They examine the very concept of God to try to determine what is involved in saying that there is a perfectly good, all-knowing, and omnipotent being. They ask: What is really involved in saying something is omniscient? Is such a concept of God a coherent one? What is involved, what is meant, by saying there is evil in the world? Must there be some evil for there to be any good, or is it only necessary to have some *idea* of evil? To ask and try to answer or resolve such problems is to engage in an analytical study of concepts. And it is this activity—this analytical study of concepts—that I take to be an activity most distinctive of philosophy. It is here that we should start when we philosophize, although I do not say that we should end here.

Is just *any* analytical study of *any* concept philosophical? Under certain circumstances it perhaps could be, but not characteristically. Only the analytical study of *some* concepts is philosophical. Which concepts are involved in philosophical activities? The ones that are most important to us! They are the pivotal concepts in our organization of thought and action, and the concepts that are, or at least seem to be, in conflict with other important concepts. Finally and most crucially, they are the pivotal concepts over which we are perplexed. These concepts are the stuff that philosophy is made of.

There are concepts that both perplex us and provide the basis of all thought and language, and these concepts are of the greatest philosophical interest. As Stuart Hampshire well puts it:

> As philosophers, we are interested in the most general features of the whole apparatus of concepts, in the different categories of thought and knowledge. If we exhaustively analyze some particular concept, it is generally as an example of a type of concept, with a view of showing the place of this type in the system of our thought, its peculiar function, and its difference from other types. We want to arrive at a general view through the particular case.[3]

Many philosophers would balk at what I have said. It should not be forgotten that there are many other definitions or characterizations of philosophy. The famous Catholic philosopher Jacques Maritain, for example, defines philosophy as "the science which by the light of reason studies the first causes or highest principles of all things—is, in other words, the science of things in their first causes, in so far as these belong to the natural order."[4] And the English Marxist, Maurice Cornforth, tells us, "Philosophy is the attempt to understand the nature of the world and our place and destiny in it. The task of the philosophers has always been to enrich the understanding and to generalize its conclusions."[5] Even more typically, many philosophers assert that "philosophy is concerned with the presuppositions of science as well as with whatever is presupposed in activities of other kinds: morals, politics, art, and so on."[6] On this view, "the task of the philosopher . . . is to express presupposed concepts and beliefs accurately and clearly, to ascertain which of the beliefs are true and which false, and if possible to define some of the concepts in terms of others of them and to derive the true beliefs from the more fundamental ones."[7] Therefore, it will be argued that to stress, as I have, the analytical study of concepts is to ignore *speculative* philosophy. But, the argument could continue, *critical* philosophy (the analytical study of concepts) is ancillary to speculative philosophy, that is, to the study of the ultimate principles in terms of which everything, including man's nature and destiny, can be understood. The ultimate task, the final goal of philosophy is to discover and articulate such ultimate principles.

While my characterization of philosophy is partisan, this one is, too.

There are many who deny that there are such principles and think that a speculative philosophy is an impossible attainment. There are others who think it is nonsense—a pseudoscience without a real subject matter. In turn, many speculative philosophers think that those who limit themselves to critical philosophy are insensitive Philistines destructive of the human spirit. I shall not take sides here, at this stage. The issue is indeed much more complex than I have made it seem.

However, later, when we examine the nature of metaphysics, we shall consider this question, but now two remarks are in order. It is evident enough that critical philosophy is an indispensable preliminary discourse to any reasonable speculative philosophy. If we do not have a clear understanding and a perspicacious display of our fundamental concepts, we cannot begin to understand, articulate, or develop a speculative philosophy based on rational grounds. And we would have no way of assessing speculative systems of philosophy. Such analysis must at the very least be our first move. This fact, about the relationship between critical philosophy and speculative philosophy, dictates what a good introductory course in philosophy must be: It should be primarily a course in philosophical problems.

Mindful of this, this book, designed as an introduction to philosophy, is a book fundamentally concerned with the basic problems of philosophy. No attempt is made to give a historical survey of the development of philosophy or an extended statement of the great speculative philosophical systems. A historical survey without a prior understanding of the nature of philosophical reasoning and without a feel for the problems discussed would be of little value; a study of philosophical systems without an understanding of the conceptual problems that gave rise to them would be equally pointless. We will be concerned, rather, with certain of the very basic problems of philosophy: freedom, God, morality, man, belief, and the limits of what it makes sense to say. Only the latter will seem remote from the problems of men. However, as I shall show, this last question emerges naturally and unavoidably from a determined consideration of the other problems. And it is these problems that pose the fundamental questions of philosophy, since they are the philosophical problems with which everyone, in one way or another, is concerned, and to which everyone, in some manner or another, has an answer. A man may not be able to articulate his answer; he may even deny that he has an answer. But his very behavior shows what he thinks about God, freedom, morality, man, and belief. It has been well said that 'What is philosophy?' is not so very different from 'What is man and his world?'. "To ask how we shall philosophize is already to ask what we shall make of ourselves."[8]

It is natural to object that in speaking of philosophy in this way, I have too sharply professionalized it, too rapidly made it into an intellectual discipline or a professional activity, and thus I have mistakenly taken it away from its primitive function in which it was a quest for wisdom and an attempt to articulate a way of life. Pythagoras thought of a philosopher as a lover of wisdom, and Plato and Aristotle thought of philosophy as a way to achieve wisdom. It has been said that we should define 'philosophy', as the ancients did, as a search for wisdom. We should not so intellectualize it as to make it an analytical study of concepts, but should regard it as the articulation of a concrete way of life.

Surely there is something wrong here. When we say that a philosopher is a lover of wisdom, what exactly is being claimed? What is it to seek wisdom? Wisdom is a very puzzling notion that, in certain moods, we are tempted to make sport of, but it is still a notion to which we are most certainly drawn. One crucial thing about wisdom was well brought out by the renowned English philosopher Alfred North Whitehead when he remarked, "You cannot be wise without some basis of knowledge; but you may easily acquire knowledge and remain bare of wisdom."[9] Wisdom does not just consist of the acquisition or systematization of knowledge, although it must rest on knowledge. In short, we cannot equate knowledge and wisdom.

What is wisdom then? If philosophy is a search for wisdom, what is it that we are searching for? If we have no idea at all, we cannot intelligibly speak of searching for it or of loving it. Yet when we try to define it, say what it is, we are in troubled waters. Wisdom (as one philosopher put it, tongue-in-cheek) "is an objectivity, a calmness, an impartiality of spirit that supposedly is highly advantageous in guiding one through the turbulence and immediacy of life's emotions." That is to say, a philosopher, as a seeker after wisdom, helps people adjust to the conflicts and tensions that are an inescapable part of human existence. There is a point to this philosopher's irony, for surely, if we take this assertion seriously, there is indeed something fishy about such a claim. I am sorry to report that philosophers are not better adjusted than most men. Philosophers are heirs to these conflicts and tensions too—sometimes even more acutely than other men. Furthermore, really expert guidance—counseling, if you please —has been taken over by the specialists: psychoanalysts, psychiatrists, mental hygienists, marriage counselors, vocational guidance people, and the like. This is not the sort of thing that one can legitimately expect from a philosopher.

When such remarks are made, it is natural to reply that attaining the kind of psychological adjustment that such specialists can help us to attain is surely not to attain wisdom. That was not at all what we were talking about. For *some* at least, *some* such psychological adjustment *may* be a necessary condition for attaining wisdom; but to attain it still is not to attain wisdom. But then again let us ask: What, pray tell, is wisdom? What would it be like to be wise? What are we searching for when we search for wisdom? If, after struggling through this book and several more, and after struggling through an intensive course in philosophy, you were finally to attain wisdom or were to fail to attain wisdom, what is it that you would be attaining, or failing to attain? How would you recognize a wise man if you saw one? How could you know or have good reason to believe that you now did or did not finally have what you were after— i.e., some modicum of wisdom?

It is natural to respond: If I knew what it would be like to be wise, I would not have to bother my head about philosophy. However, that response cannot be right, for if you had *no idea* of what you were looking for or what wisdom is, you could not be in a position to feel such a lack now or to realize, at the end of your course of studies, that you had failed to attain wisdom or come any closer to attaining some measure of wisdom. So the question remains: What are you looking for when you seek wisdom? What is wisdom? Can it be taught? Isn't there something absurd about anyone literally thinking that after he had read a book in philosophy or anything else that then he would know what wisdom is? Can you get up on your wisdom as you do on your French or your calculus by dint of diligent study? Can wisdom be acquired the way knowledge can? Is it really a philosopher's task to teach wisdom or to show you the way to wisdom or to reveal to you "the meaning of life"? Do we really know what we are asking for here, or what we mean when we talk about a search for wisdom? Is it, after all, only so much idle talk? Is it not the case that what science and ordinary observation cannot teach mankind, mankind cannot know; and is it not also perfectly evident that science, and its auxiliaries, logic and mathematics, cannot give us any of that peculiar kind of knowledge that would bring us wisdom?

These questions—the whole flood of them—are very odd questions indeed. We do not have any very clear understanding of what is being asked or what it would be like to answer such questions. If, as you read the questions, you felt "at sea," felt some matter of principle was at issue but were not clear what it was or just how one would go about trying to answer such questions, you have in reality come to feel philosophical perplexity, at least in its rudimentary stages.

Yet this is not simply the kind of perplexity that only a man in an ivory tower would have. Reflective human beings generally have wanted to make sense of their lives, to become as clear as they could about what ultimate commitments, if any, are worthy of their allegiance. This calls for some knowledge of good and evil, some understanding of what we human beings can become. And here we very much need, in any quest for wisdom, analytical study of such key concepts as good/evil, man/God, freedom/determinism. We want to understand what we can know and what we can do about what we know. When a Berkeley student, Brad Cleaveland, spoke out bitterly to his fellow undergraduates about the dulling routine of his education, of the bread-and-circus quality of much of it, he was surely right when he reminded them of the importance to them all of asking such fundamental questions as: What am I to become? What am I to give my allegiance to? What kind of society do I want to live in? Why am I at the university? What is knowledge? What is radicalism and revolt? These are questions we very much need to come to grips with in a nonevasive manner. And in achieving this, the analytical study of concepts plays a crucial role.

Herein lies the role of critical philosophy in human living, in forming what the great nineteenth-century German philosopher Ludwig Feuerbach called a truly human society, and in providing a humanistic education. And herein lies one of the key values of a liberal education. Philosophy, if pursued with passion and intelligence, can help us to see more clearly what is involved in these 'imponderable questions' that we all ask; and, thus, it can help us squarely face these questions. Along the same lines, it can help free us from the bondage of prejudice, provincialism, and illogicality and thus serve another aim of a liberal education. It can sharpen our critical outlook, so that we can come to learn to look at things—our own beliefs and commitments and those of others—with a certain restraint and skepticism. It can help us to read newspapers more critically and to see through the evasions and pomposities of politicians and other users of Madison Avenue techniques. We need to develop a sense of what a good argument and reasonable evidence look like; and we need to develop a healthy skepticism about the claims and beliefs we find in us and around us. Some philosophical doubts, as I shall show, are absurd, but a recognition of this should not obscure the fact that we need to develop a wary skepticism concerning the cultural artifacts of our tribe.

William James, that versatile and central figure in American thought, once said that we philosophize "to attain a conception of the frame of things which shall on the whole be more rational than the somewhat chaotic view which everyone by nature carries about with him under his hat."[10] This, to my mind, sums up very well what should be the aim of philosophy. The analytical study of concepts should be a means to this and to whatever else a quest for wisdom involves. This is, in brief, what I have been trying to communicate to you. Surely the stress on the ancient sense of 'philosophy' as a quest for wisdom is correct. What would be the point of attaining clarity about our fundamental concepts if this did not help us in our lives, if it did not contribute to the attainment of wisdom? We must not forget in philosophy the aim of our drive for clarity. But it also seems that we do not even have a tolerable understanding of what we are searching for when we search for wisdom. We must apply conceptual analysis to the very concept of wisdom.

Rather than tackling the concept of wisdom head on, I shall proceed obliquely by examining our concepts of man, freedom, God, morality, and knowledge. Surely if we are ever to attain wisdom or even come to grips with what is involved in attaining it, we must come to have a clear understanding of these concepts.

III

The philosopher is not alone in seeking wisdom. The poet, the novelist, the sage also seek wisdom—they also struggle with these imponderable questions. Some have thought, including so profound a philosopher as Wittgenstein, that we will find more wisdom in the poets and the novelists than we will ever find in the philosophers or get from philosophy. What are we to say to that, and how do we distinguish the philosopher from the sage?

Whatever wisdom is to be attained cannot be attained by either philosopher or sage alone; their roles are not competing but complementary. Gottfried Keller's *A Village Romeo and Juliet* or Tolstoy's *Hadji Murad* do something for me that neither Hume's *Treatise* nor Wittgenstein's *Bluebook* can do. But exactly the reverse is true as well. What we need to do first is to distinguish the philosopher from the sage.

The philosopher, the sage, and the poet all seek insight, but the philosopher does not and cannot rely on insight alone. He must rely on insight backed by reasoned argument. The heart of philosophy is argument. The conceptual analyses of philosophy typically proceed by way of argument. Unlike the novelist or poet, a philosopher, whether speculative or critical, must back up his insights with arguments or reasons. A philosopher who develops a contempt for argument and who refuses to argue or reason, but just dishes out the insight for you to take or leave—as Heidegger seems to do—has thereby ceased to be a philosopher or to engage in philosophical discourse. His social role is that of the sage and not the philosopher.

One might try to give reasons for not engaging in philosophical reasoning at all—for bringing philosophy to a halt. But that is not to just dish out the insight, as someone who was simply a sage would do, but to engage in philosophical argument to try to reason people out of engaging in philosophical activities. This is no more a *conceptual* anomaly than is a war to end all wars. In both instances one may be trying to do something that *in fact* cannot be done, but that is another matter.

The preceding question about the respective roles of the philosopher and the sage raises questions about the respective functions of philosophy, history, and literature in a humanistic education or in a truly human life. I shall comment on this as a coda to this initial chapter.[11]

The qualities an educated man needs most are *creative* imagination, *practical* wisdom, and *logical* thought. Philosophy, history, and literature are complementary in what they give us in this respect. They are all integral parts of humanistic learning, but we should come to see that they have their respective strengths and weaknesses.

The study of literature can impart sensitivity, a sense of the complexity, ambivalence, and depth of human existence; it can also develop a sensitivity to the nuances of language and a sense of scholarly care. But since such a study is strong, intensely strong, on the side of creative imagination, it tends to starve the rigorous, critical, analytical side of our nature. Here philosophy is a crucial balancing factor.

History comes closest to providing a balanced diet. It is concerned with *describing* and *explaining* how men act, at least in their socially important actions. It is often thought, however, that history is not concerned with criticizing and assessing human actions. We get descriptions of the plague that ravaged the armies during the Thirty Years War and descriptions of the plundering and raping. But besides a description of the behavior of men in concrete, living detail, and a knowledge of how we would put together the bits of evidence to make a historical narrative, we want to develop skills and a capacity for abstract thought that would enable us more readily to assess what principled differences divided the Protestant cause from the Catholic one. Here we need philosophy as an analytical study of concepts.

Philosophy has its characteristic strengths and weaknesses, too. It is surely true that the study of philosophy, more than the study of literature or history, if taken as a sole diet, leads to intellectual starvation. Philosophy, I shall argue, has no subject matter of its own. Mathematics, natural science, psychology, anthropology, politics, history, morality, art, and religion all in themselves, and in their intramural relations, provide material for philosophy. The concepts embedded in these activities perplex us, and it is the job of the philosopher to help us attain some clearer understanding concerning the working of these concepts. But without a first-hand knowledge of some of these matters—a knowledge by *wont*, so to say— philosophical study is pointless. "A course on moral and political philosophy is starvation indeed unless it is accompanied by some study of history or of the social sciences."[12]

A liberal education, if it were any good, as it usually is not, should teach us to think: to be rational, nonevasive, sensitive creatures with an increased understanding of the human predicament. We want, or should want, men capable of rigorous and objective thought; in addition we want, or should want, men with creative imagination and practical wisdom. Philosophy by itself could help produce clever sillies. All three subjects help bring out some elements of the preceding ideal, but taken by themselves they are all inadequate. To achieve a genuine education and a truly human society, we need the qualities they severally help to develop.

NOTES

1. We should not neglect the point Collingwood makes, which is that the problems the questions posed were often very different and do not readily stand cultural and historical uprooting.
2. What is meant by conceptual analysis will become clearer as we proceed.
3. Stuart Hampshire, "Philosophy and Beliefs," *The Twentieth Century* (June, 1955), p. 511. This is Hampshire's remark in a discussion on this topic with Quinton, Murdoch, and Berlin.
4. Jacques Maritain, "The Nature of Philosophy and of Theology," in Henry W. Johnstone Jr. (ed.), *What Is Philosophy?* (New York: 1965), p. 32.
5. Maurice Cornforth, "The Task of Philosophy," in *What Is Philosophy?* ibid., p. 68
6. Henry W. Johnstone Jr., in the introduction to his *What Is Philosophy?* ibid., p. 8.
7. Ibid.
8. F. E. Sparshott, "Speculation and Reflection, or: It's All Done by Mirrors," *University of Toronto Quarterly*, vol. XXXV, no. 1 (October, 1965), p. 20.
9. Alfred N. Whitehead, "Wisdom," in Marcus Singer and Robert Ammerman, (eds.), *Introductory Readings in Philosophy* (New York: 1962), p. 3. Excerpted from Whitehead's *The Aims of Education* (New York: 1929), chap. 3.
10. William James, *Essays in Pragmatism* (New York: 1951), p. 3.
11. My brief remarks on this topic were for the most part inspired by P. H. Nowell-Smith's brilliant inaugural lecture, "Education in a University" (Leicester: 1958).
12. Ibid., p. 10.

SUPPLEMENTARY READINGS
CHAPTER 1

Books

Bobik, Joseph (ed.), *The Nature of Philosophic Inquiry* (Notre Dame, Ind.: University of Notre Dame Press, 1970).
Britton, Karl, *Philosophy and the Meaning of Life* (London: Cambridge, 1970).
Collingwood, R. G., *Speculum Mentis* (London: Oxford University Press, 1924).
*Danto, Arthur C., *What Philosophy Is* (New York: Harper & Row, 1968).
*Dewey, John, *Intelligence in the Modern World*, chapters I and II (New York: Random House, 1939).
*Dewey, John, *Reconstruction in Philosophy* (Boston: Beacon Press, 1957).
Ducasse, C. J., *Philosophy As a Science* (New York: Oskar Piest, 1941).
*Gorovitz, Samuel, and Ron G. Williams, *Philosophical Analysis: An Introduction to Its Language and Techniques* (New York: Random House, 1963).
Hall, E. W., *Categorial Analysis*, part I (Chapel Hill, N.C.: University of North Carolina Press, 1964).
Heidegger, Martin, *What Is Philosophy?* (New Haven, Conn.: College and University Press, 1955).

*Asterisks here and in all the bibliographies denote relatively easy readings.

*Hirst, R. J., *Philosophy* (London: Routledge, 1968).

*James, William, *Essays in Pragmatism*, essays I and IV (New York: Hafner, 1951).

*Johnstone, Henry W., Jr. (ed.), *What Is Philosophy?* (New York: Macmillan, 1965).

Körner, Stephan, *What Is Philosophy?* (London: Allen Lane, Penguin Press, 1969).

Marcuse, Herbert, *Negations*, chapter 4 (Boston: Beacon Press, 1968).

Moore, G. E., *Some Main Problems of Philosophy*, chapter I (London: Macmillan, 1953).

Newall, R. W., *The Concept of Philosophy* (London: Methuen, 1967).

Passmore, John, *Philosophical Reasoning* (London: Duckworth, 1961).

Petrovic, Gajo, *Marx in the Mid-Twentieth Century* (Garden City, N.Y.: Doubleday, 1967).

Rhees, Rush, *Without Answers* (London: Routledge, 1969).

Waismann, F., *How I See Philosophy* (New York: St. Martin's, 1968).

Articles and Pamphlets

*Broad, C. D., "Two Lectures on the Nature of Philosophy," in H. D. Lewis (ed.), *Clarity Is Not Enough* (New York: Humanities Press, 1963).

Goddard, L., "Philosophical Thinking" (Armidale, New South Wales, Australia: Halstead Press, Sydney, 1962).

Hall, E. W., "Is Philosophy a Science?" *Journal of Philosophy*, 1942.

*Hampshire, Stuart, "The Progress of Philosophy," *Polemic*, no. 5 (1946).

Hook, Sidney, "Pragmatism and the Tragic Sense of Life," in Lionel Abel (ed.), *Moderns and Tragedy* (Greenwich, Conn.: Fawcett, 1967).

McLean, George F., "The Nature of Philosophical Inquiry," *Proceedings of the American Catholic Philosophical Association*, vol. XLI.

Mezaros, Istvan, "The Possibility of a Dialogue," in Bernard Williams and Alan Montefiore (eds.), *British Analytical Philosophy* (New York: Humanities Press, 1966).

Nielsen, Kai, "John Dewey's Conception of Philosophy," *The University of Massachusetts Review*, vol. II, no. 1 (autumn, 1960).

*Nielsen, Kai, "Linguistic Philosophy and Beliefs," in Gerry H. Gill (ed.), *Philosophy Today*, no. 2, (New York: Macmillan, 1969).

*Nielsen, Kai, "Philosophy and Education," *Journal of Education*, vol. 15, no. 5 (May, 1966).

*Passmore, J. A., "Philosophy," in Paul Edwards (ed.), *The Encyclopedia of Philosophy*, vol. 6 (New York: Macmillan, 1967).

*Passmore, John, "Philosophy in the Last Decade," Occasional Paper No. 14, 1969 (Sydney, Australia: Sydney University Press, 1969).

Pears, D. F., "The Philosophy of Wittgenstein," *The New York Review of Books*, vol. XII, no. 1 (Jan. 16, 1969).

Price, H. H., "Clarity Is Not Enough," in H. D. Lewis (ed.), *Clarity Is Not Enough* (New York: Humanities Press, 1963).

Ryle, Gilbert, "Abstractions," *Dialogue*, vol. I (1962).

Ryle, Gilbert, "Philosophical Arguments," in A. J. Ayer (ed.), *Logical Positivism* (Glencoe, Ill.: Free Press, 1959).

Schlick, Moritz, "The Future of Philosophy," and Rudolf Carnap, "On the Character of Philosophical Problems," both in Richard Rorty (ed.), *The Linguistic Turn* (Chicago: University of Chicago Press, 1967).

Simmel, Georg, "On the Nature of Philosophy," in Kurt H. Wolff (ed.), *Essays on Sociology, Philosophy and Aesthetics* by Georg Simmel et al. (New York: Harper & Row, 1965).

*Sparshott, F. E., "The Central Problem of Philosophy," *University of Toronto Quarterly*, vol. XXXI, no. 1 (October, 1961).

Sparshott, F. E., "Speculation and Reflection, or: It's All Done by Mirrors," *University of Toronto Quarterly*, vol. XXXV, no. 1 (October, 1965).

Urmson, J. O., "The History of Philosophical Analysis" and "Discussion of Urmson's 'The History of Analysis'," and P. F. Strawson, "Analysis, Science and Metaphysics" and "Discussion of Strawson's 'Analysis, Science and Metaphysics'," all in Richard Rorty (ed.), *The Linguistic Turn* (Chicago: University of Chicago Press, 1967).

I
FREEDOM AND DETERMINISM

2

HOLBACH: THE DENIAL OF HUMAN FREEDOM

I

I should now like to leap into the middle of one of the most ancient and the most harassing of philosophical subjects: the freedom of man. In wrestling with its complexities, we will come to see the crucial importance of viewing philosophy as an analytical study of concepts.

To what extent, if at all, and in what ways and to what degree are we free? Except in certain despairing or reflective moments, we certainly have the feeling that we are free, but are we really? We are agents who act, make decisions, make choices, sometimes deliberate on what we are doing, and sometimes, although not always, act in accordance with the intentions we have formed as a result of our deliberations. We have desires and wants and sometimes, although certainly not always, we are able to do what we want. Aren't such facts clear enough evidence that we humans are, at least in some circumstances, free?

Are we really? The desires we have, the languages we speak, the choices that seem feasible to us or really are open to us, even the very character we have—all these are biologically, environmentally or culturally conditioned. That I write in English and write in this very manner, that I argue in the manner I am arguing, and that you are reacting in the manner you are reacting, are all the results of matters ultimately quite external to us, matters over which, in the final analysis, we have no control.

Eugene O'Neill gave a dramatic expression to this fatalistic belief in *Long Day's Journey into Night* when he had Mary Tyrone reflect sadly:

> I suppose life has made him like that, and he can't help it. None of us can help the things life has done to us. They're done before you realize it, and once they're done they make you do other things until at last everything comes between you and what you'd like to be.[1]

17

Is this so? Is it really the case that we human beings are not in any significant way free? Or is this fatalistic attitude an evasion on our part—a rationalization—that enables us to evade our responsibilities as human beings by always excusing ourselves for the things we do? Existentialists tell us this is exactly what we are doing. Such a fatalistic attitude is for them a clear case of *bad faith*.

There are dozens of crisscrossed, involuted, complex issues here. I will start by stating, and then developing, two extreme views. One, stated starkly by Baron Holbach, a major philosopher of the Enlightenment, and Clarence Darrow, a famous criminal lawyer, tries to show that human freedom is an illusion. The other view, vividly expressed (although in different ways) by both the Russian writer Fyodor Dostoevsky and the American philosopher William James, tries to persuade us that it is better, in spite of everything, to regard man as a free agent, and that such rationalistic claims as Holbach makes can never be acceptable to man. Both these affirmations and denials of freedom are extreme and are couched in somewhat metaphorical and often unclear language. Not many philosophers would accept either view, stated as they are by these men. Of course that is not to say that neither view can be correct. Their being out of favor with philosophers should only put one on guard.

Baron Holbach was not just a philosopher who attacked doctrines of the freedom of the will. He was the most important philosopher of the French Enlightenment, and he stated in a powerful and philosophically comprehensive way the central beliefs of the Enlightenment. His *System of Nature*, published in 1770, is a systematic and highly integrated defense of materialism, atheism, utilitarianism, and determinism. As a materialist Holbach thought that only matter exists, and that mind and will are but modifications of the brain. Man and all his artifacts are completely a part of nature and are investigatable and predictable by purely scientific means. Nature is like a machine and man is a part of nature, but he is nonetheless a creature of dignity and value. Human happiness and harmony are the ultimate goals in life and are, generally speaking, attainable once man learns to live in accordance with reason and nature. In achieving this, one will of necessity come to see through his religious illusions—illusions that impede rather than further his moral development. But Holbach would not say a man had achieved happiness and harmony until that man recognized that he is completely and inescapably a determined part in the immutable, eternal order of nature. This recognition involves seeing that free will is an illusion.

In the *System of Nature* we have a thorough materialist, speculative philosophy—an utterly secular conception of man's nature and destiny. There, Holbach gives us a systematic, carefully elaborated ideology.[2] That is, he presents a propagated general outlook consciously incorporating certain values and aiming at a transformation of man and society. As his friend Diderot said, we have here "a philosophy that is clear, definite and frank . . . a philosophy . . . all of one piece."

It is this vision of man that we have inherited from the Enlightenment; and it is this picture of man and the world that religious men, romantics, and existentialists of all sorts have reacted against. Dostoevsky's *Notes from Underground,* which we will consider in the next chapter, is one such reaction. It is unrestrained and deeply ironic, but it cuts to the very core of the assumptions of the Enlightenment.

You should reflect, after you have pressed deeper into your study of philosophy, whether and to what extent a Holbachian vision of the world ought to be accepted. But for now, consider only Holbach's claim that freedom is an illusion.[3]

II

Holbach would surely have agreed with Clarence Darrow that "man is the product of heredity and environment" and that like certain machines, he is programmed. That is, his behavior is ultimately and completely determined in every respect by stimuli external to him. Darrow, in the twentieth century, put in less systematic form what Holbach argued for, systematically, in the eighteenth century. Darrow maintained that this deterministic contention is "amply proven" by the history of science and the history of man, as well as by logic and philosophy. A rational man must recognize that free will is an illusion, and must arrange his view of the world (including his view of morality) in accordance with this deterministic picture. Holbach is of the same stamp. He opens his argument for establishing the illusory nature of the doctrine of free will by proclaiming:

> In whatever manner man is considered, he is connected to universal nature, and submitted to the necessary and immutable laws that she imposes on all the beings she contains, according to their peculiar essences or to the respective properties with which, without consulting them, she endows each particular species. Man's life is a line that nature commands him to describe upon the surface of the earth, without his ever being able to swerve from it, even for an instant. He is born without his own consent; his organization does in nowise depend upon himself; his ideas come to him involuntarily; his habits are in the power of those who cause him to contract them; he is unceasingly modified by causes, whether visible or concealed, over which he has no control, which necessarily regulate his mode of existence; give the hue to his way of thinking and determine his manner of acting. He is good or bad, happy or miserable, wise or foolish, reasonable or irrational, without his will being for anything in these various states. Nevertheless, in spite of the shackles by which he is bound, it is pretended he is a free agent, or that independent of the causes by which he is moved, he determines his own will, and regulates his own condition.[4]

In short, Holbach and Darrow are maintaining that all processes are continuous sequences of causes and effects. That is to say, for any event or state E, we believe that there is some antecedent event or state—or series of events or states—such that when events or states like that occur, events or states like E must subsequently occur. This is what it means to say, as Darrow does, and as Holbach does, that "Law is everywhere supreme." There are laws for all events or states, including all human actions. (Actions are treated as a subspecies of event.) Because of this ubiquitousness of laws, free will is an illusion.

Holbach is well aware that for psychologically compelling reasons we tend to make the opposite assumption. Religion demands it; society, morality, our flattering picture of ourselves, all conspire to make us believe in human freedom.[5] It is natural to assume that without an assumption of free will, life would be a meaningless, moral chaos. If there is no free will, human responsibility also becomes an illusion; and punishment thereby becomes what Sade took it to be, merely a form of irrational torture. After all, if every action has a cause it is true of crimes as well. Thus, they all have sufficient conditions for their occurrence—conditions for which the individual can in no way be responsible. This means, or at least seems to mean, that all crimes are really diseases, and that no man can justly or justifiably be blamed or held responsible for anything. This, if we have enough imagination to translate it into the concrete, becomes a paradoxical conclusion indeed. Holbach himself does not draw such conclusions, but he is aware how natural it would be to draw them, and he is aware of the fact that such a conclusion makes most men continue to believe in free will in spite of its intrinsic improbability.

If we look at it rationally, Holbach argues, it is evident that no man is the maker of his own temperament. To be sure, he acts purposively and forms intentions, but in whatever he does he always acts in the way his strongest motives dictate. If I am wild with thirst and I spy a pond I will rush to drink; but if I am not so wild that I can still behave with some degree of rationality and have a tolerable control over myself, I will not drink from it if someone convinces me that it is poisoned. Holbach argues that in neither case do I act from my own free will, but rather from the strongest motive, which, in the case where I refrain from drinking, is the desire for survival.

I cannot prove my freedom by performing a kind of utterly gratuitous act. My very desire to prove that I am free by such an act "becomes a necessary motive" that makes me do what otherwise would be quite inexplicable. If I desperately wish to prove myself free, and if in my desperate quest for freedom I become a complete madman, I may disconfirm my critic's taunt: "One thing you won't do is jump out the window." But this, as Holbach points out, does not prove me free. It only shows that my opponent misjudged what was actually my strongest motive. He had not correctly assessed the violent Dostoevskian temperament that lay within me. But this temperament, like a milder temperament, did not come out of the blue. It, too, has its sufficient conditions. As Holbach puts it, "The actions of fools are as necessary as those of the most prudent individuals."

III

Let us ask this question: What would it be like to be a free agent? When we assert or deny that man has a free will, what are we talking about?

To be a free agent is to be able, as Holbach puts it, to move oneself by oneself. That is to say, a man is free if and only if "he determines himself without cause. . . ." There is indeed a distinctive mental activity or willing that goes with human actions; but we must not forget that the will is but a "modification of the brain" and that it, like everything else, has causes external to it that determine what and when we shall will something.

It is a myth to think of the will as some supernatural or nonnatural prime mover that is the original cause of everything a man does. The very conception of such a will, apart and distinct from nature, is an incoherent conception. We do indeed have a primitive sense of initiating an action, or of trying or striving to do something; that is no mysterious little ghost in the human machine, but rather something perfectly natural and part of the immutable natural chain of cause and effect. Moreover, *what* we will try to do and *when*, or even *that* we will strive to achieve whatever it is we want to do, is finally determined by factors outside ourselves. Thus, it is an illusion to think that man has such a nonmaterial will, independent of the laws of causality, or that man can determine his will independently of the causes by which he is moved. Forces in our cultural life and our human vanity—our strong need to distinguish ourselves from the other animals—conspire to make us believe that we are free agents, but this belief in human freedom is a myth.

That my will is as it is rather than otherwise is determined by the sum of the influences operating on me. The sum of my environment, culture, and heredity makes my will as it is, makes me will *what* I will. We do, indeed, desire what we desire, want what we want, fear what we fear; these are plain tautologies, but *what* we fear, *what* we desire, *what* we want is determined by our environment and our heredity.

Holbach sums up his own position in the following ringing tones. (We must not forget that he was not only a conceptual analyst, but was also a man propounding and proselytizing a new and perfectly secular world view.)

In short, the actions of man are never free; they are always the necessary consequence of his temperament, of the received ideas, and of notions, either true or false, which he has formed to himself of happiness; of his opinions, strengthened by example, by education, and by daily experience.

Man . . . is not a free agent in any one instant of his life; he is necessarily guided in each step by those advantages, whether real or fictitious, that he attaches to the objects by which his passions are roused: these passions themselves are necessary in a being who unceasingly tends towards his own happiness; their energy is necessary, since that depends on his temperament; his temperament is necessary, because it depends on the physical elements which enter into his composition; the modification of this temperament is necessary, as it is the infallible and inevitable consequence of the impulse he receives from the incessant action of moral and physical beings.[6]

IV

Holbach turns to a classic objection to such deterministic views. Men sometimes are able to *do* what they *want* to do; human beings do make choices, and sometimes they are not constrained to act in one way rather than another. Does this not show that sometimes men can act as free and responsible moral agents?

Holbach says it does not show that men are free. We must not "confound constraint and necessity." A man may cease to be contrained, as when he is let out of prison, without thereby gaining a free will. He still must act in accordance with natural laws even though he is beyond the prison walls. And although sometimes a man may do what he wants to do, he is not thereby free, for what he *wants* to do is not his to choose; and he would *not* do what he does in such circumstances but for the fact that he wants to do it. His actions are not really free because they are the inevitable consequence of his wants and of certain other perfectly determinate factors—factors that in the last analysis are beyond his control. Similarly, that he is "a master of his choosing" proves nothing about his freedom, for that he chooses at all and what he chooses is determined by factors that he does not control and that are external to him. Thus, according to Holbach, the ability to choose, to do what you want to do or to act without constraint, does not really establish human freedom.

What deludes man into thinking that he is free, when he does make a choice, is that he does not discern the true *motive* or cause that *sets* him in action. Yet the human will is in complete bondage to nature.

There are, Holbach argues, internal and external motives (prods to action).[7] But the thoughts that come into a man's mind are not something of which he is the master. In the last analysis our internal motives are brought about by external motives.

If this is so, why do men continue to believe in this mythical human freedom? We have already seen part of Holbach's answer. Human vanity and fear keep men from acknowledging that they are simply a part of nature. But Holbach gives another answer as well: The complexity of the human animal is such that man is not aware of and, in practice, often cannot be aware of the complex of motives that determines human action. *Ignorance of why he acts as he acts gives him the illusion of freedom.* If he were less complicated, he would perceive that his actions are as fully necessitated as is the behavior of a protozoan. As Holbach puts it:

> It is . . . for want of recurring to the causes that move him; for want of being able to analyze, from not being competent to decode the complicated motion of his machine, that man believes himself a free agent; it is only upon his own ignorance that he founds the profound yet deceitful notion that he has of his free agency. . . .[8]

This view of Holbach's may seem shocking; it may seem to some destructive of "the human spirit," although to others it may seem like a great liberation from sophistry and illusion, while to still others it may seem simply confusing. There will be those of you who will feel that somehow the issue has been begged or never properly stated. There may even be some who feel that Holbach has shown us nothing of note, for he is, in effect, preaching to us rather than critically exploring the problem by giving us an analytical examination of the concepts of freedom and human action. There is indeed a point to some of these reactions.

There are some crucial questions to start asking here: Has Holbach made his claims with sufficient clarity so that we could determine whether they are true or false? Can his claims readily be stated with a little demythologization in such a way that we would be justified in asserting that what he says is true or is at least essentially true? Furthermore, is it the whole of the truth here? Has Holbach given us good grounds for accepting what he says? If his conclusions are true, although his grounds for them are shaky, what exactly are the grounds that would give them substantial support? Has Holbach really succeeded in capturing our central concept of freedom, or is his concept a confused philosophical one? And if he has succeeded in digging out our common concept, has he succeeded in showing it to be an illusory concept?

I will make a start at coming to grips with the issues involved in these questions by examining in the next two chapters two radical rejections of such Holbachian thinking, namely the 'irrationalism' of Dostoevsky and the indirect defense of indeterminism we find in William James. By following such a procedure we will better be able to see what is involved in such a Holbachian challenge to the viability of our concept of freedom.

NOTES

1. Eugene O'Neill, *Long Day's Journey into Night* (London: Jonathan Cape, 1956), p. 53.
2. I am using 'ideology' here in a perfectly nonpejorative manner.

3. It is a prejudice of certain speculative philosophers to think that, typically, a given claim made by a philosopher cannot be examined in isolation from his other philosophical beliefs. Indeed, it is true that one philosophical question leads to another, and it is also true that as rational men we want to put the pieces together, but we can examine certain philosophical arguments made by a philosopher without examining his whole philosophical system. We can examine Aquinas' five ways to prove the existence of God without examining his theory about the relation of reason and revelation, his conception of original sin, and the like.

4. Baron Holbach, *System of Nature*, translated by H. D. Robinson (Boston: 1853), chapter XI. Original publication 1770.

5. I am not endorsing Holbach's sociological remark here but merely recording it. Surely many of our contemporaries do not think that man is in any significant sense a free agent.

6. Baron Holbach, op. cit., chapter XII.

7. To speak of 'external motive' involves a misuse of 'motive'. Here Holbach was plainly talking about what we would now call an external causative factor or force.

8. Baron Holbach, op. cit., chapter XII.

3

DOSTOEVSKY:
FREEDOM
AS IRRATIONAL CHOICE

I

Dostoevsky's *Notes from Underground* was written in 1864, slightly less than one hundred years after Holbach's *The System of Nature*.[1] In almost every respect it is fundamentally opposed to Holbach's views and to the whole attitude of the Enlightenment. Dostoevsky's most trenchant irony is directed against the idea of secular salvation through a knowledge of ourselves and through a tough-minded understanding of our world. He turns with scorn from what he takes to be the childish idea that if we can only free ourselves from a belief in Ghostly Deities and attain a genuine knowledge of the laws governing human and societal development, then at last we can achieve human happiness and a distinctive human flourishing.

Dostoevsky's Underground man will have none of this. He finds the enemy of man *within* man. And he sees this as a permanent human condition. He pictures man in all his perversity and ambivalence. He makes us see things about ourselves we would rather not see; he makes us aware of our seemingly insatiable passion for bloodshed and cruelty, chaos and destruction, and of our extraordinary love of suffering. He shows us that self-knowledge does not always lead to freedom and self-realization, for it also can be a bitter, destructive thing—something that we both desperately want and do not want. In reading him, we become acutely aware of the shadow that surrounds all human enlightenment. In effect, the persuasive manner in which he writes makes us ask questions about ourselves that we normally will not face; and in doing this we come to feel the force of the Underground man's question: Can a man of perception respect himself at all?

Dostoevsky's reaction against Holbachian ideas is a cry of the human heart against what he takes to be the extreme claims of science. It is essentially a moral and human revulsion at what Dostoevsky regards as the implications of a deterministic materialism. Dostoevsky maintains that such a materialist view, with its accompanying belief in human progress, is not only psychologically naive but also destroys the very dignity of human life. In reading *Notes from Underground* we discover that the Underground man is a fantastically tormented, ambivalent, perverse creature. For him, "consciousness is an illness—a real thoroughgoing illness." He is a man who cannot be of one piece; his ideals—his conceptions of the good and the beautiful—crumble before his actual life and his mocking, ambivalent attitudes. Yet, perversely enough, he finds intense enjoyment in his very despair and self-loathing.

Through all this monologue, this exhibitionistic performance, runs a caustic irony. How serious is the Underground man or, rather, *when* is he serious? He tells us that he has talked a lot of nonsense and that he does not mean a word of what he says. But is this itself to be taken seriously? It seems not, for surely, taking into account all his jesting, he is at the very least displaying his own disquietude, a disquietude that we as readers can hardly escape feeling as our own as well as his. What is its source? What is it that so deeply disturbs him?

Note that very soon after the Underground man's disquietude is established, quips and derisive remarks begin to appear about 'the laws of nature'; we can hardly avoid noting that what Dostoevsky says here is not unconnected with the kind of remarks we have found Holbach and Darrow making about a deterministic universe. The Underground man is affronted by the laws of nature. He wishes to flaunt them and show his contempt for them. The impossibilities with which he is confronted, the stone wall he runs up against, are the "laws of nature; the deductions of natural science, mathematics." But after all, he ambivalently remarks, like them or not, one must just accept the laws of nature. Yet, he is not going to be reconciled to them, although—and here is another turn of the screw —he recognizes that this is an absurd attitude to take. There is no one to blame, nothing that it makes sense to be spiteful about; yet the ache remains and a deep desire to spit disdainfully on the "whole legal system of nature."

Why the ache? Why is Dostoevsky so upset about science and the so-called "laws of nature"? Why is he so disturbed about principles of reason and truth that (1) would enable us to predict or retrodict—to infer in a reliably testable manner from present data what happened in the past— the behavior of men, and (2) would be principles in accordance with which men could rationally and reasonably govern their lives? The short answer is that if there were such laws and if such predictions were possible, then there would be no freedom of choice. But freedom of choice is the most precious thing. It is this that that ungrateful biped, man, longs for more than anything else. Dostoevsky will not let us forget that there is something frightful about human freedom. Yet he cannot tolerate an image of man in which freedom is denied. Although man has a very poor sense of what is to his advantage—he is too tormented, too complex for that—he does know this much: His "most advantageous advantage" is precisely the freedom to choose his own life, the ability to remain the rider and not the ridden.

In Holbach's world this would be impossible. It would be a perfectly dehumanized world, a boring, senseless Crystal Palace in which man would indeed be reduced to a machine. Man, if such a view is true, "is something of the nature of a piano key or the stop of an organ. . . ." We must not forget the Underground man stresses,

> . . . that man everywhere and at all times, whoever he may be, has preferred to act as he chose and not in the least as his reason and advantage dictated. And one may choose what is contrary to one's own interests, and sometimes one *positively ought* (that is my idea). One's own free unfettered choice, one's own caprice, however wild it may be, one's own fancy worked up at times to frenzy—is that very 'most advantageous advantage' which we have over-looked, which comes under no classification and against which all systems and theories are continually being shattered to atoms.[2]

Deeper than any desire to do what is reasonable, to discover and act in accordance with 'right reason', 'true virtue', 'the common good', whatever these may be, is the desire to have an "independent choice, whatever that independence may cost and wherever it may lead." This freedom of choice is a deeper and more profound value than truth, beauty, virtue, or even rationally advantageous choice. But in a Holbachian world, this value would be an illusion; therefore we must reject such a Holbachian world-view no matter how conclusive the evidence for it is. Dostoevsky seems to be telling us that our very conviction that we are free, even if in reality we aren't free, is more valuable than truth. Truth is a very great value indeed, but without a belief in freedom, our lives would be utterly mean-ingless. We should sacrifice truth itself to keep our 'lifesaving' belief in freedom.

This is blind irrationalism and, it is natural to reply, a pure example of man closing his eyes to reality. Truth and an understanding of one's predicament is not the only value, but it cannot be slighted that much. Without it, everything else collapses.

The Underground man is keenly aware of the objection that he is "fly-ing in the face of reality." And in a way, it should be remarked, such an accusation is unjust. The Underground man certainly wants to face up to human reality; he will not go in for the kind of evasion that claims that there are some laws of nature that mankind can never understand. He terms such a belief contemptible and senseless. Moreover, he tells us that "if desire should come in conflict with reason we shall reason and not desire, because it will be impossible retaining our reason to be *senseless* in our desires, and in that way knowingly act against reason and desire to injure ourselves."

But all the same, if it is always possible unerringly to predict what a man will do, then man is simply a piano key or the stop on an organ; his life is totally senseless. To take this lying down, simply to take it as 'a fact' that life is meaningless, surely is not something that men, or at least the overwhelming majority of men, would be prepared to do. Indeed, we do want to know and we do want to discover laws. We would like to know whether determinism is true; that is, we would like to know whether for any event, including any action whatsoever, there is some causal law or conjunction of causal laws which entails that such an event or action will take place given certain determinate antecedent conditions. We would indeed like to know whether every event has a cause, for we do have definite interests in rationality; but we must not forget that

> . . . reason is nothing but reason and satisfies only the rational side of man's nature, while will is a manifestation of the whole human life including reason and all the impulses. And although our life, and this manifestation of it, is often worthless, yet it is life and not simply extracting square roots.[3]

We want to live and to satisfy our capacity for life, not simply our capacity for reasoning. There are many things precious to us that we may never come to understand rationally. (Dostoevsky explicitly avoids making the obscurantist claim that they cannot be understood rationally.) Given these interests, we will not be "bound by an obligation to desire only what is sensible." And this caprice of ours may in reality be "more advantageous to us than anything else," for "it preserves for us what is most precious and most important—that is, our personality, our individuality." Men would prefer any absurdity, any fantastic element, against a deterministic and utilitarian world view. For by preferring this absurdity, he could "prove to himself . . . that men still are men and not keys to a piano, which the laws of nature threaten to control so completely that soon one will be able to desire nothing but the calendar." And if man really were nothing but a piano key and this were proven to him, he would purposely do something perverse, bring on himself and others any suffering or chaos and darkness so as to "convince himself that he is a man and not a piano key." He would "purposely go mad in order to gain his point," for his very humanity is necessarily linked to his freedom.

II

It is natural and appropriate to ask what all this establishes. How does it in any way refute or rebut Holbach, or challenge the key ideas and ideals of the Enlightenment? In *our context,* it would be a mistake to say that such questions are inappropriate because Dostoevsky is a consummate artist displaying the human predicament and we should restrict ourselves to noting how well he realizes his purely literary aims. It would be a mistake so to limit ourselves here, for in such a philosophical context we are precisely looking at his claims as philosophical claims or, if you will, claims about man and his estate. And surely this is how Dostoevsky wanted them to be taken. He is indeed an astounding writer— surely one of the deepest and profoundest in the whole Western literary tradition. From his anguished pen he has given us something that cannot but "get to" any sensitive person. But it is also true that there are certain perfectly evident conceptual confusions in what he says: Mathematical statements should not be assimilated to the laws of nature, and the laws of nature should not be treated as if they were legal fiats. But these confusions hardly touch Dostoevsky's main claim, that if it is true that freedom is an illusion, then life is senseless. Like Feuerbach and Marx after him, Holbach believed in determinism; that is, he believed, as we have seen, that for any event or state of type X there is a distinct event(s) or state(s) of type Y, plus a true causal law that asserts whenever X then Y. Holbach concluded that since this is so, freedom is an illusion. But he drew no nasty consequences from it. Again, like Feuerbach and Marx, he thought that as man came slowly to understand himself and as he freed himself from the oppression of superstition and from oppressive social conditions, he would create a more "truly human society" and achieve greater happiness. Dostoevsky thinks this is a snare and a delusion.[4] If determinism is true, freedom is an illusion and no truly human society is attainable; for if man is not free, his very humanity is itself something without substance—a sentimental idea of a deluded animal.

It has been powerfully argued that none of these troubling conclusions follow, for Holbach is plainly wrong, and hence Dostoevsky is wrong here as well. Freedom and determinism are quite compatible. This challenges at its very center the Dostoevskian belief that if man's behavior were exhaustively explainable in terms of laws of nature, man's personality and sense of self would be destroyed. The compatibility thesis will be examined later, but for now let us see if Dostoevsky gives us good grounds for (1) believing that freedom is not an illusion and (2) believing that even if it is, the exceedingly despairing or nihilistic consequences he draws from it actually do follow.

In examining these two questions we should first note that there is an ambiguity in Dostoevsky's very intent. Which, if any, of the following three things is he trying to do?

1. Is he trying to show that in spite of appearances to the contrary, man, after all, does have a free will?

2. Is he trying to show that most men are so irrational they will go

on believing that they have a free will, no matter what the facts are about human behavior?

3. Is he trying to show that whether or not man has a free will, it is far better, even if that belief be an illusion, to believe in free will?

I think he is trying to make the latter claim, but I am not interested here in whether an exhaustive textual analysis would bear out my belief. I am interested in trying to show that such an interpretation of Dostoevsky's thought makes his claims more fertile and interesting than they otherwise would be.[5] If, by contrast, he is taken as intending the second point, he has merely stated, informally and with little empirical backing, an interesting hypothesis in social psychology. If the hypothesis is true, it would pose an interesting problem in pedagogics—how could we, or could we, condition people so they would not be so irrational? It would not show that all human beings are caught in illusions, that freedom was possible or impossible, or that we would be dehumanized in a determinist world.

If, however, he is really arguing for the first point, he has done a very poor job of it, for he has not been able to get around Holbach's objection that the man who, in order to prove himself free, refuses in a particular instance to do what is manifestly the sensible thing to do, only shows that his *desire* to be free was stronger than his desire to be safe or happy. He still does not give us the slightest reason to believe he actually has a free will, a kind of individual prime mover, which is not a part of the causal order. He has not shown, for all his perversity or love of disorder, that his behavior is not predictable or retrodictable. But this is the only consideration in Dostoevsky that even looks like a direct argument for human freedom.

So, if we are to make much of Dostoevsky's claims, we must turn to the third interpretation. We must realize that Dostoevsky is raising what is essentially an ethical question, a question about the respective importance of man as rational animal and man as acting, feeling, and living being.

Why is it better to believe that one has a free will even if this is an utterly fantastic notion, known to be an illusion? Because, Dostoevsky would answer, freedom is what makes us human; our lives would be quite without significance if we did not *believe* we are free.

To this there are at least two important counters. First, if freedom is an utterly fantastic notion, known to be an illusion, we cannot, no matter how much we want to, make ourselves believe it. Second, and more important, if we are not in fact free, our believing we are free does not give our lives significance; it will only give us the *illusion* that they have significance.[6]

To the first objection a Dostoevskian could retort that this ignores man's infinite—or at least extensive—capacity to deceive himself, to kid himself into believing in the emperor's new clothes. Man can and frequently does rationalize to such an extent that he comes to treat as believable what in another frame of mind he knows to be unbelievable.

The second objection, however, cuts deeper, but there are two natural lines of reply. First, Dostoevsky or a Dostoevskian might respond: Well, then, it is better, far better, to live under the illusion that one's life has significance than under the clear awareness that one's life is without significance. Second, there is the subtler counter, although perhaps no better, that in talking about the 'significance of life' there is no difference between a life actually having significance and one's feeling that it has. If a person has a steadfast conviction that his life has significance, it has significance; if not, not.

Neither of these replies to my second objection is adequate. Consider the second one first. It will not withstand the test of translation into the concrete. Examples, live examples, undermine it. Consider a scholar who in reality was a crashing bore and pedant, who never succeeded in doing anything other than boring students and putting in dull and opaque terms what has been said with perception and verve by others. Such a man might devote all his energies to his work, tie up the very rationale of his existence with it, have scarcely any life apart from it; but while he might believe with all his heart his life was significant, he would, like the Professor in *Uncle Vanya*, be very much deceived. Examples of this sort are easy to multiply. One can honestly believe or feel that one's life is significant when in fact it is not.

My above response is less of an argument than a counterassertion carrying evidential force by reminding us of distinctions we make that seem at least to be quite objectively grounded. It is indeed trivially true that if one finds one's own life significant, then one's life seems significant to one. But my point is that one can very readily be deceived about the significance of one's life. Moreover, I am not just saying that *others* can and often do make a different evaluation about an agent's life than the agent himself, but beyond that, I am adding that a man—such as the Professor in *Uncle Vanya*—can easily delude himself into believing that his life has significance when it plainly does not. This should be evident enough from careful reflection on my preceding example. It is simply not true that if one feels or believes one's life has significance, that it therefore must have significance.

Consider now the first reply I have concocted for Dostoevsky. Since freedom and a sense of self—a sense of human consciousness and identity—are more precious than anything else, why is it not worth upholding even if freedom is an illusion, and will be known to be an illusion by a nonevasive student of life? Isn't such a "royal lie" absolutely essential in such a circumstance? What sense is there in being bound by an obligation to desire only what is sensible, what is rational, what is truthful, when this truth will not make you free, when it will rob your life of its significance? If someone in turn replies, "But all the same, truth is sacred, and self-knowledge and nonevasive living are the key to what it is like to be truly human," it begins to look as if we are approaching, or perhaps have already arrived at, an ultimate clash over values that can in no way be rationally resolved. The Underground man, it might be thought, has as much and as little right to his commitments as the Socratic lover of truth.

However, to make this claim concerning the irresolvability of fundamental disagreements over values would be premature. It would block inquiry too soon. There are a number of questions that we should put to the Underground man.

Why value freedom so much, why link your sense of the significance of life to freedom, if it really is an illusion? Why link your life to a falling star? Man in fact has a big brain and is sometimes inescapably prone to reflection. This being so, he indeed rationalizes, but, buffeted as is "the voice of the ego," man in the long run tends to see through at least some of his rationalizations. This being so, will he not, as does the Underground man himself, inevitably, sooner or later in the history of mankind, come to see through his myth about freedom and become as tortured and alienated as is the Underground man? There are, as even the Underground man acknowledges, other values. Shouldn't we, *if the facts are as he says they are*, forget about freedom and give whatever significance we can give to our lives through a consideration of what is worthwhile in other values? That is, in such a situation wouldn't it be better to fasten on to the other great goods of life?

The Underground man has not shown that, in such a circumstance, such a transvaluation of values would not be desirable, not just for man viewed as a "thinking reed", but for man viewed as a living, struggling individual thrust into a harsh world.

Moreover, why put such an exclusive stress on freedom? Why treat it as so infinitely precious if it leads to suffering, cruelty, chaos, and terror? Utopia—the life of the Crystal Palace—or even a bourgeois or communist life might indeed be boring, but isn't sadism, cruelty, and torture a still worse ill? Is boredom the worst thing that could befall a person? *If* we must purchase our freedom at the price of our sanity, why so value freedom? Dostoevsky has given us no reason to believe that, *in such a circumstance*, it would be such a supreme value. We are sorely tempted to go along with him because we attach the value to it that it has in normal circumstances. But if what Dostoevsky says about determinism is true, it would not, in such altered circumstances, have that value.

There is a deeper and less debatable twist to this dialectic. If, as Dostoevsky alleges, we must go mad to believe we are free, then we in reality cannot be free. A madman—a man who utterly deludes himself—

is not a free man; a deluded man has not found himself or preserved his personality. He has, to the very degree of his delusion, lost himself. Dostoevsky is indeed surely right in asserting that to be human, to be an existing individual, is not simply to be a rational animal, a thinking reed; but without rationality one is scarcely human at all.

Even putting these questions aside, there are other problems as well. If consciousness, if awareness of self, is such an illness, such a torture, why then so value a sense of being a unique individual? Why, if this be true, so prize such a grip on one's own destiny when it will lead to one's own destruction? Only on other assumptions would 'individuality' have such a high value.

Lastly, and most radically, why assume that even *if* determinism did logically commit one to the denial of free will, that determinism would, if true, and if acknowledged to be true, destroy personality and individuality? Dostoevsky assumes it. But I ask again, *why* assume it? Suppose that the behavioral sciences develop in such a way that our behavior becomes perfectly predictable. Assuming such a situation, reflect about people over fifty who have been married with tolerable happiness since their youth. Now consider this: Suppose it were true that a psychologist could have predicted with exactitude for any of these people the kind of person they would have married if he had had, as he could have had, adequate data about what they were like at the age of fifteen. Suppose further that *now* they recognize that this is so. Why should this ruin their marriages? Why should this make these marriages any the less personal or precious? It should not. Now generalize from this to other aspects of life. Why would the fact that all these aspects are predictable or retrodictable rob them of their individuality or their value? Dostovesky evidently assumes that they would, and many people terrified by *Brave New World* make the same assumption. But isn't this a piece of mythology?

It isn't predictability per se that is disquieting to a clear-headed man. What is disquieting is that predictability raises the specter of someone with the power and the requisite predictive knowledge *manipulating* us for his own ends or the ends of some institution he serves. But this is not a necessary consequence of universal predictability. Thus, it is not predictability itself, it is not 'the laws of human nature', if indeed there are any such laws, that rob us of our individuality and make us puppets of some grand or cynical or crazy design.

NOTES

1. For the cultural, ideological, and philosophical setting of *Notes from Underground*, see Robert Louis Jackson, *Dostoevsky's Underground Man in Russian Literature* (The Hague: Mouton, 1958). It also contains an extensive bibliography of commentary about *Notes From Underground*. Throughout this

chapter I have taken the Underground man to be speaking for Dostoevsky. This could be challenged, of course, but the correctness of my assumption is not crucial to my argument.

2. Fyodor Dostoevsky, *Notes From Underground*, in Walter Kaufmann (ed.), *Existentialism from Dostoevsky to Sartre* (New York: Meridian, 1957). It is interesting to reflect that in spite of their generally radically opposed attitudes, here Dostoevsky and Spinoza are in accord. See Stuart Hampshire, "Spinoza and the Idea of Freedom," *Proceedings of the British Academy*, vol. XLVI (1960), pp. 202–203.

3. Fyodor Dostoevsky, op. cit., p. 73.

4. See here Robert Louis Jackson, op. cit., chapter II.

5. I do think, however, that a textual analysis would bear out my claim.

6. There is also the further and somewhat more analytical counter to Dostoevsky to the effect that if human freedom is an illusion then it cannot be correct to assert 'Freedom is what makes us human'. This, of course, gains force only if 'human' is taken literally. That we are tempted to reject this counter —or at least feel dissatisfied with it—exhibits, I think, a tendency to take 'human' in such contexts in a normative and problematic way.

4

WILLIAM JAMES:
THE DILEMMA
OF DETERMINISM

William James, a major American philosopher and psychologist, believes, like Dostoevsky, that the implications of determinism are such that if determinism is true, morality loses its essential rationale and life becomes meaningless. He also agrees with Dostoevsky that in examining this problem we must keep constantly in mind not only the fact that man is a reasoner but also that he has deep emotional and practical needs. James stresses repeatedly that no adequate philosophy can ignore such needs. When we take these needs into account, James claims, we will come to see that a Holbachian world-view is intolerable. James's singular contribution consists in his turning these familiar considerations into a distinctive philosophical argument for accepting indeterminism.

A determinist maintains that for every event or state whatsoever (let us call it Y) there are some antecedent conditions, that is, events or states (let us call them X) such that when such antecedent conditions occur, events of type Y will occur. That is, for anything whatsoever there are sufficient conditions for its occurrence. This is what is meant by saying that every event has a cause and every action has a cause. Indeterminism, of course, is the denial of this doctrine. It is the belief that there are *some* events, including some actions, that do not have causes—antecedent conditions—sufficient to bring about their occurrence such that whenever these antecedent conditions obtain, just that type of event or action occurs.

Holbach and Darrow write as if science and philosophical analysis have indisputably established the truth of determinism. And for all his fulminations against determinism, Dostoevsky seems to assume that, from a rational standpoint at any rate, determinism is reasonably well established. James, by contrast, contends that it is impossible to prove or disprove determinism or indeterminism. And if James is right here, this would seem to entail agnosticism in this conceptual area. How, then, can

James's "The Dilemma of Determinism" be taken as a rational defense of indeterminism?[1]

In this way: James argues that if we come to see vividly some of the implications of determinism, and if we further come to recognize that there is nothing irrational or bogus about the concept of chance, we will find that it is more reasonable to adopt an indeterministic or libertarian view than a deterministic view. That is to say, we will find it more rational to assume that we have a free will than to assume the truth of determinism.

In trying to show that it is more reasonable to assume that our wills are free, James makes two very important assumptions, both of which are challengeable. (Of course, this is not to say that they are not justified.) They are as follows:

1. Where we must choose between two or more theories or beliefs, none of which can in fact be verified or confirmed, we are entitled to assume that theory or belief which appears to us to be on the whole the most reasonable of the available theories or beliefs.

2. We theorize in order to attain a scheme of things that will give us the most subjective satisfaction. (Quite in line with the general thrust of his argument, James, faced with the obvious retort that this is not the only reason we theorize, could have replied that this is the most fundamental reason we theorize.)

These two assumptions are very important for James's argument, for if determinism is both theoretically unprovable (if there is no good evidence for or against its truth) and if it runs against one's sense of moral fittingness, then, given the correctness of James's assumptions, one has a perfectly legitimate right to reject determinism. And in exercising that right, one need not at all be a romantic irrationalist or any kind of irrationalist at all.

Now, James in effect continues, determinism does not give us *subjective* satisfaction (or at least it would not if we were clear-headed), and if one inspects the matter carefully, it does not appear to be the more reasonable theory. Thus, if James is correct in his judgments and assumptions here, we are perfectly justified in rejecting determinism and in opting for indeterminism, even though we do not know, and may never be able to find out, whether indeterminism is true. In short, if an unprovable belief goes against our moral and human demands, we have a good reason to reject it and accept an equally unprovable belief that squares well with these demands.

James also stresses that it is not disagreements about the facts that divide determinists and indeterminists, but basically nonrational factors. They have, he argues, different faiths or different "postulates of rationality." It is *sentiment* that finally makes us determinists or indeterminists.

However, it is James's intent to show that the indeterminist's sentiment is the more reasonable sentiment.

To make his claim persuasive, one of the first things James must do is to explain why so many reflective people turn away from indeterminism as irrational or evasive, and then show why they are mistaken in such a reaction.

They reject indeterminism as irrational, James argues, because they have an "antipathy to the idea of chance." They feel that chance is somehow a bogus or an irrational notion that no rational man can tolerate. It is, à la the Underground man, a "suicide of reason" to believe in a chance world. Chance, they feel, is the very negation of all intelligibility, law, and order. A chance world would be a chaotic, irrational world; an intrinsically unpredictable event seems to be out of accord with a scientific conception of "laws of nature."

James argues that the concept of chance need not have such an unsavory connotation. It is in reality a purely negative notion. When we say something happened by chance, we do not say anything positive about it. We only say that it happens to be disconnected from everything else. If an event is a chance event, it is an event whose occurrence could not be guaranteed. A chance event or a chance occurrence might turn out to be otherwise. To believe in chance is just to admit that future volitions are not wholly determinate and that "the future may be other than and better than the past has been." To believe in chance is to believe that events are not so strictly connected that among future volitions there are not genuine open possibilities. In holding such a view, we reject the belief that if we only knew enough about antecedent conditions, then we would know that only one of the possibilities could be realized.

To give flesh to his claim, James translates it into the concrete by using an example. In the same spirit and to the same effect, I will give an example of my own. Suppose I am in the habit of circling around the classroom during exams. Suppose my desk is exactly in the middle of the front of the class. Suppose there are no obstacles to my walking around the class by starting from either the right or the left. Suppose further that people who have observed me in the past in the same classroom under the same conditions have observed that sometimes I start by going to the left, but on an equal number of occasions I have started by going to the right. Suppose I am sitting at my desk and on this occasion I get up and circle the room by going to the right. Now isn't it just as possible, doesn't it accord just as well with the laws of nature and rationality, for me to go to the left? Let us assume that I have circled around the room by going to the right. Suppose, as James puts it, that the powers governing the universe put the clock back with all that it contained, including me and my memories, to where I was just before I decided to get up and circle the room, annihilating the time between when I got up, circled to the right, and sat down. Imagine that everything else remains the same. Now, if you are determinists you must believe that it is impossible for me on this new occasion to do anything but go to the right. Otherwise there would be an intrinsic irrationality and chaos in the universe. But, James remarks,

> . . . looking outwardly at these universes, can you say which is the impossible and accidental one, and which the rational and necessary one? I doubt if the most iron-clad determinist among you could have the slightest glimmer of light at this point. In other words, either universe *after the fact* and once there would, to our means of observation and understanding, appear just as rational as the other. There would be absolutely no criterion by which we might judge one necessary and the other a matter of chance.[2]

Isn't it simply an unverifiable dogma to believe with the determinists that on both occasions I could have only circled by going to the right? They have no evidence at all for such a claim. My circling either to the right or to the left is equally compatible with what science and common-sense observation teaches us about the world. Neither is intrinsically irrational. That there should be such genuinely open possibilities does not commit us to any antiscientific obscurantism.[3]

James drives home this point. These alternatives, like many others that offer themselves to human beings, fit in well with "the kinds of things already here and based in the existing frame of things." How is order and rationality being upset, given this kind of discontinuity in the frame of things? We are not speaking of some 'absolute accident', some 'gratuitous act' that is absolutely irrelevant to the rest of the world. " 'Free will' does not say that *everything* that is physically conceivable is morally possible. It merely says that of alternatives that really tempt our will, more than one is really possible."[4] There is no claim that *everything* is possible or that we may not have reasonable expectations that people will act in one way rather than in another.

An indeterminist most certainly need not make such a wild claim; what he does reject is the idea that human beings could never have done other than what in fact they do. He is asserting that it is not always the case that any event Y is related to some earlier event or set of events X, such that when events of type X occur events of type Y must also occur. There are in reality some unrealized possibilities. We cannot prove that we live in a chance world, but it seems rational enough to believe that we do, for it is compatible with all our scientific and practical expectations and does not have the unfortunate corollaries that determinism has. It is of central importance to realize that we have no adequate grounds for assuming that a chance world such as James has described is an irrational one. In making it appear that it would be, both Holbach and Dostoevsky have led us down the garden path.

Yet, as James has stressed, we cannot disprove determinism either, and it does *seem* to fit in rather well with our scientific ways of thinking. It seems quite natural and almost inevitable to assume that everything has causes and that, in theory at least, if we look hard enough we will be able to discover what are the causes of a given occurrence. Although it is James's intent to argue against such claims, he sees the force in the quite natural conviction, when such reflections are engaged in, that it is absurd to say that a given occurrence has no cause as distinct from saying that we do not know its cause. And given such beliefs about the pervasiveness of causality, it is very easy to come to believe what James wishes to deny, namely, that all events have necessary causes or connections.

Why, then, according to James, should we reject determinism? Because, if determinism is true, judgments of regret and moral judgments in general become impossible or at least irrational. In fact, it looks as if morality itself becomes impossible, for it would not make sense to say that anything ought to be or ought not to be done unless it also made sense to say that at least some actions could have been different from what they in fact are. But if determinism is true, we must say that for any state, including any action whatsoever, when that state obtains certain other states must come about. Thus, nothing could have happened in a way different from the way it in fact happened, for if determinism is true, all events without exception have some definite set of determining conditions such that when these determining conditions occur, an event of the type in question must occur. If we are to be determinists, we should, like Holbach and Darrow, and unlike Hobbes and Mill, be hard determinists. That is, we should admit that no one is ultimately responsible for what he does or does not do, that no one can really help doing what he does, and that freedom and consequently morality rest on an illusion. James rejects soft determinism with scorn as "a quagmire of evasion." Freedom is not necessity understood or anything remotely like that. (In Chapter 6 the exact differences between hard determinists and soft determinists will be carefully explored.)

James admits—as we have seen—that finally the choice between determinism and indeterminism is a *personal* one. As comes out clearly in his correspondence with the British philosopher F. H. Bradley, James was fully aware of the extent to which such commitments finally rest on sentiment and of the degree to which, even among reflective and non-evasive men, such sentiments vary.[5] James grants that there are features about indeterminism that are in certain respects repugnant, but when we weigh it all, when we consider with care the moral implications of determinism, together with the complete lack of proof for it, we should say that in a deeper and more pervasive way it is more irrational to be a determinist than to be an indeterminist.

II

How much, if anything, of what James says should we accept? I would say quite categorically that James has done at least one very valuable thing: He has pointed out that those who accept indeterminism are not *ipso facto* committed to believing in some irrational, completely unpredictable world in which anything can happen. To be an indeterminist, it is only necessary to believe that it is not true that for all events there is an invariable sequence between events of the same type. This indeterminist belief may be a mistaken belief; *perhaps* analysis will someday show it to be an incoherent one—I, at least, deeply suspect it is—but given the present state of analysis, it is not an irrational, antiscientific belief that only an obscurantist could hold.[6]

James has also raised the very important question of whether determinism or indeterminism can be proven. Can they? If they cannot, is it not perfectly rational to believe in indeterminism if it makes *more sense* out of your life? To answer this question in the affirmative is not to give one to understand that, like Dostoevsky, we are going to believe it even though it is positively unreasonable to believe it. And it is to imply that since there are no good grounds for believing in its denial, and since within human beings there is a very deep need to believe in it, it is perfectly legitimate to believe in indeterminism. In fact, under such circumstances we positively should believe in it.

This is a very important point, and James's general position here is a reasonable one. But before we can be justified in accepting it, there are several points in James's claims that need careful scrutiny.

1. Is determinism really incompatible with moral freedom or the freedom of conduct? Does determinism really make life senseless? It is not at all obvious that it is so incompatible with freedom or that its acceptance does make life meaningless. Since the Greek philosopher Chrysippus (280–205 B.C.), there have been many distinguished philosophers who have asserted that determinism and human freedom *are* compatible. We cannot simply accept James's unargued claim that such a position is a "quagmire of evasion," most particularly since he states the position he rejects in an unjustifiably pejorative light. We shall examine the compatibility thesis and soft determinism in later chapters. But unless such a position is mistaken, James's claim here, and Dostoevsky's as well, collapses. Given the naturalness and greater simplicity of deterministic

assumptions, indeterminism remains what James calls a "live option" only on the assumption that if determinism is true, morality is senseless.

2. Has James actually succeeded in establishing or giving us good reason to believe that indeterminism is really more satisfactory emotionally? To be sure, it does not imply an irrational world, but does it give us the kind of freedom that we want and need for moral agency? It seems to me that it does not.

If I hold myself responsible for a certain act or for maintaining a certain attitude toward people, I must indeed believe that I am not constrained or compelled to act in the way I act—that I am my own master in the respects for which I hold myself responsible. In that way I must be a free agent in order to be a responsible agent. An indeterministic freedom would just be something that inexplicably and ineluctably happened to me. It would not be something that flowed from my character and resulted from my own deliberations and expressed my intentions. But the freedom that we want and need in our practical living—including our moral relations with others—would be this sort of freedom, not some unpredictable and quite mysterious indeterministic freedom. In order to make sense of moral action, there indeed must be a sense in which the future is genuinely open to us. That is, there must be *a sense* in which we can do other than what we do, for we cannot be complete prisoners of our past and be moral agents. But our moral acts must also be in keeping with our character, and they must be recognizable as our acts; that is, they must be in accordance with our intentions and under our control. This makes them predictable and not—as they apparently would be, if indeterminism were true—intrinsically unpredictable acts. An act for which we are morally responsible must not be an incalculable occurrence within us but something we deliberately do.[7] The freedom we are searching for and the freedom James needs to make sense of the moral life is not indeterministic freedom.

3. James simply assumes that you must be an indeterminist to believe in chance, but this is simply false. Determinists, as readily as indeterminists, can allow for chance in some perfectly straightforward sense of that term. Thus, they do not have to deny plain facts.

Consider these sentences:

(1) We met by chance in Chicago.
(2) It was by pure chance that I got this job.
(3) By chance I tuned in when Serkin was playing.

These are perfectly meaningful sentences that could be used to make true assertions. But a determinist, as well as an indeterminist, can use such sentences to make true as well as false assertions. They admit of a deterministic interpretation. Consider (3) first. What I ordinarily would mean in using 'chance' here is that the tuning in on Serkin was not deliberate, foreseen, or expected on my part. I did not notice Serkin's name in the program guide sometime before and deliberately turn on the radio to hear him. I did not even say to myself, "I would like to hear Serkin play the *Appassionata* or at least some Beethoven" and restlessly search for a station playing a Serkin recording. When I say 'by chance' I mean to deny that the situation was anything like that just described, and I am giving you to understand that I did not expect, could not have foreseen, and so on, that I would hear Serkin playing at that time and place. I imply by using 'by chance' that given the knowledge available to me at that time, I could not have predicted that I would hear Serkin when I turned on the radio. I do not at all need to deny that there were per-fectly determinate causes for my turning on the radio and for the Serkin record to be playing at that time. We can and should say similar things for sentence (2).

Sentence (1) is not radically different, and it admits of a perfectly deterministic interpretation. When I say we met by chance in Chicago, I mean to deny that we met by design, or that either of us could have expected that we would meet there, or that we had the slightest reason to believe that we might meet there. In saying that we met by chance, we could properly assert that part of what is meant is that from either a knowledge of the relevant antecedent conditions that determined my going to Chicago, or from a knowledge of the relevant antecedent condi-tions that determined your going to Chicago, it could not be predicted that we would meet in Chicago. Because of this we can say that our meeting is a 'chance event' or a 'chance occurrence'. A person with only the knowl-edge of one of these series of causes could not have predicted our meet-ing. But it should not be forgotten that the chance meeting had perfectly determinate causes, and that a person with a knowledge of both causal series could have predicted our meeting.

It is tempting to reply to such a deterministic rebuttal by saying, "You're not talking about *real chance* while James is. Surely the deter-minist can properly say what he says, but it is not really chance he is talking about. Real chance implies an actual disconnectedness in causal sequences and genuine future contingencies. It is not relative to what anyone happens to know about a given causal series."

This reply, natural as it is, clearly will not do. After all, the uses of 'chance' in the preceding sample sentences were perfectly ordinary uses of 'chance'. Why shouldn't we assume that this is what is being talked about when we are talking about chance? To assert just like that that they are not 'real chance' events begs the issue concerning what chance events are. It sounds parallel to 'They aren't real diamonds' where there is an agreed-on criterion for 'real diamonds'. But 'real chance', like 'true champions', is at best an unanalyzed term with no clear paradigms (standard examples) in ordinary life and usage. Moreover, my quite deterministically explicable sentences (1), (2), and (3) are evident paradigms of an ordinary employment of 'chance.'[8]

Beyond this, it is not at all clear that we—James or anyone else—have any clear understanding at all of what is being talked about when we speak of 'actual disconnectedness in the causal sequence' or 'genuine contracausal future contingencies'. What counts as a 'genuinely future contingency' that is not explainable deterministically? Perhaps some account of this could be given along indeterministic lines, but until a very careful elucidation is given of what is being said, we do not have anything sufficiently definite to be true, acceptable, or even false. On the other hand, we do have a perfectly ordinary and familiar set of uses of 'chance' that are quite compatible with determinism. In short, James seems to be on very shaky ground here.

4. Finally, we should ask: Is it so clear that there is no evidence at all for determinism or against indeterminism? Is it so evident that they are unprovable beliefs? If they are not, then James could not, and would not, argue that we have a right to believe here what gives us the greatest satisfaction. In such a circumstance that would indeed be a defense of superstition and irrationalism. And James would no more make such a defense than would Holbach.

It is very commonly assumed nowadays that neither determinism nor indeterminism is provable. I do not think that is nearly so evident as is usually assumed; in fact, I do not think that such a claim is even true. In the next chapter we shall examine that complex issue.

NOTES

1. See William James, *Essays in Pragmatism* (New York: Hafner, 1951), pp. 37–64.
2. Ibid., p. 45.
3. It is legitimate to argue against James that cause and effect relationships are not supposed to be rational—that is, the term 'rational' is not properly applied to them. But if this is so, it is natural to continue, 'irrational' is equally inapplicable to them and it is thus pointless, indeed senseless, to say, as James does, that either event is irrational or intrinsically irrational. I agree that such terms should not be applied to talk of cause and effect. But in the face of assertions—indeed illegitimate—that it is irrational to so speak of chance, such a denial, with its stretch of language, is intelligible and has a reasonable point.
4. Ibid., pp. 46–47.
5. J. C. Kenna, "Ten Unpublished Letters from William James, 1842–1910, to Francis Herbert Bradley, 1846–1924," *Mind*, vol. LXXV, no. 299 (July, 1966), pp. 309–331.
6. I indeed suspect that indeterministic concepts are incoherent concepts. But that this suspicion of mine is justified needs to be established.

7. I have talked for the sake of the argument here as if it made sense to speak of acts as occurrences within us. In fact I do not think that it does. If I am correct in thinking that, the general line of my argument here is further strengthened.

8. To assert that sentences such as 'We met by chance in Chicago' are paradigmatic, standard, and unpuzzling uses of 'chance' is not to deny that there are clear paradigms of what indeterminists call '*real* chance'.

5

DETERMINISM,
FATALISM,
AND PREDESTINATION

I

There is one crucial matter that we have not yet considered, namely, just what is the evidence for the truth of determinism? Holbach and Darrow evidently considered it to be overwhelmingly strong. Science, the history of mankind, logic, and philosophy, they believe, attest to its truth. Yet there are logicians, philosophers, and scientists who are not determinists. Holbach and Darrow confidently assert the truth of determinism, but, as far as I can see, they give us very little evidence for its truth. In a dramatic way they call our attention to determinism by exhibiting the depth of environmental, biological, and cultural conditioning on a man's actions, character and very conception of the world. However, a recognition of this is perfectly compatible with a *rejection* of determinism. An indeterminist needs only to say that there are no sufficient conditions for the occurrence of *some* actions such that when these conditions occur the action *must* subsequently occur. No one in his right mind is going to say that nothing is caused. Conditioning of all sorts runs very deep, but a recognition of the truth of this is compatible with an affirmation of the truth of the claim that not all actions have sufficient conditions, that is, it is not true for every action that an action of that type *must* occur when certain other events or states occur.

Holbach mainly declaims determinism. He does little to establish its truth. James thinks, as we have noted, that both determinism and indeterminism are unprovable, and John Stuart Mill and Moritz Schlick, both staunch determinists, agree with him. But they disagree about which of these unprovable assumptions is the more reasonable. (No party to the dispute thinks it is a matter of "you pays your money, you takes your choice.") James, we have seen, argues that indeterminism is the more reasonable assumption to make, and Mill and Schlick claim the opposite. I think the matter is not that simple and that it is not true that there is no evidence at all in favor of either determinism or indeterminism. It seems to me there is some reasonable evidence for determinism, at least as far as macroentities (tables, Ping-Pong balls, human beings, for example) are concerned, although, as we shall see, in the very nature of the case there could not be completely *decisive* evidence one way or the other.

Let us, for a moment, accept a simple characterization of determinism. Determinism is the belief that every event has a cause. Now, we cannot prove that every event has a cause in the same way we can prove that every red thing is a colored thing. The denial of 'Every red thing is a colored thing' is a contradiction. However, it is not contradictory, or at least it most certainly does not appear to be contradictory, to assert that not every event has a cause.

I think one of the reasons that makes some people think that determinism is almost self-evidently true is that they confuse 'Every event has a cause' with 'Every effect has a cause'. The latter, like 'Every bachelor is unmarried', is self-evidently true because it is true by definition. (Philosophers call such statements *analytic*.) But this means it reflects our linguistic usage, our determination to use words in a certain way. (I do not say that is all that it does or that it is 'language relative'. After all, the same thing could be said in German.) It exhibits the very structure, the very implicit rules or regularities, of our language. That is, with the case at hand, we *mean* by 'an effect' something that has 'a cause', so that it is senseless (meaningless) to ask whether an effect has a cause. But it is far from clear that we mean by 'event' or 'action' something that has a cause. It is not clear that 'a causeless event' or 'an action without a cause' is self-contradictory, as a 'causeless effect' clearly is. Thus, we have no good reason to believe 'Every event has a cause' is true by definition, and therefore in that way self-evidently true.

What, then, are our grounds for accepting determinism? What evidence do we have for believing it to be true? We cannot prove it, as we can a theorem in mathematics. However, since 'prove' has very context-dependent uses, our question here is (or at least should be), 'Why can't we prove it in the sense that we can give substantial evidence for believing it to be true?'.

If we say that we cannot prove it because it is an unrestricted generalization, we have said something absurd. This only means that there is a sense in which we cannot *conclusively* prove it, but a recognition of this is compatible with both the belief that we can give substantial evidence for its truth and with the belief that we could perhaps conclusively disprove it by one carefully established negative instance. If we stick to the line that no unrestricted generalization can be proven, we will be committed to saying that the statements 'All human beings capable of life have some blood' and 'All whole cows have heads' must also be said to be unprovable, for we have not and cannot examine all human beings or all cows (past, present, and future). But to maintain that such generalizations are unprovable is absurd. We have overwhelming evidence—observational and theoretical—for the truth of such unrestricted generalizations. In that perfectly legitimate sense they are so completely proven that one would have to be mad to deny they are true.

However, there is a difference between 'Every event has a cause' and 'Every human being has some blood'. The former, surface appearances to the contrary notwithstanding, is more like 'Every substance has some solvent' than it is like 'Every human being has some blood'. The 'some' in 'Every substance has some solvent' makes it immune to both conclusive confirmation or disconfirmation. If a given substance does not dissolve in any of the known solvents, the statement still is not conclusively disconfirmed, for its defender can always reply, "I didn't say 'any of the known solvents.' I only said '*some* solvent'." 'A cause' in 'Every event has a cause' means 'some cause or other' and not something definite like 'a heart,' 'an ounce of blood', or 'antecedent condition C'.

The determinist does not commit himself to anything very definite when he asserts that every event has a cause. Thus, 'Every event has a cause', like 'Every substance has some solvent', or the logically parallel statement, 'Every human being has some anxieties', is neither conclusively confirmable nor disconfirmable, and thus in a definite sense is not *conclusively* provable. However, 'not conclusively provable' does not establish that it is not provable at all; that there can be no conclusive evidence for or against the truth of the statement does not establish that there is no evidence or even no substantial evidence for or against the truth of the statement. Consider 'Every human being has some anxieties'. On both theoretical grounds and experiential grounds, it is reasonable to believe that that statement is true, although like 'Every substance has some solvent', it cannot be either conclusively confirmed or disconfirmed. Why isn't 'Every event has a cause' establishable, or perhaps even established, in exactly the same way?

There is a crucial complicating factor in 'Every event has a cause'. While 'an anxietyless human being' or 'an indissoluble substance' is perfectly conceivable, it is not clear that 'a causeless event' is conceivable. It is not clear that we know what we are talking about when we use the phrase 'causeless event'. We are very unclear as to what could count as one, and we know that if something happens it always makes sense to look for its causes. Imagine this chapter to be in the form of a lecture given over a kind of TV screen where you could not only hear and see me, but could also talk back to me by speaking in front of your TV screen. Suppose you suddenly hear a loud bang coming from the TV studios, and you ask me, 'What made that bang?' and I reply 'Nothing, it just happened'. You would not accept that. In fact, you would find my reply quite unintelligible. We may not know the cause of something, but it most surely appears to be the case that we always assume when something happens that it has a cause or, more accurately, that there are causes for its happening.

Do we even understand what it would be like not to make this assumption? It is not clear that we do. 'Causeless event' seems to be utterly indeterminate. We do not understand its use; in fact, we are not at all confident that it has a use. This being so, the very notion of a 'causeless event' is very problematical. To put the point rather differently, it is crucial for 'Every event has a cause' that there be something that could count against the claim that such a statement or putative statement is true. That is to say, we need something comparable to a substance that resisted all known solvents or a human being who, even in the most trying circumstances, never showed anxiety. In these cases we can readily conceive of some observable state of affairs that would count for or against the truth of what is being asserted. Can we do the same thing for 'an event that has no cause'? What, let us ask again, is a causeless event? What would this be like? Even in theory, what would count as one? Will we admit, for example, that there is or even could be an illness without a cause? Does it even make sense to assert 'Jones feels ill but his illness has no cause'? That certainly sounds like gobbledygook.[1]

This difficulty may arise from too anthropomorphic a reading of determinism. If we once stop thinking of 'a cause' as a label for a mysterious kind of thing or process, perhaps this difficulty would not arise. Let Y stand indifferently for any event, process, state, or action. The thesis of determinism is that for any Y whatsoever there are some sets of antecedent conditions such that when antecedent conditions of the type that were sufficient to produce Y occur again, another event (process, state, action) of type Y must also occur. The 'must' here is *not* a logical must, as in 'Every red thing must be colored', but the 'must' of causal necessity, as in 'If I am decapitated, I must die' or 'If water reaches a certain temperature under certain conditions, it must boil'. The determinist, in short, is claiming that for every event there is a 'must' that functions like the 'must' in 'If a chicken's head is cut off, it must die'. That is, he is claiming that there are sufficient conditions for the occurrence of every event, action, process, or state such that when these conditions obtain, nothing else could occur. An indeterminist must at least deny that this is *always* so. (He could deny that this is ever so, but that is patently absurd.) In speaking of 'a causeless action' or 'a causeless event' we should mean, in order to speak intelligibly, that there are some actions or events that do not have sufficient conditions; that is, there are no antecedent states-of-affairs such that if they occur the action or event in question must occur.

Problems still remain about the testability of the deterministic thesis.

Just how do we decide for a specific event, action, state, or process whether it does or does not have sufficient conditions? It would seem that in practice the only test is whether it is predictable or retrodictable. (By 'retrodiction' recall we mean 'backward-prediction'; that is, the inferring in a reliably testable manner from present data what happened in the past.)

I have carefully avoided characterizing determinism in terms of universal predictability, for there are those determinists who believe that there are certain events—individual *quanta*, for example—that are not predictable even in principle, but they still want to assert that every event has a cause. But many determinists, including Mill, define 'determinism' in terms of universal predictability. It is certainly tempting to do so, for, after all, our *evidence* for claiming that an event has a cause, that it actually has sufficient conditions for its occurrence, is our ability to predict it or retrodict it. If, alternatively, we say, "It must have a cause even though its cause cannot possibly be ascertained, no matter how much we know," have we not made determinism into an unprovable dogma after all? Is not any hope for proving determinism or for establishing it as a reasonable hypothesis tied to the hope that we can achieve ever greater accuracy in prediction and retrodiction? When Darrow claimed that the history of science attests to the truth of determinism, should we not take him as alluding to the fact that we have continued to increase the range and accuracy of our predictions? Is there any theoretical reason to believe that we cannot extend them indefinitely? Is determinism not a reasonable extrapolation from our actual practices in science and everyday life?

There are two things that need to be said here. First, there are some who will contend that when we reason in this way we are still living with the bogeyman of the nineteenth century and the nightmare of 'scientific determinism'. Scientific practice is no longer exclusively deterministic. It typically uses 'statistical laws' rather than 'causal laws'.

In physics we do not operate with deterministic assumptions on the microlevel. It is impossible in theory, and not just in practice, to predict precisely the exact position and velocity of an individual microparticle. We can predict the position and velocity of a 'swarm of quantum particles', but not of individual particles. This seems to count as a disconfirming instance of determinism when it is treated as a thesis about universal predictability. There are, however, physicists and philosophers who, while accepting the same data from microphysics as do indeterminists, place another theoretical interpretation on the data and deny that it is *logically* impossible simultaneously to predict the exact position and velocity of individual microparticles. Instead, they assert only that given the present development of physics, including its present theoretical framework, it is impossible to so predict the exact position and velocity of an individual particle. They do not deny that this is a logical possibility. The upshot of this is that microphysics does not present a clear case of a refutation of determinism.

However, even if it did, it would not do anything to show that macro-events, including human actions, were not determined. The behavior of clusters of microparticles is not so unpredictable, and from a certain perspective all large objects, including human beings, can be viewed as a cluster of microparticles.

In viewing determinism as a reasonable extrapolation from our actual practices in everyday life and science, the second point that needs to be considered here is that there seem to be certain intrinsic limitations to prediction. *Inventions* and *creative* works seem to be unpredictable in principle. But remember that a determinist who links determinism to theoretical universal predictability commits himself to the claim that on the basis of a knowledge of the state of the world at a given time and the natural laws according to which its state at any time is related to its states at other times, it would be possible to infer unerringly and exactly what the state of the world was or will be at any earlier or later time. Mill applies this to human behavior:

> . . . given the motives which are present to an individual's mind, and given likewise the character and disposition of the individual, the manner in which he will act might be unerringly inferred; that if we knew the person thoroughly, and knew all the inducements which are acting upon him, we could foretell his conduct with as much certainty as we can predict any physical event. . . . No one who believed that he knew thoroughly the circumstances of any case, and the characters of the different persons concerned, would hesitate to foretell how all of them would act. Whatever degree of doubt he may in fact feel arises from the uncertainty whether he really knows the circumstances, or the character of some one or other of the persons, with the degree of accuracy required; but by no means from thinking that if he did know these things, there could be any uncertainty what the conduct would be.[2]

It has been argued that this is a piece of mythology, for one cannot so exactly predict the occurrence of an invention or a creative work of art. That is, here we have a kind of human act that cannot be predicted. The 'cannot' here is logical and not due to any human weakness or, as Holbach and Mill would put it, to ignorance. It has been argued that for someone to have predicted the invention of the cotton gin, he would have had to be the inventor of the cotton gin and then trivially he would not be predicting its invention for he would already have invented it. For someone prior to the composing of Beethoven's Ninth Symphony to have predicted that it would be written, it would be necessary that he and not Beethoven be the composer of the Ninth Symphony. An expert musicologist, who had exhaustively studied Beethoven's life and his works prior to the Ninth Symphony, might very well have predicted that he would have written an elaborate symphony with a choral ode at the end or even something much more exact than that. But he *could not* predict it *with perfect accuracy;* that is, he could not predict the writing of the Ninth Symphony, or else he, and not Beethoven, would have been its creator.

Where an event is *entirely new,* as an invention or artistic creation must be by definition, it is not predictable *in principle* because it is not describable with exactitude prior to its invention, so we could not say with the exactitude necessary for precise prediction *what* it is that we are trying to predict. We can and do predict the general *genre,* but that is all. This shows that there are some events which are theoretically unpredictable, and this refutes determinism—or, where not linked to universal predictability, at least renders it an untestable dogma.

This argument is not sound, for, among other things, it leaves retrodiction entirely out of the picture. Once the invention is made or the creative work brought into being, we can work backward to the conditions that gave rise to it. This 'backward prediction'—retrodiction—that has not at all been shown to be theoretically impossible, and is in fact often used, shows that there are sufficient conditions for the occurrence of the invention and the creative work, just as there are sufficient conditions for all events or actions. Thus, determinism has not been refuted by this argument from creativity or shown to be an untestable dogma.

What I have tried to do here is to make the claim of determinism somewhat clearer and to show that it is not true, as it is frequently assumed, that it is an unprovable dogma. It is a vague claim, a claim that we do not *know* to be true, but it is a claim that we do not know to be false. Moreover, the thesis of determinism has not been shown to be one of the type that is so amorphous and problematical that it cannot be shown to be either true or false or probably true or false. The crucial point is to try to ascertain whether there really is good evidence for accepting determinism as being probably true. It seems to me that there is. In fact, looked at in one way, it seems to be an evident bit of enlightened common sense. Yet, as Dostoevsky and James show, it seems to have, morally speaking, paradoxical consequences. Does it really? And (1) is it, as I believe it to be, a reasonable common-sense belief and (2) is it a common-sense belief that we should accept?

II

These questions will be discussed in subsequent chapters; the remainder of this chapter will untangle determinism from two matters with which it is frequently confused, but with which it plainly ought not to be confused.

First, we need to distinguish between determinism and fatalism. *Fatal-*

ism is the point of view that claims that, for all events and actions, what happens in the future does not depend on a man's choice or action in the present. If something is fated to happen, then it will happen no matter what human beings now choose to do. Mary Tyrone, in the passage quoted in Chapter 2, exhibits a fatalistic attitude. She believes that no matter what she does now she cannot stop taking dope and that her husband cannot possibly alter his miserly ways. She generalizes that to all human behavior. The soldier is being a fatalist if he believes that a certain bullet has "his name on it" and that no matter what he does, when his time has come, it has come. What will be, will be. His death is a matter of fate over which he has no control. Oedipus was also being a fatalist when he said, "Yet I know this much: no sickness and no other thing will kill me. I would not have been saved from death if not for some strange fate."

A fatalist believes that all events are fated, that for any situation X there are certain subsequent events that are bound to happen no matter what *he* does, no matter what choices he makes or actions he takes. For everything we do, we are like Oedipus with respect to killing his father. Our present strivings to avoid certain catastrophes are utterly pointless, for our actions are never effective in altering the course of things. The only wise thing to do is to develop an attitude of complete passivity before events. Fatalism can become generalized into a feeling of futility and helplessness about all of life. Any effort to make a better world is benighted and pointless. It is out of our hands whether the future will be better or worse.

Now against such laments a determinist could quite properly say: But human actions *sometimes* do effect what will happen in the future. Freddy can pass physics if he will only buckle down for the next week. We can lessen tensions in the East if we recognize China. To say this need not imply that the government's stubbornness or folly on this issue is uncaused, or that Freddy's indolence or underachieving is not caused. It only implies that human actions, like all other events or states, affect the future. This a fatalist must deny. But in this he is surely mistaken, for he neglects to note that some events depend, or partially depend, on human choices or actions.

Even a determinist such as Holbach, who believes that past causes necessitate future consequences in a mechanical way, grants that present choices are sometimes genuinely effective in the future, in the sense that what occurs in the future depends or partially depends on them.[3] The *emotional reaction* to determinism may be very like the emotional reaction to fatalism. Since things are the necessary result of the past, they can never turn out to be different than they are. Recognizing this, one may come to *feel* helpless about what will happen in the future. Still, *the conceptual belief of fatalism is logically incompatible with determinism at a crucial point*. What is to happen in the future, the fatalist argues, cannot possibly be altered by present human actions or choices. But this is in effect a denial that certain events (our present actions or choices) are part of the causal network. *To deny this is in effect to deny the truth of determinism*. Fatalism and determinism, far from being the same thing, are in fact logically incompatible.

This will leave some people dissatisfied. There are some who have a feeling of hopelessness, a sense of fatality, that they think *must* go with determinism. I sometimes have these feelings, too. But determinism does not imply fatalism in any tolerably precise sense of the term 'fatalism'. Is there actually an intelligible claim undergirding this feeling of fatality that often goes with determinism? It is not clear that there is. We shall return to this in subsequent chapters when we discuss hard determinism.

Predestination is something else again. It should be divided into *theological* and *rationalistic* conceptions of predestination. Let us consider theological predestination first. When people speak of an event as having been predestined or foreordained to happen, they almost always, in our culture anyway, imply the existence of some purposive agent "behind" or in the universe, or at least some distinctive force in the universe—like the Greek notion of *diké*—which brings the event about or makes things happen in the way they do. There is some "guiding force" operating in or at least upon the world. That is to say, some deity brought it about or some *diké* made it happen that way. Fatalism does not logically require predestination, although in a Calvinist-type religion they as a matter of fact happen to go together. All a person need claim in order to be a fatalist is that our present actions and choices will not materially affect what will happen to us in the future. He need have no theory at all about whether there is somebody or some mysterious something behind the scenes directing the whole show.

More importantly, a determinist need not believe in predestination, for a determinist need not assume that there is a purposive agent or force behind the world or some *logos* that orders things in a definite way. He may very well not even understand what this means. He may even think it is a meaningless or at least an incoherent conception. As a determinist, he commits himself only to the belief that for any event or action, given certain conditions, such and such must happen; for example, if Smith's head is lopped off, then he must die. But the determinist need not at all believe that there must be some being who made or directs the universe in such a way that Smith's head must come off. If Smith's head is cut off, then he will die; if a given event occurs, then another given event must follow, the determinist claims. However, he need say nothing about what there must be *period* or about 'how things were in the beginning.'

We shall now briefly consider *rationalistic predestination*. Instead of

God or a *diké,* such theories commit us to the belief that there is a *Logos,* a rational principle of intelligibility or a sufficient reason, so that it is not logically possible that there could have been a different state of affairs from the actual state of affairs. Everything that is or will be is necessitated by this "rational principle." The universe has a sufficient reason. That is, if we only knew enough, if we could only see things from an eternal point of view instead of a temporal point of view, we would come to recognize that the world could not have been other than it is; that the actual world is also the *only logically possible* world. If we generalize 'Everything has a reason', we come up with such a view. But, again, a determinist need not be committed to such a rationalistic view of things. Having distinguished it from determinism, I shall ignore it, for it is very implausible and scarcely intelligible. In short, fatalism and predestination have no plausibility at all, but determinism has.

NOTES

1. 'Every event has a cause' may not be so different from 'Every human being has some anxieties' as the argument given in the preceding paragraph would have it. After all, if we always *assume,* as I have alleged, that when something happens it has a cause, then the denial of that statement must be intelligible too, unless what we are assuming is analytic. (Even then it would be 'intelligible' in the way self-contradictory statements are intelligible.) After all, we cannot *assume* something unless it is intelligible. But then we must have some understanding of a key element in the denial of my assumption, that is, 'a causeless event'.

   There is force in this counter, and if well taken it would strengthen my argument that the deterministic thesis is open to confirmation and infirmation. Yet it does seem utterly mystifying to conclude or even think that something happened but there was no cause of its happening. We have words here with no definite meaning.

2. J. S. Mill, *System of Logic,* book IV, chapter 2.

3. This is not to deny that a choice is itself always a causative factor, but it is to deny that what happens to us in the future is always determined by the choices we make.

6
THE COMPATIBILITY
OF FREEDOM
AND DETERMINISM

I

I have argued that we do not know whether determinism is true or false, although we do have good grounds for believing that determinism is not an unfalsifiable, unprovable dogma. I have also argued that it is not equivalent to and does not even commit one to a belief in either fatalism or predestination. They are highly implausible notions, while the thesis of determinism, as I have characterized it, is a plausible commonsensical belief for which there is some reasonable evidence. I added "as I have characterized it," for there are mechanistic types of physical determinism that attempt to characterize human actions in terms of purely nonsymbolic, physical movements that will not, I believe, stand up to rational scrutiny. I have not tried to identify a human action as a species of physical event; instead, I have been content to state determinism as the claim that both events and actions always have sufficient conditions for their occurrence.

I shall not try here to give a fuller characterization of determinism or try further to show how we might establish or disestablish it. However, I would not like to lull you into complacency about this. My argument about the testability of determinism is controversial; many questions concerning the logical status of determinism remain. In some respects we have only scratched the surface, but I do hope that I have done enough to shake up the common view that determinism is an 'unprovable dogma', 'a metaphysical article of faith'. And I hope I have done something to free determinism from some of its implausible metaphysical plumage and to make evident how deeply ingrained it is in reflective common sense.

What I now wish to consider is what I take to be the most significant question we can ask about determinism and human conduct: Is determinism compatible with our central beliefs concerning the freedom of conduct and moral responsibility? It was because they thought that such beliefs were plainly incompatible that Dostoevsky and James were so nagged by determinism. With such philosophers as Thomas Hobbes, David Hume, John Stuart Mill, Moritz Schlick, and A. J. Ayer—all staunch defenders of the compatibility thesis—there is a vast shift not only in argument but also in attitude. There is no *Angst* over the ubiquitousness of causal laws. There is no feeling that life would be meaningless and man would be a prisoner of his past if determinism were true. Holbach is wrong. Even if determinism is true, freedom is not an illusion. The belief that it is an illusion is a philosophical confusion resting on a failure to pay sufficiently close attention either to the actual role of our concept of freedom in our lives or to the actual nature of determinism. It is such a twin failure that generates the conflicts we have been investigating.

The crucial point to note initially is that Mill and Schlick, as much as Holbach and Darrow, are thoroughgoing determinists. But they are determinists who do not believe that freedom and determinism are incompatible. James dismissed this position contemptuously with the label 'soft determinism'. For him 'soft determinism' had an emotive force similar to 'soft on Communism'. But while a summer bachelor is no bachelor at all, a soft determinist is just as much a determinist as a hard determinist. I shall continue to use the label 'soft determinism'—although I shall not use it in any derogatory sense—to refer to the view that maintains that determinism and human freedom are logically compatible. (Sometimes in the literature they are called 'compatibilists'.) A view such as Holbach's or Darrow's, which Schlick says rests on "a whole series of confusions," I shall call 'hard determinism'. (Sometimes in the literature 'hard determinists are called 'incompatibilists', for they believe freedom and determinism are incompatible.) But both hard and soft determinists agree that every event or state, including every human action or attitude, has a cause; that is, for anything whatsoever there are sufficient conditions for its occurrence.

The at least *prima facie* surprising thing is that these soft-determinists still believe in the freedom of conduct and believe that human beings are—at least sometimes, anyway—responsible moral agents capable of acting in specific situations in ways other than those in which they in fact acted. Let us see how the soft determinist argument unfolds.

II

Morality, soft determinists argue, has or should have no interest in the determinism/indeterminism controversy. Morality is indeed vitally interested in the freedom of conduct, for it only makes sense to say that men

ought to do one thing rather than another on the assumption that sometimes they can do other than what they in fact do. If no man can do
other than what he does in fact do, then all talk of what men ought
to do or what is right and wrong is indeed senseless.[1] But to be interested
in the freedom of conduct, as morality properly is, is not at all to be interested in some mysterious and no doubt illusory 'freedom of the will'.
'Freedom' has its opposite, 'compulsion' or 'coercion'. A man is free if he
does not act under compulsion. He is free when he is able to do what
he wants to do or when his acts and actions are in accordance with his
own choices and decisions, and when what he wants to do or what he
chooses is not determined by some person, force, or some disposition,
such as kleptomania, which has gained ascendency over him. He is, by
contrast, unfree to the extent that he is unable to achieve what he wants
to achieve and to act in accordance with choices based on his own
rational deliberation because of either outside influence or psychological
malaise. 'Freedom' does not mean some scarcely intelligible state of affairs,
'exemption or partial exemption from causal law' or 'breach of causal
continuity'. To be free is to have the ability and opportunity to do what
one wants to do and to act in accordance with one's own rational deliberations, without constraint and compulsion. It is something which, of course,
admits of degrees.

Mill, Schlick, and Ayer argue that an anthropomorphic view of our
language tricks us into thinking that man cannot be free if determinism
is true. People tend to think that if determinism is true, events are in
the power of other events and a person's acts or actions cannot alter the
course of events. What will happen in the future is already fixed by
immutable causal laws. But such views rest on unrealistic, anthropomorphic thinking. They are scarcely a part of a tough-minded deterministic
world perspective.

Similar anthropomorphic transformations are made with 'necessity' and
the little word 'cause'. And this, too, leads to needless befuddlement by
causing us to misunderstand the actual workings of our language. It is,
for example, terribly easy for the unwary to confuse causal and logical
necessitation. But there is a very considerable difference in the meaning
of 'must' in 'If you cut off his head, he must die' and 'If it is a square, it
must have four sides'. In the latter case—an example of logical necessitation—'having four sides' follows by virtue of the meaning of the term
'square'. The 'must' refers to this logical relationship. In the former case,
it holds in virtue of something in the world. People also infer mistakenly
that the event or effect is somehow contained in the cause. But this mystification is hardly intelligible.

There is also, as Schlick points out, a persistent confusion between
laws of nature and legal laws.[2] The word 'law' has very different meanings in such cases. Legal laws *prescribe* a certain course of action. Many

of them are intended to constrain or coerce you into acting in a certain way. But laws of nature are not prescriptions to act in a certain way. They do not constrain you; rather, they are statements of regularities, of *de facto* invariable sequences that are parts of the world. In talking of such natural laws we often bring in an uncritical use of 'force', as if the earth were being pushed and pulled around by the sun. Putting the matter this way makes one feel as if one is always being compelled or constrained, when in reality one is not. Without the anthropomorphic embellishment, it becomes evident that a determinist commits himself, when he asserts that *A* causes *B*, to the view that *whenever* an event or act of type *A* occurs, an event or act of type *B* will occur. The part about compulsion or constraint is metaphorical. It is because of the metaphor, and not because of the fact, that we come to think that there is an antithesis between causality and freedom. It is the *manner* here and not the *matter* that causes the trouble.

Demythologized and correctly conceived, causal necessity as applied to human actions is, Mill argues, simply this: Given the motives that are present to an individual's mind, and given the character and disposition of the individual, the manner in which he will act can be "unerringly inferred." That is to say, if we knew the person thoroughly, and knew all the inducements acting upon him, we could predict or retrodict his conduct with as much certainty as we can predict any physical event. This, Mill argues, is a bit of common sense and is in reality not in conflict with our operative concept of human freedom, for even if we say that all human acts are in principle predictable, this is not to say that people are acting under compulsion or constraint, for to say that their actions are predictable is not to say or even to give one to understand that they are being manipulated by anything or anybody. Being under some sort of compulsion or constraint is what limits our freedom.

III

The natural reaction to such a belief is this: If 'causal necessity' means anything, it means that no human being could, *categorically* could, do anything other in exactly similar circumstances than what he in fact does. If determinism is true, we must believe that for every event and for every action there are sufficient conditions, and when these conditions obtain, the action must occur. Since this is so, aren't all our actions in reality under constraint and thus, after all, not really free?

Soft determinists try to show that such an objection is a snarl of conceptual confusions, and that once we untangle them we will not take this incompatibilist line. A. J. Ayer makes one of the clearest and most forceful defenses of this view. His argument will be followed here, with a few supplementations from Mill.[3]

The conceptual facts we need to clarify are these: If the word 'freedom' is to have a meaning, it must be contrasted with something, for otherwise it is quite unintelligible. If I tell you I have just bought a wok, but I cannot contrast a wok with any *conceivable* thing that I would *deny* is a wok or not assert is a wok, then I have not been able to convey to you the meaning of 'wok'. In fact, if it is not so contrastable, it is indeed meaningless. The same thing obtains for any descriptive term. Thus, 'freedom', if it is to be intelligible, must be contrastable with something. There must at least be some *conceivable* situations in which it is correct to use the word and some *conceivable* situations in which it would not be correct. Yet it is plainly not an unintelligible sound, but a word with a use in our discourse. So we must look for its nonvacuous contrast. It is here where the soft determinists' initial point is critical. 'Freedom' is to be contrasted with 'constraint' or 'compulsion' rather than with 'determinism', for if we try to contrast it with 'determinism', it is far from clear that we get an intelligible contrast. It is not clear what sort of an action we would count as a 'causeless action'. But if we contrast 'freedom' and 'constraint', the contrast is clear. So we should say that a man's action is not free when it is constrained or when he is compelled to do what he does.

Suppose I say, "There is to be no smoking in the classroom." By this act I put the people in the room under constraint. I limit their freedom. But suppose Fearless Fosdick lights up anyway and I say, "Put it out, Mister, if you want to stay in the class." I in effect compel him, or at least attempt to compel him, to put it out. Being compelled or constrained to do something may very well entail that the act has a cause. But plainly the *converse* does not hold. As Ayer puts it, "From the fact that my action is causally determined it does not necessarily follow that I am constrained to do it." This is an important point to make, for to say this is in effect to claim that it does not necessarily follow from the fact that my actions are determined that I am not free. But, as I have said, if instead we take 'freedom' and 'being causally determined' as our contrastible terms, we get no clear contrast. On the other hand, even in a deterministic world we have with our above distinction between 'freedom' and 'compulsion' or 'constraint' preserved the needed contrast.

In setting out this contrast between when a man is or is not free, it is important to ask in what circumstances I can legitimately be said to be constrained and so *not* to be free.

1. *When I am compelled by another person to do what he wants.* Such a compulsion need not altogether deprive me of my power of choice. The man who compels me in a certain way need not hypnotize

me or make it physically impossible for me to go against his will. It is sufficient that he should induce me to do what he wants by making it plain to me that if I do not, he will bring about some situation that I regard as having even more undesirable consequences than the consequences of acting as he desires. In such a circumstance I am acting under constraint and involuntarily, although it is not true that my freedom to act here is utterly circumscribed.

2. *Where a man has attained a habitual ascendency over me.* Indeed, in such a circumstance I can come to want to do what Big Brother wishes. Nevertheless, I still do not act freely because I am in reality deprived of the power of choice. And in this context this means I have acquired so strong a habit of obedience that I no longer go through the process of deciding whether or not to do what the other person wants. About other matters I may still deliberate, but as regards the fulfillment of this other person's desires, my own deliberations have ceased to be an effective causal factor in my behavior. For this reason I may properly be said to be constrained since I have lost my power of choice in these matters.

3. *In order for me to be unfree in certain respects, it need not be a man or group of men that have gained ascendency over me.* A kleptomaniac cannot correctly be said to be a free agent, in respect to his stealing, because even if he does go through what appears to be deliberations about whether to steal or not to steal, such deliberations are irrelevant to his actual behavior in the respect of whether he will or will not steal. Whatever he resolved to do, he would steal all the same.[4]

This case is important because it clearly shows the difference between the man—the kleptomaniac—who is not free with respect to his stealing and an ordinary thief who is. The ordinary thief goes through a process of deciding whether or not to steal, and his decision decisively effects his behavior. If he actually resolved to refrain from stealing, he could carry out his resolution. But this is not so with the kleptomaniac. Thus, this observable difference between the ordinary thief and the kleptomaniac, quite independently of the issue of determinism, enables us to ascertain that the former is freer than the latter.

Note that in both cases, if determinism is true, then what either individual decides to do is causally determined. When we reflect on this, we are inclined to say that although it may be true that, unlike the kleptomaniac, the ordinary thief could refrain from stealing *if he chose*, yet since there is a cause, or set of causes, which causally necessitates his choosing as he does, how can he properly be said to have the power of choice? He indeed may not *feel* compelled the way the kleptomaniac does, but neither in some circumstances does the person over whom someone else has gained an ascendency. But the chains of causation by which the thief is bound are no less effective or coercive for being invisible.

Cases are being run together in this last remark that ought not to be run together. If we keep them distinct, in each instance we have a clearer contrast between actions that are free and actions that are not free. There remains a crucial difference between the thief and the kleptomaniac, namely that *the thief can choose not to steal and his choice can be effective.* The kleptomaniac cannot do that. Again, even in a deterministic world, there is a difference between the neophyte over whom someone has gained ascendency and someone who is not afflicted with kleptomania. For the latter there is no one whose very word is law, that is, who compels action. The thief, but not the kleptomaniac, feels no overwhelming compulsion to steal; and the person who must do what Big Brother dictates will feel an irresistible compulsion to do what he dictates as soon as it goes against something he would *otherwise* very much want to do, or if his rationale for doing it is effectively challenged by someone else.

A simpler case will make even clearer how it is that the notions of compulsion and constraint give the necessary contrast with our concept of freedom and not the concept of determinism or causal necessitation. There is indeed a difference between the man who suffers from a compulsion neurosis to wash his hands and the man who gets up and washes his hands because they are in fact dirty. Both actions have causes, but not all causes are constraining or compelling causes—they are not like a compulsion to wash our hands—and it is only the latter sort of causes that makes men unfree.

IV

Yet, in spite of these evident contrasts, we are still haunted, when we are in the grip of a philosophical perplexity about freedom and determinism, by the question, or muddle felt as a question: Do not all causes equally necessitate? Is it not arbitrary "to say that a person is free when he is necessitated in one fashion but not when he is necessitated in another"?

Soft determinists reply that if 'necessitate' merely means 'cause', then of course 'All causes equally necessitate' is equivalent to 'All causes equally cause'—and that is hardly news. But 'All causes equally constrain or compel' is not true. If one event is the cause of another, we are stating that the event said to be the effect would not have occurred if it had not been for the occurrence of the event said to be the cause. But this states nothing about compulsion or constraint. There is indeed an invariable concomitance between the two classes of events; but there is no compulsion in any but a metaphorical sense. Such invariable concomitance gives a necessary but not sufficient condition for causation. It is difficult and perhaps even impossible to say what constitutes a sufficient condition. But given the frequent situations in which we speak of one thing causing another without asserting or implying a compulsion or constraint, they plainly are not further necessary conditions. (When I watch a wren in the park my behavior has causes sufficient for its occurrence, but I was neither compelled, constrained, nor forced to watch the wren.) Whatever more we need beyond invariable concomitance for causation, compulsion isn't one of the elements.

Even in a deterministic world we can do other than what we in fact do, since all 'cans' are constitutionally iffy.[5] That is to say, they are all hypothetical. This dark saying needs explanation. Consider what we actually mean by saying, 'I could have done otherwise.' It means, soft determinists argue, 'I should have acted otherwise if I had chosen' or 'I would have done otherwise if I had wanted to'. And "I can do X" means 'If I want to I shall do X' or 'If I choose to do X I will do X'.

In general, soft determinists argue, we say a man is free rather than unfree when the following conditions hold:

1. He could have done otherwise if he had chosen to.
2. His actions are voluntary in the sense that the kleptomaniac's stealing is not.
3. Nobody compelled him to choose as he did.

Now it should be noted that these conditions are frequently fulfilled or satisfied. Thus, 'freedom' has a definite contrast and application. Basically it contrasts with constraint. Since this is so, we can say when it is true or probably true to assert that a man is free, and when it is false or probably false to say that he is free. Given the truth of this, it is evident that a man can act as a free and responsible moral agent even though his actions are determined. If we are not talking about some obscure notion of 'free will' but about what Schlick calls the 'freedom of conduct', freedom is after all compatible with determinism.

V

Hard determinists characteristically respond to such arguments by claiming that such an analysis does not dig deep enough. It neglects the fact that while we are frequently able to do what we will or choose, or to do what we want or dislike doing least, in no instance in our lives are we able to will other than what we will, choose other than what we choose, want other than what we in fact want, or dislike other than what we in fact dislike. This is what Holbach was driving at when he claimed that freedom is an illusion. We indeed may sometimes have freedom of *action*, but we do not have what is really crucial, namely freedom of *will* or freedom of *choice*. A man's choices and strivings characteristically flow from his character, but, as Mill puts the argument against his own position, "his character is formed *for* him, and not by him; therefore his wishing that it had been formed differently is of no use; he has no power to alter it."[6]

Mill's response here is very instructive. Because in the ultimate resort a man's character is formed for him, it does not follow that it cannot *in part* be formed by him. We may in fact desire in one way or another to alter our personalities. We indeed may not be satisfied with our lives. And sometimes when we feel this way we are in a position to alter in some measure the course of our lives. These things are sometimes in our power. Furthermore, no one willed us to be anything in particular. That we have a certain sort of character is not the result, in most instances at any rate, of a deliberate design on anyone's part. Moreover, "we are exactly as capable of making our character, if we will, as others are of making it for us." Our personalities are alterable and in fact do change in many instances. Although we have no control over the *initial formation* of our character, we, within limits, can alter it if we want to do so.

To this the hard determinist still replies that the rub is '*If* we will or *if* we want to'. To admit this, he contends, is in effect to surrender the whole point, "since the will to alter our own character is given us, not by any efforts of ours, but by circumstances which we cannot help. . . ."

Mill agrees this is "most true," and if the hard determinist sticks here we cannot dislodge him. But, Mill goes on to say, "to think that we have no power of altering our character, and to think that we shall not use our power unless we desire to use it, are very different things, and have a very different effect on the mind." A person who does not wish to alter his character cannot *feel the depressing effect* of the hard-determinist doctrine. Mill then goes on to make the crucial observation that "a person feels morally free who feels that his habits or his temptations are not his masters but he theirs. . . ." And such a man, according to Mill, is a free agent even though he is a determined part in a deterministic universe.

I believe the general drift of Mill's remarks here are a step in the right direction, but they are not without their difficulties. And these difficulties are sufficient to require a modification of Mill's views. A man can certainly very well *feel* free and still not *be* free, *feel* that he is the master of his actions when he is not. Certain neurotic and psychotic types feel that certain things are in their power when in reality they are not. But it is here that the conditions I set forth earlier, largely following Ayer, are crucial. If a man is not being compelled or constrained by another person or institution or cataclysmic occurrence (for example, an earthquake or something of that order) and if no person, force, or disposition (for example, kleptomania) has gained ascendency over him so that he cannot think and act rationally, then when he *feels* his habits or temptations are not his masters but he theirs, in those circumstances he is indeed a free moral agent. If he is a rational agent he is responsible for what it is in his power to do; and to the degree that it is in his power to do one thing rather than another, he is correctly said to be free.

NOTES

1. The point I make here is somewhat more controversial than my exposition would give one to understand. See here W. K. Frankena, "Obligation and Ability," in Max Black (ed.), *Philosophical Analysis* (Ithaca, N.Y.: 1950).
2. Moritz Schlick, *Problems of Ethics* (New York: 1939), pp. 146–148.
3. See A. J. Ayer, "Freedom and Necessity," in his *Philosophical Essays* (New York: 1963).
4. Some criminologists and psychologists have doubts about the viability of the very concept of kleptomania. And given the complexity of the phenomena referred to when we speak of 'kleptomania', it might be alleged that we should probe deeper and use quite different arguments. This may very well be so. I have been content here to expound Ayer on this point and show that it is not unreasonable to give a soft-determinist account given such psychological phenomena.
5. The phrase is J. L. Austin's, but he denies that all 'cans' are constitutionally iffy. See J. L. Austin, *Philosophical Papers* (Oxford' 1961), chapter 7.
6. J. S. Mill, *System of Logic*, book IV, chapter 2. The relevant sections are reprinted in Paul Edwards and Arthur Pap (eds.), *A Modern Introduction to Philosophy* (New York: 1965), second edition.

7

CRIME
AND RESPONSIBILITY
IN A DETERMINISTIC
WORLD

I

I want to state and then critically assess what might seem to be the Achilles' heel of soft determinism: its concept of responsibility and punishment. I shall do this by examining Moritz Schlick's classic statement of a soft-determinist conception of responsibility.[1] First I shall state Schlick's view, then a careful and celebrated criticism of it given by C. A. Campbell, and finally I shall pursue some refinements of the soft-determinist account of responsibility that might obviate Campbell's powerful criticisms. (I would like to say parenthetically that this examination will exhibit the importance of philosophical argument and counterargument. It will show how philosophers with very different philosophical commitments can come to see that certain claims just will not wash. I know that it is tempting, after one's first contact with philosophical disputes, to conclude that it is all a matter of 'you pays your money, you takes your choice'. But here, however inconclusive the *final* result, we can, if we attend carefully to the arguments, ascertain that certain points made by the disputants are quite clearly right and certain points quite clearly wrong.)

Schlick's argument in effect shows that given the soft-determinist conception of freedom that I have articulated, the conception of the central meaning of 'responsibility' in human affairs becomes perfectly determinate. He, of course, agrees that a man is not responsible if he is not free, but in the appropriate sense of 'to be free and responsible', a man need not and in fact cannot be 'free of causal law'. Rather, Schlick argues, as does Ayer, that determinism is a presupposition for responsibility. After all, if a free act is simply a causeless act—that is, something that just inexplicably happens to us by chance—then we cannot have a motive or reason for doing it. It is not something that we have deliberately done in either a responsible or an irresponsible manner, but it is simply something that has just happened to us.

What we should do, Schlick argues, is to put aside the whole question of determinism/indeterminism and consider instead the conditions under which we would actually assign responsibility and *why* we assign responsibility. Furthermore, we should consider our fundamental *aims* in assigning responsibility and in punishing or blaming someone. Schlick remarks in this context that it is barbarous to regard punishment as "a natural retaliation for past wrongs." The behavior of someone such as Clytemnestra is something we could not tolerate in a civilized world. Punishment, Schlick argues, should become solely an educative and protective measure. Our aim is holding someone responsible, and our aim in any blame or punishment should be to try to form *motives* that will help to prevent a repetition of such acts and/or to try to protect people from the harm that might come from such acts.

We are only justified in punishing human beings who are responsible moral agents. However, in many contexts we do not actually need to punish people who in fact are proper subjects for punishment. But in thinking about punishment—in trying to decide when it is a reasonable practice—we should carefully consider the following questions: *Who* is to be punished? *Who* is to be regarded as the wrongdoer? It is evident, Schlick argues, that the "original instigator of the act need not necessarily be the wrongdoer." After all, his contribution—even when we can determine who is the original instigator—can in most instances hardly be calculated; moreover, he is generally beyond the reach of educative influence. What should be recognized instead, Schlick argues, is that a man is responsible (everything else being equal) when he himself feels responsible for the act. "The immediate consciousness of freedom" of the indeterminist is in reality nothing more than the agent's knowledge that he has acted on his own desires.

It is indeed true, Schlick acknowledges, that one's desires are a function of one's character and situation; but he argues, as did Mill, that it is anthropomorphic thinking to believe that our *desires* are imposed on us by some external power and that no one has any freedom. One is free, Schlick tells us, when one can act on one's desires and one can, generally speaking, be held responsible for such actions. These are genuinely self-determined actions. In such a situation one can say that one could have acted differently, meaning that *if* one *wanted* to, one *would* have acted differently.

Where one does something reprehensible and where one did it deliberately—that is, acted on one's desires—one can be held responsible and justly be punished, where the punishment is such that it can alter one's behavior (keep one from repeating such acts). But where no amount of blaming or threatening or punishing can alter one's behavior, the person in question is not responsible for his action—is not, in the respect in question, a free or a rational agent—and he cannot be justly punished, although he may be restrained to protect others. But if determinism is true, there are causes for both the actions of the man whose behavior is alterable by punishment and the actions of the man whose behavior is not so alterable. In neither case is there any "partial exemption from causal law." Only the man whose behavior is alterable by punishment is responsible, Schlick argues. The man whose behavior is not so alterable is not responsible. Questions of moral responsibility, and thus questions of moral freedom, perhaps even require determinism; at the very least, they are certainly not incompatible with it. In fact, as Schlick protests, the whole question of determinism/indeterminism only beclouds the issue of moral freedom and responsibility. A man, as we argued in the last chapter, is free when his behavior is not compelled or coerced; and a man is responsible for behavior which is in that way free and which can be altered by punishment. Thus, freedom and responsibility are quite possible in a deterministic world.

Both hard determinists and indeterminists such as Campbell argue that there remains a fundamental sense in which no one could do other than what one does, *if determinism* is true.[2] It is indeed true that even in a deterministic world, *if* I choose to or *if* I want to or *if* I will it, I would, under certain circumstances, do something different from what I in fact do. But what I *want* or what I *will* is still out of my hands, is still completely determined. So if we accept determinism, it remains the case that in a fundamental sense no one is actually free, and thus no one can be responsible for what he does. Given the truth of determinism, there is a *fundamental and crucial sense* in which no one could do anything other than what he in fact does.

II

You will recall that critical philosophy is primarily, if not exclusively, conceptual analysis. That is, it is the analytical study of concepts, an attempt to give us some clarity about our fundamental concepts—which are often deeply perplexing.

Keeping this analytic aim in mind, consider this: If an analysis of scientific method were such that it ended up analyzing the concept of science in such a way that none of the activities that are paradigmatic of science—for example, physics, chemistry, biology, and so on—were on such an analysis really scientific, we would have excellent reasons for thinking that something had gone wrong with our analysis. Similarly, if our analysis of responsibility and punishment is such that it makes mishmash out of even our most reflective application of those concepts in everyday life, then we would have excellent, although perhaps not decisive, reasons for thinking something had gone wrong with our analysis. But, Campbell points out, Schlick's analysis entails a number of consequences that are simply too paradoxical to be acceptable. That is to say, Campbell is maintaining that Schlick's analysis does make mishmash out of those concepts and so must be rejected as inadequate.

What are the particulars of Campbell's claim? First, on Schlick's account people could correctly be said to be responsible who are *not* ordinarily regarded as responsible agents. Second, some people who are normally taken to be responsible are not, on Schlick's theory, regarded as responsible. And, finally, there are contexts where we assign degrees of responsibility where, on Schlick's theory, we could not.

Campbell's objections need translation into the concrete. Given Schlick's analysis, Campbell claims, we could hold dogs and babies responsible for their acts. Their behavior can indeed sometimes be altered by punishment, but it is absurd to regard them as blameable or responsible. For someone to be responsible for his actions, it is not sufficient that he do something harmful and that his behavior in this respect can be altered by punishment. The behavior of some animals and babies can often be so changed, but it makes no sense to assert that they are responsible for what they have done. But on Schlick's theory, we would have to say just that. So Schlick's theory commits us to assigning responsibility where there is no responsibility. Thus, in this plain sense Schlick's theory is inadequate.

Schlick also fails to assign responsibility where responsibility clearly applies. Suppose, after the shooting of Malcolm X, his followers had shot down his murderers. The killers would then be dead so they are hardly punishable, but if we were to ask who was responsible for Malcolm X's death, it would still, everything else being equal, be correct to say that those dead men were responsible. Similarly, historians can assign responsibility for actions undertaken long ago; and a dead parent, who has warped his child's life, may still be responsible for his child's murderous acts, although the dead parent cannot be punished. We can find out who is blameable and responsible, according to Schlick, by finding out who is punishable. Dead men are not punishable, so on Schlick's theory we would be committed to saying that such people are not the agents responsible for certain wrongs. This is absurd, so Schlick's theory must be wrong.

Similarly, we assign different degrees of responsibility even where people might respond to punishment in the same way. Two students cheat. Under the threat of exactly the same punishment, they both will refrain from cheating. But suppose I discover that one comes from a destitute home where cheating, stealing, and contempt for or indifference to such distinctions has been the rule, while the other student comes from an environment in which he has been taught that one should not cheat and has not been deprived or been subject to undue duress. Even though they are both equally capable of altering their behavior as a result of punishment, still, everything else being equal, the man who has lived in such a dehumanizing and crippling ethos is certainly less to blame, less responsible for his acts, than is his fellow student.

III

Sidney Hook tries to meet these Campbellian objections while remaining within a soft-determinist framework.[3] He is not concerned to defend the *letter* of Schlick's analysis, but Schlick's general soft-determinist claim that freedom and responsibility are possible in a determined world. It is indeed true, Hook argues, that we do not blame children or animals unless we attribute intentions and a certain amount of rationality to their actions. What we need to add to Schlick's account is a condition to the effect that the agent's act was intentional or that the agent was sufficiently rational to have been capable of having foreseen the undesirable consequences of his act. When these conditions obtain, and when the act in question is actually undesirable, then, if punishment would alter his behavior in the future, we are justified in punishing him and in holding him responsible. If these conditions do not obtain, we cannot properly regard him as a responsible moral agent and we are not justified in punishing him. Children and animals, where they do not have a sufficient degree of rationality to understand the implications of their actions or where they *cannot* be said to be behaving intentionally, are not blameable or responsible even if they do stop doing those things when they are punished. And even if we in some way or other hurt them—for instance, spank, slap, or simply look disapprovingly—to keep them from doing certain things, still we cannot sensibly regard them as the justly punished wrongdoers.

We should say different things about past actions. As determinists, we can quite consistently say that Napoleon or Kaiser Wilhelm were responsible for certain of their actions. To say that they were responsible for these actions is to give people to understand (1) they were in a rational frame of mind during the period in question, (2) they knew what they were doing when they acted as they did, and (3) if they had been punished for these acts, they would have altered their behavior. Certainly such a conception, as Campbell himself recognizes, is in line with Schlick's suggestions and, what is more important, is perfectly compatible with determinism.

Similarly, we can correctly assign *degrees* of responsibility, even when two or more people are likely to respond in a similar way to punishment or when we have reason to think that one person understood more adequately than the other the implications of what he was doing or had a more adequate opportunity to have its implications pointed out to him than did the other person.

Schlick was wrong in thinking we could determine who is responsible simply by finding out whom it makes sense to punish—that is, whose behavior is alterable by blame and punishment. But he may be right in stressing that there is no point or use in blaming or punishing a person save directly or indirectly to prevent the undesirable act from being repeated in the future. Moreover, he was right in sensing that there is a perfectly reasonable rationale for punishment even in a deterministic world. In order to have society at all, as Hook points out, certain social relationships and institutional arrangements must be regarded as binding on people: People simply must not indiscriminately kill; contracts and promises must, everything else being equal, be honored; the laws or at least the central laws of the state must, everything else being equal, be respected; people's liberty and rights must be respected. Where this behavior is *not* reinforced, where it is not insisted upon, chaos will result. We will have a situation that nearly everyone will find undesirable. These regulations are necessary conditions for social life. Rational adults (and older children and adolescents) who understand what they are doing and are able to help themselves are justifiably held responsible for treating such social relationships as binding.

Consider a harmful action of an adult, rational individual. If we have good grounds for thinking that (1) he understands what he did and he did what he did intentionally and (2) he is the sort of person who can be made to desist from such behavior by punishment, then we have a very good reason to think that he could have done otherwise, if he had wanted to. Under such circumstances it makes good sense to punish him and hold him responsible for such an act. But if threats of punishment make no difference to his behavior, we have very good reasons to believe that his action was not something that he could have controlled, for even if we make it extremely unprofitable, painful, and generally undesirable for him to do it, he would do it anyway. Schlick's argument was right in principle, but mistaken in detail.

NOTES

1. Moritz Schlick, *Problems of Ethics* (New York: 1939), chapter 7. The relevant selection is reprinted in Paul Edwards and Arthur Pap (eds.), *A Modern Introduction to Philosophy* (New York: 1965), second edition.
2. C. A. Campbell, "Is Free Will a Pseudo-Problem?" in Paul Edwards and Arthur Pap, ibid.
3. Sidney Hook, *The Quest for Being*, chapter 2.

8

A CRITIQUE
OF DETERMINIST
CONCEPTIONS
OF FREEDOM
AND RESPONSIBILITY

I

In the last two chapters I have argued the soft determinist's case for freedom and moral responsibility. I find it a very appealing case, although to make it thoroughly satisfactory it would have to have a much more extended and careful statement than I have been able to give it here. Whether such a satisfactory account could be given I do not know, but I am inclined to think that some sophisticated account along these lines would be able to resolve our fundamental perplexities concerning the ancient problems of the conceptual connection between freedom, responsibility, and determinism.

However, I am acutely conscious that I have not been able to give such an account, and that no account that I have seen has seemed to me satisfactory in *every respect*, although this seems to be a feature of all philosophical argumentation. (This surely is *not* to say that one philosophical argument is as good as another. Imperfect accounts can still be better or worse.) Moreover, of late there has been a considerable dissatisfaction with the very possibility of any satisfactory compatibilist account of freedom, moral responsibility, and determinism.[1] This chapter will raise and pursue some of these difficulties.

It is natural to argue that such considerations as were brought to the fore in Chapters 6 and 7 do not push the question far enough. A man, soft determinists say, is free when he is not being compelled or constrained against his wishes (or against his rational wishes) to do a certain thing. However, this is but a necessary condition, not a sufficient condition for being free and responsible. If you are so compelled you are indeed not free, but you may not be compelled in any of these ways and still be unfree, unable to do *other* than what you in fact do. But if this condition holds—if you are unable to do other than what you in fact do—there remains an important sense in which in *the last analysis* you are not responsible for your acts. After all, consider this: The things you take to be undesirable or right or wrong arose from prior conditioning; furthermore, if you say, as Hook does, that a person must take responsibility for what is self-determined and that he is free just to the degree that his behavior is self-determined, then you must recognize that no one's behavior is really self-determined, that there remains an important sense in which nothing is really in your power. That is, no one ultimately could determine, create, or at first form his own character. Even Mill acknowledges that. The character you have, the moral ideals you hold, the beliefs you take to be feasible, were in the last analysis determined by factors external to you. Here Holbach is quite right. To have created your own character, so that your behavior could be self-determined, you would have had to be what you could not possibly have been, namely, your own father and mother. In other words, it is logically impossible for you to have originally formed your own character, and thus it is also *logically* impossible that you should be responsible for having the character you have. That is just something that you were given, like the color of your eyes or the language you speak.

Consider any present state, say your own disposition to act in a certain determinate way. Let us call that E. If determinism is true, E, like all events or states, is causally necessitated. This means, among other things, that it, like all states or events, has causal ancestors. That is to say, if D is the cause of E, there is still some causal ancestor C such that given C, D cannot but occur and thus E cannot but occur. Given a certain character—something that we are given, not something that we create—and certain circumstances, again something which is at least ultimately beyond our control, our present behavior is just as inevitable as is E, given C.

How, then, can we justifiably say our actions are self-determined or that anything really is in our power? And given this, how can we, after all, rightly be held responsible for anything? No doubt we need such moralistic talk as a device for social control, but a reflective man will see that in a way it is a swindle—that no one really can be blamed for what he does or be responsible for his actions. There is in reality neither merit nor guilt. We indeed need some scapegoats to avoid a brutal state of nature, but let us not delude ourselves into thinking that anyone can really be responsible for his actions. Our characters are formed for us and not by us, and our actions are the inevitable result of our character and our situation.

II

Such arguments, it will be replied, indicate we have lost sight of Mill's key insight that we can, if we wish, in some ways and *within certain limits,* alter our own characters. We are not, at least not in all respects, as Mill well realized, 'prisoners of fate' or 'captives of our own character'.

Here it is natural to reply that such Millian philosophers have not taken seriously the facts of depth psychology. Mill says, as we have seen, that one can alter within certain limits one's own character, if one's behavior is personally distressing and if one wants to. Well, many people *cannot:* psychotic people not at all, and neurotic people only in certain very limited respects. Consider a neurotic woman who needs a man (1) to give her the psychological comfort of having a 'father', (2) to give her the feeling that she is feminine, and (3) to give her what she consciously and understandably wants, a home and children. But she also unconsciously fears male domination; the very act of intercourse seems to her an act of submission to a male dominance—a dominance that she cannot tolerate psychologically. So her marriages and/or affairs all break up after a very short time. She consciously wants very much to get married and to stay married and to have a home and family. She does not want, so to speak, to be passed from bed to bed. Each time she gets involved with a man, she says, and no doubt believes, that this time it's for good; but with each new relation her unconscious identification of sex with male dominance and aggression soon sets in and she rejects or strikes out against her man and the whole circus starts up again. Her psychiatrist may convince her that she regards sex as a battle for dominance, and she comes to see how ridiculous this is, but affectively—emotionally—she goes on in the old way. She *cannot* use her knowledge to do what she *consciously wants to do.* She wants to alter her character. She hates herself as she is, but she cannot change. Mill (and Hook as well), it will be argued, are far too rationalistic in their treatment of this problem. Not everyone can alter his character in the desired respect *if only he wants to* badly enough. He may very much want to and still be quite unable to do so.

It seems to me that soft determinists have a perfectly adequate reply to this. Certainly not everyone is free in every respect. That ought to be a truism. This woman, in this crucial respect, is not free, but is prey to a psychological compulsion; but not everyone is neurotic in that way or to that degree. If everyone were, the very word 'neurotic' would have *no* meaning, for we would not understand how it qualified 'behavior'. It would not make a nonvacuous contrast with anything. No doubt, more people are neurotic than we used to think; and it is evident enough that the lists of crimes are becoming shorter and the lists of diseases longer; but to be able to speak of sick, that is, neurotic, behavior at all, there must be some patterns of normal behavior that are taken as the *norm.*

Where people are capable of rational deliberation and are capable of acting in accordance with their deliberations, and where they are in some reasonable measure able to do what they want, and where they are able, if they want to, and perhaps with the help of a psychiatrist, to alter their character in certain definite respects, they can quite properly be said to be free, responsible agents. Where, and to the extent, they *cannot* do that, they are then not free or responsible. But some people have this rationality and can so alter their characters and thus their behavior. Thus, some people some of the time are responsible moral agents. Freedom is a matter of degrees, but some people have a considerable degree of freedom and can be held responsible for their acts or, more accurately, for those acts in their control. And for many people the number of such acts is not inconsiderable.

It will, however, be countered that those who, within limits, can alter their character and change their behavior can only do it if they *want* to and if they are sufficiently nonneurotic to be able to help themselves or to respond to psychotherapeutic treatment. But—the objection continues —what they want or whether they are or are not *that* neurotic is, in the last analysis, out of their hands. They were not and could not be their own mother and father. In this fundamental sense, one's character is not and cannot be—logically cannot be—*self-determined*. Yet, if determinism is true, all one's subsequent behavior is the inevitable result of the character one happens to have and the situation in which one finds oneself. Consider this deductive argument deployed by Hospers in defense of hard determinism:

1. An occurrence over which we had no control is something we cannot be held responsible for.
2. Events E occurring during our babyhood were events over which we had no control.
3. Therefore events E were events which we cannot be held responsible for.
4. But if there is something we cannot be held responsible for, neither can we be held responsible for something that *inevitably* results from it.
5. Events E have as an *inevitable* consequence neurosis N, which in turn has as *inevitable* consequence behavior B.
6. Since N is the inevitable consequence of E, and B is the inevitable consequence of N, B is the inevitable consequence of E.
7. Hence, not being responsible for E, we cannot be responsible for B.[2]

Our situation is fixed for us and our characters are formed at a time when we are in no position to do anything about it. But according to Hospers, if determinism is true, everything that follows inevitably results from it. Thus, looked at in a deeper light, we need to realize that no one is *ultimately* responsible for his actions. As the classical hard determinists put it, you can sometimes do what you will but no one can *possibly will other than what he wills*. 'You will what you will' and 'You want what you want' are significant tautologies. If you had been brought up differently you might have willed differently or wanted different things. But given your concrete existential situation, you cannot possibly will or want other than what you will or want, if determinism is true.

The implications of this need a fuller consideration than most soft determinists have been willing to give. Without attempting to get to the bottom of this complex matter here, we can at least make the following remarks: From the fact that no one could create his own character, it does not follow that no one is responsible for what he does or that no human being is in any significant sense free. That would only follow if it were true that one would only be responsible and free if one could create one's own character, but there are at least two good reasons against saying that. First, making this putative criterion the criterion for 'ultimate responsibility and freedom' obscures important distinctions that we need to make in the very course of living. This will be illustrated in a moment. Second, if 'He is *not* responsible' is to make sense, it must make some nonvacuous contrast; that is, 'He is responsible' must make sense. That it be intelligible seems to be essential to the hard determinist's thesis, for he wants to assert that no one is ultimately responsible for what he does. But this, at the very least, seems to entail (1) that 'He is responsible' must be intelligible and (2) that whenever it is asserted it must always be false if hard determinism is to be established. (The hard determinist could hardly consistently maintain 'He is not responsible' is analytic or meaningless, for then his own thesis, 'No one is ever responsible', would be either empty or meaningless.) But if we can meaningfully say 'He is responsible' is false, we must understand what it would be like to meaningfully say that it is true. However, given the conditions the hard determinists present, it could only be true if one could ultimately create and determine one's character, for only if one could do that would one's behavior, given their definitions, be self-determined and thus responsible. But one could only ultimately create one's own character if one were one's own father and mother. But 'X is his own father and mother' or 'X is his own creator' is a contradiction. Thus, given the hard determinist's own definitions, nothing could possibly count as 'responsible behavior'. 'Responsible behavior' on their special use, like 'round square', is self-contradictory. But then "irresponsible behavior' or 'behavior for which one is not responsible' becomes a pleonasm or a redundancy. In reality, 'irresponsible' or 'not responsible' does not and cannot qualify action anymore than 'unmarried' qualifies 'bachelor'. But this is not the way the concepts 'not responsible' and 'irresponsible action' actually function in everyday life. Moreover, it would turn out that 'He is not responsible' or 'No one is responsible for his actions' would become tautologous, and thus it cannot have the moral and practical force Holbach and other hard determinists attribute to it.[3]

Let us turn to illustrations of the first claim against hard determinism. If a man could only be responsible or ultimately responsible if he could create his own character, then we would have to say that there was no difference, as far as responsibility and 'being in control' is concerned, between the responsibilitiy of a man who seduces a girl because he does not like going without sex for a week while his wife is having her tonsils out and the man who seduces a girl because he is responding to post-hypnotic suggestion. You would also have to say there is no difference between the responsibility of a boy who steals kites in Beverly Hills for the fun of it and a boy who steals bread in Calcutta because he is starving. Stealing because one is starving or seducing on posthypnotic suggestion is behavior that is very different with respect to its compulsiveness from stealing for kicks and seducing for minor convenience. There are good reasons for holding people responsible for the latter sort of behavior and for not holding them responsible for the former. If we accepted the hard determinist's definitions, we would have to run roughshod over these important distinctions. We would ignore the practical force of our talk about responsibility. If determinism is true, all behavior has causes, that is, conditions sufficient to bring it about. Moreover, it is true by definition that no one could have been his own father and mother. But, even though these conditions obtain, there is still an important difference between the cases just described that allows us to assign responsibility in one case and deny it in the other. Thus, if our talk about responsibility is to make sense at all—and it does make sense—*then* it makes sense even in a world where every event and every action has a cause and where there is no 'partial exemption from causal law'.

III

The preceding method of reasoning constitutes a sensible, practical answer to such hard-determinist arguments. Surely there are these differences and surely it is true that no matter what we discover about the truth or falsity of determinism or some alleged 'ultimate conditions of responsibility', these distinctions hold, and there are overridingly practical and moral reasons for continuing to make them. Thus, even in a deterministic world, talk of responsibility has a point.

Perhaps this is all that needs to be said. Surely it is evident that it is reasonable to make these distinctions and that they do need to be made. Yet a man in a philosophical bog about free will will remain, I think, obscurely troubled. 'But in the last resort. . . ,' he will continue to think; and what, after all, should we say about the deductive argument given on page 74? Unless something is wrong with it, do not the unwelcome consequences, paradoxical as they are, follow after all?

What we should do about the deductive argument is to challenge premiss (5): Events E have as an inevitable consequence neurosis N, which in turn has as *inevitable* consequence behavior B. It is simply not true. A little reflection on the fact that psychotherapy is sometimes successful makes this evident. It is not the case that *any* event E—just any event you might select—in early childhood has as an inevitable consequence neurosis N. There is a difference in meaning between 'All events have causes' and 'All events have unavoidable causes'. Determinism only commits you to the former, not the latter. Nor is it necessarily true that neurosis N has as an inevitable consequence behavior B. It all depends on the neurosis and the situation. In fact, it could not always be true or else no therapist could ever cure or in the slightest degree alter the behavior of any patient. If this were true, the whole practice of psychoanalysis or any other kind of therapy would be impossible. But since it is not, our behavior cannot be the inevitable result of our neurosis. Hospers' choice of colorful language—'inevitable consequence'—insinuates something that is not the case.

Indeed, if determinism is true, all behavior has causes. As we have seen, however, all causes do not compel or coerce, and one is not always a prisoner of one's past. Hospers gives us dramatic examples in which indeed the man in question is not free or responsible, although people who view such cases in a superficial manner might think so. But Hospers presents them in such a light that we can no longer plausibly view such cases in that way. However, he does not plausibly move from *some* to *all* or even to *most*. Why should we accept his microcosm as a model for the macrocosm?

Assume that I am compulsive. This is my neurotic hang-up. Assume that prior to lecturing, I count at least five times to be sure I have all the pages of my lecture. Finally, I note, or someone else notes, the absurdity of my behavior. As far as logic, psychoanalytic theory, common sense, or determinism go, my subsequent behavior here is not the inevitable result of my neurosis. I may very well be able to stop such absurd counting. People do alter their behavior in such ways. And if I cannot, if I have such a thing about my lecture that my behavior is in this respect unalterable, then in *this respect* I am not free. But there is not the slightest reason to think that all my behavior, much less everyone's behavior, is always the inevitable result of neurosis. A noteworthy thing about my hang-up over my lecture is that it is, behaviorally speaking, the exception and not the rule.

Furthermore, as we have already seen in another context, not *all* behavior could be called 'neurotic' or 'neurotic behavior', for if one tried to do that, these phrases would become like 'three-angled triangles', an utter redundancy. More behavior may very well be neurotic than we characteristically believe, but we must have certain paradigms of normal behavior in order to give sense to the concept of neurotic behavior. It is only verbal magic that makes Hospers' deductive argument look like an argument that would commit a rational man to believing no one can ever really be free or responsible.

Yet it remains that in 'the last resort' no one could form his own character; and whether he has the sort of character that enables him, if he wants to, to alter his character is again a matter of 'luck'. That is, it is not something in his own control. But does this not strike at the very heart of our concept of responsibility?

Moreover, a hard determinist could respond to my arguments by admitting that hard determinists have made a logical error in asserting that no one is ever responsible for what he does or that no one is guilty or no one blameable or justly punishable. These are themselves moral remarks, and they require a nonvacuous contrast. Their meaningful employment presupposes that it is possible to state under what conceivable conditions a person would be free and responsible. A reconstructed hard determinist would also admit that, in effect, hard determinists had set the criteria for human freedom so high that it is logically impossible for these conditions to obtain and thus, if such criteria are adopted, it would make no sense to say that anyone is or is not responsible. To do this is indeed, he would admit, a blunder. What we should have said instead, the hard determinist could continue, is that if one reflects carefully on determinism and the conditions of character formation, one will come to stop using the language of crime and punishment, freedom and responsibility, guilt and merit. One's whole vocabulary and way of thinking about these matters, at least during one's reflective moments, will slowly undergo a sea change, and one will come 'to see' the world differently, analogously to the way a man slowly comes to see the world differently after he has given up his religious beliefs. One will no longer talk and think in the old way.

If hard determinists would put their claim this way, I think they would be on stronger ground, although, again, the question immediately arises: Assuming we all wish to avoid a state of nature in which each man is turned against the other, is there not an evident pragmatic need, in certain circumstances, to praise, blame, and hold oneself responsible and expect responsible behavior from others? Certainly reflection on the 'springs of human action' should make one more tolerant. But note that even here we have the ubiquitous 'should'. How could we sensibly eliminate it from our lives? And, after all, a soft determinist can be tolerant, too; and should not any man, be he a hard or a soft determinist, recognize that tolerance should have its limits?

The topic of responsibility is a difficult one. Much more needs to be said than has been said here, but it has not been shown that responsibility is an impossible or a senseless notion, even if every event and every human action is caused.

NOTES

1. See A. I. Melden, *Free Action*, and the essays in Bernard Berofsky (ed.), *Free Will and Determinism*.
2. John Hospers, "Free Will and Psychoanalysis," in Paul Edwards and Arthur

Pap (eds.), *A Modern Introduction to Philosophy* (New York: 1965), second edition.

3. Some might counter that once it is seen to be a tautology a whole mode of discourse (here, our ordinary talk of responsibility) would be seen to lack an intelligible rationale. And if this is so, this could have a considerable normative impact. I think there is merit in this reply. For some of the rationale behind it, see Stuart Hampshire, "The Interpretation of Language: Words and Concepts" in Richard Rorty (ed.), *The Linguistic Turn* (Chicago: 1967).

9

PSYCHOANALYSIS AND MORAL FREEDOM

We have seen some of the basic considerations that divide hard and soft determinists over the concepts of freedom and responsibility. Hard determinists would have us believe that these concepts are in some sense empty while soft determinists are concerned to show that although every event and every action has a cause, there remain legitimate applications for the terms 'freedom' and 'responsibility'. Both sides have tried to use psychoanalysis to reinforce their claims. There are indeed certain elements in psychoanalytic thought that can be used to reinforce either view, but I believe a careful reflection on psychoanalysis—particularly on the aims and methods of psychoanalytic therapy—would indicate that it fits better with soft determinism than with hard determinism. There is, however, an understandable tendency to take a hard-determinist line concerning psychoanalysis and human freedom. Hospers does just this in the essay discussed in the last chapter. I want to say something about the kind of arguments he, and others like him, use, and then I want to sketch in the other side of the matter. First, however, something should be said about the scientific status of psychoanalysis and then about Freud's 'psychic determinism'.

There are those who would say that psychoanalysis is hardly more scientific than Christian Science; that is, it is a pseudoscience and we can justifiably dismiss it. Basic psychoanalytic claims are stated in such a loose way that they are incapable of being confirmed or disconfirmed, and there are no adequate tests as to what constitutes a cure or whether the alleged success of psychoanalytic therapy has much to do with psychoanalytic conceptions or practice. If the same sort of people who profit from psychoanalytic therapy spent, with a similar conviction, as much time and money with a Christian Science practitioner, they might very well register a similar success. All we have with psychoanalysis, some will say, is the *ersatz* religion of the therapeutic community.

There are indeed serious questions about the scientific status of psychoanalysis, although I am inclined to think that remarks of the sort I just made are far too extreme. In trying to decide what to think about such matters, we must beware of taking physics as our *sole* model for what is genuinely scientific lest we rule out such perfectly well-established sciences as geology or cultural anthropology. At the very least, we can say that reflection, careful observation, and energy of many dedicated and intelligent men have gone into psychoanalysis, and that it has become an established medical practice.

I shall assume here what I admit is arguable, that psychoanalysis has a legitimate scientific status and, what is even more arguable, that the central psychoanalytic claims are true. Working with these assumptions, I want to examine their implications for freedom and responsibility.

Freud was a determinist. In fact, he argued for something that might be called *psychic determinism*. Charles Brenner, in a popular resumé of the Freudian position, states the central thesis of psychic determinism in a succinct manner:

> The sense of this principle is that in the mind, as in physical nature about us, nothing happens by chance, or in a random way. Each psychic event is determined by the ones which preceded it. Events in our mental lives that may seem to be random and unrelated to what went on before are only apparently so. In fact, mental phenomena are no more capable of such a lack of causal connection with what preceded them than are physical ones. Discontinuity in this sense does not exist in mental life.[1]

This is sometimes taken to imply the denial of freedom and responsibility, but to deny human freedom on such a basis is just to miss the key conceptual distinctions that the soft determinists have so powerfully stressed. It is to be caught up in the kind of confusions that we discovered in Holbach.

There are, however, other considerations that actually have led some psychologists and philosophers to believe that if the Freudian conceptions are true, then no one is free, for everyone is compelled in all his actions and attitudes by unconscious motives that drive him to act in ways that are beyond his rational control. Our reasons for acting in the way we do are in reality all rationalizations.

On the contrary, I think that Freudian conceptions, if true, actually would have the reverse effect. They would extend, rather than limit, our powers of rationality. They help us to understand our own motives in a deeper way and to understand more adequately the behavior of others. In increasing our rational understanding of ourselves and others, they tend to increase our control of ourselves and to enhance our freedom rather than to diminish it. In fact, that is the central aim of psychoanalytic therapy: to increase our freedom by increasing our capacity for self-direction.

The opposite, however, is often simply assumed. That is, it is assumed that if psychoanalysis were true, the world Eugene O'Neill so powerfully depicts would indeed be the real world—man would indeed be the prisoner of compulsions over which he neither has any effective control nor even any adequate understanding. Let us trace how such an argument unfolds.

II

Someone who wished to argue in this way might begin by granting the point made in the last chapter against the hard determinist; that is, that it is nonsense to speak of 'causing one's own character' or to say that a human being to be free or responsible would originally have to be able to choose his own character. But the reply might be that there is another important notion, only recently brought clearly to light by psychoanalysis, that radically alters our concept of moral responsibility and really vindicates the hard determinist or at least indicates clearly that no man is really free or responsible. This notion is the Freudian concept of unconscious motivation. If psychoanalysis is true, all human behavior is unconsciously motivated. Even when in a calm, reflective moment we deliberate and decide to do something for reasons of which we are fully aware, our choice is in fact determined not by the reasons we give to ourselves, but by subconscious forces of which we are not even aware, still less in control. And these causes are all *compelling* causes. That is to say, they are genuine compulsions.

Moreover, it is not just the sick man who is dominated by his unconscious; all men are dominated by their unconscious compulsions. As Hospers metaphorically put it, "The unconscious is the master of every fate and captain of every soul." Surely I can say what it would be like for a man to be free. A man is a free human agent (1) if he is reasonable, (2) if he is not externally compelled, coerced, or constrained, and (3) if his actual motives are conscious ones that in his rational moments he accepts when the relevant facts are before him. To the extent one's conduct meets these conditions, one's conduct is free. But hard determinists such as Hospers maintain that no one is *in fact free,* for all our acts are actually unconsciously motivated. As a result, we are all internally compelled or constrained by unconscious psychological forces to act as we do. If this condition of servitude did not obtain, then we could say that a man was free, but unfortunately it does obtain. Our very condition, hard determinists maintain, is one of human bondage.

We have here an empirical claim that very much needs to be questioned, namely, that people are always unconsciously motivated and that no one's actual motives are his conscious motives. It seems to me that this is both false and, as R. S. Peters observes, not even a claim that Freud made or that is actually supported by psychoanalytic theory. However, I would like to let all that pass and argue instead that even if such a theory of motivation were true—and not, as it actually is, a misreading of Freud—it still would not establish that no one was ever free or responsible. That is, even if everything I do is unconsciously motivated, it still does not follow that I am not free and capable of responsible moral agency.

The *rationale* is this: Although whatever I do may be unconsciously motivated, only if my unconscious motives are *malevolent*—that is, if they make me do things I *suffer* from or make me feel *unhappy, ambivalent, remorseful, ashamed,* or something of that nature—am I in any proper sense in some degree compelled or constrained by being unconsciously motivated. Men, such as many of O'Neill's characters, who feel forced to do one thing rather than another without understanding why and while hating themselves for it, are paradigms of men who in these areas of their lives are not free. They are indeed driven men, living under obscure compulsions. But why should all, or even any, of one's unconscious motives be of that unpleasant nature? There seems to be no good ground for asserting that all or even most of them are of that nature.

Nowell-Smith, in his "Psychoanalysis and Moral Language," develops the preceding contention in an incisive way.[2] If psychoanalytic theory is true, and if it is the case that all one's behavior is determined by unconscious or subconscious motives, then 'being free' should no longer be defined as being incompatible with 'being determined by subconscious motives', for then no behavior would be properly classifiable as free and we would have to run roughshod over distinctions that we want and need very much to make (for example, distinctions between the kleptomaniac and the ordinary thief).

To gain clarity concerning this point, we need to distinguish between *craving* and *wanting*. I may want very much to attend the festival at Salzburg, but this does not mean or imply that I have a craving to do so, that is, that there is an irresistible or at least a powerful force—say, as an addiction to morphine—driving me to act in a certain way, whether I want to or not, think it desirable or not. If I am hooked on morphine I may very much want to get off the stuff, but, given the power of my craving, I know I cannot let it alone no matter how much I want to. But if I merely want to do something, even if I want to do it very much, such as going to the festival at Salzburg, I will not go if I discover a decisively good reason for not going. If I go anyway—if in that way I must go—no matter what the rational considerations, I really do have a *craving* here. It now becomes evident that it is not merely that I want to go. Psychologically speaking, I must go no matter how weighty the reasons for not going.

In both cases, if psychoanalytic theory is correct, my behavior is determined by unconscious motives. But there is a genuine and important difference between the behavior of a dope addict and a normal music lover, between the man with an irresistible craving and the man who wants very much to do something. It is the former man who is driven. His behavior, at least where the craving is irresistible, is determined by *malevolent* unconscious motives; that is, they make him do things that in his "calm, reflective moments he consciously wants not to do" or "things that lead to remorse and shame." But we are not always so driven. When we become aware of certain unconscious motives, we do not always feel shame or remorse or feel that we are being forced to do something we do not want to do. If someone were to prove to me that my deepest unconscious motive for becoming a professor was one of exhibitionism, I would indeed be shocked, but I would still not feel that my unconscious was the master of my soul, as long as I liked teaching, was convinced on rational grounds that what I was doing was useful, and had good grounds for believing that I could stop being a teacher if I came to dislike teaching.

Only some of our unconscious motives are malevolent ones—motives driving us to do things we would not do. It is one thing to feel driven to go to a bar; it is quite another to want to go to the movies—even to want very much to go to the movies. The Freudian theory of unconscious motivation does not collapse this difference, but it is where a man is *driven* by an irresistible *craving* to do what he consciously does not want to do that we say his behavior is unfree and that we are not justified in holding him responsible for such acts. But we are not all in this 'craving predicament' all of the time, and there is nothing in Freud to establish that we are. If psychoanalytic theory is correct, we should *not* say that no man is free, but that a man is free in "inverse proportion to his neuroticism." Most of us, perhaps all of us, are neurotic about some things. We have our cravings and hang-ups, and in those respects our freedom is limited. But in everything we do we are not dominated by cravings. Where our behavior is not irrational and where we are able to do what we want to do, we have free agency.

III

Suppose to this argument someone replies: But whether you feel uncomfortable when you are unconsciously motivated or not, or whether your unconscious is malevolent or not, it is still causally determined and thus you are not free. But this really is irrelevant, for it only returns again to the general thesis of hard determinism that we have already found grounds for rejecting. In effect it is simply claiming that the opposite of 'freedom' is 'determinism' and not 'compulsion'. But, as we have seen, this deprives 'free' of its nonvacuous contrast and thus of its very meaning, for without such a contrast it could not function as a descriptive term. However, 'free' does have a variety of uses in the English language; it is not a term devoid of descriptive meaning.

Another line of attack might be taken against the general argument I gave in the preceding section. Suppose it is said that when one reflects on unconscious motivation, and notes how it actually works, it becomes evident that everyone actually has a malevolent unconscious. That is to say, all of one's unconscious motivations, and thus, on this theory, all of one's actual motivations, are malevolent. This, the argument might continue, can be seen when we take into account that any man who now feels free would come to feel the constraint of his unconscious when he became even partially aware of its pervasive determining effect on his life. Only ignorance of our motives makes us feel free. But this, as Holbach stressed long ago, is a delusory freedom. Understanding of our actual motives would always make us feel constrained. Given a genuine understanding of the real springs of his action, no man would feel free. Our unconscious motives must always be apprehended as malevolent—that is, as driving us in directions that we do not want to go—when we actually come to understand how they operate. Only the lack of a true understanding of our condition gives us the delusory conviction that sometimes our conduct is not constrained.

Even if on inspection this claim turns out to be what it indeed purports to be, a thesis about human beings which directly or indirectly rests on observation, it still does not follow that there is good evidence for its truth. Let us grant that it is an empirical thesis (to use the philosopher's label for such a thesis), but it is an untested empirical thesis for which, in fact, no evidence has been given. That is, we have no reason to believe it to be true. If there were any evidence, it would be of a psychosociological sort, but no such evidence backs up these claims. So it is hardly incumbent on anyone to try to assess the evidence. It would seem that it is very unlikely that this claim is true, for it is reasonably evident that a man might, for example, be unconsciously motivated to become a surgeon because of certain sublimated sadistic impulses and later discover that he had these impulses without at all wishing to give up surgery, which after all has a point, is lucrative for him, and is something at which he is skilled. The burden of proof is certainly on the hard determinist to give us some reason for thinking all unconscious motives are malevolent.

One of the reasons we are tempted to believe 'the unconscious' is malevolent or that, if all our actual motives are unconscious, we are actually acting under compulsions, is that people who write on such mat-

ters often get much mileage out of a quite inflated and misleading vocabulary. Hospers is a good example. His metaphorical and animistic employments of language indeed make philosophy lively, but they can also
convey, through their very manner, a mood that in reality is not backed
up by argument. By a kind of verbal magic, Hospers makes us feel that
we are all captives of our unconscious, when he has not established anything of the kind. An aseptic description would convey the same information, but would not evoke fatalistic attitudes.

Let me justify my point by working with some examples from his
"Free Will and Psychoanalysis." Hospers remarks:

> The conscious life of the human being, including the conscious decisions and
> volitions, is merely a mouthpiece for the unconscious—not directly for the
> enactment of unconscious drives, but of the compromise between uncon-
> scious drives and unconscious reproaches.[3]

Note first that the very choice of the word 'drives' rather than 'wishes',
'motives', 'needs', or 'desires' conjures up Newtonian forces—a man being
pushed or pulled, being compelled or driven. But what is the empirical
justification for choosing this term rather than other more neutral terms?
To make Hospers' philosophical point, it is a strategically judicious
choice, but there are no other grounds for choosing it. Rather, by using
it Hospers can insinuate a picture of man that he has not supported by
empirical evidence. He could have chosen a more neutral word to describe
the same empirical data. However, with that more neutral description he
would not have conjured up that fatalistic picture. To proceed as he did
is surely to pass out false coin.

Take an even more blatant example from the same passage just quoted:
"merely a mouthpiece for the unconscious." Taken literally, what the
Freudian is claiming is that one's conscious thoughts and wishes are
caused by unconscious thoughts and wishes. That is, when unconscious
thoughts or wishes of a certain type occur, conscious thoughts or wishes
of a certain type will subsequently occur. But this does not make the
conscious thoughts the mouthpiece for the unconscious ones. 'Mouthpiece' has a pejorative force. When it is applied to a man—for example,
'Humphrey was Johnson's mouthpiece'—it is intended to convey the impression of someone who is not his own man, who is simply someone
else's spokesman without a will of his own. By Hospers' very choice of
words that have a certain pejorative-emotive force, a certain attitude is
conveyed toward the situation. For someone hearing these emotively
charged words, the very words tend in certain contexts to structure the
situation in a determinate way—a way, but for the choice of words, that
is not all necessary. It is again analogous to reading back into the laws
of nature the prescriptive force of legal laws and in reading into 'neces-

sitation', while speaking of causal laws, the compulsion of 'necessitation' when I say, 'You must be quiet in church.'

Hospers tried to defend his use of animistic and metaphorical language by saying it is dramatic and his case can be most clearly made by using it. This is surely so if 'clearest' is construed as 'most forceful', where this in turn is intended to convey that it can be made pedagogically exciting, can *prod* people to think, and can make his claims seem very compelling to the unwary. But his tactic here also functions to insinuate a point that has not been established by hard argument. Because of this, it is more mystifying than genuinely clarifying. Hospers makes his claim psychologically forceful by the use of such colorful language, but he does not establish it by cogent reasoning.

Let me finish my indictment of Hospers' analysis by citing another clear case of his verbal legerdemain. Hospers wants to establish that it is not just the psychologically maladjusted who are the "puppets of their unconscious," but even the plainest of plain men. He tells us that

> . . . psychiatrists began to realize, though philosophers did not, that the domination of the conscious by the unconscious extended, not merely to a few exceptional individuals, but to all human beings, that the 'big three behind the scenes' are not respecters of persons, and dominate us all, even including that *sanctum sanctorum* of freedom, our conscious will. To be sure, the domination by the unconscious in the case of 'normal' individuals is somewhat more benevolent than the tyranny and despotism exercised in neurotic cases, and therefore the former have evoked less comment; but the principle remains in all cases the same: The unconscious is the master of every fate and the captain of every soul.[4]

With respect to this passage, simply note the choice of language: 'master of every fate', 'captain of every soul', 'somewhat more benevolent than the tyranny and despotism', 'domination', 'respecters', 'big three behind the scenes'. These are all emotively charged words that cannot help but convey a certain mood to almost everyone, unless they make a deliberate effort to emotively neutralize them. It is like the difference between 'no man is an island' and 'man is a social animal'. In the passage just quoted, all the power of rhetoric is brought to bear to create an effect that an aseptic, reasonably operational description would not convey. But nothing has been done to show—that is, to establish rationally—that the 'stream of determinism' and the pervasiveness of unconscious motives makes us human puppets. No philosophical argument or empirical evidence has been deployed to show that since all our actions have unconscious motives as sufficient conditions, all human beings are compelled in all that they do and so are never free. Here the deflationary pen of a conceptual analyst is of very considerable value.

Although Hospers gets far too much mileage out of a dramatic and careless use of language, he is surely right in stressing that Freud has helped us see how the area of compelled acts is much more extensive than is usually thought. There are some very complex and very powerful unconscious compulsions. Kafka's world is no doubt not the real world, but Hospers in effect reminds us how very real it can be. Hospers is also correct in stressing that normal men have unconscious drives and compulsions, too, and that people are frequently deluded into thinking they are free when they are not. But he very much overstates and overdramatizes his claims about being compelled or driven by unconscious motives. It is one thing to say that all our acts or wishes are caused by unconscious motives; it is something else again to say that unconscious motives compel us to do all the things we do. Freud does not even claim the former, but even if he did, it would not imply the latter, and no evidence has been given for belief in the latter. We are again back to an old confusion we discussed earlier about 'necessitate'. All causes do not equally constrain or compel and in that way they do not equally necessitate, although trivially all causes equally cause and in *that way* equally necessitate, but we get no compulsion from *this sense* of 'necessitate'.

It is one thing to say 'All wants and desires have causes' and 'All wants and desires have as causes unconscious needs and wishes'. It is something altogether different to say, as Hospers does, that 'Unconscious forces drive men into wanting or not wanting whatever they want'. Hospers assumes that if the former is true, the latter is. But even if the former is true, the latter may not be true. My liking Grand Marnier may have all sorts of unconscious grounds. Perhaps I unconsciously want to show that in spite of my proletarian origins I have culture, too. But I am not driven into liking Grand Marnier as a wino is driven to seek drink. It is simply Hospers' choice of dramatic language and not anything in the facts that makes us feel as if no man could ever really be free or responsible, since, after all, we are all really puppets to our unconscious drives.

IV

Someone might argue that freedom or the concept of a free man should be treated as a kind of ideal concept or theoretical construct comparable to 'economic man' or 'genital character'. A man is free if his behavior is self-determined, and his behavior would be self-determined if his actual motives were his conscious motives. Psychoanalysis shows, however, that his conscious motives are not in fact his actual motives. Therefore, no man in reality is free or responsible, although some approach this ideal. Here we do have a nonvacuous contrast. We know what it *would be like* for men to be free and thus not constrained, although in fact none are and we do not expect anyone ever to be such a free agent. Furthermore, we should aim in that direction in therapy. Thus, 'compelled' could have a significant opposite even though no one in reality is free or responsible.

We must again consider what we are trying to do. We want to discover the conditions under which a man would correctly be said to be a free responsible agent. I grant that it is possible to develop a *different* conception of freedom in which it turns out that no one is in fact free. But to do this is in reality to give a persuasive definition of 'freedom'. That is, the person doing it has wittingly or unwittingly taken a term— for example 'freedom'—with a certain emotive force and, while retaining that force, changed its meaning. Ordinarily we use the word 'free' so that a normal man who marries the girl he wants to marry because he wants to marry her would be said to have married her of his own free will.

It is our normal practice to excuse responsibility for things such as infancy, insanity, paralysis, duress, coercion, and so on, although no list is likely to be exhaustive. No one in his right mind blames the infant who overturns the kerosene stove. But when a normal adult burns a house down in order to collect the insurance, we do blame him in normal circumstances. Our notions of freedom and responsibility develop against this concrete practical background. If we accept, however, the preceding stronger stipulative sense of 'freedom' in which it is an ideal concept never exemplified in human living, we would have to desist from holding people responsible even when they are rational individuals and when saying they are responsible tends to inhibit antisocial acts and tends to rehabilitate the actor. After all, on this stipulative definition they are not really 'free'.

Why should we change our use of the word 'free' as a result of these psychoanalytic discoveries—even assuming they are genuine discoveries— about human motivation? What practical or theoretical reason is there for such a redefinition? It is no good replying "Because now with our deeper discoveries about human nature, we see that no one is ever really free. No one really knows what he wants and no one ever really has a nonmalevolent unconscious." The 'really' tips things off here. We started out by asking if men were ever free, responsible, and so forth; we have now found sensible uses for 'He did it of his own free will', 'She is responsible for that', and the like. They would be sensible even if these psychoanalytic discoveries we mentioned were indeed genuine discoveries. Where in an ordinary sense X is rational and can *do* what he wills—that is, where he has the ability and the opportunity—we regard him as a free agent; but on any *given occasion,* he cannot possibly will what he does not will. Where we can *alter* his behavior and where he has done something wrong and where he has the ability and opportunity to learn that it is wrong, we justly can hold him responsible. Even Hospers does not wish to attack this. What possible reason could there be for saying that this freedom is not *real* freedom?

We can, of course, stipulatively redefine 'freedom' in some other way so that this ordinary garden variety is not 'real freedom', but then we would have to say that some of the apparent freedoms or illusory freedoms were freer than other apparent freedoms or illusory freedoms. In this instance we would just be bringing in the old ordinary distinctions between 'free' and 'unfree' under a new name. What possible point could there be in such linguistic gymnastics?

It seems that psychoanalytic discoveries help us to come to see why it would be reasonable to classify many things as diseases which were formerly regarded as crimes. It could help us to see that certain people we thought were blameable and responsible really were not. But the distinction between crime and disease, the distinction between free and constrained or compelled remains.[5] If the world were radically different, then it might be true that no one would be free, but the world is not this way, and our very talk about freedom and responsibility developed against this background.

V

I have tried to show how hard-determinist or quasi-hard-determinist utilizations of psychoanalysis do not do anything to establish that freedom is an illusion. In rounding off this theme, I now want to return to a consideration mentioned early in this chapter, namely, that if psychoanalytic thinking is sound and psychoanalytic practice successful, human freedom is enhanced rather than diminished. This is compatible with soft determinism, but does not commit one to it. I contend that if psychoanalysis is even roughly true, its implications do not support hard determinism, but indicate how some men at least can attain an even greater freedom and thus greater responsibility.

Psychoanalysis developed as a clinical practice used to cure neurotic people. Psychoanalysis is not just an explanatory theory of human behavior, but is primarily a set of therapeutic practices designed to alter human behavior in certain respects. The aim of therapy is, to put it bluntly, to get people to stand up on their own two feet. Freud wished to help people see the world more clearly. He tried to help them to understand themselves and their own motives; he tried to help people who wanted and needed such help to develop the ability to live their lives in such a manner that they would not be dominated by infantile fantasies, but would live lives in which they came to see the world in a more adult way. Therapy aims to help people gain greater freedom and not to convince men that they are prisoners of their own unconscious.

Like Marx, Freud believed that man could be freed to a certain extent from forces that work beneath the surface by coming to understand them.[6] Understanding, at least some of the time, brings some degree of control and some more tolerable relations with the world—although, of course, freedom is always a matter of degree.

Ideally speaking, moral standards are standards we adopt because we see their point. Even if we first get them because of social stimulation, this need not undermine them. No causal theory as to their origin need do so if they do indeed have a point. The aim of Freudian psychotherapy is to put people in a position in which they, as rational individuals, can choose their own standards, can make themselves fully autonomous moral beings.

I suppose the worry of the hard determinist remains the speculative one that the behavioral sciences may make certain discoveries about human beings and these discoveries will perhaps be used to shape personalities in such a way that they may someday lose their capacity to behave as autonomous individuals. But even if this can possibly be the case, it will not be science or psychoanalysis that can make us unfree, but rather science and psychoanalysis used by some unscrupulous or sick man. As long as people still have preferences and wants and are able to exercise those preferences, they will be free even though it is the case that all those preferences are determined. *Brave New World* is frightening not because it is a deterministic world but because in such a world opportunities that humans now have are closed to them without their even being aware of it.

We can sum up our discussion in this way. The reason that both hard determinists and soft determinists have been able to utilize psychoanalysis in support of both of their philosophical claims is that there are elements in it that seem at least to support either side. If there is anything to psychoanalysis at all, it is true that more people are unconsciously compelled in more ways than common sense or at least Edwardian common sense would have us believe. This would show that people are sometimes mistakenly thought to be capable of moral agency in certain respects when in fact they are not. However, the practice of psychoanalysis also shows how men can extend their freedom by extending their rational control over their behavior.

To understand our unconscious motives—that is, to make them conscious motives—is typically to gain control of them. This increases our range of responsible action. It liberates us, or partially liberates us, from a bondage to the way our early lives have warped our view of the world. Yet, no matter how we balance it, there is nothing in psychoanalysis to establish that human responsibility is an illusion because the unconscious is the tyrannical master of every fate and captain of every soul. This belief is as myth-eaten as a belief in the Garden of Eden.

NOTES

1. Charles Brenner, *An Elementary Text Book of Psychoanalysis*, p. 92.
2. P. H. Nowell-Smith, "Psychoanalysis and Moral Language," in Paul Edwards and Arthur Pap (eds.), *A Modern Introduction to Philosophy* (New York: 1965), second edition.
3. John Hospers, "Free Will and Psychoanalysis," in Paul Edwards and Arthur Pap (eds.), ibid., p. 82.
4. Ibid.
5. See here Thomas S. Szasz, *The Myth of Mental Illness: Foundation of a Theory of Personal Conduct* (New York: 1961), and his "The Mental Health Ethic," in Richard T. De George (ed.), *Ethics and Society* (Garden City, N.Y.: 1966).
6. R. S. Peters, *Authority, Responsibility and Education* (London: Allen and Unwin, 1959), and his "Freud and Responsibility," *The Nation* (Nov. 16, 1957).

SUPPLEMENTARY READINGS
PART I

Books

*Benn, S. I., and R. S. Peters, *The Principles of Political Thought* (New York: Free Press, 1965).
*Berlin, Isaiah, *The Hedgehog and the Fox* (New York: Mentor Books, 1957).
*Berlin, Isaiah, *Historical Inevitability* (London: Oxford University Press, 1954).
*Berofsky, Bernard (ed.), *Free Will and Determinism* (New York: Harper & Row, 1966).
*Campbell, C. A., *In Defense of Free Will* (London: 1969).
*Care, Norman S., and Charles Landesman (eds.), *Readings in the Theory of Action* (Bloomington, Ind.: Indiana University Press, 1968). Contains an extensive bibliography.
Edwards, Jonathan, *Freedom of the Will* (New Haven, Conn.: Yale University Press, 1957).
Farrer, Austin, *The Freedom of the Will* (London: Adam & Charles Black, 1958).
Hampshire, Stuart, *Freedom and the Individual* (New York: Harper & Row, 1965).
Hampshire, Stuart, *Thought and Action* (London: Chatto and Windus, 1959).
Hart, H. L. A., *Punishment and Responsibility* (Oxford: Claredon Press, Oxford, 1968).
*Hook, Sidney (ed.), *Determinism and Freedom in the Age of Modern Science* (New York: New York University Press, 1958).
Kenny, Anthony, *Action, Emotion and Will* (London: Routledge, 1963).
Lehrer, Keith (ed.), *Freedom and Determinism* (New York: Random House, 1966).
Melden, A. I., *Free Action* (London: Routledge, 1961).
*Moore, G. E., *Ethics* (London: Oxford University Press, 1912).

*Morgenbesser, Sidney, and James Walsh (eds.), *Free Will* (Englewood Cliffs, N.J.: Prentice-Hall, 1962). Contains an extensive bibliography.
*Nowell-Smith, P. H., *Ethics* (London: Penguin, 1954).
Ofstad, Harald, *An Inquiry into Freedom of Decision* (London: G. Allen, 1961). Contains an extensive bibliography.
*Pears, D. F. (ed.), *Freedom and the Will* (New York: St. Martin's, 1963).
Peters, R. S., *The Concept of Motivation* (London: Routledge, 1958).
Schopenhauer, Arthur, *Essay on the Freedom of the Will* (New York: Liberal Arts Press, 1960). Translated by Konstantin Kolenda. The German edition, 1839.
Skinner, R. F., *Science and Human Behavior* (New York: 1953).
Taylor, Charles, *The Explanation of Behavior* (London: Routledge, 1964).
*Vesey, G. N. A. (ed.), *The Human Agent*, Royal Institute of Philosophy Lectures, vol. I (1966/7), (New York: St. Martin's, 1968).

Articles and Pamphlets

Baier, Kurt, "Responsibility and Freedom," in Richard T. De George (ed.), *Ethics and Society* (Garden City, N.Y.: Doubleday, 1966).
*Berofsky, Bernard, "Determinism and the Concept of a Person," *Journal of Philosophy* (1964).
*Bradley, R. D., "Free Will: Problem or Pseudo-Problem?" *Australasian Journal of Philosophy* (1960).
Bradley, R. D., "Ifs, Cans, and Determinism," *Australasian Journal of Philosophy* (1962).
*Campbell, C. A., "In Defense of Free Will," An Inaugural Lecture (Glasgow: Jackson, 1938).
Canfield, J. V., "The Compatibility of Free Will and Determinism," *Philosophical Review* (1962).
*Clifford, W. K. C., "Right and Wrong: The Scientific Ground of Their Distinction," in his *Lectures and Essays* (New York: Macmillan, 1879).
Feinberg, Joel, "Action and Responsibility," in Max Black (ed.), *Philosophy in America* (Ithaca, N.Y.: Cornell University Press, 1965).
*Gallie, W. B., "Free Will and Determinism Yet Again," An Inaugural Lecture, The Queen's University of Belfast, 1957. Printed and published by Marjory Boyd, M. A. Printer to the Queen's University of Belfast.
Ginet, Carl, "Can the Will Be Caused?" *Philosophical Review* (1962).
Hampshire, Strawson, and Pears, essays in P. F. Strawson (ed.), *Studies in the Philosophy of Thought and Action* (London: Oxford University Press, 1968).
*Hobart, R. B., "Free Will as Involving Determination and Inconceivable Without It," *Mind* (1934).
Kaufman, Aronld S., "Ability," *Journal of Philosophy* (1963).
Lehrer, Keith, "Can We Know That We Have Free Will by Introspection?" *Journal of Philosophy* (1960).
MacIntyre, A. C., "Antecedents of Action," in B. Williams and A. Montefiore (eds.), *British Analytical Philosophy* (London: Routledge, 1966).
Ofstad, Schultzer, and Hedenius, essays in *Philosophical Essays Dedicated to Gunnar Aspelin* (Lund, Sweden: Gleerup Bokförlag, 1963). These are three

interesting essays on this topic in English by these Scandinavian philosophers.

*Oldenquist, Andrew, "Choosing, Oeciding and Doing," in Paul Edwards (ed.), *The Encyclopedia of Philosophy*, vol. 2 (New York: Macmillan and Free Press, 1967).

*Raab, Francis V., "History, Freedom and Responsibility," *Philosophy of Science* (1959).

*Smart, J. J. C., "Free Will, Praise and Blame," *Mind* (1961).

*Taylor, Richard, "Determinism," in Paul Edwards (ed.), *The Encyclopedia of Philosophy*, vol. 2 (New York: Macmillan and Free Press, 1967). Contains an extensive bibliography.

Thalberg, I., "Freedom of Action and Freedom of Will," *Journal of Philosophy* (1964).

*Thornton, J. C., "Determinism and Moral Reactive Attitudes," *Ethics*, vol. 79, no. 4 (July, 1969).

II
LOGIC
AND
TRUTH

10
TRUTH AND VALIDITY: SOME REMARKS ABOUT LOGIC

I

We have now completed our examination of 'freedom and determinism'. It is a basic problem in philosophy, and without doubt it is one of the problems that remains most resistant to an adequate solution. I have generally taken a soft-determinist line, but I should in candor remark once more that problems remain and that many able philosophers doubt that such a compatibilist account can be successfully carried out.

Particularly to be noted is a group of philosophers of quite recent vintage who, with respect to the determinism/indeterminism controversy, in effect cry, 'A plague on both your houses.' Causal explanation, these philosophers claim, and the very categories of cause and effect, are perfectly appropriate to physical movements devoid of symbolic content—for example, 'my arm went up'—but not to purposive human actions where goals and norms intervene—'I raised my arm to salute the chief'. For such actions, which are distinctive bits of human behavior, the whole language of causality, or at least the scientific conception of causality appropriate to determinism, is quite inappropriate. We should instead talk about the reasons for doing one thing rather than another. Causal explanation only becomes appropriate where every semblance of rational behavior breaks down. It is not that indeterminism is true, but that such notions do not take hold on human actions. We can no more correctly apply such categories to human actions than we can speak of stones as frivolous or serious.[1]

I have grave doubts about those aspects of action theory, as it is sometimes called, which require anything more vis-à-vis determinism than an abandonment of physical determinism. But it is a sophisticated account of human behavior, and on a more extended account of our problem it would certainly deserve careful examination. Yet these remarks should serve as a warning—only one of several that could be made—that there is much more to be said than what has been said here.

Some may think my remarks are already too extended. Given my 'inconclusive conclusions' and given the parade of argument and counter-argument concerning 'freedom and determinism,' it is natural to react: "Well, philosophy is something in which a number of philosophers hold a number of more or less conflicting opinions about very abstract matters, but you soon learn there is no way of telling who, if anyone, is right or wrong." Some might go on to reflect: "And Professor Nielsen happens to *like* soft determinism so that is where we finally settle with him when discussing this question. But another professor who happened to favor hard determinism or indeterminism would have finally settled with his hobbyhorse. After all, let us not kid ourselves, it is all a matter of how you just happen to *feel* about it. James is right: Our emotions finally determine what we will say on such matters."

This is, indeed, a discouraging attitude. Where it comes to express a settled conviction, it naturally leads either to an overt abandonment of interest in philosophy or to what in reality is also, although in a disguised way, an abandonment of genuine philosophical interest, namely, the adoption of what I call 'the great-visions approach to philosophy'.

The basic attitude here is this: These great questions are all unanswerable, but let us come to see what the great men—the towering figures of the past and present—have had to say, and let us learn simply to appreciate their wit and wisdom. Such an approach drops all serious effort at philosophical argument and criticism and stresses a kind of flabby sympathetic display of the story of philosophy that panders to popular vulgarity while, in effect, dishonoring those very philosophers whom 'the great-visions men' allegedly appreciate. This seems to me a despicable approach—I use that term advisedly. If these questions really are unanswerable, then we ought not to try to answer them any more than we ought to try to utter the unutterable. Moreover, we should not speak of wisdom here; there is no wisdom involved in trying to answer unanswerable questions, only foolishness.

However, the very assumption behind 'the great-visions approach' needs to be challenged, namely, that these questions are unanswerable and that there are no 'answers' which can be shown to be conceptual confusions and so not answers at all. The assumption needs challenging that in philosophy all genuine answers are equally unsatisfactory or, what comes to the same thing here, equally satisfactory. This does not follow from what we have seen about questions concerning freedom and determinism, and there are no good independent grounds for holding it. Moreover, it should be noted that not all philosophical questions have remained in so many respects such tough nuts to crack as has the problem of freedom. We will see when we examine the problem of God that something much more definite can be established in philosophy than what I was able to establish about freedom. I chose to begin with freedom for I wanted you to see how tangled and entangling philosophical questions can be.

Such a treatment runs the risk of leaving you with the impression that it is all a matter of personal and utterly arbitrary choice. This feeling, as natural as it is, rests on a mistake. For some philosophical questions, as we shall see, more definite answers are available, and it is not even true that no progress was made in talking about freedom. Some simple answers can be definitely ruled out; that is, everyone who will study the matter with reasonable care can see that there are answers that should be ruled out. (Reflect here on the evident difficulties in Holbach's and James's accounts, and the way that it was quite apparent that Schlick's theory needs modification.) And there are answers, although not perfectly satisfactory, that are more adequate than others; and they can be seen by open-minded people to be more adequate answers.

Note in this connection that basic philosophical questions are very general questions concerning matters that engage us deeply. Given their very nature, answers to them are most likely to remain controversial and deeply contested, but this does not mean that certain answers are not more adequate than others. It does not mean that in philosophy you can reasonably think anything that you please, or that it is all a matter of what you like. It may very well be that the time will come when we can give as definite and as generally satisfactory answers to questions about human freedom as we can now give concerning arguments purporting to prove the existence of God.[2] We want very much to have answers to these basic philosophical questions. And when we fail to give an adequate answer to them, attempts should be made again and again to do so. The only thing that should persuade us to desist from this philosophical endeavor is a knockdown argument that proves these questions are *in principle unanswerable* and thus not literally questions at all. It is only then that we should turn to cultivating our gardens.

The next basic philosophical problem we will treat extensively is the problem of God, but before we do that I want to add some philosophical tools to your think tank by saying something in this chapter about logic and in the next two about knowledge and the fixation of belief.

II

Let me commence by making some very elementary remarks about logic. In typical circumstances involving reasoning, we are trying to produce conclusive arguments, or as near to conclusive arguments as we can get for certain propositions, statements, or policies. An argument is any group of statements of which one follows or is claimed to follow from the others, which are regarded as providing grounds for the truth of that one.[3] Arguments have a certain structure. They will have a conclusion, that is, a statement or proposition affirmed on the basis of the other statements or propositions in the argument. These statements, which are affirmed as providing grounds for accepting the conclusion, are the premisses of an argument. What is a conclusion in one argument can be a premiss in another argument. No proposition taken by itself in isolation is either a premiss or a conclusion.

Examples (*P* equals premiss and *C* equals conclusion):

1. P. All people who are religious are happy.
    P. Jeanette is religious.
    C. Jeanette is happy.

But what is a conclusion in this example can serve as a premiss in the next:

2. P. Jeanette is happy.
    P. People who are happy are well adjusted.
    C. Jeanette is well adjusted.

In reasoning, we are concerned of course not only with getting arguments but also with getting valid arguments. Our first two arguments are valid arguments, but the following one is invalid:

3. P. All people who are religious are happy.
    P. Some people who are not religious are unhappy.
    C. Only if you are religious are you happy.

I wish here to say something about what makes an argument valid and to distinguish between *valid* arguments, *sound* arguments, *conclusive* arguments, and *reliable* arguments. Logic is concerned with the canons of *valid* argument. A valid argument, or, more accurately, a valid deductive argument, is an argument such that *if* the premisses are true, the conclusion cannot be false. It is logically impossible for the conclusion of a deductively valid argument to be false if its premisses are true. A traditionally central task of deductive logic—either traditional Aristotelian logic or modern symbolic logic—is to clarify the nature of the relationship that holds between the premisses and the conclusion in valid arguments so that we have clear and decisive *tests* of validity.[4]

An *inductive* argument, by contrast, does *not* claim that if the premisses are true the conclusion of *logical* necessity must be true. It claims, rather, to give some evidence for the truth of the conclusion. A good inductive argument gives a reasonable degree of likelihood or probability to the conclusion.

This is a crude example: A large and varied number of cases of sleeping sickness has been observed. In all cases the disease came about after the person had received many mosquito bites, and it is further known on independent grounds that mosquitoes are frequent carriers of sleeping sickness. Mary Jo comes down with sleeping sickness. Last week she was in the woods and was badly bitten by mosquitoes. In such a circumstance, it is natural to conclude that Mary Jo got the disease as a result of being bitten by the mosquitoes. Note that while this is a reasonable induction, it is certainly not a deductively valid argument.

We shall concern ourselves in the rest of this chapter with deductive arguments only. That is, with arguments which, when correct, are such that if the premises are true and the argument valid, the conclusion cannot be false. Such arguments hold in virtue of their form alone.

Examples:

> All men are mortal.
> Socrates is a man.
> ∴. Socrates is mortal.

> All material objects are made of blue cheese.
> The Empire State Building is a material object.
> ∴. The Empire State Building is made of blue cheese.

Both the sensible argument and the ridiculous one are equally valid. They are both of the general form

> All S's are P.
> r is an S.
> ∴. r is P.

Logic is now characteristically done symbolically. It is topic neutral, and its arguments hold by virtue of their form alone. In fact, they turn on the meanings of the constituent logical terms ('if', 'then', 'and', 'but', 'not', 'all', 'some', and so on). Consider the following:

1. If p then q.
   p.
   ∴. q.
2. If p then q.
   not q.
   ∴. not p.

These are always valid no matter what is substituted for p or q. They hold by virtue of their form alone. But the next two are invalid, for we can readily think of substitutions for p or q where the argument will not hold.

3. If p then q.
   not p.
   not q.

4. If *p* then *q*.

   q.
   _____

   p.

Example 3 is called the fallacy of *denying the antecedent*. Example: If he is a Vietcong, then he is a devil. He is not a Vietcong, therefore he is not a devil. But that is hardly true, for Hitler was a devil and Hitler was not a Vietcong. Example 4 is the fallacy of *affirming the consequent*. Example: If it is orange, then it is colored. It is colored, therefore it is orange. But that is plainly invalid.

Consider the following valid argument:

If Agnew is elected, Wallace will become Secretary of State.
Agnew is elected.
_____

Wallace will become Secretary of State.

From this, it is important to keep in mind the following things:

1. If Wallace becomes Secretary of State, it does not follow that Agnew is elected. If McCarthy or even Dick Gregory were elected, they could, as far as logic goes, make Wallace Secretary of State. If the first premiss in the above argument had read instead, "Only if Agnew is elected will Wallace become Secretary of State," then it would follow that if Wallace is made Secretary of State then Agnew was elected.

2. What we can conclude from the above argument is that if the above premises are true, then, if Wallace is not made Secretary of State, it follows that Agnew was not elected.

III

In deductive logic we are fundamentally concerned not with the truth of propositions or statements but with the deductive relations between propositions. What follows from what is the concern of the deductive logician. If certain statements are true, what, if anything, follows from them? How can we decide when an argument is valid? Logicians wish to get beyond an appeal to intuition—even if it is only a linguistic intuition—to a place where we have developed tests for validity.

It is crucial to see and to take to heart that truth and validity are distinct notions. Arguments and not statements (tautologies apart) are valid or invalid; statements or propositions are true or false, but they cannot be valid or invalid. We can have a valid argument with false statements, that is, with false premises and a false conclusion. We can have a true conclusion and false premises in a valid argument. We can have true premises and a true conclusion and an invalid argument. We can have true premises and a false conclusion and an invalid argument.

We can have false premisses and a true conclusion and an invalid argument. *The only thing we cannot have is a valid argument with true premisses and a false conclusion.*

However, the most crucial thing to see here is that from knowing *only* the truth of the premisses and the conclusion we cannot tell if an argument is valid, and from knowing *only* the validity of an argument we cannot know if its conclusion is true. The mere knowledge that an argument is valid will never enable us to determine whether any proposition is true. Logic cannot, by itself, determine truth.

IV

What has just been said is a perfectly noncontroversial truism, but it still might cause surprise on occasion. Some might exclaim: "But do you really mean logic is unconcerned with truth? It then cannot be very important!" (Part of the practical value of logic involves just seeing that such a 'then' should not be accepted.[5]) It is often terribly important, we must not forget, to determine what follows from what. 'What are the logical consequences of adopting this policy?' That is often a very worthwhile question, and a question whose answers are very hard to come by. The same, of course, holds in science: What follows if this hypothesis should be true?

However, it is indeed true that in actual living argument we are typically concerned not only with valid arguments but with sound arguments as well. *A sound argument is a valid argument with true premisses.* And, therefore, there is a true conclusion. A deductive argument fails to establish the truth of its conclusion if it is unsound. If it is *unsound*, it either is invalid or at least one of its premisses is not true.

We still need two more distinctions for, as G. E. Moore stressed, we not only want sound arguments, we want, where we can get them, *conclusive arguments* as well. *That is, we want valid arguments with premisses known to be true.* After all, our premisses might be true without our knowing them to be true. In such a situation, if our argument were valid, our argument would be a sound one, but we still would not *know* whether our conclusion were true. For this we need a *conclusive* argument—the highest *desiderata* of all reasoning.

Very often we cannot get conclusive arguments. Perhaps, as some philosophers believe, we never can. But when it is impossible to get conclusive arguments, we should seek reliable arguments—*that is, valid arguments with premisses for whose truth we have good evidence.* (Note here that reliability admits of degrees, and arguments can be more or less reliable). If certain premisses are true, or if we have good evidence for their truth, logic can help us determine the truth or reliability of other statements by enabling us to derive them from these premises. But we cannot by logic alone know or have reason to believe in the truth or even the credibility of any statement or proposition.

Our knowledge in logic is always 'iffy': If certain statements are true, then other statements are true. But we must, in order to know or have good reason to believe any statement to be true or credible, go beyond logic. How we determine the truth or the probable truth of a statement will be examined in Chapters 11 and 12. But in saying we must go 'beyond logic', I am most certainly not saying we must reject or neglect logic. Our goal as reasoners is to establish conclusive arguments; and where we cannot get conclusive arguments, we should seek reliable arguments. But to be either conclusive or reliable, such arguments must be valid, for if our arguments are not valid they cannot possibly be conclusive or reliable. (Recall that we are talking about deductive arguments.) Validity is not enough, but with invalid arguments we have nothing.

V

Logic underlies all coherent thinking. In that way it is central in the pursuit of truth.

I have defined 'philosophy' or, rather, 'critical philosophy', as the analytical study of concepts. Well, is this not just a fancy way of saying that philosophy is simply logic? To give a perspicuous display of concepts is—someone might argue—simply to show their logical interrelationships. Science and/or common-sense observation determines the *truth* or *probable truth* of statements, and philosophy—that is, logic—displays their logical interrelationships, shows us what follows from what. Critical philosophy is simply logic or applied logic. That is what an analytical study of concepts actually comes to. The rest is all simply fine talk.

To assert this would be a serious error. Philosophy certainly uses logic, and *sometimes* the primary conceptual clarification given by philosophy is this display of the logical interrelationships of statements. Often, however, and I would say typically, philosophical perplexities are quite different: They center not around whether a certain argument is valid, but around the intelligibility of certain concepts expressed by certain terms occurring in the premises of the arguments or in isolation. When, in Chapter 8, we discussed Hospers' deductive argument, this feature of philosophical argumentation came out in a natural way. The argument did not center around whether the conclusion followed from the premises, but around premiss 5. There was the straightforward empirical question of whether it was true, but, as a more typically philosophical question, there was the question about the meaning of 'inevitable' in that premiss and there was the question about whether 'all causes equally compel'. This last consideration forces us to think about 'compel', 'cause', 'necessitate', and the like. What do they mean, and how do they function in discourse? But this, I would maintain, is a different question from trying to find out what follows from what.

It is plausible to counter this claim of mine by saying that to ask 'What does X mean?' comes down to asking 'What symbols or terms are synonymous with X?' But then to say 'X means Y' or 'X does not mean Y' is literally to make a logical move via the law of identity or a principle of immediate inference. It is not the case that when as philosophers we analyze the meaning of 'democracy', 'God', 'positron', or 'freedom', we are at all content with just providing synonymous expressions, although sometimes we indeed do that. Reflect for confirmation of this on what we actually did when we discussed freedom and determinism.

Let me further confirm and illustrate more fully what I intend by discussing another example. St. Augustine faced this dilemma: Either God cannot abolish evil or He will not. If He cannot, He is not all-powerful; if He will not, He is not all-good. But Jews and Christians *must* believe that God is all-powerful and perfectly good. How can they consistently do that? How is it possible, or *is* it possible—at one and the same time— to assert honestly that there is suffering in the world and that the God of the Christians and the Jews really exists?

Let us set out what is involved rather more explicitly in the form of three propositions:

1. The world contains instances of suffering.
2. God exists—and is omnipotent, omniscient, and perfectly good.
3. An omnipotent and omniscient being would have no morally sufficient reason for allowing instances of suffering.

Let us call this triad A. Consider here what logic can and cannot do. It does tell us that (1), (2), (3) in triad A cannot *all* be true. But logic cannot tell us which one is false. Yet to decide which proposition is false, or at least which one to reject, is a crucial philosophical question, for here we have the center of the problem of evil. Let us, in trying to see how philosophical analysis is not logic or applied logic, although it often uses logic, examine how a philosophical analyst would handle the inconsistent triad A. We should note first that only proposition (1) is an empirical one. That is, it is experience that tells that it is true. It is evidently and obviously true. But neither (2) nor (3) is an empirical statement. Since (1) is an obviously true empirical statement, either (2) or (3) must be rejected, unless we want to fly irrationally in the face of the facts. But (2) is an article of faith for a Jew or Christian. Such a believer, in order to be a believer, must simply accept it, although a nonbeliever is in a position of asking whether it is more reasonable to accept (2) or (3). If a Jew or Christian is trying to give a coherent account of his faith, he must find grounds for rejecting (3) or, at the very least, he must show that (3) is not certainly true. After all, if (3) is true, then (2)— the believer's crucial article of faith—is most certainly false. And if a non-believer is to become a Jew or a Christian, he must show that it is more reasonable to believe (3) is false than it is to believe (2) is false. A little reflection should make this evident.

However, to see how we would make either choice takes us into the very heart of philosophical reasoning and shows us that it is neither the sort of reasoning we use when we test empirical hypotheses nor what we do when we do logic. Compare (3) in triad A with (4) that follows— the frustration-aggression hypothesis.

4. People who are frustrated tend to respond with aggression.

What crucial experiment would test (3) in triad A? It is far from evident that an ycould· How can we show that (3) is formally—that is, logically— in error? In the first place, it is not an argument. Compare (5), which is a genuine argument and thus is either valid or invalid.

5. If Oswald lives he will be found innocent. Oswald did not live. There-fore he will *not* be found innocent.

Logic shows us that this is an invalid argument, for it commits the fallacy of denying the antecedent. But with (3), as with Hospers' premiss 5, we have to reflect on the meanings of the crucial constituent terms. In (3) we must clarify the meanings of 'omnipotent' and 'omniscient'.

We would reason something like this: A father could have a morally sufficient reason to allow the suffering of his child if in some crucial respect he lacked the relevant knowledge or power to bring it to an end. He might also see that it was a necessary means to a higher end: He might allow his child to suffer the pain of an operation if it would save his life. To have a morally sufficient reason to allow suffering, he must know or have a very good reason to believe it is a necessary means to some much higher end, or he must lack the power to stop it, or the knowledge of how to relieve it. If these conditions do not obtain, he can have no morally sufficient reason to allow suffering.

We must now ask ourselves if this is always or necessarily so. To get an answer to this we need an analysis of the meaning of the phrase 'a morally sufficient reason to allow suffering'. What is *meant* by this? We are tempted to say that only the above conditions could count as an excuse for allowing suffering. And we are further likely to think that an omnipotent, omniscient being would have to create the best of all possible worlds. Would it not also be true that even the best of all possible worlds must contain instances of suffering? We need to ask ourselves if it is really true that the best of all possible worlds must contain instances of suffering. Neither logic nor empirical investigation will answer that question; what is needed is a conceptual analysis, a careful elucidation, of such concepts as good and evil, best of all possible worlds, and suffering. In short, we can never know whether 'suffering exists' and 'God exists' contradict each other, as do 'All swans are pink' and 'Some swans are not colored', until we have a perspicuous representation of these terms. This is a matter of analyzing their meaning, not simply of setting out their formal relationships with other terms or the formal relationships between sentences in which they occur and other sentences.

Philosophy (more accurately, critical philosophy)—an analytical study of concepts—is an attempt to clarify what is meant by certain puzzling concepts. The clarification here does not typically come from the use of logic, the formal display of the interrelationships between statements, but from an analysis or clear characterization of the meanings or functions of the constituent nonlogical, nontopic-neutral terms embedded in the perplexing statements. What we need in philosophy is a perspicuous representation of the functions of these statements in the stream of life.

NOTES

1. This is ably argued by A. I. Meldon in his *Free Action* and again in his "Philosophy and the Understanding of Human Fact," in Avrum Stroll (ed.), *Epistemology: New Essays in the Theory of Knowledge.* This position is expounded and discussed critically in some of the essays in Bernard Berofsky (ed.), *Free Will and Determinism.*
2. I should add the cautionary remark that there will no doubt be some philosophers, even among them some analytic philosophers, who will doubt that such definite answers can be given. They will point to renewed discussions concerning the ontological and cosmological arguments. However—and this is a sociological remark—there is a much wider agreement among philosophers that the proofs for the existence of God are not sound than there is about the adequacy of soft determinism. I should also remark that I am not implying that there are no unsettled questions about the concept of God. I am only referring to the attempts to demonstrate His existence.
3. I am not implying that in all arguments 'follow' is an ellipsis for 'deductively follow'.
4. The preceding is a rather simplified account of what a logician is up to. Surely a modern logician would want to say a lot more about what modern logic is about.
5. 'Unconcerned' here may mislead. Logic does not directly establish truth or try to, but 'unconcerned' has an emotive force that should not be applied in the context in which I used it.

11

TRUTH, KNOWLEDGE, AND THE FIXATION OF BELIEF: I

I

We have considered the role of logic in human reasoning and we have learned the very important fact that logic *by itself* cannot determine the truth of any matter of fact or of any substantive principle. Logic is concerned with the canons of validity—with what follows from what. In noting that an argument is *valid*, however, we do not determine whether the conclusion is true. Truth and validity are distinct notions. In knowing that the argument is valid, we know only that if the premises are true, the conclusion must be true. Logic alone cannot uncover truth, but we saw how it nonetheless could be an important instrument in the attainment of truth.

What we seek in reasoning is not merely valid arguments—although we do seek these—but *conclusive* arguments, that is, valid arguments with premises *known* to be true. Where we cannot get conclusive arguments, we seek *reliable* arguments, that is, valid arguments with premises for which we have good evidence or good grounds for believing them to be true or for accepting them.

How can we do this? How can we determine whether our beliefs are true or whether we have good grounds for believing any given assertion? Here is where the whole problem of the fixation of belief becomes crucial. What is the *most reliable method* for settling opinions? *How* can we determine which set of premises it is most reasonable to accept? In considering this, we will for the present bypass Descartes and Hume and start with Charles Saunders Peirce's famous essay, "The Fixation of Belief."[1] Peirce, who is probably the most important American philosopher of the early twentieth century, makes the following matter-of-fact observation.

Our beliefs guide our desires and shape our actions. The Assassins, or followers of the Old Man of the Mountain, used to rush into death at his least command because they believed that obedience to him would insure everlasting felicity. Had they doubted this, they would not have acted as they did. So it is with every belief, according to its degree. The feeling of believing is a more or less sure indication of there being established in our nature some habit which will determine our actions.

These habits are very strong, and "we cling tenaciously, not merely to believing, but to believing just what we do believe." Real doubt is never merely an academic Cartesian matter. If a man has a certain belief, he will tend to behave in a certain way. Doubt, like an irritation of a nerve, interrupts this action. Such irritation—the irritation of doubt— triggers the struggle to attain a state of belief. But the belief must be there first. We have a steady belief and something happens to upset it. The struggle of doubt begins. When this irritation is ended, however, the doubt ends. Hence, as Peirce puts it, "the sole object of inquiry is the settlement of opinion." Peirce goes on to add significantly:

> We may fancy that this is not enough for us, and that we seek not merely an opinion, but a true opinion. But put this fancy to the test, and it proves groundless; for as soon as a firm belief is reached, we are entirely satisfied, whether the belief be false or true. And it is clear that nothing out of the sphere of our knowledge can be our object, for nothing which does not affect the mind can be a motive for a mental effort. The most that can be maintained is that we seek for a belief that we shall *think to be true*. But we think each one of our beliefs to be true, and, indeed, it is a mere tautology to say so.

Given the terminological distinctions we have been making, Peirce is saying that in actual practice we do not seek out conclusive arguments, but reliable ones. Truth is hard to attain, but if we can discover something we believe to be true, something that will genuinely stop the irritation of doubt, we will have attained a settled opinion, put doubt to rest; and this, after all, is the real aim of inquiry or of reasoning.

II

The $64 question remains: What is the most reliable method of assuaging the rub of doubt and fixing belief? To answer this, Peirce is led into an examination of what he takes to be the four basic methods of fixing belief utilized by man throughout his checkered history. He called them the *method of tenacity;* the *method of authority;* the *metaphysical* (or *a priori*) *method;* and the *scientific (or pragmatic) method*. It is Peirce's contention that only the last method is satisfactory, for the others in reality break down in practice. I shall characterize these various methods, give Peirce's main argument for giving the grand prize to the scientific method, and then assess Peirce's claims.

The Method of Tenacity

A man uses the method of tenacity when he holds his beliefs unswervingly and dogmatically, simply because they are *his* beliefs and he *wants* to believe them. A man uses this method when he refuses to consider whether there is any evidence for or against those beliefs. He simply believes whatever he wants to believe. Anything that might be taken by someone else as disconfirming evidence is simply rejected as 'false propaganda' or 'patently untrue.' He fancies that if he constantly reiterates his pet beliefs to himself, dwelling on all that may be conducive to those beliefs, and turning with horror, contempt and hatred from anything that might disturb them, he can attain satisfaction. That is, he can avoid the irritation of doubt and free himself from the 'wolves of disbelief'.

Peirce, quite consistently with his general approach, assesses these methods strictly in terms of whether they will stand up in *practice*. Thus, he does not inveigh against the evident irrationality of the method of tenacity. After all, a man who uses this method and knows what he is doing does not propose to be rational. One advantage of this method— an advantage not to be scoffed at—is its simplicity. With it there is no anxiety or struggle of soul. And this gives its practitioners considerable peace of mind. There is for them the tranquility that follows from their "steady and immovable faith." For any question, just consider what you *want* to believe, and after that there is no further question about deciding what to believe. As Peirce puts it:

> Thus, if it be true that death is annihilation, then the man who believes that he will certainly go straight to heaven when he dies, provided he has fulfilled certain simple observances in this life, has a cheap pleasure which will not be followed by the least disappointment. A similar consideration seems to have weight with many persons in religious topics, for we frequently hear it said, 'Oh, I could not believe so-and-so because I should be wretched if I did.' When an ostrich buries its head in the sand as danger approaches, it very likely takes the happiest course. It hides the danger, and then calmly says there is no danger; and, if it feels perfectly sure there is none, why should it raise its head to see? A man may go through life, systematically keeping out of view all that might cause a change in his opinions, and if he only succeeds—basing his method, as he does, on two fundamental psychological laws—I do not see what can be said against his doing so. It would be an egotistical impertinence to object that his procedure is irrational, for that only amounts to saying that his method of settling belief is not ours. He does not propose to himself to be rational, and, indeed, will often talk with scorn of man's weak and illusive reason. So let him think as he pleases.

Unfortunately, the method of tenacity has its disadvantages as well. The social impulse is against it. In some dreadful moment of lucidity, its devotees will see or are very likely to see that other men's opinions are quite as good as their own. This will shake their confidence in their own beliefs. They will then be forced—psychologically forced—whether they like it or not, to seek some extrapersonal rationale for their beliefs. In short, they cannot—as a matter of fact—keep up their own secure confidence in such a simple method of fixing belief.

The Method of Authority

The method of authority is really the method of tenacity institutionalized. It is superior to the method of tenacity because, through institutional control by the state and/or the church, what is taught and what can be read or said can be carefully controlled. Through mystery, miracle, and authority the method of authority can win the hearts and minds of the great masses of people.

Again, such a method has its characteristic advantages. We indeed have the comfort of "Big Brother." Everything can be known and everything can be decided for the individual. Thus, he need not be a "masterless man" who must somehow decide for himself how to orient his life in an alien world. By using this method, he can avoid the agony of personal decision and the rub of doubt and the struggle to attain beliefs he has reasoned out on his own. The others are with him, so he has the blessings of human solidarity. He need only *goad* his will to be in tune with his institutionally fixed Absolute. And with an alert method of authority, there will be a kind of good Pavlovian conditioning to keep tootle straight on the tracks, no matter what, from cradle to grave. With luck—given a certain development in science—we might even be able to help out the individual by fixing up his genetic structure after the manner of Brave New World.

Unfortunately, man's big brain messes things up for him. Unless we have some superlative *1984*, it will, as a matter of fact, be impossible for the state to regulate beliefs or opinions on everything. It may be left up to the individual to decide whether it is more rational to assert that fish bite best when the wind is in the west and least when the wind is in the east or vice versa. In short, it is difficult to construct a total faith, and to maintain total ideological thought control. And it is such failures in achieving thorough thought control that make room for the rub of doubt. Some men will start to wonder if the received laws are right. Is 'X is true' really always equivalent to 'Big Brother says X'? In the struggle to fix belief—that is, in the struggle to avoid the unpleasantness of doubt—they will, as a matter of fact, come to seek some new, more objective method for settling opinion. They will seek some extrapersonal and extrainstitutional method that will not only produce an impulse to believe but will also enable them to decide what propositions are to be believed.

Some deviants from the cultural norms will take the attitude that they will not accept anything "that seems to be determined by caprice." They will not remain satisfied with whimsical beliefs, whether they are their own or those of their local belief and taste setters. They will be the troublemakers in the culture. However, it remains doubtful whether they can bring the masses with them, for, as Peirce remarks, perhaps the vast majority of people will always fix their beliefs by the method of authority, being *content to remain intellectual slaves*. As a matter of anthropological fact, however, it will also remain true that every society will produce its heretics who will question the established order of things, who will— even when they are strongly tempted to—not warm themselves at the tribal campfire. And these critics of society will, even for what Peirce regards as the larger masses of intellectual slaves, disrupt the established order of things. This, given man's very biological makeup, his degree of intelligence, cannot—again, as a matter of fact—fail to be true. Thus, the *method of authority*, like the *method of tenacity*, will break down in practice.

The Metaphysical Method

(Peirce sometimes refers to this as the *a priori method* or the *method of intuition*.) This is the method of traditional philosophers. Descartes and Spinoza—Continental philosophers of the seventeenth century—can be taken as exemplary cases. Philosophers, let it be noted, have typically been the ones who have *not* been able to bend their 'cultural knee'. They have usually, in some sense, stood outside the tribal circle and either scoffed at or, as Descartes and Kant did, tried somehow to find a higher rationale for their central tribal beliefs. Typically, they have never been able to accept, consciously at least, the method of authority as such. Yet, the beliefs sanctioned by authority still have a powerful hold on them.

Philosophical rationalism has always operated on the principle that belief should be fixed by an 'appeal to reason'. Rationalists tell us that we are only to believe what is clear and distinct to our unencumbered reason. This, they argue, is the way to fix belief. This method alone will end the quest for certainty. It will take us beyond the idols of the tribe and finally give us intellectual peace. We should, as Descartes stressed, examine all our beliefs and accept only those that embody "clear and distinct" ideas.

An idea is clear if it is an idea or concept that will be recognized whenever it is encountered. This means nothing more, Peirce contends, than that we have a familiarity with the idea in question. But this familiarity may be merely a subjective *feeling* of mastery, which may signify no real mastery at all. That is, one may feel that he is clear about something and yet be quite mistaken.

A distinct idea is one that after dialectial examination contains nothing that is not clear. That is, it must not only be clear at the outset, but it must also "sustain the test of dialectical examination." Yet, Peirce asks, how do we distinguish between something that seems clear and distinct and also really *is* clear and distinct, and something that seems clear and distinct but really *is not* clear and distinct? We seem to have no firm ground to stand on here at all.

Peirce presses us to ask: How do we know whether our clear and distinct beliefs are actually correct beliefs? Saying that a clear and distinct belief is in accord with reason or agreeable to reason does not make it so. Might not a belief be clear and distinct and still be mistaken? How do we know when a belief is in accord with reason and is thus a belief we might assert as a premiss in a reliable argument? What is our test for correctness in this dialectical examination? Peirce ironically remarks of the phrase 'in accord with reason': "This is an apt expression; it does not mean that which agrees with experience, but that which we find ourselves inclined to believe."

This metaphysical method has a far more objective, far more attractive sound than the method of tenacity or authority. Peirce argues, however, that this is misleading, and in practice this method has always been a failure. In spite of its rationalistic sound, it

> . . . makes inquiry something similar to the development of taste; but taste, unfortunately, is always more or less a matter of fashion, and, accordingly, metaphysicians have never come to any fixed agreement, but the pendulum has swung backward and forward between a more material and a more spiritual philosophy, from the earliest times to the latest.

The *a priori method* in reality does not, according to Peirce, go beyond the *method of authority* in any essential respect, since with it we have no test for what is actually agreeable to reason. For any question of fact or substantive principle, we have no way to distinguish, by the use of such a method, between what we merely believe is agreeable to reason and what actually is agreeable to reason. So what we as individuals think is agreeable to reason will, in reality, unless we are cultural rebels, turn out to be that which our culture patterns, implicit or explicit, have accustomed us to approve of or accept. And even if we are rebelling against our tribal folklore, the direction of our rebellion will be set by our particular mores and by our individual feelings. There is no way by such a dialectical examination to distinguish between 'X really is in accord with reason' and 'X merely seems to be in accord with reason'. But this means that the statement 'X is in accord with reason', like 'free' for a hard determinist, has no nonvacuous contrast, and so it is a term devoid of any determinate meaning. It purports to be descriptive, but in fact it is not. Thus, it is useless in deciding how to fix belief.

However, people, or at least a significant number or group of people, will sooner or later see through this method of fixing belief. In short, the metaphysical method, like the method of tenacity and the method of authority, breaks down in practice. That is its fundamental defect. There is a large number of people who, when they see "any belief of theirs is determined by any circumstance extraneous to the facts, will from that moment not merely admit in words that that belief is doubtful, but will experience a real doubt of it, so that it ceases to be a belief."

They require that their belief should not rest on something purely conventional or personal, but should be founded on something that has some external permanency. They want something objective, that is, something publicly determinable. They want a method such that if it is applied diligently, "the ultimate conclusion of every man shall be the same." The scientific method, Peirce claims, gives them such a foundation. It alone will serve as an adequate method for fixing belief.

III

What remains to be done, however, is to give a characterization of scientific method that will show that this is actually so. In "Fixation of Belief," Peirce states in a rather cryptic way what he means by 'the scientific method'. Its fundamental tenet, according to Peirce, is this:

> There are real things, whose characters are entirely independent of our opinions about them; those realities affect our senses according to regular laws, and, though our sensations are as different as our relations to the objects, yet, by taking advantage of the laws of perception, we can ascertain by reasoning how things really are, and any man, if he have sufficient experience and reason enough about it, will be led to the one true conclusion. The new conception here involved is that of reality.

Peirce contends that the scientific method is the only method that actually enables us to correct and check our conclusions. There is with the scientific method a public check on whether what I believe to be so really is so. If I fix my belief in this way, my statements and beliefs are all taken as hypotheses: that is to say, they are all *open* to a public test—to confirmation and disconfirmation. The man who will use this method cannot claim a belief to be true or justified and *deny* that there is publicly ascertainable evidence for it. If I fix my beliefs in this way, I must state my claims in such a way that they are open to such a *public check*, and if I claim that a statement warrants belief, I must have *tested* and *confirmed* it, or I must have good reasons to believe that others have tested and confirmed this statement. If others try the same tests and they do not work out, then my belief cannot correctly be said to be justified.

Scientists do not want simply to amass facts about the things around them. They endeavor to make sense of these facts. They want to develop theories of great generality with predictive reliability and capability of generating many predictions. In this way, their explanations gain general explanatory power. They are not tailor-made for the particular case. They attempt to see the old things in a new way; that is to say, they develop new ways of organizing phenomena so that what appears to be inexplicable and irregular will be seen to be quite explicable and regular.

Scientific explanations, as distinct from those explanations utilized by the other methods of fixing belief, are put forth tentatively and provisionally. They are subject to repeated tests. The scientist seeks to state his hypotheses in such a way that they admit of disconfirmation. That is to say, he tries to state them in such a way that experiments can be conducted such that, depending on the results of these experiments, his hypotheses will be either confirmed or disconfirmed.

If the hypothesis is that frustrated people will respond aggressively, he will try to state it in such a way that one can say, "If I do so and so, that will frustrate people, and then I will observe they do such and such." If in a number of carefully controlled situations they are observed not to do such and such when so frustrated, then the hypothesis in question is disconfirmed. Those hypotheses that have great generality and predictive fertility finally become laws in the corpus of science when they have withstood repeated attempts at disconfirmation. The crucial point is that all explanations must be subject to test, direct or indirect, if they are to rate as scientific explanations and scientific methods of fixing belief. Sense experience, but not just an individual's sense experience, is the ultimate test of a scientific explanation or theory.

However, we must not forget here that frequently in science our tests are *indirect*. Testing Newton's laws or Einstein's theory is not like looking out the window to see whether it is raining or sticking your big toe in the water to see if the water is cold. Rather, these scientific claims are only tested indirectly. But indirect testing is a method we are all perfectly familiar with since we use it repeatedly not only in science but in everyday life as well. Suppose a student writes a term paper on Peirce and he comes up with some complicated ideas that I suspect have been plagiarized from a source he has not cited. Let us say the source does not occur in his bibliography, but that in his term paper several crucial passages stating a complex argument are, with minor variations, identical in wording to the crucial arguments of the source not cited. I now check with the library and discover that the student in question has checked out this book. I have used an indirect test of my hypothesis, 'B took his major criticisms of Peirce from book A'.

The indirect test here is indeed not completely decisive. The student may have taken out the book and never looked at it or never read the part that contained those criticisms, and by coincidence thought of the same criticism and put it in very similar language. But this is highly unlikely, and I have very good grounds for confronting the student concerning it.

Such indirect testing is standard practice in science, and it is crucial to remember that Peirce is claiming that if a belief is not either directly or indirectly *tested*, we do not really have good grounds for accepting it as true, although in some circumstances we may take it as a reasonable hunch. Moreover, a belief that is neither directly nor indirectly *testable* cannot possibly be an objective belief. And, as we have argued, only such objective beliefs will in practice finally satisfy men—will finally ease the rub of doubt and thus adequately fix belief.

Let us look at this matter of fixing belief from a slightly different angle. Man, the social animal that he is, cannot for long avoid conflicts of opinion and attitude. Doubt is an irritant, and it will continue to plague men. There is no way of dispelling doubt in general, but the scientific method alone affords us a method of relieving *specific* doubts that arise in the course of living. Such a method will not give us certainty, but it will give a greater measure of truth than any alternative method. It is, as Cohen and Nagel (men very much in the Peircian tradition) put it, "the only way to increase the general body of tested and verified truth and to eliminate arbitrary opinion." If we want to arrive at any measure of truth, it is well to clarify our ideas by asking for the precise meaning of our words, and to try to check our favorite ideas by so formulating them that they occur in statements capable of experiential (and quite public) test by those who will take the trouble to investigate the matter.

We should fix all our beliefs in this manner. We should not accept the plaintive cry that there is some private way of mystic intuition that will enable us to fix belief, or the claim that "the heart has its reasons that reason does not know." That people should make such appeals is understandable enough, but they will not lead us to truth. The little truth we can garner will be gained by the rather more mundane method of science.

Peirce points out, however, that using the scientific method of fixing beliefs has its disadvantages; it sometimes disturbs one's peace of mind, for it often leads one to question tribal taboos, and this brings on the scorn of the mob, or, where one is silent, it causes one to feel alienated and estranged from one's society. It is not only that "hell is others" but, as Peirce puts it, often "a man torments himself and is oftentimes most distressed at finding himself believing propositions which he has been brought up to regard with aversion."

However, *if* a man *wishes* his opinions to coincide with the facts, he must use the method of science. Furthermore, in case after case, in situation after situation, he will suffer if he does not *attend to the facts*, if he does not *reverence the truth*. Finally, Peirce adds an ethical argument:

> To avoid looking into the support of any belief from a fear that it may turn out rotten is quite as immoral as it is disadvantageous. The person who confesses that there is such a thing as truth, which is distinguished from falsehood simply by this, that if acted on it will carry us to the point we aim at and not astray, and then though convinced of this, dares not know the truth and seeks to avoid it, is in a sorry state of mind indeed.

Is this always so? Is it never the case that a man ought to hide the truth from himself? From Socrates to Freud we have been prepared to commit ourselves to truth at any cost. I, too, feel a strong emotional inclination to side with Peirce here. But in a cool hour I ask myself if we can be so sure that this is right for everyone no matter what his circumstances. Imagine a very old country priest who begins to have his doubts, and let us assume for the sake of this example that his doubts are justified and his faith is without a rational ground. But suppose his whole life is tied to his vocation as a priest and that he is a good priest who helps others. Is it so certain that he should press through to the truth? This point plainly needs discussing. Moreover, it may be generally true that many people are better off with their illusions.

There is another point that certainly should prove embarrassing for Peirce. How would we use the scientific method for fixing Peirce's ethical judgment here? How would we use it to show that Peirce's commitment to truth was the correct view and the other view was that of a man in a sorry state of mind with a warped sense of moral judgment? What crucial experiment or set of experiments could be run here that would decide the matter one way or another, that would not, as James would put it, ultimately involve an appeal to a person's sentiments, to what he would commit himself? It is not at all evident that scientific method would be able to fix our belief here.

However, in fairness to Peirce we should regard his moralizing at the end as an aside. The crucial question is this: Has Peirce shown that the scientific method is the sole adequate method for fixing belief, the sole method that will stand up in practice? We shall turn to a critical examination of this point in the next chapter.

NOTES

1. This classic essay has been reprinted in various places, including Phillip P. Weiner (ed.), *Values in a Universe of Chance: Selected Writings of Charles S. Peirce* (Garden City, New York: Doubleday Anchor Books, 1958). All references to Peirce in this chapter are to that essay.

12

TRUTH, KNOWLEDGE, AND THE FIXATION OF BELIEF: II

I

How much of the "fixation of belief" should we accept? Where we are talking about questions of empirical fact, it seems to me that Peirce's claim is essentially right. This is not to say that there are not crucial additional complexities that Peirce did not notice—particularly where we are talking about questions of social and institutional fact—but the thrust of his argument clearly seems to me to be in the right direction. When we want to know what happened in the world or what assertions concerning what happens in the world are credible, the scientific method of fixing belief, characterized in the broad manner in which Peirce characterized it, is the sole reliable method. When we want to know what to *expect*, as distinct from knowing what to *do*, such a method is the only adequate method for fixing belief.

A speculative philosophy or a metaphysics *as a kind of* superscience is ridiculous. But human beings have a whole battery of interests: We do not only want to know what the empirical facts are, we also want to know what to do. Not all questions we want to ask are questions of fact. And it is at least *arguable* that there are facts other than empirical facts.[1]

Moral questions engage us: Is it really wrong to struggle to make one's way to the top without regard for others? Can it ever be right to say: My country right or wrong, but still my country? We ask similar questions about literature and art. Must all good fictional characterization have a basic fidelity to human nature? Is lyric poetry the highest form of literary expression?

Consider these statements: ' "My country right or wrong, but still my country" is a vile sentiment', 'All good fiction must have a basic fidelity to human nature', 'Lyric poetry is the highest form of literary expression'. Now compare them with 'The typewriter is green', 'Ireland has no native snakes', 'Frustrated human beings tend to respond aggressively'. We know what it would be like to fix beliefs concerning the latter lot scientifically because we know what counts as evidence for statements made by the use of such sentences. But for the moral and aesthetic utterances, the matter is quite different. We have no clear idea how, if at all, they could be confirmed or infirmed. It is not evident that we could give evidence for or against them in the sense that, apart from the human attitudes we agents take toward them, we could simply confirm that they indeed were so or not so.

We do not even know what it would be like to make a probable judgment here. It is far from clear that they are scientifically or experientially testable by public observation. At the very least, Peirce has not given us the slightest reason to think that this is so. There are many who think moral and aesthetic utterances have a very different status and that such moral and aesthetic utterances do not make claims that can be scientifically fixed. Peirce does not show that this is not so.

Consider—normative questions apart—religious questions: (1) Is there a God? (2) Were His most crucial revelations given to Mohammed? Has there been or could there have been a crucial experiment or set of experiments here? To put it conservatively, it seems very difficult to conceive of what it would be like to fulfill these conditions, and after all these centuries is this simply due to the poverty of human imagination? Again, it is difficult to believe that this is so. Could one in any way publicly verify (1) or (2), that is, fix belief here by the use of what Peirce calls the scientific method? Perhaps, but the burden of proof most surely rests on Peirce to give us some good reasons for believing that this is so.

Let us turn to the affairs of men. Suppose someone asks: (1) Did the Nuremberg trials have a genuine legal basis? (2) Does the state have the right to enforce questions of private morality?

How could the method of science—basically the method of systematic observation, hypothesis construction, and experimentation—settle such questions? Unless, after the fashion of the Germans' use of *Wissenschaft*, we extended the use of 'science' far beyond its normal confines, we have no idea of how to uncover scientifically—basically by the use of hypothesis construction and experimental testing—answers to those questions.

Perhaps there are many reliable methods of fixing belief, some of which are applicable in one context and some in another. After all, one would hardly expect to find the experimental method applied in pure mathematics or logic. There the *a priori method* seems to be quite appropriate. What method is reliable, it is reasonable to argue, depends on the subject matter.

Not all philosophers would acknowledge such a plurality of methods. Peirce and Dewey would argue that the scientific method of fixing belief can be extended to these areas as well. Here we must use creative ingenuity to come to see how such an extension can be made.

Dewey, in particular, has argued that until we come to work out its application in such spheres, we will have no way of objectively fixing belief in those areas.[2] Others argue that this is in effect to treat science as a "sacred cow," and that it is impossible and unnecessary to extend scientific method to those areas in order to have an objective way of fixing belief.[3] Still others argue that this extension of scientific method cannot be carried out, and since it cannot be carried out, there can be no objective fixation of belief for such matters.[4]

It is certainly not obvious that such an extension of the scientific method can be made, but it is also true that I have not shown that it cannot be made. All I have done here is to raise questions. Crucial tests of whether such a Peircean program can be carried out will arise when we discuss both the topic of religion and the topic of morality. But that the scientific method can be the sole adequate method here for fixing belief seems implausible on the surface, at any rate. The burden of proof surely rests on the Peircean to demonstrate how this is possible.

II

Now I want to discuss the question of whether philosophy can become a science. I have argued that philosophy is not logic, and I shall now argue that neither is it science. That is, I want to argue that we cannot extend to philosophy itself the Peircean method of fixing belief by use of the scientific method. If we are to remain wedded to the claim that the only adequate method of fixing belief is the method of science— where 'science' does not come to have the wide meaning of *Wissenschaft*—then we must become therapeutic positivists and argue either that what constitutes a philosophical problem or a philosophical answer should be radically altered or that all philosophical problems are in reality pseudoproblems resting on linguistic or conceptual confusions.

But why not treat philosophy as a science? Leaving questions of philosophical ethics or law aside for the present, why not use Peirce's method for resolving philosophical questions? Are they not questions of fact? Is it not a question of fact whether or not every event has a cause? Should it not be painfully evident that we should use the method of science to resolve that question? It is indeed a highly speculative question of fact, but nevertheless a question of fact, that is, a question about empirical states of affairs.

I must squarely face such questions. Why can philosophy not be a science? Would it not indeed be a good thing to put an end to all the loose talk and acrimonious dispute that goes with untestable claims? Should not philosophers at long last resolve to get rid of the atmosphere of the seminary and take on the ways of men of science? Then, and only then, will philosophy reconstruct itself. There is a point to such a claim, but there is confusion in it as well.

On the side of those who would make philosophy a science, it needs to be noted that where there is a genuine advance in any intellectual subject, there is a disappearance of 'schools of thought' in which one expects and needs a diversity of viewpoints and in which the disputants strive to win converts and to defend themselves from their intellectual enemies. And, it should be observed, it is just this that happens when intellectuals debate on large cultural topics. They form schools of thought and they unwittingly become ideologues.

This has happened in philosophy as well, and to an extent it still happens. I am not at all suggesting that *The Partisan Review* or *The New York Review of Books* cease operation; there is indeed an evident need for this kind of discussion and it most definitely has a point. It helps form a critical awareness about our society that is most necessary. But in philosophy we need to get beyond ideological debate and ideological stances. Moreover, the existence of 'schools of thought' is an embarrassment in science, and it *ought to be* in philosophy. There are signs— although not terribly reliable ones—that in Anglo-American and Scandinavian philosophy the battle of "isms" may at long last be stumbling to a halt. Discoveries of a sort are made and some agreement is reached by competent researchers in restricted areas.[5] But this does not make philosophy a science in a straightforward sense.

However, I shall argue that it is a mistake to regard philosophy as either a deductive science, such as geometry or logic, or an empirical science, such as physics or biology. This should be obvious, but I fear even the obvious has, at times, been doubted. Let me indicate why philosophy is neither a deductive nor an empirical science.

Why not cast philosophy in a deductive mold with theorems, proofs, and questions to be decided yes or no? For one thing, proofs require premisses.[6] Whenever such premisses have been set up in the past, even tentatively, the discussion at once challenged them and shifted to a deeper level. And where there are no proofs, neither can there be theorems.

Perhaps there are certain premisses that are self-evident, the denial of which would be self-contradictory. They, it might be thought, are acceptable premisses for first principles in philosophy. But then they would be analytic premisses, what Hume called relations of ideas, and from analytic premisses alone no synthetic conclusions could follow. Thus, they would tell us nothing of substance about the world, since nothing at all would be excluded. That is to say, no conclusions about what the world is like would follow from them and no conclusions about how we are to act, how we are to live and die would follow from them either.

These remarks may seem obscure to some. An analytic premiss is an analytic statement that serves as a premiss in an argument. An analytic statement is one whose denial is self-contradictory, or what comes to the same thing, a statement that is true by definition. Examples will make my meaning clearer: 'Puppies are young dogs' and 'Puppies are young'. Note the former is a definition—the 'are' functions as the sign of equality —and the latter is deducible from the definition. Similarly, 'Every effect has a cause', discussed when we examined determinism, is analytic. It also follows from the definitional statement 'An effect is an event or action that has a cause.'

By contrast, synthetic statements are those that are not true by *definition* and are not statements derivable from definitions alone or statements the denials of which are contradictory. Examples are 'Puppies are tail-waggers', 'Puppies are hard to train', 'The causes of the Civil War are hard to discern', 'The cause of Napoleon's death is unknown'. These synthetic statements are statements of the kind Hume called "matters of fact." He believed that all synthetic statements are statements of empirical fact.

What is meant by saying that analytic statements tell us nothing and exclude nothing can be seen from working with an example. 'Puppies are young dogs' would normally be used to teach someone the meaning of 'puppy' or to amplify his understanding of the term. If he did not understand that puppies are young dogs, he could not understand or at the very least could not adequately understand the word 'puppies' and so he would not understand or at least at all adequately understand the sentence 'Puppies are young dogs'. But if he understands, or at least if he at all adequately understands, the meaning of 'puppy', he already understands they are young dogs from a knowledge of the meaning of the word alone. Thus, 'Puppies are young dogs' tells him nothing about the world beyond what he would get from a knowledge of the meaning of the word 'puppy'. In this crucial way, analytic statements tell us nothing.

I would only qualify this by saying that analytic statements can give us added information about our language and about the nature of the concepts expressed by such sentences. Moreover, analytic statements do not exclude anything either, for while we know very well what a world would be like that excludes tail-wagging puppies and what a world would be like that includes them, we do not have the least understanding of what it would be like for there to be a world in which puppies are not young dogs. That, given the meaning of 'puppy', is inconceivable.

Analytic statements are not only said to be vacuous in the manner just discussed, but they are also said to be *a priori*. In saying they are *a priori*, we are saying they are statements the *truth* of which holds independently of experience. Most analytic philosophers believe that all and only analytic statements are *a priori*. However, some philosophers, following Kant, think that in addition there are synthetic *a priori* statements, for example, 'Every event has a cause' or 'Nothing can be both red and green all over'. The crucial thing to keep in mind at this stage is that at least the bulk of *a priori* statements are analytic and the bulk of synthetic statements are empirical. It is with them that we have firm, paradigmatic senses of 'analytic' and 'synthetic', and with analytic statements alone we get clear cases of *a priori* truths.

Given the preceding claim about *synthetic a priori* statements, perhaps the premisses or at least one of the premisses in a philosophical argument could be synthetic and *a priori;* and if this were so, then certain conclusions of substance could follow from such premisses. But even assuming there is some tolerably clear sense in which we can justifiably assert there are *synthetic a priori* statements, we would still have the problem of validating them. Suppose two different philosophers came up with two different and conflicting *synthetic a priori* statements. The statements cannot both be true. Both philosophers regard their statements as being clear and distinct and as being in accord with reason. But here, as Peirce stressed, since we lack any kind of a genuine test at all, we cannot decide which one *is* really clear and distinct and which one *merely seems* so; if they are synthetic *a priori* statements, we cannot decide which claim is actually in accord with reason and which claim merely appears to be in accord with reason.

There seems to be no way of deciding what could possibly count as being right or wrong here. There is no agreement that there are any *synthetic a priori* statements; there is no agreement as to *which* statements are synthetic *a priori* statements; there is no agreement how, if there were, we could establish some to be true and others false; there is no agreement in what sense, if at all, they would be self-evident; and, finally, there is no agreement about their role or lack thereof in a philosophical system.

Yet, someone still might say, "But can you prove there are no *synthetic a priori* statements? Or, more generally, can you prove there are no proofs in philosophy?' And the answer is *no*. As the contemporary British philosopher Waismann rightly remarks, "Such a proof, if it were possible, would by its very existence establish what it was meant to confute." He goes on to say:

> Why suppose the philosopher to have an I.Q. so low as to be unable to learn from the past? Just as the constant failure of attempts at constructing a perpetual motion machine has, in the end, led to something positive in physics, so the efforts to construct a philosophical 'system', going on for centuries and going out of fashion fairly recently, tell their tale.[7]

We have good reasons for saying there are no proofs in philosophy, but this does not entail that there are no *arguments*, good reasons, or plausible reasoning in philosophy. There are. But the attempt to make philosophy into a deductive system with self-evident axioms, postulates, and so on, simply will not do. In that very rationalistic sense of 'proof', there are no proofs in philosophy.

Even if philosophy cannot be a deductive science, why can it not be an experimental science? Why is it impossible in philosophy to fix belief as Peirce advocated? Why could not some of the premises be simply general statements of fact that have been confirmed to one degree or another, or are at least statements of fact that are confirmable in principle? We could, of course, stipulate that certain empirical statements such as 'Men tend to be aggressive', 'Both Communist and non-Communist countries are developing in strikingly similar ways', and 'The Universe is expanding' be called philosophical statements. No doubt many very different kinds of statement have been called 'philosophical statements', and doubtless some of them have been vast and exceedingly vague or sometimes simply truistic empirical generalizations. However, such statements and empirical statements in general have usually *not* been regarded as 'philosophical statements'. Philosophical perplexity has not often been generated around statements that in a reasonably evident sense are verifiable (confirmable or infirmable) in principle. Yet it is only statements that are either directly or indirectly verifiable (testable empirically) that clearly serve as acceptable factual assertions in a system of thought that would fix belief by the scientific method. But in their typical instances, at any rate, philosophical statements are not such empirical statements and philosophical questions are not empirical questions.

To see how this is so, it is well to look at a sampling of questions that have been commonly regarded as philosophical. Philosophers characteristically ask questions such as the following:

1. Do we perceive material objects or do we perceive only sense data? And how do we recognize a sense-datum? What is there that's not a sense-datum?

2. Do we have knowledge of other minds or of the feelings of others?

3. Is something good or evil because we approve or disapprove of it, or do we approve or disapprove of it because it is good or evil?

4. If God is all-good and all-powerful, why is there evil? Is not all evil in the final analysis merely appearance? (And another philosopher asks: But is not the *appearance* of evil itself an evil? And is there not an infinite regress from which we cannot escape?)

5. Are moral judgments really scientific hypotheses? (Alternatively: Are they really statements at all? Can there, Russell persists in asking, really be ethical knowledge?)

6. Is time reversible?

7. Did the universe have a beginning in time or is it eternal?

8. Do not all men in the final analysis seek only what they take to be their own happiness? Can we ever really ascertain the true nature of happiness?

9. Are there universals or is there just the name in common between utterly distinct particulars? What is 'a particular' really? And—after all—what is there? Is to be to be a value of a bound variable?

10. Can there be a thought that is not expressible in language? What is thinking, anyway? Can machines think?

11. If a man's choices are determined, can he be a responsible moral agent? Can a man be free and determined? What is freedom really? Can we ever justifiably punish another man? Are all crimes really only diseases?

12. What is the meaning of life? What is the point of human existence? How should I live if I am to live well?

These are typical philosophical questions and no doubt in certain respects are very different, but they also appear to have some very important features in common. As Isaiah Berlin remarks, these "questions tend to be very general, to involve issues of principle, and to have little or no concern with practical utility." Indeed, there is something very peculiar about these questions. The man who seriously entertains them is not very sure what exactly he is asking or what would count as an answer. As Ludwig Wittgenstein, perhaps the most important philosopher in the twentieth century, was given to saying, the man who honestly asks a philosophical question is like the man who is adrift, who does not know his way around; he asks the sort of question that paradoxically brings itself into question.

In philosophy there seem to be no self-evident premises to which we can appeal from which we could deduce answers to these questions, and our other great instrument of human knowledge, empirical investigation, seems equally helpless to supply us with answers. If I ask myself 'Did I leave my car at Union Square?', I know what to do in order to verify that, and I know 'Is a car really an automobile?' to be a self-answering question. Nor do I have any trouble with 'Is smallpox a disease?' or 'Can there be a cure for cancer?' But what about 'Are all crimes really only diseases?' Well, people once thought that acts we now say are caused by kleptomania, alcoholism, or even insanity were crimes. But by now most of us have become accustomed to acknowledging, as I put it in an earlier chapter, that the list of crimes gets shorter and the list of diseases longer. In the light of this we ask ourselves if perhaps there really are no crimes and if maybe no one is really free. And if no one is ever really free, how is crime possible? Now, what crucial experiment or empirical investigation could I conduct to answer this question? I am not even sure what the question really asks. I am not even sure in what sense it really is a question. I do not know what would be taken as an answer to it such that if I did construct a hypothesis and make deductions from the hypothesis and try to verify the observation statements that I deduced from my hypothesis, I would know whether or not I had answered the original question. How *could* all crimes really be diseases? Do not the words 'crime 'and 'disease', like the words 'good' and 'bad 'and 'approve' and 'disapprove', have meaning only when they can be significantly opposed to each other? The idea of any straightforward empirical test for whether all crimes are really diseases seems utterly fatuous. And it is even more fatuous for some of the more traditional problems. What kind of experiment would prove or give substantial evidence for the truth of falsity of the claim that there are universals, sense-data, material objects, thoughts that could not be expressed in language, a meaning to life, and the like?

We know in a general way what kind of empirical observations would help us answer 'Are there snakes in Ireland?', 'Are educated women undersexed?', 'Was there a Civil War in the United States in the nineteenth century?', 'Is Einstein's theory superior to Newton's?', and 'How should I mend my boy's sled?'. But we are not at all clear about how to answer 'Are there material objects in the universe?', 'Are educated women really women?', 'Did the universe have a beginning in time?', 'Are the predictions of scientists more reliable than the claims of shamans?', and 'How should I live and die?'.

Empirical knowledge is in some degree and in some sense relevant to the answering or dissolution of those questions, but they are hardly straightforward empirical questions to which we could give straightforward or even crooked empirical answers. These questions, which bring themselves into question, are not ones that could be answered by constructing an 'experimental philosophy' in which a number of empirical statements stood as the basic premises.

We might reconstruct philosophy, as Dewey sometimes seems to suggest, by putting aside these questions and by asking and answering quite different questions in their stead. And this may well be a reasonable thing to do, for there is indeed something queer and unrealistic about philosophical questions. Rather than answering or even dissolving therapeutically the philosophical questions, this Deweyian approach simply bypasses them, and gives the word 'philosophy' a radically new meaning. However, this, in turn, would need to be philosophically justified in a more standard sense of 'philosophically justified'.[8]

It is just these strange and haunting questions that bring themselves into question, that have traditionally been the main philosophical questions; and it is to these that we must address ourselves when, in any ordinary sense, we ask philosophical questions. They are expressive of deep conceptual dilemmas that are often, although not always, generated by a failure to understand the logic of our own language or the relations between our language and some technical language that has been developed. They are not questions that require an empirical investigation of our world, and we will not dissolve or relieve these dilemmas by constructing some very general scientific theory and calling it 'philosophy'.

We do not answer 'Do I ever really know what is in the mind of another?', taken as a philosophical question, in the way in which we answer 'Do I ever know if my car is out of gas?'.

III

In concluding this chapter, let me take a live example to illustrate the point I am trying to make about philosophical argumentation. Moreover, I want to show how philosophy, while being neither logic nor an empirical science, can, as conceptual analysis, relieve important perplexities.

Jean-Paul Sartre tells us that "man is a useless passion." In spite of his political activism, in spite of his courageous commitment to the Left, there emerges from Sartre's plays, novels, and philosophy a despairing, utterly bleak picture of man and his lot. Man, as Sartre pictures him, is indeed a useless, rather humdrum passion. Life, given this picture, is absurd.

Perhaps Sartre is right. Man's cruelty to himself is only outstripped by his cruelty to others. Life could be something beautiful; instead, for most at least, it is inhumane, degrading, and ugly. We fight brutal wars that need not be fought; we brutalize people in a senseless and inhumane way; we have a great industrial civilization, yet many people live in poverty, sloth, and ignorance. More people than we care to remember live in dull, vicious stupidity, while others buy bigger and faster cars so they can kill themselves in ever greater numbers, stuff themselves with an ever more international cuisine so that they can have heart attacks with ever greater frequency, and fly to every corner of the earth so they can find a Hilton hotel where everything is just as it is at home.

Men are sufficiently indifferent to the conditions of life of their brothers to allow themselves to live in gaudy, senseless luxury while, practically under their noses, people live in poverty and filth, and mass starvation becomes an ever greater world problem. There are the stupid, ugly rich and the stupid, ugly poor, both living, for the most part, utterly vapid, senseless, stultifying lives. Any slight tendencies to creativity or sensitivity in that rational animal we call man are usually stamped out before he reaches thirty. It is things like this (and they could easily be multiplied) that prompt one to assent to Sartre's claim that man is a useless passion.

This picture of man is indeed Sartre's, but there is also something in Sartre's conception of man that is much more controversial and mystifying. In making his assessment of man, Sartre wants something independent of individual and even social resolve in virtue of which man can be said to be a useless passion. It is not just a brute empirical fact that man is a useless passion, but a metaphysical necessity. The crucial Sartrean argument for his claim about man is this: Man has no *essence*, no essential nature; there is nothing he *must* be. In this sense man is contingent;

and, given a realistic, nonevasive conception of what man is, he could not be other than contingent. Since man is contingent, by definition, no decision of his, no manipulation of language however artful, can remedy his contingency, and therefore all his actions collapse into meaninglessness.

However, it is just here where philosophy as conceptual analysis is important, for a little attention to logic and to the concept of contingency should make it evident that this famous Sartrean ground is no ground at all for being pessimistic about men. Sartre may revere words, may marshal them with great dexterity, but all the same his argument here is absurd. Sartre tells us that he prefers detective novels to reading Wittgenstein, but what is indeed evident is that Sartre very much needs to study Wittgenstein. Even if man cannot remedy his contingency, it *does not therefore follow* that all his actions are meaningless. A doctor who closes a man's wounds and relieves a man's pain is as contingent as those Nazi doctors who performed sadistic and senseless 'medical experiments' on concentration camp victims, but his act in relieving suffering is not meaningless or senseless while theirs is. The men who first took freedom rides and led voter registrations are as contingent as those American capitalists who bought diamond necklaces for their dogs while they employed child labor seven days a week, twelve hours a day. But the actions of the freedom riders were meaningful—that is, significant—while the actions of those capitalists were senseless acts that deny the humanity of others and give the lie to the humanity of their authors. There is no logical connection between a man being contingent and his acts being meaningless, insignificant, or worthless. We human beings all must die, and in that sense love between human beings cannot but come to an end, but this enhances its worth rather than detracts from it. The Sartrean 'therefore' is simply gratuitous.

There is in Sartre's account as much trouble with 'contingency' as there is with 'therefore'. There are various context-dependent senses of 'contingency 'and its opposite 'necessity'. 'Contingency', in talking about man, if it means anything at all, means that man is born, will live a short while, and then will die, and that his birth, his lifespan, and so on, depend upon features of the universe that are not at all inevitable. But Sartre also means that since man is not a divine artifact or a created being, he can therefore have no essence—there is nothing he was *cut out to be*, there are no absolute values he could simply discover. Man is what he makes of himself; his *values* are those decisions to which he commits himself, those plans he undertakes. But why should this contingency make man a useless passion? Although man must die, there are still the joys of the world, including the joy of seeing others discover these, and there remains the task of relieving the awful burden of human suffering.

For reasons of the sort I outlined above, our experience with our fellows hardly makes us confident of human love, goodwill, or even human rationality. But this has nothing at all to do with our contingency, and in fact only if we are contingent can there even be the slightest hope that we could come to live in a way that is somewhat more humane, somewhat less senseless.

Perhaps there are good reasons for saying man is a useless passion. My study of history and my view of contemporary life hardly incline me to generalizations about the *goodness* of man. Man is, as far as I can see, neither *naturally* good nor bad; he can, and usually does, become a little of both. His circumstances, his chance meetings, and his own acts made in the light of these circumstances, very much affect the direction of his moral development. But Sartre's general *claims* about human contingency give us *no reason at all* to conclude dramatically that man is a useless passion; they give us *no reason* for despair about man.

I attempted in the last section of this chapter to illustrate with reference to a celebrated contention by an internationally famous author how philosophy, while being neither logic nor empirical inquiry, can say something important about ultimate human concerns and in this way help fix belief. What it does in this instance is deflationary, but in ridding us of one alleged basis for a kind of cosmic despair about the human condition, it hints at what would count toward a meaningful life.

Philosophy is neither logic nor science. It should not, after the fashion of Plato or Spinoza, erect vast philosophical systems claiming a distinctive kind of philosophical knowledge. But for all that, it can continue to have an important and seminal role in our lives.

NOTES

1. I argue in my *The Quest for God* that it is a mistake to believe there are facts other than empirical facts.
2. See, for example, his *The Quest for Certainty* or his *Reconstruction in Philosophy*.
3. See G. E. Moore, *Principia Ethica*, or W. D. Ross, *The Right and the Good*.
4. A. J. Ayer, *Language, Truth and Logic*, or Bertrand Russell, *Religion and Science*.
5. This hardly proves enough, for while we are trying to transcend purely ideological debate, it is also evident that we need an overview which, though it should perspicuously display categories, also includes a *Weltanschauung*.
6. Gilbert Ryle, "Philosophical Arguments," and F. Waismann, "How I see Philosophy." Both are reprinted in A. J. Ayer (ed.), *Logical Positivism*.
7. F. Waismann, op. cit., p. 346.
8. I have elucidated and assessed this conception of philosophy in my "John Dewey's Conception of Philosophy," the *University of Massachusetts Review*, vol. II, no. 1 (autumn, 1960).

SUPPLEMENTARY READINGS
CHAPTERS 10 THROUGH 12

Books

*Barker, Stephen, *The Elements of Logic* (New York: McGraw-Hill, 1966).
*Chisholm, Roderick M., *Theory of Knowledge* (Englewood Cliffs, N.J.: Prentice-Hall, 1966).
*Clark, Romane, and Paul Welsh, *Introduction to Logic* (Princeton, N.J.: Van Nostrand, 1962).
*Copi, Irving, *Introduction to Logic* (New York: Macmillan, 1961).
Copi, Irving, *Symbolic Logic* (New York: Macmillan, 1966).
Descartes, René, *Philosophical Writings*, translated by Elizabeth Anscombe and Peter Geach (Edinburgh: Thomas Nelson, 1954).
*Gorowitz, Samuel, and Ron. C. Williams, *Philosophical Analysis* (New York: Random House, 1965).
Hume, David, *An Enquiry Concerning Human Understanding* (Oxford: Clarendon, 1902).
Jeffrey, Richard, *Formal Logic: Its Scope and Limits* (New York: Holt, Rinehart and Winston, 1964).
Kant, Immanuel, *Prolegomena to Any Future Metaphysics*, translated by L. W. Beck (Indianapolis, Ind.: Bobbs-Merrill, 1962).
*Lemmon, E. J., *Beginning Logic* (London: Nelson, 1965).
Lewis, C. I., *Mind and the World-Order* (New York: Dover, 1929).
Locke, John, *Essay Concerning Human Understanding* (London: J. M. Dent, 1961).
*Mates, Benson, *Elementary Logic* (New York: Oxford University Press, 1965).
Moore, G. E., *Some Main Problems in Philosophy* (New York: Macmillan, 1953).
Quine, W. V. O., *Methods of Logic* (New York: Holt, Rinehart and Winston, 1962).
*Salmon, Wesley, *Introduction to Logic* (Englewood Cliffs, N.J.: Prentice-Hall, 1963).
*Scheffler, Israel, *Conditions of Knowledge* (Chicago: Scott, Foresman, 1965).
Strawson, P. F., *Introduction to Logical Theory* (London: Methuen, 1960).
*Suppes, Patrick, *Introduction to Logic* (Princeton, N.J.: Van Nostrand, 1960).
*Woozley, A. D., *Theory of Knowledge: An Introduction* (London: Hutchinson, 1960).
*Yolton, John, (ed.), *Theory of Knowledge* (New York: Macmillan, 1965).

Articles and Pamphlets

Broyles, James E., "Charles S. Peirce and the Concept of Indubitable Belief," *Transactions of Charles S. Peirce Society*, vol. 1, no. 2 (fall, 1965).
Firth, Roderick, "Phenomenalism," in Max Black (ed.), *Philosophical Analysis* (Ithaca, N.Y.: Cornell University Press, 1950).
Frankfurt, Harry G., "Descartes' Validation of Reason," *American Philosophical Quarterly*, vol. 2, no. 2 (April, 1965).
Gettier, Edmund, "Is Justified True Belief Knowledge?" *Analysis* (1963).
Griffiths, A. Phillips, "On Belief," in A. P. Griffiths (ed.), *Knowledge and Belief* (New York: Oxford University Press, 1967).

Lewis, C. I., Nelson Goodman and Hans Reichenbach, "The Experiential Element in Knowledge," *Journal of Philosophy*, vol. XLIX (1952).

Marhenke, Paul, "Phenomenalism," in Max Black (ed.), *Philosophical Analysis* (Ithaca, N.Y.: Cornell University Press, 1950).

*Popper, Karl R., "On the Sources of Knowledge and of Ignorance," in J. N. Findlay (ed.), *Studies in Philosophy* (New York: Oxford University Press, 1966).

Price, H. H., "Some Considerations About Belief," in A. P. Griffiths (ed.), *Knowledge and Belief* (New York: Oxford University Press, 1967).

*Quinton, Anthony, "The Foundations of Knowledge," Bernard Williams and Alan Montefiore (eds.), *British Analytical Philosophy* (London: Routledge & Kegan Paul, 1966).

*Quinton, Anthony, "*A Priori* and the Analytic," in P. F. Strawson (ed.), *Philosophical Logic* (New York: Oxford University Press, 1967).

*Strawson, P. F. "Meaning and Truth" (Oxford, England: Inaugural Lecture at the University of Oxford 1969).

III
THE
CLAIMS
OF RELIGION

13

PHILOSOPHY
AND RELIGION:
A PREAMBLE

I

In discussing God and religion, it is difficult to know where to start. Almost all of us in one way or another are taken up with religion, even if this consists of a steadfast rejection of religious beliefs and attitudes. It is a rare man who is utterly neutral about religion. But the questions concerning religion that genuinely engage us are often very diverse.

At one end of the spectrum, there are some who cannot bring themselves to think seriously about religion in other than psychological or sociopsychological terms. Such people are usually convinced that man is essentially a religious animal. His present torment is that he is thrust into a world in which 'God is dead'; that is, into a culture where our superannuated conception of a god somehow 'out there' is coming to seem utterly unbelievable and unacceptable, but no new conception of God or conception of the object of religious reverence has replaced it. We are in a spiritual interregnum. This, they believe, is our central religious predicament; unable to survive without religious commitment, we must adjust religious dogmas to the realities of our post-Christian, post-Judaic era. We must somehow work out a new way of life, or radically alter the old one, so that we can come to have a religious commitment without a belief in a transcendent God or any other such obscure conception.

For others, the crucial question is: Do we need religious myths to make sense of our lives? Must we have some nonrational ideology to give significance to our existence? Neither of these groups is interested in the *literal* claims of religious belief, but in what they 'really mean' *for* us; that is, what role do they actually play in human living, how do they keep us going in the hell that may be our lot?

There are, as well, a myriad of other stances toward religion. We have so far mentioned only some stances of the 'extreme Left' of religiosity.

At the other end of the spectrum, there are those—particularly those who have rather orthodox backgrounds—who want to know quite literally: Can we *know* or can we have any good grounds for believing that the God of the Biblical tradition actually exists? Here, believers 'on the Right' have a religiosity that in part is metaphysical. They believe they have some tolerably coherent conception of this 'Wholly Other Creator'. They want to know whether their faith is in any sense grounded in reason. Can we, they want to know, in any way come to know or have good grounds for believing that the Biblical God exists? And if such knowledge or such rationally grounded belief is impossible, do we have good reasons for accepting God simply on faith?

I shall start with the first of these questions in the next chapter, then go in later chapters to the latter one. Finally, I shall consider some more radical questions about the intelligibility of God-talk—talk to, of, or about God. I proceed in this way because these later, more current questions gain force only if we are already convinced that we cannot know that God exists and that the traditional conception of God logically, although not psychologically, is one great cultural myth on a par with a belief in Santa Claus. Questions about the intelligibility of God-talk are logically prior to such questions, but they are not usually psychologically prior.

If you are convinced that in the twentieth century any literal belief in God is impossible, think again and make sure that you are not caught in a kind of secular dogma of your own. Some powerful philosophical arguments have been directed against God-is-dead theology by orthodox thinkers. E. L. Mascall's *The Secularization of Christianity* is the most notable example. Perhaps this very secular attitude is itself a cultural myth that cannot withstand rational scrutiny. At the very least, earn your right to disbelief by coming to know whether we can have any good grounds for believing that the God of the Biblical tradition exists! When we have some reasonable answer about that, it will be time enough to worry about what to do about a post-Christian era.

II

Our first question is: Can we show that there is a God, or can we have any reasonable grounds for believing that there is a God? In considering arguments trying to establish that it is in fact true that there is a God, we shall be concerned with whether it is in fact true that there is a *transcendent* God. That is to say, is there an individual who exists now and who always existed and always will exist; who cannot begin to exist or cease to exist, and who thus existed prior to the world and continues to exist apart from the world, is in no way dependent on the world; and who in some sense created the world, sustains the world, and can bring about changes in it?

There remain, however, important prolegomena here. Some analytic philosophers have raised this question: Is 'Is there a God?' a proper question? That it is a grammatically correct question does not prove that it is a proper question. There are questions that are in some sense grammatical that are still nonsensical—for example, 'How fast does time flow?', 'Does virtue run faster than laughter?', or 'How tall is God?'.

When J. J. C. Smart first wrote his much discussed essay "The Existence of God," he thought that 'Is there a God?' was an improper question.[1] He later came to change his mind, but many people feel the way Smart felt then. Given the importance of his claim, I want to state and briefly examine it.

Smart draws an analogy between 'Does God exist?' and 'Do electrons exist?'. He wants to say—or, rather, at that time wanted to say—that they are both logically improper questions.

> In order to acquire the concept of an electron we must find out about experiments with cathode ray tubes, the Wilson cloud chamber, about spectra and so on. We then find the concept of the electron a useful one, one which plays a part in the mass of physical theory. When we reach this stage, the question 'Do electrons exist?' no longer arises. Before we reach this stage, the question 'Do electrons exist?' has no clear meaning. Similarly, I suggest, the question 'Does God exist?' has no clear meaning for the unconverted. But for the converted, the question no longer arises. The word 'God' gets its meaning from the part it plays in religious speech and literature, and in religious speech and literature the question of existence does not arise. . . . So within religion the question 'Does God exist?' does not arise, any more than the question 'Do electrons exist?' arises within physics. Outside religion the question 'Does God exist?' has as little meaning as the question 'Do electrons exist?' as asked by the scientifically ignorant. Thus I suggest that it is possible to hold that the question 'Does God exist?' is not a proper question without necessarily also holding that religion and theology are nonsensical.

Smart's plausible yet not unpuzzling argument received a sharp rebuttal from J. A. Passmore.[2] Passmore first points out that we should not, as Smart's argument requires, assume that the world is divided up into only two classes of human beings: the unconverted and the converted, the people outside the circle of faith and the people inside it. There is a third class, the *de*converted. "After all," Passmore writes,

> very many atheists were once Christians. At some point within religion the question of God's existence must have arisen for them; just as, to carry on Smart's example, questions about the existence of the ether or of absolute space, or of absolute time, arose within physics. No doubt one has to give

up religion . . . if one comes to the conclusion that God does not exist, while one does not have to give up science after deciding that the ether does not exist. But this is not the point; which is simply that questions about God's existence can and do arise *within* religion.

Moreover, Passmore continues, if Smart's argument had any force it

would give complete protection to nonsense of the most diverse kinds. Consider, for example, the conception of a 'Germanic soul'. Then, it could be argued, "if you are not a true German, you cannot understand what the existence of a 'Germanic soul' involves; if you are, its existence is simply taken for granted as a condition of a True-Germanic way of life; the question whether it exists, then, can never arise, but statements about it are nevertheless not meaningless." If one is really prepared to maintain that questions like 'Do ghosts exist?' can never be properly asked except by those who whole-heartedly believe in ghosts, and therefore will not want to ask this question, then no doubt religion is 'saved'—but so is every form of superstition.

This argument convinced Smart and led him to abandon his claim. Smart remarks with admirable candor, "Mr. Passmore's criticisms of my lecture on the Existence of God are well taken and I now agree almost whole-heartedly with them." Specifically, he has come to agree with Passmore that 'Does God exist?' and 'Do electrons exist?' are proper questions to be answered yes or no.[3]

There is, incidentally, a worthwhile moral to this beyond its argumentative importance. Arguments sometimes are convincing in philosophy. It is not, James and Bradley to the contrary notwithstanding, a question of sentiment ruling the roost so that the philosopher always works up bad arguments for what he would believe anyway.

III

There are, however, certain theologians of a neoorthodox or existentialist persuasion who reject any consideration of 'the proofs' on quite different grounds. The eminent German theologian Rudolf Bultmann is a typical example." He begins his essay "What Sense is There to Speak of God?" by claiming:

If by speaking 'of God' one understands *to talk 'about God'*, then such style of speaking has no sense at all; for in the moment when it happens the subject (*Gegenstand*), God, has been lost. For when the thought 'God', is thought at all, the implication is that God is the Almighty, i.e., the reality controlling everything. But this thought is no thought at all when I *talk about* God—that is, when I regard God as an object of thought toward which I can take a position; when I adopt a point of view from which I stand indifferent to the problem of God; when I suggest propositions concerning

God's way and reality which I can reject or, if they are illuminating, accept. Anyone who is moved by proofs to have faith in God's *reality* can be certain that he has comprehended nothing of the reality *of God;* and whoever thinks to proclaim something of God's reality by means of evidences of God is debating about a mirage. For every 'talking *about'* presupposes a standpoint apart from that which is being talked about. But there can be no standpoint apart from God, and for that reason God does not permit himself to be spoken of in general propositions, universal truths which are true without reference to the concrete existential situation of the one who is talking.

It makes just as little sense to talk about God as it does to talk about love. In fact, it is impossible to talk about love unless the talking about love be itself an act of love. All other talking about love is no speech of love, for it takes a position outside love. In short, a psychology of love would be something quite different from speaking about love. Love is no given situation (*Gegebenheit*) *for the sake of which* (*woraufhin*) something done or something spoken, something not done or not spoken, is possible. It comes into being only as a condition of life itself; it only *is* in that I love or am loved, not as something secondary or derivative (*daneben oder dahinter*).

There is sincerity and intensity here, but it remains the case that these remarks by Bultmann are thoroughly confused. First, consider his analogy with love. He is claiming that it makes no more sense to talk about God than it does to talk about love. Talk about love must itself be an act of love. But it is absurd to say we cannot talk about love. Many poets and novelists have done it with power and conviction. Recall the depiction of the relation between Kitty and Levin and Anna and Vronsky in *Anna Karenina,* or the relation between Natasha and Prince Andrew and Natasha and Pierre in *War and Peace,* or again in a different way old Prince Bolkonski's relationship—stormy as it was—with his son and with his daughter Mary. Similar illustrative detail could be taken from Stendhal, George Eliot, Shakespeare, Donne, and a host of others. Moreover, in no straightforward sense (and perhaps not in any crooked sense either) are their remarks about love acts of loving.

When I assert that we often torture those we love—remember old Prince Bolkonski's relationship with his daughter Mary—and that often unwittingly we love a projected image of all our ideals rather than the person who is the purported object of our love, I make two perfectly intelligible and perhaps true statements about love that most certainly are not themselves acts of love. So Bultmann's analogy is utterly broken-backed. And with the collapse of his analogy we have lost a major rationale for saying that we cannot speak of God or that we cannot speak of God if our attitude toward him is one of indifference.

What could be salvaged from Bultmann's remarks is this: As a matter of psychological fact, one who has never loved could say or understand precious little that was significant about love, and similarly one who has never felt his own finitude, his own contingency, could have little under-standing of talk of God. This seems to me very likely to be true, but it does not mean that we must now actually love to talk intelligibly about love. What is the evidence that even a bitter or even a very cynical man, who had once loved deeply, could not speak with considerable under-standing about love, or that an atheist, who had well known the tempta-tion to believe, or had been a believer once himself, could not speak with considerable perception about God? Neither Bultmann nor, as far as I know, anyone else has given us good reason to believe that it is impossible or even difficult for an atheist to do that. We do not have to be fat to drive fat oxen to market.

Bultmann's analogy apart, why should it be that if we talk about God, "God has been lost"? After all, God is a transcendent reality. It is not like talking about a *quantum* particle that may be affected by observing it, or about a purely psychological reality that may be affected by our re-lation to it. In Bultmann's own words, we are talking of "the Almighty, i.e., the reality controlling everything." God is transcendent to the world and utterly self-sufficient. He is not affected by my cognizing Him. That He becomes an object *of thought* does not make Him an object any more than thought becomes an object because it is an object of thought. To think otherwise is simply to pun on 'object'. Nor does it make God finite or my concept of God a concept of a finite God, because I adopt a point of view toward God—unless, in order for God to be almighty, everything must be God. But this would lead to a pantheism that Bultmann surely wants to avoid.

As a committed believer, I can and indeed must take my God to be my Almighty Sovereign, and still, as a philosopher or theologian, I must reflect about God. Anselm and Aquinas did this, and Bultmann has done nothing to show any inconsistency or incoherence in such a practice. Thus, he has done nothing to show that "anyone who is moved by proofs to have faith in God's reality can be certain that he has comprehended nothing of the reality of God." As long as we do not identify God with everything that is, there is no reason why we could not take a standpoint apart from the reality talked about, even when that reality is God. An almighty being who controls everything could allow that. Bultmann has given us no reason to believe that God does not allow that or that we cannot make general statements about God. In fact, Bultmann himself does just what he says cannot be done when he tells us "God is the al-mighty." Note that this was done in the course of doing a bit of philos-ophy and that it was not tied to any existential situation.

Moreover, it is not true that in making God an object of thought "I adopt a point of view from which I stand indifferent to the problem of God. . . ." I may ask these questions about God in anguish and with hope.

Shatov in Dostoevsky's novel *The Devils* is a good example of a man who does just that. He breaks with his nihilistic and unbelieving past in the sense that he accepts the whole Christian way of behaving and the Christian's attitudes. In short, he opts for the Christian *Weltanschauung* (world-view). His difficulty is that he does not believe in God. When taxed concerning his belief, he can only stammer, "I want to—I shall believe." He is anything but indifferent to God. He is a man waiting with longing for a sign—something that will make belief in God sufficiently credible to make it believable. He has the agapeistic (selfless-love) attitudes and commitments of a Christian, but he has a different intellectual apperception of the world. Surely, many men are in just this human predicament: They want with all their hearts to believe in God but they cannot.

Bultmann has not given us the slightest reason for believing that there are no general propositions or universal truths concerning God. Nor has he given us any good grounds for believing that no question can arise about God's existence or nonexistence. Finally, he has not given us grounds for believing, as he asserts in a later passage, that we *sin* when we make an honest effort to try to find some evidence for the existence of God. Bultmann utterly fails to show that we cannot sensibly ask the question 'Is there a God?'.

IV

Given Bultmann's years of careful work in Biblical studies and his comparative philosophical naiveté, it is not surprising that his remarks here should be confused. The reason his Biblical studies could lead him astray in this context is this: Disbelief for someone in the Biblical world characteristically did not connote the intellectual skepticism to which we are accustomed. It was rooted not in such intellectual disbelief concerning the reality of God or the intelligibility of the concept of God, but in a disbelief in His effective saving Presence. In the world of the Bible, people who reacted against a belief in God came to feel that God had turned His face from them, that God no longer cared about them.

This difference in attitude has been well characterized by the English theologian John Baillie in his *Our Knowledge of God*. Baillie points out that speculation about the existence of God is entirely foreign to both the Old and New Testaments. It was through the Greek philosophers that speculation about the existence of God came into Jewish religious thought. Specifically, it came into Judeo-Christian culture in the first part of the first century A.D. with Philo of Alexandria, a Jew who tried to combine Hellenistic philosophy with Judaism. Utilizing the conceptual tools of

Greek rationalism, Philo tried to prove the existence of God. Such speculation is utterly foreign to the Bible. As Baillie puts it:

> All through the Old Testament it is assumed that the knowledge of God rests, not on cosmological speculation, but on the revelation of Himself which He has vouchsafed—on the theophanies of Mount Sinai, on the laws He gave to Moses, on the words He spoke to the prophets.[5]

In this respect our world and "the world of the Bible" reflect radically different *Weltanschauungen*. The problem that the Biblical writers faced was not that people would have no belief in God at all, but that they should believe in too many gods. "None of the Old Testament writers treats of the existence of deity as if it were an open question or in any sense problematic. They betray no consciousness that there were any in Israel who denied it." Where we get a turning from God in the Old Testament, as well as in the New, it is not through theoretical dissent from the proposition 'There is a God' but, as I said earlier, from a disbelief in His effective Presence and interposition. Their problem was not 'What gods, if any, exist?', but 'What gods must I worship?'.

The disbelief Jesus deplored was "not intellectual persuasion of God's nonexistence," but something that was wont to "consort with the most undoubting intellectual persuasion of His reality, namely, that men who though incapable of doubting Him . . . lived as though He did not exist." Even late in the Bible there is this same attitude. The writers of the Epistles recognized, of course, "that saving faith in God the Father and in Jesus Christ His Son must include belief in God's existence as a necessary part and implication of it . . . but such a purely intellectual acceptance, though it must enter as a component part into a truly living faith, is held to be of little or no value in itself." They simply assumed a belief in such a reality; what they were concerned with was the attitude toward this assumed reality. In particular, they were concerned with man's repeated rebellion against God.

Neoorthodox theologians, thinkers such as Niebuhr, Barth, Brunner, and Bultmann, keeping close to the world of the Bible, see disbelief as sin, as rebellion against God. They do not see it as most centrally a question of incredulity concerning the reality of the Divine, but as a waywardness of the heart, a double-mindedness toward a Presence that men in their heart of hearts cannot deny. This is no doubt true for some forms of disbelief. But there are too many Shatovs, too many humble and honest seekers after God, who would believe but cannot because for them belief in God has become, intellectually speaking, too much like a belief in the reality of Santa Claus. For them, the problem of the existence of God is a genuine problem.

Sometimes this tendency to intellectual disbelief is halted, as it is for

Baillie himself, not by any proofs but by *a sense of the Presence of God.* Baillie remarks:

> . . . for the New Testament, as for the Old, God is One who is directly known in His approach to the human soul. He is not an inference but a Presence. He is a Presence at once urgent and gracious.[6]

Compared to this knowledge, Baillie argues, the best argument is, as it were, a "sorry substitute," "a superfluous addition." This sense of the Presence of God, he claims, is overwhelming and makes all argument pro and con but the tinkling of empty cymbals.

Here we have what in reality is an appeal to religious experience, but this appeal also raises evidential claims that we must consider. Many have had such experience but do not believe that it was an experience of God. It also should be noted that many, including many fideists, have no such compelling awareness of the Presence of God. Like Kierkegaard, they are filled with doubts but still they believe. Others are filled with doubts and do not believe. For these last people, to recapture the world of the Bible is not enough; they need, if such can be given, some evidence that the Biblical stories are not *simply* myth or *merely* myth. They may well recognize that myth, like poetry and metaphor, has an important role to play in human living—after all, religion is not science or a metaphysical system. They also realize, however, that to be a Jew or Christian involves not only acting in a certain way but also an acknowledgment *that it is a fact that there is a God*—a Transcendent Reality—who created the world and upon whom the world is utterly dependent. They understandably want to know whether there is any good evidence at all for believing that it is true that there is such a Transcendent Reality upon whom the world is utterly dependent. For this reason a consideration of the proofs and a consideration of the evidential value of religious experience becomes crucial. Thus, the question 'Is there a God?' is far from an idle question, a question merely symptomatic of the intellectual pride of the man who asks it.

V

Before considering the reasons philosophers have given for saying that we could in some sense prove the existence of God, there are a few further points we ought to note.

First, as J. J. C. Smart points out, if the arguments for the existence of God are shown to be unsound, it does not *follow* that God does not exist. What does follow is that the arguments do not disprove the atheist's claim that God does not exist or answer the agnostic's question about the existence of God by showing that God does exist. To show that an argument is invalid or unsound is not to show that the *conclusion of the argument is false*. It is only to show that the argument does not warrant our asserting the conclusion to be true. All the proofs of God's existence *may* fail, but it still may be the case that God exists. It may still even be the case that God's existence will someday be proved, for someone may think up a new proof that will not fail. That such an argument has yet to emerge gives us reason to be skeptical, but it does not give us sufficient grounds for saying that it is impossible to give such an argument. In short, to show that the proofs do not work is not enough, by itself, to destroy faith. It still may be the case that there is a God.

After all these years of religious discussion, if none of the proofs work, we are in a position to assert justifiably that since the proofs are unsound, it is not correct to assert that belief and unbelief are on a par and that in such a situation one can justifiably believe what one wants to believe. Rather, in such a situation belief is on the defensive, and the burden of proof is on the believer to give us some reason for believing in God. After all, if there is *no evidence* for the existence of God, then the probability that He exists is very low. We most certainly cannot justifiably assert that belief in His existence is on a par with disbelief, if there is no evidence at all for believing that He exists.

We cannot, strictly speaking, disprove the existence of Santa Claus or unicorns, either, but the probability of their existence is, to put it conservatively, rather low. If there is no evidence that there is a God, we can have no rational reason for believing that He exists, while we have very good reasons for believing that He does not exist, namely, that there is no evidence at all for the existence of a putative reality bearing the extraordinary descriptions given to God. Thus, it is not fair to assert, given the failure of the proofs, that belief and disbelief are on a par. If the proofs fail and if the appeal to religious experience provides no evidence that there is a God, the burden is on the believer to provide some other reason for belief in God.

Finally, we should note that the classical arguments are very brief and, further, that they are statable, *assuming the meaningfulness of the premisses*, in the form of valid arguments. For example, if there are contingent beings then there must be a necessary being; there are contingent beings; therefore, there must be a necessary being. This is a perfectly valid argument; the question is, is it a sound, conclusive, or even reliable argument? In short, our problem is to try to give conclusive arguments or at least reliable arguments for the existence of God. (Recall that a conclusive argument is a valid argument with premisses *known* to be true. A reliable argument is a valid argument with premisses for whose truth we have good evidence.) In short, our task is to see if we can find a conclusive or reliable argument for making it reasonable to believe that there is a God, that is, that there actually exists what Jews and Christians have traditionally referred to as their Lord and God.

NOTES

1. J. J. C. Smart, "The Existence of God," in Antony Flew and Alasdair MacIntyre (eds.), *New Essays in Philosophical Theology.*
2. John Passmore, "Christianity and Positivism," *Australasian Journal of Philosophy,* vol. 35 (1957).
3. J. J. C. Smart, "Philosophy and Religion," *Australasian Journal of Philosophy,* vol. 36, no. 1 (1958).
4. Rudolf Bultmann, "What Sense is There to Speak of God?" *Christian Scholar* (1957).
5. It could be argued with some plausibility that the Book of Ecclesiastes is at least a partial exception to Baillie's generalization. See John Baillie, *Our Knowledge of God* (London: Oxford University Press, 1939), p. 121.
6. *Ibid.,* p. 125

14

ST. ANSELM
AND THE ONTOLOGICAL
ARGUMENT

I

The ontological argument, alone among the classical arguments for the existence of God, is a purely *a priori* argument. That is to say, the truth of its premises does not depend on experience. It is the core of the argument and a source of its fascination to maintain that anyone who has an adequate understanding of the meaning of the word 'God' can come to see, simply from carefully reflecting on the meaning of 'God', that it is self-contradictory to assert 'God does not exist' or 'God exists *only* in the understanding', that is, 'God is only my idea or my tribe's idea'.

Anselm lived from 1033 to 1109. He was not simply a philosophical theologian, but also became the Archbishop of Canterbury. The argument with which we are concerned was formulated in 1077. Essentially the same argument was later reformulated by Descartes, Spinoza, and Leibnitz. It has been criticized and reformulated repeatedly ever since Anselm originally formulated it. Only a few years ago, a distinguished analytical philosopher, much to the surprise of many people, defended one of Anselm's formulations of the argument, and another philosopher has recently published two books devoted to its statement and defense.[1] In short, this very compact and very ancient argument has held a fascination for philosophers.

I am also aware that many people on first hearing it are quite unimpressed and feel confident that somehow it must be subterfuge, while others will be caught up with it in spite of its *a priori* nature. Part of its fascination is that, if correct, it does something that most people think is impossible, namely, it establishes the existence of something nonconceptual from purely conceptual considerations. In other words, from being clear about a certain concept we can see, if the ontological argument is correct, that a certain reality must exist. The soundness of the argument would establish that we should not always, as Peirce would have us do, fix all our beliefs by an experimental method. If we get clear about the very meaning of the word 'God', we will come to understand that there must be such a reality.

Some of you may be inclined to think that this surely is the trick of the week, for one plainly cannot go from words to the world or from concepts to reality. But this is just what is at issue, for Anselm wishes to argue that while in all other cases it is indeed true that such a bridge cannot be made, in the case of God, and in the case of God alone, we can make this bridge. To understand clearly what it is to believe in God is to understand that God must necessarily exist.

In the preface to the *Proslogion*, Anselm tells us that it is a "meditation of the grounds of faith." He, as a loyal Christian, "seeks to understand what he believes." Let us go back in time and note carefully Anselm's own way of putting his central claim.

> O Lord, you who give understanding to faith, so far as you know it to be beneficial, give me to understand that you are as we believe, and that you are what we believe.
>
> We believe that you are something than which nothing greater can be conceived.
>
> But is there any such nature, since 'the fool has said in his heart: God is not'?
>
> However, when this same fool hears what I say, when he hears of this something than which nothing greater can be conceived, he at least understands what he hears.
>
> What he understands stands in relation to his understanding, even if he does not understand that it exists. For it is one thing to stand in relation to our understanding; it is another thing for us to understand that it really exists. . . . Therefore, even the fool is convinced that something than which nothing greater can be conceived at least stands in relation to his understanding, because when he hears it he understands it, and whatever he understands stands in relation to his understanding.
>
> However, that than which a greater cannot be conceived can certainly not stand only in relation to the understanding. For if it stood only in relation to the understanding, it could be conceived to be also in reality, and this would be something greater. Therefore, if that than which a greater cannot be conceived only stood in relation to the understanding, then that than which a greater cannot be conceived would not be something than which a greater cannot be conceived. Obviously this is impossible.
>
> Therefore, something than which a greater cannot be conceived undoubtedly both stands in relation to the understanding and exists in reality.[2]

Since God, by definition, is that than which nothing greater can be conceived, then God must necessarily exist. Anselm goes on to say that if one has an improper understanding of the *meaning* of the word 'God', or no understanding of it at all, one can indeed think that there is no

God, but "No one . . . who understands what God is can think that God is not." Whoever correctly understands that "God is that than which a greater cannot be conceived" at least "understands that He exists in such a way that even for thought He cannot not exist." To conceive of God correctly, Anselm tells us, is to conceive "of something which cannot be conceived not to be." For if it could be conceived not to be, it could also be conceived to have a beginning and an end. But this is "impossible for that than which a greater cannot be conceived. Therefore, whoever really conceives of this conceives of something which cannot be conceived not to be."

Many people, as remarked at the beginning of this chapter, are inclined to believe that this is word-twisting. One cannot, from examining the nature of our signs and symbols, determine that what they refer to exists. It is absurd to think we can go like that from words to the world. Perhaps. But what exactly is the argument against it? I shall lay out Anselm's argument step by step in somewhat more modern terms and see what can be said against it.

One preliminary first, however. To the surprise of philosophers, the distinguished Protestant theologian Karl Barth, in an influential book, has argued that we should not take Anselm's remarks as a philosophical argument to prove God's existence, but only as a theological exercise to gain a better understanding of how God exists.[3] According to Barth, Anselm aims only at understanding God's existence, not at demonstrating it. Moreover, Barth maintains, it is an understanding that can be had only within the context of faith.

Indeed, as we have seen from the passage initially quoted, Anselm begins with an invocation "O Lord, you who give understanding to faith . . ." and when he has completed his argument, he remarks at the end of chapter IV, "My thanksgiving to you, good Lord, my thanksgiving to you. For what I first believed through your giving I now understand through your illumination so that now, even if I did not want to believe that you exist, I would be unable not to understand it." Anselm was a monk writing for faithful monks and not a Christian philosopher trying to convince a Bertrand Russell or Jean-Paul Sartre. For Anselm it was indeed a matter of faith seeking understanding. And it is certainly true that his faith does not depend on his argument. If Gaunilo or some other monk had succeeded in convincing him that his proof was invalid or unsound, he would simply have admitted failure and gone on believing as before.

Anselm held on faith that God exists and that he has such and such a nature. His proof does not arise out of doubt but out of intellectual curiosity, or, I would say although Barth would not, out of a philosophical but not a religious craving to see if he could prove that God exists and what such a proof would come to. His attitude toward God is in a relevant sense comparable to the attitude of a modern philosopher of science toward electrons. Such a philosopher would indeed not deny that there are electrons, but he might work very hard to give an analysis of what is meant in asserting that electrons are real things. Anselm does not doubt that there is a God, but he attempts to analyze what could be meant in asserting or denying that God exists.

However, this does nothing to show that Anselm's argument is not a proof or an attempted demonstration of God's existence. To talk about his motives for writing it, or the context of faith in which it is written, is one thing; to talk about the logical structure of his actual arguments is another. It is well known that the validity of a belief is independent of its origin. The arguments, as we have them, do take the form of proofs, and they thus can be inspected for their validity and conclusiveness. Anselm's motives for presenting them cannot affect that. Whether they arose in the context of faith or in the battle between belief and unbelief, they are either valid or sound arguments or invalid or unsound ones. And their soundness can just as well be discussed in altered religious circumstances.

Moreover, Anselm does speak in his preface of searching for an argument "sufficient in itself to prove that God truly exists, and that he is the supreme good, needing nothing outside himself, but needful for the being and well-being of all things." That Anselm and his fellow monks would not dream of giving up their belief in God if Anselm's argument was faulted is not to the point. Anselm's argument purports to be an argument of universal validity. That is to say, Anselm argues, if anyone understands properly the meaning of the word 'God', he must see that it is self-contradictory to deny that there is a God. The only way this is tied to historical circumstances is through the meaning of the word 'God'. If the meaning of the word radically changed so that 'God' was no longer characterized as that than which no greater can be conceived, was no longer conceived as the highest reality, then the argument, even if sound, would not establish that there was a reality answering to this new conception of God. But this in turn would not affect Anselm's argument concerning his conception of God. Moreover, Anselm's conception of God most surely appears to be the traditional Judeo-Christian concept of God. Given that traditional conception of God, Anselm claims universal validity for his argument. In fact, it should be what I have called a conclusive argument. And thus, if it is indeed conclusive, it should be accepted by believer and nonbeliever alike.

Barth's remark about it, applying only within the context of faith, is a misleading way of saying that if the word 'God' is not correctly understood, the argument would not be seen to be conclusive. We must first see what Jews and Christians mean by the word 'God'. When we see what they mean, we see, according to Anselm, that given this concept, it cannot be the case that God does not exist. Thus, we have a proof, and a purely *a priori* proof, of the existence of God. The question is: Is it a sound argument?

II

In fine, I take Anselm's claim to be essentially this: If you understand what God is—if you understand how 'God' is correctly used—you cannot conceive that God does not exist. God, by definition, is "that than which a greater cannot be conceived." He who thoroughly understands this assuredly understands that this being so truly exists that he cannot consistently be conceived not to exist, even in our conceptualizations of him.

Let us delineate Anselm's arguments somewhat more explicitly.

1. God (by definition) is a being than which nothing greater can be conceived.

2. The above is intelligible; that is, we *understand* it when we hear it.

3. It is one thing for an object to be in the understanding (that is, to be conceivable); it is another thing to understand that the object actually exists.

4. The atheist ("the fool") believes that he can conceive of God—God exists in his understanding—but that there is no actual referent for the word 'God'. That is, he believes that he can conceive of God as not existing. God only exists, he says, in his understanding.

5. But "that than which nothing greater can be conceived" cannot exist in the understanding *alone*, for to conceive of a being existing *only in the understanding* is not to conceive of a being than which nothing greater can be conceived, for clearly a being existing in reality would be a greater being than a being, like a unicorn, which was simply a human conception, which existed in the understanding alone.

6. Thus, to say 'a being than which nothing greater can be conceived is a nonexisting being' is to utter a *self-contradiction*.

7. Since this is so, a being than which nothing greater can be conceived must exist.

8. Since God (by definition) is that than which nothing greater can be conceived, then God must exist.

This argument can be set out in a simpler form where—assuming the intelligibility of its premises—it is plainly a valid argument.

A being than which nothing greater can be conceived must actually exist or not be the greatest being that can be conceived.
God is that than which nothing greater can be conceived.

God must actually exist or not be the greatest being that can be conceived.

God (by definition) is the greatest being that can be conceived.

God must exist.

Essentially the same argument could also be put in a hypothetical form.

If God is that than which no greater can be conceived, then God must exist or else He would lack something and not be that than which no greater can be conceived. But God (by definition) is that than which no greater can be conceived. Therefore, God must exist.

A later Cartesian formulation of the argument—also valid—would run as follows:

If God is a perfect being, then God possesses the attribute of existence. God (by definition) is a perfect being. Thus, God possesses the attribute of existence.

If something possesses the attribute of existence, then it exists. God possesses the attribute of existence. Thus, God exists.

These various versions of the ontological argument for the existence of God certainly appear to be valid, if we can justifiably assume that the premisses are intelligible. But the crucial question is whether they are conclusive arguments or even reliable arguments. That is, are they valid arguments with premisses known to be true or with premisses that we have good and sufficient reasons for accepting?

I wish to claim that the ontological argument, including the various forms I have just given you, is neither a conclusive nor a reliable argument. The above arguments all suffer from what I take to be a common mistake. They implicitly or explicitly take existence to be an attribute, property, or characteristic. This is most obvious in the last Cartesian formulation, but it is implicit in the other formulations as well.

My first task—moving from counterassertion to argument—is to show that my claim is correct and that existence is not a characteristic or property of things. The word 'exists', unlike 'growls' or 'smells', does not function as a descriptive predicate that characterizes anything. Existence is not a property or attribute that something could lack! Existence never characterizes or enlarges our *concept* of anything. To say that so and so exists is a way of asserting that our concept has application or exemplification. That is to say, it is a way of saying that there is at least one of whatever it is that we are talking about. The concept of something is not amplified or made greater by saying that there actually exists something of which it is a concept. The concept is not greater or more perfect because it is exemplified, that is, the word expressive of the concept actually refers to something. Rather, when it is exemplified we know that it actually applies to something. Our *concept* of God is not amplified by our knowing that He exists. To say that 'X exists' is to give one to understand that X has denotation, that X refers to something. But this does not describe or characterize X, and thus existence is not an attribute or characteristic of X.

This in substance is the famous Kantian argument against the ontological argument, namely, the argument that existence is not a property or attribute of anything. It is the claim that the word 'exists', unlike 'growls', 'red', or 'hard', does not actually function as a predicate; that is, it does not function as a descriptive word, such as 'growls' or 'red', which actually describes or characterizes something.

Now, as G. E. Moore pointed out, this is not to stay that 'exists' does not take a predicate place in some grammatically well-formed sentences.[4] After all, we can and do say things such as 'God exists', 'God does not exist', 'Mermaids do not exist', 'Ghosts do not exist but pygmies do'. But when philosophers have said that the word 'existence' is not a predicate and that existence is not a property, they have meant to assert that the grammatical form of statements in which 'exists' sits in the predicate place can be misleading, for 'exists' in such statements does not stand for a property (characteristic, attribute) as 'growl', 'red', or 'hard' do. There is no characteristic, existence, that 'exists' refers to that some or all things have or can have, as there is a characteristic redness that all or some things can have and which would, if they had it, delineate (characterize) these things in a certain specific way.

This is fine and convenient theorizing, it is natural to respond, but how do we, or *do* we, know that it is so? How are we to determine whether existence is or is not a characteristic of reality? How do we know that it does not function like 'red' and 'growls' to characterize things? The best way of determining this, and the only way as far as I can see, is by examining the uses of 'exists' and by comparing them with the uses of paradigmatic property words such as 'red' or 'growls'.

Consider the following sentences.

A.   There are some missile bases in Cuba and they are dangerous.

B.   There are some missile bases in Cuba and they exist.

Note that A is a perfectly intelligible sentence and the last part of the conjunct, 'they are dangerous', is informative. B, on the other hand, is nonsense, or at least redundant. That is to say, the last part of the conjunct, ('they exist'), adds nothing to the first part. It just repeats and does not add anything new. But if 'exists' stood for a characteristic, the last part of the conjunct should be no more superfluous than the last part of the conjunct in A. But it is plainly superfluous, as anyone familiar with English can tell from inspecting A and B. Thus, 'exists' does not function as a word standing for a characteristic, but, as the 'There are' form makes more explicit, it simply asserts that there are some of whatever it is that we are talking about.

Consider the following sentences:

    C. Some missiles in Cuba are not controlled by Russians.

    D. Some of the Russian jet bombers are not assembled yet.

    E. Some missiles do not exist.

    F. Some Russian jet bombers do not exist.

Some sort of metaphorical or joking context apart, E and F are plainly nonsense, while C and D make sense. Again, the moral is clear: If we try to treat existence as an attribute, property, or characteristic of things, we produce nonsense.

Consider one last appeal to usage:

    Tame tigers growl.

    Tame tigers exist.

The first sentence is ambiguous. It could mean (1) all tame tigers growl, (2) most tame tigers growl, or (3) some tame tigers growl. It is important to note that (1) or (2) cannot be true unless it is true that some tame tigers growl. That is, (3) must be true for the first two to be true.

Now look at the second example. Like the first, it cannot possibly be true unless some tame tigers exist. But note that the second sentence is not ambiguous in the way we have just noted that the first is. In point of fact, it is not ambiguous at all. To say that tame tigers exist is just to say that some tame tigers exist, and to say this is simply to say that there are some tame tigers. 'Tame tigers exist' could not mean 'All tame tigers exist' or 'Most tame tigers exist'. These sentences are nonsensical. If 'exists', like 'growls', actually characterized or described tame tigers, it would be a further question whether it characterized some, most, or all of them. But 'All tame tigers exist', unlike 'All tame tigers growl', is nonsense; and 'Most tame tigers exist', unlike 'Most tame tigers growl', is also nonsense. 'Tame tigers exist' always means, and only means, that there are some tame tigers. Once we see this, once we take to heart how very different it is from 'Tame tigers growl', it will be apparent to us that 'exists', unlike 'growls', is not a label for a property or characteristic of things.

Such linguistic evidence gives us good reason to believe that although 'exists' sometimes functions in a predicate place in a sentence, it does not function as a property word, it does not predicate any property or characteristic of anything. That is, 'exists', unlike 'growls', is not a quality, attribute, or property of anything. To say that so and so exists is not to amplify our concept of it, is not to characterize or describe it, but is to say that it actually applies to something. But—and this is crucial—whether or not it applies to something cannot be seen from examining the concept itself.

Some might try to counter the above argument by saying that sometimes 'Tame tigers exist' does not mean 'There are some tame tigers', but 'Tame tigers are extant', where 'extant' has as its opposite 'extinct'. 'Extant' and 'extinct' are said to describe or characterize tame tigers. But 'extant' or 'extinct' no more characterize tigers than does 'exist'. Knowing that they are extant would not at all help us to identify them: it would not help us pick them out from among the other entities in the universe. It would only tell us that there actually are some now. That is to say, 'Tame tigers are extant' is just another way of saying that now there are some tame tigers.

A similar try might be made by maintaining that 'Tame tigers exist' actually has the force of saying 'Tame tigers are not mythical creatures'. 'Mythical' is a word characterizing unicorns, and 'nonmythical' characterizes tigers. Since 'Tame tigers exist' does the same work as 'Tame tigers are nonmythical', 'exists' also functions as a descriptive term. However, saying tame tigers are not mythical does not describe or characterize tame tigers. Rather, it is a way of saying that there actually are some. Knowing they are nonmythical would not help us identify them in the way that knowing that they growl or they are yellow would. To know that a unicorn is a mythical creature is not to know what it is like beyond knowing that the concept unicorn has a place in mythology; and to know that is to know that a unicorn is not a bit of the furniture of the universe— that there are no unicorns.

Consider one last example to drive home the point. Let us say that I go fishing in Tibet and while there I discover a new kind of fish called a 'tok'. On returning home I try to characterize it for you. I say that a tok is a long fish with large scales and sharp teeth. Toks break water frequently and fight doggedly. In short, toks are long, silvery, surface-feeding fish that inhabit the mountain streams of Tibet. I might amplify my remarks by saying that toks are silvery green and yellow. This would indeed add to my initial characterization of toks. But if I said "In addition, toks exist," I would not add to my characterization of toks. In setting out, after my return from Tibet, to characterize toks, it is presupposed, if you take at face value my characterization, that toks exist— that there are some toks. If I then told you they were only imaginary fish, my story would simply be a bad joke. In saying that toks exist, I do not add to my characterization of toks as I do when I say that they are green and yellow. To say that so and so exists is not to amplify our concept of it or to characterize it, but to say that our concept applies to something, that is, it is exemplified and I am giving one to understand that my subject expression has denotation. But whether or not it applies to something, whether the word in question has denotation, cannot be seen or determined from examining the word or concept itself. We cannot in this way build a bridge to the world from words expressive of our concepts.

Let us now apply this directly to the ontological argument. God, to be a perfect being, must possess all attributes that can consistently go together. But, so the ontological argument goes, existence is an attribute, so He could not lack that without lacking something. Thus, an absolutely perfect being must exist since we do have a concept of such a being. But since existence is *not* an attribute, it is not an *attribute* that a perfect being or any being might lack or possess. Rather, the relevant question is: Is there a denotation—an actual referent—for 'perfect being'? But that cannot be determined by examining the word or the concept expressed by the phrase 'perfect being'. Again, since existence is not an attribute, it is not something that a being than which nothing greater can be conceived could either have or lack. Thus, a being than which no greater can be conceived will not fail to be a being than which no greater can be conceived, if it does not exist, since existence is not a property or characteristic that it might either have or fail to have.

The concept is not altered by whether what it signifies actually exists or whether or not we know that it applies to something. My concept of a dime is not affected by whether I actually have one. Moreover, given that a concept may have application to something, whether a concept actually applies to something can never be determined from examining the concept itself.

In short, to say 'X exists' comes down to saying 'X actually refers to something'. But whether it actually refers to something can never be determined from determining its sense (its function in the language). The only thing we could know, as in the case of 'round square', from knowing its sense is that such a word could not possibly apply to anything. But from knowing that a term could *possibly* apply to something, refer to something, we cannot determine whether in fact it does refer to something. Thus for all its seeming logical necessity, the ontological argument fails.

NOTES

1. N. Malcolm, "Anselm's Ontological Arguments," *Philosophical Review* (1960), and C. Hartshorne, *Man's Vision of God* and *The Logic of Perfection*.
2. All the direct quotes from Anselm are from *A Scholastic Miscellany*, vol. X, LCC, Eugene R. Fairweather (ed.), published in the United States by Westminster Press (Philadelphia: 1956). Used by permission.
3. Karl Barth, *Anselm: Fides Quaerens Intellectum*, translated by Ian Robertson.
4. G. E. Moore, "Is Existence a Predicate?" in A. G. N. Flew (ed.), *Logic and Language*, series II. Some qualifications to Moore's thesis are made by D. F. Pears in his "Is Existence a Predicate?" in P. F. Strawson (ed.), *Philosophical Logic*. But Pears's thrust is in a Moorean direction and his argument does not require any important modification in the argument of this chapter even if his argument is conclusive.

15

ST. ANSELM
REVISITED:
ARGUMENT
AND COUNTERARGUMENT

I

I have attempted to refute the ontological argument using a modernized reformulation of the Kantian critique which (1) claims to show that the ontological argument presupposes that existence is an attribute, and then (2) proceeds to argue that existence is not an attribute.[1] However, even on the assumption that my refutation is correct, the argument about whether there is a sound ontological argument should not stop there, for it has been argued with considerable force that there is a distinct argument in St. Anselm that does not assume existence is an attribute or a perfection. Thus, this other form of the ontological argument is not undermined by the standard Kantian objections.

An important contemporary analytical philosopher, Norman Malcolm, has developed this argument of Anselm's in a sophisticated way.[2] I want to examine Malcolm's argument.

Malcolm agrees that existence is not an attribute or a perfection. But, as I said, he thinks that there is an argument in Anselm that does not turn on those considerations. When Anselm speaks of God, the being, a greater than which cannot be conceived, he says:

> And it so truly exists that it cannot be conceived not to exist. For it is possible to conceive of a being which cannot be conceived not to exist. Hence, if that, than which nothing greater can be conceived, can be conceived not to exist, it is not that than which nothing greater can be conceived. But this is a contradiction. So truly, therefore, is there something than which nothing greater can be conceived, that it cannot even be conceived not to exist.
> And this being thou art, O Lord, our God.

It is Malcolm's contention that Anselm is here claiming two things. (1) A being whose nonexistence is *logically* impossible (a logically necessary being) is greater than a being whose nonexistence is logically possible. (2) God is a being than which a greater cannot be conceived. Malcolm stresses that the second point is a logically necessary proposition. It is what I call an analytic statement: a statement the denial of which is self-contradictory and a statement true by definition. The same thing is true for such statements as: God is the greatest of all beings, God is the most perfect being, God is the supreme being. They simply hold in virtue of the very meaning of 'God' in Jewish and Christian God-talk. We would not call something God or Our God which we did not believe had those features anymore than we would call a married man a bachelor.

There is, however, a problem concerning Anselm's first point. What is the meaning of 'greater' in Anselm's phrase? It appears, Malcolm reminds us, to mean "exactly the same as 'superior', 'more excellent', 'more perfect'." But what is meant by such phrases? Is it simply that it exists that makes something more perfect or superior? It would certainly seem to be a mistake to say so, for while it is better actually to have friends than to merely think you have, it is better to think you have cancer than actually to have cancer. It is the *character* that something has, not whether it exists or not, that makes it good or bad, superior or inferior. Malcolm accepts this, but he takes Anselm to be saying *not* that existence is a perfection but that *necessary* existence (the *logical* impossibility of nonexistence) is a perfection. Something is greater, superior, more perfect if it *necessarily* exists than if it merely contingently exists.

How does Anselm prove this? Why is it so? Or is it so? Malcolm's argument goes roughly like this. We can come to understand what is meant here by 'a greater' by reflecting on the notion of dependence. Many things depend on other things. And surely if X depends on Y, then there is an evident sense in which Y is greater than X. If we "reflect on the common meaning of the word 'God' (no matter how vague and confused this is), we will come to realize that it would always be incorrect to say that God's existence should, *in any way*, depend on anything." Whether we believe in God or not, we must believe that the "maker of heaven and earth (if there is such) and of all things visible and invisible (as said in the Nicene Creed) cannot be *thought* of as being *brought* into existence by anything or as *depending* for its continued existence on anything." God (by definition) is an absolutely unlimited being. But (as we have seen) being a dependent or limited being is a comparative defect. A being that is not limited and not dependent on another being is a greater being than one that is so limited or dependent. The greatest conceivable being must be a being absolutely unlimited. But God (by definition) is such a being.

An absolutely unlimited being cannot be a being that could be prevented from existing, or a being that might cease to exist. Furthermore, it could not be the case that it might just happen that such a being did not exist. If something just happened to exist it would not be eternal and thus not an absolutely unlimited being. To say 'It just happens to be' implies 'It might not have been', but it is inconsistent to say of a being that is eternal that it might *not* have been.

Anselm makes the subtle point that if you can conceive of a certain thing and this thing *does not* exist, then, if it were to exist, its nonexistence would be possible. This, Malcolm argues, would make it into a noneternal and dependent being, for its existence would depend on certain conditions. By contrast, to be an eternal being, and not just a being with everlasting duration, is to be a logically necessary being. But a being that couldn't not exist could not be dependent on anything else. Such a being must be an eternal, completely independent being. If there is such a being (as we have seen) it is greater than any contingent being, a being whose nonexistence is logically possible. And this is what Malcolm set out to establish in the first section of his essay, that is, that a noncontingent being is greater than or superior to a contingent being.

We can now, Malcolm contends, accept both points in Anselm's argument. That is, the following two claims appear to be true. (1) There is an important and fundamental respect in which a being whose nonexistence is logically impossible (a necessary being) is a greater being than a being whose nonexistence is logically possible. (2) God (by definition) is a being than which a greater cannot be conceived. Thus, we are in the position to assert that it is a necessary truth that God is a necessary being, and as such is a greater or more perfect being than any contingent being possibly could be.

It is also evident from the above that contingent existence or a contingent nonexistence cannot have any application to God. It makes no more sense to speak of God in these terms than it does to speak of stones as being happy or sad. That this is so can be seen from some further considerations independent of my previous argument. The following two statements can be seen to be necessary truths—that is, analytic statements—by anyone who has an acquaintance with English and a tolerable acquaintance with God-talk.

1. God could not contingently not exist, for if He does not exist now He could never come into existence.

2. He cannot contingently exist, for if He exists now He cannot cease to exist.

That these are analytic can be determined by reflecting on the very use, the very meaning, of the expression 'God'. The God of the Bible, death-of-God theologians to the contrary notwithstanding, could not literally die, although commitment to Him or belief in Him could die in men's hearts and minds. Anything that literally died or that we took to be a being that could die would *thereby* not be called 'God' by a Jew or a Christian. Nor could anything that simply came into existence be the

God of the Biblical tradition. He is from everlasting to everlasting; He could not come to be or start existing anymore than a puppy could be an old dog.

Thus, when we are talking about that than which no greater can be conceived, we are talking about something that, if it exists, has necessary existence, for such a being is conceived of as an eternal being and an eternal being is by definition a being that could not come into existence or go out of existence or in any way cease to exist. Even the notion of endless duration is not correctly applied to it, much less equivalent to it, because that would imply that it was conceived in temporal terms. It simply does not make *sense* to speak of an eternal being coming to exist or ceasing to exist.

In this context Anselm is not treating existence as a property or attribute, but he is taking *necessary* existence and *contingent* existence as properties or attributes; and he is taking necessary existence as a defining property of God, just as having three sides is a defining property of a triangle. Thus, in this argument he avoids the traditional criticism that the ontological argument makes the fatal assumption of taking existence to be a property when it is not. But with the qualifiers 'necessary' and 'contingent' we do get a characterization of what we are discussing. That is, although existence is not a property, necessary existence and contingent existence are properties.

In short, what Anselm has shown is that if God exists His existence is necessary. Anselm should be understood as claiming that an eternal being, a being than which no greater can be conceived, cannot possibly be conceived not to exist. Thus, Malcolm claims, God's existence is either logically necessary or logically impossible. Since this is so, "the only intelligible way of rejecting Anselm's claim that God's existence is necessary is to maintain that the concept of God, as that than which no greater can be conceived, is self-contradictory or in some other way nonsensical." But that it is self-contradictory or in some other way nonsensical does not appear to be so. 'God' has a well-established use in the language. People understand—even though they may disbelieve—talk about their Almighty Father in Heaven, the creator of the heavens and the earth. It is not like uttering 'Johnson slipshod generate motionless cataracts' or 'Humphrey sleeps slower than Wallace'. Moreover, 'God is the creator of the heavens and the earth' most certainly does not appear to be a contradiction. It is not like 'Fathers are not males'. God's existence must therefore be logically necessary. And thus it is self-contradictory to assert, 'There is no God'.

Malcolm's restatement of Anselm has been aptly condensed into the following argument:

1. If God, a being a greater than which cannot be conceived, does not exist, then He cannot come into existence. For if He did He would either have been caused to come into existence or have just happened to come into

existence, and in either case He would be a limited being, which by our conception of Him He is not. Since He cannot come into existence, if He does not now exist His existence is impossible.

2. If He does exist He cannot have come into existence (for the reasons given), nor can He cease to exist, for nothing could cause Him to cease to exist, nor could it just happen that He ceased to exist. So if God exists His existence is necessary.

3. Thus, God's existence is either impossible or necessary.

4. It can be the former (that is, God's existence can be impossible) only if the concept of such a being is self-contradictory or in some way logically absurd.

5. Assuming that this is not so (that is, assuming our notion of God is logically sound),

6. it follows that God necessarily exists.

II

The first thing to do in examining Malcolm's defense of Anselm is to consider, apropos propositions (3) and (4) above, whether, after all, God's existence is impossible because the concept of God is self-contradictory or in some way logically absurd. To what may be the surprise of non-philosophers at any rate, many philosophers do maintain that the very concept of God is logically absurd because it is in some way meaningless, and a few think it is self-contradictory.[3]

In the fourth section of his essay, Malcolm turns to this kind of objection. I shall examine this issue by considering Malcolm's answer to this objection. He admits that he cannot demonstrate that the concept of a being a greater than which cannot be conceived is not self-contradictory, but then again he cannot prove that it is not self-contradictory to maintain that there are material things or that we see material things. All he can do by way of argument about these points is to knock down particular arguments given by philosophers who try to maintain that these three concepts (God, material thing, seeing a material thing) are self-contradictory. He has no idea of what it would mean in general and without reference to some particular kind of reasoning to demonstrate that these concepts are not self-contradictory. Moreover, they all have a fixed place in our language and an established place in our lives. Thus, there should be no general presumption that they are self-contradictory. The burden of proof is on the skeptical philosopher to give us some reason to think that they are.

Malcolm maintains that a similar thing should be said for the claim that they are meaningless or in some way logically absurd. God-talk has an established role in human speech. Indeed, God must be taken to be a mystery by religious believers, but He is not taken to be so mysterious that talk of Him becomes meaningless or utterly incoherent. Believer and nonbeliever alike indicate they have some understanding of the term 'God', because both readily recognize that it is senseless to say 'God likes coffee' or 'God was born yesterday and weighed five pounds'. Those are not the blasphemous remarks of a man who curses God, but the senseless remarks of someone who has not caught on to God-talk at all. Anyone with even a very superficial contact with Judaism, Christianity, or Islam and with an acquaintance with English can see that if he will but reflect for a moment. If anyone with a tolerably proper grasp of English seriously gave voice to such utterances, he would clearly indicate by his very linguistic behavior that he had no understanding of God-talk. In short, while we have no understanding of 'Envy lies potatoes', we do have *some understanding* of 'God loves all His creation'.

In this plain sense Malcolm is clearly right: We have *some understanding* of God-talk even though (I would add) it may very well be that there is also a sense in which God-talk, or at least some crucial segment of it, is in some important respect meaningless or logically absurd. However, given that Judaism and Christianity are ongoing modes of life with accepted forms of speech, the onus is surely on the critic to give some particular and powerful argument for saying that, appearances to the contrary, the concept of God is meaningless or logically absurd. (We shall consider in Chapter 20 just such an argument.) Thus, in lieu of such a powerful argument it seems reasonable to assume that the concept of God is not self-contradictory or in some way logically absurd.

At any rate, on the not implausible assumption that the concept of God is not defective in either of these ways, let us see if Malcolm has actually given us a conclusive or reliable argument for believing there is a God. Malcolm thinks he has established that 'There is no God' is a necessarily false statement and that 'There is a God' or 'God exists' is an *a priori* truth. Malcolm believes he has established that it would be self-contradictory to deny that God exists. Has he established any such thing?

III

It is crucial to determine whether Malcolm has been able to surmount successfully certain very commonly accepted criticisms of some of the positions that he advocates. There is, for example, the very generally held view that logical necessity applies to statements or propositions and not to things, no matter how extraordinary these things may be.[4] Thus, while the concept of God has not been shown to be self-contradictory, the concept of a logically necessary being is senseless since (by definition) only a statement and not a being can be self-contradictory. Moreover, if we identify God with a logically necessary being, as Malcolm does, then the very concept of God is also senseless. We cannot intelligibly assert logically necessary existence.

Closely linked with this view is the position derived from Hume and held by most analytic philosophers: Any assertion of the existence of something can be denied without logical absurdity.[5] That is, for any statement that genuinely functions to assert the existence of something, we can without self-contradiction deny that statement. If Jones asserts that there is X or X exists, he is giving us to understand that 'X' refers to something, and we can without contradicting ourselves always assert that there is no X—that 'X' does not refer to anything. We can always negate the proposition in question. Whatever can be conceived of as existing can also, as far as logical possibilities go, be conceived of as not existing. No statement of such a form can be a logically necessary statement. Logical necessity depends only on our symbolism or on the relationship between concepts. In short, necessary truth reflects our use or employment of words.

It is such considerations that make it evident that no being or existent can be logically necessary. If I assert that there is a so and so or that so and so exists, you can always deny that statement without contradicting yourself. It is only propositions such as 'Puppies are young dogs' or 'Red things are colored' or 'Every effect has a cause' that *can* be logically true, and they are never *existential* propositions (propositions that assert the existence of something). Thus, there can be no logically necessary beings or logically necessary existence. If Anselm and Malcolm are right, a Divine existence, if there is any, is to be taken to be a logically necessary existence. But for the reasons just given, such a Divine existence is not merely incredible but it is after all impossible.

Malcolm remarks that what is at the very heart of these criticisms of the ontological argument and what is essential for their success is (1) the belief that since logical necessity reflects our use of words and (2) that since propositions or statements and not things are logically necessary, every proposition or statement of the form 'X exists' must be contingent. People who use this argument, Malcolm remarks, then conclude that since this is so, our concept of God is indeed very problematic. To conceive of God is to conceive of a logically necessary being, and this requires that 'God exists' or 'There is a God' be logically necessary truths rather than propositions that could be significantly denied. But, as we have seen, all propositions of the form 'X exists' or 'There is an X' are contingent. Since this is so, 'God exists' or 'There is a God' must, in order to be intelligible, also be contingent, and therefore can be significantly denied. Thus, they conclude, the requirement that 'There is a God' be a logically necessary truth must be mistaken, and thus it must be possible to say without contradiction that 'There is no God'. Whatever the subject of discourse, it must be possible, as Hume thought, to

assert that it is not true that there is anything of the sort that you mention, whatever it may be that you care to mention. Thus, since God is
conceived of as a *logically necessary being* in Anselm's conception of
Him, the preceding establishes that God can no more exist than can a
round square. If we follow Anselm's line of reasoning to the bitter end,
we come to a very different conclusion than the one Anselm would lead
us to. We come to see that there can be no God. We have, given Anselm's
assumptions, unwittingly produced an ontological *disproof* of God's existence.[6] If God must be conceived of as a logically necessary being, then
the concept of God is a self-contradictory concept.

Malcolm replies that the claim that no existential statement is a logically necessary truth is just a dogma and is not rooted in our actual use
of language. Moreover, if we really take seriously the view that logical
necessity reflects our use of words, we must "Look at the use of words
and not manufacture *a priori* theses" about them. In the Nineteenth
Psalm, we get a use of language that clearly shows that in the Christian
religion God is actually conceived of as a necessary being. It says: "Before
the mountains were brought forth, or ever thou hadst formed earth
and the world, even from everlasting to everlasting, thou art God."

Here we find expressed in the Bible, Malcolm contends, the idea of
necessary existence and the idea of the eternity of God—ideas "essential
to the Jewish and Christian religions." The very existence of such discourse refutes the claim that statements of the form 'X exists' are never
logically necessary and that this contingency of existential propositions
reflects our fundamental conventions of language, for here we have a
standard use of language in which 'God exists' or 'There is a God' are
logically necessary statements such that it would be *contradictory* to assert
that there is no God.

There is, however, at least one argument that refutes Malcolm's claim.
This argument contends that Malcolm has unwittingly punned on the
different uses of 'necessity'.[7] Malcolm's quotation from the Bible shows
that Jews and Christians conceive of God as an eternal being, as a wholly
unlimited being. It does not show that God is conceived of as a *logically*
necessary being. God's existence is thought to be necessary in the sense
that God is conceived to be unlimited and eternal: He could not just
happen to exist, come to be, cease to be, begin to be, and the like. Since
eternity is not mere endless duration, we cannot even conceive of a non-
existent *God* anymore than we can conceive of a nonexistent *eternal*
being. That would be like trying to conceive of eternal beings that are
noneternal. But this does not establish that there are eternal beings and
it does not establish that there is a necessary existence. Moreover, God is
conceived of as having necessary existence in that He is conceived of as
that which everything else depends on while not being dependent on anything Himself. But this does not in the slightest establish that God's

existence is *logically* necessary or even that we know what it would be like for a being or for being to be *logically* necessary in contradistinction to knowing what it would be like to say that a proposition or statement is logically necessary.

In speaking of God, Malcolm at .this crucial juncture only speaks of necessary existence; he does *not* speak of *logically* necessary existence. But this seemingly innocuous shift in his argument is of the most considerable moment, because in different contexts we mean different things by 'necessary', 'impossible', and even 'inconceivable'. It is impossible for me to write this textbook in Russian, but not logically impossible. It is necessary that I have lungs to live, but not logically necessary. It is inconceivable that Frank O'Connor can carry the Empire State Building to Albany on the palm of his hand, but not *logically* inconceivable. You perfectly well understand what we would have to do. There are physical necessities, psychological necessities, legal necessities, moral necessities, perhaps even spiritual necessities as well as logical necessities.

'An eternal being cannot cease to exist or begin to exist' is parallel to 'A bachelor cannot get divorced or have a wife'. Both statements are *a priori* truths: analytic statements the denial of which is self-contradictory. They are logically necessary statements, while 'Decapitated human beings quickly die' is not a logical necessity but is an evident physical necessity. 'Eternal beings cannot be conceived not to exist' is also an *a priori* truth and a logical necessity. It parallels 'Perpetual motion machines cannot run down'. But even though perpetual motion machines cannot run down, there may be no perpetual motion machines; and even though eternal beings, if there are any, cannot fail to exist—that is, cease to exist—and in that way cannot be conceived not to exist, it remains true that there may be no eternal beings. *Eternally it might be the case that there are no eternal beings.*

When we say 'Eternal beings cannot fail to exist' we mean that 'If a being is eternal it cannot fail to exist'. But this does not commit us to the claim that there are any eternal beings, although it does commit us to the claim that if it is true that there are no eternal beings it is timelessly true that there are none.

Malcolm has shown that we conceive of God as having independent existence, eternal existence, and unlimited existence. But Malcolm has not shown that the statement 'There is a God', like 'There are no married bachelors', is a *logically* necessary truth and that 'There is no God' or 'It is false that there is a God' are contradictions. To do this he would have to give us some reason for thinking that 'There is an eternal being', 'There is a being upon whom all other beings depend but who depends on no one itself', and 'There is an unlimited being' are logically true and that it is self-contradictory to deny them. Malcolm has not given us good grounds for believing that they are self-contradictory. He has given us no adequate grounds for denying, as self-contradictory, what most certainly appears to be at least a logical possibility, namely that there is no X such that X is eternal, independent of all else, and unlimited.

Malcolm maintains that one gets caught in a contradiction if one tries to assert that *if* there is an eternal being then it necessarily exists. To say that is in effect to say, 'If there is an eternal being and he might not exist then he necessarily exists'. To so assert 'he might not exist' and 'he necessarily exists' is to assert *p* and not-*p*. Thus, Malcolm argues, the locution 'If there is an eternal being then he necessarily exists' is incoherent because self-contradictory. Yet it is plainly presupposed in my argument in the previous paragraph.

Malcolm's defense here is not successful, for 'If there is an eternal being then it necessarily exists' can readily be understood in such a way that it is not a contradiction. When such an utterance is made, there need be no assertion and denial that God necessarily exists. The terms 'necessary' and 'necessarily' have different meanings in different contexts. When I say that an eternal being necessarily exists, I say that it timelessly exists. That is to say, I give to understand that such a being could not come to be or exist now and then cease to be. We cannot conceive of such a reality as being at all subject to the vicissitudes of time. In that sense it is necessary, but when I say there might be an eternal being, the 'necessity' that is the opposite of 'might not be' is not the necessity that goes with being eternal or even an eternal, independent, and unlimited being. Rather, it is the *logical* necessity that goes with statements or propositions. I am only saying that it is logically possible that 'There is an eternal being' might be false. This gives one to understand that 'There is an eternal being' is a contingent proposition and not a logically necessary, analytic one. To say 'An eternal being does not exist' is in effect to say 'There is nothing that answers to the description "eternal being"'. Logically we can infer from this that since there is none now, there never was one and there never will be one. But there is no reason to think that logic rules out the possibility that it is eternally the case that there is no eternal, independent, unlimited being; that is, that there is no being a greater than which cannot be conceived. Perhaps there is such a being, but there is nothing to show that it is self-contradictory to deny that there is such a reality. Even on Malcolm's subtle reformulation, the ontological argument fails.[8]

This, I should add, is only one of many criticisms that could be (and have been) made of Malcolm's argument—or, if you will, of Malcolm's statement and defense of an Anselmian argument—although I think it is the most central criticism. His essay has been subject to several powerful and sustained criticisms.[9] Malcolm, after the manner of G. E. Moore, has remarked that he does not "know that it is possible to meet all of the objections," although, "on the other hand" he does "not know that it is impossible either."[10] But the criticism I have voiced here, which in turn is a simplified version of a criticism that has been voiced, is absolutely central. Until and unless Malcolm can give us some slight reason for thinking it can be met, it would most certainly appear evident that the ontological argument, even in his subtle formulation, is an unsound argument. It is immensely instructive about the concept of God, but it gives us no adequate grounds for believing there is a God or that God exists.

NOTES

1. Kant's central arguments are in the section entitled "The Impossibility of an Ontological Proof of the Existence of God," in his *Critique of Pure Reason*. That the actual formulation of Kant's own argument plainly has defects and is subject to a variety of interpretations is brought out in the symposium on Kant's refutation of the ontological argument in *The Journal of Philosophy*, LXIII (1966). What in effect is a contemporary restatement of what I take to be the sound core of the Kantian arguments is effectively used by W. I. Matson in his examination of the ontological argument. See W. I. Matson, *The Existence of God*, pp. 44–55. I have ignored here another standard difficulty in the ontological argument, namely, its unjustified assumption that existence is a perfection.

2. Norman Malcolm's "Anselm's Ontological Arguments" is conveniently reprinted in John Hick (ed.), *The Existence of God* and Alvin Plantinga (ed.), *The Ontological Argument*.

3. J. N. Findlay's "Can God's Existence Be Disproved?" in A. Flew and A. MacIntyre (eds.), *New Essays in Philosophical Theology*, and Ronald Puccetti's "The Concept of God", *Philosophical Quarterly* (1964), present two contemporary arguments to establish this point. L. Feuerbach, most notably in his *The Essence of Christianity* and in *The Essence of Religion*, attempted in the nineteenth century to establish that the concept of God is incoherent. In my *The Quest for God* I try to use analytical techniques to make the same point. Anthony Flew makes similar arguments in his *God and Philosophy*.

4. In the context of theological discussion, this is effectively argued by J. J. C. Smart and by J. N. Findlay in their contributions to the collection of essays previously cited: *New Essays in Philosophical Theology*.

5. David Hume, *Dialogues Concerning Natural Religion*, part IX.

6. J. N. Findlay, op. cit., has powerfully articulated that argument.

7. See Terence Penelhum, "On the Second Ontological Argument," *Philosophical Review*, LXX, no. 1 (January, 1961), and T. P. Brown, "Professor Malcolm on 'Anselm's Ontological Arguments'," *Analysis* (October, 1961).

8. Some of the difficulties in Malcolm's arguments here, plus a link between such arguments and the considerations that I shall raise in Chapter 21, are incisively discussed by Robert Coburn in his "Professor Malcolm on God," *Australasian Journal of Philosophy* (1963).

9. Some further criticisms of Malcolm's argument not previously mentioned include Raziel Abelson, "Not Necessarily," R. E. Allen, "The Ontological

Argument," Paul Henle, "Uses of the Ontological Argument," Gareth B. Matthews, "On Conceivability in Anselm and Malcolm," Alvin Plantinga, "A Valid Ontological Argument?" all in *The Philosophical Review,* vol. LXX (January, 1961); Jerome Shaffer, "Existence, Predication and the Ontological Argument", *Mind,* vol. LXXI (July, 1962), and Jan Berg, "An Examination of Ontological Proof, *Theoria,* vol. XXVII (1961).

10. See the footnote on page 162 of his *Knowledge and Certainty.*

16

AQUINAS
AND THE FIVE
WAYS

I

The ontological argument is a purely *a priori* argument and it fails. We need to look in a different direction for a sound argument for the existence of God. St. Thomas Aquinas, the traditional intellectual hero of the Roman Catholic Church, does just that. Like St. Anselm, he was a loyal medieval monk who tried to give a rational demonstration of the existence of God. Again, as with Anselm, it was a matter of faith seeking understanding, but the way in which Aquinas thought one could come to know that God exists was radically different from the way Anselm thought this was possible.

Aquinas rejected the belief that one could come to know that God exists from becoming clear about the concept of God. Rather, the existence of God is demonstrated from His *effects* in the world. It was Aquinas' conviction that God has revealed Himself to man in a thousand ways. If we will but carefully reflect on certain very common experiences, we will come to see that God most certainly does exist. The relevant facts about the world are not esoteric facts that only a person with very considerable scientific or philosophical training could discover. And they are not facts—if indeed there are such facts—that only a person with certain 'mystical intuitions' or a distinctive 'existential temperament' could discover. The relevant facts are facts plainly at hand for anyone, facts with which Neanderthal man could have been acquainted perfectly well. To come to know that God exists, it is maintained, is a matter of carefully noting what else must be true if it is true, as it plainly is, that things are moved, that events have causes, that organisms are born and die, that some things are worse than other things, and the like. If we carefully follow the implications of these empirical truisms, Aquinas and modern Neo-Scholastics argue, we will come to see that God exists.

It is natural to react that since even Neanderthal man no doubt was acquainted with the facts just alluded to, it then must be very easy to prove the existence of God. But plainly it is not easy, so something must be wrong with Aquinas' contention. The quite proper reply that Aquinas would make is that while the facts are plainly before one, the proper interpretation of these facts is not at all evident. That is to say, it is not easy actually to recognize that God exists since such states of affairs obtain. The intellectual difficulty is in understanding what else must be true given the preceding empirical truisms.

Aquinas, of course, accepted Scripture—meaning by this he accepted the Old and New Testaments—as the revealed word of God; but he recognized that only if we can demonstrate that God exists can we know that there can be a Divine Scripture at all. Once we know that God exists, we can accept many other things on faith—for example, the doctrine of the Trinity. But unless we are to build on a house of cards, we must at least be able to demonstrate that God exists and this, as the French Thomist Etienne Gilson puts it, can only by done by starting from "the consideration of God's effects."[1] We start, Gilson contends, from some thing or situation empirically given in sense knowledge and go on to "infer a non-empirically given existence." It is *only* from such an actually given empirical existence that we could "legitimately infer a non-empirically given existence."[2] So Aquinas' central question becomes: Can the affirmation that there is a God assume the form and acquire the status of a scientifically demonstrated conclusion?

In his *Summa Theologica* Aquinas gave five distinct demonstrations of the existence of God. We shall consider only two: 'the second way' and 'the third way'. By common consent they are taken to be his most powerful arguments for the existence of God. If they are not sound, there is little reason to believe that Aquinas has actually established the existence of God. In effect, however, I shall discuss 'the fifth way' in the next chapter under the rubric 'the argument from Design'. And 'the first way'— the argument from motion—is in all but externals identical with 'the second way', the argument from causality. The problems that arise about the argument from motion are essentially the same as the problems that we shall uncover in examining 'the second way'.

I shall, as I go over these two arguments, first state Aquinas' own formulations and then give a more compact formulation of my own that lays bare the essentials of the argument. I shall then criticize the argument and continue to reformulate it in the light of those criticisms in a persistent search for a formulation of arguments that can give us a sound or at least a reliable argument for the existence of God.

My putting Aquinas in a somewhat streamlined dress follows the practice of many modern Thomists. It is justified by the fact that Aquinas seemed at least to attach no particular significance to the exact letter of his formulations, for in various places he stated essentially the same arguments in different ways. Moreover, he did not always give all five arguments.[3]

It should also be kept in mind that many contemporary Thomists or Neo-Scholastic theologians and philosophers tend, as Ronald Hepburn has well put it, to see Aquinas' various arguments, themselves borrowed from various sources, as a "single thrust of argument that aims to show the derivativeness and dependence of the world as we experience it, and to lead to an awareness of the wholly different mode of being of the God who upholds (who 'must' uphold) the world by his creative might."[4] We must ask, looking at the arguments singly and then thinking about them together, if they at all achieve that, and if they give us a sound or even a reliable argument for a single First Uncaused Cause that causes all else but is itself not caused or a necessary being—an unlimited, eternal reality—upon whom all other things are dependent but which is dependent on nothing itself.

As Aquinas was very well aware, this surely is not all of what we mean by 'God', but it is an essential part of our meaning. No matter how much we as Jews or Christians stress that God is truly other, that He is in large measure incomprehensible to finite minds and that Divine Reality is utterly transcendent and mysterious, we must mean at least what Aquinas means in his theological characterization of God, unless the concept of God is to undergo a radical sea-change from what it has meant in the Jewish and Christian tradition. At our present juncture the crucial question is: Do we even have good grounds for believing that such a reality as Aquinas tries to characterize exists?

Both 'the second way' and 'the third way', as well as Aquinas' 'first way', are appropriately labeled *cosmological* arguments for the existence of God. That is, they are arguments that purport to demonstrate the existence of God from premises asserting some highly general empirical facts about the world. Let us commence by quoting Aquinas' own statement of 'the second way'.

> The second way is from the nature of the efficient cause. In the world of sense we find there is an order of efficient causes. There is no case known (neither is it, indeed, possible) in which a thing is found to be the efficient cause of itself; for so it would be prior to itself, which is impossible. Now in efficient causes it is not possible to go on to infinity, because in all efficient causes following in order, the first is the cause of the intermediate cause, and the intermediate is the cause of the ultimate cause, whether the intermediate cause be several or one only. Now to take away the cause is to take away the effect. Therefore, if there be no first cause among efficient causes, there will be no ultimate, nor any intermediate cause. But if in efficient causes it is possible to go on to infinity, there will be no first efficient cause, neither will there be an ultimate effect, nor any intermediate efficient causes; all of which

is plainly false. Therefore it is necessary to admit a first efficient cause, to which everyone gives the name of God.[5]

His argument can be reexpressed in the following compact form where it is (assuming the *intelligibility* of the premises) plainly a valid argument. The point is, is it a *sound* or even a *reliable* argument?

> If there are causes in the world, then there must be a first uncaused cause to make all this possible.
> There are causes in the world.
> _____
> Therefore there must be a first uncaused cause to make all this possible. This first uncaused cause that causes everything else but is not itself caused we call God.

In trying to determine whether this argument is conclusive, sound, or even reliable, we should note that it is the first premiss that is most obviously open to challenge. Consider:

> If things are caused in the world, then there must be a first uncaused cause to make all this possible.

Why? Why couldn't there be an infinite series of caused causes instead? There cannot, Aquinas argues, because then it would have been impossible for the causal order to have got started in the first place. And if that were so, then even now there would be nothing, for something cannot come from nothing. There plainly is something, so there must be an uncaused cause that caused everything else. That is, there must be an uncaused cause that got everything started in the first place.

This, it will be replied, begs the question. Why must things 'have got started in the first place'? Why must there have been 'a first place'? Why could there not be an infinite series of caused causes? An infinite series is not a long or even a very, very long *finite* series. The person arguing for an infinite series is not arguing that something came from nothing, nor need he be *denying* that *every* event has a cause. He is asserting that we need not assume that there is a *first* cause that started everything. Only if the series of causes were finite would it be impossible for these to be something if there were no first cause or uncaused cause. But if the series is literally infinite, there would be no need for there to be a first cause to get the causal order started, for there always would be a causal order since an infinite series can have no first member or being. We indeed may not know that there actually is an infinite series of caused causes, but Aquinas has not given us anything approaching an adequate reason to believe that there is not one or that it is more reasonable to believe that there is a finite series than to believe that there is an infinite series. The burden of proof is surely on him to rule out the possibility of an infinite series or to give us some reason to think it less likely than a finite series culminating in a first cause. It is just this that he has failed to do.

Do not be tricked into thinking that it is more reasonable to believe that there is a First Uncaused Cause than to believe that there is an infinite series of 'caused causes' because the former belief seems more 'natural'. Remember that from childhood on we have heard about 'in the beginning'. If you had been brought up among the educated elite in the Soviet Union, you would have heard other stories and other things would be more familiar to you and would seem more natural. The crucial question is, logically speaking, is there any reason to believe that one assumption is more reasonable than the other? Aquinas has given us no reason to believe this.

Moreover, even if this causal argument were a conclusive one, it still would not (1) prove what a Theist wants, namely that there is a *single* first cause or (2) establish the present existence of this first cause.

Defenders of the causal argument will at this point in the dialectic insist that we need to distinguish between *causes in fieri* (efficient causes) and *causes in esse* (sustaining causes). The former is a factor that brings about or helps bring about a determinate effect. A cause *in esse* is a factor that keeps or sustains or at least helps keep or sustain an effect in existence. If I build a sailboat I am its cause *in fieri;* the materials that keep it in existence are its *cause in esse*. Sometimes the *cause in fieri* and the *cause in esse* are the same. A candle is the *cause in fieri* of the light it produces. (The light comes from the candle.) But it is also the *cause in esse* of that light, for the candle must continue to exist for the light to exist. But even here the two kinds of causes remain conceptually distinct.

Aquinas, it can be argued, is—or at least should be—concerned with *causes in esse* and not with *causes in fieri*. He is denying that there can be an infinite series or an infinite hierarchy of *causes in esse*. But it is indeed perfectly possible that there might be an infinite series of *causes in fieri*. Yet that there can be *such* an infinite series of causes, we are given to believe, would not hurt the basic structure of Aquinas' reasoning. On this interpretation of Aquinas, his argument, if correct, would establish the *present* existence and not simply the *past* existence of a first—that is, an uncaused—cause.

There are, however, other objections to this way of stating the argument. It is not implausible to claim that every event in the universe has a cause, meaning by that a *cause in fieri*. But is it plausible to argue that all subatomic particles have a *cause in esse*? Consider atoms, electrons, mesons, and the like. What do they depend on for their existence? It does not seem to be the case that the most fundamental particles have a *cause in esse*. Indeed, as Norman Kemp Smith has put it, a minimal conception of the Divine must be a conception of something upon which all things rest. But why think that subatomic particles rest on or depend on something more fundamental? Why *must* such physical realities or why *must* the fundamental particles of physics depend on anything at all? The argument from causality would have us believe that it is some kind of conceptual necessity that there must be such a causal dependence. But no reason has been given to justify a belief that such a causal dependence obtains here.

Even if my way of putting the matter here is somehow mistaken, it remains the case that once again the *infinite* regress question returns like the repressed. In denying that there is a *first cause in esse*, the critic need not be denying that what the defenders of the causal argument call a *first cause in esse* is a *cause in esse* or even (necessarily) that everything must have some *cause in esse*. He need only deny its 'first causiness.' In fact, he need not deny that there is a first *cause in esse*, but merely in good Kantian fashion maintain that the defender of the causal argument has no more established that there is such a first *cause in esse* than he has established that there is a first *cause in fieri*. In both cases an infinite series of caused causes is at least as plausible a conception. It may indeed be true that everything in the world depends on something external to it, is sustained by something else. However, this does not establish or give us any reason to believe that there is some *first* cause that, directly or indirectly, sustains everything else but is not itself sustained by anything. It could just as well be the case that there is an infinite series of caused causes, all sustained by something else. Remember that a genuinely infinite series is not just a very, very long finite series; if it is truly infinite, there cannot be a first member that sustains all the other members. No reason has been given for thinking such an infinite series is impossible or even unlikely and that there must be a first cause on which everything else ultimately depends.

III

The argument, however, would not stop here, for contemporary philosopher-theologians such as Copleston and Mascall—both of whom work out of what is essentially the tradition of Aquinas—would argue that even if (as a matter of fact) there were an infinite series of *causes in fieri* or *in esse*, this would *not* do away with the need for an *ultimate* first cause to give a complete explanation of the world.[6] Why, it now needs to be asked, is a series of 'phenomenal causes' (as Copleston calls them) an insufficient explanation of the whole series? Because to explain fully the existence of the *series* itself we need to postulate a *'transcendent cause'* of the series—something beyond or distinct from the causes in the series of 'phenomenal causes'.

There are, however, serious and crucially damaging objections to this view. First, 'series' is not a word that stands for something that might have a cause. It is absurd to ask for the cause of the *series* as distinct from asking about the cause of its individual members. The word 'cause' has no meaning here. Suppose there were a multiple car accident involving four cars. Car 1 ran off its lane and hit Car 2 head on. This made Car 2 suddenly halt, and Car 3 was going so fast it could not halt in time and so it piled into Car 2. Car 4, in turn, had defective brakes and was going so fast that it could not stop in time either, so it hit Car 3. Now we have given the causes of the various collisions. To ask for the cause of *the series*—if the question is sensible at all—could only be to ask who *initiated* the series, namely, in this instance to ask why the first car hit the second car. But this is still to appeal to a 'phenomenal cause' and not some 'transcendent cause'. To ask in any other way what caused the series is to ask a senseless question of the order of my asking why did the class come on Tuesday after I had discovered the cause of each member coming.

There are further difficulties. Reference to 'transcendent cause' begs the question, and more importantly still, no meaning has been given to 'transcendent cause'. To believe A causes B as in "Decapitation causes death' or 'Prolonged lack of sleep causes nervousness' involves believing that there are two independently ascertainable classes of events A and B, and that whenever events of type A occur, events of type B occur. But in order for us to assert that A is the cause of B, they must be independently specifiable so that it is possible to assert correctly that A has been observed and that whenever A occurs B occurs as well. None of this works with a so-called 'transcendent cause', for if A is transcendent it cannot be observed. Moreover, Aquinas and his modern followers claim one can *only* know God through his effects. This makes the so called transcendent cause (part of what we mean by 'God') in principle unobservable. And if it is *in principle* unobservable, then we can never be in a position to know what it would mean to say it was the cause of anything because we could not *independently* specify or identify it. This independent specification or identification is essential for our being able to justifiably assert that a causal relation obtains between two events or things. If we cannot even say, as we cannot in this case, what it would be like to give such an independent specification, then we cannot even intelligibly speak of a causal relation in such a context.

Finally if 'transcendent cause' is to be identified with 'God', such 'a cause' by definition is a unique reality. But to assert a causal relation—for example, 'Decapitation causes death'—we need classes of events with more than one member to justify our saying A causes B. Recall that to assert a causal relation between A and B commits one to the claim that whenever an event of type A occurs, an event of type B occurs. But where something occurs that is by definition a unique event, we could not sensibly say that. For all these reasons it makes no sense at all to speak of a 'transcendent cause'.

IV

At this point—if the defender of the cosmological argument does not give up—it is natural to shift from the causal form of the cosmological argument ('the second way') to another form, namely to the argument from the contingency of the world. (Aquinas' 'third way'.) This is one of the reasons why it is usually claimed that the argument from contingency is the more fundamental argument. A defender of the cosmological argument might concede that a series is indeed not a kind of thing over and above its members, and that it does not make sense to ask for the cause of the *series*, except in the innocuous sense already specified.

When people confusedly ask for a cause here they are really asking for an explanation—the *raison d'être*—of the entire series. They are not, in all strictness, asking for its cause. They are in effect noting that a series of 'phenomenal causes' (composed of contingent beings) is *not* really fully or completely explained or made 'intelligible' unless we invoke the conception of a necessary being. As Copleston puts it, "What we call the world is intrinsically unintelligible apart from the existence of God." And God, by definition, is a necessary being.

It is in such a manner that we come to rely, in trying to state a sound form of the cosmological argument, on the argument from the contingency of the world. Aquinas states the argument as follows:

> We find in nature things that are possible to be and not be, since they are found to be generated, and to corrupt, and consequently, they are possible to be and not to be. But it is impossible for these always to exist, for that which is possible not to be at some time is not. Therefore, if everything is possible not to be, then at one time there could have been nothing in existence. Now if this were true, even now there would be nothing in existence, because that which does not exist only begins to exist by something already existing. Therefore, if at one time nothing was in existence, it would have been impossible for anything to have begun to exist; and thus even now nothing would be in existence—which is absurd. Therefore, not all beings are merely possible, but there must exist something the existence of which is necessary. But every necessary thing either has its necessity caused by another, or not. Now it is impossible to go on to infinity in necessary things which have their necessity caused by another, as has been already proved in regard to efficient causes. Therefore we cannot but postulate the existence of some being having of itself its own necessity, and not receiving it from another, but rather causing in others their necessity. This all men speak of as God.[7]

As Aquinas states it above, the argument from contingency presupposes the soundness of the causal argument. But this can be avoided, and the logical core of Aquinas' argument can be stated as follows: All around us we see contingent beings. That is, we see beings that might not have existed, such as physical objects, rainbows, human beings, and the like.

In saying they are contingent, we are implying that we can conceive of the universe without conceiving of this or that physical object. The Brooklyn Bridge, the Grand Canyon, and even earth itself are not necessary existents. The various things that they are all might very well not have been. Human beings—to take one kind of contingent being—depend for their existence on other contingent beings. But we still need to give an explanation of their existence, for because they are contingent they do not have their reason for existence within themselves. To account for these contingent beings—to make contingent being intelligible—we must postulate a necessary being, a being that has the reason for its existence within itself. In short, it is evident enough that there are contingent beings, but the very existence of such contingent beings implies the existence of a necessary being.

This argument can again be put in a still briefer form and in such a way that it becomes plain at a glance that, if its premisses are intelligible, it is a valid argument.

> If there are contingent beings then there is a necessary being.
> There are contingent beings.
> _____
>
> Therefore there is a necessary being.

The central question: Is this a sound argument?

There are many problems with such arguments. One, as should be apparent from our discussion of the ontological argument, is with the very concept of a necessary being. Is it an intelligible concept? Kant remarks in *Critique of Pure Reason*:

> In all ages men have spoken of an absolutely necessary being. There is, of course, no difficulty in giving a verbal definition of the concept, namely that it is something the non-existence of which is impossible. But this yields no insight into the conditions which make it necessary to regard the non-existence of a thing as absolutely unthinkable.

Such a cosmological argument cannot be a sound or a reliable argument if the reference to necessary existence in the argument is to a logically necessary being. 'A logically necessary being', as we have seen in the previous chapter, is as contradictory as a 'round square'. Logical necessity applies only to propositions, that is, to statements that can serve as premisses in arguments. Beings cannot be premisses. A being, eternal or otherwise, cannot be *logically* necessary, for only a proposition or statement—something, as I remarked, that could serve as a premiss in an argument—can be *logically* necessary. If we say that *since* there are contingent beings there *thus* must be a logically necessary being, that is, a being whose nonexistence is inconceivable (logically impossible), we have made a logical mistake. There is and can be no *logically* necessary existence to be contrasted with contingent existence in such a way that a logically necessary existence could be a property of God and contingent existence, by contrast, a property of other realities. This is so because it is self-contradictory to speak of a being whose nonexistence is *logically* necessary. For 'There is a God' to be analytic (self-evident) *in itself* although not necessarily self-evident to us, and for 'There is no God' to be contradictory, just this is necessary. But this is impossible, for it is self-contradictory to speak of a being whose existence is logically necessary. As Hume well put it: "Whatever we conceive as existent, we can also conceive as non-existent. There is no being, therefore, whose non-existence implies a contradiction." Thus, we cannot conceive "of a being which cannot be conceived not to exist. . . ." The ontological argument, as we saw, broke down here, and the cosmological argument will break down at this point too, if its defenders insist on trying to construe God as a logically necessary being.

V

This, however, need not finish off the argument from contingency. 'Necessary' and 'contingent' are context dependent, systematically ambiguous terms. God could be a necessary being without being a *logically* necessary being. Given the fact that, as a matter of fact, we do know that there are contingent beings—a truism about the world although not a *logical* truism—do we not then, after all, have this reliable argument for the existence of God: If there are contingent beings, then there is a necessary being. There are contingent beings. Therefore there is a necessary being. Thus, we know such a necessary being or God actually exists. It is indeed true that to deny that there is such a being is *not* self-contradictory, but a necessary being is still a being whose nonexistence is so unthinkable that he is necessary in some other way. Such a being has sheer *factual* necessity.[8]

This needs elucidation. The kind of necessity we are talking about when we speak of God is the necessity that would go with being a completely unlimited being—a being upon which everything else depends, but which is itself not dependent on any other reality. Such a being, as a sheer matter of fact, is eternal, incorruptible, indestructible, and the creator and sustainer of all other beings. In saying it is eternal we are saying that it never came into existence and that it shall never cease to exist. Surely this is a type of necessary existence.

Even given this elucidation of 'contingent being' and 'necessary being', some traditional difficulties remain. Why should we assume that *because* there are contingent beings there *must* be a necessary being, as there must be a hill since there is a valley? There are valleys in the land, but that there is no high ground above it is nonsense. But *must* there actually be a necessary being—if there are contingent beings—or is it only necessary that we have some concept of what would count as 'a necessary being'? *If* we assert that there actually must be a necessary being, the question immediately arises: why so? Why could there not be an infinite series of contingent beings each dependent on the other *ad infinitum?* Why multiply entities beyond need and assume that there must be some being or reality that is totally unlimited and independent of all else? It certainly seems more reasonable to operate on this assumption: Wherever possible, take the simpler explanation. In this situation assume no more than that there is an infinite series of such contingent beings!

Still more fundamental difficulties remain with the argument from contingency. It is far from clear what must be the case for it to be true or false, or even probably true or false, that there is a being who is totally unlimited or independent of all other beings. It is not evident that we have any criteria in virtue of which we could identify such a being, or that we know when to assert or deny that there is such a being. And while we very well may never be able to prove that there is an infinite series of contingent beings (with no necessary being upon which they are all dependent), it is a much simpler assumption to make, for we need not postulate the existence of such an odd being, 'world ground' or 'Wholly Other Transcendence'—putative conceptions so obscure that their very intelligibility is in question.

VI

At this point it has been argued (by Copleston, for example) that although there possibly might be an infinite series of contingent beings each of which depended on something else for its existence (none containing within themselves the reason for their own existence), still even if we proceed to infinity in that sense, we still have no *ultimate explanation* of why anything exists at all. That there is something rather than nothing becomes just an amazing and wondrous fact, but without the assumption of a necessary being we have no explanation for it. We have no explanation of *existence* at all. Without the postulation of a necessary being, we can have no total explanation of existence to which nothing further can be added; although without it we can, and of course do, know that things exist, for there are (so we affirm) an infinite series of contingent beings. However, even though we know *that* they exist, we do not and cannot, without the assumption of a necessary being, know *why* they exist. Their existence has not been made intelligible to us. They are just brute facts.

When Bertrand Russell remarked in response to this kind of argument that in asking for such a total explanation, "You're looking for something which can't be got, and which one ought not to expect to get," Copleston replied, not unreasonably, "To say that one has not found it is one thing; to say that one should not look for it seems to me rather dogmatic." To this Russell responded, "Well, I don't know. I mean, the explanation of one thing is another thing which makes the other thing dependent on yet another, and you have to grasp this sorry scheme of things entire to do what you want and that we can't do."[9] Copleston's point in return would be to claim that *if* we are to have an adequate explanation of existence or reality we would have to be able to answer just such a question, otherwise man's lot in the world is as absurd and irrational as Camus thought when he wrote *The Myth of Sisyphus*.

One might challenge both Copleston and Camus by arguing that such a claim rests on a misconception of what an explanation is and does, misconstrues what it is to make "reality or phenomena intelligible." The claim redefines an 'adequate explanation' and 'a complete explanation' in an obscure and arbitrary way.

In this context Paul Edwards sensibly argues, "Normally, we are satisfied that we have explained a phenomenon if we have found its cause or if we have exhibited some other uniform connection between it and something else."[10] If we find what factors make something occur, we have given an explanation of it; if not, not. An explanation is adequate or complete when we can list the factors that brought about the event.

Suppose we are trying to explain why in 1968 Humphrey received the Democratic party nomination for President rather than McCarthy. We could point out that Humphrey had the support of President Johnson, that he had the party bosses and the party apparatus behind him, that he supported the Democratic Administration's policies (including their war policies), and that he had the support of important financial interests in the country. The reasons McCarthy failed to gain delegate support are also evident. He was regarded as something of a maverick, he alienated delegates by refusing to flatter them and by holding himself aloof, he opposed the Administration, and he was thought too radical by many. We could give further factors of that sort filling out the picture more completely and explaining by exhibiting a coherent *pattern* of events. If someone complained that such an explanation was superficial, we could go on to show how Johnson gained ascendency over the party apparatus, why important financial interests wanted Humphrey rather than McCarthy and how this is related to America's empire, the Vietnam war, and the like. To explain McCarthy's reaction to the delegates and the delegates' reaction to him, we could characterize the kind of men that become delegates, the extent and nature of antiintellectualism in America, McCarthy's own background, and so on. In explaining Humphrey's nomination we would appeal to facts of this sort. In carrying it further—giving a more complete explanation—we might explain the causes of antiintellectualism in America by displaying similar facts about the people who immigrated to America and their role in founding the country and their relation to Europe.

Note, however, that to explain completely why Humphrey was nominated, we need not explain how the earth was formed or go back to some first cause or necessary being. That we bring out contingent factors and make no reference to a necessary being in no way indicates that our explanation is in any way defective. It may be defective because we did not mention enough contingent factors, include the right kinds, or arrange them in a sufficiently perspicuous pattern; but our explanation is not defective or incomplete because it does not mention a necessary being or show why there is something rather than nothing.

To this rather commonsensical reply, it could in turn be said: Indeed, to explain in the preceding manner may be the way one gives an adequate or a complete explanation of the occurrence of a *given event*, such as the nomination of Humphrey, the assassination of Kennedy, the dislike of Johnson, the brutality in Chicago during the convention, the failure of Phillip Phillippos in Philosophy 62, and the like. However, it is no explanation at all of why there is anything at all. It still remains just a brute but mysterious fact that anything at all exists. We still have not been given an explanation of existence—of why there is anything of any sort—much less an adequate or complete explanation of existence. Indeed, 'Why is there anything at all?' is an odd question, but in certain philosophical and perhaps even religious moods it is natural to ask: Why is it that any of the things that make up the universe actually exist? They do, of course, but *why* is this so? There might have been nothing at all!

If we say, as some have, 'Well, why shouldn't there be something?' or say, as Russell has, "Well it just so happens that there is something," we have only avoided the question—deliberately or otherwise—but have not tried to answer it or establish that it is a pseudoquestion. We might try to block this admittedly peculiar question by claiming it is unanswerable in principle and so no genuine question at all, because the statement 'There is and will be nothing' is either self-contradictory or in some other way meaningless. But by that very logic we are required to say that 'There is and will be something' is either analytic or meaningless. It most certainly does not appear to be either. Defenders of the argument from contingency will argue that only if we assume that there is a necessary being that has within itself the reason for its own existence—a being that did not just happen to exist—can we adequately explain why there is something rather than nothing.

VII

The argument need not and should not stop here. Even *if* we grant that how it came to be that there are any contingent beings at all is inadequately explained if we do not assume that there is a necessary being, it does not at all follow that there actually is such a necessary being. It would only follow that there is a necessary being if it were true that there is a complete explanation that would give us an adequate explanation of why anything exists at all. Why should we assume or even believe that we actually have such an explanation?

It is certainly very natural to reject the principle of sufficient reason and to say that it has not been established that there must be or even that there is (if only we could discover it) an explanation for everything. Some events or states of affairs may never be explained. There may even be some things that are inexplicable.[11]

Ninian Smart in his *Philosophers and Religious Truth* tries in a limited sort of way to defend the principle of sufficient reason.[12] He points out that it always appears quite possible to ask why a given state of affairs exists rather than some other state of affairs. "Indeed," he asks, "is it not our normal hope that any given state of affairs can be explained?" It is certainly our normal hope and expectation, and there may even be no conceptual bars against asking why anything exists at all. It is without doubt an odd question, and perhaps it is quite pointless to ask it. It does not follow, however, that the sentence forming the putative question is incoherent or logically absurd. But the fact, if indeed it is a fact, that such a question is logically in order establishes nothing about whether we have good grounds for expecting that we will find such an explanation, expecting that there actually is—let alone *must* be—an explanation for everything, including an explanation of why there is anything at all.

It is also important to remind ourselves again that we must not forget what an extraordinary question is being posed. We are asking: Why is there anything at all, or why is there a universe at all when, as far as logical possibilities go, there might have been nothing? Assuming that we can make *some* sense of that question (and I think we can), we need to stress again how very universal it is. From the fact that it is plausible to expect an answer to such diverse types of question as 'Why is there no hot water today?', 'Why did the 1848 Revolution fail?', and 'Why are there photons?', it does not at all follow that we should expect an answer—recognizing how very different it would have to be—to the (putative) question 'Why is there anything at all?'. Even if we look on the cosmos, as Ninian Smart does, as a vast pattern of events, no one—neither Smart, Copleston, nor anyone else as far as I know—has given us any good reasons at all for thinking we have grounds for believing there is even a tolerably adequate explanation of why there is a cosmos.

In addition, note that with this stress on 'ultimate explanation' and the principle of sufficient reason, there has occurred a very important sea change in the cosmological argument. It turns out that the amended argument is not what it appears to be. It is *not:* If there are contingent beings, then there is a necessary being. There are contingent beings. Therefore,

there is a necessary being. Rather, it is: If there are contingent beings and
if we have a *complete explanation* of why there is anything at all, then
there is a necessary being. There are contingent beings. *And there is such
a complete explanation of why there is anything at all.* Therefore, there
is such a necessary being.[13]

Again I ask, why should we assume that there actually is such an
explanation? What evidence do we have for the existence of such an
explanation?[14] Why should we believe that if only we look long enough
and reason carefully enough and (perhaps) take the 'right' attitude toward
our world, we must discover such an explanation? Do we have any good
grounds at all for such an expectation? To *assume* there is or there must
be such an explanation begs the very point at issue: To assume that there
actually is such a complete explanation is to assume that there is a necessary being, since only a necessary being would be said to explain adequately why there is something at all rather than nothing. But it is exactly
the existence of this necessary being that we are trying to establish. We
cannot pull ourselves up by our own bootstraps.

We tend to overlook the completely question-begging nature of such
a cosmological argument because of a crucial ambiguity in the use of
'explanation' in such an argument. When 'explanation' is used in the
normal ways—when we try to find the cause of, the rationale for, or the
purpose or function of something—it is very natural (although perhaps
mistaken) to assume that all phenomena have explanations of at least one
of the preceding types. A stick in the water appears to be bent, Humphrey
was nominated although he was clearly not the candidate best qualified
for the job, the Russians are ahead of us in missile building, Fred up
and left his wife after all these years. We assume that there are causes
or reasons for these events or actions. Moreover, whether we have found
explanations for them or not, we assume that such occurrences or actions
can in one way or another be explained. This is not to say that 'why
there is something rather than nothing' must have an explanation, or that
all events must be explainable in the very peculiar sense that someone
such as Copleston requires, that is, the sense that would require us to
invoke a necessary being to make 'reality around us intelligible'. To say
there must be such an explanation begs the very question at issue. We
only have the right to conclude that such a necessary being, or God, exists
if we have good grounds for believing that there actually are such ultimate
explanations. Furthermore, we can only assert that there are such explanations by *assuming* that there is a necessary being or God, although it is the
existence of just this being that the argument from the contingency of
the world was designed to establish.

For these reasons it seems to me that the cosmological argument collapses in its two major forms: the causal argument and the argument
from the contingency of the world. Again we are left without a demon-

stration of God's existence. Neither singly nor together do these cosmological arguments give us good grounds for believing that the world is derivative from or dependent on a transcendent reality or a wholly different mode of being who upholds and gives significance to man and the world by His creative might.

NOTES

1. Etienne Gilson, *The Christian Philosophy of St. Thomas Aquinas*, p. 51.
2. Ibid., p. 61.
3. Ibid., pp. 45–65.
4. Ronald Hepburn, "From World to God," *Mind*, vol. LXXII, no. 285 (January 1963).
5. Thomas Aquinas, *The Summa Theologica*, Question 2, Article 3. The translation used is Anton C. Pegis' updating of the English Dominican translation. See Anton C. Pegis (ed.), *Basic Writings of Saint Thomas Aquinas*, vol. I, (New York: Random House, 1944), p. 22.
6. F. C. Copleston, *Aquinas* (Baltimore: Penguin Books, 1955), chapter III, and E. L. Mascall, *He Who Is* (London: Longmans, 1943), chapters V and VI.
7. Thomas Aquinas, op. cit., pp. 22–23.
8. This interpretation of necessary existence has been forcefully argued by John Hick in his "Necessary Being," *Scottish Journal of Theology*, vol. 14, no. 4 (December, 1961). That Aquinas construed necessary existence in this manner has been convincingly argued by Patterson Brown, "St. Thomas' Doctrine of Necessary Being," *The Philosophical Review*, (January, 1964).
9. Bertrand Russell and F. C. Copleston, "The Existence of God—a Debate," in Paul Edwards and Arthur Pap (eds.), *A Modern Introduction to Philosophy*, (second edition).
10. Paul Edwards, "The Cosmological Arguments," in Donald R. Burrill (ed.), *The Cosmological Arguments*. See also in the same volume Terence M. Penelhum, "Divine Necessity."
11. This is not to assert, as those who defend the category 'miracle' do, that there are events or states of affairs that cannot be explained scientifically. Rather, it is only to assert that we do not know that it is the case that everything will be explained or that everything can be explained.
12. Ninian Smart, *Philosophers and Religious Truth*, p. 102.
13. Paul Edwards, op. cit., pp. 119–120.
14. If we say 'Because we know there is a necessary being of the requisite sort' we have begged the question at issue.

17

THE ARGUMENT
FROM DESIGN

I

While this argument is often called a proof or demonstration of the existence of God, it actually does not in its typical formulations take the form of a demonstration. Rather, the argument from design is an argument from the observed order in the universe—or, as some would say, the observed order of the universe—to the *hypothesis* of a supreme orderer or designer of the universe.

The argument from Design is not a demonstration of the existence of a cosmic orderer. Rather, it is an inductive, empirical, would-be scientific argument. That is to say, it is not an argument such that if its premises are true its conclusion cannot be false. The natural theologian will say, if he is wise, 'This is an argument in which we invoke the hypothesis of a Supreme Being in order to account as adequately as possible for certain observations we have made of the world.' This hypothesis and this hypothesis alone, he is claiming, adequately accounts for the observed order in the world.[1] However, 'proof' is often used in several rather different senses and I will continue referring to it as 'a proof'.

Simply stated, the argument from Design goes like this: Look about you. Note the order and perfection of certain natural beings. Birds regularly find their way from the Antarctic to the Arctic. Fish on the bottom of the sea have lights. Dogs in the Arctic have long hair; dogs in the tropics have short hair. Note the careful coordination of eye, ear, and opposable thumb in the human animal. Recall the remarkable complexity of the eye of insects. Note the behavior of ants, bees, homing pigeons, and the like! Note the predictability of eclipses and the regularity of the movements of the starry sky. Consider, to put it more generally, the vastness of our universe and its amazing regularity. If we consider all these things, if we really dwell on them, we *cannot* reasonably conclude that it all *just happened to be,* and it is also clear enough that this amazing matching of part to part exceeds any possible human contrivance. To explain adequately this order or design—these remarkable regularities of copresence and succession—we must assume that the universe was created by an infinite, wise, and powerful designer. That designer we call God.

The English philosopher William Paley in his *Natural Theology* (1802) gave a formulation of the argument from Design that was immensely popular and influential. It had a wide acceptance in intellectual circles during the nineteenth century. Moreover, Paley's work served as the metaphysical underpinning for many of the scientists who stubbornly and bitterly resisted Darwin in the first years after the publication of the *Origin of Species* (1859). Ironically enough, David Hume's *Dialogues Concerning Natural Religion,* published in 1779—twenty-three years *before* the publication of Paley's *Natural Theology*—radically and powerfully criticized arguments of the type made by Paley. And it is sad to note that there is little in Paley's argument to exhibit that he was aware of how damaging Hume's criticisms were to his claims. Yet during the nineteenth century, as far as educated popular consciousness went, Paley's arguments carried the day.

Hume's arguments, you should note, are perfectly general ones and are not at all dependent on any particular empirical findings or on biological theories such as Darwin's theory of natural selection. In examining the argument from Design, I wish for the most part to utilize what are essentially Humean points. First, however, I would like to say something about the argument from Design and Darwinian conceptions since it is often thought that the theory of natural selection plainly gives the argument from Design its *quietus.*

II

Darwin's theories—and most particularly the doctrine of natural selection—do in a sense refute Paley and those like him, for they give a naturalistic hypothesis to account for the facts of orderliness and orderly change and development in the world. Thus, if this Darwinian hypothesis is at all plausible, it is not true that only the design argument accounts for the order in the world. And it is a good methodological principle to use wherever possible the simplest set of principles, categories and/or hypotheses that will satisfactorily account for the facts, although we must not forget that what counts as 'satisfactorily accounting for the facts' is often a very contested or at least a very contestable matter. Since this is so, the correct application in a given case of such a principle of scientific simplicity is not a simple matter. However, it has been argued with some considerable persuasiveness that the Darwinian hypothesis is clearly the simpler hypothesis and that it accounts for the facts at least as adequately. Therefore, between the two competing hypotheses the Darwinian hypothesis is to be preferred.

Like many others, I am strongly inclined to think this is so. But I attach little strategic importance to this argument one way or another, for it seems to me that there are general logical or conceptual difficulties in the Design argument that topple it regardless of whether any theory of natural selection or any modern improvement of it does or does not adequately account for the degree of orderliness we discover in the world.

However, I will first briefly consider the import of Darwinian conceptions on the argument from Design.

The *Origin of Species* was written in 1859 and it caused, as is well known, a great stir in Victorian England. It was thought to conflict with the Christian conception of Creation, the doctrines of the Fall and Redemption, the doctrines of the human soul and immortality. If what Darwin said was so, it was widely believed, man is in reality only a developed ape and not God's pride and joy, the crown of all His creation. However, as has been frequently pointed out, these religious doctrines, taken less woodenly and less literally, were felt by non-Neanderthal religious people to be quite compatible with a general evolutionary account of things.

It was, however, the doctrine of natural selection that provided the real sticking point. Richard Owen, Darwin's chief scientific opponent during that period, vigorously opposed him on this issue while accepting a general evolutionary picture of things. Thinking along much the same lines as did Paley, the scientists of Darwin's time were convinced that the organic structures of nature could not be adequately explained without reference to a Designer who ordered the world in that way.

Natural selection, you will recall, is that process whereby certain organisms with characteristics that help them adapt to their environment tend to survive and transmit their characteristics, while other members of the same species that have fewer adaptive characteristics tend to die out. This leads to the survival of what, biologically speaking, are the fittest members of the species. By this is meant that those members of the species that happen to have characteristics most adaptive to their environment tend over a long period of time to survive, and in the course of generations there is a development in the species toward a greater degree of adaptability. This general point can be expanded in this way: For any given population, the number of individuals born is in excess of the number that can be supported as full-grown individuals in the ordinary environment of the population in question. Hence, there must occur a struggle for existence. Where among individuals of a certain species their biological structure varies in a more adaptive direction, individuals of that type, Darwin argued, had a better chance to survive. In nature all sorts of variations are produced at random, including many that are more abortive than beneficial. It is entirely due to the contingencies of the situation—temperature, rainfall, and so on—which forms tend to be more adaptive and thus to survive. As Alvar Ellegard puts it:

> . . . the wonderful fitting of means to ends, formerly explained as due to Divine Guidance, either directly through a miraculous creation, or indirectly through secondary causes, now appeared as the automatic result of a process of trial and error. It was not necessary for any Intelligence to plan suitable changes in the organisms, since blind, unintelligent chance would suffice to produce the random variations that Darwin required. The adaptation was a hit and miss affair, and it worked because the hits would be preserved as a matter of course in the struggle for existence.[2]

Darwin, unlike his fellow scientists, had no need to appeal to Purpose and Design to explain the wondrous complexity and adaptability in biological organisms. This struck at the very heart of the nineteenth-century conception of man and life. With people such as Paley—and this view was extremely common—*biology* had always furnished the best evidence of God's benevolence. With Darwin, as Ellegard nicely put it, "it was as if the witness for the defense had turned witness for the prosecution." If indeed, as it is now generally believed, the basic process underlying variations in the species is a random one, then it follows that it is a mistake to argue as Paley did that from noticing the marvelous adaptations in the organic realm one was justified in concluding that the world was designed. However, this does not mean that it is false that it is designed. It only means that Paley's arguments do not show that it was designed.

III

It seems to me that a naturalistic hypothesis such as Darwin's is plainly the more reasonable one. However, I do not want to rely on that argument, for there will always be those who will believe that a modern-day Paley could make a revised edition of his *Natural Theology* to accommodate natural selection and maintain that the very complexity and subtlety of the natural laws governing the evolutionary process itself manifest God's Design, that is, show that there is a first Designer who created the world for providential ends. I think such talk about 'the evolutionary process' evades the specific issue about natural selection, but I do not wish to argue this point. Rather, I wish to claim that there are purely abstract arguments, at least as old as Hume, that utterly demolish the argument from Design.[3]

1. Supposing we must postulate a designer to account adequately for the orderliness of the universe, this postulation, even if justified by the evidence, does not establish the existence of a Creator or the existence of

the God of Judaism and Christianity or even a world-ground upon which all things depend. At best it would only establish the existence of a finite, although still powerful, orderer or designer, or a group of orderers or designers. Thus, we need to be quite clear that even if the postulation of a designer is justified, we have not established that (1) there is an infinite orderer or designer, (2) there is only one orderer or designer, and (3) our designer or designers still exist, any more than the existence of a watch implies or in any way establishes the present existence of a watchmaker.

2. As Hume points out, the evil—the suffering—in the world puts into question the truth of the claim that this is a world designed and governed by an all-powerful, all-wise, and all-good being. Certainly the array of disorders in the world is such that we would not and could not reasonably conclude simply from observing our world that it was created or designed by such a power.

3. We indeed do see traces of order and disorder in the universe. But since, as Peirce put it, universes are not as plentiful as blackberries, we have no way of telling whether the *universe itself* or even the *part we know of it* is or is not disordered, for we have nothing to compare the universe with. Thus, we cannot justifiably make such a judgment.

To this the contemporary theologian William Tennant replies in his *Philosophical Theology* (volume II, chapter IV) that while indeed there is no logical relation here and while it is true that we cannot make a judgment of mathematical probability that the world is so ordered or has design, all the same there is here an "alogical probability which is the guide of life." This, Tennant thinks, is the basis of "all scientific induction." But we must be wary here, for the relationship between the universe and its alleged ground is said by Tennant to be unique. And this is surely very different than the ordinary case. When Robinson Crusoe judged from a footprint in the sand that a man was on the island, he had some evidence to go on. There was an antecedent probability that he had judged correctly, based on statistically relevant samplings, between the occurrence of footprints in the sand and the treading of human beings. We have no such antecedent probability about the order of the universe.

This is true, Tennant agrees, but he maintains that in both situations there is also reliance on an "alogical probability." How did Crusoe, Tennant asks, originally get his knowledge "as to the existence of fellow men who not only make footprints but also supply service and friendship?" Tennant tells us that this knowledge "seems to have been mediated in much the same way as is the teleologist's belief in God." This remark seems to me totally without rational merit, even assuming we know what is meant by an 'alogical probability'. There is something that Crusoe can directly observe or verify, in virtue of which he could attain his knowledge about men and his principles. However, we cannot directly observe God, or Divine Causation. Moreover, if we could so observe or encounter God or the Divine Presence, we would not need the argument from Design. The *origin* of our belief in our fellow men "may very well be ultimately an affair of human psychology and life . . . ," but such a belief and the statements asserting that belief are perfectly open to empirical check. There is direct verification here. We can fix these beliefs by means of the scientific method. But this is *not* the case with God and if it were we would not even need the argument from Design, for then we could directly verify God's existence.

IV

Let us go on to the new set of arguments. If, in trying to defend the argument from Design, it is maintained that the universe exhibits a purpose, what is this purpose? How could we detect it? What conceivable observations would establish that the universe either had or did not have a purpose? For a moment we will stop talking about the problematic notions 'the universe has a purpose' or 'the order of the universe' and take the *prima facie* less troubling notion 'order in the universe'. Pursuant to that, consider these two statements:

A.   If one notes order in the universe then there is a God.

B.   If one starves rats for sixteen days then they will die.

The defender of the argument from Design is treating A, as far as its logical status goes, as being on a par with B. Both are allegedly empirical hypotheses, although A is a more general and a grander empirical hypothesis. But they both presumably are open to confirmation and disconfirmation.

Now actually consider them. With B we can carry out certain operations and they will have empirical consequences which will test the truth of B. But A is quite different. It looks testable but it is not. B is a genuine empirical hypothesis, and to be so it must to some degree be disconfirmable by negative instances and we must be able on the basis of it to make predictions or retrodictions. B has such empirical, directly observable consequences—if the stated operation is carried out, the rats will cease to breathe and move, and after a time will start to smell. All this is directly observable. Since such directly testable consequences are derivable from B, we are prepared to say that it is an empirical hypothesis. But what directly testable statements can we derive from A? What would we have to see, hear, feel, or touch, in order to apprehend or be aware of God? Moreover, if we could say what we would have to do to make such observations we would not need the argument from Design, for we would know what we would have to have, know what it would be like to be directly aware of His presence—and we would not have to infer His existence from the order in the universe or from the alleged order of the universe.

Such an argument will in turn be countered by the claim that it is 'naively empirical' and out of touch with actual scientific practice. Indeed, empirical hypotheses must be empirically testable—they must have observable consequences—but they need not have *directly* observable consequences and they need not be confirmable or disconfirmable in isolation from other empirical hypotheses. That is to say, it is not each individual hypothesis that must be directly verifiable (confirmable or infirmable); the verification can be much more indirect. There can be hypotheses with unobservables which, as part of a cluster of systematically related hypotheses, are not themselves verifiable, although within that domain there must be some hypotheses that have directly testable empirical consequences.

Much of this is surely correct, although there is also some conceptual confusion here. First, we logically could not speak of 'indirect verification' or 'indirect test' here if we ruled out the *logical possibility* of direct verification. If it made no sense to speak of 'direct verification' in this domain, it would make no sense to speak of 'indirect verification' either because, by failing to contrast with anything, 'indirect' in such a context could not (logically could not) qualify 'verification'. Second, and more directly to the present point, A is neither verifiable in isolation as is B nor is A a part of a systematically related cluster of hypotheses such that we know what it would be like to even very indirectly verify or confirm A and disconfirm or infirm not-A. Since this is so, A is plainly not what it purports to be, that is, a genuine empirical hypothesis.

Consider now C, another way of stating the claim of the Design argument.

C. If there is a supreme Designer of the universe then the universe will be ordered.

Try to take C on analogy with B as an empirical hypothesis. Perhaps, in seeking the argument from Design's necessary empirical anchorage, it is more plausible as a hypothesis than is A. But our old question returns: how is C empirically testable? What would it be like to find an ordered universe? Compare finding an ordered universe with finding Uranium 255 or fragments of Sputnik 1. Order is hard to find, not because there is not much of it, but because we do not know what it is. It is not that we are justified in saying that the universe is disordered or chaotic. Rather, we do not know how to use 'order' or 'disorder' *in such a context*. The concept of order has no application here. Thus, we do not know what it means to say that the universe is either ordered or disordered. For this reason we are not in a position to carry out any empirical tests to confirm or disconfirm C. In fine, C is not stated in a sufficiently determinate way to be either confirmable or disconfirmable and thus C is devoid of empirical content. Since this is so, C cannot be an empirical hypothesis.

There is another related difficulty in the argument from Design. It is not unreasonable to argue that whether or not you see order depends on how you look at whatever is before you. If there are lots of blobs of color on a piece of paper and some of them are crimson, orange, and scarlet, then the crimson, orange, and scarlet blobs will have some determinate relations to the other colors. Are we to say then that the colors exhibit order or not? That depends on how you look at it. You can, if you try hard, probably find 'order' in anything, if you consider it in a certain way. And you can probably find 'disorder' in anything if you consider it in other ways.

Note also the vagueness of the claim that the universe exhibits order. What is *meant* by saying 'The universe is ordered' or 'There is a purpose to the universe'? What would the universe be like if it were *not* ordered or if it did *not* have a purpose? As was pointed out, we cannot empirically test 'If there is a supreme designer of the universe then the universe will be ordered' because we do not know what the criteria are that would distinguish an ordered universe from a disordered one.

In an attempt to make the claim made by the theologian more precise, we might claim:

D. If there is a supreme designer of the universe then the universe will be arranged in such a way that it obeys the laws that scientists have so far discovered and will in the future discover.

But what sense, if any, is there in speaking of 'obey' here? Laws of nature, as we have seen when we discussed Schlick's views on freedom and responsibility, are not orders to be obeyed or disobeyed. When we discover phenomena that will not fit in with a law or a hypothesis, we suggest another hypothesis, modify our original hypothesis, or simply (although rarely) abandon our original hypothesis. Moreover, a genuine scientific hypothesis deals with a specific subject matter, not with everything.

To avoid the difficulties in D, a theologian might try still another reformulation:

E. If there is a supreme designer of the universe then the universe will be such that scientists will continue to discover laws that will enable them to predict and retrodict phenomena with ever increasing reliability.

In its specification of the problematic term 'ordered universe', this statement implies a definition of 'ordered universe', but there is no particular reason to accept this definition. It surely is not a lexical definition reporting ordinary usage. However, if one does adopt it to give some sense to 'an ordered universe' as distinct from 'a disordered universe', it should be immediately apparent that such order does not evidence a supreme designer, or any designer or orderer at all. There are many natural processes and some cultural products—for example, sound shifts within natural languages—that are predictable or retrodictable but do not at all require, in order to make their predictability and retrodictability intelligible, the postulation of a supreme designer. Even if (as seems likely) scientists continue with ever-increasing scope to predict and retrodict more reliably and systematically, this does not establish or even make probable the claim that all the phenomena they predict have a designer. Note there is nothing conceptually awry about denying the implication in E, that is, denying that the 'if-then relation' holds. The burden of proof is surely on the defender of the argument from Design to show why it does hold. But this has not been done.

V

It should also be noted that the argument from Design rests on faulty analogical reasoning, that is, the analogy between an artifact and its designer and the universe and God. If we find something that looks like a watch or like any artifact, we should indeed say that it probably had a maker or designer, for it is a member of a class of objects (watches or artifacts) and at least some of us have at other times *observed* that watchmakers make watches or people design objects similar to what we have observed. Since the object we have run across is very like the thing we have seen designed, we can judge with a reasonable probability that it too was designed. But with God and the universe the analogy is not close enough to be convincing, for what is said to be the effect (the ordered universe) is *entirely unique and singular*. Since it is not comprehended under any species or class, we can have no basis at all for making the judgment that it has or has not a designer. Since God and the universe are both unique and singular, we cannot have any such empirical basis for saying that God designed the universe or caused it to come into existence.

Against this argument, which is essentially an argument given by Hume, it can be argued that a defender of the argument from Design need not argue from the universe-as-a-whole but only from noting certain parts of it. We see specific and striking evidences of design or at least order in the universe, and to account adequately for such design or order we are compelled to assert that there must have been a designer of it all. It could not just have happened that way. To account for these marvelous things we must postulate a maker or a designer.

At this point it is crucial to ask the following question: a maker or designer of *what*? We have two alternatives. We may say the ordered parts of the universe, or the universe-as-a-whole. If we say 'the ordered parts of the universe', where are we? The ordered parts can properly be said to have many designers, and some of them need not require a designer at all for a proper explanation of their occurrence. We have many purely naturalistic explanations available for the ordered part of the universe. Some of them most surely must be defective in certain specific ways, but they are simpler than the "supernaturalistic explanations" and have at least as much claim on our belief. Let us not multiply conceptions beyond need! If, alternatively, we say 'the-universe-as-a-whole', we are back with our original difficulties. Since universes are not as numerous as blackberries, we have no basis for claiming that the universe is ordered or not ordered. We have no 'other universes' to compare this universe with in virtue of which we could make the comparison. If we inspect with even tolerable care 'the universe', it is evident enough that the idea of there being more than one universe is unintelligible. In fact, 'The universe is ordered' and 'The universe is not ordered' are both lacking in factual or cognitive import, for they clearly have no truth conditions: We do not know what could count for or against their truth. Since in making such utterances we have no idea of what would count toward establishing their truth or falsity, we should say that they are pseudofactual statements. That is, they are putative statements of fact that do not have the logic of statements of fact.

VI

Let us assume for the sake of continuing the argument that there is some difficulty in what was said above. There are still further gaps in the argument from Design, some of which Hume brought to the fore.

God is very unlike a watchmaker or any kind of designer in the following important respect: God, as the maker of the world, the creator and sustainer of the universe, was supposed to have created or made the universe from nothing (whatever that may mean), while the watchmaker, architect, or any other designer creates his design from material that already exists. He does not make something from nothing. (This is even true of the tune the musicmaker makes.) Thus, we have another crushing disanalogy. The watchmaker analogy gives us no idea at all of what it would be like or what it could mean to make a world from nothing.

There are further crucial disanalogies between how a watchmaker or designer works and how God purportedly works. God, it is said, lays down or creates the laws of nature. The designer exploits already existing laws of nature. From the fact that there are natural laws and that we can make predictions and retrodictions, it does not follow that there must be some external design and some designer. There is no cosmic significance to be attached to the fact that the events occur in the order they do rather than in some other order. For anything to happen at all, events must occur in *some* order.[4] If we have some independent grounds for believing in God, we might ask why it was that He ordered the universe in the way He did, but independently of this there is no reason to believe that such order as we find exhibits the work of an orderer or designer.

NOTES

1. Sometimes the phrase 'observed order *of* the world' is used rather than 'observed order *in* the world.' Such a verbal difference may seem inconsequential, but in reality—as we shall see—it is of considerable moment.
2. Alvar Ellegard, "The Darwinian Theory and the Argument from Design," *Lychnos* (1956), p. 182.
3. I do not go into this, but even talk of 'the evolutionary process'—as if there were some identifiable unitary process called 'the evolutionary process'— radically departs from anything that is genuinely scientific. See Stephen Toulmin, "Contemporary Scientific Mythology," in Toulmin et al., *Metaphysical Beliefs* (London: 1957).
4. Someone might counter that no matter what happens—what conceivably could happen—events must occur in some order. Hence if I accept that, I cannot consistently say that we cannot know whether the universe is orderly or disorderly. If I am right in my argument that events must occur in some order, I have an *a priori* proof that the universe is and must be in order. The correct reply is that I do not accept that; rather, I have a proof that the concepts of order do not apply to the universe as a whole, for no matter what the universe is like on such an account, I would still have to say, if I used these terms at all, that it is orderly. But then 'orderly' would no longer qualify universe.

18

THE APPEAL
TO RELIGIOUS
EXPERIENCE

I

Many people who are not at all convinced by the traditional proofs of the existence of God still feel that there is a more direct, immediate, and certain knowledge of the existence of God than anything that could be given by such a speculative proof, even if a sound one could be found. They believe that a religiously sincere person can come to know that there is a God by direct experience of His presence. Such people, it is believed, know Him immediately and directly as a person, as a Thou. This claim is usually linked with a stress on the importance of revelation, either as a direct personal revelation or as the records of such personal encounters left in the Scriptures.

John Baillie, to take an illustrous contemporary example, claims that "our knowledge of God . . . rests on revelation of his personal Presence as Father, Son and Holy Spirit." And this in turn rests on the fact that someone has had a personal encounter with the Divine. If one has such an encounter or such a confrontation, all argument becomes superfluous and pointless; if one has not, no description can convey the reality of such an encounter and no argument can establish that there are such encounters. Without the requisite experience one is utterly at sea, but after such an encounter one becomes more certain of God's reality than of anything else. Yet certainly this is not via an inference from our experience of finitude or contingency to a necessary being or unconditioned being. It is rather a matter of *direct experience*.

The people who have such a compelling experience of God apart, one can reasonably contend that religion, and some form of religious experience, is a universal phenomenon, culturally speaking. Here is what the distinguished anthropologist and linguist Edward Sapir in his *Culture, Language and Personality* has said.

. . . religion in some sense is everywhere present. It seems to be as universal as speech itself and the use of material tools. It is difficult to apply a single one of the criteria which are ordinarily used to define a religion to the religious behavior of primitive peoples, yet neither the absence of specific religious officers nor the lack of an authoritative religious text nor any other conventional lack can seriously mislead the student into denying them true religion. Ethnologists are unanimous in ascribing religious behavior to the very simplest of known societies.[1]

People who argue that we have a direct experience of God or the Divine also frequently argue that this experience is unique, since the Divine Reality is by definition unique. It will not be possible, they maintain, to describe the compelling touch of God otherwise than as the compelling touch of God. Moreover, this sense of the Presence of God is something that is as directly given to man as is the capacity to see light or hear sound. This directly felt *experience* is, for the one who has it, compelling and self-authenticating, and this direct awareness of God makes his world and his existence *intelligible* as nothing else can. The self is unified, finds its identity, or achieves its homeostasis by means of this experience. Such an experience enables the man who has it to overcome feelings of estrangement or alienation. No purely secular experience can match in this manner his religious experience. The man who has this religious experience has a firm conviction that he is utterly impotent without God, but that with God—with the mysterious reality he encounters—his life gains a meaning.

Philosophers, it is often argued, typically overrationalize religion. They try to treat it as either metaphysics or ethics. But the experience of the infinite mysterious reality that is God is not grasped through conceptual thought or some intellectual intuition. Our awareness of God is given in the immediacy of feeling. It is principally a feeling of utter dependence on an infinite and mysterious wholly other reality, a reality which does not admit of anything other than an inadequate conceptualization. It is in our heart, in our feelings, that we know God, and not in our minds. God—the infinite totality, the wholly other reality—transcends the reach of our concepts; God is an object of feeling and faith rather than of intellection. And without such feelings of dependence there can be no sense of the presence of God and no understanding of religion at all.

This view, classically articulated by Two German theologians, Friedrich Schleiermacher *On Religion: Speeches to Its Cultured Despisers* (1799) and Rudolf Otto *The Idea of the Holy* (1917), tries to give a foundation for faith in religious experience, which would subvert the need for an appeal to proofs for the existence of God. If they are right we do not need these rationalistic demonstrations, for in his own sense of creatureliness and dependency man has a direct awareness of the Divine Presence.[2]

II

I shall now try to set out the logic of this claim. That such putative knowledge of God is grounded in feeling does not mean that in arguing that this is so—as Schleiermacher, Otto, Baillie, and Kemp Smith do—that their arguments themselves do not have a certain logical structure and hence are open to appraisal. Consider (1) 'I have a direct experience (encounter or apprehension) of God, therefore I have a sufficient reason to believe that God exists'. This statement might be taken to entail the claim that it is contradictory to assert (2) 'I have had a direct experience of God, but God does not exist'. Thus, to assert that I have a direct experience of God commits me to the assertion that God exists.

Indeed, if one does have a direct experience of *God*, then God does exist. But this way of putting it begs the substantive issue at hand, for the whole question is: Does the *feeling* that one is in the presence of God or the *sense* of the presence of God actually establish that one is in the presence of God? How does one move—or does one legitimately move—from the *psychological* fact to the *ontological* reality? After all, the following remarks are *not* self-contradictory. (3) 'I feel that I am in the presence of God but there is no God.' (4) 'My experience is that of the compelling reality of God, but in reality God does not exist.' We must beware of just automatically attaching a cosmic significance to our pious feelings. Yet aren't these experiences reliable evidence that God exists? If a large number of people have the same experience under varied conditions, do we not have very good grounds for claiming that what they say they experience really exists? Wouldn't we indeed have to have very powerful contrary reasons for denying that their claim is a valid one? Given the fact that religious experience is nearly universal, the burden of proof is surely on the skeptic to show that the believer's claim is defective.

III

Historically there have been many such skeptical arguments. One weak argument that has in fact been very influential is the claim that mystics, religious visionaries, and prophets have been very neurotic and thus their reports of their experience cannot be relied upon. In appraising this contention we should first note that the fact that these are unusual experiences cannot itself be used as a sufficient warrant for the claim that the people who have them are therefore neurotic. That is to lift oneself up by one's own bootstraps and to go in a very small and vicious circle. Here we need some *independent* criteria for who is neurotic and who is not. Moreover, as a matter of fact, many religious mystics lived perfectly normal lives. The only unusual thing about them was their very intense religious experiences.

For the sake of the argument, let us suppose what is contrary to fact: such mystics and visionaries are invariably neurotic. It still does not follow that since they are neurotic what they think they experience—that is, the supernatural—does not exist. The experiences are such that they may very well make a person a little cracked, or perhaps it takes a somewhat cracked person to have such experiences, for after all they are supposedly very extraordinary.[3] *But the validity of a belief is independent of its origin.* Why should these psychological facts show that the person who has the experience does not actually encounter a Divine Presence? Why does it show, or does it show, that there is not anything supernatural answering to his experience? The answer to these rhetorical questions is that it does not.

Moreover, to argue in the way our critic of the appeal to religious experience has been arguing is to take as paradigmatic the highly unusual religious experiences of mystics and people who have visions. However, they are hardly typical cases of what it is we are talking about when we talk of religious experience. In claiming that religious experience gives man a knowledge of God, one need not be referring to these very unusual religious experiences. Rather, one could argue that most human beings who have feelings of alienation and dependence and who feel as if they were in the presence of a mysterious infinite Thou who cares for them and protects them, have no idea of what it would be like to have the 'nonsensuous apprehension of the unity of everything' claimed by the mystic. That is to say, they have no idea of what it would be like to have the sort of experience that is said to be the mystics' fundamental religious experience or consciousness. But the feeling of creatureliness and dependence so well described by Schleiermacher and Otto appears to be universal, and if it actually is—if it really cuts across religions and cultures—we plainly cannot dismiss it as the experience of a few crazy people.

It is also sometimes claimed that these religious experiences are simply disguised sexual predicaments—warped sexual desire gives these experiences the structure they have. But sexual desires can hardly be a sufficient condition for the occurrence of the experience, for many people with very strong and even with very warped sexual urges do not have religious experiences. Even if they did, this would not establish that they were only about sex and not about God. Perhaps, since sex is a relatively permanent drive in human beings, God took this sure route to show His presence to man: to reinforce the idea of God, to stamp it in, so that everyone would have it.

In sum, the preceding arguments against the claim that religious experience puts us in contact with God are not sound arguments, although they have convinced many uncritical people. *If* this is the best the skeptic can do, the believer need not be unduly worried.

IV

The dialectic of the argument should not stop here, however, for the skeptic can reply that the origin of these religious beliefs, the manner in which they are taught, the false beliefs about man and nature which they embody, all militate against their being acceptable beliefs. They arise out of desire and fear; teachers, parents—a variety of authority figures—drill children in religious doctrines at an early and impressionable age. These teachers have authority over the children when they are very much at the same stage of development, intellectually and emotionally, as the savages among whom these beliefs first arose. Moreover, the authority figures who teach this belief attach great importance to the acceptance of it. You are sinful, evil, somehow wayward if you do not accept these beliefs. This indoctrination at such an impressionable and dependent age leaves its emotional effects. In short, we need to recognize that children are simply drilled to interpret their experiences in a certain way, and thus on good Pavlovian principles it becomes perfectly natural—in many instances one might say almost inevitable—for them to believe in God or Atman-Brahman or whatever tribal deities are around. But we have been given no good grounds for believing that such experiences really put them in touch with God or Atman-Brahman or the Divine, however much they may come to feel that this is so. Surely, we need to be given reasons for believing that such experiences, no matter how valuable and how invigorating they may be to the people who have them, actually put people who have such experiences in touch with some cosmic spiritual presence—a presence that our religions speak of in various highly symbolic and inadequate ways.

Religious experiences are indeed real, distinctive experiences that have changed the destiny of men and nations. This much must be granted by any unbiased man. But why should we think that they really put us in touch with a supernatural or transcendent reality or state? Their origin, persistence, and rationale can be explained naturalistically. And where we can explain something on a simpler basis, we ought always to explain it on that basis. To accept the theistic explanation or reading of these experiences involves the assumption of some very peculiar, hardly intelligible concepts. Why do this if the experiences can be accounted for without such assumption? The reason for making this theistic assumption is that this is how most, although not all, of the people in our culture who have such experiences so account for or interpret their experiences. But that they interpret them in this way can in turn be accounted for in terms of the conditions under which they arose and the way in which religious doctrine is presently taught to impressionable children. Why multiply entities beyond need?

It is indeed true, as Broad stresses, that modern science has "almost as humble an ancestry as contemporary religion."[4] It is also true that most of us take it, as we do religion, pretty much on authority; but science has developed techniques to check its claims. Anyone who will take the trouble can utilize them in criticizing and correcting what he accepts more or less on authority from science. Religion, by contrast, makes an ultimate appeal to *authority* that even the experts must accept. That one encounters God in these experiences and not Shiva or the promptings of one's own superego is *finally* decided for adherents to a religion by *authority*. There are indeed tests that one can make concerning the genuineness of the alleged religious experience, and there are practices one can engage in that will generally lead to the having of such experiences, but those who faithfully carry out the practices and do not have the 'blinding insight' are said to be somehow religiously defective. This shows that the test for the genuineness of the experiences is only a test in name, for if one does not, after faithfully carrying out the appropriate religious practices, have such an experience of the supernatural or the numinous or have a sense of the presence of God, one is then automatically judged defective in one's perception. The reality of the numinous is assumed from the very beginning. It is not really an experiential matter at all. But then the alleged empiricism of the religious apologists who make an appeal to religious experience is actually false coin.

Something else needs to be said in this context. Perhaps the relation of the believer to the nonbeliever is like the relation of the sighted man to blind men in a society of blind men, all of whom have been blind since birth. Could we not reasonably say about the claims of any of our particular religions what C. D. Broad has said, namely, that any claim on their part "to have complete or final truth . . . is too ridiculous to be worth a moment's consideration" and still be skeptical, as Broad is, that "the whole religious experience of mankind is a gigantic system of pure delusion"?[5] Using an analogy with the blind, how can we be so sure that it is not reasonable to claim that men who have religious experience are not in touch with a cosmic, spiritual presence?

This analogy is superficially appealing, but if we think it through it will be seen to have too many defects. Blind people, as well as color-blind and tone-deaf people, can come to recognize that they are blind, color-blind, or tone-deaf. There are objective, agreed-on tests about this accepted by all informed parties. In a society of blind people they could come to recognize indirectly through the use of physical tests (spectroscopic analysis and the like) that the sighted man who was dropped into their culture was making true statements when he claimed that different objects had different colors, and they could come to see by the rapidity and ease with which he made these discriminations that he had some faculty they did not possess. There is nothing parallel to this check in the appeal to religious experience. Many people have the experiences Schleiermacher and Otto characterize as religious experiences, and yet in having these experiences they are not in any way aware of God or a Divine Presence. Like Matthew Arnold, Thomas Hardy, and George Eliot they have feelings of alienation, creatureliness, and dependence, but they remain secularists utterly unaware of the presence of something infinite upon whom they can depend. In short, they have the characteristic reaction that constitutes religious experience but they have no awareness of God. However, they do not agree that they are 'the blind ones' and that people who maintain that having these experiences puts them in touch with a Divine Thou are 'the sighted ones'. And what we need to note here is that there are no agreed-on tests concerning who is or who is not religiously blind, who is and who is not suffering from illusion.

If the religious apologist appealing to religious experience retreats to the claim that religious experiences are *self-authenticating,* he must face a host of difficulties. If this is his claim, the analogy with the man with normal sight who can identify colored objects directly breaks down, for if I as a person with normal sight assert that I see a bluebird over there, I cannot legitimately maintain that my claim is self-authenticating. What others see or do not see, what science can determine, very definitely affects the veracity of my claim. The only place where I can even plausibly claim that my assertions are self-authenticating is where they are utterly psychological. That is to say, if I had asserted 'It *seems* to me that there is a bluebird over there' instead of 'I *see* a bluebird over there' or 'There is a bluebird over there', then it is rather plausible and perhaps even correct to assert that my claim about what I *seem* to see is self-authenticating. I can be mistaken about what I see but not about what I seem to see. In order to get something that is self-authenticating, we have something that is psychological and subjective and no longer an existential claim about what there is in the world or what allegedly 'sustains the world'. Surely the person who makes an appeal to religious experience wants and needs to make an existential claim and not merely a psychological and subjective claim. But by appealing to the analogy of seeing or hearing and the like, all we legitimately can claim to be self-authenticating are purely psychological nonexistential claims. The conclusion we should draw by resolutely carrying out the preceding analogy is that so-called self-authenticating religious claims based on such an appeal to religious experience are purely psychological, nonexistential claims. Of course, this is not what the religious apologist wanted or needed.[6]

If in response to this the religionist making an appeal to religious experience maintains that these disanalogies reveal how *sui generis* (unique unto itself) religious experience is and that it cannot properly be compared to any other experience, then he has indeed abandoned the analogy and can no longer compare a 'God-blind man' with a blind man, a society of blind men, a color-blind man, and the like. If, alternatively, he gives up his claim that the claims of religious experience give us an awareness of God and that these claims are self-authenticating, then he must face the difficulties previously mentioned. Many people have religious experiences, but by no means do all careful observers who have such experiences agree that in having these experiences they are having an encounter with God or some cosmic Divine Presence. To maintain that our religious experience gives us such a direct knowledge of God confuses the experience itself with a specific interpretation of that experience. But we have seen that this interpretation is not mandatory. Others interpret these experiences naturalistically in an utterly secular framework. Such a naturalistic interpretation has the advantage of being simpler, for it does not postulate in interpreting the experience some 'Transcendent Reality' that transcends the empirical realm. Perhaps such a naturalistic interpretation is somehow mistaken; perhaps it is not really simpler than the theistic interpretation. But the essential point is that they are both interpretations and that there is no agreed-on test for deciding which, if either, is the correct interpretation.[7]

Given all these difficulties, it is apparent that the appeal to religious experience does not give us adequate or even nearly adequate grounds for believing in God. Appeals to religious experience seem simpler and more direct than do traditional proofs of the existence of God, but in reality the appeal to religious experience involves, although in a more surreptitious manner, equally problematical metaphysical constructions.

NOTES

1. Edward Sapir, *Culture, Language and Personality*, (Berkeley and Los Angeles: 1950), p. 121.
2. In addition to Schleiermacher and Otto, Norman Kemp Smith in his *The Credibility of Divine Existence*, pp. 375–397, John Baillie in his *The Sense of the Presence of God*, and H. D. Lewis in his *Our Experience of God* develop such claims.
3. C. D. Broad, *Religion, Philosophy and Psychical Research*. The sections relevant to our considerations are reprinted in W. B. Alston (ed.), *Religious Belief and Philosophical Thought*, pp. 164–172.
4. Ibid.
5. Ibid.
6. In an acute and detailed manner, C. B. Martin has made a similar criticism. See chapter V of his *Religious Belief*.
7. See Herbert Feigl, "Empiricism Versus Theology," in Paul Edwards and

Arthur Pap, *A Modern Introduction to Philosophy*, first edition (Glencoe, Ill.: The Free Press, 1957), Kai Nielsen, "Christian Positivism and the Appeal to Religious Experience," *The Journal of Religion*, vol. XLII (October, 1962), and Kai Nielsen, *Contemporary Critiques of Religion* (London: Macmillan, 1971), chapters III and IV.

19

THE WILL
TO BELIEVE

I

We have seen that neither religious experience nor the three most powerful proofs for the existence of God give us good grounds for claiming to know or to justifiably believe that God exists. Since this is a very fair sample (to put it conservatively) of the arguments that could be deployed to establish God's existence, we have good grounds for believing that we should answer negatively our first questions concerning religion, and assert that we do not know that there is a God. We do not even have adequate grounds for believing that God exists. From this we should conclude that no man who wishes to accept only beliefs for which there is good evidence should believe that there is a God, for we have no rational demonstration of God's existence and we have no substantial evidence for His existence in virtue of which we could justifiably claim that we have grounds for believing that there is a God.

Many believers as well as nonbelievers would assent to that. In fact, many orthodox Protestant theologians would welcome this conclusion as making room for faith by freeing religion from rationalistic pretensions.

Thus, our second question arises: Granted that we do not know God exists and do not have any grounds for believing that God exists, are we justified in accepting the Biblical God purely on faith?

Both William James, who did pioneer work in the psychology of religion, and Soren Kierkegaard, among the profoundest religious thinkers of any time, have given us classical defenses for believing purely on faith. I shall examine their arguments, starting in this chapter with William James and passing on in the next chapter to the more radical views of Kierkegaard.

Let us step back a moment to get an overview of James's justification by faith.[1] The whole tradition of modern philosophy, both rationalist and traditional empiricist, sets philosophy in a very intellectualist tradition that contends with Descartes—in one phrasing or another—that to think philosophically is to accept as true only that which recommends itself to reason. What recommends itself to reason may mean what is checkable by sense experience or what is known to be true by the 'clear light of reason'. That is to say, the alternatives are the empiricist's claim that we can properly claim to *know* to be true only those ideas that have been verified—checked by what Peirce called "the scientific method"—or the rationalist's claim that we can and must pass beyond the fallibilities of sense experience to what is clear and distinct to the reflective mind. But behind this disagreement lay a common agreement on the part of both rationalists and empiricists that we must fix our beliefs and policies of conduct by what can be known by reason. The empiricists differ from the rationalists principally because the former limited the scope of reason to what admits of verification or to what can be inferred from such verifiable statements solely with the aid of purely formal logical principles. But both empiricists and rationalists agreed that "to be unphilosophical . . . is to be seduced by the enticements of will, which beckons men beyond the boundaries laid down by Reason into the wilderness of error."[2]

Nineteenth-century agnosticism expressed this intellectualistic stance with peculiar moral fervor. W. K. Clifford in his "Ethics of Belief" expressed it succinctly when he said, "It is wrong everywhere and for anyone to believe anything upon insufficient evidence."

James was convinced that this conviction, so central to traditional philosophy both rationalist and empiricist, was in effect irrational and destructive to the human spirit. We must come to recognize, James stressed, that philosophies are not "just intellectual constructions but that they are always expressions of certain basic hopes, fears, expectations and desires."[3] We are not simply abstract intellects or a kind of natural computing machine. We are men with hearts, prejudices, fears, hopes, ideals. There are burning practical questions concerning what to do and what attitude to take toward what is done, and we must somehow resolve them. In the last analysis we are more concerned with the practical question, what is to be done, than with the theoretical question, what is it that exists and why does it exist. Any philosophy that refuses to come to grips with such questions of *Weltanschauung* will not long gain acceptance from reflective human beings.

II

In "The Will to Believe" James develops this theme and gives it a special application to questions of religion. James makes it very clear at the outset that he is not abandoning the tough-minded position of empiricism.

Wherever there are intellectual considerations that would allow us to verify or scientifically check the truth or the probable truth of one statement as opposed to another, we ought to do so. We ought to avail ourselves of the scientific method of fixing belief where there are scientific considerations or conceivable experiments that would establish the truth or falsity of such a belief. But in those grinding dilemmas of life where our options are live, forced, and momentous and where *the issue is such that it cannot by its very nature be decided on intellectual grounds*, in such situations and in such situations alone, our "passional natures" may legitimately decide what we are to believe. If the truth of statements such as 'We are immortal', 'There is a God', 'God is good', 'The best things are the more eternal things', or 'The universe is a Thou and not an impersonal it' cannot be decided by intellectual considerations one way or another, we have the right to believe them if our passional nature demands or requires it. To behave in this way in such a situation is entirely reasonable. To take the Clifford-Huxley 'out' and to moralize "do not decide but leave the question open" is, in effect, to determine a certain course of action and not really to remain neutral. If our need to have a religious faith is strong, then, *where there is not even tolerably adequate evidence* either for or against God's existence, it is perfectly rational for us to believe that there is a God.

James sometimes even puts the matter in a still stronger way. Where there is no evidence to show that God does not exist, we can use Pascal's argument about the wager. That is to say, we may reasonably stake all we have on God's existence, for if we win in such a case we gain eternal beatitude; if we lose, we lose nothing at all. "If there were an infinity of chances, and only one for God in this wager, still you ought to stake your all on God; for though you surely risk a finite loss by this procedure, any finite loss is reasonable if there is but the possibility of an infinite gain." James's more typical and more modest claim is that where the evidence balances out, and where the matter at hand is of great practical importance, and where the option is a momentous and forced one, we can legitimately and rightfully believe what we *want* to believe. We need not assume that beliefs are always or even typically under our control, but James is claiming that where they are under our control we can legitimately believe what we want to believe when the above conditions obtain.

James could not accept Thomists' or orthodox rationalists' arguments for the existence of God. He assumed, as do most modern thinkers (including theologians), that Kant and Hume had shown such proofs to be unsound. He studied with great sensitivity the varieties of religious experience, but concluded his classic *Varieties of Religious Experience* (1902) with the claim that "the attempt to demonstrate by purely intellectual processes the truth of the deliverance of direct religious experience is absolutely hopeless." That in our religious experience we do encounter or in some way come to know a Divine Reality is one of those beliefs that cannot be decided by intellectual considerations. But here, James argues, we may legitimately let our *hearts* decide what we are to believe. If we want to believe that we encounter God or Atman-Brahman, we are perfectly justified in doing so. This does not mean, James is careful to add, that we can believe any old superstition we want to believe. Where there is good evidence against a belief, as there often is against certain sectarian doctrines, we most surely ought not to believe them.[4] Many matters that are called religious can be scientifically and empirically settled, and when they can, we must turn—if we are to be reasonable— to the method of science. Here James is in complete agreement with Peirce. But where beliefs cannot be so settled and where they are momentous options for us, they are the legitimate objects of faith.

III

For most of us religion becomes a problem some time in our lives. Whether or not to become religious or to remain religious becomes a momentous, forced, and live option. We have an option when we need to make a decision between two or more alternatives. Some options are not forced ones, for example, 'Either love me or hate me'. After all, you could be perfectly indifferent. But some options are forced, for example, 'Either accept this truth or go without it'. Here there is no alternative. There is no possibility of not choosing, for there is "no standing place outside of the alternatives."[5]

Religious options, James argues, are forced. So-called agnosticism is *in effect* an atheism or a nonbelief. Consider this case. Suppose a man is brought up in such a way that he becomes a kind of 'Graham Greene Roman Catholic'. He has all kinds of intellectual trouble with his faith, but he still has a strong need to believe—to remain a faithful Roman Catholic—and he wants very much to believe. Suppose further that there is nothing of an intellectual kind that can resolve his doubts. In this context he has a genuine option: Either leave the Church or stay in it and go to Mass and make his Easter duty, and so on. He cannot do both, and he cannot avoid both. He may stay in the Church, go to Mass, and so forth, or he may leave like James Joyce and become a nonbeliever or join some other religion. If he refuses to do either of these things, he has in effect chosen to become a sort of quasi-agnostic. He waits, occasionally goes to Mass, resolves to go but never in fact goes to confession. But this is itself a definite course of action and it is incompatible with being a Catholic. He has more than one alternative, and in that sense James oversimplifies the situation, but as Sartre also points out, in such practical situations one cannot *not* decide. As Easter approaches he has a forced option: Either remain a Catholic and make your Easter duty or leave the Church.

James would hardly be concerned with questions concerning the merits of remaining in the Catholic Church, for he would surely regard that as a narrow sectarian matter. But James did believe that religious options generally have that logical character, including even the very general option to believe or not to believe in God. And it was such general issues that he thought were of the utmost human importance. With these 'overbeliefs', as he called them, we have forced, momentous, and live options. And over the overbelief theism, James opts for belief in God, and he takes this belief to be a reasonable belief even for an empiricist. If a man needs a belief in God—and James did and he thought all men did—and if we do not have good evidence for the claim that God does not exist, then it is not unreasonable to believe in God. This is not a defense of superstition, however, for to accept a superstitious belief or hold a superstitious belief is to accept or hold a belief that is *contrary* to the evidence. James will no more sanction that than will Peirce or Hume. But where, after carefully examining the evidence, the religious belief and the nonreligious belief in question are seen to be equally compatible with the evidence, one can without being at all superstitious, irrational, or obscurantist believe what one most deeply *wants* to believe. Why on earth not? To refuse to believe in such a situation because by believing one might be duped is to be infantile. That kind of indecisiveness is plainly neurotic.

IV

In my account of "The Will to Believe" I have deliberately left out many of the particulars concerning what James considers faith, religion, and belief in God to be. In my judgment they involve most of the obscurities, confusions, and ambivalences of liberalism in religion. I have only utilized that part of James that any Jewish or Christian believer might not reject in connection with a justification by faith for his belief in God, that is, a reality transcendent to the world and upon whom the world depends.

James's essay, as might be expected, has engendered considerable criticism, some of it quite irresponsible. Of the more responsible criticism, Morris Cohen's is both representative and instructive.[6] Cohen claims there "may be more wisdom and courage as well as more faith in honest doubt than in most of the creeds." He contends that James is mistaken in believing that eternal salvation depends on making a religious commitment. If our life is indeed eternal we will have many occasions for religious commitment. Given "the endless variety of religious creeds" held by various people to be "essential for our salvation," why not take a skeptical attitude until there is some reasonable ground for accepting one rather than another? Instead of accepting one, as James (according to Cohen) would have us do, it is better to remain aloof and skeptical, since the various creeds cannot establish the authority of their individual claims. Given their conflicting nature, it is better, Cohen tells us, to "leave them all alone and console ourselves with the hypothesis . . . that the starry universe and whatever gods there be do not worry about us at all, and will not resent our enjoying whatever humane and enlightened comfort and whatever vision of truth and beauty our world offers us."

I am in the curious position of being inclined to agree in attitude with much of what Cohen avers while remaining quite unconvinced that he has done anything to meet James's central claims. Cohen's telling points, it seems to me, are either on the periphery or against a straw man. In the first place, James was plainly not concerned with specific creeds such as Judaism, Christianity, and Islam. The sort of general religious commitment, such as belief in God, that James took to be essential to make sense of one's life, does not commit one to such specific religious doctrines. Perhaps that is a deficiency in James's account, but that is another matter. James was no more arguing for a commitment to the doctrinal formulations of any of the great religions than was Cohen. James was arguing for the right to make a commitment to an undifferentiated and, I must say, very vapid theism. He was talking about a very vague kind of theism or religiosity that hardly would be condemned as such by any religious man in the Western tradition, although many such men do believe that such an undifferentiated theism could not even begin to carry us far enough to lead us to anything recognizable as religious faith. Cohen's searching question, 'Why accept one faith rather than another?', would become relevant where we would have to go further, if indeed we would have to go further. In "The Will to Believe," James has nothing to say about this; but to criticize him for that is in effect to ask that he write on a different topic than the one to which he addressed himself. But James, I repeat, might continue to argue with at least some plausibility that in order to give significance to one's life it is enough to believe that the eternal things are the best things and that the universe is not simply an impersonal it, but somehow a personal Thou. And it is indeed true that many people find religious solace in such an undifferentiated theism. They are too suspicious of the doctrines of particular faiths to remain even remotely orthodox Jews or Christians, and they are too imbued with the spirit of religious tolerance to accept the exclusive claims to truth of Judaism or Christianity. The doctrinal schemes and sometimes even the moral codes of traditional religion are unacceptable to them, but they do need or at least think they need a theistic conception of things. Such metaphysical religiosity may have its deficiencies, but it is not likely to get one into a very severe ethnocentrism.

More importantly, when Cohen cautions us to adopt a kind of agnosticism and wait until the evidence is in, he misses James's crucial point, namely, that for the beliefs he is talking about—the beliefs he calls overbeliefs—we cannot establish whether they are true or false, rationally justified or unjustified. If it were possible to get evidence for their truth or falsity, Cohen might very well be right, for in such a circumstance part of what it means to hold a rational belief is to hold a belief that is determined not by the will or by authority but by the available evidence. And it is a truism to say that we ought to try to be rational. Indeed, in such a context it might very well be true that we should wait until the available evidence is in or at least be very tentative about our beliefs in lieu of good evidence. But we need faith just where the issue is momentous, where there is no question of getting evidence, and where there is no other way of deciding the issue on intellectual grounds. James is defending our right to believe what we will concerning these humanly central, passion-engendering, *untestable* overbeliefs. It is here and only here where James's doctrine is relevant.

Cohen could shift his grounds and argue, as some have, that such untestable beliefs are meaningless or cognitively meaningless, and thus not genuine beliefs. But he does not and his actual argument, if it is to have any force at all, must assume that these overbeliefs are meaningful. If they are meaningful and if they are as completely untestable, as James believes them to be, then talk about doubt and waiting for evidence is all sham, for in such a situation there can be no evidence for their truth or falsity. If we are going to accept them at all, we must accept them on faith. In such a context James poses this question for us: If indeed these beliefs are crucial to give sense to our lives, if the very possibility of our salvation is linked with them, why not simply accept them on faith since there can be no evidence against them? There is nothing to be doubted here, for that would imply that we could come to find out whether they are true. Instead they are, so to speak, up for subscription. Why not subscribe to them if they and they alone can really give significance to our lives? To here be a yea-sayer rather than a nay-sayer is both reasonable and humane.

V

I think, as by now should be evident, that there is much more to this essay than has usually been thought, and *if* James could successfully defend a number of his key presuppositions, he would have a very compelling claim indeed. But it is just in defending these that James would have very considerable difficulties.

The first questionable assumption is his treating belief and disbelief as if they were on *a par* intellectually. We have seen in previous chapters that there is no even nearly adequate evidence for the belief that there is a God. In fact, from a purely cognitive point of view, the reasonable assumption to make is that there is no God. It is not that the grounds for belief and disbelief cancel each other out and that as rational creatures we must remain agnostic from a purely intellectual point of view. If that were true, James's case would be much stronger. But that is not the case. Rather, viewed intellectually, to believe that there is a God is on a par with believing there are ghosts. Both are fantastic constructions that scandalize the intellect and test our credulity. If it were not the case that culturally and often personally so much emotional and ideological investment goes into religious belief, the central tenets of Judaism and Christianity would be no more acceptable to modern men than a belief in fairies. William Golding and Lewis Namier are certainly correct in stressing that there are deep mythical and nonrational forces at work in man and that they profoundly affect his view of the world. It does not follow, however, that they are something to be believed in; or that all our viewing of the world must be or should be essentially mythical; or that, vis-à-vis religion, belief and disbelief are on a par and one can legitimately believe what one wants to believe. James does assume they are on a par, but his assumption is very questionable. For his position to be viable, James would have to give his belief that they are on a par considerable evidential support. But he nowhere attempts to do this, and it is not at all evident that it could be done.

The second assumption James makes that needs challenging is that man needs religion for his life to have significance. James assumes that life is without meaning or at least is without its full significance if there is no God. Morality, he assumes, would lack any foundation at all, or at least would be without adequate foundation in a Godless world. In an essay "Reflex Action and Theism," James argues that materialism can never be an ultimate philosophy—presumably meaning by that an adequate ultimate philosophy—because materialism gives us "a solution of things which is irrational to the practical third of our nature, and in which we can never volitionally feel at home."[7] It will never satisfy us in our heart of hearts, for it would give us a world without value. But it has satisfied some, and some have thought it gave us 'a rational world' in which human values are not without a point.

Chapters 20 and 22 will attempt in some detail to rebut such Jamesian beliefs.[8] It suffices here to say that James simply assumes them. Historically (recall Holbach and Hume, for example) many people have made exactly the opposite assumptions. Materialism has been a liberating doctrine for many, as it was for Holbach, Feuerbach, and Marx. It answers for many people what James calls "the practical third" of their natures. Not all men have Dostoevskian-Pascalian temperaments. James mistakenly reads his predicaments into mankind at large. There are indeed many men such as James, but not all men see the world or need to see the world in that manner. If we do *not* see the world in that manner, if we do *not* feel that if God is dead nothing matters, then the rationale for 'opting for God' which James develops is undermined.

There is a third assumption that James makes that is also questionable, but unless what James assumes here is so his basic argument is again undermined. James assumes—and must assume to make his argument work—that belief in God is perfectly intelligible, that is, that we know what it would be like for God to exist but that we just do not know and cannot come to know whether in fact there is such an ultimate reality. He assumes in the same vein that we know what it *means* to assert that the universe is not a mere it but a mysterious Thou. In this he misses what to many people is the most perplexing and skepticism-inducing aspect of religions such as Judaism and Christianity: that central strands of the God-talk that are integral to these religions are so obscure that these core doctrinal claims seem to many so near to being meaningless that not enough can be made of them to make theistic religious belief possible for an individual who reflects on what he is saying and trying to believe.

This conviction is not always articulated in exactly this way or held so definitely. But, incidentally, it is something like this that accounts for the brief but extraordinary appeal of the death-of-God theology. It was felt by many people who wanted very much to remain within the Church that now they could do so in good conscience and not believe in such fantastic constructions as God and immortality. That other fantastic constructions were required by the radical new theology only gradually became apparent. Even within the mainstream of Jewish and Christian thought, to say nothing of secular thinking, it is the question concerning the very intelligibility or coherence of religious discourse that is for many the central stumbling block to faith.[9] But James simply assumes that such God-talk is in place as it is, and he rather conventionally worries about whether we could know that the claims of religion are true and if not whether we are justified in accepting them on faith. At an even more basic level, we are faced with the crucial problem of whether there is, for nonanthropomorphic theistic religions, anything that could even count as 'religious truth' or as true religious claims. Such questions will be examined in Chapter 21. Here it should suffice to note that James's account is undermined unless there is a sense in which religious utterances of the kind relevant to his account are properly characterizable as being either true or false.

NOTES

1. The title "The Will to Believe" is an illbegotten title and James came to wish later that he had given his essay one of several other titles. One of these, most appropriately to my mind, was "A Defence of Faith." See R. W. Beard, "'The Will to Believe' Revisited," *Ratio*, vol. VIII (December, 1966), p. 170.
2. John Passmore, *A Hundred Years of Philosophy* (first edition), p. 95.
3. William James, "The Sentiment of Rationality." This essay should surely be read in conjuction with "The Will to Believe."
4. It is failure to keep in mind this obvious point that vitiates so many criticisms of James's defense of a policy about certain beliefs. A philosopher as distinguished as Bertrand Russell makes just this error in his *History of Western Philosophy*. Beard quite rightly refers to it as "an almost grotesque misrepresentation." Beard, op. cit., p. 174.
5. Beard in his perceptive essay shows that there are some unclarities and errors in James's concepts of a forced option and a genuine option. They are of a technical nature that need not detain us here. Beard provides reformulations that can be reasonably taken to capture James's basic intent and that avoid these technical difficulties. Ibid., pp. 176–179.
6. Morris R. Cohen, *The Faith of a Liberal*, pp. 357–361. It is reprinted under the title "Religion and the Will to Believe," in Marcus G. Singer and Robert R. Ammerman (eds.), *Introductory Readings in Philosophy*.
7. In William James, *The Will to Believe and Other Essays*.
8. I also do this in some detail in my *Ethics Without God*, forthcoming. And there is a powerful argument for this point of view in Ronald Hepburn's *Christianity and Paradox*, chapter 8.
9. This is brought out by essays I, II, VI, and X in Antony Flew and Alasdair MacIntyre (eds.), *New Essays in Philosophical Theology*; Terence Penelhum, "Faith, Fact and Philosophy," *Toronto Quarterly* (1956); William Blackstone, "The Status of God-Talk," *Journal for the Scientific Study of Religion*, vol. V, no. 3, (1966); Bernard Williams, "Has 'God' a Meaning?" *Question* (February, 1968); and notably by two eminent theologians, Ninian Smart and John Hick, in their respective inaugural lectures, "Theology, Philosophy and the Natural Sciences" (Birmingham: 1962) and "Theology's Central Problem" (Birmingham: 1967).

20

FAITH
AND REASON

I

Given the conceptual incongruity of what we are talking about in speaking of God—that is, an infinite person who transcends the world and is yet utterly unlimited—and given the fact that there is no evidence for the existence of such an anomalous reality, the evidence points very decidedly to the conclusion that there is no such reality. And as James himself stresses, a rational man should tailor his beliefs to fit the evidence. One can only justifiably believe what one wants to believe, he maintains, when the evidence balances out between the conflicting positions or when there can be no evidence either way. But in the religious situation the evidence strongly favors disbelief.

It is here that Kierkegaard enters. In a passionate, perceptive, and keenly intelligent way, he defended the right—in fact, the human necessity—of taking a leap of faith, even in such a situation. He tells us in his *Journals* that he is overwhelmed by doubts. He stresses that a belief in God is a scandal to the intellect, a manifest absurdity, but all the same to ward off despair and to give sense to our lives, we must take the leap of faith, we must believe in something that intellectually speaking we recognize to be absurd. Kierkegaard assaults the very fundamental ideals of the enlightenment, the world-historical perspective of a Hegel or Marx, and the assumptions of liberal Christianity. As he stresses in his *Concluding Unscientific Postscript*, it is only by being subjective and rejecting the myth of objective truth in such domains that one can grasp religious truth. We can never prove or establish or even come to understand the Divine by reference to worldliness. We cannot through study, through gathering evidence by amassing facts, by careful reflection or philosophical analysis make the transition from the world-historical to the subjective, that is, the agent's commitment to God. It is here that fideism has hit rock bottom.

To be a fideist is to believe that religious belief cannot be based upon demonstrative knowledge, empirical investigation, or some set of rational principles uncovered by philosophical reflection, but that it rests *solely* on faith. Religious knowledge is completely beyond the limits of man's finite understanding. But, a fideist would argue, we are hounded by heaven; our very human condition drives us to faith if our lives are to have any meaning at all. Our wills are indeed free, and we can in our pride turn from God. If we do, however, we will in effect destroy ourselves by destroying all hope for a meaningful existence. Without faith, a sensitive and nonevasive man will be caught in the spite and self-laceration of the Underground man, but out of his despair he will finally come to realize his helplessness. Despair finally drives the human animal to accept God through faith alone. Reason, Kierkegaard argues, clearly shows the absurdity, the intellectual affrontery, of Christian belief; the compelling necessities of life drive those who are not evasive about themselves to belief.

Johannes Climacus (one of Kierkegaard's philosophical pseudonyms) vividly presents the scandal to the intellect involved in Christianity. In *Philosophical Fragments* (chapter 5) Climacus tells us that the supreme merit of Christianity is that it goes beyond all other religions in its flight to the absurd. In averring that 'Jesus is God' it excels all other religions in asserting the occurrence of the impossible. With this central assertion, Christianity, proudly flying its paradox, becomes *the* sole claimant to the title of "total absurdity." An Incarnation is logically impossible, but the true "knight of faith" will believe in it all the same.

We must put aside all Faustian vanity and no longer seek knowledge of Divine Existence. Out of one's despair, and with an infinite trust, one takes the leap of faith—one accepts on trust the authority of Jesus and the Bible as the revealed word of God. We take this leap while realizing that the historical Jesus is lost in the extreme uncertainty of distant history. The Bible, as Bishop Nygren likes to emphasize, is inevitably interpreted when used as a source of doctrine and religious inspiration. The Bible no more speaks for itself than historical facts speak for themselves. And considering that there are literally thousands of religions, most of which claim to reveal Absolute Truth, revelation (more accurately an *alleged* revelation) cannot carry its own guarantee. Furthermore, there can be no warrant for the contender for revelation from within itself, for any claim that it made would be subject to doubt unless this contender for revealed truth were already *accepted* as the record of God's self-disclosure.

Kierkegaard does not run from any of these difficulties, and in his replies the purity of his fideism becomes apparent. As an orthodox Christian, Kierkegaard takes the Incarnation to be the central tenet of Christianity. That Jesus is the son of God is something Kiergekaard takes on trust, and he is uninterested in all historical evidence or analytical argument for or against this belief. In *Training in Christianity* and in *Philosophical Fragments* (chapters 4 and 5), Kierkegaard argues that the historical records of events in Palestine in the first century, Biblical knowledge (no matter how accurate) about the character, moral teachings, and miracles of Jesus are all irrelevant to the only crucial claim about Jesus— namely, that Jesus is God. Historical events would be about an individual man, and our knowledge of them would never attain certainty. And even if they did, they would give us no grounds for a belief that Jesus is *God*. A philosophical analysis of the doctrine would also not help, for at best it could only give us an elucidation of what could be *meant* by saying that 'God has appeared in history'. It could not show the really crucial thing, namely, that He really had appeared in history. We can only accept the Incarnation on faith; that is, accept it in spite of the fact that there is absolutely no evidence for it.

Revelation is in no better position. We can only make the leap of faith with fear and trembling, for we can have no rational assurance that what we accept as God's revealed Word is not a siren song of the Devil, purely an expression of our own or a culturally defined (mass) neurosis, or an arbitrary, idiosyncratic faith. There is no rational warrant for the belief that if one studies a little more, examines religion a little more closely or honestly, one will finally have some grounds for belief. Even if one engages in this study with the determination of a Faust, one will get nowhere. To think that one might so discover God is an illusion that is itself a kind of evasive "double-mindedness" that enables one indefinitely to postpone making the leap of faith. There is nothing to be discovered. One must simply act, for there are and can be no rational grounds for Christian belief.

Kierkegaard does not balk at such 'facts'. He argues in his *Philosophical Fragments* that if we think about God and if we consider the central importance of freely accepting or rejecting God, the point of the total mystery and absurdity of the Incarnation will become apparent. God is like a king who wants to marry a poor maiden, but only if she loves him for himself alone. In order to ascertain what her attitude toward him is, the king must approach her incognito to avoid captivating her with his splendor or forcing her into a decision that takes into consideration his station. God is in a similar predicament vis-à-vis man. If we had good grounds for believing that the Incarnation had actually occurred, we might be frightened by God's power or seduced by God's rewards into believing in Him; hence, it is only to be expected that God would come incognito to get a fair test of the authenticity of our faith. Thus, it is perfectly understandable that God would make his Incarnation completely a matter of faith, that he would offer *no* evidence for the fact that the Incarnation has occurred.

This is fideism at its maximum purity. I suspect there are some Christians, as well as others, who will say that by taking it in such purity we have revealed its absurdity. A counter to this is that belief is now perfectly protected from the "wolves of disbelief." It has stared rational criticism straight in the face and simply rejected it. It has refused to play "the reasoning game in religion." Religion is *not* something to be reasoned about, it is not something that in its basic aspects is subject to rational scrutiny and assessment.

Indeed, many Christians who would turn their backs on questions of the analysis of religious belief and have no interest in proofs or disproofs of the existence of God would not go as far as Kierkegaard. They would grant that finally one believes on faith, but there are some 'signs' of His presence. Christianity is not the complete absurdity Kierkegaard claims. It is indeed true that the signs of Divinity are always ambiguous and that they are never rationally compelling; there neither can nor should be a foolproof proof for the existence of God. It is even true that there is no agreed-on method for resolving these questions, but this does not mean that such matters are *completely* beyond the scope of reason.

I do not wish to take sides in this family quarrel between pure and impure fideism. They both have their characteristic strengths and weaknesses. However, there is one advantage to pure fideism that is worth mentioning. In putting religion completely beyond the pale of rational assessment, pure fideism (unlike impure fideism) *appears*, at any rate, to be in a better position to evade the difficulties raised for Christian belief by a philosophical analysis of religious claims. The philosophical burden of this chapter will be to show that this is not so; that both pure and impure fideism face difficulties not envisaged by Tertullian, Pascal, Hamanan, Kierkegaard, or Barth; and that unless theologians and reflective believers want to advocate complete obscurantism and mystagogy, they need to face these difficulties.[1]

II

The skeptical critic at first appears to be utterly disarmed by such a fideism. It looks as if anything he could say would automatically be question-begging. Kierkegaard maintains that reason cannot in any fundamental way determine whether we should or should not make a religious commitment. If I then point out that Christianity or a belief in God is absurd, a dyed-in-the-wool Kierkegaardian will, of course, heartily agree. Belief in God is indeed a scandal to the intellect. It is absurd. Looked at in terms of 'objective truth', it is like believing in Santa Claus or fairies. But he will go on to stress that where we are speaking of human existence—of what we are to make of man, of how we are to live and die— no objective knowledge is possible.[2] In short, Kierkegaard would surely accept Luther's judgment that "Whoever would become a sound believing Christian must tear out the eyes of his reason." But he would add that this is true for all ultimate commitments, secular as well as religious. Reason cannot tell us the true ends of life. It is not just the religious man who is in that predicament; we all are. We cannot, Kierkegaard repeats over and over again, discover by reason or the use of our intelligence how we are to live and die. Rational argumentation can do no more than make us cognizant of the alternatives before us. It cannot tell us or even relevantly guide us in making our fundamental choices. It is not that Kierkegaard thought that reason was of no value, for it is reason itself that "shows us that in the end the choice of the individual must be sovereign." Reason shows us that reason cannot determine the ends of life. But it remains true that what people who take a world-historical point of view want reason most of all to do, reason cannot do. That is, we want reason to determine how it is that we should live and die, but it cannot.

There is something tough-minded and appealing about this, but we must not let Kierkegaard enchant us into accepting this fideism uncritically. The first thing we ought to ask in trying to appraise such a fideism is this: If belief in God is so absurd, why believe in God? Indeed, it may be the case that we have to believe in something, have some set or cluster of ultimate commitments, but why believe in something one recognizes to be absurd? If anything is evident in morality and in life, it surely is that one ought *not* to believe in what is *unreasonable*. It may indeed be true that reason cannot uniquely determine or ascertain what we are to believe and how we are to act given the alternatives available to us. But this gives us no warrant for believing what we know to be absurd. To believe in an absurdity is a veritable paradigm of what one ought not to do.

Moreover, if to believe in the Incarnation is literally to believe in a contradiction, then indeed there can be nothing to believe in, nothing to accept on faith, any more than one could take it on faith that there are round squares when one knows that a round square is a self-contradictory conception. If Kierkegaard has simply engaged in hyperbolic overstatement here, and if the concept of an incarnate God or the concept of God is not literally a contradiction but only a patent absurdity, we could as far as logic is concerned believe in God. But why believe in a patent absurdity? If a man wishes to be rational he cannot believe in what he acknowledges to be an absurdity. It is a perfect case of what he ought not to do.

If Kierkegaard in turn flings out the challenge 'Why be rational?', then the reply should be that the very question 'Why?' commits one to asking for reasons for one's actions, and that in turn presupposes a commitment to trying to be rational.[3] One might argue, and argue rationally, concerning whether in *everything* one does one ought in every respect to be rational. Perhaps sometimes one ought to take a vacation simply because one wants to, even though one cannot afford it and there are no over-riding reasons for taking a vacation then. It may be a good thing some-times to give in to whim. It is no doubt a mistake to calculate too nicely or ratiocinate everything. But here we are plainly using reason to attempt to determine what is the proper scope of reason. 'Why be rational *ever?*' makes no sense, because to ask *why* is to ask for a reason and to pre-suppose that one is prepared to be guided by reasons. Simply to refuse in this overall sense to be be guided by reason is utter madness. It is an attempt to deny one's humanity—that is, to reject one of the distinctive capacities of the human animal, namely, one's capacity to guide one's action by intelligence. We suffer sufficiently in the natural course of things, but to act in accordance with Kierkegaard's directives is a way of virtually assuring suffering and distress. If this is what it is à la Kierke-gaard to make life more difficult, let us by all means not make life more difficult.

There is another error in Kierkegaard that needs to be noted. Not everything that is not rational is irrational. My preference for cherry pie over apple pie is not rational, but neither is it irrational. It may very well be rational *not* to look for or expect a reason for everything. It may be in a large sense rational to act sometimes on whim or to do what is nonrational. That is, it is not the case that there is a compelling reason for everything that human beings legitimately do. To think that there must be is rationalism gone mad.

We have very good grounds for believing that some choices are non-rational, that is, that they are just choices—choices made for no reason. But if a choice is really irrational or absurd it is *contrary* to reason. If something is actually contrary to reason, it can never, exactly by the very definition of what reason is, be something that we ought to do. More-over, in saying that reason cannot determine the ends of life, why acknowledge more than that reason cannot uniquely determine the ends of life? But this acknowledgement would not entail or support the claim that our ends of life are irrational or absurd, but only that we do make and properly make some nonrational choices. This does not even remotely justify, sanction, or excuse making irrational choices.

III

Suppose someone were to argue that Kierkegaard's point could be freed from such entanglements by saying that what is essential to his point is the claim that questions about human existence and about God are such that they cannot be fixed by the scientific method. Instead, feeling and a stark subscription to a way of life are crucial. Kierkegaard leads us to see that in reflecting about religion and about life we must simply make a decision about how we are to live without having any grounds for our decision. If we push it to its limits, reason—that is, honest and informed human reflection—leads us to recognize that such fundamental beliefs are simply up for subscription. That is to say, it will become evident that one's fundamental decisions here are and must be nonrational.

Logically speaking, this means that our choices here are like the choice between apple pie and peach pie, but emotionally speaking it is very different, for one's whole life orientation is radically at stake in the making of such decisions. Moreover, there is nothing irrational or in any way disreputable about making nonrational choices in a nonrational manner. The mistake on the part of the philosophers is to look for proof and reasons where there can only be—depending on the type of nonrational considerations—stark choice, questions of taste or sensibility, decisions of principle, or conversion or commitment.

I would in turn challenge such a claim by questioning whether a believer can justifiably regard all his basic religious commitments as being so thoroughly nonrational. We need to step back and examine the structure of a portion of Kierkegaard's argument to understand the relevant considerations here. Kierkegaard's central problem is 'What is it to be a Christian in Christendom?'. He turns all the power of his very incisive irony and psychological perceptiveness against the claim that it is easy to be a Christian in Christendom. This preoccupation leads to a stress on 'the how' and not on 'the what' in Christian belief. In a way this is perfectly proper, for it brings out clearly that to be a Christian essentially involves having a set of commitments personally held with inwardness and passion and not just, or at all, being an adherent to a kind of primitive philosophical system or *Weltanschauung*. It is only from a world-historical point of view that Christianity can be looked upon as a *Weltanschauung*. A Christian cannot take his own Christian point of view to be a world-historical point of view. Yet with this very stress on 'the how', Kierkegaard simply evaded perfectly legitimate questions about *what* is to be believed. These questions cannot be evaded, however, if *Christianity* is to be our faith or if *God* is to be the object of our commitment.

Consider *what* makes something a religious belief or a Christian belief. It cannot be just the passionate inwardness Kierkegaard so stressed, for moral and aesthetic beliefs can have that quality as well. To isolate and identify Christian belief, belief in God, or even religious belief, we must say something—scandal to the intellect or not—about 'the what' as well as 'the how'. With apple pie and peach pie, one can talk about what one prefers. Concerning questions of moral and social policy, it might finally come down, in trying to decide what to do, to a bare subscription to a way of acting. But in typical cases at least, we still perfectly well understand *what* we are deciding to do, or at least by diligent study we can come to understand *what* we have resolved to do.

When one says 'God is incarnate in Jesus' or 'God could never be incarnate' or 'Nirvana cannot be attained by seeking it' or 'God shall raise the quick and the dead', one cannot, from a *believer's perspective*, be taken to be just expressing one's feelings or to be simply obliquely saying something about how one is to act. These statements most certainly appear to be claims of a very mysterious sort about how things are. They most certainly appear to be sentences used to make statements. And if something is a statement it is either true or false.[4] (And with statements, 'objectively true' or 'objectively false' is redundant.) Yet to take Kierkegaard's favorite example, it is absurd—childishly absurd—as Kierkegaard himself stressed about this example, to assert that God is incarnate in Jesus, for to make this putative assertion is to give one to understand that the infinite was given embodiment in the finite, the unlimited in the limited, and the eternal in the temporal. From any rational point of view, it is not merely nonrational but *irrational* to believe in contradictions. To be embodied in the finite or in the temporal, the infinite or eternal must thereby cease to be what it purportedly is, namely, an infinite, unlimited, eternal being. Moreover, our reason cannot grasp what it is for something to be an unlimited, eternal, or infinite being.

To believe in such realities is not merely nonrational but positively irrational, for we have purported claims here that we do not understand. Taken in a straightforward manner they appear at least to be patent contradictions, but we are counseled against taking them in such a literal way. And then we do not know what to make of them. We do not understand what it is we are supposed to believe or commit ourselves to. Yet we are to take these claims to be eternal truths, although we do not understand what would constitute grounds for their truth. We do not even understand what we are supposedly asserting when we make such utterances.

Yet knowing they are absurdities, Kierkegaard glories in these absurdities. However, if *everything considered* they are absurd, they ought not to be believed.

IV

It is natural to retort at this point that Kierkegaard should not be interpreted as asserting that *everything considered* they are absurd. Rather, they are absurd from a strictly intellectual point of view or from what Kierkegaard likes to call a world-historical point of view.[5] But when we take an existential point of view, that is, when we consider the whole existing individual with all his needs, we can see that it is not at all absurd for him to accept these beliefs which from a purely theoretical, objective, or world-historical vantage point are absurd. To put it as bluntly as possible, without religious commitment—in fact, for Kierkegaard, without a specific Christian commitment—there is only despair and sickness unto death. With such a commitment there remains hope for God's mercy and grace and for life everlasting, even though these concepts have scarcely any meaning; without such religious commitment there is for the nonevasive man only despair at the utter insignificance of life. Because with a belief in Christ there is no utter loss of hope and of significance, it is not at all absurd to accept these objectively absurd beliefs purely on faith. Indeed, as knights of faith, we must crucify our intellects, but this is not absurd when it is the only way it is possible to have hope. And it is the only way possible to have hope, for only by believing this scandal to the intellect can we make life meaningful.

Why, I would respond, think that life is meaningless or pointless without a belief in God? I do not believe in God and I am utterly devoid of the slightest religious conviction, but I do not find life meaningless and I see no reason why I should find life meaningless.[6] There remains for me all that love, friendship, and human comradeship can bring. This is something so precious that it hardly bears talking about in sober philosophical prose. It is not that there is anything mysterious here, but that to talk about it in other than a platitudinous way is to become autobiographical or concretely descriptive. Yet it is something of immeasurable human value, and it can remain completely untouched by one's religious affiliations or lack thereof.[7]

In addition to this there remain the pleasures of living—the pleasures of companionship, of love, and of working together at a common task. Life under some conditions is intolerable, but whether it is or is not intolerable has nothing to do with the absence of God. Rather, physical ills apart, when it is intolerable it is largely due to the inhumanity of man to man. But our world is not always the world of *Who's Afraid of Virginia Woolf?* In our Godless world there is joy and love and understanding and a million sources of varied kinds of pleasure. One of the reasons Tolstoy and George Eliot have such a profound effect on us and do not strike us merely as nineteenth-century figures but as human beings who make profound and natural testaments to their fellow human beings is that even in a world that knows all the horrors that our world knows, there are these sources of joy, love, and understanding to which we respond quite spontaneously even when we remain devoid of religious commitment. In short, there is much, even in a world without God, that gives life verve and resonance. And in solidarity with one's fellow human beings one can find sources within oneself to endure what must be endured, to bear what must be borne. The dignity of man is not at all contingent upon there being a God. And if a secular point of view is correct and life must inexorably come to a quite unequivocal end for each of us, this only enhances the value of life.

Kierkegaard is profoundly convinced that his life would be meaningless without God, but it does not follow from the fact that he believes this that it would in actuality be meaningless. It is perhaps a correct psychological insight to claim that his believing it to be meaningless might *help make* it meaningless for him and for people he convinced by his powerful rhetoric. But if he could bring himself to have an open mind on the subject, he could come to see the reasons I have already given that his life need not be meaningless without such a belief. Moreover, even if without a belief in God *Kierkegaard's* life would be without significance, given his psychological predispositions, it does not follow that his particular psychological predicaments apply or even should apply to man at large. Kierkegaard was a profound thinker; he was often both psychologically and conceptually perceptive. But to maintain or to suggest, as do some of his disciples and admirers, that not to share Kierkegaard's predispositions here is somehow *necessarily* to have a shallower appreciation of life is surely a bit of blind parochialism. There are men in our culture who live dedicated, meaningful lives, such as the doctor in Camus' *The Plague,* and yet are quite without religious belief. There are whole cultures without a concept of God or immortality that are as old as Christianity. There is no reason to think that these human beings saw their lives as a Wasteland.

In short, even if reason is as utterly impotent about the ends of life as Kierkegaard avers and as I shall challenge when we later discuss ethics, it does not follow that life is meaningless. And most certainly it does not follow that only by a leap of faith to a belief in God can we endow life with meaning.

V

Kierkegaard or a Kierkegaardian might reply that since reason cannot aid in deciding between conflicting human aims or ends, one clearly can reasonably believe whatever one wants to believe. From a cognitive point of view, belief and unbelief in such a circumstance are both equally worthy and equally unworthy of our acceptance. This would certainly constitute a considerable shift in attitude for a Kierkegaardian. But even if, for the sake of argument, we accept such a relativism, it does not give us anything like an adequate rationale for being fideists.

Proceed in Kierkegaard's manner! Stop trying to think like a world-historical thinker and take an existential point of view! Take such relativism to heart! Become fully aware of the vast array of *Weltanschauungen* all up for arbitrary subscription! Now consider. If this is our situation, if this really is what one must face as a nonevasive individual, you will hardly be able to claim with a straight face that your Christian belief is true or normative for all men, for you will then see that it is perfectly arbitrary to hold that your belief is preferable to the beliefs of others or in any sense more justified or more worthy of belief. Recognizing and taking to heart the fact that you do not properly understand what is involved in your belief and that there are myriad other conflicting claims to 'ultimate truth' and 'ultimate significance', rationally just as well warranted or just as ill warranted, you cannot, as a reasonable individual, claim any special significance for your own belief. If you defensively reply, "Why be a reasonable man then?" we can and should retort that we have already seen that it is senseless to ask: Why be a reasonable individual?

Rationality is indeed limited, but the recognition of this is not a good ground for taking a Kierkegaardian leap in the dark to the God of Abraham, Isaac, and Jacob. Since such a Kierkegaardian leap is simply a leap in the dark to something acknowledged to be rationally absurd, it could also just as well be a leap to national socialism, a snake cult, the Ku Klux Klan, or anything that might thoroughly engage one's emotions. The recognition that this is so surely makes it apparent that it is not true, as Kierkegaard maintains, that "the conclusions of the passions are the only reliable ones." It is obviously the case that some conclusions of the passions are not reliable. But Kierkegaard need not deny that, for he is claiming that *only* conclusions of the passions are reliable, not that *all* conclusions of the passions are reliable. Surely many of the conclusions of the passions that we would reject—and Kierkegaard would reject as well—are conclusions of the passions that are plainly contrary to reason. Belief in Christianity is the exception for Kierkegaard. But why should it be the exception? Doesn't his making it the exception reveal more about Kierkegaard than about man's predicament?

It seems to me that it does, and that Kierkegaard has given us no good grounds for believing that the conclusions of the passions are the only reliable conclusions. That we should not neglect, ignore, or simply negate what our passions prompt us to do is one thing—something that is surely so—but that we should not rely on our heads and our intelligence but only on our passions is something else again—something that most certainly is not so. There can be 'a festival of life' without such irrationalism.

Kierkegaard surely did us a service in ironically lashing out at those who in some rationalistic phantasmagoria make a philosophical system everything, and in a mindless way live in a little shack by the side of it. But Kierkegaard utterly overreacted to rationalism and the historicism (historical relativism) of Hegel. A life is neither free nor distinctively human that does not use reason in appraising the ends of life. Kierkegaard brilliantly used reason to try to establish that reason was helpless in such contexts. Perceptive and profound as his attack on the ideals and presuppositions of the Enlightenment are, they fail all the same. Even if I am somehow mistaken in that contention and I remain too thoroughly and rigidly a child of the Enlightenment, it remains the case that Kierkegaard utterly failed to show that to make sense of life or morality, a sensitive and nonevasive man is driven to a belief in God. Even if reason is impotent in determining the ends of life, it does not follow that we should become knights of faith.

Pressed in this fashion, Kierkegaard could fall back on a mere irrationalism. He could cry with Luther "reason is a whore"—"You must part with reason and not know anything of it and even kill it; else one will not get into the kingdom of heaven." I could, of course, ask for the particulars, ask what grounds he has for his radical value judgment and why it is we must 'know nothing of reason'. But given such an outburst, it would be apparent that Kierkegaard would not be prepared to listen to reason—to reflect about the matter at all. (I do not suggest that this was his actual temperament, but that that might be a reaction of Kierkegaard or a Kierkegaardian under such a dialectical strain.) At such a point there can be no further argument or rational discussion with such a man, although I can point out to others that such a fideism is gratuitous, irrational, and inhuman. Man should indeed avoid *hybris*, but neither should he demean or deny his distinctive powers. Kierkegaard was a profound man, but when with Luther he urges man to obey God blindly, absurdly, without recourse to reason, he denies those very fundamental qualities in us that make us human.

NOTES

1. I would like to add that fideism is not a creature of Kierkegaard's tortured consciousness but is a very old and pervasive approach in Christian thought. Richard Popkin has beautifully documented this in his "Theological and Religious Scepticism," *The Christian Scholar*, vol. XXXIX (June, 1956), pp. 150–158 and "Kierkegaard and Scepticism," *Algemeen Nederlands Tijdschrift Voor Wijebegeerte En Psychologie*, vol. 51 no. 3, pp. 123–141.
2. D. Z. Phillips, "Subjectivity and Religious Truth in Kierkegaard," *Sophia*, vol. VII, no. 2 (July, 1968), pp. 3–13. Or even if some is possible it is of little value in such domains. For an exposition of this see Mary Warnock, *Existentialist Ethics*, pp. 5–11.
3. I have shown why this must be so in my "Linguistic Philosophy and 'The Meaning of Life'," *Cross Currents*, vol. XIV, no. 3 (summer, 1964), pp. 313–334. Moreover, if it is alleged that I am arguing with a straw man here and that a true irrationalist or nonrationalist would not ask for reasons for being rational, but would simply say, "Don't bother me! I don't want to be rational," I would respond by asserting that he, unlike Kierkegaard, has

opted out of the reasoning game altogether, and he is being a genuine irrationalist and not just a nonrationalist. Such a position is self-destructive, as we have seen in discussing Peirce in Chapter 11. Moreover, Kierkegaard was committed to using reason to show that there were many crucial things in life—including the dispute between belief and disbelief—that could not be so resolved.

4. This seeming unassailable assumption, I should add, has been challenged by ordinary language philosophers such as John Austin (cf. his *How to Do Things with Words*) and by logicians such as Nicholas Rescher (cf. his *Many-Valued Logic*). I am far from convinced of the force of these arguments against such a commonsensical claim, but that conviction is no substitute for argument. So here again we see another issue that needs further discussion and argument.

5. Soren Kierkegaard, *Concluding Unscientific Postscript*, pp. 75–77, 88–90, and 120–123. D. Z. Phillips, op. cit., pp. 4–5, clearly expresses the core of Kierkegaard's distinction here.

6. See here Kurt Baier, *On the Meaning of Life*. This has been conveniently reprinted in *Philosophy For a New Generation*, A. K. Bierman and J. A. Gould (eds.), (New York: Macmillan, 1970).

21
MEANING
AND TRUTH:
THE SIGNIFICANCE
OF GOD-TALK

I

It has been said that philosophically sophisticated and even not so sophisticated contemporary men have been more troubled with questions of *meaning* than with questions of *truth-finding* vis-à-vis religion.[1] By that certainly cryptic and perhaps obscure remark I mean that while they, as native or fluent speakers of the language (in our case English), have no trouble in forming well-formed English sentences in which 'God' and the like occur, they all the same feel they can make nothing of the putative concepts supposedly expressed by their God-talk. It need not be that God has become dead in their hearts, but that even when they have the urge to believe, when they want to find an overall rationale for their lives and grasp the sorry scheme of things entire, they still can make nothing of very fundamental segments of God-talk.[2] Try as they will they cannot figure out what it is all about. The words seem quite meaningless to them. They are prepared to accept a certain amount of mystery but not utter incoherence or gibberish. The question is: Is God-talk actually unintelligible or at least incoherent, or have such sceptics failed to view it in the right manner? That is, does Jewish or Christian religious discourse and particularly the key links in this discourse make sense, even rough sense?

To discuss this question properly we need to clarify the distinction between questions of meaning and questions of truth-finding. Suppose someone asks me: 'Are there any Moslems at Fordham?' or 'Are there squirrels on Korcula?' or 'What is the freezing point of champagne?'. Here no problem of *meaning* is likely to arise. I know what is being asked for, but I do not know the correct answers to these questions, although I know what I must do to find an answer. Thus, in such situations we clearly have questions of truth-finding.

Now consider the following (putative) questions: 'Can you have a pain and not be conscious of it?', 'Is time reversible?', 'Is there a distinctive "poetic truth" or "musical truth" only expressible by poetry or music itself?'. Here the normal response is, or at least should be: What is being asked for? What do you mean? It is not, as in the first batch of questions, that we know what is *meant* but do not know the correct answers. Rather, our problem here is that we do not understand what is being asked. We do not know what, if anything, would count as an answer to such questions (putative questions). At the very least they require careful interpretation before we understand what it would be like to answer them or to have an answer to them. And an interpretation here means an explanation of their *meaning*. Thus, with these last questions we do not have questions of truth-finding but questions of *meaning*.

It is also true that questions of meaning are logically prior to questions of truth-finding. If someone asserts 'Time is reversible' or 'Truth is timelessly transcendent' or 'Humphrey sleeps slower than Nixon', I must understand what is meant by these putative statements before I can go about trying to determine whether they are true or false. When someone says 'Time is reversible' or 'People have unconscious pains' we cannot say yea or nay, for we do not understand whether his supposed statement is even true or false because we do not understand what he is trying to assert. In fact, to understand such utterances as statements is to understand what it would be like for them to be either true or false, probably true or false, or at least what would count for or against their truth or falsity. That is, if we understand that they actually assert something, we understand that if such and such happens, then they would be true or probably true; but if such and such happens instead, then they would be false or probably false.

For you to understand 'People have unconscious pains' (to understand both that it *asserts* something and *what* it asserts), it is necessary for you to understand under what conditions such a putative statement would be true or likely to be true, and under what conditions it would be false or likely to be false. For someone to explain what he means by 'People have unconscious pains', he must explain under what conditions the statement would be true or probably true, and under what conditions it would be false or probably false, or at the very least he must be able to describe what counts for and against its being true. If no distinctive experiences are relevant to its falsity, we cannot understand what is being asserted or denied. In fact, under such circumstances nothing can be asserted or denied. The sentence may very well have some other function in the language and thus in all probability have a meaning in some sense, but we still do not understand it as being used in such a manner so as to constitute a genuine bit of fact-stating discourse.

II

Now we can return to God-talk. Religious questions and religious utterances of the sort central to the claims of Judaism and Christianity typically raise questions of *meaning* rather than questions of *truth-finding*. It is these logically prior questions of meaning that are our most fundamental stumbling blocks vis-à-vis religion, not questions of truth-finding. I do not want to be misunderstood. Surely we want to know the truth about our religions; that is our end, or at least it ought to be. But religious claims cannot possibly be true unless they are intelligible, and many of the key sentences in the corpus of religious discourse appear at least so near to being meaningless, so incoherent, so devoid of factual intelligibility, that we are blocked on the logically prior question of meaning.[3] This is a deeper explanation of why the various so-called proofs of God's existence could not get off the ground.

Consider such statements as have occurred in the traditional attempts to demonstrate the existence of God. 'Since there are contingent beings there must be a necessary being', 'There are contingent beings but no necessary being', 'The universe has a beginning', 'The universe is without beginning or end', 'The universe has a cause', 'The universe has no cause', 'The universe is an ordered whole', 'The universe is not an ordered whole'. What are we really asserting when we try to use these sentences to make statements? What conceivable experiences would count for or against their truth or falsity?

It is far from clear that anything would or could. 'The universe is an ordered whole' and 'The universe is not an ordered whole' both seem to be equally compatible with anything and everything that could conceivably be experienced. If you think you believe the universe is an ordered whole, what would you have to experience that would make you change your mind or even weaken your belief? If you cannot say at least to the extent of giving some indication of what you would have to experience, then *what* is the difference between your believing that the universe is an ordered whole and your not believing it is an ordered whole? If you cannot specify what one states and the other does not, if you cannot show some conceivable differential in experience between them, then pray tell what is the difference between them? How can you for yourself distinguish them other than in a *purely verbal* manner? And if there is only this purely verbal difference, then is there really a difference between them or are they *ersatz* statements masquerading as genuine factual statements? (In speaking of the latter, I am speaking of statements that are true or probably true if such and such occurs or obtains, and are otherwise false or probably false.)

Compare 'The universe is an ordered whole' or 'The universe has a cause' with a genuine factual statement, for example, 'There are squirrels on Korcula'. I do not know whether there are or are not, but if I actually believe that there are and I assert that there are, if you believe me and if you think my statement is true, you know what differential in experience makes you believe the statement to be true, and you know what you have to experience in order to be justified in believing it to be false. And so it is with all genuinely factual statements.

This is not the case, however, with 'The universe is an ordered whole' or 'The universe has a cause'. Orthodox believers want to say that it is true—that it is a fact—that the universe is an ordered whole. But such a sentence seems to lack all factual content, to be devoid of the kind of intelligibility it must have to make a true or false statement of fact. We have no idea of what we would have to experience or fail to experience in order to have some idea of whether it is true or false. Men who try to assert it and men who try to deny it do so in the face of the same experimental and experiential evidence. Neither the yea-sayers nor the nay-sayers can cite even a conceivable differential experience that would justify either a yea-saying or a nay-saying, or even distinguish the alleged claims made by the partners to the dispute.

Leave aside such abstract metaphysical-theological sentences—after all, some Kierkegaardian believers refuse to take them as legitimate parts of Christianity—and consider some sentences that play a key part in the actual religious life of Jews and Christians. Consider 'In the beginning was the word and the word was God', 'God shall raise the quick and the dead', 'God created man in His image and likeness', or 'God is our loving Father'. What would we have to experience in order to have the slightest reason to think any of these supposed statements are true or false? Imagine that you somehow persist after your body has long ago rotted away.[4] This sentence itself may be unintelligible or incoherent, but let us assume for the sake of the discussion that you know what it would be like to survive bodily death. But even then, would you know or even have grounds for believing it was *God* who had raised the dead? Do you have any idea what it would be like to see God or to have a vision of God? If you do, you should be able to describe what that would be like, or at least to give some tentative indication of what that would be like. You cannot legitimately say, 'Well, you will know what it is like then (in the hereafter),' for if you do not have any idea now what it is that you must see or encounter to encounter God, how will bodily death help you?

If I had *no* idea of what a mountain was like I would not, on being taken to the Himalayas, be able to recognize them as mountains, for I would not at all know what to look for in order to see mountains. In the case of the Himalayas someone might say, 'Well, the Himalayas are what you will see when you look north from Darjeeling on a clear day.' But I cannot legitimately say anything parallel to that when it comes to speaking of God. I cannot intelligently say, 'God is what you will see when you awaken from bodily death,' for people who believe in immortality believe that when they awaken 'on the other shore' they will encounter other things as well—other blessed souls, for example, or, depending on where they are, other damned souls. Presumably, in either case there will be a whole new world for them with all its trappings. If they have no idea of what it would be like to see God or encounter God *now*, they will then not be any better off, for they cannot know whether or not they have actually encountered Him there. To be simply told that God is what you will encounter when you 'awaken from bodily death' will not do, for upon awakening you will encounter many things. So how can you tell whether it is God you are encountering if you now have no idea of what it would be like to encounter God?[5]

It will not even help to be told 'God is what you will encounter there that is utterly unlike anything you have ever encountered before'. 'Utterly unlike' is the tricky phrase in this context. What in such a context counts as 'utterly unlike'? If the alleged experience of God is taken to be so utterly, utterly other that we have no idea of what will constitute this experience when we have shuffled off our mortal coils, then even in such a situation we will not know that it is *God* we have encountered or stood in the presence of. Many things, including our loved ones, will be very different, and we have not been told how unlike something must be in this context to be 'utterly unlike'.

Someone might respond, "Well, although our loved ones will be very different in the hereafter, God is that which is so utterly different that unlike other realities which are identifiable in the hereafter as the same reality as realities with which we are presently acquainted, God is not *in any way* like anything we have experienced." But then we have no criteria in virtue of which the referent for 'God' can be identified. We can only say what God is *not*. But now God is no longer distinguishable from 'nothing at all'. If, instead, we do specify somewhat more definitely what will count as being 'utterly unlike' in such a context, then we must already, at least vaguely, spell out to some extent what sort of a concept we have of God. Indeed, given the above experiential appeal, for such talk to be intelligible we must be able to articulate at least in general terms what would constitute a Divine encounter.[6] Then our original question returns: Do you have any idea at all of what this would be like? I do not think that you do.

III

So if we are going to speak coherently of a 'Divine Encounter' or a 'Beatific Vision' after the death of the body, it is crucial that we now have some idea of what would constitute such an encounter or such a vision. What does count as a Divine Encounter? How do you fill out the directions such that after the 'death of the body' you would have the slightest reason to believe that what you encountered was God? Remember that you must specify the relevant experience asceptically in nonreligious terms so that someone who had no understanding of religion could recognize his experience as the requisite experience. If you do not do that you go in a vicious circle. You explicate what is problematical in terms of something equally problematical. We are trying to understand what God-talk means, to understand what reference is made by such putatively referential terms as 'God' and 'the Divine'. To try to explicate them by equally opaque and problematical terms will not help. If they cannot be explicated—and no one seems to know what it would be like to do it—'God shall raise the quick and the dead' and the like most certainly seem to be factually unintelligible (without determinate factual content).

Think concretely and nonevasively about this. Whether you are or are not a believer, ask yourself what it would be like to encounter, experience, see, or have a vision of God. I do not think you can say what it would be like unless you so anthropomorphize God that He becomes something with a kind of gigantic body.

Such a God would plainly be a religiously inadequate concept of God. If that were your God, you would be believing in an idol. From a religious point of view it would be blasphemy to believe in such a God. However, as soon as you try to spiritualize God, as soon as you deanthropomorphize your concept of God so that you try to think of a 'Pure Spirit', you no longer have the remotest idea what it would be like to have a vision of God. Thus, you do not understand what it means to say 'God raised the quick and the dead' or 'God is the maker of the heavens and the earth'. 'God' becomes a kind of empty word to fill in the blank before '——— raised the quick and the dead', '——— made the world', and the like.[7]

If you think that is too quick or the notion of an 'empty word' itself too obscure, consider this: If you profess to believe in God, what would lead you to give up your belief if you did encounter this reality, or see it, or have a vision of it, now or hereafter? If you profess not to believe, meaning by that you believe that it is *false* that there is a God or false that God is the maker of the heavens and the earth, what is it that would lead you to abandon your disbelief and say, 'I have been wrong; it is indeed true that there is a God' if you did encounter it, see it, or have a vision of it now or hereafter? I do not believe that either such a believer or such a nonbeliever can answer that question. But if they cannot, and if you cannot, then are not such beliefs *ersatz* beliefs, for are not your putative statements of belief devoid of factual content? I believe they are.

IV

Let us consider one further case to drive home the point that the very meaning of religious utterances involves a serious problem that is logically prior to the problem of the truth of religious claims. Consider 'God loves His children'. This (or so it would seem) is quite parallel to 'Jones loves his children'. But we know what counts as evidence for or against the claim that Jones loves his children. With God it is very different, however. Six million of His children are brutally murdered in a few years in Germany, some five hundred thousand to a million more during an anti-Communist frenzy in Indonesia, and another million in Vietnam. Yet God does not in any way act to prevent such slaughters. An earthquake kills thousands in Turkey, millions starve in Brazil and India and Biafra, yet our Heavenly Father does nothing. An earthly father who allowed such things to happen to his children when he could prevent them would never be properly called 'a loving father'. Yet no matter what horrors befall man—'God's children' to adopt once more the idiom—believers do not retract their claim that God loves his children.

This is not how we use 'Jones loves his children'. If Jones tortured them to death—not to save their souls and not in order to prevent their undergoing even a worse torment and death at the hands of someone else, but just for 'kicks'—he could not possibly correctly be called 'a loving father'. If we tried to do that, 'love' would either no longer be functioning as a descriptive term, that is, it would no longer characterize anything, or it would now be used in a way opposite to its normal employment. Where we are talking about human love, 'loving' marks out some differential in experience such that certain things count toward establishing that someone acts in a loving manner and certain things count against it. For this reason it could not be correct in *all* conceivable circumstances to assert that Jones loves his children. But believers so use 'God loves His children' that it is perfectly correct to make this putative assertion in all conceivable circumstances. Then what is the difference between 'God loves His children' and 'God does not love His children'? In what way does God's love differ from God's anything, if 'God loves His children' is to be asserted no matter what happens? If any action of God must (logically must) be a loving action, then loving no longer qualifies action and it becomes meaningless to say either 'God loves His children' or 'God does not love His children'.

Moreover, and independently of the preceding points, loving involves action, and how could a 'bodiless person' (assuming we know what that means) act? 'Bodiless action' seems quite meaningless, but if that is meaningless then 'God's actions' or 'The acts of God' is also meaningless. If such phrases are meaningless, then 'God loves His children' is meaningless.

Because of considerations of this sort, the central claims in Jewish and Christian God-talk seem to be devoid of factual intelligibility. But it is surely this kind of intelligibility that Theistic belief requires, for Jews and Christians must take it to be a fact that God loves His children, that God shall raise the quick and the dead, and most fundamentally of all that there is a God.[8]

V

It is a popular tactic in religious apologetics to try to escape this difficulty about the meaning of key religious utterances by saying, 'You must take them on faith. Faith must precede understanding. Do not get caught up in the speculative games that some philosophers play'.

There is, however, a fundamental confusion in this apologetic tactic when applied to questions of *meaning* as distinct from questions of *truth-finding*. If the fideistic believer in question already understands the *meaning* of these utterances but does not know if what they assert is true, it is at least intelligible, although perhaps irrational (apropos our arguments in the preceding chapter), to make a fideistic appeal after the fashion of Pascal or Kierkegaard. He might in such a circumstance accept them on faith without conceptual impropriety. But if he literally does not understand them—cannot make out what they claim—then he cannot take them on faith no matter how desperately he may want to do so, for he does not understand *what* to take on faith.

Suppose I say, "The Neckar thinks." You say, "What does that mean? What are you talking about?" I reply, "Never mind, just take it on faith." But this makes no sense. You cannot possibly fulfill my request, for you do not know *what* to take on faith—what to do to accept it humbly on trust. In order to be able to do that you would have to understand the meaning of the utterance in question. Only if you already understand what it means can you possibly take it on faith. Thus, faith cannot precede understanding, and one cannot settle these perplexing and harassing problems concerning meaning by an appeal to faith.[9]

VI

There is another kind of objection to what I have been arguing that is perhaps less likely to occur to someone who has not engaged in an academic study of philosophy. It is an even more powerful and more central objection than any we have hitherto considered in this chapter, although it is still an objection that can be met, in my opinion. The objection is this: In my argument I have assumed, without making it explicit, a certain criterion of meaning—a certain doctrine about what it makes sense to say. But it has frequently been argued that this criterion is in effect an empiricist dogma that is far too narrow, too parochial to be acceptable.

I simply have dogmatically assumed, it will be argued, that a proposition is devoid of factual meaning (factual content or significance) if there is not at least some conceivable evidence for or against the putative proposition in question.[10] This in turn assumes that we cannot possibly know that a factual proposition is true or false unless we have some empirical evidence for or against it. Note 'empirical evidence' appears at least to be a redundancy. But, it is countered, it is just this that is the hidden dogmatic assumption in my argument. It simply takes 'empirical facts' to be a redundancy and 'metaphysical facts' to be an unintelligible collocation of words. This simply dogmatically rules out by stipulation—by *definitional fiat*—any possibility of knowing what is the case, what is so, nonempirically. And it is here that we have an unjustified empiricist dogma.[11]

This complex issue cannot be discussed here, although we shall discuss it in later chapters when we consider the verification principle. But we should note how very essential abstract questions of meaning are to philosophy—to concrete, live philosophical problems that harass people. Central difficulties—although not all the difficulties—in the proofs for the existence of God turn on questions of what it makes sense to say. Questions about the intelligibility or coherence of God-talk are at the very heart of philosophical reflections about God. And whether it makes any sense for you to remain Jews, Christians, or Moslems depends on large measure on such abstruse considerations.

This may seem like an arrogant claim, but note that if my *argument* about God-talk is correct, sentences such as 'God created the heavens and the earth', 'The universe has a cause', and 'God loves mankind' are without the kind of intelligibility they must have if Judaism, Christianity, and Islam are to contain a viable set of beliefs. That is, they purport to be factual statements and yet, if my argument is correct, they are actually devoid of factual intelligibility. Perhaps my criterion of factual intelligibility is in some way too narrow. We return quite naturally and unavoidably to abstract and indeed difficult questions of meaning.

Without arguing in this chapter whether my criterion of factual intelligibility is too narrow (although I shall so argue later when we discuss verifiability), I ask you to consider carefully the following questions: What would it be like to know that something is so—that something is a truth about the universe—nonempirically?[12] You know 'Puppies are young dogs' and 'Wives are women' are true without making any observations, because their truth is determined by our linguistic conventions. In short, they are analytic, but as such—as we have seen—they are nonrevelatory about the nature of the world. Consider this question very seriously: What (if anything) can you know about the nature of your world that does not *in the last analysis* rest on observation? Ask yourself honestly and nonevasively what nonempirical knowledge you have of anything. If you reply that you have an 'intuition of being', 'a grasp of a Pure Divine

Thou that is not an it', 'an encounter with God', 'a revelation of Divinity', 'an awareness of the truth of Being, the Encompassing or of metaphysical facts', ask yourself honestly if you do really have such encounters, intuitions, and the like.

Think carefully about what is involved here and about the meaning of the constituent terms in these obscure phrases. Could you really have an *encounter* with a *transcendent* being? Then how could it be transcendent? After all, when we say God is transcendent, we are trying to say that He is transcendent *to the world*. And if you say 'But God is both transcendent and immanent and so He can after all be encountered', you again have the old problem of anthropomorphism and of a being that is properly called 'God' still having a body, for unless this assumption is made what is *it* that becomes immanent? Think carefully about the meaning of your words in such contexts. Ask yourself if you really have anything like genuine knowledge or understanding here.

I am confident that you do not. I think you are using 'empty words' devoid of sense. I think that if you will reflect carefully on what you are saying in such contexts, you will come to see, in Hume's celebrated phrase, that what you are saying is "all sophistry and illusion." But my final remarks here remain basically *ad hominem*; they are fundamentally of value only in getting you carefully and sceptically to reflect on your own discourse and your own claims when you engage in God-talk. My remarks are designed to prod you to try to do what I think you will fail to accomplish, namely, to make sense of the central strands in your own religious discourse. Any further argument on this issue would take us into a discussion of the scope and the suitability of what philosophers call the verifiability or testability criterion of meaning. Keep in mind, however, that in the arguments I have deployed here I have only utilized it as a *criterion* of *factual intelligibility* (factual significance).

Remember also that Jews and Christians must believe that it is a fact that there is a God, that He created man, that He protects man, and the like; taken as claims about an anthropomorphic being—'a God up there'—they are patently false factual claims, and this is now widely recognized by believers and nonbelievers alike. Spiritualizing the Deity, as we now do, we gradually get putative claims that go beyond any conceivable confirmation or disconfirmation, either direct or indirect, and thus we get a claim that is devoid of factual intelligibility. As I pointed out, my 'thus' will surely be challenged, and the merits of this challenge will have to be discussed in subsequent discussions of the verifiability criterion.

For the present I shall end this discussion with this question: If you are either a believer or a nonbeliever who believes that it is false or probably false that there is a God, what would you have to experience, now or 'hereafter', in order for you to come to change your mind? If neither believer nor nonbeliever can say, and if—to put the point in a somewhat weaker way—no experience actual or conceivable is relevant to the truth or falsity of your beliefs, just what are you believing or disbelieving? Do you really understand what you are trying to assert or deny when you engage in God-talk? I doubt very much that you do.

NOTES

1. The central considerations here are well expressed in some of the essays in A. Flew and A. MacIntyre (eds.), *New Essays in Philosophical Theology.* I owe the terminological distinction here to Professor Adel Daher. Note also the references in footnote 9 in Chapter 19.

2. The phrase 'God-talk' may suggest a disrespectful or abusive attitude toward religion on my part, but this was not my intent. 'Religious discourse' is too wide a term, for there are religions without God. 'Talk about God' and 'Talk of God' are too narrow, for I want a term to cover all reference to God.

3. That reasonably orthodox believers at least take them to have such factual intelligibility is shown by John Hick, "Christianity," vol. 1 of Paul Edwards (ed.), *The Encyclopedia of Philosophy;* by I. M. Crombie, "The Possibility of Theological Statements," in Basil Mitchell (ed.), *Faith and Logic,* and by F. C. Copleston, S.J., *Contemporary Philosophy,* chapter VII.

4. I do not mean to suggest that I think that immortality is a coherent concept, and I only suppose for the sake of the argument here that it is. For an extended and careful discussion of immortality see Terence Penelhum, *Survival and Disembodied Existence.*

5. I have developed this argument fully in my "Eschatological Verification," in George Abernethy and Thomas Langford (eds.), *Philosophy of Religion* (second edition).

6. I have brought out some of the difficulties in the very idea of such an encounter in Chapter 18. Ronald Hepburn in *Christianity and Paradox,* chapters 3 and 4, exhibits more fully the incoherence of such theological claims.

7. Axel Hägerström has some important things to say about the concept of an empty word in his *Philosophy and Religion.*

8. Note the references in footnote three in this connection.

9. I have elaborated this point more fully in my "Can Faith Validate God-Talk?" in Martin E. Marty and Dean G. Peerman (eds.), *New Theology No. 1,* pp. 131–149. I have blocked similar appeals to revelation in my "The Primacy of Philosophical Theology," *Theology Today,* vol. XXVII (July, 1970).

10. The claim I defend here has been sharply argued for by Robert Hoffman in his "Theistic Religion as Regression," *Insight,* (winter, 1966) and responded to in the same issue by John J. Lakers, Ferdinand Etzkorn, and Alden L. Fisher. Note also Hoffman's reply in the subsequent issue. For a clear statement of some standard arguments that maintain this is an empirical dogma, see F. C. Copleston, S.J., op cit., chapters 1 through 4, and E. L. Mascall, *Words and Images,* pp. 1–14. The latter is reprinted in George Abernethy and Thomas Langford (eds.) *Philosophy of Religion* (second edition).

11. This objection has been forcefully argued by F. C. Copleston, S.J., in his

debate with A. J. Ayer. See A. J. Ayer and F. C. Copleston, "Logical Positivism—A Debate," in Paul Edwards and Arthur Pap (eds.), *A Modern Introduction to Philosophy* (2nd ed.).

12. I also discuss this issue in some detail in my *Quest for God.*

SUPPLEMENTARY READINGS
CHAPTERS 13 THROUGH 21

Books

Allen, Diogenes, *The Reasonableness of Faith* (Washington, Cleveland: Corpus Books, 1968).

*Alston, William P. (ed.), *Religious Belief and Philosophical Thought* (New York: Harcourt, Brace & World, 1963).

Aquinas, Thomas, *Philosophical Texts*, edited and translated by T. Gilby, (Oxford: Oxford University Press, 1951).

*Blackstone, William T., *The Problem of Religious Knowledge* (Englewood Cliffs, N.J.: Prentice-Hall, 1963).

Diamond, Malcolm L., and Thomas V. Litzenburg, Jr. (eds.), *Theology and Verification* (Indianapolis, Ind.: Bobbs-Merrill, 1970).

Feuerbach, Ludwig, *The Essence of Christianity*, translated by George Eliot (New York: Harper & Row, 1957).

Feuerbach, Ludwig, *Lectures on the Essence of Religion*, translated by Ralph Manheim (New York: Harper & Row, 1967).

*Flew, Antony, *God and Philosophy* (London: Hutchinson's, 1966).

Flew, Antony, and Alasdair MacIntyre (eds.), *New Essays in Philosophical Theology* (New York: Macmillan, 1955).

Hägerström, Axel, *Philosophy and Religion*, translated by Robert T. Sandin (London: G. Allen, 1964).

*Hepburn, Ronald, *Christianity and Paradox* (London: C. A. Watts. 1958).

*Hick, John (ed.), *The Existence of God* (New York: Macmillan, 1964).

Hick, John, *Faith and Knowledge*, second edition (Ithaca, N.Y.: Cornell University Press, 1966).

Hick, John (ed.), *Faith and the Philosophers* (New York: St. Martin's, 1964).

*Hick, John, *Philosophy of Religion* (Englewood Cliffs, N.J.: Prentice-Hall, 1963).

High, Dallas M. (ed.), *New Essays on Religious Language* (New York: Oxford University Press, 1969).

Hook, Sidney (ed.), *Religious Experience and Truth* (New York: New York University Press, 1961).

Hume, David, *Dialogues Concerning Natural Religion*, edited and with an introduction by Norman Kemp Smith (Indianapolis, Ind.: Bobbs-Merrill, 1947).

Kierkegaard, Soren, *Concluding Unscientific Postscript*, translated by David F. Swenson (Princeton, N. J.: Princeton University Press, 1941).

Kierkegaard, Soren, *The Sickness Unto Death*, translated and with an introduction and notes by Walter Lowrie (Garden City, N.Y.: Doubleday, 1955).

*MacIntyre, Alasdair, and Paul Ricoeur, *The Religious Significance of Atheism* (New York: Columbia University Press, 1961).

*Matson, Wallace I., *The Existence of God* (Ithaca, N.Y.: Cornell University Press, 1965).

*Mitchell, Basil, "Neutrality and Commitment" (Oxford, England: Inaugural the University of Oxford, 1969).

Mitchell, Basil (ed.), *Faith and Logic* (London: G. Allen, 1957).

Paley, William, *Natural Theology* (Indianapolis, Ind.: Bobbs-Merrill, 1963).

Penelhum, Terence, *Survival and Disembodied Existence* (New York: Humanities Press, 1970).

Phillips, D. Z. (ed.), *Religion and Understanding* (Oxford: Basil Blackwell, 1967).

*Pike, Nelson (ed.), *God and Evil* (Englewood Cliffs, N.J.: Prentice-Hall, 1964).

*Reardon, B. M. G. (ed.), *Religious Thought in the Nineteenth Century* (London: Cambridge University Press, 1966).

Religion and Humanism (London: British Broadcasting Corporation, 1964).

Santoni, Ronald E. (ed.), *Religious Language and the Problem of Religious Knowledge* (Bloomington, Ind.: Indiana University Press, 1968).

Talk of God, Royal Institute of Philosophy Lectures, Vol. 2: 1967–1968 (New York: St. Martin's, 1968).

*Toulmin, Stephen, Ronald W. Hepburn, and Alasdair MacIntyre, *Metaphysical Beliefs: Three Essays* (London: SCM Press, 1957).

Articles and Pamphlets

Clarke, B. C., "Linguistic Analysis and the Philosophy of Religion," *Monist*, vol. 47, no. 3 (spring, 1963).

Cody, Arthur B., "On the Difference It Makes," *Inquiry*, vol. 12 (winter, 1969).

Daher, Adel, "God and Logical Necessity," *Philosophical Studies*, vol. XVIII (The National University of Ireland, 1969).

Daher, Adel, "God and Factual Necessity," *Religious Studies*, vol. 6 (1970).

*Hick, John, "Theology's Central Problem" (Birmingham, England: Inaugural Lecture at the University of Birmingham, 1967).

Levin, David Michael, "Reasons and Religious Belief," *Inquiry*, vol. 12 (winter, 1969).

Miller, John F., "Theology, Falsification, and the Concept of *Weltanschaung*," *Canadian Journal of Theology*, vol. XVI (1970).

Nielsen, Kai, "The Intelligibility of God-talk," *Religious Studies*, vol. 6, (1970).

*Nielsen, Kai, "In Defense of Atheism," in Howard Kiefer and Milton Munitz eds.), *Perspectives in Education, Religion and the Arts* (Albany, N.Y.: State University Press of New York, 1970).

*Nielsen, Kai, "Language and the Concept of God," *Question*, no. 2 (January, 1969).

Nielsen, Kai, "On Fixing the Reference Range of 'God'," *Religious Studies*, vol. 1 (October, 1966).

Nielsen, Kai, "On Speaking of God," *Theoria*, vol. XXVIII (1962, part 2).

*Nielsen, Kai, "Religious Perplexity and Faith," *Crane Review*, vol. VIII, no. 1 (fall, 1965).

*Penelhum, Terence, "Faith, Fact and Philosophy," *Toronto Quarterly* (1956).

Phillips, D. Z., "From World to God," *Aristotelian Society*, supplementary vol. XLI (1967).

*Phillips, D. Z., "Religious Belief and Philosophical Enquiry," *Theology*, vol. LXXI (March, 1968).

*Phillips, D. Z., "Subjectivity and Religious Truth in Kierkegaard," in Jerry H. Gill (ed.), *Philosophy Today*, no. 2. (London: Collier-Macmillan, 1969).

Smart, Ninian, "Interpretation and Mystical Experience," *Religious Studies*, vol. 3, no. 1 (1967).

*Smart, Ninian, "Theology, Philosophy and the Natural Sciences" (Birmingham, England: Inaugural Lecture at the University of Birmingham, 1962).

Thornton, J. C., "Religious Belief and 'Reductionism'," *Sophia*, vol. V, no. 3 (October, 1966).

Williams, Bernard, "Has 'God' a Meaning?" *Question* (February, 1968).

Yandell, Keith, "Empiricism and Theism," *Sophia*, vol. VII (October, 1968). Comments by Kai Nielsen.

IV

JUSTIFICATION
AND
ETHICS

22

MORALITY
AND GOD

I

There are certain fundamental conceptual problems that have in one form or another perplexed and harassed man throughout his history. They are by no means the only basic philosophical problems, but they are the ones that have the most immediate human relevance. Freedom, God, and morality have remained perennial problems for the human animal; what I am, what can I do, what can I know, what ultimate commitments (if any) are worthy of my allegiance, are questions that can arouse anxiety and demand attention.

I have tried to say something about what we can do (about the extent and nature of our freedom of conduct) and about what we can know, including whether we can know that there is a God. I have argued that there is moral freedom even in a deterministic world, and that we do not have good grounds for believing there is a God or for accepting Judaism or Christianity or any religion of that order. I wish now to turn to questions about the foundations of morality: Must we or should we as rational beings be as skeptical about the foundations of morality or the objectivity of even the most reflective moral beliefs as we should be about the claims of theistic belief? It is to this question or rather cluster of questions that I now turn.

In the present chapter I want to begin this inquiry and to finish off some unfinished business from our discussion of religion. When we discussed the fideistic arguments of James and Kierkegaard, it became evident that one central fideistic gambit—or appeal, if you prefer—was the claim that to make sense of one's life, to find a humanly tolerable basis for morality, we must believe in God. I said then that this is an assumption that needs justifying. I wish here to examine its rationale and in the course of that examination to argue that the assumption made by James and Kierkegaard is not justified. In doing this I wish to put aside all our previous skeptical questions about the truth and the coherence of God-talk. *For the sake of the argument of this chapter,* I am willing to assume that it not only makes sense to postulate such 'a reality' but that it is indeed true that there is one infinite Creator of all other things; that there is an infinite, uncreated, eternal, personal reality transcendent to the world, who created all that exists other than Himself, and who sustains and protects all His creation. I, of course, do not believe that there is such 'a reality', but I want now to consider whether it is the case that only if such 'a reality' exists can morality have an adequate foundation.

More generally, is it true—as many theologians, religious apologists, and even some secularists maintain—that the viability of moral beliefs is dependent on a belief in God?[1] That is, is it the case that without such a religious commitment morality is groundless and life is without significance? If this is indeed so, it might very well be better to take 'Kierkegaard's out' and, since religious discourse has *some* kind of sense, make with fear and trembling the leap of faith, hoping against hope that one's religious formulas are sufficiently intelligible so that such a faith will not be a self-defeating, senseless act. This leap of faith, as our examination of Kierkegaard has brought out, is, even more than he acknowledged, a very risky undertaking. Thus, it is of the utmost importance to discover if morality requires a belief in God.

I want to examine the claim, so frequently made by both believers and nonbelievers alike, that the very possibility of a significant life and an adequate morality stand or fall with a belief in God, that is, an infinite transcendent Creator of the heavens and the earth. Give up a belief in God, it is claimed, and morality becomes either unintelligible or thoroughly inadequate. This apologetic claim has several forms. Some theologians argue that there can be no morality without a belief in God; others claim the milder thesis that a secular ethic—any secular ethic—is inadequate when compared with an ethic inspired and informed by theistic commitments.

To me, both of these claims seem groundless. It seems to me that just the reverse is true; that is, a certain amount of moral insight, which logically speaking is prior to and logically independent of religion, is necessary for us even to understand and accept the God of the Biblical tradition. I shall also argue that it is not true that religious moralities are superior to all or even to most secular moralities. There are indeed some religious moralities—for example, a Quaker morality, let us say—that are superior to some secular moralities—for example, the moral code of Stalin or de Sade. But secular morality at its best has not been shown to be inferior to religious morality at its best; and in its *theoretical foundations*, secular morality, I shall argue, is far more adequate. When Reinhold Niebuhr claims that religious ideas are the ultimate basis for moral standards and that Christian faith is the essential foundation of any adequte morality, he says something that is flatly contrary to the truth.

Such confident declamation on my part, as well as on Niebuhr's, may seem unseemly in philosophy. I engage in it to make it evident where I stand and to make explicit the claims and counterclaims that need to be *argued* (reasoned out).

There is a preliminary that should be attended to in order to avoid an elementary confusion. It is customary within the Jewish, Christian, and Islamic religions to distinguish between religious cults, religious moral codes, and religious creeds or doctrines. It would of course be absurd to maintain that morality is independent of religious *moral* codes, for they are themselves distinctive types of morality. What the claim concerning the logical independence of morality from religion comes to is the claim that morality, including religious morality, is logically independent of religious doctrine or religious creeds. That is—to put the point more precisely—the claim is that we cannot deduce what we ought to do or discover how we ought to live from coming to know that there is an infinite all-knowing, all-powerful being who created us and who wills and commands that we do certain things. From such fundamental nonevaluative statements of religious doctrine, I shall argue, we cannot derive any moral claims at all or find in them any adequate ground for moral belief, let alone the sole morally and humanly acceptable foundation of morality.

II

It is customary to ask people who argue for the independence of morality from religion, 'Well, where did you *get* your moral beliefs if not from your religion?' The answer should be, 'From my parents and teachers—the people who surrounded me in my childhood'. But this is obviously not the answer that the questioner wanted. Perhaps he wanted to know where moral ideas and a sense of moral obligation come from in the first place. Are some of them innate? Did they all arise through social stimulation? Did they come from God or what not?

What must be seen is that the answer to this, whatever it is, is not very important morally or philosophically. It seems to me most reasonable to assert that because of a certain fairly evident biological homogeneity in *homo sapiens,* certain things always cause pleasure or pain and would consequently come to be said to be good or bad, and certain things are wanted or needed and certain things feared or hated and consequently would come to be said to be right or wrong. It should be quickly added that these "root natural goods" are indeed deeply affected by social stimulation. Yet, it is in some such way that moral ideas arise and take hold on people. But, as I said, how they arise is unimportant; what is important is their present status and function.[2]

Do moral claims admit of objective justification, or in the last analysis are they merely the expression of the feelings of those who make them? If they are *merely* the expression of the whims of mortal will, then they do not and cannot make a significant claim to truth. Yet, that we would not have any moral ideas except for the fact that we have certain emotions or attitudes does not at all establish that moral ideas are simply expressions and evocations of emotions or attitudes that in turn tend to stimulate action. That fact, if it is a fact, only establishes something about how moral ideas come about. We must not forget that the *origin* of a belief does not determine its truth or falsity. That Hitler or Stalin first thought of a certain contention does not *ipso facto* make it false. There is one crucial question to ask about any serious claim, no matter where or how it arose: Is there evidence or grounds for its truth or falsity? With respect to moral beliefs we must ask: However our moral beliefs arose, is there or is there not evidence for their truth? Is there any reason to believe that any moral claim, or at least any fundamental moral claim, is true? The central question is: Are any moral beliefs or commitments—including our most precious ones—objective, or are they all subjective?

I should say a little about what would count as a 'subjective' or 'objective' judgment here. A moral utterance and thus the belief or attitude expressed by that utterance is subjective if it *merely* expresses or describes (or both expresses and describes) the attitudes or feelings of the utterer or his cultural group, and is simply used by him or them to evoke or invite similar attitudes in others. If all moral judgments are as they are characterized here, they cannot correctly be said to be true or false in a manner that would make their truth or falsity independent of the particular and contingent attitudes of the maker of the moral judgment or of the people in his cultural circle.

To claim that some moral judgments are objective is to claim that there are some moral judgments that are either true or false and that their truth or falsity does not depend on the peculiarities of the person who makes the judgment or the culture to which he belongs. The particular contention we need to examine here is the claim that moral judgments can be objective and true only if these moral judgments are somehow rooted in or based on a belief in God.

III

Consider the old conundrum: 'Is something good or obligatory because it is willed or commanded by God, or is it willed or commanded by God because it is good or obligatory?'.

If we take the latter alternative, goodness or obligatoriness is not logically dependent on God. God commands or wills something because it is good or obligatory; but then there is something that God acknowledges to be good or obligatory that in no logically essential way depends on God. It would be good or obligatory even in a world without God.

Suppose instead we take the first alternative. Something is good or obligatory because it is *willed* or *commanded* by God.[3] But why does the fact, or does the fact, that something is willed or commanded create an obligation or make something good? If a commandant of an air base orders everyone to take exercises at 4:30 A.M. every morning, it does not follow that what he commands is good. If I tell my wife *not* to wear lipstick, it does not follow that her not wearing lipstick is a good thing. If a Hitler, Franco, or Stalin commanded something or proclaimed that a certain thing must be done, it certainly would follow that people under their control would find it prudent to obey. It does not at all follow, however, that they have a moral obligation to obey, or that what was commanded, enjoined, proclaimed, ordered, or willed was the morally right thing to do—good or desirable from a moral point of view. These edicts, commands, or orders in and of themselves cannot make something good or obligatory.

If we drop the fearsome three and turn to God the case is different. It is *God's* commanding it or *God's* willing it or *God's* ordaining it that makes all the difference. Why does this make a difference? It makes a difference because *God* is the perfect good, and being the perfect good He could not command or proclaim what, everything considered, is evil.

It is indeed perfectly true that any Jewish or Christian religious believer who has a tolerable grasp of his faith must believe that.[4] He must believe that or he will no longer be even a remotely orthodox Jew or Christian. But *how* does the believer know that God is good? It is clear that this is an odd question. This is not something that a believer asks himself; he just takes it for granted that God is good. It is one of the 'givens' of the confessional group of which he is a member. Still, how does he *know* that this infinite maker of the world is good? What justification does he have for this assumption? And if to be a Jew or Christian commits him to making this assumption, what justification does he have for remaining a Jew or a Christian, given that he must make this assumption to remain in the circle of faith. (Recall vis-à-vis James and Kierkegaard that it was claimed that we were driven to God to make sense of morality. But in trying in turn to justify that claim, we seem to be driven to morality to justify our religious commitments.)

To dig out the central issue here, let us consider the status of 'God is good'. Is it nonanalytic and in some way a substantive claim? Is it analytic? Or does it have some still different anomalous status? (Remember that an analytic statement is a statement the denial of which is self-contradictory—for example, 'A bachelor is unmarried'.)

Let us first take it to be a substantive, nonanalytic claim. Taken in this way, it is quite appropriate to ask the believer what reason he has for believing it to be true. Suppose he says that his experience in life has made it evident to him that God is good. That is, he finds it impossible to deny that God is good after reflecting on and taking to heart the fact that God gave man life and sustains his life, that the world is ordered and beautiful, that the Divine Scriptures have great power and dignity, and that the way of life advocated by Judaism and Christianity is profoundly appealing.

Now let us assume what is indeed questionable, namely, that we do owe our existence to God, that the world is ordered and beautiful, and that the way of life advocated by Judaism and Christianity is profoundly appealing. Reflection on these facts (putative facts), let us assume, indeed does make it apparent that God (the infinite Creator of the heavens and the earth) is good. But this very argument shows, as clearly as anything can, that the believer has criteria logically independent of his belief that there exists an infinite Creator of the world, in virtue of which he decides that that infinite being is good. In coming to know that the infinite Creator of the world is good, or in justifying his belief that such a reality is good, he uses an independently derived criterion to judge that the person revealed to him in the Scriptures is good, that that person or power to whom we ultimately owe our lives is good, and the like. *Even if* his claims here were plainly and obviously true, it would still be the case that he had to use his own moral insight in making this judgment. Any other human being in a similar situation would have to do so as well. That is to say, to make this judgment we must use a moral criterion not logically grounded in our belief in God.

It is much more plausible to take 'God is good' to be analytic. If it is analytiç, then 'God is good', like 'A square is four-sided' or 'A wife is a woman', is a statement the denial of which is self-contradictory. On such a reading it does not make sense to ask how we know that God is good, for 'God is good'—like 'A bachelor is unmarried'—is true by definition.[5] And in this way, it is tempting to argue, we can see that morality is essentially dependent on religion.

It is just in this last claim that the believer makes his most subtle mistake. The actual facts are just the reverse. To understand as fully as a human being can what it is 'to believe in God', one must first have an independent understanding of and a criterion for what is good. In showing that this is so, I need not invoke any moral convictions of my own or invoke any 'saving myth' or *Weltanschauung*. I can establish this point simply by noting certain morally neutral features of the logic of language. The considerations here are strictly logical or conceptual and do not involve a moral commitment or any ultimate concern on my part.

'God is good', when used in Jewish and Christian religious discourse, does seem to me to be analytic in most of its employments. But now compare it with two logically parallel analytic statements: 'A square is four-sided' and 'A wife is a woman'. Neither of these statements is a definition though they are true *by* definition. The predicates in each case partially define the subject.

Notice first that in order to understand what was meant by a 'square' we would first have to understand the meaning of 'a four-sided figure'. Similarly, if we did not already know what a woman was, we could not understand what was meant by 'wife'. We have a parallel case with 'good' and 'God'. If we did not first understand what was meant by 'good', we could not possibly understand the Jewish and Christian concept of God. Nothing would or could be called 'God' in such a religion unless it were thought to be *worthy* of worship. We might be afraid of and awed by a great power who spoke out of a whirlwind; we might be fearful that such a being would destroy us or torment us, and so we would obey him. But simply by recognizing that he was a mysterious power, force, or necessary being, no matter how powerful, we would not know or have grounds for believing that such a reality was *worthy* of worship.

Under most circumstances, a necessary but not a sufficient condition for judging anything to be *worthy* of worship is to judge it to be *good*.[6] But we could not properly call any reality, being, unconditioned ground of being, foundation of the earth, or 'World-Ground', God unless we knew or had good reason to believe that it was *worthy* of worship. We could not even know or have a good reason to believe that such an unconditioned ground of all finite reality was good—let alone worthy of worship —from noting its necessity, power, or mysteriousness. That is, from simply knowing that there is a transcendent reality that is the supreme or absolute or unconditioned ground of all other being, we could not know or even have good grounds for believing that that reality was worthy of worship or was even good.

Within Jewish and Christian religious discourses, however, to call something 'God' is to give to understand that it is worthy of worship. But to know that a reality is worthy of worship, we would have to understand already what was meant by 'good' and to have a criterion of goodness. Since this is so, in this most fundamental respect at least, a minimal moral understanding or grasp of what is good and evil must be logically anterior to and logically independent of any knowledge or belief that there is an unlimited, eternal being who is the maker of the world and who is worthy of worship. So even if there is an infinite, all-powerful, necessary being who created man and proclaimed laws for man to obey, it does not follow that man's knowledge of good and evil is logically dependent on the existence of such a reality.

It might be replied that I am ignoring an important element in the believer's account, namely, his claim that if there were no God, man would not exist, so in that way man could not know good and evil. This causal dependence, however, does not imply logical dependence. It is crucial to note that for any man who would or could exist—or taking men who do now exist—they could not know that there is a God or even understand what the word 'God' means in Jewish and Christian discourse unless they already had some moral understanding or understanding of good and evil that has no *logical* dependence on their having a concept of God or on there actually being such a reality. It is in this fundamental sense that even in a theistic universe moral beliefs are independent of and not founded on religious ones.

Theologians conceive of the world in a topsy-turvy way. It is not that morality is dependent on belief in God. Quite the reverse. Without a logically prior moral understanding, man could have no grasp of the Judeo-Christian God. This can be seen from a logical examination of the very concepts in question. That some theologians and some plain folk think otherwise only attests to the fact that they are confused.

IV

It has been maintained that my preceding argument in effect ignores the possibility that 'God is good' may be neither analytic nor synthetic. Actually, 'God is good' may have some quite different status. Why assume all propositions must be one or the other? 'Orthodox Jews fast on the day of atonement' would be difficult to classify properly as either analytic or synthetic. It is not self-contradictory to assert, 'Martin is an orthodox Jew but he did not fast on the day of atonement', and several orthodox Jews not fasting on the day of atonement would not disconfirm our generalization. Thus, this obviously intelligible proposition seems to be neither analytic nor synthetic unless we are going to call it—simply giving a label to something not understood—'synthetic *a priori*'.[7]

Perhaps it is a mistake to maintain that anything as fluid as a natural language could be so neatly dichotomized. At least I will not argue for it here, and my argument for the independence of morality from religion will not turn on the assumption that analytic *a priori* or synthetic *a posteriori* are exhaustive alternatives. Yet, when we examine the actual use of 'God is good' in Christian and Jewish religious discourse, it certainly appears in its standard employments to be functioning analytically. It does not make sense for a Christian or a Jew to say, 'God ordained it but it is evil', 'It is God's will but it ought not to be done', or 'I believe in the Father, Son, and the Holy Ghost but they are evil forces'. Anyone who understands Jewish and Christian God-talk knows that within such universes of discourse and forms of life it is not open to someone who uses

'God' as Jews and Christians do to ask whether God is good. Such a putative question is as closed as the supposed question 'Are fathers males?'. 'God is evil' or 'God is not good' is self-contradictory for one who uses language as Jews and Christians do.

Such a defense of the analyticity of 'God is good' within Judeo-Christian religious discourse seems to me reasonable and very likely correct, but I am not entirely confident that it is unassailable, so let us not assume it in our discussion in this section. Perhaps 'God is good' has some different hitherto unspecified logical status. Let us consider the following alternative and consider its implications for grounding moral beliefs on a knowledge or well-grounded belief that God exists.

The alternative I have in mind is one urged by Patterson Brown in his "God and the Good".[8] 'God is perfectly good', he maintains, is neither a moral judgment nor an analytic one. Instead, it is the ultimate moral criterion for a Jew or a Christian. A Jew or Christian is morally obligated to do whatever God commands, and not to do whatever He prohibits. Rather than comparing 'God is perfectly good' to 'A square is four-sided', it should be compared to 'The scratches on the platinum-eridium bar in Paris are one meter apart'. Brown argues that this proposition "cannot accurately be characterized as either empirical or necessary." It is indeed true that given our actual metric standard, a table is a meter wide if and only if its edges would be coincident with the scratches on the Parisian bar were they brought together. But there is, Brown avers, no possible measurement—that is, confirmation or disconfirmation—of the statement 'The scratches on the bar in Paris are one meter apart'. Yet the meaning of 'meter', that is, 'the unit of length of the metric system', does not determine the truth of 'The scratches on the bar in Paris are one meter apart'. Other and conflicting criteria of metric length are perfectly compatible with the meaning of 'meter'. Rather than being either analytic or synthetic (here empirical), 'The scratches on the bar in Paris are one meter apart' simply states a standard. Moreover, the statement is plainly true, that is, what it states is so, although it asserts neither an empirical fact nor a definition nor anything that follows from a definition. What it does do is state the standard or criterion of metric measurement.[9] Yet, note it is true—and this is indeed peculiar—*because it is stipulated to be true.* Similarly, for Jews and Christians, Brown maintains, 'God is perfectly good' is neither analytic nor itself a moral judgment, but is a statement of the ultimate moral criterion in Judaism and Christianity.

Brown is perfectly correct in maintaining "that no one could properly be called a 'Jew' or 'Christian' if he felt free to disobey God on ethical grounds, or brazenly defended as good things which God condemned, or who was willing to pass independent judgment on God's actions or commands." That God willed it or ordained it, morally speaking, settles the matter for a Jew or a Christian. As a Jew or a Christian he has no moral alternative but to try to act in accordance with what he takes to be the will of God.

However, a Jew or a Christian is a man first and a Jew or Christian afterward. Becoming or remaining a Jew or a Christian means, among other things, *adopting* or continuing to *opt* for a certain way of life; it involves *adopting* or *opting* for a distinctive moral view of the world, and a belief *in*—as distinct from a belief *that involves*—an *affective* attitude toward God (the Creator of all finite things) and indeed a trust in Him.[10] But whether by one's own reflective decision one becomes a Jew or a Christian or whether one has simply imbibed it very much as one did one's mother tongue and continues as a member of a confessional group to hold to one's religious commitment, one must (logically must) as a man have made an even more fundamental moral or normative commitment in *becoming* or *remaining* a Jew or a Christian. That moral or normative commitment is that something could be and indeed is *worthy of worship*, and moreover, that what is worthy of worship is this infinite, transcendent, uncreated, eternal, personal Creator and sustainer of all finite things.[11] That is, in order to remain or become a Jew or a Christian, we must not only believe that such a reality exists but we must also come to believe that it ought to be worshiped, that is, that it merits worship.

Whether or not a given Jew or Christian is aware that this is an operative assumption in his belief is not crucial. What is crucial is that an analysis of the structure of his belief or the structure of Judeo-Christian discourse indicates that, acknowledged or not, such an assumption is operative.

My central point is that even if we know that a transcendent, absolute Creator of the world exists, we cannot from a statement asserting that such a reality exists derive (deduce) that such a reality is *worthy* of worship or that morally speaking we ought to do what such a reality wills. In becoming or remaining a Jew or a Christian, we do indeed decide that such a reality is *worthy* of worship and that His will is morally authoritative for us and in our judgment should be morally authoritative for all mankind. In *believing in* God, we *commit* ourselves to acting on His edicts. However, to come to believe in God—as distinct from simply knowing or believing that an infinite, transcendent Creator of the world exists—involves a decision or recognition on our part concerning what is *good and evil*, concerning what if anything is *worthy* of worship. This, as we have seen, cannot be derived from knowing that there is an infinite and all-powerful Creator of the heavens and the earth. To know whether we should use the laudatory label 'God' for such a creator and *believe in* such a creator necessarily involves an independent assessment on our part of what is good and evil. It must be an assessment in which we employ our own moral awareness, for it cannot simply be a conclusion that can be derived from the knowledge that an infinite, all-powerful Creator of the world exists. In fact, this logically prior moral understanding is necessary for one to become a Christian in Christendom.

V

Some theists might grant much and perhaps even all of what I have just argued and still claim that when we work out a morality in concrete detail and link it with a way of life, we will come to see that the only adequate morality is a morality grounded in a belief in God. They will grant that without some independent understanding of morality we could have no knowledge of God at all. But given this knowledge and given a perceptive grasp of the human condition, we will come to appreciate why it is that no purely secular morality can be adequate to man's needs. Man is a religious animal. Without a belief in God his life will remain fragmented and meaningless.[12]

Why should this be so? Or is it so? It can be argued reasonably enough, Dostoevsky notwithstanding, that all human beings seek happiness, and that human happiness is only obtainable in a world in which men can have some sense of what they are and why they are alive. But, many Christians and Jews will argue, if men do not view themselves as children of God, created by God with a purpose and with the hope of eternal life, no *true* happiness, no genuine sense of direction, is possible for them.

It should be noted that such a conception is very ethnocentric. There are religions—systems of salvation—that have no conception of God and of man as a creature of God. Theravada (Hinayana) Buddhism is a crucial case. There are other religions, for example, Confucianism, where belief in a deity or deities is extremely peripheral. Yet these religions have for a long time given orientation to men's lives and a sense of purpose to human existence. Similarly, as J. S. Mill has pointed out in his splendid essay "The Utility of Religion," the Greeks did not find their fundamental moral orientation in their religion.[13] Cultures such as the Theravadin communities of Ceylon and Burma have existed from time immemorial without a morality or a sense of life-orientation grounded in a belief in God. Once we recognize this, it should be apparent that only our "sacred culture"— that is, our local culture patterns—and our early indoctrination keep some of us from finding a meaningful life in a godless world.

There is nothing in human nature unadorned by our particular "sacred culture" to support the claim of St. Augustine, Pascal, Newman, and Tolstoy that man can find happiness and a direction in life only through a belief in God and in personal immortality. There are cultures without a belief in God or any kind of cosmic power and without a conception of personal immortality. And in these cultures men have lived their lives with as much sense of direction and with as much happiness as have Jews, Christians, and Moslems, even in the greatest ages of belief in the West. Why should we assume that there is something about us, apart from our early indoctrination, that makes it necessary that we believe in God to give direction to our lives? And in this connection we should not forget that there have been men at all times and in all places who have refused to warm themselves by their tribal campfires. Some of them have been fragmented men living dislocated lives, as have many men with a steadfast faith in God. But not all such nay-sayers to their "sacred culture" have felt so dislocated.

St. Thomas Aquinas is sometimes interpreted as claiming that while logically speaking morality is independent of religion and precedes religion, when dwelled upon deeply it leads to a belief in God. To have the kind of universality necessary to substantiate it, Aquinas' claim needs to be assessed from a cross-cultural point of view. But even a superficial cross-cultural evaluation makes it evident that what Aquinas claims to be the case plainly is not so.

That aside, even within our culture, if we are honestly empirical about such matters, it is apparent that Aquinas' claim is just not true. For some men, indoctrinated in a certain way, scrupulous and sensitive moral reflection does as a matter of fact lead them to believe in God; for other men, indoctrinated in another way, it does not. A student of mine in a first course in philosophy once wrote in a term paper, "Do I call on God in vain? Is He a concept of fantasy like a gremlin or gnome?" Yet, no doubt with anguish and turmoil of heart, this student went on to say, "I want to believe. I need to believe. Still the question gnaws at me, 'Is there a God?' " Surely this is a real and common enough human predicament.[14]

There is no doubt that some people, to preserve their mental equilibrium, very much need to believe in God. Many are not quite that bad off, but they would feel fragmented and dislocated without a belief in God. I recall conversing with a psychiatrist once after I had given a lecture on "Freud and Religion." This psychiatrist, who specialized in analyzing ministers and priests, was quite adamant in stressing that many people simply needed to believe in God. That is to say, people with certain psychological problems and a certain indoctrination very much need their religion. But this psychiatrist, who had been brought up as a Jew, found no need for religious belief for himself. What he was concerned to stress was that while many people do not need religion to give direction to their lives, some people would go to pieces without their belief in God.

This psychological reality must be faced by anyone who candidly and honestly examines whether it is true that an adequate morality needs to be a theistic religious morality. The religious person—the person with a Pascalian personality—must be careful not to move from 'I need to believe in God' to 'Man needs to believe in God' or even to 'I need a belief in God or my life will be pointless'. He may need a belief in God and he may *feel* that his life must be without purpose or without point if he gives up his belief in God. It does not *follow*, however, that his life will be without purpose if he does give up his belief in God. There can be purpose *in* life and one's life can have a purpose, even if one was *not* made for a purpose. One's life can have a purpose if there are things that are *worthwhile* doing and things that can bring joy and happiness. In a world without God there can be joys—love and friendship, for example. And it seems to me platitudinous to remind you that even in a godless world there remain all the joys of experience. That for each of us all these experiences must someday come to an end does not diminish their value but makes them all the more precious. Even in a world without God, we still have the task to relieve the awful burden of human suffering and degradation. There are people in India, Brazil, Vietnam, Biafra, South Africa, Mozambique, and the United States—to name a few conspicuous places—who are at this very moment suffering horribly and dying. There are men in some of these places who are doing things that dehumanize them and dehumanize their victims. Can this activity be justified or even excused? Is it an evil means we must tolerate in order to prevent a still greater evil? or do these things have no justified point or excuse, and never can—God or no God—have such a point or excuse?

Human suffering is evil. To inflict or tolerate it must always require a very considerable defense in a world where man is taken to be something of value. Our lives and the lives of our fellow humans are sufficiently important for us to think hard about these matters and to act nonevasively. All actions are not equivalent in a godless world. In such a world there are human concerns that plainly call forth our commitment.

In such a struggle against human suffering and against human degradation, one can find a sense of self and a sense of purpose. We need neither God nor the afterlife to give direction to our lives and to know something of human happiness. Men need not be made for a purpose in order for life to have a purpose and a point.

NOTES

1. Graeme de Graaff rightly points out that in considering this question we need to have clearly before our minds a distinctive concept of God or else our discussion will generate more heat than light. If to be moral is simply to live in *agapé*, and if to live in *agapé* is to believe in God, and if this is all that belief in God comes to, then indeed to be religious is to be moral and to be moral is to be religious. Atheists are converted by stipulative redefinition, but then there is and can be no problem at all about founding morality on a belief in God. I have taken the characterization of God of mainline Judeo-Christianity—the conception of God we saw

Anselm and Aquinas articulating—and I have posed my question in terms of that central conception of God. Graeme de Graaff gives a useful survey of the various problems posed in considering God and morality in his essay of that title in I. T. Ramsey (ed.), *Christian Ethics and Contemporary Philosophy* (New York: 1966), pp. 31–52.

2. See P. H. Nowell-Smith, "Morality: Religious and Secular," in I. T. Ramsey (ed.), ibid., pp. 95–112.

3. The point here would not be affected if we talked instead of what was demanded, ordained, or proclaimed by God. There are, as de Graaff points out, evident defects in a command theory of morality which are independent of considerations of religious morality. But the problems raised in this chapter concerning any religiously grounded morality do not rest on assuming what de Graaff calls a 'God's commands view of morality.' Graeme de Graaff, op. cit., 31–35.

4. To my amazement I have heard some students, under pressure of the kind of conceptual considerations raised in this chapter, deny that. Patterson Brown, however, has clearly shown, what seems evident anyway, that Jews and Christians do not and cannot question the perfect goodness of God, on pain of ceasing to be Jews and Christians. Patterson Brown, "God and the Good," *Religious Studies* (April, 1967), pp. 274–275. Whether this is unequivocally so for all the conceptions of God in the Old Testament is another matter.

5. Note that to be analytic a statement does not have to be a definition, but it must be true by definition.

6. I say 'under most circumstances necessary' for I do not wish to rule out demonolatry, that is, the worship of evil spirits, as unintelligible; I do not want to say 'The evil shades merit our worship, our celebration of the Black Mass' is self-contradictory. If we allow God-talk, as we now are, there is no reason not to allow demon-talk. However, it is not a possible (conceptually or logically possible) claim within Jewish-Christian religious discourses. There it is ruled *a priori* and by definitional fiat. A Jew or Christian cannot assert that something is *worthy* of worship or *merits* worship without giving you to understand that it is good. I owe this example to Professor Patterson Brown, though he tries to make, mistakenly in my judgment, the opposite point with it.

7. Someone might well reply that I am mistaken in thinking that 'Orthodox Jews fast on the day of atonement' is not analytic. It elucidates a characteristic of orthodox Jews *in general* and it would be self-contradictory to deny that orthodox Jews do not fast on the day of atonement. There is a condition of being an orthodox Jew (of being a member of the class of orthodox Jews) such that we could say 'fast on the day of atonement' is an expression standing for a defining characteristic of orthodox Jews taken as a class. But vis-à-vis some individual, say Martin, it does not function in this way. It applies to him if he does such and such and not if he does otherwise. Thus, 'Martin is an orthodox Jew but he did not fast on the day of atonement' is not self-contradictory. Rather, it is an empirical claim. But this does not show, as my argument in section IV of this chapter claimed, 'Orthodox Jews fast on the day of atonement' is not analytic.

8. Patterson Brown, op. cit., pp. 269–276.
9. See Brown's argument for this. Ibid., p. 271.
10. I argue in some detail in my "On Believing that God Exists," *The Southern Journal of Philosophy*, vol. 5 (fall, 1967), pp. 167–172, that there is an important difference here, that in religious discourse 'belief that' is logically presupposed by 'belief in,' and that belief in God involves having a certain attitude toward God. See also J. J. C. MacIntosh "Believing In," *Mind* (July, 1970).
11. That this question is a subject of lively moral debate rather than simply something everyone assumes is shown in articles by H. J. McCloskey and Charles Hartshorne in *The Southern Journal of Philosophy*, vol. 2 (winter, 1964), pp. 157–168.
12. John Hick in part IV of his *Faith and Knowledge* (second edition) argues in this way, and Alasdair MacIntyre once did too in his *Difficulties in Christian Belief*. I have attempted to refute their specific claims in my "An Examination of an Alleged Theological Basis of Morality," *The Illiff Review*, vol. XXI, no. 2 (fall, 1964), pp. 39–49 and in "Morality and God," *Philosophical Quarterly*, vol. 12, no. 47 (April, 1962), pp. 129–137. MacIntyre has indicated his own reversal of his position in Alasdair MacIntyre and Paul Ricoeur, *The Religious Significance of Atheism*. See also Antony Flew, "Two Views of Atheism," *Inquiry*, vol. 2 (winter, 1969).
13. This essay, together with "Nature," his important criticism of natural law conceptions of ethics, is reprinted in Marshall Cohen (ed.), *The Philosophy of J. S. Mill*. A similar argument to the central argument of this chapter is reprinted in J. B. Schneewind (ed.), *Mill's Ethical Writings*, pp. 81–82.
14. Americans and Canadians brought up amidst American and Canadian religiosity should not overemphasize the pervasiveness of this among educated Westerners. One should reflect on the remark of the Norwegian philosopher Herman Tennessen that "Atheism is extinct in the more advanced parts of the world—for lack of opposites. A serious atheist is considered in Scandinavia a slightly ludicrous bore. The myths are neither pompously condemned nor solemnly repudiated, but rather conceived as sweet and charming subjects for art and poetry—like old-fashioned steam engines and antique hot-water bottles. Needless to say, the myths have in this form totally lost all consolation potentialities." Herman Tennessen, "Happiness Is for the Pigs: Philosophy versus Psychotherapy," in *Journal of Existentialism*, vol. VII, no. 26, (winter, 1966/67), p. 200. And such an attitude about belief in God can coexist side by side with an intense and brooding concern about 'the meaning of life'—as in Ingmar Bergman's films or Pär Lagerkvist's novels and plays.

23

ETHICS
AND CULTURAL
RELATIVISM

I

We have seen how it is not possible to ground moral beliefs in religious beliefs. From coming to know (if indeed such a thing is possible) that there is a transcendent being who created the world and who sustains our existence and created us for a certain end, we still cannot determine or ascertain what, morally speaking, we ought to do and what we ought to seek. A nagging doubt now hoves into sight: If our moral claims do not have an objective basis in a belief in God, then what, if any, objective basis do they or can they have? Perhaps they are just expressions of feeling or, as Kierkegaard avers, brute subscriptions to principle. This raises for us a most—perhaps *the* most—central philosophical question about morality: Is there any objective and rational basis for moral belief? That is, are there any moral claims that are true or at least validated in such a way that their truth or validation does not depend on the personal or cultural idiosyncrasies of the person making the judgment?[1]

In pursuing this question let us look at it from another angle. Bluntly stated, a general question that deeply affects us when we reflect on morality and on our lives is this: How should human beings live? Among the many conflicting ideals, what standards of conduct and what ideals of life should we make or keep as our own and try to act in accordance with?

There are many who think that in putting it this way I have already begged important questions. I have assumed that in morals we can show that some given moral ideal or moral standard, or set of moral standards and ideals, can be shown or can be known to be correct. This, some will argue, is impossible, for these ideals and standards are all relative. We talk about correct moral standards, but in reality they are all historically and culturally contingent standards. They are simply the ideals and standards of a particular culture or class and they cannot be cross-culturally validated. We cannot as moralists or as moral philosophers speak for man generally, but at best for a particular culture or class at a particular time and place.

Philosophers who seek to establish a rational and objective basis for morality must squarely face this question of relativism. Nietzsche thrusts this problem at us in an incisive way at the beginning of Part V of his *Beyond Good and Evil*. He remarks that we have nothing that even approximates a 'science of morals', and that before we could have one we would need to do something moral philosophers have not done, namely prepare a typology of morals. In seriously thinking about ethics, Nietzsche avers, we need to develop a keen curiosity about actual moral differences— about other peoples and other times. We should, if we are to treat our question seriously, develop a historical and anthropological understanding. As Nietzsche puts it himself, for a long time we need "to collect material, to conceptualize and arrange a vast realm of subtle feelings of value and differences of value. . . ." But, he goes on to say, it is just this that moral philosophers have been unwilling or unable to do.

> Just because our moral philosophers knew the facts of morality only very approximately in arbitrary extracts or in accidental epitomes—for example, as the morality of their environment, their class, their church, the spirit of their time, their climate and part of the world—just because they were poorly informed and not even very curious about different peoples, times and past ages—they never laid eyes on the real problems of morality; for these emerge only when we compare *many* moralities. In all "science of morals" so far one thing was *lacking*, strange as it may sound: the problem of morality itself; what was lacking was any suspicion that there was something problematic here. What the philosophers called "a rational foundation for morality" and tried to supply was, seen in the right light, merely a scholarly variation of the common *faith* in the prevalent morality; a new means of *expression* for this faith; and thus another fact within a particular morality; indeed, in the last analysis a kind of denial that this morality might ever be considered problematic—certainly the very opposite of an examination, analysis, questioning and vivisection of this very faith.[2]

It is the belief of many who think about such matters that if one would honestly carry out this typology of morals, one would arrive at a complete ethical relativism. It is only our ignorance and ethnocentrism that keep us from arriving at that conclusion. That is to say, we should be led from such an examination to believe that we could not but accept the contention that what is right or even desirable for one individual or society need not be right or desirable for another, even when the situations in question are similar. Such a claim seems to many to be a truism that any man who is tolerably well informed and the least bit perceptive must just accept. Even in similar situations not only the actions but the very moral standards by which actions are appraised need not be the same to be equally correct. The Swedish philosopher Axel Hägerström graphically conveys this sense of relativism.

> Herodotus relates that the Persian king, Darius, put the following question to some Greeks, who were visiting in his court: 'For what price would you be willing to eat the dead bodies of your fathers?' 'Not for anything in the world,' came the answer. Whereupon Darius called in some representatives of an Indian tribe, among whom that which was abhorrent to the Greeks was the custom, and he asked them for what price they would be willing to burn the dead bodies of their fathers. They vigorously repudiated every thought of anything so horrible. The author applied this in the following way: If one showed all possible customs to men and asked them to choose out the best, each one would select those which he himself happened to follow. A similar proposition among the Greeks, which undoubtedly originated in the time just preceding the Sophists, is the following: If one allowed men to cast into a pile the customs which they regarded as good and noble, and afterwards permitted each one to choose out of the pile those which seemed to him to be base and outrageous, nothing would be left over, but everything would have been distributed among them all.[3]

In short, it is the belief of many that the facts concerning the diversity of morals uncovered by anthropologists give undeniable substance to the thesis of ethical relativity. But it is also the belief of many others that more recent work in anthropology has so qualified the thesis of cultural relativism that it will no longer support ethical relativism. In this chapter I want to examine these claims. It will be the burden of my argument to establish that anthropological discoveries cannot by themselves establish either ethical relativism or its opposite. I agree with Nietzsche that we should not take morality simply as something *given*, and I further agree that in developing a moral philosophy we need a typology of morals. But neither a wide diversity of moral belief nor a thorough *de facto* convergence of moral belief is sufficient to establish ethical relativism, absolutism, or the claim that there are objective moral beliefs.

II

Let us now see how this is so. Anthropologists often stress the radical diversity of our moral beliefs. In 1903 the French anthropologist Levy-Bruhl in his *Ethics and Moral Science* contended that moral codes and systems "are merely rationalizations of custom." What *is done*, he argued, is right. Where a given culture has a rule that all twins are to be killed at birth—or, as in some places in the Amazon, that all captured children of an enemy tribe are first to be adopted and then, during adolescence, to be eaten ceremonially by the families that adopted them—such mandatory social practices are right (morally obligatory) for that society. Morality,

Levy-Bruhl maintained, is simply the body of rules that actually determines conduct in any society. Social structure and expected behavior vary enormously among different cultures; thus, morality—the normal, sanctioned behavior—also varies extensively from culture to culture.

Thirty years after *Ethics and Moral Science* was published, the American anthropologist Ruth Benedict, with a much greater store of anthropological information at hand, made the same type claim. "Morality," she tells us, "differs in every society, and is a convenient term for socially approved habits." In a way that would bring chills to one affected by G. E. Moore, she calmly tells us, 'It is morally good' means the same as 'It is habitual'; and what is habitual for the Tapirape is not habitual for the Papago or the American. In a culture that conditions people to amass property and wealth and directs people to seek success, the attainment of extensive property and power will be good. In a society in which contemplation and fidelity to one's ancestors are stressed above all, the attainment of wealth and power will not be so highly prized. Confronted with an extensive variety of cultures, anthropologists have been impressed until very recently with the differences in human nature and moral rule rather than the similarities. Levy-Bruhl, Boaz, Benedict, and Mead are the classical sources here.[4]

However, in the recent past there has been a shift in anthropological thinking about cultural relativism, and now we find such eminent anthropological authorities as Kroeber, Linton, Redfield, and Kluckhohn emphasizing that there are common denominators amid the variations.[5] There are what they like to call 'universal values'. Kroeber and Kluckhohn remark that "to say that certain aspects of Nazism were morally wrong, is not parochial arrogance. It is—or can be—an assertion based upon cross-cultural evidence as to the universalities in human needs, potentialities, and fulfillments and upon natural science knowledge with which the basic assumptions of any philosophy must be congruent." They speak of a "raw human nature" and the "limits and conditions of social life." They claim that it is proper to speak of a "common humanity," and our common humanity can serve as a basis for a morality that is *not* completely culturally relative.

Amid incredible variation in human ideals, there are some commonly accepted standards and ideals of a very general but still fundamental nature resting on a pan-human consensus. There are certain very general moral principles that all normal members of all cultures take as authoritative. The incest taboo is universal, all cultures regulate sexual behavior, all cultures have some property rights, and no culture tolerates indiscriminate lying or stealing. All cultures believe that it is good as a general rule to preserve human life; they draw a distinction between 'murder' and 'justifiable homicide', such as execution, killing in war, in religious ceremonials, and the like. As Redfield points out, there are no societies where mothers are not obliged to care for their children. Neglect of her own child, or abuse of her own or another's child, is universally taken to be wrong. And in all cultures children also have obligations to their parents, although the exact nature of these obligations varies considerably from culture to culture.

More generally, there are no cultures without moral codes; and, as Linton points out, these codes always function to ensure "the perpetuation and successful functioning of the society," although *sometimes* the relevant social unit may be all of mankind. This commitment to societal survival takes pride of place—all societies have something very like our right of eminent domain—but "within the limits set by the priority given to a society's needs, all ethical systems also seek to provide for the physical needs of individuals." Man needs society, but he also has familial needs, and he has a need for protection from what Linton calls "ego injury" as well as physical injury. All moral codes serve both to protect society and such individual needs, although where there is a conflict an individual's needs are secondary to those of the society.

In sum, there are deep-rooted needs, distinctive capacities, and characteristic human attitudes that are perfectly universal. 'Universal values' are said to be based on these needs, and on these values rests a cross-culturally valid, objective morality.

It is indeed true that just what is to count as 'incest', 'murder', 'neglect', 'abuse', and the like is culturally relative to an astounding degree. For the Romans, killing one's parents was the most unspeakable of evils, but for pre-Christian Scandinavians it was (and for the Eskimos of the more recent past it still is) a duty in order to set them up in heaven with a reasonably intact and properly functioning body. But anthropologists stress that amid this exuberant variety of moral belief we still always find concern in all tribes to preserve life. Moreover, there remains some overlap among cultures concerning what is to count as 'murder' and what is to count as 'justified killing'. Similar things could be said for 'incest', 'neglect', 'abuse ', and the like. There are, as Kluckhohn concludes, "pan-human universals as regards needs and capacities that shape . . . at least the broad outlines of a morality that transcends cultural difference."

It is Kluckhohn's and Linton's belief that this convergence is not just a fortunate circumstance. Kluckhohn goes so far as to claim that it is a "presumptive likelihood" that certain very general "moral principles somehow correspond to inevitabilities given the nature of the human organism and of the human situation." We humans have many variable needs, but "some needs," Kluckhohn argues, "are so deep and so generic that they are beyond the reach of argument; pan-human morality expresses and supports them."

There are several difficulties here. Linton, Kluckhohn, and Redfield are partially aware that an ability to formulate very general moral principles acceptable to all normal members of all cultures establishes very little, for we can always find some common denominator for such formulations if we delete enough detail. We have not discovered anything very interesting or significant when we find out that all normal people in all cultures regard some patterns of sexual behavior as bad and some ways of eating as desirable, and that all cultures have some concept of murder. To say that murder is wrong and eating is good is at best minimally informative. Paul Taylor in his acute criticism of this trend in anthropological thinking is perfectly correct in saying, "What an ethical absolutist wants to know is . . . whether it is right to let a person die of neglect when he can no longer contribute to a society's economic production, whether it is right to kill unwanted infants, whether monogamy is the best sexual institution, whether a person ought to tell the truth under specified circumstances, and so on."[6] If we are troubled by ethical relativism, we generally want to know things of this order: Are there some nonethnocentric objective reasons for our moral belief that we ought not to kill a child whom we do not want? We want to know whether our very strong convictions here could be established as sound, and conflicting convictions extant in other cultures shown to be wrong.

There is an additional difficulty for any view that seeks to base morality on some common human nature. Even if there are universal human needs, why should they be satisfied? We all have needs for companionship and sexual satisfaction. Universal as such needs are, however, they can be so modified and controlled as to become almost nonexistent. Furthermore, I can ask myself whether I should shun companionship and become self-absorbed, or whether I should become more outgoing and gregarious. A certain amount of contact with others is almost inevitable, but beyond the bare minimum should I seek a life full of friends and the resources of society or should I live in relative isolation? Would it be better for a reflective young man to try to become another Thomas Merton and seek the "voices of silence" and renounce the joys of the flesh, or should he have wife, family, and the art of conversation? Discoveries about universal human needs are not sufficient to resolve questions like these. The fact that people universally have sexual urges does not tell us whether we should make our present sexual patterns more or less permissive. After we find out what the needs of man are, we still have to find out which needs should be allowed to flourish and in what way, and which needs should be inhibited. In seeking a more adequate culture, in attempting to decide whether one way of life is better than another, anthropological discoveries *by themselves* can give us no new directions. From the fact that there are such universal human needs, we cannot deduce any categorical moral proposition at all.[7]

Neither group agreement nor difference in moral belief or attitude establishes a theory of ethical relativism or objectivism. Ethical relativism is the contention that what is right or good for one individual or society need not be right or good for another even when the situations in question are similar. But universal agreement concerning a moral belief does not establish the soundness of that belief. The soundness of a moral belief does not depend simply on the number of people who believe it, but on whether adequate justifying reasons can be given for holding it. If reasonable people assent to it, we have some reason for assenting to it, but whether a person is either reasonable or a rational moral agent is not dependent on whether or not his beliefs, attitudes, and actions are in accordance with those of the majority or some very general consensus. Even if a universal concurrence in moral belief and attitude were discovered, the ethical relativist could still claim that this agreement does not rest on rational grounds but merely on a contingent and fortuitous similarity or uniformity in what is approved. The ethical relativist or a Nietzschean iconoclast could reasonably argue that although the agreement is extensive it is quite arbitrary, for it has no rational basis. Since it is reinforced by early and persistent social stimulation, it is very persuasive and often very compelling psychologically; just as many of the literati and quasi-literati started to admire Kipling simply because T. S. Eliot did, so many people come to approve what they approve because from a very early age they have been told *it is to be approved*. This generally makes for agreement rather than disagreement. But if some others come to have different and conflicting moral beliefs, the fact that most do not have these moral beliefs and attitudes does not constitute a sound basis for asserting that the minority is wrong. That there are what Linton calls "universal values" only proves that people tend to agree about some very general moral judgments. It says nothing about who (if anyone) is right or which moral views (if any) are sound.

In sum, I wish to say that anthropological facts about the divergence, convergence, or complete coincidence of the moral beliefs of different cultures neither establish nor refute ethical relativism. People and whole cultures could be in radical disagreement about what they ought to do and moral relativism would not be established. But if it could be shown that a considerable number of contradictory moral claims were equally *sound* and that moral codes were in logical conflict but were still equally *well justified*, then ethical relativism would be established. The rather common assumption that if men do share moral beliefs then conventionalism and relativism are false, is itself false.

III

It is vital in such discussions to distinguish between *ethical relativism* and *cultural relativism*. The latter is simply the *factual thesis* that different peoples often have differing moral standards and/or ideals and sometimes these conflict in a very fundamental way. Ethical relativism, by contrast, is itself the *moral* or *normative* claim that what is right or good for one individual or society need not be right or good for another even when the situations in question are similar.

What is crucial to see here, and what is missed by both sides in the dispute between the anthropologists that has just been discussed, is that even if the factual thesis of cultural relativism is true, it does not follow that ethical relativism is true. We do not derive from this purely factual thesis—that is, cultural relativism—any normative thesis at all. In fact, cultural relativism in no way establishes ethical relativism; one could, as either an ethical absolutist or an ethical objectivist, perfectly well accept cultural relativism. And one would not thereby be committing oneself to the view that the moral standards of every group were equally correct or even equally correct for them. As a cultural relativist, one holds no view at all about what if anything constitutes a *correct* moral standard or a *justified* moral ideal. (I will distinguish between 'ethical absolutism' and 'ethical objectivism'. Both, of course, constitute a rejection of ethical relativism, and both are compatible with cultural relativism. By 'ethical absolutism' I mean the claim that there is one eternally true moral code that is to be applied unvaryingly to all men everywhere. By 'ethical objectivism' I mean the view that maintains that some moral arguments are reliable and there is some reliable moral knowledge. An ethical objectivist maintains that there are, even among fundamental moral judgments, some moral judgments whose truth or falsity does not depend on the peculiarities of the person who makes the judgment or on the culture to which he belongs, but are ascertainable by a rational agent from any culture who is apprised of the relevant facts. I distinguish between 'ethical absolutism' and 'ethical objectivism' because, while I think the former very implausible, I believe the latter to be defendable. If there is to be a reasonable alternative to relativist and subjective theories, it will have to be some form of ethical objectivism. What is important to determine, if we can, is whether ethical objectivism is a more plausible view than ethical relativism, ethical skepticism, or subjectivism. Emotionally—giving vent to our moral feelings— most of us would very much want some form of ethical objectivism to be true. But do we really have good grounds for believing it to be true?)

Now we need to ask this question: If the anthropological facts about agreement or disagreement in morality do not establish or refute ethical relativism, what would establish it?

It is sometimes thought that the truth of ethical subjectivism in any of its forms would establish ethical relativism. Subjectivism concerning morality is the view that there is no way of rationally resolving fundamental moral disputes, for fundamental moral judgments or ultimate moral principles cannot correctively be said to be true or false in such a way that any rational agent, apprised of the relevant facts, will agree about their truth or falsity. Subjectivism has at least two forms, which need to be assessed separately. The first, which I shall label 'naive subjectivism', has been definitely and clearly refuted—as I shall show. The second form, which I shall label 'nonnaive subjectivism', is a more difficult view to refute.[8]

Naive subjectivism: Moral judgments are merely autobiographical judgments about the attitudes or feelings of the person making the judgment.

Nonnaive subjectivism: Moral judgments do not assert facts but express the attitudes or feelings of the person making the judgment and are used by him to evoke or invite similar attitudes in others and to stimulate action.

Even if it were true that there is this conceptual connection between subjectivism and ethical relativism (and this is questionable, to put it mildly), there are good reasons for rejecting subjectivism. Naive subjectivism is demonstrably false, and nonnaive subjectivism is very probably false.

There is a short linguistic argument that is quite decisive against naive subjectivism. Reflect on these two statements:

A. It is wrong to kill.
B. The idea of killing, as a matter of psychological fact, arouses in me an antiattitude toward killing.

If naive subjectivism is true B is a translation of A. In fact, if naive subjectivism is true, both statements are equivalent in the strong sense that they not only have the same truth conditions but have the same *meaning*. They plainly do not have the same meaning or the same truth conditions, however, for I can surely say, without *contradicting* myself, that the idea of killing arouses in me a disposition *not* to kill and a feeling of detestation toward killing, but all the same I ought under certain circumstances to inhibit that disposition and those feelings. That is, a man might perfectly well acknowledge both that he detests killing and further acknowledge that sometimes it is not wrong to kill. It *might* be absurd to say that, but it plainly is not self-contradictory. *Since* I can say that, statements A and B cannot be identical in *meaning;* since they are not identical in meaning, naive subjectivism must be false. (Recall that for naive subjectivism to be true, both statements must have the same meaning.) Moreover, what would establish the truth of B is reasonably evident, but what—if anything—would establish the truth of A is not at all evident. If both have the same meaning, however, what would establish the truth of one would establish the truth of the other.

Exactly the same would be true of the following statement: If Swenson utters, 'Harassing others is evil', this means, according to a naive subjectivist, 'I, Swenson, have a tendency to disapprove of the harassment of others'. But 'Harassing others is evil' most surely does not mean *that*, for the following statements are most certainly not contradictions: 'I, Swenson, have no tendency to disapprove of harassing others, but harassing them may be evil all the same' and 'Even if I, Swenson, were dead, harassing others would be evil'. Yet if the naive subjectivist's equivalences actually held, such statements would be contradictory. Since they plainly are not contradictory, naive subjectivism must be false.

We have narrowed our field slightly. We have seen that neither cultural relativism nor naive subjectivism by themselves or together are sufficient to establish ethical relativism. The former does not show that ethical relativism is true or well grounded, for even if cultural relativism is true, it remains as compatible with either ethical absolutism or ethical objectivism as it is with ethical relativism. In short, an ethical absolutist or objectivist could quite consistently accept cultural relativism as a correct account of what people generally *take* to be right and wrong.[9] Naive subjectivism does not support ethical relativism because naive subjectivism is false.

However, we still have nonnaive subjectivism in the running. Beyond that, we should note that perhaps the major reason for accepting ethical relativism is the reason advanced and argued for in the opening chapters of Edward Westermarck's *Ethical Relativity*. The reason is just this: No one has been able to articulate convincingly and defend either an absolute or an objective morality. Not even the foundations of such a moral system have been convincingly set out. That is to say, nobody has been able to state an acceptable objective rationale or ground for moral belief; nobody has been able to show how we could justify a universally binding moral code. It is this that leads many to a reluctant acceptance of ethical relativism.

Edward Westermarck has argued, as have others, that attempts to establish an objective ethic all suffer from crucial conceptual defects. After attempting to establish this, he proceeds to give an explanation of why all attempts must be failures by elucidating and defending a form of nonnaive subjectivism.[10] His view in turn commits him to what is sometimes called *meta-ethical relativism*, namely, to the view that there are no sound procedures for justifying one moral code or even one set of moral judgments as opposed to another code or another set of moral judgments. Two moral codes, although they conflict, may be equally 'sound'; two or more moral claims, even when they are conflicting may be equally 'justified'. Furthermore, there is no way of rationally resolving fundamental moral disputes, for fundamental moral judgments or ultimate moral principles cannot correctly be said to be true or false in such a way that any rational agent, who is appraised of the relevant facts, will have to agree on their truth or falsity.

It is this cluster of claims that is thought by many to provide a convincing support for ethical relativism. Do they, if true, provide good grounds for ethical relativism? If true, whether they support ethical relativism or not, they certainly refute ethical absolutism and ethical objectivism. The point is, however, are they true or at least more rationally acceptable than any of the alternative views that would support ethical objectivism, or should we remain agnostic about the whole affair of morality?[11] It is to these considerations that we will turn in the next three chapters.

NOTES

1. I add the alternative 'or at least validated' for those who think that it is a conceptual blunder to speak of moral claims as being either true or false but still believe that some moral claims have greater rational warrant than others. Henceforth, I will simply speak of their being true or false. For anyone who believes this mode of speech to be misleading, the substitution of 'validated' or 'rationally vindicated' for 'true' will not substantially affect my argument. I have elucidated and defended speaking of moral claims as being true or false in my "On Moral Truth," in Nicolas Rescher (ed.), *Studies in Moral Philosophy* (Oxford: 1968) and in my "Problems of Ethics," in Paul Edwards (ed.), *Encyclopedia of Philosophy*, vol. III.

2. Friedrich Nietzsche, *Beyond Good and Evil*, translated by Walter Kaufmann, pp. 97–98.

3. Axel Hägerström, *Philosophy and Religion*, translated by Robert T. Sandin, p. 71.

4. See here particularly Ruth Benedict, "Anthropology and the Abnormal," *Journal of General Psychology*, vol. 10 (1934) and her *Patterns of Culture*; Edward Westermarck, *Ethical Relativity*; and Melville Herskovits, *Man and His Works*.

5. See here Ralph Linton, "Universal Ethical Principles: An Anthropological Approach," in R. N. Anshen (ed.), *Moral Principles of Action*; Robert Redfield, "The Universally Human and the Culturally Variable," *The Journal of General Education*, vol. X, (July, 1957); C. Kluckhohn, "Ethical Relativity, Sic et Non," *Journal of Philosophy*, vol. LII (1955); and Margaret Mead, "Some Anthropological Considerations Concerning Natural Law," *Natural Law Forum*, vol. VI (1961.)

6. Paul Taylor, "Social Science and Ethical Relativism," in his *Problems of Moral Philosophy*.

7. This needs to be qualified. There are contexts—as I explain in my "Morality and Needs"—where 'need' functions as a moral or normative term and then, of course, there is no question of a purely factual or nonmoral statement entailing a categorical moral judgment. See my "Morality and Needs," in J. J. MacIntosh and S. C. Coval (eds.), *The Business of Reason*.

8. See the last two essays in G. E. Moore's *Philosophical Studies* and the chapter entitled "Naive Subjectivism" in Paul Edwards, *The Logic of Moral Discourse*.

9. See Walter Stace, *The Concept of Morals* and Paul Taylor (ed.), *Problems of Moral Philosophy,* pp. 41–66.

10. Edward Westermarck has been unduly neglected by moral philosophers and grossly misinterpreted as a naive subjectivist. The article on Westermarck in the *Encyclopedia of Philosophy* corrects these errors and makes it evident that Westermarck is not a naive subjectivist.

11. For two sophisticated statements of this view, see John Mackie "A Refutation of Morals" in Paul Edwards and Arthur Pap (eds.) *A Modern Introduction to Philosophy* (second edition) and Jonathan Harrison, "Ethical Skepticism," *Aristotelian Society Proceedings,* supplementary vol. XLI (1967). But also note what is in effect an attempt to deflate these claims in L. G. Miller's "Moral Skepticism," *Philosophy and Phenomenological Research,* (1961–62).

24

SEARCH
FOR A STANDARD: I

I

Our arguments in the last chapter have made it evident that we do not know that ethical relativism or the more sophisticated forms of subjectivism are true. We should not overlook the point, however, that from what we have so far established, we do not know them to be false, either. A conclusive way of refuting ethical relativism is to show that certain sufficiently comprehensive and fundamental moral principles or standards are true or at least rationally justified. (I say 'sufficiently comprehensive' for they must provide standards that would serve as systematic action guides.) To see if such a refutation is justified, we should begin in our search for a standard by examining some of the fundamental standards of the classical ethical theories. If we can see that one of these fundamental standards is true and sufficiently comprehensive, ethical relativism and subjectivism are refuted. Even if nothing as decisive as this is achieved, it remains true that to the extent that we can show—if indeed we can show—that one of these classical principles or standards is more reasonable than the others, to that extent ethical relativism and subjectivism are weakened.

Consider the following very popular candidates for justified fundamental principles of morality:

1. *The appeal to nature or to human nature:* Man has the rule of right within his own nature. All he needs to do is to find out what he really is—what his essential nature is—and then he will discover what he ought to do and what he ought to be.[1] This argument has a respectable lineage. It received its classical formulation in Cicero's *De republica* and its equally classical refutation in J. S. Mill's essay "Nature."[2] It is an appealing view, but it has standard and I believe crippling difficulties. Once we give up a certain rather traditionalist belief in God, according to which man was

created for a purpose and thus has a function and hence an essential nature, the very notion of 'an essential human nature' becomes problematic.

A fountain pen *must* have certain characteristics in order to be a fountain pen, a heart *must* have certain characteristics in order to be a heart, and a man must be able to do certain things in order to be a teacher. But 'godless man' has no function, was not cut out to be anything. There indeed may be certain characteristics that are *in fact* common to and distinctive of all actual human beings. It is not evident, however, that there are any distinctive features or set of features that all those things and only those things that could correctly be called 'human beings' must have in virtue of which, if something has it, we have to call that something 'a human being' and if that something does not have it, we cannot correctly call it 'a human being'. It is not even an *a priori* truth—and it may not be unambiguously true at all—that only human beings could have a language or a culture.

Moreover, while we can find out what a good fountain pen is by finding out what pens are for, we cannot find out what a good man is by finding out what men are for, for men are not for anything. Similarly, we can find out what a good janitor is by finding out what role janitors are supposed to play in society, but we cannot in an analogous manner speak of man's role in society. Man *qua* human being has no such role. Men do not in such a functional sense have an 'essential nature' in virtue of which we can, by coming to understand it, come to know what is right or desirable. And if to speak of man's 'essential nature' is merely to speak of all those characteristics that *in fact* are common to and distinctive of all human beings and only human beings, we, in discovering those features, do not *ipso facto* discover something desirable.[3] Perhaps, as Nietzsche thought, "man is something to be surpassed"—perhaps man's behavior patterns, given his irrationality and inordinate love of cruelty, are something to be changed or surpassed.

There is a further and distinct consideration that needs to be examined. If all those things men do and can do are regarded as 'natural'—as expressive of what man essentially is—then 'acting in accordance with his nature' cannot be a standard for appraising action. On such a reading of 'natural', the alleged standard 'Do what is natural' or 'Act in accordance with your nature' is compatible with anything and everything man does and can do. Since this is so, doing what is in accordance with one's own nature cannot guide conduct at all, because a person can never derive from it or in any way intelligibly conclude from it 'Do this and avoid that'· In doing anything at all, one is acting in accordance with 'nature'. Given such a conception of what man essentially is, one cannot fail to act in accordance with one's own nature no matter what one does or fails to do.

If the standard is weakened by taking 'nature' to stand for what men *characteristically* do, then we have simply a built in defense of the status quo. Any innovation would have to be wrong; what is habitually done would have to be the thing to do. And if an innovation eventually became the thing done, it would simply in virtue of that become right, although it remained the wrong thing to do while it was still an innovation. Given such an appeal to human nature, there would be no point at all in examining what the innovation actually is. In virtue of knowing that it was an innovation, we would know that it was wrong. But this standard appears to be utterly arbitrary and antipathetical to all human creativity, and no reason has been given for accepting it. It is indeed a general action guide, but not one a reflective man would accept.

The appeal to nature might be given a still different interpretation. Doing what is in accordance with your own nature can be contrasted with doing what is conventional or a result of human contrivance. But even with this contrast, it still does not follow that doing what is natural is always the desirable thing. Wearing clothes, fixing one's teeth, making medical discoveries are human contrivances and in the requisite sense 'not natural', but it is at least arguable that they are desirable. To do only what in that sense is natural would keep us back in the pre-Stone Age— a mixed blessing even in our age of alienation.

If to follow 'the rule of right within one's own nature' is to say that conscience should be the standard of action—the fundamental action guide—it must be pointed out that the conscience of mankind by no means speaks with one voice. Some of the cruelest, vilest things in the world have been done as a result of the promptings of conscience. Furthermore (and less dramatically), the demands of conscience are frequently rationalizations in our own favor. Conscience, as George Eliot vividly portrays in her novels, is often an artful aid in an unwitting distortion of our appreciation of moral considerations.[4] Following one's conscience can become an effective way of rationalizing acting for one's personal aggrandizement. One acts selfishly and ruthlessly but, through the mechanism of conscience, one comes to feel that although the effects may be harsh on others, one is doing one's duty in acting in accordance with the dictates of conscience.

In spite of this—for such rationalization surely is not the rule—it would normally be the case that an agent in deciding what to do would rightly follow his own conscience. But if again and again acting as his conscience dictates clashes with the moral convictions of others and/or brings about disastrous results—causes avoidable misery, suffering, and injustice—a reasonable human being will surely come to question accepting what his conscience urges as his decisive action guide. A man cannot be confident that he has come to know what is the right thing to do by finding out what his conscience dictates.

Such considerations lead us to realize that man does not and cannot find the rule of right from within, that is, from simply clearly and non-evasively seeing what he is. We have as our ancestors an incredibly vicious strain of tree shrews; and although we are indeed the first terrestrial animal to understand the mechanism of evolution and we have conquered every other form of life on earth, we still wage war with napalm, fragmentation, and radiation bombs, torture our fellow human beings in incredibly sick and brutal ways, continually and deliberately slaughter beings who do not threaten us, and remain largely indifferent to the misery and starvation of others. So even if we find out what we 'really are' or what 'our essential nature is', there is still the further question of how we are to act or what rule of life is generally desirable. I do not want to deny for a moment that an understanding of the distinctive needs, wants, and pervasive preferences of the human animal is of utmost importance in deciding how we ought to live and what ways of life are desirable, but I am arguing that we cannot discover or justify a fundamental moral standard by simply coming to know what we are.[5]

2. *The principle of utility:* One ought to act in accordance with that principle which approves or disapproves of every action whatsoever, according to the tendency it appears to have to augment or diminish the happiness of the individuals whose interests are in question. In short, the rightness or wrongness of an action is judged by its consequences. Actions are right or wrong depending on whether they have good or bad consequences. And, for the classical utilitarians, to have good consequences is to have consequences that are at least as pleasant on the whole as the net consequences of any alternative course of action open to the agents in such contexts; to have bad consequences is to have consequences that on the whole are more unpleasant than any of the alternative actions open to the agents involved.[6]

'Happiness' here is taken to be an umbrella term for the aggregate of pleasures and enjoyments, and 'unhappiness' for the aggregate of pains and disagreeable states. A man whose life had been replete with pain, suffering, and anguish could not correctly be said to have had a happy life; if a man's life had been rich in varied enjoyments and pleasures, it could not correctly be said to be an unhappy life. It was Bentham's and Mill's essential claim that the fundamental standard of conduct that ought to be adopted is the one that asserts that the action which ought to be followed is that action which will bring about, of the alternatives possible, the greater quantity of happiness. In short, an action ought to be done, according to the classical utilitarians, if and only if it, at least as much as any of the possible alternatives, maximizes the total amount of pleasure of those persons affected by the action.

Usually, at any rate, the greatest total happiness will be brought about by seeking the greatest happiness for the greatest number. But the ultimate moral principle remains: Seek the greatest measure of total happiness (pleasure) that it is possible to achieve. That should be the ultimate rationale of all our moral actions and all our moral practices.

To such a position—a position usually called hedonistic utilitarianism—it is sometimes objected that we have and can have no common measure of happiness. One man's pleasure is another man's poison.

However, while 'happiness' is vague and the sources of happiness are varied, it is not true that happiness is such a problematic concept that we cannot say anything that would be met by a large measure of agreement. It is evident enough that people who have just been napalmed or been in an auto accident are normally not happy. And it is not just physical pains but also other painful experiences concerning which there is considerable agreement. A man whose children have just died, whose wife has just left him, or who has lost his home and means of security, normally is not happy. And it is as evident as anything can be that the prisoners in the Nazi concentration camps or the people who starved in Biafra were far from happy while they were going through those experiences. There are indeed hosts of doubtful cases, but it also remains true that we can observe children in a park or couples walking along on a Sunday afternoon and gain a tolerably shrewd idea of which children are happy or which couples are happy and which are not. It is not true that we are on utterly swampy ground here, that we can have no common measure of happiness.

More generally, how can we know what will make a man happy? By finding out what ends he seeks or tends to seek. Underground men—as our earlier discussion of Dostoevsky evidenced—will indeed complicate matters, but a man will be happy (if anything will make him happy) when, given that he is a rational man and tolerably well informed about his condition, he is able to do what he wants most to do. Often we do not know what this is or we are ambivalent about it. But we cannot correctly say that this is always the case and that of happiness and unhappiness there is no common measure.

In the light of this discussion, it is well to reformulate the principle of utility in a somewhat different way. (Here we are following A. J. Ayer.) "We are always to act in such a way as to give as many people as possible as much as possible of whatever it is that they want."[7] How do we know that this principle is true, or do we even have reason to believe it or any of the other formulations of the principle of utility are true? Before we go into this, consider an important rival principle, the Kantian one.[8]

3. *Kantian moral principle:* "So act as to treat humanity, whether in thine own person or that of another, always as an end, never merely as a means." Kant's principle might be stated in a fuller and perhaps a clearer way as follows: We are always to act in such a way as to treat human beings (including ourselves) as individuals (as persons) deserving

of respect in their own right and never merely as means (simply as instruments to be used for certain ends). This is indeed a moving principle. But again, how do we know, or do we know or have reason to believe, that such a principle is true?

4. *Combined Kantian and Utilitarian principle:* We might even combine Bentham and Kant in the following manner: For any situation whatsoever we are always to act in such a way as to give everyone involved— treating each man as a person deserving of respect in his own right—as much as possible of whatever it is that the person wants that is compatible with his treating his fellow men as persons.[9] Again, however, how do we know, or do we know, that this principle is true? That it in effect gives voice to some of our most central and cherished sentiments is not enough to show it to be true.

II

Displayed for you, admittedly without their rather complicated contexts, are some of the central principles of classical ethical theory. There is indeed much that could be said about all of them. Concerning each one of them, and any other ultimate principle that might be offered as well, our original question—like "the return of the repressed"—continues to haunt us: How do we know, or do we know, that any of these standards are true or rationally justified? What reason have we to believe that they are true or rationally justified? We must not confuse our wishes with our quest for objective reality. Can we actually develop a reliable argument in which one of these principles follows as a conclusion? Can we prove or confirm or establish the truth or probable truth of any of these ultimate principles?

We are on slippery ground here, but one thing at least is evident: there is one familiar sense in which they cannot possibly be proved. That is, we cannot demonstrate or deductively establish them. They all purport to be ultimate principles, but if they are ultimate principles they cannot follow from any other principles or they would not really be ultimate. To try to prove or demonstrate an ultimate principle in this direct way is as foolish as the attempt to prove an axiom. Anyone who attempts this logically impossible feat shows that he does not understand what is meant by the phrase 'ultimate principle'.[10]

Both Bentham and Mill recognized and indeed stressed the preceding reasonably obvious truth. They went on to argue that although the principle of utility, as an ultimate principle, is not susceptible to direct proof, it is susceptible to an indirect proof. Ultimate principles, they both argued, can be reasoned about and justified, even though they are not capable of demonstration in the logically conclusive way in which theorems can be demonstrated.[11] Bentham maintained that the "natural constitution of the human frame" is such that men on most occasions in their lives habitually and often unwittingly defer to the principle of utility in the ordering of their actions, although they may never have heard of it or stated explicitly (let alone with any precision) what their actions show to be their basic principle of action.

In trying to establish indirectly the principle of utility, Bentham considers what he takes to be the alternatives to the principle of utility and tries to show how they are thoroughly inadequate candidates for ultimate moral principles. He points out that if we oppose the principle of utility with what he calls "the principle of sympathy and antipathy," we do not oppose it with a principle at all but with what in reality signifies the negation of all principle. The 'principle' of sympathy and antipathy asserts that independently of whether the course of action diminishes suffering, it should be done if we happen to approve of it or if it is approved of, and should not be done if we happen to disapprove of it or it is not approved of. Bentham points out that "what one expects to find in a principle is something that points out some external consideration, as a means of warranting and guiding the internal sentiments of approbation and disapprobation." Thus, the principle of sympathy and antipathy is in reality no principle or standard at all. By contrast, the principle of asceticism—that is, the principle that approves of an action when it tends to diminish happiness and disapproves of an action when it tends to augment happiness—is such a constant principle. It is indeed a genuine moral standard or action guide. Moreover, there is no demonstration that it is false any more than there is a demonstration that the principle of utility is true, but that this is so simply results from its being a logical characteristic of an ultimate principle. To recognize the truth of this logical point does not at all commit us to deny that there are arguments for or against the principle of asceticism, as well as arguments for or against the principle of utility. When considering such conflicting ultimate principles, the lack of direct proof does not mean that there are no arguments—and indeed sometimes very reliable arguments—for or against such principles. We have no good reason to think that reason becomes wanton when we come to ultimate principles simply because they cannot be proved by being deduced from anything. That no such demonstration is possible does not preclude, as J. S. Mill put it, that "considerations may be presented capable of determining the intellect either to give or to withhold its assent to the doctrine. . . ." In such a context, Mill adds, this is equivalent to proof.

Given this kind of proof or vindication of ultimate principles, arguments for rejecting the principle of asceticism are obvious enough. As Bentham put it, let but "one tenth part of the inhabitants of this earth pursue it consistently, and in a day's time they will have turned it into a hell."

The principle of asceticism does give us a ground for punishing and reprobating the vile pleasures of cruel and sadistic men, but so does the principle of utility, for the pleasures of these men do not stand alone. If the greatest attainable happiness is man's moral goal, and considering the fact that the realization of such cruel and sadistic pleasures is most certainly followed by such a "quantity of pain that the pleasure in comparison of it, is as nothing," we have very good utilitarian grounds for roundly condemning such actions. In short, the principle of utility has all the advantages of the principle of asceticism with none of its manifest disadvantages. Neither principle is capable of direct proof, that is, logical demonstration. However, there certainly are obvious reasons for preferring the former to the latter.

It will be replied that there are other candidates for the first principles of morality besides those Bentham considers, and these principles are also opposed alternative principles to utilitarianism. Moreover, Bentham notwithstanding, they are not reducible to the former principles, that is, to the principle of utility, asceticism, or sympathy and antipathy. The following principles are such alternatives, and we need to consider whether we should accept any of them in preference to the principle of utility, and whether the principle of utility can in any objective way be shown to be a superior standard to these alternatives.

1. Every man is to be treated as an end (as a person) and never as a means only. (This is the Kantian principle previously referred to.)

2. The end of moral endeavor should be human self-realization.

3. Human liberty should be the goal of the ethical life.

4. The pervasive practices of our lives as social beings, for example, promise-keeping, truth-telling, good faith, kindness, and consideration, should together—no practice taking pride of place—provide our standard of action. What is in accord with them, is the thing to do.

Utilitarians often reply that such principles are too indeterminate to serve as effective action guides. For example, it is not clear what it is to treat a man as an end or as a person, or—as in the case of the fourth alternative—the standard is not sufficiently comprehensive or complete to constitute a definitive overall action guide. New situations will arise that are not covered by the practices, and such a pluralistic conception of fundamental moral principles will not even hint at a suggestion of what principle of action should guide us in such circumstances. Moreover, rules of action implicit in the practices can conflict. For example, sometimes I cannot avoid harming a person if I tell him the truth. But in such circumstances, given the last pluralistic principle, I have no grounds for choosing one way of acting rather than another. Utilitarianism, by contrast, gives us a general rule of guidance in such situations. And while it is indeed true that it is moving to speak of treating someone as an end or as a person, what more does this high-sounding talk mean than that one should not disregard his interests? What is it to have regard for someone's interests but to consider his needs, wants, and desires as something that, everything else being equal, should be satisfied? To treat him as a person is to recognize that his well-being or happiness is to be acknowledged and considered along with the well-being and happiness of others—each person counting for one and none counting for more than one. That is to say, we are to put equal value on the interests of everyone involved. But this, utilitarians argue, takes us back to utilitarianism. Talk of treating men as persons unpacks, where it is intelligible, into the utilitarian notion that the maximum possible increase in human happiness for everyone without exception is the central aim of morality.

The idea that human liberty should be the goal of the ethical life is also a questionable alternative to utilitarianism. It is indeed true that human liberty is a very precious thing. But it is plainly not the only great good, and there are the conflicts between liberty and equality. Is it not right—perhaps even an obligation—to rein in liberty when it causes widespread social harm (human misery and deprivation)? Was it not right to limit the liberty of the industrialists by making laws about child labor, working conditions, and hours? It seems quite evident that in doing this we did the right thing. At the very least, some very powerful arguments in defense of liberty would have to be made against such a counterclaim. Liberty, in short, is seen to be a value, but as precious as it is, it is not the only or the highest value in the firmament of values. In trying to decide how we should live and what moral considerations have the most stringency, the value of liberty may in certain situations be outweighed by other moral considerations. I am not at liberty to drive my car with defective brakes even if I want to, for fear of the harm it may do to others as well as to myself. And even if I do not care about myself in this respect, that others may be killed counts decisively against my doing this. Here considerations of suffering and harm ('illfare', if you will) outweigh considerations of liberty.

If it is replied that these restrictions on the liberty of others are themselves only rationally made in the name of a greater overall liberty for everyone, it should in turn be replied that this is not so. People hospitalized because of automobile accidents caused by being hit by cars with defective brakes indeed have their liberty severely curtailed by being so harmed, but it is not at all evident that by restricting people's liberty to drive with defective brakes less total liberty is restricted than by alternative social arrangements. And even if it could be established that by allowing people to drive with defective brakes or by allowing child labor more overall liberty would be achieved than by acting on alternative social policies, it does not follow that this is what should be done. Such practices still could be condemned, and naturally would be, because of the suffering they caused. Moreover, it is surely morally arguable that some human liberty should sometimes be sacrificed for the ideal of equality.

I do not claim to have established that in the 'hierarchy of values' considerations of equality or of human suffering should always or even ever take precedence over considerations concerning human liberty. Perhaps no such 'hierarchy of values' can be rationally established. But I have said enough to make it evident that taking human liberty as one's ultimate standard is indeed to place oneself on dubious ground. 'To maximize liberty' certainly does not appear to be the goal of all rational moral endeavor, although liberty is plainly one of the great human goods.

The notion of self-realization (alternative 2 on page 277) is at least equally problematical. What is it to realize yourself? Some speak of actualizing your potentialities. Well, you have many potentialities; they can hardly all be actualized. If it is said in reply that you should actualize those that are most distinctively human, we are back with the problems discussed when we spoke of an appeal to human nature. We also have to remind ourselves that there is no clear notion of what is 'distinctively human'. In addition, it is not evident why, even if something is uniquely human (as Aristotle and Kant both took human reason to be), it is something overarchingly desirable. D. H. Lawrence was no doubt a 'wild man', but he did give us something to 'think on' here.

Alternatively, if we say that to achieve self-realization is to achieve a distinctive human flourishing, we must inquire whether there are any criteria of human flourishing that are not basically utilitarian and hedonistic. After all, what constitutes human flourishing? Presumably, and minimally, it would have to be that which minimizes human harm and maximizes human well-being or welfare. But how are we to understand these notions except in terms of what would answer to human interests, satisfy human needs, and give human beings pleasure? Again we are back to essentially utilitarian and hedonistic criteria.

The point of my arguments in the last few paragraphs has been to maintain that while there are indeed principles alternative to the principle of utility, they all seem to either reduce to or to be dependent on the principle of utility, or are principles whose inadequacies are evident.

It could be and has been replied that the principle of utility is equally problematical and unclear. J. S. Mill tells us that the object of virtue is the "multiplication of happiness." But how do we 'multiply happiness' or even make objective assessments about the *extent* of happiness? And do we know or even have adequate reasons for believing that it is the objective of virtue? Many have denied that it is the sole objective of virtue, and some have denied that it is the objective of virtue at all, or even that virtue can have any objective, goal, or rationale. For Bentham and for Mill, underlying all their other claims is the claim that pleasure and enjoyment—and pleasure and enjoyment alone—are intrinsically good, that is, worth having for their own sake. However, we must stress the fact that some have not accepted this claim concerning intrinsic goodness and others are agnostic about it.[12] Hedonistic utilitarians must show that these people are somehow mistaken about this. That most people think that this hedonistic claim is so (if indeed most people think that) would not establish that it is so, any more than a convergence in human customs would establish that the customs in question are desirable.

How do—or do—Bentham and Mill know that pleasure and enjoyment alone are intrinsically good? They seem to offer no way at all of determining or ascertaining that, and we seem to be up against a wall here. Consider just how you would prove or give some sound reason for believing that pleasure is the *sole* intrinsic good, or even that pleasure is good. It indeed seems like the merest truism to say that pleasure is good— although not a truism at all to say that it is the *sole* intrinsic good. But even for this truism, what evidence do we have to establish its truth? More fundamentally still, what would it be like to have evidence here? We seem to be at an utter loss. Yet, it also appears evident that pleasure is good. What are we to say to a doubting Thomas? It looks as if the utilitarian claims are as unfounded as the other claimants to the title 'ultimate principles of morality'.[13]

III

We can afford to take the axioms of pure mathematics as arbitrary starting points, and in applied mathematics we can assess the different axiomatic systems by their fruitfulness or utility. But such a utilitarian appeal is one of the things up for grabs in ethics. There is dispute—and indeed, intense *moral* dispute—over the very starting point. We cannot settle the dispute along conventionalist lines, for moralists are not willing to take their ultimate principles as being simply conventions or stipulated arbitrary postulates. Too much hangs on their acceptance. The practices that are required or judged desirable are determined by the particular principles taken as ultimate moral principles, together with our knowledge of what is in fact the situation in question. But since these are the principles by which we embody our most precious commitments about how we are to live together, we cannot be content, when faced with a fascist or a racist with opposed values, simply to treat the conflict as a matter to be amicably resolved on the tolerant policy 'you pays your money, you takes your choice'.

We can hardly remain content with 'an ethics of pure arbitrary postulate', yet we seem not to know how to validate our ultimate moral principles. Any objective ethic must be able to answer the question: How do we know what is right? We seem at a loss for an answer here. It is often assumed that it is a logical feature of moral judgments that there must be good reasons why any and every moral agent should do what is morally right and wrong. It is frequently maintained that the best life and the most rational life is the moral life. But to know that this is so—rather than to make it an article of faith—we would at least have to know in some objective fashion what is right and wrong. We do not seem to be able to establish that we have such moral knowledge. The fact that we have strong moral commitments does not establish this. Perhaps there is no common agreement on what constitutes human good and harm. Perhaps they are a function of our particular custom-encrusted moralities; and it may be true that there are no nonquestion-begging criteria for which of these moralities is the correct morality or the closest to a true moral ideal. In fact, the very notion of 'a true moral ideal' may turn out to be a moving but empty notion.

IV

It is indeed true that we know things to be true that we may not be able to demonstrate to be true. If what we argued—following Hume—about the ontological argument is correct, no matter of fact is capable of logical demonstration.[14] All statements of fact can be denied without inconsistency. For example, though I cannot in this sense demonstrate that I am typing now or that my automobile keys are on my desk, I do know, and you can also know in the appropriate circumstances, that I *am* now typing and that my automobile keys *are* on my desk. In fact, we know many things to be true by observation. But while we can tell through observation that Nixon has black hair, we cannot tell simply through observation whether Nixon is a good man or a conscientious President, or whether his policies for America and for the world are policies we ought to accept. One can find out by making observations that most Swedes are Protestants and that most Austrians are Catholics; but one cannot simply find out *by observing what is the case* that pleasure and pleasure alone is intrinsically good or that we ought to love one another. You know how to ascertain the truth of 'The Neckar runs through Heidelberg', but you do not know what to observe to determine the truth of the claims that 'Pleasure is good' or 'We ought to love each other'. For fundamental moral claims, the two great instruments of human reason—logical demonstration and empirical inquiry—seem to be insufficient methods of attaining truth.

Moreover, it will not do to try to fix our standard and resolve our perplexities in a *definist* manner.[15] Suppose we try to say that any of the following propositions is true by definition because it is analytic.

1. The ultimate end of action is to achieve the greatest possible happiness for the greatest number.
2. Happiness is good.
3. Pleasure is good.
4. Satisfaction of desire is good.
5. Enjoyment is the sole intrinsic good.
6. Life is good.
7. What people want, they ought to have.
8. What people take an interest in must be intrinsically desirable.

It is evident, however, that if any of these propositions is analytic, it could not serve as an action guide, and thus it could not serve as a moral principle. Take what most certainly appears to be an analytic utterance: 'Murder is wrong'. (For it to be analytic, 'murder' would have to mean, as it ordinarily does, something like 'wrongful killing'.) If 'Murder is wrong' is analytic, it has the same meaning as some such utterance as 'Wrongful killing is wrong' or 'Wrong killing is wrong' or 'Unjustifiable killing is wrong'. But such utterances do not serve as action guides because they are compatible with anything that may happen.

Suppose a man is having an affair with his secretary and the man's wife kills him in a fit of jealousy. From simply knowing that murder is wrong, we cannot know that killing is murder. Suppose, to take another example, a soldier's superior officer orders him to shoot a prisoner, and the soldier knows that if he does not shoot him he will himself be shot. If the soldier shoots the prisioner under such circumstances, has he murdered him? Or what if a man is very careless about repairing his brakes, and with these defective brakes he cannot stop quickly enough and hits and kills a pedestrian. Has he murdered him? Or take something that unfortunately is very common: People are killed in war. Have they been murdered? Many regard former President Johnson as a murderer. Is he really a murderer?

We know that murder is wrong by definition, but we cannot simply conclude from the fact that someone has killed someone that he has murdered him, and from knowing the analytical truth 'Murder is wrong', we cannot know which killings are actually murders. In this crucial way, 'Murder is wrong' is contentless and not action-guiding. We need an independent criterion for what killings are murders. Where 'Murder is wrong' is analytic, it cannot be an action guide, and the same would be true of any of the eight propositions just listed if they actually were analytic. If they are analytic—true by definition—they are not action guides and so are not ultimate moral principles.

It should be further pointed out, as G. E. Moore in effect did in the early parts of his *Principia Ethica*, that such propositions are not analytic, or—to put the present point more cautiously—they most certainly do not appear to be analytic. When a hedonist claims 'Pleasure is good', he is not saying 'Pleasure is pleasure' or 'Pleasure is pleasant'. And it is not unintelligible to ask if pleasure is good, and one does not *contradict* oneself if one denies that pleasure is good. If 'Pleasure is good' were analytic, it would be as senseless to ask if pleasure is good as it is senseless to ask whether bachelors are unmarried. And as one contradicts oneself when one denies that a father is a male parent, so one would contradict oneself when one said that pleasure is not good—if 'Pleasure is good' were analytic. However, while it is absurd to assert that pleasure is not good, it is not self-contradictory. But if the question about the goodness of pleasure is an open one, and if it is not self-contradictory to deny that pleasure is good, then 'Pleasure is good' is not analytic.

Similar things can be said about the other seven sentences in the list. We can intelligibly ask if life is good and even conceive of some circumstances in which it is not. And we can intelligibly ask (as many have), as far as logic is concerned, whether the ultimate end of action is to achieve the greatest possible happiness for the greatest number. That is no more a closed question than is 'Is pleasure good?' or 'Is the satisfaction of desire good?'

It may be replied that this Moorean argument is inconclusive because perhaps, like some complicated mathematical formula or like 'A menseless man is a man destitute of decorum', some of these propositions are *covertly* analytic. That is, they are actually analytic, but most people or at least many people are not sufficiently clear about their correct definition—and thus not sufficiently clear about their meaning—to regard them, when they think about them, as statements the denial of which is self-contradictory. Thus, someone might ask in all innocence, "Is a menseless man really destitute of decorum?" That is, he might unwittingly treat such a closed question as if it were an open question. Surely, the fact that we—that is, most native speakers—treat such a question as an open question does not settle the question whether 'A menseless man is a man destitute of decorum' is analytic. This much should be evident. But the force of the Moorean arguments is to point out that such propositions, as the preceding eight, certainly seem to be synthetic even to native and reflective speakers of the language, since it appears to be the case that they can be significantly denied and that open questions can be formed with them, and that since this is so, the burden is on the critic to show that they are analytic—that what appears to be an open question is actually a closed one. Furthermore, the old point remains that if any of these eight propositions can be shown to be analytic, they could not serve as action guides and hence as either ultimate or nonultimate moral or normative principles.

V

As moral agents we need to answer the questions 'How should I treat other people and what expectations may I have of them?' and 'What are the things that should be valued above everything else?'. We are stuck with these questions. We have seen that we cannot answer them simply by appeal to our conscience or to the anthropological facts about what people do. So we go in search of an objective and rational moral standard. Up to this point our quest has had most equivocal results, for it would appear that the classical ultimate standards all have fairly evident defects and that no method has been articulated for the attainment of moral knowledge or even to show that it is possible to attain moral knowledge. Some form of moral skepticism or subjectivism would seem very likely to be the correct account of the matter.

Is this really the case? When we read of an instance in our society where two men offered a girl a ride home after a dance, proceeded to drive her out into the country and then took turns raping her, robbed her of all her money, and then made her walk home coatless through the freezing winter night, do we not know, without any doubt at all, that they did something not only morally wrong but plainly vile? And when we read that ten thousand people starved every day in Biafra and none of the great powers did anything in a serious way to stop this, and the two opposing sides made political capital out of it, do we not know that such actions are wrong? Is there any doubt about these matters at all? Is not any moral theory that cannot show that we do indeed know such things are wrong as mistaken as is any epistemological theory that cannot show we know that there are tables and chairs and the like?

Yet, such an appeal to cases is tricky in philosophy. Both of these examples seem to me to carry with them an evident moral. But two other philosophers felt considerable doubt about the second example, and it could be that I have just not looked long enough to find a reflective and knowledgeable person who would have doubts about the evident correctness of my moral evaluation concerning the first example as well. Yet surely justification must come to an end at some point in moral reasoning, and would not the final check come against cases of that sort? Are they all that doubtful? Would a reflective person doubt the moral evaluation I made concerning them at any time other than when he was engaging in philosophy?

One should indeed be skeptical about moral skepticism. Is there not in the above skeptical argument a kind of failure to appreciate the force of the kind of moral realism with which Kingsley Amis confronts us so compellingly in his novels? Yet, can we—remembering the great range of human differences that Nietzsche referred to—be quite so confident about what is in effect an application of what has been called 'the paradigm case argument'? Still, to go around again, do we not quite plainly know that certain actions are wrong?[16] Is it the case that we can be certain about morality but not certain about moral theories? But again, we should be haunted here by the fact that men of good conscience in different times and places have had very different moral convictions, and representative figures of different cultures appear at least to have held these very different moral beliefs with equal sincerity and conviction. This does not show, as we saw in the last chapter, that they were all equally correct, but it also does not show that any were mistaken either. This fact should make us wary in applying a paradigm case argument here to meet the challenge of ethical scepticism. We should go back to the lists and see if we can discover or develop an objective moral standard that rational and nonevasive men can accept.

NOTES

1. This view has many statements from Cicero and Aquinas down to Erich Fromm. For a sophisticated contemporary statement of it see W. D. Falk, "Morality and Nature," *The Australasian Journal of Philosophy*, vol. XXVIII (September, 1950), pp. 69–92.

2. Mill's essay has been frequently reprinted and anthologized. See Marshall Cohen (ed.), *The Philosophy of John Stuart Mill*, pp. 445–488, and Marcus G. Singer and Robert R. Ammerman (eds.), *Introductory Readings in Philosophy*, pp. 262–279.

3. For the sake of the discussion I assume what is indeed arguable, namely, that there are such distinctive features.

4. George Eliot's *Middlemarch* abounds in examples. See Book Two, chapter 18; Book Six, chapter 61; and Book Seven, chapter 70.

5. I have tried in some detail to examine critically the appeal to human nature in "On Taking Human Nature as the Basis of Morality," *Social Research* (summer, 1962) and "Conventionalism in Morals and the Appeal to Human Nature," *Philosophy and Phenomenological Research*, (1962). I have criticized natural law conceptions in my "An Examination of the Thomistic Theory of Natural Law," *Natural Law Forum*, vol. 4 (1959) and in my "The Myth of Natural Law," in Sidney Hook (ed.), *Law and Philosophy*. However, for another side of the matter see Alan Donagan, "The Scholastic Theory of Moral Law in the Modern World" in *Aquinas: A Collection of Critical Essays*, A. Kenny (ed.).

6. Jeremy Bentham, *An Introduction to the Principles of Morals and Legislation* (1789), and J. S. Mill, *Utilitarianism* (1861). J. J. C. Smart in *An Outline of a System of Utilitarian Ethics*, attempts to do for our time what Mill did for his, and Jan Narveson in *Morality and Utility* attempts in a detailed and careful way to defend what is roughly a Millian utilitarianism that carefully takes into account developments in contemporary analytical philosophy.

7. A. J. Ayer, *Philosophical Essays*, p. 267.

8. Immanuel Kant, *Fundamental Principles of the Metaphysics of Morals* (1785).
9. Arthur E. Murphy, *The Uses of Reason,* chapter 1, part II. The core of this has been reprinted in Marcus G. Singer and Robert R. Ammerman (eds.), *Introductory Readings in Philosophy.* See particularly p. 394 for an elucidation and defense of this blending of Kantian and utilitarian claims.
10. Bentham clearly recognizes this. See chapter I of his *An Introduction to the Principles of Morals and Legislation.*
11. Bentham, ibid., argued for this in chapter I, and Mill in chapter IV of his *Utilitarianism,* op. cit. The basic rationale of their argument here is brilliantly elucidated and defended by E. W. Hall in his "The 'Proof' of Utility in Bentham and Mill," *Categorial Analysis,* pp. 106–132. Hall also refutes some long-standing but mistaken criticisms of Bentham and Mill.
12. A good selection of the representative arguments pro and con about this occur in Paul Taylor's anthology *Problems of Moral Philosophy,* pp. 407–451. It is also discussed by John Hospers under the heading 'hedonism' in his *Human Conduct.*
13. I have argued as if 'utilitarianism' was an ellipsis for 'hedonistic utilitarianism'. This is indeed not so, for there are nonhedonistic utilitarians. The classical utilitarians, however, were hedonistic utilitarians. Many of my criticisms of utilitarianism apply to both forms, although some apply to hedonistic utilitarianism alone. But a nonhedonistic, pluralistic utilitarianism gets into additional difficulties similar to those who argued for principle 4, page 277, and those utilitarians who are intuitionists run afoul of the difficulties in intuitionism discussed in the next chapter. There is a fashionable distinction between act-utilitarianism and rule-utilitarianism which I have also not discussed. Act-utilitarianism is the view that the necessary and sufficient condition for the rightness of any particular act is that it maximizes an intrinsic good—on hedonistic accounts, pleasure—which is thought to be wholly present in individual experiences. Rule-utilitarianism, by contrast, argues that the necessary and sufficient condition for the rightness of any particular act is that it is in accordance with a *rule* which of all the possible alternative rules applicable in such situations would, if consistently acted on in such situations, maximize an intrinsic good—on hedonistic accounts, pleasure—which is thought to be wholly present in individual experiences. I have not distinguished them here or discussed the relative merits of these two different types of utilitarianisms for two reasons. (1) There are powerful arguments advanced by R. M. Hare in *Freedom and Reason,* by Jan Narveson in *Morality and Utility* and by David Lyons in *Forms and Limits of Utilitarianism* which give us good grounds for thinking that any form of rule-utilitarianism that approaches acceptability collapses into act-utilitarianism. However, that the argument is complex and that rule-utilitarianism is not plainly dispensable is made evident in Gertrude Ezorsky's "A Defense of Rule-Utilitarianism," *The Journal of Philosophy,* vol. LXV (September, 1968) and in Richard Brandt's "Some Merits of One Form of Rule-Utilitarianism," *University of Colorado Studies,* no. 3 (1967). (2) Whatever the comparative merits of the two utilitarianisms, powerful reasons for not accepting any form of utilitarianism

have been given by Lyons, op. cit., by John Rawls in "Justice as Fairness," *Philosophical Review*, vol. LXVII (1958) and by A. I. Melden in "Two Comments on Utilitarianism," *Philosophical Review*, (October, 1951) and in "Utility and Moral Reasoning," in Richard T. De George (ed.), *Ethics and Society*. These arguments have led me to abandon utilitarianism. See Chapter 26. Given the precariousness of the utility of the distinctions between the two utilitarianisms, given limited space, and given the fact that there are crucial criticisms applying to both forms of utilitarianism, I did not in the text distinguish them. For a simplified account of these distinctions and the relative merits of each, see Paul Taylor (ed.), *Problems of Moral Philosophy*, pp. 139–153, John Hospers, *Human Conduct*, pp. 311–337, and Michael D. Bayles (ed.), *Contemporary Utilitarianism*, pp. 1–12. In claiming, as I do, that to assert 'Pleasure is good' is to assert a truism, this indeed gives you to understand that I think the principle Bentham called the "principle of asceticism" is absurd.
14. Chapter 15, section IV.
15. See W. K. Frankena, "The Naturalistic Fallacy," in Philippa Foot, *Theories of Ethics*; E. W. Hall, *Categorial Analysis*, pp. 109–122; George Nakhnikian, "On the Naturalistic Fallacy," in Hector-Neri Castañeda and George Nakhnikian, *Morality and the Language of Conduct*; and C. Levy, "G. E. Moore on the Naturalistic Fallacy," in P. F. Strawson (ed.), *Studies in the Philosophy of Thought and Action*.
16. This kind of skepticism about moral skepticism is powerfully argued by R. F. Holland, "Moral Scepticism," *Aristotelian Society*, supplementary vol. XLI (1967), pp. 185–198. But to come to see that there are problems about this commonsensical approach, see Jonathan Harrison, same volume, pp. 206–207.

25

SEARCH
FOR A STANDARD: II

I

We saw toward the end of the last chapter that ultimate moral principles were not to be construed as empirical statements of fact or hypotheses open to confirmation and disconfirmation. That something is right or wrong or good or evil is never something that simply could be established by observation or by inference from observation. Our central ways of knowing—that is, by logical demonstration, simple observation, and by the use of experimental design—seem not to be sufficient in themselves, either singly or jointly, to establish the truth or falsity of basic moral claims.

Faced with these difficulties, some distinguished and indeed toughminded philosophers have suggested that we must appeal to intuition to establish ethical first principles. I am no 'partisan of intuitionism' myself, and I am fully aware of the antipathy, distrust, and in some places settled disbelief that intuitionism arouses. But given the breakdown or at least apparent breakdown of the more standard methods in ethics, given the at least partial force of arguing from paradigm cases as I did at the end of the last chapter, and given the fact that intuitionism has been defended by some distinguished philosophers, we should see what can be said for this method. Can we come to know in some intuitive way what is right or wrong? Can such a method of ethics enable us to arrive at a sound or reliable objective moral standard or set of moral standards?

We should first try to understand what is involved in intuitionism in ethics. It is the claim that we have a faculty of moral insight, or at least that we have cognitive moral insights, by means of which we simply directly recognize the truth of certain fundamental moral principles or judgments. It is usually identified with a special '*a priori* insight'. Such an intuition is *not* a kind of feeling or hunch, but it is thought by intuitionists in ethics to be a rational faculty or capacity. It reveals to us necessary moral principles that are as self-evidently certain as the axioms of logic and mathematics. But unlike analytic statements they are supposed to give us an objective knowledge of moral reality. (In some sense they are supposed to be both synthetic and *a priori*.)

Samuel Clarke, a seventeenth-century exponent of intuitionism, put the intuitionist claim in this confident way.

> [Basic moral principles] are so notoriously plain and self-evident, that nothing but the extremest stupidity of mind, corruption of Manners, or perverseness of Spirit can possibly make any Man entertain the least doubt concerning them. For Man endowed with Reason to deny the Truth of these things, is the very same thing as if . . . a Man that understands Geometry or Arithmetic, should deny the most obvious and known proportions of Lines or Numbers, and perversely contend that the Whole is not equal to all its parts, or that a square is not double to a triangle of equal base and height.[1]

Clarke, and Thomas Reid as well, are confident there are intuitions that moral agents could not seriously and honestly bring themselves to doubt. Ewing, a twentieth-century intuitionist, is not nearly so confident. He recognizes at the outset that one of the main reasons people are led to deny the objectivity of ethical belief is that in reasoning about ethics, "we are very soon brought to a point where we have to fall back on intuition, so that disputants are placed in a situation where there are just two conflicting intuitions between which there seems to be no means of deciding."

Ewing nevertheless defends an appeal to intuition as the sole means of attaining truth concerning fundamental questions of ethics and as an escape from subjectivity. Ewing even argues that "all reasoning . . . presupposes intuition." To see Ewing's grounds for such a claim, note what he says about deductive reasoning. I cannot argue 'A therefore B' and 'From B, C follows' without

> seeing that A entails B and B entails C, and this must either be seen immediately or require a further argument. If it is seen immediately, it is a case of intuition; if it has to be established by further argument, this means that another term, D, must be interpolated between A and B such that A entails D and D entails B, and similarly with B and C, but then the same question arises about A entailing D, so that sooner or later we must come to something which we see intuitively to be true, as the process of interpolation cannot go on *ad infinitum*. We cannot therefore, whatever we do, get rid of intuition if we are to have any valid inference at all.[2]

Concerning this it will be surely objected that the 'intuition' Ewing is talking about in such a situation is 'linguistic intuition'—a knowing how to employ certain words in our language. When I 'see immediately' that if A is to the right of B and B is to the right of C then A must be to the right of C, I am doing nothing more extraordinary than indicating that I understand the meaning of 'to the right of'. In just the same way I indicate my understanding of the meaning of the word 'puppy' when I recognize that puppies are young dogs, or my understanding of the use of 'red' when I recognize immediately that red things must be colored.

The same thing holds about entailment in Ewing's case.[3] I exhibit, in recognizing such truths, my understanding of my language and an understanding that any equivalent terms in other languages must function in the same way. The mastery of a language consists fundamentally in coming to know how to operate with the terms in question. The connections are all analytic, and there is no need whatsoever to appeal to intuition. Even if one does continue to talk in this misleading manner about 'intuitions', what must be recognized is that the intuitive claims made in ethics are not that certain analytic statements are true, as in the preceding cases, but that certain synthetic statements—statements not true by definition—are true.

Ewing argues that it is not only in logic and mathematics and with analytical statements that we need intuitions but in all other areas of reasoning as well. Ewing make the surprising claim that even in arguing about questions of fact we need at various key points to appeal to intuition. Ethics, he maintains, is not at all that unique in this respect. If we are not suspicious about the appeal to intuition concerning matters of fact (as we should not be after we have examined the matter), we should not be suspicious about it in matters of morality.

Let us examine Ewing's argument that we appeal to intuition even in deciding complex factual issues. An illustration will help make determine what Ewing is contending. Historians still argue about whether it is or is not a fact that Germany lost two thirds of its population during the Thirty Years War. Some believe that they did and some believe that they did not. In deciding which belief is the more probable, different people will make different judgments, giving differing weights to the different considerations. In making such judgments a historian will finally have to rely on his own estimate of the weight of the various considerations that count for and against the claim that Germany lost two thirds of its population during the Thirty Years War. And this in turn rests on the individual historian's 'insight into their nature'. Sometimes, in making such judgments, we can calculate the probabilities, but sometimes we cannot. Often, according to Ewing, we either 'see' or do not 'see' which is the more likely, and we cannot prove that what we are convinced of is so.

Surely there is something wrong with this way of talking about and conceiving the situation. The word 'see' is but a metaphor here. Moreover, if there were something that we could literally see, we would not have to rely on insight. Indeed, dropping the useless metaphor of 'seeing' here, we can say that in some judgments of probability we have to rely on our insight, meaning by that our past experience. Beyond that, in such circumstances we must simply make a decision of principle about what to believe without any substantial grounds for deciding one way rather than another. But there is no call to speak of some distinctive nonempirical cognitive faculty here, or to speak of an *a priori* insight. That Germany lost two thirds of its population during the Thirty Years War purports to assert a fact. It makes an empirical claim and as such it is confirmable or infirmable. If certain new records were unearthed or several very unimpeachable chronicles were discovered, such a claim could be disconfirmed or at least infirmed by something that is quite plainly observable. That is to say, there are certain observable states of affairs that we can quite readily conceive of, which, directly or indirectly, would count as empirical evidence for the truth or the falsity of such a claim.

There is a very considerable difference, however, between basic judgments of value and questions of fact. As Ewing himself is concerned to stress, basic judgments of value are not so confirmable or disconfirmable while factual statements are. What, for example, would confirm or disconfirm either 'Pleasure and pleasure alone is *worth* seeking for its own sake' or 'I know it is not in your advantage, but you ought to do it all the same'? What would we have to see, hear, smell, touch, weigh, measure, or count in order to confirm or disconfirm these judgments? They most certainly appear to be completely unverifiable even in principle. At least in this crucial respect there is not the parallel that Ewing stresses between judgments of fact and judgments of value. There is nothing analogous in the rest of our experience that would justify our speaking of 'moral intuitions' as a source of moral knowledge.

II

Let us look at another point that Ewing makes in defense of intuitionism. He tries to take some of the mystery away from the notion by showing that *in a way* intuitions are testable, and that we can distinguish between genuine and *ersatz* intuitions. This is important because what are taken to be intuitions frequently conflict, and, if the appeal is not to degenerate into a subjective one, we must have some reliable method in virtue of which we can distinguish 'real intuitions' from merely 'ostensible intuitions', authentic intuitions from inauthentic ones.

Ewing contends that we can be mistaken in our intuitive judgments because our intuitions may be distorted to a degree because they arise (1) from a lack of adequate experience with the matter about which we make the judgment, (2) from "intellectual confusions of some sort," (3) from "failure to attend adequately to certain aspects of the situation or of the consequences," and (4) from "psychological causes such as those with which the psychoanalyst deals." But if our intuition is not distorted in any of these ways, we must say that what is intuitively evident to us is a genuine intuition, an intuition we must accept as true. (That is, statements expressing such intuitions must be said to be true.)

To see a little more adequately why someone might maintain this, let us examine an ethical dispute. In doing this, keep in mind that initially one might very well think that the following principles are intuitively true. However—or so it is claimed—a consideration of their consequences will cast doubt on that.

> The ultimate end of all moral action is to seek the maximum amount of happiness possible.
>
> The ultimate end of all moral action is to seek the maximum amount of satisfaction of desire.

Secularists with even mildly benevolent or kind dispositions are inclined, at least on first hearing such utterances, to opt for a principle like the above utilitarian principles. What could be better than a world of happy people, and obviously the more happiness the better. But now consider this consequence. Suppose we say quite plausibly that happiness mainly consists of the satisfaction of desire or of enjoyment. Then, consistent with what we said above, we would go on to say the more satisfaction of desire there is in the world the better. If we say this, we would seem to be committed to saying that there cannot be anything evil or even wrong with the enjoyment or pleasure derived by a large enough audience—say Madison Square Garden filled to capacity—watching the torture of an unemployable man whom nobody loved. According to our preceding principle, the badness of the situation should diminish as the size of the audience and consequent total enjoyment increases. But our very benevolent attitudes—to say nothing of our moral sensibilities—prod us into rebelling at that judgment. Actually, we are inclined to say—inconsistently with our above general principle, that is, the more happiness the better—that the situation grows worse when more people enjoy and take pleasure in such torture. The more people who enjoy it, the worse it is. It is bad enough if a few do, but it is worse still if many do. This is surely 'the verdict' of our moral feelings. Reflecting on these consequences, we may no longer accept in an unqualified way our initial judgment. Yet, it is just this judgment that seemed initially to be certain. It might be argued that on examination, however, we come to 'see' that it is not a genuine intuition.

In such a manner we can correct what Ewing calls our 'intuitions'. Ewing also points out that even after such corrections are made, there remain conflicts in intuition. Even after the reasoning involved in the above case, we might still get the following ethical argument.

A: There is something evil, intrinsically evil, about taking pleasure in the pain of others that in no way is a function of its effects.

B: (a Millian hedonistic utilitarian): To take pleasure in the pain of others is evil because of its effects. That is, it tends to lead to sadistic behavior on the part of such people, but there is nothing wrong with the pleasure per se.

A: Even taken by itself, such pleasure is evil. Even if the punishment of such sadists has no utilitarian value, still they *deserve* to be punished, and ought to be punished for taking such pleasure in the suffering of others.

B: Such an attitude, such a desire to punish, is understandable but irrational all the same, for it only heaps suffering on suffering. It does nothing at all to alleviate suffering.

A: Oh, yes, it does. It assuages the feelings of those who have been made to suffer or of those who are indignant over the suffering. But even if it did not serve that function, they simply ought to suffer because they *deserve* to suffer for what they did.

B: To inflict even more suffering to lessen one's indignation at needless suffering is not worthy of a rational man. To inflict pain deliberately where that pain will not relieve a still greater pain or misery is always irrational.

A: Not always. The perpetrators of the vilest crimes at Belsen deserve to suffer for what they did quite apart from whether their behavior will be altered by their being made to suffer, or whether society will receive any benefit at all.

B: I abhor what they did as much as you do. The bestiality of it sickens my heart and fires my indignation. But to inflict even more suffering to no purpose is utterly without justification.

Here we have a very fundamental conflict in ethical commitments. Whose intuitions are we going to rely on, A's or B's? How would we decide this issue if we were intuitionists? How is Ewing going to decide which, if either, intuition is a genuine intuition? In a similar vein there are those who will argue that never under any circumstances should one punish, sacrifice, or even harm the innocent. Others will say that circumstances might arise in which, for the protection of all, we must, even from the point of view of morality, sacrifice or harm the innocent.

In the preceding case we have several conflicting yet very fundamental moral principles. Both the utilitarian principles and the principles of their opponents fit into a tolerably coherent system of ethical principles. The utilitarian principles are the simplest, but why prefer the simplest? The utilitarians may gain simplicity of theory by oversimplifying the complexity of the moral life. Intuitionism seems to be completely helpless here. How can we in these circumstances know whose intuitions are the *genuine* intuitions?

Sometimes even within a given normative ethical system there are conflicting moral statements, for example, p and not-p. Logic tells us that both cannot be true, but we also feel that both are intuitively certain. If we are intuitionists, how do we know which to choose in the situation where both p and not-p cohere equally well with the other principles in our moral system? In such a situation and given such an ethical theory, there is no objective way of deciding between p and not-p.

An intuitionist might admit all these difficulties as genuine difficulties in his account and agree that in many situations we have no way of deciding which of the alleged intuitions are genuine—after all, the moral life is complex—but he might counter that no other ethical theory is any better. Such facts, he might continue, do not refute or even seriously count against intuitionism; they merely attest to the complexity of the moral life. Moreover, concerning fundamentals, what more can we realistically say than what G. E. Moore said, namely, that good—taken now as the most fundamental ethical concept—is a unique unanalyzable moral concept? Either you are directly aware of goodness or you are not. If you are directly aware of it, you know, although you cannot prove or give evidence for the goodness of x; if you are not, you are not, and that's the end of it.

The problem remains that different people with conflicting views claim to be aware of what is good. They all claim to be directly aware that so and so is intrinsically good (worth having for its own sake), but they frequently differ about what this so and so is. If we say that some of these people are *morally blind*, we get into a number of well-known difficulties. There is no exact analogy between being color-blind and being 'morally blind' in virtue of which we can give a clear, objective meaning to the concept of moral-blindness. There are tests for whether a man is color-blind or tone-deaf. There are no tests for moral-blindness. People who are color-blind or tone-deaf can be brought to realize and accept that they are color-blind or tone-deaf, but people (generally speaking, at least) will not admit, even to themselves, that they are morally blind.

If we give up this analogy, there is no force to our talk of 'moral-blindness'. Moreover, we must simply say, if we are intuitionists, that we have conflicting intuitions about what is right or good with no way of deciding which intuitions are *genuine* intuitions.

Intuitionists claim that their ethical theory is more objective than the competing ethical theories. It alone holds out a genuine claim to objective ethical knowledge. But is it in reality more objective? It seems to me that in reality intuitionists are just as subjective as the subjectivists they criticize, for over fundamental ethical disputes, like the ones we have characterized, the intuitionists are not able to show us who is right or how we or the disputants are capable of ascertaining who has the genuine or real intuition in such a situation. (If they *both* have genuine intuitions, then there can be equally correct but conflicting intuitions. But then we hardly have a viable conception of a genuine intuition or a basis for an objective morality.) Instead of frankly admitting, as do the subjectivists, that there is a conflict of attitudes here, a different set of moral commitments, they simply redescribe this state of affairs in terms of a conflict of intuitions. Calling a whore a strumpet does not make her any the less a whore.

III

Ethical naturalism is a theory that maintains that moral statements are a distinctive type of empirical factual statement and that moral terms are equivalent to purely empirical terms. That is to say, 'good' has the same meaning as 'pleasure' or 'answering to interests' or 'making for survival' or some more complicated set of purely empirical terms. And to say that so and so ought to be done and that so and so is a duty would presumably mean that certain social demands were being made, or at least these terms would be defined in terms of 'good' or 'morally good', and this term would in turn be defined in purely empirical terms. If such a naturalistic program is indeed a correct account of morality, then—depending of course on what the correct naturalistic definition is—'Happiness is good', 'Answering to interests is good', or 'What makes for human survival is always good' would be analytic, but we have already seen the mistakes in such a claim.[4]

G. E. Moore maintained in his *Principia Ethica* that any attempt so to define 'good' is in error, for it commits something that Moore called "the naturalistic fallacy." There has been a considerable dispute about what exactly is this alleged fallacy and whether it is a fallacy or even a mistake.[5] I will take it here to be the claim that it is always a mistake to claim an identity between any empirical qualities or relations and any set of fundamental moral concepts such as good, right, or ought. The same point, or a very similar point, might be put more linguistically: 'Good', 'right', or 'ought' in their moral employments never have the same meaning as any purely empirical terms or set of purely empirical terms. Whatever naturalistic definition is proposed for 'good' (to take a key example), it always makes sense—it is never a purely *verbal* mistake—to ask 'Is X good?', where X is a term standing for such purely empirical characteristics or relations, and it never is self-contradictory to deny that X is good.[6] But, if this is so, the alleged identity of meaning could not obtain.

I neither want to deny that there are difficulties with such an account nor maintain that ethical naturalism, even when it is characterized as I have characterized it here, has been definitely refuted. But ethical naturalism is, to put it mildly, in a very controversial and problematical position, and our remarks in the last chapter about the failure of analytical moral utterances to serve as action guides should indicate that it is not a very promising position. However, that remark is itself controversial philosophically. I do not think it would be profitable or crucial to pursue this to the bitter end here.[7]

What I think is evident, however, is that moral judgments are not simply statements of fact that can be known to be true or false in the way one can know 'The watch is on the desk' or 'Irishmen tend to vote Democrat' is true or false. It is certainly mistaken or at least misleading to say there are no moral facts. (After all, is it not a fact that Hitler was an evil man or that pointless suffering should be avoided?) But people who asserted that there are no moral facts pointed misleadingly to an important contention whose falsity is not at all obvious, namely, that 'good', 'right', 'ought', or 'This is good', 'That ought to be done', 'This is the right thing to do', 'Civil disobedience in such a context is not just a right, it is a duty' do not in their moral employments stand for occurrences or states in space and time that might simply be observed or noted by a dispassionate spectator of the actual. It is not true that if such and such is observed or noted, one must assert that 'This is good' is true or 'That ought to be done' is true and if such and such is not observed or noted, we must say that it is false. It is not the case, it is claimed, that we can simply independently of our moral convictions and attitudinal sets determine moral truth or falsity by observation and logical deductions from our observations.[8]

Such a claim appears at least to be well supported. In the crucial sense specified, moral statements do not appear, at least, to state facts, but what is a fact is that people make moral judgments, for example, 'Jones believes that double parking is wrong', 'Felicia believes one ought only to sleep with one's own husband', 'Americans believe Communism is evil'.

Thus it would appear at least to be true that moral claims or statements cannot simply be known to be true or false as one can know 'The cat is on the mat' or 'An unbalanced force acting on a body will cause it to accelerate' is true or false. These nonmoral statements are verifiable, that is, directly or indirectly confirmable or infirmable. But we cannot confirm or disconfirm moral claims through observation. As we have seen, we cannot know them to be true by intuition, either. Thus, we seem to be bereft of any basis in terms of which we can gain a knowledge of good and evil or of right and wrong.

IV

Such considerations have given considerable force to subjectivism and ethical skepticism.[9] That is, many believe there can be no rational decision procedure for adjudicating fundamental moral disagreements, since fundamental moral judgments and ultimate moral principles cannot correctly be said to be true or false in such a way that any rational agent, who is apprised of the relevant facts, will agree about their truth or falsity. Naive subjectivism attempts to show why this must be so, but we have already seen that naive subjectivism is false. But nonnaive subjectivism remains in the running, and given the inadequacies of classical ethical theories and the failure of intuitionism and ethical naturalism, it requires our attention. It also shows, if it is a correct account of morality, that and why our preceding claim about moral truth must be so, for if moral utterances merely express the attitudes or feelings of their utterers and are consciously or unconsciously (unwittingly) used by them as persuasive devices to evoke or invite similar attitudes in others, then moral utterances cannot make objective truth claims.

It should be kept in mind that this claim is being made about the ultimate or fundamental moral principles or claims. Given agreement concerning them, subjectivists can agree that we can in favorable circumstances attain rational agreement about nonfundamental moral judgments being true or false. However, if any form of subjectivism is a correct account of morality, the truth of these nonfundamental moral propositions is always dependent on a contingent and nonrational agreement concerning ultimate moral principles. To see what is involved here note this example.

A: You ought to stop smoking.

B: Why?

A: Because smoking causes cancer.

B: So what?

A: Cancer is no laughing matter. It can be very painful and it frequently kills.

B: What's so bad about that?

A: Don't be stupid or just argue for argument's sake. Pain is bad and life, under most conditions anyway, is a very precious thing.

This, I admit, is an almost ludicrously artificial moral argument. People like B—if indeed there are such people—test our "willing suspension of disbelief." The example suits our purposes, however, for it brings out how, if a certain line of argument or resistance is taken concerning a very ordinary moral judgment ('You ought to stop smoking'), then a fundamental moral judgment ('Pain is bad and life under most conditions anyway is a very precious thing') will have to be elicited in quick order for its support. More realistic examples of moral argument would show the same thing only less quickly, for the argument there is more complex. Our example will do to show that moral judgments presuppose for their validity fundamental moral judgments.[10]

It is the claim of nonnaive subjectivists in ethical theory that such fundamental moral judgments are not really judgments at all, but in reality are either (1) simply emotional expressions or expressions of attitude or commitment of the utterer or (2) and more plausibly, that although they superficially appear to be either true or false moral statements, they actually are expressive and/or evocative of the emotional commitments or conative responses of the people in the cultural group of the person who makes the putative judgment.[11] The crucial claim of such a subjectivist is that moral utterances are basically emotional or conative responses and are no more capable of being true or false than 'yippie' or 'ouch' or 'shut the door'.

Such subjectivists would go on to argue, as Hume did, that in the last analysis it is our feelings, our attitudes, and not our reason and intelligence, which are decisive in our decision that something is good or bad, right or wrong, *worth* doing or seeking or *not worth* doing or seeking.[12] *Emotion* is central in morality. To come to have a certain moral point of view is basically to come to have a certain set of attitudes and to react affectively in a certain manner. It is not to come to have a distinctive kind of knowledge or gain a certain intellectual insight. Bentham is mistaken; we cannot escape appealing to 'the principle of sympathy and antipathy'. It is a bit of mythology to think that we have an objective, external moral standard not grounded in our feelings. Reason is but a slave or servant of the passions. It can tell us how to attain what we desire or how to harmonize desires, but it cannot tell us which *ends* of action to make our own. In fact, it is not only true that the rightness or goodness of an action or principle cannot be discovered by reason, but it is also true that reason can never finally move us to action. Only an emotion can *motivate* us to do anything. At best, reason can show us that there are some things we simply must do in order to attain something we want. But the ultimate *ends* of action are determined by our *feelings*. Kierkegaard was on solid ground when he claimed that reason could not determine or ascertain the ends of life. Fundamental moral judgments are really only expressions of emotion, and since this is so, there can be no question of some knowledge or rational understanding of the 'true ends of life'. Such talk can only be evasively ideological, for there is nothing to be known or doubted here.

Moral utterances, according to such an account, are thus neither true nor false, for they literally do not assert anything but simply function to express and evoke feelings and stimulate action. They are indeed frequently stated in the indicative form and *appear*, as 'ouch' and 'yippie' and the like do not, to make statements that are either true or false. But here their grammatical form misleads us. Compare

1. Jean *ought* to have left him.
2. Jean *did* leave him.

There are morally neutral, plain facts which can confirm the second statement, namely, we can determine by empirical investigation that she has lived with her mother and has not seen him for the last two years. No doubt we cannot ascertain this with certainty in most instances, but in many cases the probability is very high that what we report as the empirical facts are the facts. But with the first statement the situation is altered. Suppose—to take an absurdly radical case—the relevant empirical facts are these: He strikes her frequently, he gets drunk with the boys and spends everything he has earned, without consulting her withdraws from their joint bank account money she earned, frequently beats up their child, and sleeps with her sister. These facts would indeed strongly incline one to believe that Jean ought to have left him. But they would not commit one to that logically. That is, one does not contradict oneself if one asserts these facts and denies that she ought to leave him; they are compatible with the moral judgment that she ought not to leave him. One could well imagine a devout Catholic or Jew asking herself, "But really, all the same, should I leave him? After all, he is my husband. Is it right for me to leave him? I did vow something about for better or for worse, until death do us part." Perhaps people should not so reason. I certainly think they should not. But her remarks are not unintelligible.

Moral utterances, such subjectivists could continue, function very differently than do statements of fact in spite of their similar grammatical form. In their most typical and most crucial employments, moral utterances are used to guide conduct, to prescribe a course of action. In such employments they are used to tell people to *do* something; they do not simply or at all tell people that something is the case. They tell us to *make* something the case, but of course if we did not know something about what is the case, we could not know what to make the case or how to do it. The crucial conceptual fact is that moral utterances typically function to tell people to do something rather than to explain behavior or describe conduct.

It is this, together with their related emotive or dynamic function, that is, expressive and evocative function, that makes them normative utterances. Note that there is a very considerable difference between saying something is green and saying something is vile, or saying somebody did something and saying he should do it. In most contexts, to say that something is green or to say that somebody did something is simply neutrally to describe something; to say that it is vile or that it should be done is to express an attitude and to attempt to evoke a similar attitude in others and, in many cases at any rate, to indicate that a certain course of action is to be followed. Words such as 'vile' and 'should' have a dynamism—a trigger function—that words such as 'green' and 'did' lack, and it is in virtue of this trigger function that they are *normative*. The moral life is essentially the emotional life, and since moral utterances and terms are so expressive and evocative of emotion, they cannot be the vehicles of impersonal truth and thus they cannot make objective claims. An understanding of moral discourse will lead one to see why some form of subjectivism must be true. There can be no moral knowledge—no knowledge of good and evil—no matter how much we may wish there were, for there are no objective facts that could confirm or infirm fundamental moral claims—for example, 'One ought always to be fair in one's dealing with other people'—and thus give us some reason to believe that even our most reflective and heartfelt moral beliefs are either true or false.[13]

V

We could and in a fuller account should challenge the detail of this theory.[14] In stating it as I did, I was often on thin ice. It is indeed defective in many ways. But perhaps it could be reformulated so very similar problems about the objectivity of moral claims would arise. I am not going to challenge such a theory in any thorough or detailed way, but I will simply note one crucial difficulty and then I will, principally in the next chapter, sketch in the bare bones of a more adequate theory that could, like the phoenix, arise from the ashes. That is, it is a theory that takes due account of this subjectivist challenge and concedes much— perhaps too much—to it, and yet avoids the difficulties noted by subjectivists in previous objectivist accounts. It accounts for the same linguistic facts nonnaive subjectivists account for, and it shows how there can be a rational decision procedure in ethics.

Note first that nonnaive subjectivists, while they maintain that they could not deductively prove or confirm any fundamental moral claim, do admit that reasons are given for moral judgments. They point out that moral judgments are distinct from imperatives, commands, expressions of wishes, exclamations, and the like in that it always makes sense to ask of any moral judgment whatsoever what reasons there are for asserting it.[15] Yet it remains true that we cannot confirm or infirm a fundamental moral judgment or deduce it from nonmoral judgments. What then, subjectivists properly ask, makes a reason a good reason for a moral claim? How do the reasons for the moral conclusion support the moral conclusion? The answer, according to such subjectivists, is that they only support them psychologically. Such subjectivists stress that whatever in fact determines our attitudes is a good reason for our moral judgments. Whatever moves or prods us to act as the moral claim prescribes is by definition a good or relevant reason for the moral claim in question.

This is a reductio ad absurdum of giving a reason for a moral judgment. To see how this is so, it would be well to look at a case. Suppose I promise to help the Salvation Army distribute pledge envelopes and then

I do not do it. My wife reminds me that this is something I ought to do since I promised. Suppose I say, 'I don't see why I should.' Puzzled, she asks why I say that. I reply, 'Because my big toe itches.' Suppose my charisma with her is such that she comes to agree in attitude with me and now agrees that since my big toe itches I should not distribute the pledge envelopes. But if she has been *moved* by this fact—that is, the fact that my big toe itches—she has been moved by what, logically speaking, is a veritable paradigm (model) of an irrelevant consideration. Yet, on such a subjectivist or emotivist account, it would be a good or a relevant reason for a moral judgment simply because it turned out to be *psychologically* effective. However, as our paradigm brings out, this is not a sufficient condition, let alone a necessary and sufficient condition, for a reason to be a good (that is, a relevant) reason for a moral judgment. By arbitrary definitional fiat these subjectivists or emotivists collapse crucial conceptual distinctions between advice and propaganda, between establishing a point and *getting* someone to do something, between terminating an argument and *proving* a contention.[16]

A nonnaive subjectivist or emotivist could counter that in the preceding context and contexts similar to that, 'relevant' is itself an evaluative, emotive term. 'Relevant consideration' in such a context means nothing more than 'a consideration that the speaker is *moved* to accept in determining his attitude'. But, as the preceding paradigm example shows, this is plainly not all that 'relevant consideration' means in such contexts. Recall exactly what these emotivists were trying to do: They were trying in a normatively and morally neutral manner to characterize how our moral discourse actually works. However, just as the most superficial reminders of usage show that 'X is true' does not mean 'X is believed with good warrant', so by the same evident considerations of usage it can be made plain that 'X is a morally relevant reason for doing Y' does not mean 'X is a consideration the speaker is moved to accept in deciding to do Y'. Just as it is perfectly correct to state, 'Although he believed X with good warrant, X turned out to be false', so it is perfectly correct to say 'X moved the speaker to do Y but X, morally speaking, is a perfectly irrelevant reason for doing Y'. We could not intelligibly say this if the equivalences of meaning asserted above actually held.

Noting that 'morally speaking', 'irrelevant', 'correct' and the like are evaluative terms is not to the point as a rebuttal, for evaluative or not, emotive or not, such linguistic and conceptual regularities as are revealed in the preceding examples indicate that these terms also have determinate criteria that limit what we can and cannot say with conceptual propriety when we use them.

The argument in the preceding paragraphs shows that there are determinate criteria for what, logically speaking, can count as a good or relevant reason in ethics, and that the emotivist and nonnaive subjectivist accounts do not correctly characterize the way moral discourse functions here.

Emotivists have not argued in the way I am about to characterize, but an emotivist might shift his ground and say, alternatively to what has been said so far, that a reason is a relevant reason for a moral judgment only if it is stated by way of a premiss which, when combined with another premiss, validly entails the moral judgment in question. He could assert this and still consistently continue to insist that this only obtains when the other premiss (usually a major premiss) is itself a value judgment, devoid of truth value and expressive and evocative of human attitudes. If such evaluative premisses are accepted, he would continue, there can be relevant reasons in moral argument; if not, there cannot be. And if not, we simply have in the last analysis one attitudinal stance set against another. In such a situation there is nothing to argue about, nothing to prove. In reality, 'proving an ethical claim' or 'objectively justifying an ethical claim', he could go on to maintain, is an empty notion. There is no 'proving to be done' or 'justification to be carried out', except in the trivial sense of deducing one evaluative utterance from other premisses, at least one of which is equally expressive and evocative and devoid of truth value. The chain of reasoning must come to an end, and we are finally left with such expressive and evocative major moral premisses devoid of truth value, for which no reasons, justification, or proof of any sort can be given.

Yet again, if p is a moral premiss, it would seem to be the case that it is always perfectly in order (as a logical point, at least) to ask for reasons for accepting that moral principle—for accepting what it claims as being so. Unless the nonnaive subjectivists can articulate some sound argument for believing that there is a certain class of cases—to wit, certain very fundamental moral judgments for which such a request for reasons is logically out of order—it would at least appear to be the case that their position has been faulted. Yet Ayer is perfectly correct in asserting that one cannot deductively prove or inductively establish a fundamental moral principle.

What has gone wrong? What is left out of the subjectivist's or emotivist's account? These subjectivists have failed to take proper note of the fact that morality is a practical activity and that we can and do reason about what *to do* as well as about what is the case. Moral questions, as we have noted, are fundamentally questions about what to do. In reasoning about conduct—in engaging in what some people rather misleadingly have called 'practical reasoning'—we are reasoning about what to make the case, or about what to do, or about what attitude to take toward what is or has been the case. Our concern with what is the case in morality is subordinate to our concern with what to do about it or what stance to take toward it. That is, in reasoning morally we are concerned with what is the case to the extent that such concern is relevant in establishing what it is that we are *to do*. Moral knowledge, if indeed there is any, is for the most part knowledge about what to do or to have done, about what is good to seek, or about what one ought to be or have been. (I say 'for the most part', for in asserting that someone has an admirable character, we appear at least to be making an assertion about what is the case, although nonnaive subjectivists (emotivists) would, of course, construe that utterance quite differently. But we can safely ignore that complication and say: Moral utterances are primarily concerned with what to do.)

There is, as far as I can see, no sound reason to assume that such practical discourse—primarily 'a telling to' discourse rather than 'a telling that' discourse—is more untrustworthy or subjective than theoretical discourse. It is just different, with a different rationale and a different role in the stream of life.

Such a claim is further reinforced when we recall that reasoning in any domain—mathematics, science, law, morality—is a limited context-dependent mode of reasoning. To know what constitutes a good move in chess, a good play in football, a legally valid judgment, or a good military strategy, one needs to understand the overall *rationale* of the activity in question. Note that if an explanation provides a lucid representation of the relevant phenomena, is a systematic explanation that coheres well with the laws, validated theories, and other explanations of the scientific corpus in question, and if it has considerable predictive power, it will be said to be a good scientific explanation. That this is so is evident from knowing the overall rationale of science. Analogous arguments have been and should be made for morality.[17]

Thus, a first move in providing a viable alternative to ethical scepticism or subjectivism is to understand clearly the functions or purposes of morality in human living. This is the key to getting some reasonably determinate general answers as to what constitutes a good reason in moral reasoning. Only if there are fairly determinate answers to the following questions will it be the case that there is a definite pattern to moral reasoning and a set of reasons that unequivocally constitute good reasons in ethics. And unless this is so, subjectivism or ethical skepticism will remain the option a nonevasive man will have to accept.

The questions we need to face center in this cluster: What central role or roles does morality play in human living? Why is it that we have a moral code, any moral code, at all? What is the point of having a morality, any morality, at all? To know what would count as a justification of a moral proposition, we must have answers to such questions. Understanding a concept involves grasping its functions, coming to see its role in the stream of life, understanding what is characteristically done with it and through it. This is what we must do with moral concepts, for until we so understand them, we cannot know if moral claims can have the kind of objectivity we desire. It is to this task that we will turn in the next chapter.

In this section I have tried to set the stage for that task by indicating that to answer these questions is crucial if anything is to be made of moral objectivism, that conceiving of moral discourse as a form of practical discourse takes account of the linguistic facts highlighted by nonnaive subjectivists, and that subjectivism itself cannot account for a feature of moral discourse that it acknowledges to be an integral part of that discourse.

NOTES

1. See the selection from Samuel Clarke in vol. II of L. A. Selby-Bigge (ed.), *British Moralists*. The crucial claims made by Thomas Reid are in his *On The Active Powers of Man* (1788). There is a central brief selection from Reid's ethical writings in Paul Edwards and Arthur Pap (eds.), *A Modern Introduction to Philosophy*, pp. 288–297.

2. A. C. Ewing, *The Definition of Good*, chapter I. See also the selection from Ewing in Paul Edwards and Arthur Pap (eds.), op. cit., pp. 310–320. Ewing later in his *Second Thoughts in Moral Philosophy* has tried to abandon intuitionism, but, as D. H. Monro shows in an examination of this book, many of the assumptions of intuitionism remain. See D. H. Monro, "Critical Notice," *Australasian Journal of Philosophy*, vol. 38 (December, 1960), pp. 260–274.

3. By 'entailment', philosophers mean a relation between statements such that to say one or more statements entail another statement is to say that the last statement follows validly from those statements. One or more premisses entail a conclusion if and only if it is logically impossible that the premisses should be true and the conclusion false.

4. Chapter 24, section IV.

5. G. E. Moore, *Principia Ethica*, chapter 1. For discussions of the naturalistic fallacy see A. N. Prior, *Logic and the Basis of Ethics*, pp. 1–12. (This important critique of Prior's is reprinted in Rosalind Ekman (ed.), *Readings in the Problems of Ethics*, pp. 118–126.) W. K. Frankena, "The Naturalistic Fallacy," in Philippa Foot (ed.), *Theories of Ethics;* George Nakhnikian "On The Naturalistic Fallacy," in Hector-Neri Castañeda and George Nakhnikian (eds.), *Morality and the Language of Conduct.* C. Lewy, "G. E. Moore on the Naturalistic Fallacy," *Proceedings of the British Academy*, vol. L (1964) gives an excellent elucidation of what Moore was claiming; and working with an unfinished draft for a new Preface to *Principia Ethica*, he gives us some of Moore's second thoughts about the naturalistic fallacy. This important essay has been reprinted in P. F. Strawson (ed.), *Studies in the Philosophy of Thought and Action*.

6. It is not clear what Moore thought he was trying to deny could be naturalistically defined. If we read his thesis linguistically, it is 'intrinsic good' that could not be naturalistically defined, but his argument could be extended to other fundamental ethical terms.

7. I have pursued it further in my "Problems of Ethics," in Paul Edwards (ed.), *Encyclopedia of Philosophy*, vol. III.

8. This is clearly argued by Axel Hägerström in "On the Truth of Moral Propositions," in his *Philosophy and Religion*, pp. 77–96, and by A. J. Ayer, "On the Analysis of Moral Judgements," in his *Philosophical Essays*.

9. For two recent sophisticated book-length defenses of subjectivism in ethics, see J. Hartland-Swann, *An Analysis of Morals*, and D. H. Monro, *Empiricism and Ethics*.

10. Sidney Hook, following some leads given by John Dewey, has interestingly and plausibly tried to resist the idea that in actual argument we get pushed into the position of having to fall back on such fundamental moral claims. See chapter II of his *The Quest for Being*. His arguments, however, have been very fundamentally and carefully challenged by Richard Brandt in chapter II of his *Ethical Theory*. For a good selection of John Dewey's ethical writings, see John Dewey, *Intelligence in the Modern World*.

11. Important brief statements of this position occur in Bertrand Russell, *Religion and Ethics*, chapter IX; A. J. Ayer, *Language, Truth and Logic*, chapter VI; John Mackie, "A Refutation of Morals," in Paul Edwards and Arthur Pap (eds.), *A Modern Introduction to Philosophy*; Alf Ross, "On the Logical Nature of Propositions of Value," *Theoria* (1945); and Ingemar Hedenius, "Values and Duties," *Theoria* (1949).

12. David Hume, *Treatise on Human Nature*, (1739), and P. H. Nowell-Smith, *Ethics*. See my "Hume and the Emotive Theory," *Philosophical Studies*, vol. XIX, (1970: The National University of Ireland).

13. Many of the authors (Ayer and Stevenson most particularly) who hold such a position or something very close to it, would object to being called subjectivists. They identify 'subjectivism' with what I have called 'naive subjectivism' and they are indeed not subjectivists in *that* sense of 'subjectivism'. They also point out that they are engaging in meta-ethics and not normative ethics and that meta-ethical claims are *morally neutral* and hence they could not be subjectivists. (Meta-ethics examines the meaning or use of moral terms or utterances and attempts to elucidate the logic of moral reasoning. Normative ethics is concerned with the justification of fundamental moral claims and in that general way with the establishment of what is right or wrong, good or bad, and with examining whether it is possible to articulate and defend an objective moral code. In the chapters on ethics I do both meta-ethics and normative ethics. But I have not systematically distinguished between the two activities in the text, and indeed in situations where one is concerned with the logic of moral reasoning, it is not easy or perhaps even necessary to do so.) I would agree that one cannot deduce normative ethical statements from meta-ethical ones, but meta-ethical theses have normative implications all the same. If I accept the meta-ethical thesis that moral utterances are neither true nor false but are simply expressive, it is irrational for me to believe that there are natural moral laws. That is to say, it is irrational of me, for example, to believe the normative ethical claim that it is true that human beings ought never to commit suicide. See A. J. Ayer, "On the Analysis of Moral Judgements," in his *Philosophical Essays*, and Charles Stevenson, *Facts and Values*, pp. 71–93. I have eluci-

dated and defended my claim that meta-ethics has normative relevance in my "Problems of Ethics," *Encyclopedia of Philosophy*, vol. III.

14. I have attempted this in my "Problems of Ethics."
15. See, for example, A. J. Ayer, "The Analysis of Moral Judgements," in his *Philosophical Essays*.
16. This point is well made by Paul Edwards in *The Logic of Moral Discourse*, R. M. Hare in *The Language of Morals*, and W. D. Falk in "Guiding and Goading," in Rosalind Ekman (ed.), *Readings in the Problems of Ethics*.
17. Stephen Toulmin argues this with considerable force in his *An Examination of the Place of Reason in Ethics*.

26

ON MORALITY
HAVING
A POINT

I

Moral discourse, like any other mode of discourse, has a limited scope. Not all talk about what is right or wrong, good or bad, or about what should or should not be done is moral talk. When I ask about the right way to carve a turkey, whether ballet is a better art form than opera, or whether I should put oil in my car, I am not asking moral questions. When are questions about normative matters moral questions? The best way to answer this is to come to understand the distinctive roles of morality in human living. Once we see the overall rationale or function of morality, we can come to understand readily enough what questions are moral questions, what considerations are moral considerations, and what reasons can count as good reasons in ethics. Most centrally of all, we must try to ascertain what is the fundamental point of having such a form of life. What is the point (the underlying *raison d'être*) of having moral institutions, practices, and rules? Rather than try to catalogue all rationale for morality I will state and explain a central one, a rationale that would remain central no matter what additional ones morality may have. It is in virtue of this rationale that one can come to understand that —and why—certain reasons must be good reasons in ethics.

We should start by reminding ourselves that we have many diverse and frequently conflicting wants and needs. Given these wants and needs and given the fact that we are active striving agents, we cannot but come into conflict with each other on certain occasions. When we do, we need some socially recognized device more pervasive and ubiquitous than the law—and without which the law itself could not for long operate—to adjudicate these inevitable human conflicts. The adjudication must be such that the parties in question, if they reason rationally, will regard it as equitable, and it must be sufficiently comprehensive and stable so that the agents involved could form some expectations concerning ranges of permissible human behavior vis-à-vis each other. It is just such a role that morality plays in the stream of life; that is to say, morality is that sort of system of social control. Such a way of putting it may, for the literary and tender-minded, sound too computerizing. However, if you will reflect dispassionately, you will see that (1) the characterization of morality is apt and (2) it does not dehumanize. It is the *type* of social control that makes something dehumanizing, not the very fact of social control.

Now the prime question is, of course, what kind of system of social control? Morality is—or so I would maintain—a system of social control that functions primarily equitably to adjudicate conflicting wants, needs, and human aims in such a way so as not only to make societal life possible and tolerable but also to diminish as much as possible human harm and suffering.[1] To a very considerable degree the very *raison d'être* of morality is to adjudicate between the frequently conflicting and divergent desires and interests of people, in order to give everyone as much as possible of whatever it is that each one will want when he is being rational, when he would still want what he wants were he to reflect carefully, and when his efforts to satisfy his own wants are constrained by a willingness to treat the rational wants of other human beings in the same way.[2] (Remember the good life is not simply the moral life; morality is a necessary feature—not, however, a logically necessary one—but still a minimum feature in a rich and a good life. One may be a morally good man—a man of intelligent actions and conscientious will—and remain in many ways an incomplete human being, far from being able to live what Feuerbach and Marx called a 'truly human life'. Without morality man is indeed dehumanized, but even with moral commitments he may remain a sadly defective human.)

It can be objected that to characterize the overriding or underlying function of morality in this way is arbitrarily to pick one function of and rationale for morality from among many. There are other ways of guiding conduct, there are other means of social control, and morality has other roles in human living.

The remark about an arbitrary selection apart, this is perfectly true. But it is also true that usually, typically, and understandably there has been concern, when morality has been at issue, to adjudicate and in some way harmonize conflicts of interest and divergent needs in such a way that life together remains or becomes humanly tolerable. As Hobbes showed, it is intolerable and perhaps even impossible for man to live outside of society. We all have perfectly rational self-interested motives for living in society, and we all—or nearly all of us—sometimes at least desire happiness and security. Given this desire and given the understanding that happiness would be either impossible or radically lessened if we did not live in cooperative social groups, we can quite readily come to recognize the value of life in society. However, given our need for happiness and given the brute fact that without society this need could not be satisfied, we, if we even have a minimal amount of rationality, would continue to opt for a life in society. What kind of society are we to seek, if we are intelligent and informed and if we could alter society to best fit our desire for happiness? Where it is evident that we need each other, where it is plain that we need the cooperation of others in order to achieve even a tolerable measure of happiness, and where there is a *rough* equality of strength and intelligence between human beings, we would reasonably desire a world in which conflicting desires and interests were adjudicated and harmonized in such a way so as to give everyone as much as possible of whatever it is that each one wants and would still want on rational reflection when he was prepared to consider the wants of his fellow human beings in the same way.

My saying that this is the kind of system of social control we would want, if we were being intelligent, surely does not make it so. What are the grounds for my claims? I start with the truisms that we want to be happy, that we want to satisfy our desires, and that we realize that we need others in order to do that. As George Eliot put it, "Men's lives are as thoroughly blended with each other as the air they breathe. . . ." In stressing our desire for happiness, I am not suggesting that we are all always or even usually motiviated by selfish desires. It is evident enough that there are both thoroughly unselfish and thoroughly selfish people— the Dinah Morrises and Hetty Sorrells—and that most of us are somewhere between these two extremes.

I am saying, however, that even starting from a purely 'selfish base', a rational person will in reality recognize the value of human cooperation. What are the optimal conditions for human cooperation?

In a world where man is the kind of animal in which all adult human beings are of roughly equal strength and intelligence, and where positions of coercive political power remain precarious, the conditions in which most people will be best assured of maximum cooperation are the ones decisive in the system of social control I have outlined. In turn, the conditions of maximum cooperation between men is the condition most likely to be conducive in most circumstances and in the long run to an individual's maximum satisfaction of desire. Even so, of course, an individual may not be happy, but—unless he is very powerfully and securely placed— such a system of social control gives him a better chance of being happy than any alternative social arrangement. The restrictions imposed by such a system of social control on his doing what he wants are the minimal ones compatible with social justice and a respect for human well-being; he may do what he wants as long as it is compatible with other people also doing what they want to do when they are behaving rationally and when they are acting under the same restraint. And where two or more people cannot all do what they want, a moral agent must be bound by a fair decision concerning whose wants should have pride of place in such a situation.[3] Thus, if two people both want to go to a play and there is but one ticket left, the person who arrives first should have the ticket, everything else being equal. In a world where each person is allowed to do whatever it is that he wants that is compatible with the others doing the same, and with a respect for the well-being of others, one would get maximum cooperation. This would enhance to the fullest extent for almost all people their chance of being happy, and so to the extent they are being rational, they would opt for such a system of social control.

Indeed, if they were motivated purely or primarily by self-interest *and* if they were in very secure positions of power or privilege, they would not opt for such a system but would rationally prefer a system of privilege. I am not saying that we could on grounds of self-interest alone justify such a system of social control to all men irrespective of how they are placed in society, but I am saying that for the vast majority of men, situated as most men are situated and could be expected to be situated, enlightened self-interest would unequivocally support a preference for such a social arrangement.

The Nietzschean objection that such an attitude betrays the attitude of the slave—the fearful, cringing, weak man incapable of self-discipline and decisive action—seems to me mistaken. The attitude embedded in the norm I have characterized would be a rational attitude for a strong or weak man; unless (as Nietzsche did not) one simply meant by 'a strong man' a Himmler-type with an overweaning desire to dominate others. But a man whose strength lay in his intellectual and moral discipline and in his self-overcoming would have no need to trample on others and would recognize that the general optimal conditions for such self-overcoming would include such a system of social control, although it would include much more as well.

It is indeed true that not everyone who has set forth a system of social guides and constraints has so reasoned. Hitler's infantile apocalyptic code most certainly does not square with it; but more and more men, either in theory or in practice, have come to reason (or at least to profess to reason) in accordance with the system of social control I have characterized. It is a central element in the actual moral codes of many societies. Given a pervasive *desire* for happiness on the part of human beings, given the recognition that even a precarious happiness is impossible outside a cooperative society for any but a privileged and powerful few, and given the rough physical and intellectual equality of human beings, such a conception of the central function or rationale of morality becomes manifestly reasonable.

II

It will be objected: Suppose one does not care much about happiness, suppose one does not regard happiness or security as good? In fact, you might remind me that earlier I pointed out that the statement 'Happiness is good' is not analytic and that we could not prove or verify that happiness is good. Now, it is natural to object, in a moralistic mood you sneak it in, so to speak, through the back door. But I have not tried to prove that happiness is good. It seems to me evident enough both that happiness is good and that most people *regard* happiness as good and, except in purely theoretical contexts, would regard any dispute about this as fatuous. In fact, they regard 'Happiness is good' as a truism. (That happiness is the *sole* good or the *highest* good is, of course, another matter.) Moreover, it is of course true that the fact that people regard happiness as good does not prove that it is good or even show that we know that it is good. I did not try to show that, and I *need* not show it. What I did claim was this: People desire, as a very central end of action, those things that they think will bring them happiness, and they can be brought to see that unless they live in a reasonably cooperative society, there is small chance of their getting any measure of what they want. They can further see, if they will reflect carefully, that generally speaking it is in the interests of everyone that the distinctive social controls and restraints which constitute a central portion of morality have, as their overall and underlying function or rationale, the regulation of society so that everyone can have as much as possible of whatever it is he on reflection and when he is being rational wants, that is compatible with a like treatment of all other men.

Where it is in fact *impossible* to satisfy the interests of everyone, one should satisfy the most *inclusive* set of interests that would involve the minimum sacrifice of individual interests. Rational human beings, even purely self-interested humans, would come to see, given our evident need for society, that such a society would *generally* be in the best interests of everyone alike. Given that men are rational—although of course, they often are not—and given that they desire happiness, they will seek a society in which this general touchstone, as to how to guide behavior, will be the central function of ethics or morality. (That irrational men will not desire such a system or that some people will not be sufficiently clearheaded to see that it is the best system of social control does not, of course, tell against the correctness of my argument here, although it does raise questions of pedagogics.)

Given the acceptability of such an overall function of ethics, we can successfully refute meta-ethical relativism. Meta-ethical relativism is, in turn, a key rational support for ethical scepticism, subjectivism, and ethical relativism. In saying this I do not for a moment mean to deny that there are situations where we will remain in moral perplexity. However, we now have at least a very general standard in accordance with which we can appraise specific moral codes and the moral rules and the social practices that give these codes and rules their full substance. Where we can conceive of a specific practice, alternative to the extant one, which if adopted would genuinely give the people who would be involved more of what they on reflection would want when they are being rational and are dealing fairly with their fellows, we can correctly judge that that practice would be a better practice than the extant one—would be the practice that, everything else being equal, we *ought* to adopt. Normally, but not always, our specific moral judgments will be made in accordance with those practices, that is, the moral practices we have adopted. Without such practices our moral freedom would indeed be an anguished freedom as some existentialists tell us. Moreover, since without such practices we would always need to calculate or in some way reason out what we should do in specific situations, our ability to act as moral agents, or to act *decisively* as moral agents, would, in effect, be paralyzed. That we have a stable set of practices and rules to utilize in moral reasoning is absolutely essential to morality. Morality cannot be identified with those practices, but without them we would not have something recognizable as a morality.

Morality, however, is not simply "my station and its duties," and there is nothing so sacrosanct about these practices or the rules attached to them as to put them beyond the scope of moral assessment. In circumstances where there is some reason to think that acting in accordance with them would work against human interests, taking all relevant effects into consideration (including long-range effects), we can and should refuse to reason in accordance with them. In other cases we can replace them with alternative practices that answer more adequately to human interests.

III

This statement needs a much fuller and a rather more qualified statement than I can give it here, but this much should be apparent: We have reasonable grounds for rejecting subjectivism, ethical skepticism, and ethical relativism. Whatever the logical status of moral utterances, we have—given such an overall rationale for morality—an objective criterion for justifying the adoption of one moral code or one set of institutions or practices rather than another, or for making one moral judgment rather than another. It may indeed not be determinate enough always to give us a rational decision procedure when we must decide between conflicting codes or practices, but sometimes we can, reasoning in accordance with it, rationally decide what we are to do. We are not simply thrown back on how we happen to feel. Moreover, note that this conception of the function of ethics meshes perfectly with the principle I stated as an ultimate principle of morality combining Kantian and utilitarian claims.[4] That is, it fits well with claiming that for any situation whatsoever, we should always act in such a way as to give everyone involved as much as possible of whatever it is that each person wants that is compatible with treating everyone as persons. There is something evidently important to morality about both the Kantian and the utilitarian claims, but they both are also subject, as we have seen, to fairly evident difficulties. This combination joins their sound elements and avoids, by its qualification of each, difficulties in both utilitarianism and Kantianism. And the reason we should have such a principle is made evident when we consider it in the light of the function of ethics.

We are now in a position to see that some moral arguments can be reliable, and there can be some moral judgments whose truth or falsity does not depend on the idiosyncrasies of the person making the judgment. Thus, if I assert 'Civil rights workers ought to be kept out of Mississippi', and if it can be shown that adoption of this maxim, rather than some alternative, would answer less adequately to the interests of *everyone*—blacks, whites, reds, yellows, and so on—then this maxim should not be adopted; if it would answer more adequately to their interests, it should be adopted. Many times we cannot, as a matter of fact, tell for some rule or practice what its consequences or probable consequences will be, but sometimes we can have a well-founded belief here. As Peirce and others have made us aware, we do not get certainty in science, either. Even without certainty, however, we can reliably fix scientific beliefs. Similarly, if we attend to the wants and needs men actually have or could reasonably be expected to have, and if we attend to that very central role of morality in society that we have characterized in this chapter, we can see that in morality, as in science, we can also objectively fix belief. In neither area are we stuck with the method of tenacity or authority; in neither area do we have something that is merely a subjective matter of taste.

It is certainly natural to object here that I have not gone beyond platitudes. I have not shown how we can objectively answer the really harassing, nasty, and perplexing problems of moral belief and commitment that disturb all thoughtful and conscientious men. I have not shown how we can gain insight—to say nothing of having given my mite of insight—into how we can properly grapple with these harassments. But I did not try to do so. Rather, I did try to block a very general skepticism concerning morality that would claim that any clear-headed, nonevasive man would have to be some sort of moral sceptic, subjectivist, or ethical relativist. I have tried to show, or rather suggest, how morality could have a rational foundation, how there could be moral knowledge, and how moral propositions could be objectively true or false. I tried to establish that it is not the case that in morals it is all just a matter of 'you pays your money, you takes your choice'. I have not tried to exhibit how we could resolve deep moral perplexities—surely we could not even begin to do that without a detailed consideration of the actual situation giving rise to the moral perplexity—but I have tried, as opposed to the sceptic, to show that there is a rationally and objectively establishable limit on what we may legitimately do.

Once we have seen that morality as a whole is not a house of cards, we are in a position, free from a conviction that there can be no objective argument here, to examine concretely and in detail the specific moral perplexities that bedevil us. And it is indeed here where we must go beyond the philosopher's armchair; it is here where we need detailed and sophisticated knowledge of man and society. With respect to these specific moral perplexities, we can sometimes, when we so reason, get an answer; but *sometimes*, as things stand, we will end up just having to decide how we are going to act or to what we are going to commit ourselves. *Sometimes* we will just have to commit ourselves without knowing whether our commitment is the best one we could make. And this is indeed agonizing, for so much turns on our decision in such contexts. Although we will not in such a circumstance be able to give a reason for our choices, we can still make our choices reasonably—that is, thoughtful choices made after carefully reviewing the relevant facts and taking to heart what we do know. But that sometimes we must do this—that we must just decide without being able to justify our decision—is not unique to morality and to questions of value. And it does not show that these moral decisions or commitments, let alone *all* moral decisions or commitments, are forever beyond the pale of rational assessment.

IV

The argument should not end with that purple passage, for there remains a particularly disturbing kind of objection that needs to be answered. Someone might grant that I may very well be right in what I have said about the function of morality and the structure of good reasons attendant on that function, but I have not yet touched the problem of the single individual trying to decide how he is to live—trying to decide what order of priorities to adopt in his own life. And I am not talking here about the Undergroundling or the 'Kierkegaardian', who is prepared to fly in the face of reason; I am talking of the man who is resolved to be guided by reason, who has what has been called a 'commitment to rationality'. Can we show this individual that simply considering his own point of view, if he is to act rationally, the best thing for him to do is to adopt that moral point of view most nearly in accord with the system of social control characterized above?

We must be clear about what we are asking here. I am not *now* trying to establish that from 'a god's-eye point of view' or from an ideal or disinterested observer's point of view, the best life and the most rational life is a moral life that squares best with the kind of system of social regulation I have characterized. I have already tried to establish that, considering society at large, we should adopt such a system of social control. But the question I am now asking is a different one. It is a question about what is the most rational thing for an *individual* to do when he is trying to decide what order of priorities are to count most heavily *for him* in the conduct of *his life*. He could very well agree that such a system of social control is a most desirable thing to have in society, since life for most people, including himself, would be less miserable with such a system of control in force than if it were not in force. But granted the desirability of its being in force, why should he not simply take advantage of its being in force, acting in accordance with it when it is in his interest to do so and not acting in accordance with it when it is not in his interest to do so? Why is it—or is it—irrational for him, or for any solitary individual, to take such an amoral point of view when he can be quite confident that most others will not and when he keeps secret his resolution to act in such a manner?

It is evident that by so acting he is being immoral, since he is persistently and self-consciously free-loading by accepting the benefits of a society organized on a moral basis without accepting any of its responsibilities or liabilities, the general acceptance of which is essential to the functioning of the very institutions he accepts as plainly desirable. He takes advantage of the goodwill and commitment to morality of others without exhibiting goodwill himself or taking any of the risks or sharing the burdens essential to the continued existence of the system of social control that is admittedly beneficial for all. This kind of unfairness is the quintessence of immorality.

That is evident. But this is simply to expose the nerve of the problem. Of course he acts unfairly, but remember he does not intend to act fairly or morally but only to act in such a way that his interests will not be damaged. Morally speaking, he most certainly should not so act, and it makes no sense to ask 'Why should one be moral?' where the 'should' has a moral force.[5] That is like asking 'Why should you do what you should do?'. However, not every use of 'should' is a moral one, and the question still remains: What reason is there for an individual to adopt a moral point of view?Why should he do what, morally speaking, is the right thing to do? How can we show—or can we show—that doing what is ethical is the rational thing for him to do and that it is irrational for him to adopt instead the point of view of an enlightened individual egoist?[6] (Such an individual egoist indeed need not be Plato's or Gide's immoralist who cannot control his passions.)

We can put the problem in a somewhat different manner. A man may agree that in some contexts we clearly know how we as moral agents ought to act, but he may wonder what reasons (if any) can be given for doing what he and we acknowledge we are *required* to do, morally speaking. That is to say, what reason is there for an individual, living in an ongoing moral community, to do what he honestly regards as the right thing to do? If everyone or even a considerable number of people failed to take a moral point of view, then life would indeed become intolerable. But if I am not a public figure and if I am a reasonably discreet and rational individual, living in a society committed to a moral point of view, my behaving in a nonmoral way will not cause social chaos or in any way make community life intolerable. Thus, to prove that society, that is, the people who make up society, have a legitimate interest in morality will not show why I, as an individual in such a society, should be moral. Surely I must seem to be a good fellow, but what reason is there for me to be a morally good man? Why in such a situation should I not allow my self-interest to override the moral demand that the interests of everyone involved have an equal claim to be taken into consideration? Why should I be moral? (The 'should' here cannot, of course, have a moral force.)

People do feel perplexed about this, and initially at any rate, we do not know what to say. In certain moods some of us even come to feel that here we are up against a deep 'existential surd', which reveals that there is an element of the arbitrary at the very heart of morality.

However, some very able philosophers have argued that nothing like this follows, for the very question, 'Why should I be moral?' is a pseudo-question.

One such attempt to show that this is so is made by John Hospers in his *Human Conduct*. His argument is brief and to the point. I want to state it, show why I think it fails, and illustrate how by failing just as it does it leaves standing in all its starkness the question 'Why should I be moral?'. A man who tries to ask this question, Hospers argues, is prey to conceptual confusion, for such a person is in effect asking for a self-interested reason for doing what is not in his self-interest. This is like asking for a yellow banana that is not yellow. As Hospers puts it:

> Of course it is impossible to give him a reason in accordance with his interest for acting contrary to his interest. That would be a contradiction in terms. It is a self-contradictory request, and yet people sometimes make it and are disappointed when it can't be fulfilled. The skeptic shows us an example in which he would be behaving contrary to his interest and asks us to give him a reason why he should behave thus, and yet the only reasons he will accept are reasons of self-interest.[7]

An 'answer' to such a 'question' would need to claim that there is a self-interested reason for doing what is not in one's self-interest, and this is surely a contradiction.

Hospers' argument does indeed clearly show that if we are *reasoning morally*, 'It's the right thing to do' or 'It's the morally best thing to do' is the final sort of justification we can give for acting in one way rather than another. In such a situation there is no justifying what is right. We simply should do it because it is right. Sometimes what is right and what is in our rational self-interest coincide and sometimes they do not, but one can never, from a moral point of view, justify acting immorally by proving that it is in one's self-interest. It is a truism that, morally speaking, we should always do what is right, but it is also a truism that from a self-interested point of view an individual should always do what is in his self-interest. From a moral point of view, moral reasons are by definition decisive; from the point of view of self-interest, self-interested reasons are by definition decisive. Moral considerations count even from that vantage point, but there they can never override considerations of enlightened self-interest.

We can now ask what is surely the central question: What would it be like to establish that one point of view rather than another was the more rational or the best for a free, intelligent, and thoroughly nonevasive individual? It looks as if there could be no nonquestion-begging answer one way or another here. From a moral point of view moral reasons are superior; from a self-interested point of view self-interested reasons are superior. Yet these two alternative points of view present themselves to an individual. They are there before him, and in the situation Hospers describes, he must simply choose between two alternative ways of acting— ways of acting that can have very different consequences. Looking at the matter strictly from an individual's point of view, where there are no self-interested reasons for doing what is right, it is logically impossible that there could be any nonquestion-begging reasons for adopting one alternative rather than another. In effect, Hospers' analysis clearly brings out why this is so. In such a context, a person faced with such alternatives must just make a decision concerning how he will act and how he wishes to live.

While there are, or at the very least may be, specific situations in which we can find no objective reason for acting as a moral agent rather than as a man who is looking out for number one and only number one, we must take care not to draw the mistaken conclusion that this shows that there can be no reasons of an objective sort for adopting, as an overall life policy, a moral point of view, as distinct from a purely egoistic point of view. It is one thing to say that there are some situations in which doing what is right will not bring one happiness and will not serve one's rational self-interest, but it is another thing again to claim that a man who made egoism the maxim of *all* his actions would be happy or would, by consistently acting on this maxim, in reality serve his own self-interest. That this would be so is very questionable.

It is indeed a mistake to assert that being immoral always leads in the long run to misery; it is also a mistake to deny that immoral behavior sometimes leads to greater happiness. But such a recognition does nothing to establish that the man who has consistently and thoroughly reasoned according to purely egoistic principles would not be unhappy. It is only in our tribal folklore that *all* acts of immorality lead to regret and misery. Occasional immoral acts are quite compatible with a happy life for the immoralist, but a thorough and consistent pattern of wrongdoing will, as the world goes, make for him and for those about him a little circle of misery.

So while we can see that in asking 'Why be moral?' one need not be falling into conceptual confusion, we can also see how the considerations raised in the previous paragraph, when thought through, take the sting out of the 'Why be moral?' question. Viewed purely in the abstract, there indeed is and can be no nonquestion-begging answer to the question 'Why should I be moral?'. However, for human beings as we find them and as we are likely to find them in the future, with the needs, personalities, and wants that they have or even are likely to come to have, consistently failing to act in accordance with a moral point of view will lead to a miserable life for the person who so acts. In short, there are solid self-interested reasons for a man not to override moral considerations. Indeed, *only* to be a man of good morals is not, as Kant stressed, to be a morally good man, but there are generally good self-interested reasons for becoming genuinely unselfish and for becoming a moral agent. We have good reasons, as individuals in a system of social control which is at least predominately moral or morally directed, not only to support that system of social control *or* some better moral system of social control, but also generally to act in accordance with a moral system of social control ourselves.[8] And there are decisively good reasons, considering society at large, why moral systems of social control should prevail.

On the part of most people, there may indeed be a kind of Kantian or Platonic wish for a more absolute and more determinate objectivity for moral beliefs than the one I have just outlined, and it indeed is to be hoped that a more probing examination of morality could give us a more determinate ground for a belief in the objectivity of morals. It would be desirable to have a rationally justified conception of the foundation of morality so that by utilizing it we could uncover objective grounds in accordance with which conflicts concerning, say, the desirability of Communist versus Liberal ideals, could be objectively assessed.[9] But even if we can go no further than we have gone here, we can still without mystification or evasion keep the wolves of subjectivism, ethical relativism, and moral scepticism safely at bay.[10]

I have taken seriously Nietzsche's contention that we should take morality as something that is problematic. Surely our own tribal morality is problematic (that should be evident enough), but I have tried in a tough-minded fashion to establish that (1) by examining the key role that morality plays in the life of man, we can discern a rationale for rational, nonevasive men—Nietzschean 'supermen', if you will—having and sticking with the system of social control I characterized in this chapter, and (2) there are good reasons why an individual—including such 'Nietzschean individuals'—should act in accordance with the moral point of view embedded in that system of social control.

NOTES

1. I do not, of course, intend to deny that suffering can on occasion have a moral value, although I would like to add that many Christian moralists and Russian novelists overdo this. But I am denying the value—moral or otherwise—of suffering that will not in turn help, directly or indirectly, to diminish the sum total of human suffering or serve to improve the quality of human living, that is human well-being and human welfare.

2. It is important to recognize that I am not sneaking in an alien and contested moral criterion with my use of the word 'rational'. In speaking of a man behaving rationally, I need say no more for my purposes here than that a man behaves rationally when he is a man who has a sense of his own interests and has the ability to act in accordance with his interests and will act in accordance with his own interests where moral considerations, considerations of friendship and/or family do not intervene (what he will do when such considerations intervene I leave open), is willing to listen to evidence, and is willing to grant that if X is a good reason for B doing Y in Z, it is also a good reason for anyone else relevantly like B and similarly situated. That is not all that is meant by 'behaving rationally', but such a characterization is all that is intended by my use of 'behaving rationally' and my other references to 'rational'.

3. A fair decision procedure would in turn be a decision procedure which would (1) give such persons, everything else being equal, equal treatment and (2) be made in accordance with the principle that we should seek to maximize situations in which there is an achievement of the wants of everyone where the achievement of any given individual's wants respects the rights of the rest of humanity to have their wants satisfied as well.

4. Chapter 24, section II.

5. Stephen Toulmin aptly shows how such a question can be senseless in *An Examination of the Place of Reason in Ethics*, pp. 160–165. For a further defense of this position, see also A. I. Melden, "Why Be Moral?" *The Journal of Philosophy*, vol. XLV (Aug. 12, 1948), pp. 449–456. The appropriate section from Toulmin together with my comment designed to show how, all the same, Toulmin fails to block the 'Why Be Moral?' question is reprinted in Rosalind Ekman (ed.), *Readings in the Problems of Ethics*, pp. 350–364.

6. By an 'individual egoist' I mean a man who reasons and acts according to the following maxim: Where questions of choice or voluntary action arise, I ought always to do what will most further my self-interest.

7. John Hospers, *Human Conduct*, p. 194.

8. This is not remotely intended as an oblique defense of the moral status quo. In fact, I think such a defense is utterly untenable.

9. For difficulties here see W. B. Gallie, "Liberal Morality and Socialist Morality," in Peter Laslett (ed.), *Philosophy, Politics and Society*, first series. But also note C. B. Macpherson, "The Maximization of Democracy," in Peter Laslett and W. G. Runciman (eds.), *Philosophy, Politics and Society*, third series, as providing evidence that some headway can be made.

10. For a further development of the leading arguments of this section see my "Why Should I Be Moral?" in Kenneth Pahel and Marvin Schiller (eds.), *Readings in Contemporary Ethical Theory*. But see also the article by J. C. Thornton in the same volume.

SUPPLEMENTARY READINGS
CHAPTERS 22 THROUGH 26

Books

Aristotle, *The Nicomachean Ethics*, translated by J. A. K. Thompson (London: G. Allen, 1953).

Baier, Kurt, *The Moral Point of View* (New York: Random House, 1965).

Bayles, Michael D. (ed.), *Contemporary Utilitarianism* (Garden City, N.Y.: Anchor Books, 1968).

Bentham, Jeremy, *The Principles of Morals and Legislation* (New York: Hafner, 1948).

*Brandt, Richard, (ed.), *Value and Obligation* (New York: Harcourt, Brace & World, 1961).

Butler, Joseph, *Sermons and Dissertation Upon Virtue*, reprinted in *British Moralists*, L. A. Selby-Bigge, vol. I and II (Indianapolis, Ind.: Bobbs-Merrill, 1964).

Cohen, Marshall, (ed.), *The Philosophy of John Stuart Mill* (New York: Modern Library, 1961). Contains "Utilitarianism," "Nature," and "Utility of Religion."

*Ekman, Rosalind (ed.), *Readings in the Problems of Ethics* (New York: Scribner, 1965).

Ewing, A. C., *The Definition of Good* (New York: Macmillan, 1947).

Ewing, A. C., *Second Thoughts in Moral Philosophy* (London: Routledge, 1959).

Feinberg, Joel (ed.), *Moral Concepts* (London: Oxford University Press, 1970).

*Field, G. C., *Moral Theory* (London: Methuen, 1921).

Foot, Philippa (ed.), *Theories of Ethics* (London: Oxford University Press, 1967).

*Frankena, William K., *Ethics* (Englewood Cliffs, N.J.: Prentice-Hall, 1963).

Gosling, J. C. B., *Pleasure and Desire: The Case for Hedonism Reviewed* (London: Oxford University Press, 1969).

Hare, R. M., *The Language of Morals* (Oxford: Clarendon Press, 1952).

*Hospers, John, *Human Conduct: An Introduction to the Problems of Ethics* (New York: Harcourt, Brace & World, 1961).

Hudson, W. D. (ed.), *The Is-Ought Question* (London: Macmillan, 1969).

*Kamenka, E., *Marxism and Ethics* (New York: St. Martin's, 1969).

Kierkegaard, Soren, *Either/Or*, vol. I and II (Garden City, N.Y.: Doubleday, 1959).

Kierkegaard, Soren, *The Sickness Unto Death*, translated by Walter Lowrie (Garden City, N.Y.: Doubleday, 1955).

*MacIntyre, Alasdair, *A Short History of Ethics* (New York: Macmillan, 1966).

MacIntyre, Alasdair (ed.), *Hume's Ethical Writings* (New York: Collier Books, 1965).

Monro, D. H., *Empiricism and Ethics* (Cambridge: Cambridge University Press, 1967).

*Moore, G. E., *Ethics* (London: Oxford University Press, 1912).

Moore, G. E., *Principia Ethica* (Cambridge: Cambridge University Press, 1903).

Murphy, A. E., *The Theory of Practical Reason* (La Salle, Ill.: Open Court, 1965).

Nagel, Thomas, *The Possibility of Altruism* (London: Oxford University Press, 1970).

Narveson, Jan, *Morality and Utility* (Baltimore, Md.: Johns Hopkins Press, 1967).

Nietzsche, Friedrich, *Beyond Good and Evil*, translated with commentary by Walter Kaufmann (New York: Vintage Books, 1966).

Nietzsche, Friedrich, *On the Genealogy of Morals*, translated by Walter Kaufmann and R. J. Hollingdale (New York: Vintage Books, 1967).

Nowell-Smith, P. H., *Ethics* (London: Penguin Books, 1954).

*Oldenquist, Andrew (ed.), *Readings in Moral Philosophy* (Boston: Houghton Mifflin, 1965).

Plato, *The Republic*, translated by F. M. Cornford (New York: Oxford University Press, 1945).

Prichard, H. A., *Moral Obligation* (London: Oxford University Press, 1968).

Prior, A. N., *Logic and the Basis of Ethics* (Oxford: Oxford University Press, 1949).

*Ramsey, Ian T. (ed.), *Christian Ethics and Contemporary Philosophy* (London: SCM Press, 1966).

*Robinson, Richard, *An Atheist's Values* (Oxford: Clarendon Press, 1964).

Ross, W. D., *The Right and the Good* (Oxford: Clarendon Press, 1930).

Schneewind, J. B. (ed.), *Mill: A Collection of Critical Essays* (Garden City, N.Y.: Anchor Books, 1968).

Sidgwick, Henry, *The Methods of Ethics* (London: Macmillan, 1874).

*Sidgwick, Henry, *Outlines of the History of Ethics* (London: Macmillan, 1886).

*Smart, J. J. C., *An Outline of a System of Utilitarian Ethics* (Melbourne, Australia: Melbourne University Press, 1961).

Stevenson, Charles L., *Facts and Values* (New Haven, Conn.: Yale University Press, 1963).

Stocks, J. L., *Morality and Purpose* (London: Routledge, 1969).

*Taylor, Paul (ed.), *Problems of Moral Philosophy* (Belmont, Calif.: Dickenson, 1967.

Thomson, Judith J., and Gerald Dworkin (eds.), *Ethics* (New York: Harper & Row, 1968).

Toulmin, Stephen Edelston, *An Examination of the Place of Reason in Ethics* (Cambridge: Cambridge University Press, 1950).

*Warnock, G., *Contemporary Moral Philosophy* (New York: St. Martin's, 1967).

*Warnock, Mary, *Existentialist Ethics* (New York: St. Martin's, 1967).

Wolff, Robert Paul (ed.), *Kant: Foundations of the Metaphysics of Morals,* translated by Lewis White Beck (Indianapolis, Ind.: Bobbs-Merrill, 1969). Text and critical essays.

Articles and Pamphlets

*Ayer, A. J., "On the Analysis of Moral Judgements," in his *Philosophical Essays* (New York: St. Martin's, 1963).

Baier, Kurt, "Moral Obligation," *American Philosophical Quarterly* (1966).

*Blake, R. M., "The Ground of Moral Obligation," *Ethics* (1928).

*Blake, R. M., "Why Not Hedonism? A Protest," *Ethics* (1926).

Brandt, Richard M. "Some Merits of One Form of Rule Utilitarianism," *University of Colorado Studies, Series in Philosophy* (1967).

Broad, C. D., "Egoism as a Theory of Human Motives," *Hibbert Journal* (1949–1950).

*Dennes, William R., "Knowledge and Values," in Lyman Bryson (ed.), *Symbols and Values: An Initial Study* (1952).

*Falk, W. D., "Morality, Self and Others," in Hector-Neri Castañeda and George Nakhnikian (eds.), *Morality and the Language of Conduct* (Detroit: Wayne State University Press, 1965).

*Falk, W. D., "Moral Perplexity," *Ethics,* vol. 66 (January, 1956).

Findlay, J. N., "The Structure of the Kingdom of Ends," in his *Value and Intentions* (New York: Macmillan, 1961).

Foot, P. R., "Goodness and Choice," *Proceedings of the Aristotelian Society,* supplementary vol. 35 (1961).

Foot, P. R., "Moral Arguments," *Mind* (1958).

Foot, P. R., "Moral Beliefs," *Proceedings of the Aristotelian Society,* vol. LIX (1958).

*Foot, P. R., "The Philosopher's Defense of Morality," *Philosophy* (1952).

Frankena, William J., "The Concept of Morality," *University of Colorado Studies, Series in Philosophy* (1967).

Frankena, W. K., "Some Beliefs About Justice," The Lindley Lecture, 1966 (Department of Philosophy, University of Kansas).

*Hägerström, Axel, "On the Truth of Moral Propositions," in his *Philosophy and Religion* (London: George Allen & Unwin Ltd., 1964).

Hampshire, Stuart, "Ethics: A Defense of Aristotle," *University of Colorado Studies, Series in Philosophy* (1967).

Hampshire, Stuart, "Fallacies in Moral Philosophy," *Mind,* vol. LVIII (1949).

*Hospers, John, "Reasons and Ethical Egoism," *The Personalist,* vol. 51, no. 2 (April, 1970).

*Nielsen, Kai, "An Examination of the Thomistic Theory of Natural Moral Law," *Natural Law Forum,* vol. IV (1959).

*Nielsen, Kai, "Ethics Without Religion," in Paul Kurtz (ed.), *Moral Problems in Contemporary Society.*

Nielsen, Kai, "God and the Good: Does Morality Need Religion?" *Theology Today,* vol. 21 (April, 1964).

Nielsen, Kai, "Justification and Moral Reasoning," *Methodos* (1957).

Nielsen, Kai, "Why Should I Be Moral?" *Methodos* (1963).

Rawls, John, "Justice as Fairness," *Philosophical Review* (1958).

Rawls, John, "The Sense of Justice," *Philosophical Review* (1963).
Rawls, John, "Two Concepts of Rules," *Philosophical Review* (1955).
Taylor, Paul, "The Ethnocentric Fallacy," *The Monist* (1963).
Taylor, Paul, "Four Types of Ethical Relativism," *Philosophical Review* (1954).

V
MIND
AND
BODY

27

METAPHYSICS
AND THE MIND/BODY
PROBLEM

I

In the first chapter I gave an admittedly partisan characterization of philosophy as an analytical study of concepts. I explicitly remarked that I do not believe philosophy should be limited to such an activity and that traditionally it has not been so limited. However, I did argue that it was a central activity in philosophy and that it was at the very least a crucial first step in philosophy. So far this has been primarily just what we have been doing; that is, we have been concerned with analyzing certain very fundamental concepts such as the concepts of freedom, determinism, responsibility, belief, knowledge, God, good, and morality. We have seen that these very crucial human conceptions, when we reflect about them, are perplexing and paradox-engendering. In trying to understand them—in trying to determine what it is to be free, to believe in God, to have knowledge, and the like—we discovered that it is all too easy to find oneself driven to adopting views that are excessively paradoxical or, as in the case of the freedom of action, we come to be utterly perplexed about how something we know to be the case could possibly be the case.

In talking about freedom, determinism, and responsibility, and in talking about morality, I attempted to carry through a typically analytical philosopher's strategy: I attempted to correct the distortion caused by various unbalanced views of the function of such key concepts and make plain the actual mode of operation of the philosophically perplexing concepts. In doing this, I attempted to show that there were no adequate grounds for a radical scepticism about human freedom or morality even in a deterministic world. In talking about the concept of God, I did something rather different, for there, after an attempt to elucidate, in the course of discussing Anselm and Aquinas, the actual operation of the concept of God in Judeo-Christian discourse, I tried also to show (1) that there was no evidence for the existence of such an alleged Divine reality and (2) that the very concept of God was an incoherent notion expressive of conceptual confusion. Although conceptual analysis was put to different work in these different conceptual areas, conceptual analysis remained at the very heart of our philosophic endeavors.

I now wish to turn to the mind/body problem, the cluster of problems revolving around the ancient question of whether the human mind is in some sense a different kind of entity from a body, and whether it is the case that man in reality is nothing more than an extremely intricate physical mechanism. These questions are also questions of critical philosophy and call for a careful analytical study of the key perplexing concepts. It will also be appropriate here to go back to the distinction we made in the first chapter between critical philosophy (the analytical study of concepts) and speculative philosophy, for in the context of the mind/body problem, questions of speculative philosophy and the rival claims of speculative philosophies come readily to the fore. Speculative philosophy, recall, entangles us in metaphysics—in a set of claims about the nature of 'ultimate reality'. (However, as philosophical claims, they are also claims allegedly resting somehow on reason and argument.) In fact, it will no doubt be felt by many that in the course of doing critical philosophy I have already made several metaphysical claims. Determinism and atheism, it will be said, are themselves metaphysical claims. In asserting, as I did, that neither indeterminism nor hard determinism adequately account for man's capacity to act as a responsible moral agent and that the concept of God, depending on just how we conceive of God, is either devoid of literal significance or signifies something that does not exist, I have, it will be claimed, committed myself metaphysically. I have in effect engaged in speculative philosophy and I have not simply engaged in a neutral and aseptic linguistic analysis of some of our fundamental concepts. (Like Strawson and a host of other philosophers, I have assumed—to put it as Strawson does—that "linguistic usage is the only experimental datum which we possess that is relevant to inquiry about the behavior of our concepts."[1])

In tackling our next problem, the mind/body problem, I want to do two things simultaneously, although the second will take a subordinate place to the first. I will examine the problem for its own sake as one of the primary problems of philosophy, but, while doing that, I will also examine what it would be like to engage in an articulation and defense of a set of metaphysical propositions. Speculative philosophy, as I noted in Chapter 1, is itself in a very precarious intellectual position. Its very legitimacy as an intellectual enterprise has been plausibly called into question. Yet, it would *seem* at least that in engaging in philosophical argument about God and human freedom, we are driven into taking metaphysical positions. The topic is important enough and worrying enough to explore.

However, first I would like to say a little more about what is involved in speculative philosophy or metaphysics. Metaphysicians do not want to assert only isolated metaphysical propositions such as 'Only material things, events, or processes exist' (a form of materialism). They want to articulate and rationally defend a coherent system of such statements about 'ultimate reality'. While speculative philosophers are very often 'religious philosophers', there are philosophers, including influential contemporary ones within the analytic camp, who are committed to going beyond critical philosophy to what has been called speculative philosophy, or what one of them prefers to call "synthetic synoptic philosophy." These philosophers want a non-religious scientifically oriented philosophy. They are committed to a Peircean way of fixing belief, 'a scientific image of man', and to what they regard as 'the scientific world-view'.[2]

J. J. C. Smart is one of these philosophers, and he has articulated a conception of a metaphysical and synthetic approach to philosophy in the opening chapter of his *Philosophy and Scientific Realism*.[3] Moving from an earlier purely critical approach to philosophy and without, of course, ceasing to be critical, Smart remarks, "Philosophy, it now seems to me, has to do not only with unravelling conceptual muddles but also with the tentative adumbration of a world view." He regards it as a central task of philosophy to articulate "a coherent and scientifically plausible world view." In philosophizing we must not only think clearly, as critical philosophy indeed would have us do, about the nature of the universe and the principles of conduct, but we must also think *comprehensively* about them. Thinking comprehensively, Smart would have us believe, carries us over into metaphysics and to the effort to outline a "synoptic view of the world." Indeed, we must eliminate nonsense to attain such a coherent and comprehensive world-view, but that remains only one element in articulating such a world-view. In addition, "it is the business of the philosopher to decide between various synoptic hypotheses on the grounds of plausibility." That is to say, Smart maintains, that there are various synthetic and fundamental claims about the world, which philosophers can decide for or against on grounds of scientific plausibility, which are not themselves empirically testable.

Smart cites two examples: 'Only minds and mental events are ultimately real' and 'The universe, replete with false memory traces in the brain, light rays in interstellar space and the like, began to exist ten minutes before I began writing this sentence'. The essential philosophical task, according to Smart, is to prune our ordinary and uncritical world-view of incoherent, false, and implausible claims and to replace it with a systematic rational reconstruction of our fundamental conceptual scheme —a reconstruction that will give us a true and synoptic picture of the world. In stressing, as it does, that its claims must square with a scientific view of the world, and in its distrust of what Smart regards as common-sense anthropocentricity as well as theism, Smart's own metaphysical account is indeed a particular kind of metaphysic, but the general attempt to give a comprehensive and synoptic view of the world is common to the metaphysical task of all speculative philosophies.

It may very well be possible and perhaps even desirable to grapple with the philosophy of mind without engaging in such metaphysical disputes or without engaging in any 'metaphilosophical' digressions about the possibility or plausibility of metaphysics. Whether this is so or not is a controversial issue in the philosophy of philosophy. But, as we have already noted, questions of a fundamental sort with a very metaphysical appearance seem naturally to arise when we worry about whether the mind is a different kind of entity from the body. To think this is to commit yourself to dualism, that is, to the claim that both minds and physical things exist and that they are realities of a radically distinct order. Acts of consciousness, for example, have physical associates, but consciousness itself is entirely nonphysical. Dualism is opposed by idealism and by materialism. They both claim that there is only one kind of ultimate reality. Idealism is the claim that only minds and mental realities exist or (in somewhat more sophisticated forms) only minds are *ultimately* real. (Note that in the latter formulation the conflict with dualism becomes more oblique.) Materialism maintains that only physical things or realities exist or have independent existence or (again in a somewhat less crude form) that conscious experiences and indeed the whole range of 'the mental' are not correlated with brain states but are identical with or are identified as brain processes, the undergoing of brain processes, and/or with stretches of human behavior. (These are crude formulations and will be refined later.)

These various metaphysical claims are themselves embedded as central elements in a system of statements concerning what is alleged to be 'ultimate reality'. We try through such a system of statements to "see the sorry scheme of things entire" and to attain a *rational Weltanschauung* —a picture of life that also provides a way of life.

The crucial question: Is such an activity a rational one? Are there any objective criteria of success here, or is the very effort to adumbrate a metaphysic a conceptual confusion so that a rational man should come to see that the heart of such a rationalistic endeavor is itself irrational? We can begin to broach these problems by attempting to see if there are any reasonable grounds for choosing between dualism and materialism. (I shall ignore idealism here, not because I believe it so easy to refute it— anyone who has ever tried in a nonquestion-begging way to refute

Berkeley will not think that—but because it is difficult to take such a view seriously. Materialism and dualism, by contrast, are serious contenders for our minds and our souls.)

Reflect about a systematic philosophical position (a synoptic philosophical view). If what I have said vis-à-vis religion is roughly right, materialism becomes an attractive position, if one is going to adopt any metaphysical stance at all. Given the radical implausibility and/or incoherence of the claims of religion, materialism along with atheism gives us a unified world-view. However, there are dualists who are atheists and there are some philosophical theists who maintain that they are not dualists. And it is indeed evident enough that one could quite consistently be a dualist and remain an atheist. Moreover, the very possibility of immortality seems at least to be tied to dualism. That is, if dualism is false, man cannot in any literal sense be immortal, although dualism could be true without its being true that man is immortal. Note further that if dualism can be shown to be a false or an incoherent position, it would certainly *appear* at least to be quite irrational to be a theist of any kind. Thus, even in our struggles to articulate a coherent and acceptable ideology or *Weltanschauung*, such obstruse metaphysical questions are not without their relevance. It may be the case that they might finally be shown to be of only an apparent relevance because they in reality only intrude conceptual confusion into real questions about articulating *a way of life*. But this does not appear to be so, and such a claim would itself have to be established by conceptual analysis.

II

We need first to gain a better understanding of the alternatives vis-à-vis arguments about the body and the mind, and we need a more adequate characterization of materialism and dualism. We need to realize that there are different kinds of dualism and materialism, some highly implausible and others philosophically attractive. We must seek the most plausible form of both theories that we can find, and then see if they can withstand rational scrutiny.

The need to do this for materialism is particularly acute, for as an eminent contemporary dualist, Curt Ducasse, rightly points out, *taken in a certain way*, both idealism and materialism are demonstrably false.[4] Suppose we say without qualification that materialism is the view that *only* material things or processes exist. Then, as Ducasse puts it, materialism is "demonstrably false since, besides material things and events, there exist also thoughts, feelings, desires, hopes, etc., which are events of the kind denominated 'mental' not 'material' and therefore are mental and not material for the same reason that a boy named 'John' not 'James' by his parents is John and not James."[5] (For a similar reason Ducasse rejects idealism, taken as the "ontological hypothesis" that "only minds and mental events exist.") Taking a very short way with dissenters, Ducasse concludes that it is perfectly evident here that the only plausible 'ontological claim' to make about 'what there is' is a dualistic one that holds that there are "on the one hand material things and events, and on the other minds and mental events . . . and . . . that neither can be 'reduced' to the other. . . ."

Surely things cannot be as simple as that. Materialists and idealists may have been mistaken, but they were typically intelligent and informed men who would not so fly in the face of reason as to deny these truisms. And sure enough, a contemporary materialist (D. M. Armstrong) who agrees with Smart in thinking that "we can give a complete account of man in purely physico-chemical terms," starts off his inaugural lecture "The Nature of Mind" with the remark, "Men have minds, that is to say, they perceive, they have sensations, emotions, beliefs, thoughts, purposes, and desires." Surely this is common ground for all philosophers—materialist and nonmaterialists; this is, so to speak, the given (it is what is given to philosophical discussion). The problem, as Armstrong goes on to remark, is "What is it to have a mind? What is it to perceive, to feel emotion, to hold a belief, or to have a purpose?"[6] Armstrong proceeds, as does Smart, to give an account very different from Ducasse's. So our first order of business is to try to articulate more adequately what it is to be a materialist or a dualist.

Dualism received its classical statement in the writings of the French rationalist René Descartes (1596–1650). For him there were two radically different substances: the physical, which is in space and is not conscious, and the mental, which is conscious and is not in space. Descartes remarked in his *Principles of Philosophy* (I: liii):

> Extension in length, breadth and depth constitutes the nature of corporeal substance; and thought the nature of thinking substance. For every other thing that can be attributed to body presupposes extension and is only some mode of an extended thing; as all the properties we discover in the mind are only diverse modes of thinking.

And in his *Meditations* (VI) he made a remark that could well be taken as expressing the core of the dualist position:

> Because on the one hand I have a clear and distinct idea of myself, in as far as I am only a thinking and unextended thing, and so on the other hand I possess a distinct idea of body, in as far as it is only an extended and unthinking thing, it is certain that I, that is my mind by which I am what I am, is entirely and truly distinct from my body and may exist without it.

Descartes' particular way of stating dualism is subject to various objections, but perhaps the core of his claim—and the core of the dualistic claim—could more generally and less vulnerably be put in this way: There are at least two radically different kinds of reality, existence, or phenomena: the physical and the mental. (There *may* be other things or 'nonthing' realities—rainbows, for example—that are neither. The force of dualism does not rest on its being an exhaustive distinction but on the mental and the physical being exclusive, radically distinct realities.) Physical phenomena or realities are extended in space and are perceptually public or, like electrons and photons, are constituents of things that are perceptually public. The latter cannot be a theoretical fiction, as *perhaps* a neutrino is, but to be a constituent of what is perceptually public must be in a series like the ones given by Max Born—for example, stars, planets, mountains, houses, tables, grains of wood, microscopic crystals, microbes, and all the way down to things of the same basic type only very, very much smaller.[7]

Mental phenomena or realities, by contrast, are unextended, not in space, and are *inherently* private. That is, it is *logically* impossible to literally observe them, although we can take note of them when they are our own. Given that we understand the meanings of the words 'pain' or 'sudden thought', that one has such an experience is something quite directly given to the person having the experience and to that person alone. A mental reality is a reality that in a psychological sense can only be *directly* known by one person—namely, the person who has it—and it is a reality such that nothing can override his honest avowal that he is in pain or that he has just thought of something or someone, where it is granted that he understands the meanings of the terms involved. To be a dualist is to believe that the physical and the mental are radically distinct in this manner.

The heart of the dualist claim is that the 'raw feels' (pains, sudden thoughts, desires) that we are directly and incorrigibly conscious of are inherently private, while brain states and other physical realities are public. A dualist believes that there are substantial entities designated by the term 'mind' that are radically different from physical entities or physical realities. They need not be 'mental *things*' or 'immaterial *objects*', since such notions *may* be contradictory or incoherent, but on a dualist account they must be mental nonthings: mental events of integrative nonphysical capacities or realities that are somehow identified with conciousness and whose very reality consists in being perceived, felt, or experienced. As Ducasse puts it:

> . . . whereas the *esse* (the being) of a tornado does *not* consist in its being experienced, the *esse* of fear does, on the contrary, consist in its being experienced.
>
> Just this, then, is the ultimate criterion of the 'mental' or 'psychical' character of something experienced: If something experienced is a connate accu-

sative of the experiencing, as is the case with fear, or pain, or blue or bitter taste, etc., then, *eo ipso*, it is 'psychical,' its *esse* is its *experiri*, and the experiencing is *intuent* experiencing.[8]

III

We should note the distinct point that dualism has two varieties. There is the view held by Descartes and by most contemporary dualists, *dualistic interactionism*, which maintains that the body causally acts on the mind and the mind causally acts on the body. Opposed to this is *dualistic psychophysical parallelism*. Such a dualism, like interactionism and all forms of dualism, claims that mind and body are radically different kinds of realities, but goes on to add that being such radically different kinds of realties they cannot possibly interact—there can be no causal relations between them—but the histories of each are nevertheless parallel. I shall not discuss the relative merits of interactionism and parallelism. They both have notorious difficulties, but of the two it is, I believe, fairly evident that interactionism is the least implausible.[9] Given the evident difficulties in each and given the alternative of some form of materialism, it is more important to try to see if there are grounds for preferring any form of dualism to materialism. Only if that is so, and if materialism in its most adequate formulations can be shown to be even more crippled by difficulties than is dualism, is there a need to return to a worry about the relative merits of interactionism and parallelism.

Materialism could perhaps be best generally and broadly characterized as the view that only those entities postulated by physics (including those entities that will be postulated by future and more adequate physical theories) are ultimately real. The force of 'ultimately real' here is to say that all other realities, if such there be, depend for their existence on these physical realities, but these physical realities do not depend on any other realities for their own existence.

This broad characterization of materialism allows for at least two types of materialism. Both of these types have been important in the history of materialism. The first kind of materialism is called '*reductive materialism*'. Hobbes and Holbach gave classical expression to this view, and among contemporary philosophers it is held by Elliot, Smart, and Armstrong. It is the view that there is nothing in the world over and above or other than those entities postulated by physics—including, of course, those entities that will be postulated by future and more adequate physical theories. A crude and inaccurate way of putting this position is to assert that matter alone is real.[10] Reductive materialism maintains that what is taken to be mental and distinct from the physical is really a type of physical reality, that is, what is designated or denoted by mental or psychological terms is really something physical. On such a view we can in principle give a complete account of man in purely physiochemical terms. All our conscious experiences or states of consciousness or sensations are actually certain bodily states. Rather than being correlated with certain bodily states, they are those states themselves. With such a view, man is nothing more than a complicated physical mechanism. Psychological terms really refer to types of behavioral reaction or to tendencies to behave in certain ways, or to physiological events or processes.

Besides reductive materialism we have *epiphenomenalism* (sometimes called emergent materialism or evolutionary materialism). Although they were not terribly concerned with such issues, Feuerbach, Marx, and Engels were materialists of this type; it was defended in some detail by T. H. Huxley in his "On the Hypothesis That Animals Are Automata and Its History" in his *Methods and Results;* and among contemporary philosophers, Santayana and Hardie have argued for such a view.[11] Epiphenomenalists agree with dualists that mental events, processes, and attributes are distinct from physical events, processes, and attributes. But they are still materialists, for they agree that all ultimate realities are physical and argue that psychological realities arise from physical realities and are dependent on physical realities for their continued existence. Mental realities are held to be a by-product or offshoot of physical realities. As one version put it, "the successive states of the mind are by-products of a succession of events in the cortex." Mental states are caused by physical states—mainly, if not exclusively, by brain processes—but they themselves can exert no causal influence in the physical world. There is no causal interaction between mind and body. Mind is indeed not a thing or a process, but is incidental to the body and could not exist without the body. Bodies can exist, however, without the mind.

It is in conceptual order to call this a form of materialism, for although it does not identify the mental with the physical (and thus is not a reductive materialism), it does treat the physical or those entities postulated by physics as the only entities that are ultimately real. That is to say, physical realities are the only realities, according to epiphenomenalism, which have any independent existence.

One should also classify logical or analytical behaviorism as a type of materialism, although strictly speaking it is but a particular form of reductive materialism. However, it is usually discussed apart from arguments about reductive materialism. In turn, it should be distinguished from *methodological* behaviorism, which makes no metaphysical claim at all but merely proposes as a scientific methodological restriction to limit one's study to behavior in studying the psychology of human beings. This, of course, is perfectly compatible with being a dualist or epiphenomenalist. *Qua* methodological behaviorist, one takes no position on such metaphysical questions. One does not say that mental operations or mental events are just bits of human behavior or that there are no nonphysical mental realities. Rather, one adopts a scientific program that limits psychological study to the study of behavior and, where relevant, to the central nervous system, on the ground that there we have intersubjective phenomena amenable to scientific examination while this is not true of purely inner experiences.

Logical or analytical behaviorism, by contrast, clearly does make a metaphysical materialist claim. It is the claim that mental events or processes are nothing but movements of different parts of the body or tendencies or dispositions to behave in a certain way. It is implicit in my preceding remarks that such an analytical behaviorism often combines with a brain-state theory. Sensations such as pain and itches or the having of an afterimage are treated as being identical with brain processes or the undergoing of distinctive brain processes, while such things as thoughts and rages are treated behavioristically as distinctive bits of human behavior. With such a combination we have a comprehensive reductive materialist account of mental phenomena.

IV

These are the traditional positions. Our central question is to see if we can determine which view is the most plausible—or at least the least implausible. We must also, in line with a sceptical attitude toward metaphysical claims, ask if any of these positions are sufficiently intelligible to be believable. Perhaps such metaphysical talk is as incoherent or as near to being meaningless as is nonanthropomorphic God-talk. (In my reference to 'God-talk', I presuppose the basic correctness of my arguments in Chapter 21.)

My strategy in the next few chapters will be as follows: I shall start with an examination of *reductive materialism* which, *prima facie* at least, is an attractive view to many educated twentieth-century people living in what is sometimes called (rather question-beggingly and ethnocentrically) 'the advanced countries'. I shall first state reductive materialism in the traditional and rather unsophisticated form that one encounters it in Hugh Elliot's *Modern Science and Modern Materialism*. Then I shall state a set of criticisms of such a view. Until very recently, these criticisms have convinced most philosophers that no such form of materialism is acceptable. In fact, such criticisms have led many philosophers to think that it is almost self-evidently false that 'the mental' can be identified with some subset of 'the physical'. This is thought in some quarters, although not in all, to require a reasonable man to opt for some form of dualism. I shall then examine this claim and the arguments for a revitalized and more sophisticated form of materialism that attempts to overcome these principled objections to materialism. Finally, I shall make a tentative attempt to appraise the comparative merits of these two metaphysical views. In doing this I shall also examine the attempt to show that there is really nothing at issue here and that both materialism and dualism, perpetuating conceptual confusion, simply live on by taking in each other's laundry.

As you follow through the arguments in the next few chapters, you should pause to ask yourselves if these various views about mind and the nature of 'ultimate reality' are not simply different ideologies, in a Marxian and pejorative sense of 'ideology'. Are these different metaphysical positions only differing 'picture preferences' or mythologies emotionally solacing to some, but actually distorting to the man who wishes to gain a perspicuous and realistic representation of how things are? In short, are they simply bits of disguised mythology, or is there any objective sense in which we can give evidence or reasons for or against one or another of these conflicting views? I do not mean to insinuate here a view of my own, but to put this way of viewing the matter before you and to suggest that, looked at in a certain way, it is also a central question concerning the possibility of any future metaphysics.

NOTES

1. P. F. Strawson, "Analysis, Science and Metaphysics," in Richard Rorty (ed.), *The Linguistic Turn*, p. 324.
2. Clear brief statements of this occur in J. J. C. Smart, "Man's Place in the Universe," *The Humanist*, vol. 74, no. 3 (March, 1959); D. M. Armstrong, "The Nature of Mind," *Question*, no. I (February, 1958); Wilfrid Sellars, "Philosophy and the Scientific Image of Man," in Robert G. Colodny (ed.), *Frontiers of Science and Philosophy*.
3. J. J. C. Smart, *Philosophy and Scientific Realism* (1963). It is instructive to contrast Smart's synoptic and metaphysical conception of the province of philosophy with the purely critical conception of philosophy adumbrated by Moritz Schlick in 1932 in his "The Future of Philosophy," reprinted in Richard Rorty (ed.), op. cit., pp. 43–53. Both philosophers are tough-minded and analytical and want a scientifically oriented philosophy, but in 1932 Schlick was convinced that synoptic philosophy was dead, while in 1963 Smart saw it as a crucial ingredient in the future of a scientifically oriented philosophy. For a searching critique of Smart's attempt to work out a synoptic philosophical theory, see Joseph Margolis, "Some Prospects of Synoptic Philosophy," *Ratio* (1965), pp. 105–121. Margolis's essay in my judgment shows more about the inadequacies in Smart's particular attempt to articulate a synoptic philosophical view than it does to show that such an endeavor is itself a mistaken one.
4. See C. J. Ducasse, "In Defense of Dualism," in *Dimensions of Mind*, Sidney Hook (ed.).
5. Ibid., p. 133.

6. D. M. Armstrong, "The Nature of Mind," *Question I* (February, 1968), p. 70.

7. Max Born, "Physical Reality," *Philosophical Quarterly*, vol. 3 (1954), pp. 139–150.

8. C. J. Ducasse, "Minds, Matter and Bodies," in J. R. Smythies (ed.), *Brain and Mind*, p. 95.

9. Probably the best elementary discussion of this occurs in James W. Cornman and Keith Lehrer, *Philosophical Problems and Arguments*, pp. 203–239. There is also a good elementary discussion of it in Paul Edwards and Arthur Pap (ed.), *A Modern Introduction to Philosophy*, pp. 174–185, 203–216, 220–227, 256–260, and in Richard Taylor, *Metaphysics*. C. D. Broad, *Mind and Its Place in Nature* (1925) and C. J. Ducasse, *Nature, Mind and Death* (1951) give detailed careful analytical accounts of this problem.

10. This inaccurate statement of materialism makes it plainly vulnerable to the criticisms developed by Ducasse against claiming that "to be real is to be material." That is indeed an unempirical and unjustifiable dogma. Noises, numbers, moral distinctions, smells, beauty are all real and they are not material. (Noises and smells are physical, but that is another matter.) See C. J. Ducasse, "Is Life After Death Possible?" in Paul Edwards and Arthur Pap (eds.), *A Modern Introduction to Philosophy*, pp. 258-259. My more sophisticated statement of reductive materialism avoids this objection.

11. For a brief but clear argument for epiphenomenalism see W. R. F. Hardie, "Bodies and minds," in Paul Edwards and Arthur Pap (eds.), *A Modern Introduction to Philosophy*, pp. 220–227. For a critique of epiphenomenalism see Brand Blanshard, "A Verdict on Epiphenomenalism," in Frederick C. Dommeyer (ed.), *Current Philosophical Issues*, pp. 105–120.

28

THE DUALISTIC
CRITIQUE
OF SIMPLE
MATERIALISM

I

If a human being has a mind in addition to his body, what is this mind that is more than, that is distinct from, his body? The word 'mind' seems to refer to something, and if it does not refer to something in the body, what does it refer to? If we say 'a private something we are directly aware of in being conscious', what is this nonphysical private thing, process, or nonphysical nonthing? In point of fact, what is a 'nonphysical entity or process'? Here we are talking about a 'physical something'. But in so doing we are explicating the obscure and mystifying with what is itself at least as obscure and mystifying. Moreover, we speak of 'ourselves' (some even speak of 'the self') and of 'I', and we speak of 'the human spirit' and of 'the mind'; some talk about 'spirits' or 'the soul'. What do we *mean*, what are we talking about here? What the mind, the spirit, the self is, is indeed perplexing.

As we have already indicated in the previous chapter, no matter what philosophical position we take, it is evident to reductive materialists and dualists alike that there is a sense in which there plainly are mental realities and there plainly are physical realities. We all know that air, water, iron, watches, human and animal bodies, solidity and liquidity, drying, combustion, melting are physical realities and are correctly denominated by the terms 'material' or 'physical'; and even if we believe that mental or psychical realities are a distinctive type of physical reality, we still all know the sort of items that should be denominated by such terms as 'mental' or 'physical', for example, sensations, thoughts, feelings, moods, emotional attitudes, dreams, mental images, cravings, desirings, memories, beliefs. That we have minds is evident enough, for it is a plain fact that we have sensations, cravings, thoughts, images, and the like. No philosopher—no man in his right mind (if such a pun be permitted)—

has ever tried *in this sense* to disprove the existence of the mind. Thinking of such a proof would refute what it purportedly aims to establish. (Things stand differently with 'the soul'. With 'the soul', as with 'God', we are troubled not just by its analysis but by whether it stands for or signifies any kind of reality at all.) It is one thing to know what we have in mind, but it is another altogether to know what we *mean* by the concept of mind, to have a clear conception of what it means to say we have 'a mind'. Moreover, the admission that we know we have a mind and that there are mental phenomena does nothing at all to establish which theory of mind is correct.

If we grant that there is a quite unassailable sense in which there are mental realities, our problem is: What is the correct conceptualization of them? Those who have been impressed by what Peirce called the scientific method of fixing belief, and we who think that this is the only reliable way of gaining knowledge of or tenable beliefs about matters of fact and who would seek a scientifically oriented philosophy, are very tempted to accept some materialist account of 'the mental'. But is it the case that these mental realities are in actuality nothing but a very distinctive type of physical reality such as brain processes or a distinctive form of behavior or a disposition to behave in a certain way? What do 'pain', 'consciousness', and 'anger' refer to? What is it to have a sudden thought? What are these mental events?

II

Hugh Elliot in his *Modern Science and Modern Materialism* (1921) defends reductive materialism in the context of an overall materialist *Weltanschauung*.[1] He attempts to defend three central metaphysical propositions, to show how they hang together, and to exhibit their implications. He, like most materialists, defends determinism. There is in nature a uniformity of causal law and man is unequivocally a part of that nature. This natural world has a unity and a self-sufficiency and can be and indeed should be understood mechanistically.

With such a defense of mechanism goes his second major metaphysical proposition, namely, the denial that the universe has a purpose or that man was designed or created for an end or even that there is in nature any natural teleology, that is, any purely natural purposes. It is indeed true that men engage in goal-directed behavior, but Elliot claims this behavior can, in turn, be explained mechanistically.

His third metaphysical proposition—and indeed the one with which we are presently concerned—is that "there exists no kind of spiritual substance or entity of a different nature from that of which matter is composed." A "bodily organism is a complex machine" and a mind is not a shadowy entity but a "sum-total of cerebral conditions." The very unity of consciousness "finds its exact parallel in the unity of the nervous system." There is no need to posit some nonmaterial entity to parallel this nervous system, but we should simply identify consciousness with the workings of this nervous system. "A conscious state is a specific neural functioning."

It is indeed true that to "the ordinary observer . . . nothing can be more remotely and widely separated than some so-called 'act of consciousness' and a material object." After all, we are simply immediately and indubitably aware of being in pain or of having a sudden thought, and our pains and sudden thoughts do not in such an awareness appear as cerebral processes. This much Elliot readily admits. But he goes on to remark that here we are deceived, for "mental manifestations and bodily manifestations are not two different things, as generally supposed, but one and the same thing appearing under different aspects."[2] Thus, although we are directly aware of mental phenomena, the acts of consciousness of which we are so aware do not attest to the reality of nonmaterial entities. In reality, our raw feelings are "transformations of matter and energy." Elliot tries to establish that

> every event occurring in the Universe, including those events known as mental processes, and all kinds of human action or conduct, are expressible purely in terms of matter and motion. If we assume in the primeval nebula of the solar system no other elementary factors beyond those of matter and energy or motion, we can theoretically, as above remarked, deduce the existing Universe, including mind, consciousness, etc., without the introduction of any new factor whatsoever. The existing Universe and all things and events therein may be theoretically expressed in terms of matter and energy, undergoing continuous redistribution in accordance with the ordinary laws of physics and chemistry. If all manifestations within our experience can be thus expressed, as has for long been believed by men of science, what need is there for the introduction of any new entity of spiritual character, called the mind?

It is Elliot's belief that there is none. As nonevasive men operating with scientific attitudes about the world, we should not multiply entities beyond necessity. A mind as a separate entity—a kind of ghost in the machine—is "such a superfluity" to be whisked away by Occam's razor.

It is important that Elliot's position not be misunderstood. Conscious states are indeed direct data of experience to the person who has them. We cannot reasonably deny this. That is, we are aware of being in pain, having sudden thoughts, and the like. But "there is no direct datum of experience to the effect that [a conscious state] is anything different from certain cerebral processes."

We have here, as we have in Hobbes's *Leviathan* and Holbach's *The System of Nature*, an overall statement of a materialist view of the world.

Determinism, mechanism, and the identity of the mind and the body do not logically require each other, but they do go very well together into what at least appears to be a coherent way of looking at the world, a way that can free one from false hopes and help one to overcome the anthropocentricity that puts man at the center of everything.

Materialism is a view of the world that makes way for a humanistic and secular outlook, but it is a chastened humanism, for it certainly reinforces the view that man is not of transcendent importance in the scheme of things.[3] All varieties of dualism and idealism, materialists have often argued, are anthropocentric doctrines that surreptitiously serve to comfort man against the Galilean revolution, and the even more staggering developments in cosmology and the theory of biological evolution. Dualistic views of the world afford a psychologically comforting escape from the unequivocal recognition, increasingly suggested by modern science, that "man is nothing but a very complicated physiochemical mechanism which has developed from simpler mechanisms through the operation of natural selection." A dualistic view of the world cushions us from what to many seems a bleak view of man, where man is taken to be a "vast arrangement of physical particles," and his behavior is thought to be "in principle explicable in terms of the physical laws of Nature and the positions and motions of these particles."[4] In short, what Gellner calls the compulsive insight of materialism is that what exists—including the mind—must exist in space and occupy a part of it, and that all else can only be an aspect of it.[5]

This has been thought by many careful thinkers not to be an insight but a secular dogma; and most certainly not, as Elliot thinks, the verdict of science, but a bit of metaphysical plumage ideologically attached to science. I think it is indeed fairly evident that Elliot has done little in the way of effective argument for his position, although he has articulated briskly where he stands. The philosophical point is not to preach, insinuate, or merely assert materialism, but effectively to argue for it. After all, as I have remarked, materialism is thought by many to suffer from crippling conceptual difficulties. It is to them we must now turn.

III

Consider again how we distinguished in an ordinary and noncontroversial way between 'the mental' and 'the physical'. What is physical is what is directly or indirectly perceptually public. As Ducasse puts it, "the same tree, the same thunderclap, the same wind, the same dog, the same man, etc., can be perceived by every member of the human public who has normal vision." If something does not have this characteristic, or if something is not a constituent of objects that have this characteristic, as are electrons or mesons, they would not be called 'physical objects' or 'physical processes'. But it is confidently and indeed plausibly claimed that it is evident that sensations, feelings, thoughts do not have this property that would allow us correctly to call them a kind of physical reality. In fact, we call them 'mental' because they are *inherently* and not just contingently private.

We cannot literally perceive or observe what is called a 'mental reality' —for example, a pain, a state of anxiety, a thought—as we can look at or observe a person's mole or even his liver. The individual who has the pain, the feeling of anxiety, or the thought can be directly aware of them, but no one else can. Several people, however, can directly observe an individual's mole or even his liver. His mole and his liver are not things to which he has private access. In fine, I may directly observe your mole or your liver, but I cannot directly observe your sensations or feelings. I can indeed observe your behavior or facial expressions, but I cannot directly observe whether you actually have a pain or that you are seeing a pinkish afterimage. After all, you may act as if you are in pain when you are not. But you, by contrast, are in a totally different relation to your own pain. You have a privileged access to it that you do not have to your mole or to your liver. That is to say, you have a direct awareness of your own sensations, feelings, or images. They, unlike physical objects or processes, are realities you can know that you are having in a way that I cannot; it is *logically* impossible that I could be directly aware of your sensations, thoughts, or moods in the same immediate and incorrigible way you are aware of them. Given that you understand the meaning of 'headache', you, when fully awake, cannot doubt that you have a headache. It makes no sense at all to say, 'I think I have a headache. Let me investigate.' You have privileged access to your sensations and feelings that I do not have.

Such an asymmetry does not obtain, however, for your moles or your liver or any nonmental reality. I may indeed be directly aware of a small growth in my throat that others can only with difficulty observe. But the obstruction in my throat is not ultimately and inherently private, while my pain and images are. I may *make* them public in the sense that I can *tell you* what they are; or, as in the case of pain, I can indicate by my behavior that I am in pain. But my pain is not identical with my pain behavior, and I can simulate the behavior without the pain. I cannot show you my pain or my image as I might show you my mole or my bruise. In that way mental events are inherently and ultimately private. They are not physical objects or processes that can be observed; they are not public or physical at all, but a private nonthing that most of us are aware at times of having. It is this feature that distinguishes mental realities from physical objects and makes them a unique and irreducible kind of reality.

In making this argument for dualism against reductive materialism, I have relied on two things: (1) reminding you of your own experience and (2) reminding you of what our everyday mental concepts and mental discourse is like and making you aware of how badly the materialist conceptualization of those concepts fits with this reality. In doing so I have appealed neither to the obstruse categories of some speculative metaphysics nor to the complexities of science, but to something that is as much a matter of everyday experience as the distinction between sight and sound. This appeal to the pervasive experience of mankind is indeed used to defend a dualistic view of the world, but the defense involves no flight to a mysterious metaphysical enchanter. That is to say, I have not had to involve myself in obscure talk about 'a simple substance' or 'unextended being'; I have not had to appeal to obscure Scholastic or Cartesian concepts. I have only pointed out that given this logical feature of our concept of pain, of thought, or of images (all paradigmatic mental phenomena), it could not be the case that a pain, sudden thought, or image was a distinctive type of brain process or bodily state. A brain process is perceptually public, while, as we have seen, pains, sudden thoughts, and images are not. Since this is so, reductive materialism is plainly false.

This is the most central criticism that dualists make of reductive materialism, but it is not the only important criticism. They also point out that while dualistic conceptions no doubt arose out of early animistic and superstitious circumstances and were fired by religious pressures and hopes, they still can be defended on quite independent grounds. People could have, and some do have (for example, C. D. Broad), a very non-religious view of the world and still remain dualists. Rather, a commitment to dualism involves the steadfast recognition that mental concepts and physical concepts have a very different logic. Someone who understands the roles that mental concepts and physical concepts play in the stream of life comes to understand that while the brain can be weighed and brain processes can be measured, no question can arise in a tolerably similar sense about weighing or measuring thoughts or sensations. My brain might be pickled but not my sensations.

There is no question of experimental design here. In understanding the logic of the concepts in question, one understands that there must be these differences. The differences are shown in the very use of the respective concepts. Thus, mental states cannot be identical with physical states. Thoughts, emotions, sensations, and the like are qualitatively quite unlike patterns of impulses in a brain, and therefore cannot be identical with them. It surely seems false to our own very intimate understanding of what a sensation or feeling is to say that they are material, publicly observable phenomena. Moreover, we not only experientially balk, we conceptually balk as well. It seems as if we have something that is very close to a self-contradiction in saying that mental phenomena are really material, for that seems at least to be saying that all nonmaterial phenomena are really material. It seems as if we are saying that a reality that has no shape and size and is not perceptually public really has shape and size and is perceptually public. Our experience and our sense of the logic of mental concepts militate against our accepting reductive materialism.

Dualists and reductive materialists alike note that there are close correlations between mental states and certain brain states. If one's C-fibres are stimulated one feels pain; if certain nerve centers are deadened one feels nothing at all. One can be wired up so that one can be made to feel in turn sleepy, hungry, angry, and energetic by the decisions of an electrode operator. This not only brings visions of Brave New World, but leads some to think that materialism must be true after all. And it may indeed be the case that thoughts and emotions always occur along with certain contractions and dilations of blood vessels and with certain occurrences in the brain, but this does not mean or even establish that mental events are bodily processes. We certainly do not *mean* when we say that we are in pain that our C-fibres are being stimulated or any such thing about our brains; a plain man and even a not so plain man in the Middle Ages, if indeed not now, may know next to nothing about his brain, never have heard of C-fibres and the like, but he does know what pain is and he does know what fear and anguish are. Since this is so, 'X is in pain' cannot have the same meaning as 'X's C-fibres are being stimulated'.

Thus, even if we establish one-to-one correlations between certain brain states and certain sensations or emotions, this does not establish an identity between them. In fact, only if there was *not* an identity could any correlations be established. To say X is correlated with Y implies that X and Y are not identical. So, if we hold that sensations or thoughts are really identical with brain states or brain processes, we cannot speak of their being correlated, for you cannot correlate something with itself.

IV

This is not Elliot's line of defense, but some materialists faced with such arguments, and in reality (although perhaps unwittingly) actually switching their argument, have argued that sensations and feelings must be brain states because they are caused by brain states. But then one thing is apparent, namely, that the brain processes or states that cause the sensations and feelings cannot be identical with the sensations or emotions themselves, for something cannot be the cause of itself. Thus, the sensations and emotions are, so to speak, left dangling and mysterious on such a materialist argument. There are indeed complex questions about what kind of causal relations would or could obtain there, but we shall not explore these. No matter what we say on that score, we are still left, if we try to maintain a reductive materialism, with a need to show how the sensations and feelings caused by the brain states are indeed themselves really states of the brain.[6] At best we have shown that they are caused by certain brain states, but we have not shown that they are brain states or even what it would be like to establish that they are themselves brain states.

In our arguments in the preceding part of the chapter, we have shown that sensation talk or talk of feelings is not logically equivalent to talk of brain states or bodily states; the terms in question do not have the same meaning. And when one is in pain or when one has a sudden thought, it does not seem to be the case that one is undergoing a certain brain stimulation. Thoughts and sensations certainly do not seem to be material. How can we show, or what would it be like to show, that these mental terms really stand for physical realities? We seem to be utterly at a loss here. To anything the materialist can point to, the dualist can speak of correlations between brain states and mental phenomena. And since mental states are inherently private—known directly only by the agent himself—there is no way of intersubjectively verifying or establishing that mental phenomena really are what they seem to the agent not to be, namely, physical realities.

Such arguments have led many philosophers to think that reductive materialism is almost certainly false or incoherent; that, in spite of its simplicity and attractiveness and in spite of the way it would help integrate our modern progressive, humanistic and godless world-view, it remains a metaphysical dogma of the Children of the Enlightenment and not a closely reasoned philosophical view.

V

We seem forced, if we would be tough-minded, to abandon reductive materialism as we abandoned theism, and to accept, whether we like it or not, some variety of dualism or at least epiphenomenalism. But such moves are intellectually unpalatable as well, for then we must commit ourselves to maintaining that there are some very strange nonextended and inherently private entities or realities which in some mysterious way interact with the body or work in some parallel harmony with the body.

Contemporary dualists such as Broad, Price, and Ducasse have worked hard to take away what appear to be the paradoxical features of dualism and to render it an acceptable view to the scientifically minded. Broad, for example, reminds us not to envisage the mind as "a little man inside the brain." The mind is not a kind of esoteric, private object. It is not inside or outside anything, Broad argues, for no such criteria apply to it. To ask where the mind is or to ask for the location of thoughts, Broad and many others argue, is to show that one does not understand mind-talk—that one does not understand what sort of a concept the concept of mind is. The mind is not, like an electron, a very, very little thing. It is not literally a thing or a process at all. Therefore, to go around trying to visualize the meeting place of the mental and the physical is to fail to understand what the mental is, for it can have no spatial location at all and thus cannot have a meeting place with the brain. Nor can there be a gap or a chasm between them. To think that there might be is just a confusion.[7]

In reply to the frequently voiced objection that the dualist's way of taking experience makes it something ineffable and incommunicable, Price argues that one can impart the private information one gets to others because, having like experiences, they can understand your introspective reports even though they may not believe that what you say is true and have no independent way of ascertaining that what you say is so. Furthermore, Price also could have very well made Ducasse's point, that although each of us acquires his vocabulary for mental realities by hearing certain sentences uttered by other people when they or we are behaving in a certain way, for each of us severally the words denote a particular kind of inherently private event we are experiencing when we behave in a certain way. (Note, we could not learn what pretending was until we understood what it was *not* to pretend.) An acceptance of such a privacy and privileged access does not commit us to a 'mystical' notion of ineffability or to some conception of an inherently 'private language'.

It seems to me that we have reached this stage in the dialectic concerning arguments about materialism and dualism: that the concept of mind appears to be a very different concept from physical concepts, and materialism seems to be very much on the defensive. To continue clinging to it under such circumstances certainly leaves the strong impression that one is caught up in one of the irrational beliefs of disbelief. To be a reductive materialist (or so it would seem at least) is to be caught up in an irrational total ideology that is simply the converse of theism. However, appearaces may be deceiving here. As I remarked earlier, in the past few years materialism has made a comeback sparked by some theoretical psychologists and some philosophers of science. In the next chapter we shall consider whether they can answer what appear to be the unassailable criticisms of dualists and state reductive materialism in a logically acceptable manner.

VI

Some may wonder, in view of the manifest difficulties in both reductive materialism and dualism, why I have neglected that other form of materialism, epiphenomenalism. Why not, while remaining essentially within the materialist camp, regard mental events as the by-products of certain physical processes? As more complicated physical processes develop, consciousness arises as a causally ineffective by-product of these physical processes. That is to say, when physical processes evolve to a certain level of complexity, consciousness emerges. In short, why not regard "all states of consciousness," as did T. H. Huxley in his *Method and Results* (1893), as "immediately caused by molecular changes of the brain-substance."[8] Our mental states, Huxley goes on to tell us, "are simply the symbols in consciousness of the changes which take place in the organism." Physical processes cause states of mind, but are not identical with states of mind; states of mind, however, do not cause bodily events, but are simply the causal by-products of an uninterrupted series of physical events.

For someone who wanted a scientifically oriented philosophy, it could be pointed out that epiphenomenalism both squares well with our evolutionary picture of man and allows us, in scientifically explaining behavior, to use purely physicalist laws, that is, scientific laws which utilize only purely physical concepts. The latter assertions hold, since in giving causal explanations of human and animal behavior we know (if epiphenomenalism is true) that mental events do not causally effect anything at all. Thus, we can explain behavior in purely physical terms. Epiphenomenalism does not share the difficulties inherent in dualistic interactionism; it does not try to explain how mental events can causally influence events, since it denies that such a causal relation obtains; and it does not require a *deus ex machina* as does psychophysical parallelism to explain mind-body regularities. After all, according to epiphenomenalism, mental events and states are causal by-products of physical processes.

Why then reject epiphenomenalism, and why have I not given it a more central place in my examination of the mind/body problem? My reasons are very simple: Epiphenomenalism shares the most crucial difficulties of all forms of dualism, namely, it must postulate a conceptually irreducible, utterly nonphysical psychical something. It is this postulated entity that is so conceptually problematic. Whether or not it is regarded as a by-product of physical processes or as an equal partner does not very much matter vis-à-vis the question about the problematic status of such a nonphysical entity or reality. Such a form of materialism is a doubtful advance over reductive materialism.

Epiphenomenalism also inherits the traditional problems of dualistic interactionism about there being causal connections between such different orders of reality. Even assuming that there can be causal relations between brain states and mental states (which we are now assuming to be of a different order than brain states), there are distinct difficulties for epiphenomenalism. Consider these two sentences:

1. Having a serious toothache causes me to go to the dentist.
2. Believing the child would be returned caused me to deliver the ransom money without notifying the police.

On occasion such sentences are surely used to make true statements. But if this is so, is it not evident that epiphenomenalism is false, for here we have a mental state causing a physical state? It is not always the case that only physical states or events cause mental states or events.

However, it would be the height of absurdity to think that epiphenomenalists were so stupid that they are not perfectly aware that sometimes these two sentences are used to make true statements. They would maintain that appeal to mental states as causative factors is redundant here. That is, for the first statement, conditions other than having the pain will cause the trip to the dentist. So 'cause' really does no work. Referring only to 1 now, given the close correlation of brain states and pain states and the dependence of the latter on the former, it is the case that we can, in explaining behavior, dispense with any reference to pain and explain the pain behavior only by reference to brain states and behavior. This shows the reference to pain states in sentences such as 1 is scientifically superfluous, and thus it does not count, as it appears to, as a disconfirmation of the epiphenomenalist thesis. Assuming, as surely seems evident, that a similar treatment could be extended to 2 and like sentences, we have surely not refuted epiphenomenalism by our parade of examples.

It has been shown, however, that such considerations at best establish the meaningfulness of the epiphenomenalist thesis, but do not establish its truth.[9] We have simply assumed that we could explain the trip to the dentist without reference to the pain or without taking note of the pain when we talk as we did above in 1, but we do not know that this is so. We know the conditions under which epiphenomenalism could be true, but we have no reason to think it actually is true. Moreover, as has been pointed out, even if a drug cut out the pain and we went to the dentist when the state of decay normally associated with the pain occurred rather than as a result of feeling the pain, this hardly shows the truth of epiphenomenalism.[10] It merely shows that there is a brain state *other* than the one correlated with the pain, and that this brain state can also cause trips to the dentist. As Scriven states, it "demonstrates plurality of causes, not the inefficacy of an alleged cause," (the pain). Moreover, it is also evident that the pain, whether we did or did not have what is taken to be the accompanying brain state, leads us to do things such as going to the dentist. That we could give another account of our actions in physiological terms for certain scientific purposes only shows that we can give a complementary account of what happened. It does nothing at all to show that feeling the rasping ache of a toothache cannot, as common sense would have us believe, lead to a trip to the dentist. Thus, given that we allow, as both dualism and epiphenomenalism do, that there are at least two kinds of reality (physical and mental), there is no good ground for claiming that physical events cause certain mental occurrences while denying that the mental can cause physical occurrences. Epiphenomenalism appears plainly to be a view of the mind that can hardly survive critical examination. The really crucial choices are between dualistic interactionism and some form of reductive materialism, including logical behaviorism.

NOTES

1. Substantial portions of Elliot's book are reprinted in Marcus G. Singer and Robert R. Ammerman (eds.), *Introductory Readings in Philosophy*.
2. This variety of reductive materialism has sometimes been called the double-aspect theory. It has been given a powerful contemporary statement by R. J. Hirst, *Problems of Perception*, chapter 7, and in his contributions to *Human Senses and Perception*, chapter 15 (edited by G. M. Wyburn, R. W. Pickford, and R. J. Hirst), and in chapter 9 of G. N. A. Vesey (ed.), *The Human Agent*. G. N. A. Vesey has exhibited the genealogy of such a theory and criticized it in his contribution to the same volume.
3. This is done by J. J. C. Smart in the last chapter of his *Philosophy and Scientific Realism*.
4. J. J. C. Smart, "Man's Place in the Universe," *The Humanist*, vol. 74 (March, 1959), p. 21.
5. E. A. Gellner, "French Eighteenth Century Materialism," in D. J. O'Connor, *A Critical History of Western Philosophy*, p. 295.
6. Questions about the kind of alleged causal relations involved are discussed in the references cited in note 9 Chapter 27.
7. The kind of confusion involved here is beautifully illustrated by John Tyndall in his "The Limitations of Scientific Materialism," reprinted in Paul Edwards and Arthur Pap (eds.), *A Modern Introduction to Philosophy*.
8. T. H. Huxley, *Method and Results*, p. 244.
9. See here Kurt Baier, "Pains," *Australasian Journal of Philosophy*, vol. 40 (May, 1962), pp. 1–23, and Michael Scriven, "The Limitations of the Identity Theory," Paul K. Feyerabend and Grover Maxwell (eds.), *Mind, Matter and Method*, pp. 191–197.
10. Michael Scriven, op. cit., pp. 195–196.

29

IN DEFENSE
OF REDUCTIVE
MATERIALISM

I

We have seen that reductive materialism has many difficulties. Not even its most ardent defenders would deny that. It seems very implausible to say that what we notice in 'inner experience' are brain processes. Yet, it is felt by these materialists that it is even more implausible to believe in nonphysical entities or realities. It is, they believe, too much a jar to our modern scientific understanding of the world to believe that any fundamental account of what there is would have to include irreducibly psychical somethings. Philosophers such as Smart and Armstrong argue that in spite of the conceptual difficulties in materialism, a materialist cosmological picture should be defended on grounds of scientific plausibility. The belief is that if we follow out the world view which we get from science, we will be strongly inclined toward materialism. We will indeed not be committed to a cosmological picture which is wedded to the billiard-ball conceptions of physics of the nineteenth century, but to a world-view in which energy and matter are not sharply distinguishable and to a world-view that holds that there is nothing in the world other than those entities that are and will be postulated by physics.[1]

This seems to many—it certainly seems so to me—to be a tough-minded, clear-visioned, and nonevasive approach to the world. (In the first section of Chapter 30 I shall examine the charge that it is a mindless and dogmatic Scientism.) Yet, tempting as it is to hold such a view, unless we can free it from the kind of conceptual difficulties discussed in the last chapter, we appear to be accepting it by a kind of act of animal faith.

Note exactly what we as materialists would be maintaining. We would be believing that everything that exists is physical. We would have a systematic world-view that would take us beyond the plain man's implicit metaphysics of body and soul and would plausibly construe sensa-

351

tions, thoughts, the having of afterimages—things that seem *not* to be a part of a purely physical scheme of things—as being in reality either dispositions to act in a certain way or as brain processes. It is indeed true that when we are in pain or have a sudden thought we do not notice brain processes—that is, we do not notice that they *are* brain processes—but the reductive materialist can and must consistently argue that they are brain processes all the same. And for those who want a rational synoptic picture of the world that squares with what we do know and with what is scientifically believable, it is intellectually comforting to think, as Quine puts it, that physics investigates the essential nature of the world, biology describes a local bump, and human psychology describes a bump on the bump. Once we are aware that such a view is perfectly compatible with a humane ethic and the recognition of the moral dignity of man, materialism is indeed attractive.[2]

Materialism is compatible with soft determinism and indeed even with indeterminism—after all, most present interpretations of microphysics are indeterministic. And it squares perfectly well with the view of ethics I developed in earlier chapters. However, although such a materialist *Weltanschauung* may be attractive, again the question is, is it finally an intellectually coherent account of mental phenomena? It appears from what we have so far argued that it is an unsupported dogma with gross conceptual difficulties. The efforts of the new materialists, in keeping with the critical role of philosophy as conceptual analysis, is to show that alleged crippling conceptual difficulties—the *a priori* difficulties—are indeed not crippling difficulties, or at least that they are not as severe as the difficulties in dualism or epiphenomenalism. If this can be established, if the charges that materialism is conceptually incoherent can be shown to be mistaken or at least that the alleged difficulties are less telling than the difficulties in the other accounts of the mind, then on grounds of scientific plausibility we are justified in opting for reductive materialism.

II

Let us turn to the core arguments that try to salvage materialism and then to the arguments against these arguments. Let me add, as a cautionary note, that in philosophy this issue remains a hotly debated one. There are very able and analytically oriented philosophers with a healthy respect for science on both sides of this issue; there are several varieties of materialism; and not all rejections of materialism, at least in the view of the people making the rejection, commit them to some version of dualism or epiphenomenalism.[3]

I shall start my account of how the reductive materialists hit back by characterizing the arguments of U. T. Place and J. J. C. Smart. The parts of their theories I shall examine mutually support each other and present in a straightforward manner a defense of materialism.[4]

Smart admits that a sophisticated analytical behaviorism may carry us part of the way. (He has in mind the work of the contemporary linguistic philosophers Ryle and Wittgenstein, who would not regard themselves as behaviorists but whom he regards, not implausibly, as behaviorists in spite of themselves; that is, look at their analyses rather than at their disclaimers.) To say that someone is intelligent, sad, afraid, or angry is to say something about what he is disposed to do. To say, for example, that someone is thinking of what he is doing while he is driving is to say, or at least to imply, that he has a tendency to behave behind the wheel in certain distinctive ways. One cannot correctly say that he is thinking of what he is doing unless he does behave in these characteristic ways.

If this behavioristic account—assuming what is arguable although still plausible—is correct, such an account would establish materialism, if it could be extended to cover all mental concepts. But the sailing is not nearly that smooth. The contemporary American philosopher Roderick Chisholm in his *Perceiving* has shown that behaviorism, to put it conservatively, has difficulties in adequately analyzing belief sentences.[5] And, as Smart points out, it even more obviously fails for sensations and images. It is here, if materialism is to be vindicated, that we need the brain-process theory. Suppose, to deploy the argument for that claim, that someone hits me on the head and I 'see' stars, or suppose I have an orange and yellow afterimage. When I say later and reflectively that I saw stars or when I remark, 'I see a yellowish afterimage,' my utterances are reports and they are very unlike 'Ouch' or 'Oh, it hurts', for they are not simply verbal replacements of behavior. Rather, they are reports of purely inner experience. It is this fact of the mental life that analytical behaviorism does not account for adequately.

Smart and Place want to demystify these reports and the inner experiences they report by showing that there is no reason why we should not take these inner experiences to be brain processes and nothing more. We do not need to believe in any ghostly inner realities that could not be characterized in scientific terms. Smart and Place, like other contemporary materialists, do not try to prove or establish that each type of inner experience is actually a distinctive type of brain process. That would be for physiologists to establish by experimental investigation, and that is surely only establishable (if establishable at all) when physiology and science in general are far more advanced than they are now. What Smart and Place must do is to show that there are no valid conceptual bans against materialism such that such a case could not be validly made.

Taking up this philosophical challenge, they attempt to show that there are no valid philosophical reasons why materialism should not be true. They try to show that it is not incoherent or logically misplaced to believe that such a set of identities can be discovered. In short, they try to show that reductive materialism is a plausible account of how things might be. It would be up to science to show that they are that way, for science alone gives us a reliable method of fixing beliefs about matters of fact. But, as Smart rightly stresses, if we could give a coherent account of how reductive materialism might plausibly be true, it would be quite readily accepted by very many people at any rate, for the existence of some postulated concept of a nonphysical purely psychical reality is very mystifying indeed. If such a set of arguments for reductive materialism could be shown to be sound, it would be an enormously important philosophical breakthrough, for it would now be established that we are not logically compelled to assume the existence of "an irreducibly psychical something" to account adequately for the full range of human experience.

Let us now consider Smart's particular analyses of such mentalistic talk. The crucial thing is to determine what kind of occurrence we report by the use of such sentences as these:

1. My afterimage is greenish.
2. I have a sharp pain in my back.

Being in pain involves being distressed, and indeed this characteristically involves certain distinctive bits of behavior. But it involves something else as well, namely, that there is an immediately felt sensation that we do not have in some other cases of distress. For example, contrast the second sentence with 'His deception was painful to me'. How can Smart show that it is plausible to believe that the experience of being in pain or having an afterimage is a brain process? What are the grounds for asserting 'being aware of a greenish afterimage' and 'sharp pain in my back' stand for distinctive brain processes? Recall that dualists and epiphenomenalists say that both sentences 1 and 2 report the "nonphysical correlates of brain processes." Brain processes may even cause sensations, but brain processes and sensations are never identical. Smart's opponents argue, as we have seen, that the sensations and images are so qualitatively different from brain processes that they can hardly be different names for the same reality. And when we honestly consider the raw quality of our sensations—looking at it as we experience them as agents—this indeed seems to be so.

Smart believes he can avoid this difficulty and make it evident that such psychological predicates (hereafter called p-predicates) can be shown to stand for brain processes. Smart remarks of his thesis:

> It is not the thesis that, for example, 'after-image' or 'ache' means the same as 'brain process of sort X' (where 'X' is replaced by a description of a certain sort of brain process). It is that, in so far as 'after-image' or 'ache' is a report of a process, it is a report of a process that *happens to be* a

brain process. It follows that the thesis does not claim that sensation statements can be *translated* into statements about brain processes. Nor does it
claim that the logic of a sensation statement is the same as that of a brain-
process statement. All it claims is that in so far as a sensation statement
is a report of something, that something is in fact a brain process. Sensations are nothing over and above brain processes.[6]

In the very statement of his thesis he has avoided certain of the traditional
objections to reductive materialism. He has avoided objections turning on
the point that (1) p-predicates do not have the same meaning as physical
terms (hereafter m-predicates) and (2) they could not refer to the same
thing since one can understand p-predicates without understanding anything about physiology at all. Smart's claim is that they just happen
to refer to the same thing, just as 'black' and 'schwarz' happen to refer
to the same thing even though English-speaking people may not understand 'schwarz' and German-speaking people may not understand 'black.'
Terms can even have a different meaning, as do 'evening star' and 'morning star', and still refer to the same thing. This could very well be the
case for p-predicates and m-predicates. However, the new materialists
make it plain that they are not claiming that if we are clear about what
p-predicates really mean, we will see that they have the same meaning
as m-predicates. 'Pain' and 'brain-process X' have different meanings but
refer to the same reality.

Still, this does not resolve the initial problem. Since 'the feel' of the
psychological experience to the agent is so different from anything he
knows about brain processes, it would seem unlikely they could actually
refer to the same thing. Smart, as we have already seen, grants that when
we are aware of our pains or notice afterimages, we do not notice that
they are brain processes. But this obtains in conceptually unpuzzling cases
as well. I might know someone by acquaintance—say the man in the
apartment next to mine—without knowing something crucial that is true
about him, for example, that he is the new professor of economic history.
I might even know quite a bit about the new professor of economic history—namely, know the conditions under which he has been appointed,
his views on Marx, Pareto, and the like—but never having seen him or
a picture of him, I would not know that the man I see in the morning
coming out of his apartment is the new professor of economic history.
The man I see each morning is the professor of economic history, but
I do not notice that. That is, I am not aware of that fact. Similarly, my
aches and afterimages may be brain processes even though I do not notice
that they are brain processes.

Granted this fact and that the uses of p-predicates and m-predicates
seem to be so very different, how does one know—or does one know—
that the p-predicates really refer to brain processes, where there is some
situation, as with an ache or afterimage, where we would naturally speak

of an inner experience? Smart—although not all reductive materialists have followed him here—attempts to give a translation of sentences such as the preceding two examples into sentences using only *m*-predicates.[7] He maintains, "Our talk about immediate experiences is derivative from our language of physical objects. This is so even with much of our language of bodily sensations and aches and pains. A stabbing pain is the sort of going on which is like what goes on when a pin is stuck in you."[8]

'Ache', however, functions somewhat differently. To say, "I have a terrible ache in my stomach," is to say, "What is going on in me is like what is going on when I groan, yelp, etc." We learn to use these words with reference to such outward public occurrences and then, as we gradually gain a fuller mastery of such talk, we learn in certain circumstances to inhibit our propensity to groan, and the like; and to regard those experiences which we have when we have such propensities—which are indeed very like the experiences we have when we groan, and so on—as likewise being aches and pains (of a certain sort).

The crucial point is that we can characterize what is going on in an utterly physicalistic language, that is, a language containing no *p*-predicates at all and with *m*-predicates taking the place of *p*-predicates. The translated sentences refer to public states of affairs (bits of human behavior); these—say, writhing in pain—occur only when certain brain processes are stimulated and have as their immediate explanation the stimulation of certain brain processes. Since this is so, it is plausible to think that what is referred to by the equivalent sentence with the *p*-predicate and what is referred to by the sentence with the *m*-predicate are the same.

Smart, following Place, refutes a common but plainly fallacious argument that is likely to be invoked here. Dualists and other opponents of reductive materialism are likely to respond that the *p*-predicates and the *m*-predicates could not possibly refer to the same reality. Where the *p*-predicate is 'greenish afterimage' it refers to something that is green, whereas the neurophysiologist looking into our brains is very unlikely to see anything that is green or greenish. Thus, what is referred to by the *p*-predicate could not be identical to what is referred to by the *m*-predicate. But to argue in this way is to commit the *phenomenological fallacy*. As Smart nicely puts it:

> To say that an image or sense datum is green is not to say that the conscious experience of having the image or sense datum is green. It is to say that it is the sort of experience we have when in normal conditions we look at a green apple, for example. Apples and unripe bananas can be green, but not the experiences of seeing them. An image or a sense datum can be green in a derivative sense, but this need not cause any worry, because,

on the view I am defending, images and sense data are not constituents of the world, though the processes of having an image or a sense datum are actual processes in the world. The experience of having a green sense datum is not itself green; it is a process occurring in grey matter. The world contains plumbers, but does not contain the average plumber; it also contains the having of a sense datum, but does not contain the sense datum.[9]

Smart has not established that the appropriate p-predicates refer to brain processes, but in keeping with his aims he has broken down some crucial philosophical objections that maintain that it is *a priori* impossible for this to be the case.

III

There remains a further, perhaps less obvious difficulty, but a difficulty that many feel to be overwhelming, namely, the difficulty connected with the nature of the identity between sensations and brain processes and conscious experiences and brain processes. Smart has asserted that sensations are brain processes. But what of the status of that very statement? Smart, denying that there is an identity of *meaning*, of course, denies it is analytic. That is, unlike 'Fathers are male parents', it is not true by definition. Yet according to Smart it does assert an identity—an identity that just happens to be the case. But what kind of identity, and how is such an identity established? That is, what would have to be the case or fail to be the case for it to hold or not to hold?

Smart says that the identity is strict. It is like the identity in 'Lightning is an electrical discharge'. He calls it 'strict' for he does not mean just that the sensation is somehow spatially or temporally continuous with the brain process or that the lightning is spatially or temporally continuous with the discharge, but that the lightning and the discharge are one and the same thing and the brain process and the sensation are one and the same thing. It is not contradictory on Smart's account to deny that they are the same thing or else the identity would be a logical one and not, as Smart claims, a *de facto* identity. However, Smart is not very clear about exactly what this *de facto* or contingent identity is or how we could determine when it holds.[10]

U. T. Place, from whom Smart took his point of departure in arguing for reductive materialism, is a little more helpful in his "Is Consciousness a Brain Process?"[11] Consider the following statements, which assert an identity but not a logical identity (they are not analytic).

3. His table is an old packing case.
4. Her hat is a bundle of straw tied together with a string.

5.   A cloud is a mass of water droplets or other particles in suspension.

6.   Lightning is a motion of electric charge.

These four statements involve the 'is' of *de facto* (contingent) identity. They do not assert an identity of meaning, but in asserting 'X is Y' they assert that X and Y stand for the same thing. The dualist mistakenly argues from the fact that 'consciousness' and 'being a brain process' do not have the same meaning to the claim that they cannot therefore have the same extension, that is, refer to exactly the same thing. But this argument from meaning is surely mistaken, for by the very same token we would have to say of statement 3 that a table cannot be an old packing case, since there is nothing self-contradictory in supposing that someone has a table but is not in possession of an old packing case.

There is an important difference, however, between statement 3 and this statement:

7.   Consciousness is a brain process.

Note that statement 3 is particular while 7 is universal. But statements 5 and 6 also assert universal although nonanalytic statements of strict identity. Moreover, note that we say very different things about clouds and water particles in suspension, and thus the terms have different meanings, even though they still refer to the same things. Exactly the same thing is true, Place argues, about consciousness and brain processes. They have different meanings, but 'pain' and 'stimulation of C-fibers' both refer to the stimulation of C-fibers, just as 'George Washington' and 'the First President of the United States' refer to the same person.

There is an important difference between statements 5 and 7. In 5, the cloud case, the identity of what is referred to by the two expressions is established by the continuity between the two sets of observations as the observer moves toward or away from the cloud. By contrast, in the case of brain processes and consciousness, 7, there is no such continuity between the two sets of observations. There is nothing so flatly empirical and observational. A closer introspective scrutiny of one's sensations will never reveal the passage of the nerve impulses over a thousand synapses in the way a closer scrutiny of a cloud will reveal a mass of tiny particles in suspension.

At this point the comparison between statements 6 and 7 becomes crucial. 'Lightning is a motion of electric charges', Place argues, is a more aptly parallel case with statement 7 and best brings out the nature of the identity. We can observe lightning, but we shall never be able to observe the electric charges in the same direct way. In statements 6 and 7 the verification of what is said to be identical is very different than in the earlier cases. If in the case of statement 6 we can see what justifies saying that the two sets of observations are observations of the same thing, perhaps we can gain some insight concerning what we could reasonably mean in maintaining that pains are the stimulation of C-fibers or, more generally, consciousness is a brain process and nothing else.

First note that for neither statement 6 nor 7, nor for any other *de facto* strict identity, is it *sufficient* that there be what, prior to the assertion of the identity, are called systematic correlations between the two sets of observations. There are systematic correlations between the movements of the tides and of the moon, but this does not lead us to say that records of levels of the tide are records of the moon's state. We speak instead of a causal connection between independent events or processes. Something is needed for *de facto* identity different from systematic and/or causal correlation. Our old point remains that if Y is to be correlated with X it cannot be identical with X, although we could say that what was taken to be a systematic correlation is now seen to be an identity or has now been identified as being one and the same thing. But then how do we decide when we have an identity rather than a systematic and/or causal correlation?

Place maintains that there is such an identity and that the two observations are observations of the same event "in those cases where the technical body of scientific theory provides an immediate explanation of the observations made by the man in the street." If we could immediately and exactly make new and correct predictions concerning the occurrence of conscious states on the basis of our knowledge of brain processes, we would have good evidence for such a *de facto* identity. This will obtain if the introspective observations reported by the subject are such that for each type of observation reported by the subject there is always the observation of a distinctive type of brain process such that when and only when these distinctive brain processes occur will that type of introspective report, if asked for, be made. If this obtains, then brain processes would be the immediate explanation of the observations, and thus we would be justified in concluding that there is a *de facto* identity of brain processes and consciousness.

Thus, we seem at least to have a reasonable account of the alleged *de facto* identity between consciousness and brain states of a certain type. Remember that neither Smart nor Place, nor any materialist with whom I am acquainted, maintains that they have established such an identity. Rather, they have tried to show that there is no *a priori*, conceptual philosophical reason why there could not be such an identity: an identity which, if it were to be established, would have to be established scientifically. They only maintain that once the philosophical objections to it are overcome, it is evident that it is more reasonable to believe that there actually is such an identity than to assume there are some peculiar ghostly realities and odd laws linking these unique psychological nonthings or nonphysical processes or states with physical realities.

IV

Now I want to try to assess the correctness of these new statements of reductive materialism, which has many able defenders and many able critics as well.[12] Its tenability is now very much in dispute among critical philosophers.

It has been objected that the criteria for and the nature of the contingent identity that reductive materialists talk about has not been made nearly clear enough to make possible an unproblematic statement of the theory. Until this has been done, the mind/body identity claim is not sufficiently coherent to be establishable as true or false.[13]

One attempt at remedy here would be to maintain that we could correctly say that X is identical with Y if and only if every nonlinguistic property of X is a property of Y and conversely.[14] If the morning star is indeed identical with the evening star, then it follows that, literary conventions notwithstanding, the evening star appears in the morning and the morning star appears in the evening, even though some people may not notice that the evening star appears in the morning. If they are identical, the evening star has all the nonlinguistic properties the morning star has and vice versa. In claiming that sensations or thoughts are in fact identical with brain processes, reductive materialists must be claiming that what in fact is a property or characteristic of one is in fact a characteristic of the other, just as what is in fact a characteristic of Churchill is also a characteristic of the Prime Minister of England during World War II. That is to say, it just happens to be the case with a *de facto* identity that what is a property or characteristic of what is referred to by the term 'pain' is also a property or characteristic of what is referred to by 'brain process X'.

However, the following argument is turned against reductive materialists. My knowledge that I am in pain is incorrigible, while this is not true of anything we can know about brain states or brain processes. It is nonsense for a fluent speaker of English who has learned to use 'pain' correctly to say, 'I have a pain unless I am mistaken.' It is not at all nonsense, however, to say, 'My c-fibers are being stimulated unless I am mistaken' or 'I am having brain process X if I am not mistaken.' Sensations, as we found the dualists arguing all along, have an inherently private quality, in contrast with brain processes or brain states which are public. So the terms in question not only have different meanings but also refer to different things, as can be seen from the fact that they are not contingently identical since they do not have identical characteristics.

A closely related point causes trouble for the reductive materialist. For anything that may properly be called 'a sensation', the person allegedly having the sensation is the *final authority* on whether or not he has it.

If he cannot be shown to be lying, to have misspoken himself, not to have mastered the language in question, or to have failed to understand what is being said, then he is the final and unchallengeable authority on whether something hurts him or tickles him. But being the final authority in such circumstances, whether he has it or is undergoing it is not a property of a brain process or a brain state. Then brain processes cannot be identical with sensations, for, as we have seen, one thing is identical with what purports to be another thing if and only if whatever is a property or characteristic of whatever is denoted by the first term is a property or characteristic of what is denoted by the second term and vice versa.

Moreover, given this criterion, for *de facto* identity, there seems to be an insuperable difficulty for reductive materialism—namely, that we, for example, ascribe properties to pains which we do not ascribe to brain processes. Pains can be described as being unbearable, sharp, or throbbing, but brain processes cannot be so described. Note that no phenomenological fallacy is committed here, for it is the painful experience that is of this nature. It is not true that either the brain process or the undergoing of a brain process (whatever exactly that means) is unbearable, sharp, or throbbing.[15] Moreover, brain processes can be publicly observed, spatially located, irreversible, or swift. But if either the pain is identical with a certain brain process or the experience of having the pain is identical with undergoing a certain brain process, then in both cases the things said to be identical will have the same properties, properties of purely literary or simply conventionally cultural ways of talking about them aside. We can see from the preceding that they do not have the same properties, however, so they are not even *de facto* identities. (The qualifiers about literary and conventional ways of talking serve to block the type of objection that would remind us that we speak of pain being detestable but not of C-fiber stimulation being detestable.)

It is not clear to me how or even that reductive materialists can answer this last criticism. Perhaps they could give another criterion for *de facto* identity, claiming that this one is too strong.[16] Indeed, it has been said by one reductive materialist that "the identity theory need not and must not claim that experiences and brain processes have identical characteristics, including spatial extent, still less that elements of each coincide."[17] Rather, it is argued, the core of the reductive materialist's identity claim is that a given type of sensation and a certain kind of brain process, or the undergoing of a certain kind of brain process, are one and the same thing. Properties such as being intense, nagging, throbbing, and unbearable are *subjective* properties having crucial importance only from the agent's point of view. They are unnecessary for the theoretical identification of the same realities from the point of view of science.

This *may* be a satisfactory answer or the beginnings of a satisfactory answer. Yet, we should be aware that in talking about theoretical identification, we have introduced a new notion—'identification by stipulation' —in place of our old claim to show what it would be like to establish a *de facto* identity. That is, it does not report a discovery such as the identity of the morning star and the planet Venus, but represents, in the light of our contemporary scientific understanding of man, a reasonable conceptual proposal to start treating sensations as being identical with certain brain processes or (on an alternative formulation) the having of these sensations as being identical with the undergoing of certain brain processes. What we actually do is to say that sensations are to be identified as brain processes. But then we have not established a contingent identity or shown what it would be like to establish such an identity; we have not shown what it would be like to establish that sensations are or are not the same things as certain brain processes or that the experience of having a sensation is the same thing as undergoing a certain brain process. We have instead committed ourselves by *fiat* to conceiving of sensations in a somewhat new way. Such an identity by convention or an identification by convention does not refute the dualist or epiphenomenalist, for he may not choose to adopt the reductive materialist's convention. Moreover, reductive materialists such as Smart, Place, and Armstrong want to establish that sensations are nothing over and above brain processes, that inner mental states, as Armstrong puts it, are just purely physical states of the central nervous system.[18]

What does it *mean* to say they are one and the same thing if they have different properties? And since we are talking of psychological realities, which we are trying to identify as a type of physical reality, how can it be correct to dismiss such evident properties of these realities as intensity or being throbbing as merely 'subjective'? 'Subjective' here seems out of place. At least we must be given a nonquestion-begging criterion for what counts as 'a subjective property'.

I do not want to suggest that I think these objections are unanswerable, although at present at any rate I do not know how to answer them. Most fundamentally, the reductive materialist must work out a suitable conception of a contingent identity so that it is clearer what he is claiming when he maintains that sensations and brain processes are one and the same thing or that states of consciousness and bodily states are one and the same thing. And he must answer the problems about (1) the alleged inherent privacy of the mental as against the public quality of the physical and (2) the corrigibility of statements about purely physical realities as against the at least apparent incorrigibility of such statements as 'I have a headache'. I shall return to these last considerations later in this chapter and I shall also try to offer another criterion of contingent identity. First, however, I want to state and examine Norman Malcolm's critique of reductive materialism, a critique thought by many to refute decisively reductive materialism.

V

Malcolm's essay "Scientific Materialism and the Identity Theory" also represents in sophisticated form the kind of rejection of all traditional philosophical accounts of the mind/body problem—dualism and epiphenomenalism as well as reductive materialism—that is characteristic of philosophers who have come under the influence of Wittgenstein. What they maintain is that these dualist and materialist claims are not false but so problematic as to be close to being meaningless. Malcolm claims, characteristically, that it is pointless to talk about 'mental events' or 'conscious experiences' or 'inner experiences', for these terms are "almost exclusively philosopher's terms" and have no established meaning or use. But if reductive materialism is a true account of mental processes, then it must be the case that a sudden thought or the experience one has when one has a sudden thought is a brain process or the undergoing of a brain process. This surely would be true at least for the comprehensive form of reductive materialism that identifies thoughts and consciousness with inner processes and in turn identifies these inner processes with brain states. Malcolm attempts to establish that to claim such an identity between sudden thoughts and brain states has no sufficiently clear meaning so that we could say it is either true or false, and thus we cannot justifiably accept reductive materialism.

Malcolm argues that the identity theorists—and Smart in particular—have given no clear sense to the notion of contingent identity that is so central to their claim. (After all, if they fall back on an identity of *meaning*, they will fall prey to the traditional objections outlined in the previous chapter.) Working with their examples (examples of the type we have already given), Malcolm tries to ascertain what could be meant by 'contingent identity', for example, the identity we intend when we say that 'General de Gaulle is the tallest Frenchman' is a statement of identity. Malcolm goes on to remark that to speak of 'contingent identity' in tolerably clear terms, it at least must be the case that if something X is in a certain place at a certain time, then something Y is strictly identical with X only if Y is in that same place at that same time.[19] If 'contingent identity' is to have any determinate meaning at all, this would appear to be a necessary condition for such an identity.

Malcolm's claim here about contingent identity is down-to-earth and most certainly seems to be plainly right. His rule is indeed a good one to use in determining if we have a contingent identity. Now, the obvious move is to test 'Sudden thoughts are brain processes' against this rule. Malcolm does this and argues that it fails the test. Suppose I am shaving in the morning and I hear the sound of a truck pulling up outside my house and suddenly remember that I have forgotten to put the milk bottles out. This is the having of a sudden thought if anything is. Now this sudden thought or the having of the sudden thought is, according to reductive materialists, a brain process. I indeed know when it occurred, but I do not and cannot know where it occurred, Malcolm argues, for in our ordinary discourse we can attach no meaning to the notion of *determining the location of a thought,* sudden or otherwise. Accordingly, it makes no sense to either assert or deny that it takes place inside my skull. Malcolm maintains that when this is thought through, it is seen in effect to be a crushing blow to reductive materialism. The contingent identity claimed by reductive materialists is governed by the rule that if X occurs in a certain place at a certain time, then Y is contingently identical with X only if Y occurs in the same place and at the same time as X. But now Malcolm springs his trap:

> I surmise that his [Smart's] so-called 'strict identity' is governed by the necessary condition that if X occurs in a certain place and at a certain time, then Y is strictly identical with X only if Y occurs in the same place at the same time. But if X is a brain process and Y is a sudden thought, then this condition for strict identity is not (and cannot be) satisfied. Indeed, it does not even make sense to set up a test for it. Suppose we had determined, by means of some instrument, that a certain process occurred inside my skull at the exact moment I had the sudden thought about the milk bottles. How do we make the further test of whether my *thought* occurred inside my skull? For it would have to be a *further* test: it would have to be logically independent of the test for the presence of the brain process, because Smart's thesis is that the identity is *contingent.* But no one has any notion of what it would mean to test for the occurrence of the thought inside my skull *independently* of testing for a brain process. The idea of such a test is not intelligible. Smart's thesis, as I understand it, requires this unintelligible idea. For he is not satisfied with holding that there is a systematic correlation between sudden thoughts and certain brain processes. He wants to take the additional step of holding that there is a 'strict identity'. Now his concept of strict identity either embodies the necessary condition I stated previously, or it does not. If it does not, then I do not know what he means by 'strict identity', over and above systematic correlation. If his concept of strict identity does embody that necessary condition, then his concept of strict identity cannot be meaningfully applied to the relationship between sudden thoughts and brain processes. My conclusion is what I said in the beginning: the identity theory has no clear meaning.[20]

In sum, if Malcolm is right, then to assert that a sudden thought is a brain process is to assert something that is without meaning. Thus, to assert 'Consciousness is a brain process' is also to assert something without meaning, or at least with such a problematical meaning that it could not correctly or justifiably be said to be either true or false or even probable or improbable. Therefore, reductive materialism is a conceptually incoherent claim that cannot reasonably be accepted.

Malcolm's arguments here, just as his arguments about the ontological argument, are important. While it seems to me that it is less evident that he is mistaken here than it is with his challenging arguments about the ontological argument, I still think there are grounds, although hardly conclusive ones, for thinking he is mistaken here as well. There are two important and quite different lines of argument concerning Malcolm's criticism of the identity theory.[21]

1. The majority of defenders of reductive materialism agree with Malcolm that as things stand now we do not know what it would be like to test or in any way ascertain where a sudden thought is located when that test is independent of testing where a brain process is located. That is to say, we do not know how to test whether or not a sudden thought is located inside the skull. Furthermore, they agree with Malcolm that we do not now speak of thoughts either being in or failing to be inside the skull.

However, they go on to add that if our knowledge of neurophysiology develops in a certain direction (as it might very well develop), then it would become natural to start speaking of the experience of having a thought as something that was going on in one's head. The knowledge that would be relevant and that would justify talking in that way and of generally so talking about experiences would be a knowledge of the truth of predictions of the following sort.

1. When and only when someone is in brain state a (the name of some determinate brain state) will he be having a sudden thought.

2. When and only when he is in brain state b will he be having an itch.

3. When and only when he is brain state c will he be having a sharp, stabbing pain.

If we had massive and systematically related and exact information of that sort and knew or had very good empirical grounds for believing it to be true—that is, genuine, reliable information—then it would be natural to come to speak of a pain as something that was located in one's brain or of a sudden thought as being located in one's brain. We would come to identify it as a brain state. Such sentences would then become perfectly intelligible and unproblematic, and we would have no hesitation about acknowledging where a man's sudden thoughts or pains were. Thus, utterances that at present are deviant would become nondeviant without the terms in question changing their meaning.

Certainly, the argument continues, to understand each other at all we must start from ordinary usage. But we must not have an exaggerated respect for the merely contingent forms of this discourse. At a given time in its history the very structure of our ordinary discourse may enshrine false beliefs. Under such conditions it is indeed difficult to recognize that they are false, but once this recognition is made and is culturally established, the discourse itself will change or begin to change. New experiences or new knowledge may lead us to speak quite intelligibly in altered ways. Utterances which at a given time are logically odd (conceptually problematic) will cease being so, for example, 'unconscious thoughts'. The sentence 'The having of a sudden thought is the having of a brain process' is now a very odd sentence indeed. We are not clear what we would be asserting if we were to assert it. It has no clearly established role in human discourse. But with the scientific development that I just mentioned, it would (or at least it could) become a natural and perfectly intelligible and unproblematic thing to say. With such a development, to speak of the experience of a sudden thought occurring inside one's skull would also become perfectly natural.

However, this does not end the argument, for Malcolm, anticipating this, has a rebuttal ready. He says that if we came to talk in that way we would no longer be operating with our present concept of a sudden thought, but with some *new* concept in which the meaning of 'sudden thought' had become something quite different. But, Malcolm continues, it is irrelevant to bring in such a development and to talk of these new concepts, for that is not to talk about what is at issue, namely, whether our concept of a sudden thought is a concept of something contingently identical with a brain process or—to put it more accurately—the concept of something which, when we had the experience of what is characterized by that concept (the concept of a sudden thought), we would have had something identical with undergoing certain brain processes. In other words, the problem arose about our common and everyday concept of a sudden thought and not about some future and quite different concept that we might someday come to have. After all, it is our actual concept of a sudden thought that is relevant here and not some fancied, future concept with a quite different meaning. But, Malcolm reiterates, given our present concept, it makes no sense to ask where a sudden thought is.

Malcolm's reply will not suffice, for he has not *established* that if we started talking about the locations of sudden thought, and if we started to say that the experience of having a sudden thought is an experience that goes on in our heads, we would be giving 'sudden thought' a *new* meaning—that it would become a new concept. Language, as linguists have taught us, is both highly systematic and very flexible. It can absorb many new sentences without its stock of words changing in meaning. Sentences that are deviant, sentences that many of us do not properly understand, become perfectly intelligible to native or fluent speakers once they have certain new experiences and/or given new technological developments. Consider these examples. (1) 'He went halfway around the world'. When everyone thought the earth was flat, this utterance would have been deviant; people would not have understood it. But once the earth was understood to be approximately spherical, it became perfectly intelligible. But, with due respect to Malcolm, none of the words in that sentence changed their meanings when the deviant utterance became nondeviant and plainly intelligible. (2) (To a person in New York): 'He talked to me last night from London'. Before the invention of the telephone, this would not be understood. Now it is a perfectly straightforward sentence. Yet none of the words have changed their meaning. In a similar manner, reductive materialists could argue against Malcolm that given a certain development of science, the following sentences would become perfectly nondeviant, readily understood utterances.

4.   Pain is identical with the stimulation of C-fibers.

5.   Having a sudden thought is having a brain process of type A.

6.   The thought occurred inside my skull.

We can understand in a general way what sort of scientific developments are necessary for us to be in a position to reasonably assert whether reductive materialism is true (probably true) or false (probably false). Given the kind of scientific development reductive materialists envision, statements 4, 5, and 6 would become perfectly intelligible to the plain man. Yet none of the fundamental terms in question would have taken on new meanings. Thus, Malcolm has not established that the mind/body identity theory has no even tolerably definite meaning, that is, that we have no idea what it would be like for its claims to be true or false.

2. The foregoing is enough to undercut Malcolm's central argument and to give reductive materialism a new lease on life. But there is a very different claim that makes even fewer concessions to Malcolm. This claim should be considered, especially since it is important in its own right. Anthony Quinton—although not in connection with Malcolm's arguments —has maintained, correctly I believe, that "mental entities have a real if indeterminate position in space."[22] He remarks in this context that the truth of this claim does not establish an identity of thoughts and brain processes. He also makes it evident that he does not mean this is so only for some future developed concepts of thought, feeling, or sensation, but for our present concepts. He remarks:

> If it were necessary that mental entities should not be spatial, if the ascription of spatial characteristics to them were contradictory or nonsensical, it would have been disastrous for the identity theory. For it claims that mental entities do have a precise location in space.

Here he clearly is in agreement with Malcolm, but unlike Malcolm he does not think it is a misuse of language, or a remark without meaning, to assert that a sudden thought is inside the skull. Merely considering our ordinary way of talking, there are good reasons for saying "that mental entities have at least a rough position in space of a kind which here, as in other cases, scientific inquiry may render more precise."[23]

I do not know whether this will surprise the plain man, but it is a departure from what most philosophers would be willing to commit themselves to. Therefore, we most particularly need to look for the support for this claim. Surely, as Quinton himself points out, the objects of direct, introspective awareness *qua* objects of direct introspective awareness (pains, thoughts, wishes, desires) do not reveal spatial properties. However, there is one reason—to Quinton an overriding reason—for attaching spatial location to mental states, in spite of the fact that we are not directly aware of their having a spatial location: If we did not so locate them we could not individuate them. The dualist, Quinton argues, must "admit that if experiences are radically non-spatial it is logically possible, whether or not it ever actually happens, that one and the same experience should occur in the history of two distinct selves."[24] But then the dualist has lost his ground for claiming that mental experiences are inherently private. My wife and I might both hear, starting at the same time and ending at the same time, a peculiar buzz coming from our radio. Suppose as a result we have qualitatively indistinguishable feelings of annoyance also beginning at the same time and ending at the same time. How can we, except by locating the experiences spatially, justify the commonsense and indeed scientific belief that we have two experiences of annoyance here rather than one? Quinton argues that we cannot.

It has been replied by Vesey that it seems not to have occurred to Quinton "that experiences are individuated by reference to the people whose experiences they are."[25] Unless I miss some subtlety in Quinton's argument, this commonsense reply by Vesey seems at least to be adequate. We can individuate experiences by reference to the people who have them. To distinguish one thought from another (no matter how qualitatively alike they are), we need not be able to say that thought *a* has such and such spatial location and thought *b* has such and such spatial location. We merely must be able to say that a given person has thought *a* and another person has thought *b*.

While Quinton's argument that we must speak in the way he claims to individuate experiences is not sustained, it remains the case that a reference to a person involves a reference to a body; and to recognize that should also involve the recognition that we must locate experiences as the experiences of certain people. Such a recognition in turn makes it understandable, although not logically necessary, that we should come to speak, as I believe we actually do, of an experience being in the same place as the person who has it. That is, it is natural in ordinary discourse to speak in this way—to treat the whole person as the locus of his conscious experience. And remember there are physical realities such as smells—say the smell left by a skunk even after he has been taken away and buried— that are not *material* objects, although they have a spatial location and are *physical* realities. "Perhaps," as Quinton well puts it, "we should not have any conception of space unless there were visible and tangible things, but it does not follow from this that only the visible and the tangible is in space."

In this respect heat and noises are like smells. In our commonsense discourse, they all have a rather indeterminate location in space, and as science develops they gain a more determinate location. Similarly, common sense locates experiences in the bodies of their owners, and as science develops it is likely that they will be more precisely located as brain processes. In spite of what Malcolm says, there is no *a priori* impossibility about this. In fact, given the way neurophysiology has been developing, it is very likely that definite centers in the brain are the location of sensations and sudden thoughts. Thus, Malcolm is mistaken in thinking that he has shown that reductive materialism is not a sufficiently intelligible theory to have theses that could be known to be true or probably true or false or probably false. If there were a perfect spatio-temporal coincidence between what we call mental states and brain states, we would be justified in believing that reductive materialism was the correct conception of the world.

VI

It should also be noted that if Quinton's contention here is correct, that is, that thought and sensations have a spatial location, we may now also have a simple but still adequate answer to the problem discussed earlier in this chapter about contingent identity. The criterion of identity, Quinton remarks, is "rough spatio-temperal coincidence (which if perfect would, of course, be an entirely sufficient criterion of identity) supported by concomitant variation of properties."[26]

This criterion, unlike the criterion I offered, would allow for a variation of properties. Note that with Quinton's criterion, we could avoid our problem discussed earlier about the apparent differences in properties of pains or afterimages (or, if you will, the experience of each) and brain states. Following Quinton in our treatment of the *de facto* identity claim, to assert such an identity we need not assert that all attributes, characteristics, or properties attributed to mental states must also be attributed to brain states. Note further that if we adopt the criterion about 'same characteristics' rather than Quinton's criterion, the same type of argument that is made against the contingent identity of pains and brain processes could be made against the identification of physical smells or sounds with some state of the molecules in the region of the smell or sound in question. We no more say that the molecules stink or are unbearable than we say that the brain processes are dim or nagging. But in the smell and sound case that does not keep us from claiming a contingent identity between, on the one hand, molecules in a certain region and in a certain arrangement and, on the other hand, smells or sounds. If we are justified in claiming such an identity in the sound and smell cases, why not claim a similar identity for sensations or conscious states and brain processes?

It appears to be the case that no good argument exists for *not* treating the cases as parallel or for denying that we have a good criterion for identity here. That we talk about pains differently from the way we talk about brain processes, or that we talk about molecules differently from the way we talk about smells or sounds, only indicates what should be evident anyway: We use language for different purposes and give many different types of explanation for different purposes and provide distinct accounts of the same reality for diverse purposes. It does not show that what is being talked about may not in fact be one and the same thing or that we do not have an intelligible criterion for showing that they are one and the same thing. This argument assumes, of course, that Quinton is basically on solid ground in his argument discussed in the preceding section about the spatial position of mental entities. If he is not right about that, then we would have to fall back on some of our earlier characterizations of identity or search out—to continue to defend reductive materialism—some further sense of 'identity'.

I want now to turn to some unfinished business from section IV of this chapter, namely, the problems raised about the alleged inherent privacy and incorrigibility of 'the mental' as distinct from 'the physical'. It is upon such questions that many able philosophers think that all forms of reductive materialism are shipwrecked.[27]

One important line of reply a materialist can make is to take the bull by the horns, so to speak, and deny that sensations and thoughts are utterly private in any sense other than the irrelevant sense that I cannot have your sensations or thoughts—although I may have sensations like yours and I may think of the same thing you are thinking of. In the same vein one may go on to deny that there are incorrigible sensation reports or incorrigible mentalistic truth claims, for instance, claims such as 'My head aches', 'I am very tired', 'I am thinking of my grandmother', or 'My afterimage is greenish blue'.

This denial of any inherent privacy or complete incorrigibility may at first blush seem quite implausible: plainly a bit of materialist love's labor lost. Actually, however, it can be made quite plausible, and I am inclined to believe that it constitutes an adequate rebuttal of this traditional refutation of reductive materialism.[28]

The argument goes like this: Given the fact that science has not yet established explicit identifications between specific types of sensations and specific types of brain processes, we in practice use what the speaker avows—sincerely says—as our criteria for his being in pain or having any other sensation. But even here that is a relative matter. If a man were cut wide open and was kicking around and rasping through clenched teeth, 'It doesn't hurt. It doesn't hurt,' we would (to put it mildly) doubt his report. We would either think that for some inexplicable reason he was lying, was out of his mind with pain, or did not properly understand 'hurt', as a foreigner might not. In fact, we do not always accept a man's say-so as the final ground for asserting whether or not he is in pain. Similar arguments could be made for other sensations, and the argument could be extended to mental talk generally. (Note how much easier it is for 'being angry'. People who are plainly angry often deny they are angry.) Such claims do not seem to be wholly incorrigible, and their relative incorrigibility can be readily accounted for as we have accounted for it.[29]

To continue arguing in the same general direction, imagine that we are living in an advanced scientific culture in which for a long time empirical generalizations about sensations have been subsumed under neurophysical laws, and direct manipulation of the brain has become firmly established as the sole method of relieving pain. Moreover, in this culture they have used encephalographs for ascertaining whether someone was in pain for a very long time and with thorough reliability. Such a picture is no doubt fanciful, but it still is perfectly intelligible. In such a culture, encephalographs indicate pain processes that are taken to be or are identified as brain processes. This has long since become noncontroversial. Now if a given subject, let us call him Fred, thinks he has no pain on a given occasion when the encephalograph plainly indicates that a pain process is occurring, Fred—and the other properly enculturated members of his culture as well—would plainly question whether he really properly understood the concept of pain. We would not just unquestioningly accept his report as veridical. Remember, we are imagining here a very technological society replete with portable encephalographs that also function as teaching machines to teach plain talk to children in this society. If one man *in such a culture* and on one occasion, or even a few scattered men on very infrequent occasions, did not respond as they and people generally in that culture expect them to, that would not lead them to abandon well-confirmed scientific theories about the identity of brain processes and sensations. What a person avows or says he is feeling or sensing need not, regardless of the circumstances, be an unquestionable final criterion for whether he has the sensation or feeling in question. Thus, we have lost our grounds for claiming that there is something characteristically inherently private about sensations—that sensations have an inherent privacy while brain processes do not.

It is natural to object to this argument in this way: Suppose our neurophysiological theory tells us that every time a person is in pain the C-fibers in his brain are stimulated, and they are only stimulated when he is in pain. Suppose that in our fictitious culture this hypothesis is well confirmed and has been confirmed for a very long time. Further, suppose we are living in such a culture and we have a portable encephalograph that we always carry around with us. Suppose it registers C-fiber stimulation. I notice that every time a pin is stuck in me I feel pain, and at the same time my encephalograph registers C-fiber stimulation. Suppose I also know, as does every other normal adult in this culture, that this is universally the case with people and that I (and the others as well) have grown up using C-fiber stimulation as registered on the encephalograph as one of the key criteria for the proper application of 'in pain'. Now suppose that on a given occasion a pin is stuck in me and I feel pain and yet—wonder to behold!—no C-fiber stimulation is registered on my encephalograph. I surely would not doubt that I had no pain or doubt that I properly understood 'pain', but I would doubt, many would say, that being in pain was just the stimulation of C-fibers. I would of course first think that something had gone wrong with my encephalograph, but if I checked it and experts checked it and later used different encephalographs and the same thing continued to happen, I would confidently stick with my own 'felt pain' against the results of the machine and the claims of the experts. If we look at it from our own point of view—the agent's point of view—we can see in our own case that we would never let any theoretical claim override our own direct felt awareness, given the fact that we had mastered the talk in question (pain-talk and the like). In that crucial way sensations are very different from brain processes and so could not possibly be identical with brain processes.

Smart has explicitly replied to such an objection as follows:

> If the sort of situation which we have just envisaged did in fact come about, then I should have to reject the brain process thesis, and would perhaps espouse dualism. If I felt a pain I could not reject the assertion that I had a pain. My reply is that I do not think that any such situation would in fact occur. It should be recalled that I put forward the brain process thesis as a factual identification, not as a logically necessary one.[30]

This seems to me an entirely reasonable, commonsense reply to such an objection. Materialism is a speculative claim. But if (subject to the qualifications mentioned earlier) science establishes what we *now* call repeated, exact, and systematically integrated correlations between brain processes and sensations and between brain processes and conscious acts of various sorts, would it not be the case that we should, if we wished to behave intelligently, stop talking of correlations between them and refer instead to a *de facto* identity? Wouldn't we start identifying mental processes as processes of the nervous system?

Given the comparative infancy of neurophysiology, we indeed rely in our culture (in normal circumstances, at least) on the honest avowal of the person involved that he is in pain. If we are convinced that he is sincere and that he understands properly the use of 'pain' and other bits of sensation talk, we let his avowal stand. But this still is a relative final authority; it is not a final authority come what may, for if in certain odd situations he either avows or denies he is in pain, we will not accept his avowals at face value. We will believe that something has gone wrong. The example of the man cut open, writhing, and rasping, 'It doesn't hurt,' clearly brings this out.

Moreover, even in our own case we could come to have doubts. Richard Rorty aptly shows this with the converse of the example discussed before.[31] Again the context is the same scientifically developed society. That is to say, we have a world in which for a long time empirical generalizations about sensations—taken simply now as sensations— have been subsumed under neurophysiological laws, and for a long time direct manipulation of the brain has been the exclusive method of relieving pain because it is by far the most reliable pain reliever. For as long as most people can remember, children in such a culture habitually used portable encephalographs-cum-teaching-machines, which help them learn more rapidly the proper use of sensation talk as 'ache', 'pain', 'tickle', and the like. The machines have been so programed that whenever the appropriate brain process occurs they will murmur the appropriate term.

Now suppose a man who has learned pain-talk this way burns himself with his cigar, but thinks he feels no pain even though the encephalograph says that the brain processes with which we have learned to identify pain did occur. Remember, this is something he is involved with himself; he is watching his own encephalograph and he honestly avows to himself that he is not in pain. Thus, there is no problem here of lying. With his own pain he does not have the usual means of eliminating observational error. It is not like his seeing a boat on the horizon when all the ship's sensitive instruments indicate that there could not possibly be a ship on the horizon. With reference to such a situation, Rorty argues with considerable force that neither we nor the man himself would take his own authority as final for whether or not he has a pain. In such a culture, he would initially begin to suspect that he did not know or did not adequately understand what pain is—that he had not properly mastered pain-talk or (to put the point in an alternative manner) had not got a proper hang of the concept of pain. Recall that he exhibits pain behavior when he is burned and the encephalograph indicates pain, but he does not think he actually feels what he feels when he is struck, cut, raked, pinched, and the like. After all, he would (or at least should) reflect, not all pains feel alike, and perhaps he is not really adequately acquainted with all the varieties of pain. This indeed is strange, but in such a culture what was happening to him is exceedingly strange and he would, as Hume put it in another context, have to balance improbabilities against improbabilities.

It is not that we are claiming that someone who knows what pain is can be mistaken about being in pain. Rather, in situations like the preceding one the question would arise whether the person having such an unusual experience adequately knew what pain is, and this question would arise for the agent in question himself as well as for the spectator. Thus, we have not established that there is anything inherently incorrigible about pain reports such that the agent must always have the final say as to whether he is in pain and the like. And we thus have no grounds for claiming that pains are distinct from brain processes because they are inherently private. That claim rests on the claim that the sincere avowal of 'I am in pain' cannot be overridden or be mistaken, while 'My C-fibers are being stimulated' can. But there *are* ways such an avowal can be mistaken and can be overridden. Thus, this crucial objection to reductive materialism fails.

NOTES

1. J. J. C. Smart, "Materialism," *The Journal of Philosophy*, vol. LX, no. 22 (Oct. 24, 1963), pp. 651–662.
2. See J. J. C. Smart, *Philosophy and Scientific Realism*, chapter VIII.
3. Some recent important discussions of these problems include: Paul Feyerabend, "Materialism and the Mind-Body Problem," *The Review of Metaphysics*, vol. 17 (1963), pp. 49–67; Jerome Shaffer, "Mental Events and the Brain," *Journal of Philosophy*, vol. 60 (1963), pp. 160–166; Joseph Margolis, "Brain Processes and Sensations," *Theoria*, (1965); Wilfrid Sellars, "The Identity Approach to the Mind-Body Problem" and Richard Rorty, "Mind-Body Identity, Privacy, and Categories," both in Stuart Hampshire (ed.), *Philosophy of Mind*; G. N. A. Vesey, "Agent and Spectator" and R. J. Hirst, "Mind and Brain," both in G. N. A. Vesey (ed.), *The Human Agent*; the essays by Quinton and Beloff in J. R. Smythies (ed.), *Brain and Mind*; T. Nagel, "Physicalism," *Philosophical Review* (1965); D. M. Armstrong, *A Materialist Theory of Mind*; C. F. Presley (ed.), *The Identity Theory of Mind*; and Keith Campbell's masterful summing up of the central issues in his critical notice of "The Identity Theory of Mind," *Australasian Journal of Philosophy*, vol. 46 (August, 1968), pp. 175–189. Many of these essays are reprinted in John O'Connor (ed.), *Modern Materialism on Mind-Body Identity* (New York: Harcourt Brace Jovanovich, 1969), and in C. V. Borst, *The Mind/Brain Identity Theory* (New York: St. Martin's Press, 1970).
4. U. T. Place, "Is Consciousness a Brain Process?" and J. J. C. Smart, "Sensations and Brain Processes," in V. C. Chappell (ed.), *The Philosophy of Mind*. Smart's essay is also reprinted in Paul Edwards and Arthur Pap (eds.), *A Modern Introduction to Philosophy*.

5. Roderick Chisholm, *Perceiving*, pp. 168–173.

6. J. J. C. Smart, "Sensations and Brain Processes," in Paul Edwards and Arthur Pap (eds.), *A Modern Introduction to Philosophy*, p. 231.

7. Neither Paul Feyerabend nor Richard Rorty follows him here. See references in note 3 above.

8. J. J. C. Smart, "Materialism," *The Journal of Philosophy*, vol. LX (Oct. 24, 1963), p. 654.

9. Ibid., p. 653.

10. That there are difficulties in his characterization of identity is also evident in his latest attempt at a characterization of the identity in question, although it is also clear from an examination of that work that he regards Malcolm's arguments as making too many verificationist assumptions. (Malcolm's arguments are in sections V and VI of this chapter.) See here Smart's remarks and the discussion of his thesis in C. F. Presley (ed.), *The Identity Theory of Mind*, and see Keith Campbell's perceptive remarks on this discussion in Campbell, op. cit., pp. 183–187.

11. U. T. Place, op. cit., pp. 101–109.

12. Besides the articles by Place, Smart, Quinton, Hoffman, and Rorty discussed in this article, note the references in note 3 above.

13. Norman Malcolm, "Scientific Materialism and the Identity Theory," *Dialogue*, vol. III (1964), pp. 115–126. I have only stated and criticized a very central argument in Malcolm's critique of Smart. There are other significant criticisms raised by Malcolm, although for our purposes they are less important. For an important, but I think only partially successful, point-by-point rebuttal of Malcolm's arguments, see Robert Hoffman, "Malcolm and Smart on Brain-Mind Identity," *Philosophy*, vol. XLII (April, 1967), pp. 128–137.

14. It is not unreasonable to object that 'nonlinguistic property' is too problematical to be useful here. This may be so, or at least perplexities might remain here, but my examples and the context make its meaning sufficiently clear for it to be of some value at least. In the terminology of logical theory, I am talking about an 'extensional property', but there is no brief nontechnical elucidation of what that means.

15. I add the cumbersome phrase 'undergoing of a brain process' in order to accommodate Robert Hoffman's modification of Smart's thesis.

16. Anthony Quinton, "Mind and Matter," in J. R. Smythies (ed.), *Brain and Mind*, and R. J. Hirst, "Mind and Brain," in G. N. A. Vesey (ed.), *The Human Agent*.

17. Hirst, op cit., p. 176.

18. D. M. Armstrong, "The Nature of Mind," *Question I* (February, 1968), p. 82.

19. Malcolm, op. cit., p. 117.

20. Ibid., pp. 119–120.

21. Hoffman, op cit.; Quinton, op. cit.; Rorty, op cit.; Hilary Putnam, "Minds and Machines," in Sidney Hook (ed.), *Dimensions of Mind*; David Cooper, "The Fallacies of the Linguistic Philosophy," *The Oxford Review* (Hilary, 1968).

22. Quinton, op. cit., p. 213.

23. Ibid., p. 214.
24. Ibid., p. 212.
25. Vesey, op. cit., p. 154.
26. Quinton, op. cit., p. 214.
27. See Price's and Ducasse's essays in Sidney Hook (ed.), *Dimensions of Mind*, op. cit.; Ducasse's essay in J. R. Smythies (ed.), *Brain and Mind*; and Kurt Baier, "Pains" and "Smart on Sensations," both in *Australasian Journal of Philosophy*, vol. 40 (May, 1962).
28. This is powerfully argued for by Richard Rorty, op. cit, pp. 49–60.
29. J. L. Mackie and D. M. Armstrong have also made powerful arguments concerning such incorrigibility claims in the *Australasian Journal of Philosophy*, vol. 41 (May, 1963) and in the *Philosophical Review*, vol. 72 (October, 1963) respectively.
30. J. J. C. Smart, "Brain Processes and Incorrigibility—A Reply to Professor Baier," *Australasian Journal of Philosophy*, vol. 40 (May, 1962), p. 68.
31. Rorty, op. cit., pp. 57–60; and Stephen J. Noren, "Smart's Materialism: The Identity Theory and Translation" and J. H. Chandler, "Incorrigibility and Classification" both in the *Australasian Journal of Philosophy*, vol. 48 (May, 1970).

30

SCIENTIFIC
PLAUSIBILITY
AND MATERIALISM

I

In the last chapter I attempted a defense of reductive materialism. It should be kept in mind that I did not attempt to prove that reductive materialism is true, but that there are no demonstrably sound philosophical objections to reductive materialism. That is to say, I tried to show that the various philosophical objections do not establish its falsity and that there are no sufficiently convincing grounds for rejecting materialism as a conceptual muddle. This, if successful, is a considerable accomplishment, for it has often been thought—sometimes even by eminent philosophers—that reductive materialism is plainly an untenable view.

However, even if I have been successful in this enterprise, surely the obvious question remains: Why accept reductive materialism rather than dualism, or why not remain agnostic about all such metaphysical doctrines? That materialism can be stated coherently, such that it is not undercut by analytical objections, does not show that it is the correct view of the world. Why be a reductive materialist?

The answer I would give—and this is the answer given by Smart, Place, and Armstrong as well—is that it seems to me a more plausible world-view than any of its competitors. I do not deny that there are difficulties in it. I am by no means entirely satisfied with the arguments I made in the last chapter. Also, I have not seen a statement of reductive materialism that has seemed thoroughly convincing, although I do believe, as I have tried to demonstrate, that some contemporary variants of materialism have made effective answers to what until a few years ago seemed to most people who had thought about the matter with some care to be crushing criticisms of reductive materialism. So, while I find features of materialism that certainly give me pause—mostly connected with the concept of identity, the privacy argument, and the question about the spatiality of sensations—I find even more difficulties in the opposing views or nonviews. Since this is so, and since these nonmaterialist views do not square as well with my preanalytic hunches about how things are as does reductive materialism, I continue to opt for reductive materialism.[1]

There is a different consideration that should be brought to the fore. Smart and Armstrong give a distinct and indeed important reason for accepting reductive materialism, namely, that it fits in better than do any of the alternative world-views with our scientific image of man and the world. This needs some comment, and in making this comment here I want to follow an argument made by D. M. Armstrong in his inaugural lecture "The Nature of Mind."[2]

The weight of scientific evidence, Armstrong contends, goes in the direction of viewing man as a physicochemical mechanism. Since this is so, "we [as philosophers] must try to work out an account of the nature of mind which is compatible with the view that man is nothing but a physiochemical mechanism." However, it is natural to remark that this is the grossest Scientism. Why should we accept the authority of science— indeed, of present-day science—for our image of man rather than that of religion, common sense, philosophy, or literature and art? By now, it is evident enough from what has been argued in earlier chapters why we should not accept the authority of religion, but this still leaves a very wide field. Why should we accept the authority of science for our image of man?

Armstrong's answer is down-to-earth, instructive, and squares with the Peircean arguments made in Chapter 12. He remarks:

> . . . if we consider the search for truth, in all its fields, we find it is only in science that men versed in their subject can, after investigation that is more or less prolonged, and which may in some cases extend beyond a single human lifetime, reach substantial agreement about what is the case. It is only as a result of scientific investigation that we ever seem to reach an intellectual consensus about controversial matters.

Thus, like Peirce, although clearly limiting his claims to questions of fact, Armstrong regards the scientific method as the most reliable way to fix belief, and the results arrived at by the application of this method the most reasonable basis for belief. Scientific judgments are fallible, but over questions of fact such judgments are more reliable than any other judgments. Moreover, it is a question of fact whether sensations are brain processes or whether a person is a nervous system clothed in flesh and bones, although what exactly is being asserted may be very much in need of philosophical (conceptual) clarification. Armstrong points out, what surely seems evident enough, that in other disciplines such as philosophy, theology, or literary criticism there has been a notable failure to "achieve an intellectual consensus about disputed questions among the learned." He goes on to ask rhetorically: "Must we not then attach a peculiar authority to the discipline that can achieve a consensus? And if it presents us with a certain vision of the nature of man, is this not a powerful reason for accepting that vision?"

Smart, who takes a point of view similar to Armstrong's, anticipates an objection that Armstrong does not discuss. We indeed may be justified, it is noted, in accepting the authority of science in most situations, but where we have a logical demonstration that some putative factual claim could not indeed be a factual claim, it is far more reasonable to accept the demonstration than the alleged scientific claim. Philosophical reasoning, the objection continues, is demonstrative and no considerations concerning what it is plausible to believe in the light of the development of science can be rationally pitted against a logical demonstration.

The reply Smart makes seems at least to be both important and correct. "This objection," he remarks, "confuses demonstrability and certainty."[3] Theorems in mathematics and logic are demonstrable, but we can never be certain in making such demonstrations that we have not made a slip. Thus, fallibility comes in here as well as in empirical science. Moreover, mathematics and mathematical logic are in reality a formal part of science, and while again in mathematics and mathematical logic there is a consensus, in philosophical reasonings, by contrast, even when they take the form of demonstrations, there is not this consensus. Philosophical arguments "are notoriously slippery, and philosophers are rarely unanimous. It therefore seems to me to be optimistic of philosophers to suppose that their *a priori* arguments give a higher order of certainty than do considerations of scientific plausibility."[4]

There is, however, a different and less easily answered objection, which neither Armstrong nor Smart considers. It should be agreed that over questions of fact, including questions of fact about the nature of man, science is our final arbiter, fallible though it is. But, it will be objected, the questions we have been considering are not questions of fact but conceptual questions masquerading as questions of fact.[5] When we claim that sensations are brain processes or that a human being is a nervous system clothed in flesh and bones, our statements are pseudo-scientific and not genuinely scientific. Scientism is not the view that questions of fact must be testable by the scientific method, but the naive view that simply accepts as assertions of 'scientific fact' the exuberant metaphysical claims with which many scientists and some 'scientifically oriented philosophers' bedeck scientific claims. Such mind/body identity claims are just bits of metaphysical plumage and are no operative part of any scientific discipline. It is one of the jobs of critical philosophy to watch for such metaphysical parasites and to make it evident that they are not part of the corpus of science. A sober-minded philosophy must indeed square with scientific fact and genuinely scientific beliefs, but it need not accept science's metaphysical hangers-on. Science, Armstrong to the contrary notwithstanding, does not provide us with a certain vision of the nature of man. That is not its line of business.

However, why treat the claim that man is, as Smart puts it, "nothing but a very complicated physiochemical mechanism which has developed from simpler mechanisms through the operations of natural selection" as part of the metaphysical plumage of science? Why is it not a plausible although speculative scientific belief?

The answer often given to this is that it is not and cannot be a scientific belief because it is untestable and/or because what exactly it allegedly asserts is so unclear that such a belief cannot be fixed on scientific grounds. Both dualism and reductive materialism are compatible with the same body of empirical facts. There is no conceivable experiment we could run that would verify (confirm or disconfirm) either the dualist or the materialist claims, and thus neither claim can be a scientific one. Smart himself—antiverificationist though he is—remarks, in good Peircean spirit, that "scientific beliefs have always to be tested against the facts."[6]

II

It is worthwhile noting why dualism and reductive materialism (and epiphenomenalism as well) are said to be untestable beliefs. It will be agreed by all parties that conscious experiences as far as we know never occur without a certain determinate brain activity. It is further agreed that the conscious experience and the determinate brain activity occur at the same time, and when someone has a certain conscious experience, that same person has a certain determinate brain activity and the conscious experience and the determinate brain activity are correlated spatially or occupy the same space. (Note that in the last part of the previous sentence we have alternative descriptions and they both commit one metaphysically, but as far as I can see there is no philosophically neutral way of talking here.) Moreover, it is agreed that "from electroencephalograms and other devices, activity in certain parts of the brain starts and stops as a sensory experience or a mental activity like working out a problem starts and stops, and it varies with variations in the experience. . . ."[7] In short, there is a wide agreement that, as far as we can determine, a properly functioning brain is essential for all forms of consciousness. The sensations we have and the functioning of our central nervous system are closely integrated.

Such phenomena lead reductive materialists to assert a contingent identity between mental activity and/or certain brain processes or stretches of human behavior. However, dualists and epiphenomenalists accept the same data but speak instead of systematic correlations between the brain and the mind. That is, there appars to be no disagreement about the empirical, experimental facts, but a disagreement over how to *interpret* these facts. Smart acknowledges this. He remarks of epiphenomenalism—and he has said the same thing of dualism—that "there is no conceivable experiment which could decide between [reductive] materialism and epiphenomenalism."[8] Whatever empirical facts the reductive materialist uses to show connections between what are conventionally called 'mental phenomena' and brain activity, the dualist and epiphenomenalist can and will speak of correlations. The issue—one's initial expectations notwithstanding—seems *not* to be an experimental or experiential one. However, this seems at least to lead to difficulties similar to the difficulties in non-anthropomorphic God-talk discussed in Chapter 21. Like 'There is a God' (as used by a sophisticated theist) and 'There is no God', the statements 'Man is nothing but a very complicated physicochemical mechanism' and 'Man is not simply such a mechanism but has a mind distinct from his body' appear to be factual claims, but since they both can be asserted in the face of the same empirical evidence (both actual and conceivable), there seems to be no way of determining which, if either, is true or false or even probably true or false. That is to say, like the parallel bits of God-talk, their truth value is utterly indeterminate. This has lead some analytical philosophers to be agnostic about such claims on the grounds that it is at best irrational and at worst unintelligible to be asked to accept theories without even being told what it would be like to find out whether their central claims are true or false or even probably true or false.

I would say here (although I do not think Smart or Armstrong would go along with this) that if it is indeed the case that no observation or set of observations could *possibly* be relevant to the truth or falsity of dualistic claims or reductive materialist claims, then the theses should be given up, for they are pseudotheses. But I do not think this condition of utter untestability in principle obtains vis-à-vis materialist and dualist claims. What does obtain—and this is a familiar feature of fundamental theoretical scientific claims—is that there is no crucial experiment that would decisively establish either. Furthermore, given the present state of conceptual confusion about mental states, it is not even clear what would or would not count as evidence for or against these claims. But there is no *conceptual ban* on looking for evidence here, as there is with analytic statements or with imperatives.[9] That nothing would decisively establish (verify) either that sensations are brain processes or that sensations are not brain processes does not mean that such claims are not weakly confirmable or infirmable. We saw in the last chapter how this worked with our science-fiction example of a developed scientific culture where pain-talk was taught in part by the use of an encephalograph-cum-teaching-machine which registered the stimulation of C-fibers. Smart told us under what conditions he would reject the brain-process thesis, namely, under the scientific conditions and in the scientific culture described in the last chapter, if he felt what he was confident was pain from the feel alone when there was clearly no registration of C-fiber stimulation.

One central philosophical task on the part of both dualists and reductive materialists is to state their theses with sufficient precision so that it becomes more evident what observations are relevant to their truth or falsehood and thus to make it clearer what they are claiming. There is much to be done here, and at present such claims are not, as a matter of fact, testable. It is not very evident what would test (confirm or infirm) them, but it is also true that it is not established that they are in principle untestable (nothing could—logically could—either confirm or infirm them) and thus that there are adequate grounds for rejecting them as pseudotheses.

While there is no logical or conceptual ban on testing (confirming or infirming) such fundamental materialist theses, it may still be objected that they are too speculative—too practically untestable—and too general to be an operative part of science. Such materialist claims do no scientific work, are not a part of and cannot become a part of the corpus of any scientific discipline, and should in that sense be regarded vis-à-vis science as metaphysical plumage. That is to say, they are metaphysical plumage in the sense that they are scientifically supererogatory while still making intelligible cosmological claims. To assert the thesis of mind/body identity, to assert that a human being is simply a complicated nervous system clothed in flesh and bones or that man is only a physicochemical mechanism, is not to make scientific claims but to bedeck the austere corpus of genuine science with metaphysical or at least nonscientific trappings.

Such austerity itself is suspect, however. This view of science is too operationalistic. In science, people sometimes make bold speculative claims. These claims often turn out to be very important in the development of science, yet when they are first made and often for a long time after that they cannot be tested in practice, although they are testable *in principle*. There is not the sharp dividing line between genuinely scientific claims that the preceding objection presupposes.

Yet, it will in turn be objected that such 'speculative scientific claims' as we have been discussing must, while remaining speculative, stay on the fringes of science. With such speculative claims there is not the consensus of trained investigators essential to give them the kind of authority characteristic of science. It simply confuses matters to extend to these speculative claims the charisma of operative scientific claims.

It could and should be replied that the distinction in such a context between what is science and what is not is not sharply delineated. If my preceding arguments have been correct, the mind/body identity thesis is still testable in principle and is thus subject to what Peirce characterized as a scientific method of fixing belief. Yet, it still is misleading to speak, as Smart and Armstrong do, of mechanism and mind/body identity claims as carrying the authority of science. With such claims there is not the authoritative consensus necessary for claims to become unequivocal parts of science. Even if most scientifically oriented philosophers think of 'raw feels' and sudden thoughts as brain states, this does not make such a belief an operative part of science. Even what it is that we are allegedly stating when we try to assert such materialist beliefs is sufficiently indeterminate to make the scientific status of such putative factual assertions problematic. A purest scientific methodologist might very well not regard them as even speculative scientific beliefs.

The reply I think Armstrong and Smart would make is that they are speculative claims which, given a certain development of science, could become scientific, that is, part of the corpus of a given science. All the same, however, it is not evident that reductive materialism is a view required by the development of science. It may be that science will remain agnostic about such general claims. Yet, reductive materialism is a view readily suggested by a scientific way of looking at the world, and dualism—with its claim that there are inherently private, nonspatial, non-physical realities—seems to be quite antithetical to a scientific attitude. This *may* be a metaphysical impurity which is no part of a rigorously scientific attitude. We must try to avoid confusing scientific mythology with science.[10] We must not ignore Ryle's claim that dualism rests on a category mistake, on a failure to understand the actual mode of operation of our mentalistic talk. Dualists take 'mind', 'pain', 'sensation', 'sudden thought' to be thing-words that they believe refer to recondite ghost-like things, devoid of spatial locations yet still mysteriously controlling bodily machinery. But such notions are incoherent and indeed make 'the mental' mysterious and unknowable through a nonperspicuous representation of mental facts. Materialism, it is often claimed by linguistic philosophers, takes the dualist myth too seriously and in response creates a countermyth. Neither mythology has any scientific plausibility, neither is required by a scientific point of view and in reality both are obscurantisms parading either as common sense or as a generalization from scientific discoveries about man.

Materialists should ponder this kind of critique harder than they have, but still I do not think the acceptance of such a therapeutic analysis is mandatory for a reasonable and well-informed man. Quite apart from the fact that Ryle has never made clear what constitutes a category mistake, the most salient fact about such an atempt to dissolve the mind/body problem by conceptual analysis is that it is far from evident that Ryle and Wittgenstein have been able to exorcise successfully the ghosts of dualism.[11] Their own claims seem either surreptitiously to rein-troduce dualistic assumptions or to fall prey to the difficulties inherent in analytical behaviorism. Moreover, it is not obvious that dualist claims are utterly *meaningless* and that there are no 'inner experiences' which would remain very mysterious realities indeed but for reductive materi-alism.

III

If things stand as I have argued, and if it is the case that the issue between reductive materialists, dualists, and epiphenomenalists is not an experimental issue in the crucial sense I have specified, it becomes important to ask again: Why be a reductive materialist and why claim that if one accepts the authority of science one should be a reductive materialist? Isn't reductive materialism the kind of speculative issue about which science is quite neutral?

Smart's reply at this juncture is the same as Hugh Elliot's and other reductive materialists. He appeals to considerations of *scientific simplicity*. Reductive materialism is preferable to dualism or epiphenomenalism because it is a simpler and more economical hypothesis that still accounts as adequately as do the other hypotheses for the experiential facts. The dualist says that "there are two entities that always occur together, where the physicalist (reductive materialist) says there is only one."[12] If both claims are equally compatible with the experimental evidence and with the corpus of scientific theorizing, it is better on grounds of scientific simplicity to accept the reductive materialist claim. If we accept dualism we would have to have very complicated scientific laws with a very puzzling parallelism between neurophysiological events and psychical events. This would complicate enormously our scientific picture. Thus, simply on grounds of good scientific methodology—that is, that we should not multiply entities or conceptions beyond need—we should not accept dualism or epiphenomenalism, but should accept reductive materialism. This is the cash value of our talk of scientific plausibility. While the issue between dualism and reductive materialism is not a straightforward experimental issue, reductive materialism—for one who adopts a scientific outlook—should be one's view of the world, if the defense against the *a priori* arguments designed to show that reductive materialism involves incoherent claims is successful.

Is there a comeback that the dualist could make to the appeal to the prin-ciple of scientific simplicity or to what has been called Occam's razor? Have we not nearly as good grounds for not believing in nonextended, nonphysical psychical entities as we have for not believing in ether? Dualists, however, have defended themselves along these lines.[13] When we talk about not multiplying, postulating, or assuming entities or conceptions beyond need or beyond necessity, our remarks are elliptical. When we say that it is not necessary to assume the existence of some entity or other, we must mean, if we are saying anything coherent at all, that it is not necessary for some purpose or other. And when we specify those purposes, we will see that reductive materialism is not in such a clearly superior position.

If we are philosophers our purpose might be to list the basic types of reality; and we might mean, when we talk of not multiplying conceptions beyond need, that the assumption of such a 'nonextended mental reality' was not necessary for 'a listing of everything there is'. But this, it is replied, clearly begs the question between dualists and reductive materialists. The dualist is trying to maintain that there is more than one kind of basic reality and that there is a kind of basic reality that is in no way a physical reality. To say we need not put his phenomena on a complete list of what there is already assumes what is at issue, namely, that among the kinds of basic reality that there are, there are no nonextended psychical realities.

There is, however, a more plausible specification of purpose available to the reductive materialist, and it is the one that Smart and Armstrong actually take, namely, that it is not necessary to assume the existence of such nonextended realities for the purpose of scientific explanation. We no more need them than we need a conception of Zeus in a scientific world picture. To this, one dualist has replied:

> Although it is true . . . that science should assume no more entities than are necessary for its theoretical explanations, it is not at all obvious that if an entity or kind of entity is scientifically superfluous we should conclude that it does not exist.[14]

Moreover, there is an important difference between electrons and nonphysical psychical realities. The first is a theoretical entity (an entity deliberately postulated for scientific explanation) and the second is not. The second, it is argued, is something of which we are all directly aware. We should indeed accept the existence of theoretical entities only if they are scientifically necessary, but there are no good grounds for taking the same attitude toward nontheoretical entities. Moreover, dualism leaves open the possibility (or so it would seem) that mental realities could survive the destruction of physical realities, while reductive materialism, if true, eliminates that possibility. But then this materialist theory, which has not been established to be true by empirical investigation, rules out something, on grounds of simplicity, which is essential for the purpose of theistic religions: a belief in immortality. However, given the need to believe, which is surely deep enough, there is indeed a need to multiply entities, namely, the pervasive human need to be able to hope that immortality is true. So while it may not be necessary for the purposes of scientific explanation to invoke nonphysical psychological entities, it clearly is for these human purposes. Also, since these nonscientific considerations make no antiscientific or contrascientific claim, the preceding considerations of scientific simplicity are overridden.

By now we have doubled back on ourselves and have returned to where we were at the beginning of the chapter, when we discussed Armstrong's appeal to the authority of science. Surely, given the needs of a certain kind of religious point of view and perhaps even *a certain kind* of commonsensical point of view, there is a need to postulate nonextended psychical realities. But they are, as we have seen, a conceptual hindrance and a needless complication in a scientific world outlook. (I assume here what needs to be questioned, that there is such a thing as 'a *scientific* world outlook' or 'a *scientific* vision of the nature of man'.) However, if we are convinced (1) that over questions of *fact* the scientific method of fixing belief is the most reliable method of fixing belief, (2) that science is more likely to enable us to attain a true view of things—a truer conception of what there really is in the world—than any other discipline, and (3) the truth claims of religion are illusory, then viewing man in purely physical terms is the most reasonable way of viewing man.

I have argued in earlier chapters that the truth claims of religion are illusory. I have also argued in Chapter 11 that the scientific method is the most reliable one for fixing belief concerning questions of fact, and that in science alone we attain the kind of consensus of the learned concerning *what is the case* that is essential for our attaining reliable beliefs. What science tells us is the case may indeed not be the case, but over questions of fact there is no more reliable source of knowledge or justified belief than what we can attain from science. If I have been right in these arguments, and if I have been correct in my refutations of the *a priori* arguments against reductive materialism, then reductive materialism should be a central plank in our scientific view of the world. In working out that view of the nature of mind most compatible with a scientific world-view, we may indeed come into conflict with some of the beliefs of common sense or of religion. Then, given what we have said about the authority of science, so much the worse for these religious or commonsense beliefs.

NOTES

1. I mean nothing esoteric by 'preanalytic hunches'. I am simply talking about the fact that typically before one engages in an analysis of a concept one has some definite beliefs about that concept. I shall return in the first section of Chapter 31 to some of the broader implications raised by my remarks.
2. D. M. Armstrong, "The Nature of Mind," *Question I* (February, 1968), pp. 70–72.

3. J. J. C. Smart, "Philosophy and Scientific Plausibility," in Paul K. Feyerabend and Grover Maxwell (eds.), *Mind, Matter and Method*, p. 386.
4. Ibid., p. 387.
5. Ludwig Wittgenstein in his later philosophy constantly exposed this kind of confusion.
6. Smart, op. cit., p. 389.
7. A. J. Hirst, "Mind and Brain," in G. N. A. Vesey (ed.), *The Human Agent*, p. 168.
8. Smart, "Sensations and Brain Processes," in Paul Edwards and Arthur Pap (eds.), *A Modern Introduction to Philosophy*, p. 235. In his "Philosophy and Scientific Plausibility" cited in note 3, Smart remarks: "The dualist simply says that there are two entities that always occur together, where the physicalist says that there is only one entity. No observation or experiment could, I think, refute the dualist" (p. 381).
9. The point about conceptual bans has been put very well by I. M. Crombie, "Theology and Falsification," in Antony Flew and Alasdair MacIntyre (eds.), *New Essays in Philosophical Theology*, pp. 125–130.
10. On the importance of this see Stephen Toulmin, "Contemporary Scientific Mythology" in Stephen Toulmin, Ronald Hepburn, and Alasdair MacIntyre (eds.), *Metaphysical Beliefs*.
11. See C. S. Chihara and J. A. Fodor, "Operationalism and Ordinary Language: A Critique of Wittgenstein," in George Pitcher (ed.), *Wittgenstein*; J. N. Findlay, "Linguistic Approach to Psychophysics," *Aristotelian Society Proceedings* (1951); A. C. Ewing, "Professor Ryle's Attack on Dualism," *Aristotelian Society Proceedings* (1952); and Bertrand Russell, "What Is Mind?" in his *My Philosophical Development*.
12. Smart, "Philosophy and Scientific Plausibility," op. cit., p. 381.
13. Cornman's contribution to James W. Cornman and Keith Lehrer, *Philosophic Problems and Arguments*, pp. 261–267.
14. Ibid., p. 265. See also J. W. Cornman, "Mental Terms, Theoretical Terms and Materialism," *Philosophy of Science*, vol. 35 (March, 1968).

SUPPLEMENTARY READINGS
CHAPTERS 27 THROUGH 30

Books

Anderson, Alan R. (ed.), *Minds and Machines* (Englewood Cliffs, N. J.: Prentice-Hall, 1964).
Armstrong, D. M., *A Materialist Theory of Mind* (New York: Humanities Press, 1968).
*Chappell, V. C. (ed.), *The Philosophy of Mind* (Englewood Cliffs, N.J.: Prentice-Hall, 1962).
Descartes, René, *Philosophical Writings*, translated by Elizabeth Anscombe and Peter Thomas Geach (Edinburgh: Thomas Nelson & Sons, 1954).
Ducasse, C. J., *Nature, Mind and Death* (La Salle, Ill.: Open Court, 1951).
*Feigl, Herbert, *The 'Mental' and the 'Physical'* (Minneapolis: University of Minnesota Press, 1967). Good bibliography.

Feyerabend, Paul K., and Grover Maxwell (eds.), *Mind, Matter and Method* (Minneapolis: University of Minnesota Press, 1966).

*Fodor, Jerry A., *Psychological Explanation* (New York: Random House, 1968).

*Hampshire, Stuart (ed.), *Philosophy of Mind* (New York: Harper & Row, 1966).

Hoffman, Robert, *Language, Minds and Knowledge* (New York: Humanities Press, 1970).

*Hook, Sidney (ed.), *Dimensions of Mind* (New York: New York University Press, 1960).

O'Connor, John (ed.), *Modern Materialism: Readings on Mind-Body Identity* (New York: Harcourt Brace Jovanovich, 1969).

Presly, C. F. (ed.), *The Identity Theory of Mind* (Queensland, Australia: University of Queensland Press, 1967). Excellent bibliography.

Ryle, Gilbert, *The Concept of Mind* (New York: Barnes and Noble, 1949).

*Shaffer, Jerome A., *Philosophy of Mind* (Englewood Cliffs, N.J.: Prentice-Hall, 1968).

Smart, J. J. C., *Philosophy and Scientific Realism* (New York: Humanities Press, 1963).

Smythies, J. R. (ed.), *Mind and Brain* (New York: Humanities Press, 1965).

*Vesey, G. N. A. (ed.), *Body and Mind* (New York: Humanities Press, 1964).

Vesey, G. N. A., *The Embodied Mind* (New York: Humanities Press, 1965).

*White, Alan R., *The Philosophy of Mind* (New York: Random House, 1967).

Wisdom, John, *Other Minds* (Oxford: Basil Blackwell & Mott, 1965).

Wittgenstein, Ludwig, *Philosophical Investigations*, translated by G. E. M. Anscombe, second edition (New York: Macmillan, 1958).

Articles and Pamphlets

*Armstrong, D. M., "The Nature of Mind," *Question I* (February, 1968).

*Baier, Kurt, "Smart on Sensations," *Australasian Journal of Philosophy*, vol. XL (1962).

*Blanshard, Brand, "A Verdict on Epiphenomenalism," in Frederick C. Dommeyer (ed.), *Current Philosophical Issues*, (Springfield, Ill.: Charles C. Thomas, 1966).

*Blanshard, Brand, "The Nature of Mind," in Sidney Hook (ed.), *American Philosophers at Work* (New York: Criterion Books, 1956).

*Bradley, M. C., "Sensations, Brain-processes and Colours," *Australasian Journal of Philosophy*, vol. XLI (1963).

Cornman, J. W., "Mental Terms, Theoretical Terms and Materialism," *Philosophy of Science*, vol. 35 (March, 1968).

*Ducasse, C. J., "The Method of Knowledge in Philosophy," in Sidney Hook (ed.), *American Philosophers at Work* (New York: Criterion Books, 1956).

Feyerabend, Paul, "Materialism and the Mind-Body Problem," *Review of Metaphysics*, vol. 17 (1963).

Lewis, David K., "An Argument for the Identity Theory," *The Journal of Philosophy*, vol. LXIII (Jan. 6, 1966).

Lewis, H. D., "Mind and Body—Some Observations on Mr. Strawson's Views," in H. D. Lewis (ed.), *Clarity Is Not Enough* (New York: Humanities Press, 1963).

MacIntosh, J. J., "Memory and Personal Identity," in J. J. MacIntosh and S. Coval (eds.), *The Business of Reason* (New York: Humanities Press, 1969).

Medlin, Brian, "Materialism and the Argument from Distinct Existences," in J. J. MacIntosh and S. Coval (eds.), *The Business of Reason* (New York: Humanities Press, 1969).

*Place, U. T., "Is Consciousness a Brain Process?" *British Journal of Psychology,* vol. XLVII (1956).

*Place, U. T., "Materialism as a Scientific Hypothesis," *Philosophical Review,* vol. LXIX (1960).

Putnam, Hilary, "Brains and Behaviour," in R. S. Butler (ed.), *Analytical Philosophy,* 2nd Series (New York: Barnes and Noble, 1963).

*Shaffer, Jerome, "Could Mental States Be Brain Processes?" *Journal of Philosophy,* vol. LVIII (Dec. 21, 1961).

*Smart, J. J. C., "Materialism," *Journal of Philosophy,* vol. LX (1963).

*Smart, J. J. C., "Philosophy and Scientific Plausibility," in Paul K. Feyerabend and Grover Maxwell (eds.), *Mind, Matter and Method* (Minneapolis: University of Minnesota Press, 1966).

*Smart, J. J. C., "Sensations and Brain Processes," *Philosophical Review,* vol. LXVIII (1959).

Stevenson, J. T., "Sensations and Brain Processes: A Reply to J. J. C. Smart," *Philosophical Review,* vol. LXIX (1960).

Strawson, P. F., "Persons," in his *Individuals* (London: Methuen & Co., 1959).

Taylor, Charles, "Mind-Body Identity, A Side Issue?" *Philosophical Review* (April, 1967).

VI
MEANING
AND
METAPHYSICS

31

ON ELIMINATING
METAPHYSICS

I

We not only examined materialism and dualism to see what could be said about the mind, we also examined them to see what we could say about the comparative merits of metaphysical schemes. In varying degrees these competing and conflicting metaphysical schemes are all systematic. They attempt to articulate and argue for an abstract and coherent statement of a general picture of life. One of the reasons the arguments between dualists and materialists are so intractable is that linked with each theory is a whole set of philosophical beliefs of considerable importance. It is no accident that Holbach, Elliot, and Smart, as reductive materialists, are also atheists, utilitarians in ethical theory, and determinists. It is much easier for a dualist than a materialist to believe in contracausal freedom and an inner but scientifically nonidentifiable self that initiates human actions but is itself not determined by physical causes. We can indeed be dualists without believing in such a self or in such indeterministic or contracausal freedom, but without a belief in mental realities not identifiable with physical realities—that is, not identifiable as brain processes or as bits of distinctive human behavior—we could hardly take as even remotely plausible such a conception of 'the self'. And surely, if a man is a materialist, there is no way for him to believe in God, and it is not surprising to discover that Price and Hick, both believers in the possibility of immortality, are theists.

There are less obvious but equally important links between different philosophical beliefs which cut to the very heart of one's philosophical methodology. A dualist will give credence to a 'metaphysics by introspection' in a way a materialist utterly rejects. By this I mean (to translate into the concrete) that a dualist will, as we have seen, argue that anxiety, joy, or sadness are predicable of mental states but cannot intelligibly be predicated of a brain process, and so mental states for that very reason cannot be identified with brain processes. The dualist just takes it to be intuitively true that it is unintelligible to assert that a neural condition would constitute a person's state of anxiety. If we will attend to what we are aware of when we feel anxiety, we will see that it is not at all to be aware of anything neurological. This is what I call a 'metaphysics by introspection', and it involves a philosophical methodology that materialists reject. (Not that they must or even should argue that to be in a state of anxiety is just to be in a certain neural condition. That people characteristically behave in certain ways also enters in.)

Materialists will start with the deliverances of common sense and introspection but will not attach such decisive philosophical importance to them as dualists do. Similarly, and more important, dualists and critics of materialism, such as Malcolm, attach an ontological priority to everyday concepts, where philosophers such as Smart and Armstrong give an ontological priority to scientific concepts on the ground that science forces us to see the world differently and more truly than we would with a purely commonsense view of things. Facts such as these should make it evident that to have a metaphysical view involves having a cluster of interrelated beliefs. It is not an utterly piecemeal affair.

However, the logical links between these different metaphysical beliefs that make up metaphysical views of the world are not so tight that all those views which normally go together *must* go together. Sartre is a materialist and an atheist but he rejects determinism; Ducasse is a dualist but he is also a determinist; Broad is an atheist but he rejects reductive materialism. There was even a philosopher of some renown, McTaggart, who was an atheist and believed in immortality. Moreover, these various claims, metaphysical and ethical, are often not so tightly linked that a materialist cannot in consistency be an indeterminist, or that a dualist cannot be an atheist.

Certain general philosophical views plausibly go together, however, such as reductive materialism, mechanism, determinism, atheism, utilitarianism (or a modification away from it, similar to the one I argued for in Chapter 26), and egalitarianism. Surely this is as it should be, for if we wish to go in for metaphysics at all we want to gain a view of 'the sorry scheme of things entire' that is as plausible and as correct as possible. However, we must not so lust for a coherent, unified picture of reality that we will accept what seems on careful review an incoherent belief, merely because it is an essential link in or fits well with our overall scheme of things. If a given metaphysical scheme has a particular concept as an integral element, say a concept of an immortal soul (taken as a simple, indivisible, and indestructable substance), and if conceptual analysis reveals this concept to be incoherent, then it is plainly evident that the metaphysical scheme of which it is a part is correspondingly weakened.

It is sometimes maintained against what I have just argued, and indeed against the whole problem-oriented approach of this book, that metaphysical schemes cannot be appraised piecemeal but must be appraised as a whole. I agree that even when we are very sceptical about achieving this, we finally want or should want to put ourselves into a position in which a metaphysical system could be appraised as a whole. However, prior to this desired but very ideal state, it is necessary and essential that we engage in piecemeal criticism. A materialist metaphysics such as Holbach's or Smart's argues for mechanism, mind/body identity, determinism, atheism, and utilitarianism. These are distinguishable claims, and before we can have good grounds for accepting such a scheme as a whole, we need to be clear about the nature of these separate claims and the grounds for accepting them as true or at least as more plausible claims than their rivals. The analysis I have given of determinism, theism, morality, and the mind/body identity theory has put us in a far better position to appraise the plausibility of complete metaphysical systems than if we had simply started to examine these systems as a whole.

In fact, it is difficult to understand what it would be like to examine metaphysical systems as a whole *without evaluating their several parts*. Indeed, there will come a point at which, after making an examination of the several metaphysical and conceptual claims of a metaphysical system, we will try to put the whole thing together and appraise it as a whole. This would seem to be a matter of first examining the conceptual interconnections of the various claims—for example, is determinism incompatible with the making of rational moral claims, and is a belief in a mind/body identity incompatible with a belief in God? Then, if and where there are logical incompatibilities or at least conceptual clefts or tensions, we would have to consider the *comparative* coherence and well groundedness of separate metaphysical claims. If we were very convinced that the ontological argument for the existence of God was sound and that belief in God was incompatible with accepting the mind/body identity thesis which we thought was more plausible than the other theories of mind (although less well grounded than the claims of theism, supported as they are by a sound ontological argument), then it would appear at least to be more reasonable for us to reject the mind/body identity thesis and remain theists. But we would only be justified in doing this if we in turn thought—and thought rightly—that belief in the soundness of the mind/body identity thesis was less well grounded than the belief that there is an incompatibility between believing in God and accepting the mind/body identity thesis.

In this way we can weigh the relative merits of parts of metaphysical schemes as we work toward making an overall appraisal of the scheme as a whole. Such reasoning should always be tentative, and it rests finally on considerations of plausibility. It is also apparent that it presupposes the utilization of conceptual analysis and a careful examination of the particular metaphysical claims in question. There is no shortcut in making reasonable assessments of competing metaphysical schemes.

However, it is natural and reasonable to be sceptical of the appeal I have made here and in the last chapter to considerations of plausibility. An important element of cultural determination and at least an apparent cultural relativism enters here. I—and Smart and Armstrong as well—indeed have an initial propensity to accept materialism because of our very secular and nonreligious attitudes. By contrast, a similarly educated twentieth-century Presbyterian living in urban America would tend rather to have a very deep-seated propensity to accept some form of dualism. What such a person would take to be initially plausible, commonsensical, and reasonable in this domain would be just the reverse of what I, and many like me, take as a commonsense, reasonable, plausible starting point. That is to say, prior to engaging in philosophical analysis and/or metaphysical system construction, all of us—or at least almost all of us—carry to these analyses a primitive proto-philosophy (a loose cluster of fundamental beliefs which we are in some sense committed to and regard with varying degrees of conviction as being correct or at least more plausible than their alternatives).

There can be, and are, radically different proto-philosophies even among philosophers who share a very similar philosophical method. Analytic philosophers, for example, vary enormously in their proto-philosophies. *Broadly speaking,* my philosophical method is similar to that of such philosophers as Price, Ducasse, Broad, and Hick, and I respect their analytical work very much. But our views about what it is plausible to believe differ radically. When I hear Price, Ducasse, and Broad talking of 'out-of-the-body experiences' or 'ectoplasm', or Hick talking of a 'reconstructed spiritual body' in a 'resurrection world', I feel very much the way I feel when I read about the Azande's discourse about witchcraft substance or about the Dobuans and their magical yams, or the Tiwi's conception of the land of the dead. That is to say, I feel that serious belief in such 'realities' is not really possible.[1] To me, the very extravagance of such beliefs makes it difficult to take them as beliefs that one might plausibly entertain as live options. One indeed might play a little intellectual game and see if one could give some sense to such talk or catch on to the language game and form of life of the people who talk in this way, but I find it in a psychological sense quite impossible to regard them as serious options for a man in the twentieth century. But then I also know, as a matter of sociological fact, that such beliefs are serious options for some educated, reflective men of this century, that these philosophers are in earnest about what they believe, and that they reason cautiously and exactly and understand and utilize careful philosophical argumentation. Philosophy for them, as for me, is rooted in an analytical study of concepts. The fact remains—or at least it seems to be a fact—that our proto-philosophies are so very different that when we come to appraising metaphysical systems, in spite of using a common method in philosophy, we make radically different judgments of plausibility.

Thus, we are faced with the very sceptical question: Is it just that we start with fundamentally different presuppositions here and that there is no legitimate way of arguing or reasoning about them? First, it should be noted that although we do start with different proto-philosophies and with different assumptions about what is plausible, we still have a common method of conceptual analysis. (We could differ rather considerably about *what* it is plausible to believe, without having a different concept of plausibility.) We can bracket, so to speak, the presuppositions we make, and thus work *inside* a position. Using conceptual analysis and working from inside, we can appraise a rival metaphysical claim. This is exactly what I did with the ontological argument and the cosmological argument, and this is what Malcolm did with the mind/body identity theory. Unless it can be shown, as it has not been shown, that conceptual analysis is itself not a neutral philosophical tool, at least this much can be done. That is to say, a man who had accepted materialism as a kind of proto-philosophy might very well come, if he were convinced of the soundness of Malcolm's or Ducasse's conceptual analyses of the mind/body identity claim, to reject materialism as incoherent. In fact, it is evident that this is what he should do if he were thoroughly convinced of the correctness of either of their analyses.

The same thing happens vis-à-vis belief in God in any typical course in the philosophy of religion. Some people who initially come to the course with Jewish or Christian proto-philosophies become convinced on conceptual grounds alone that such beliefs are incoherent. Thus, we can rationally work out of a proto-philosophy or radically alter or supplement it by employing conceptual analysis.

However, it should be replied that although this is true, it is not so obviously applicable *at the level we are discussing*, for there we are trying to make, in the manner described, a tentative appraisal of *whole* metaphysical schemes partly by assessing the relative plausibility of rival metaphysical claims within the competing metaphysical schemes. To tie down what is at issue, it is important to give an example. Suppose on conceptual grounds alone we are convinced that the cosmological argument for the existence of God has some merit, that is, that it is a reliable argument or that at least it appears to be more reasonable than any of the criticisms of it. Further suppose that we are also convinced that the mind/body identity thesis is a more plausible claim than any of its rivals, that is, that the argument for it is a reliable one. Carrying conceptual analysis as far as we can go at a given time, we come to these conclusions. And now we try in such a situation to decide which metaphysical scheme to accept. Shall we be theists or reductive materialists? Which is the more plausible view to accept tentatively? (One could not reasonably be anything other than tentative about the acceptance of a whole metaphysical framework.)

I do not think we simply have to fall back on our respective protophilosophies in such a situation. We surely should consider how the theistic claims and the materialist claims fit in with other metaphysical claims and with our methodological or normative principles, for example, mechanism, immortality, morality, determinism, methods of determining truth and warranted belief, conceptions of intelligibility and rationality, and the like. Surely it is more rational to accept, where the plausibility of the conflicting beliefs is nearly equal, that belief which fits in best with those other beliefs we take to be plausible. However, it remains true that we do keep falling back on considerations of plausibility, and what people at any given time take to be plausible seems in part at least to be culturally and even individually determined. This is indeed a problem, but we must also remember that (1) it is only in part culturally and individually determined and (2) we can keep on using conceptual analysis to constantly reexamine those metaphysical claims or normative claims we take to be more or less plausible. We are not in an utter ethnocentric or egocentric bind here.

II

There is a further more radical problem about metaphysical claims that came into prominence during the period between World War I and II. It was argued by some philosophers that metaphysics is to be eliminated, for all metaphysical utterances are literally meaningless or at least devoid of cognitive meaning. Metaphysical utterances attempt to go beyond the bounds of sense and thus can have no literal meaning. In reality they are emotive cries expressive of notational confusions and emotional hang-ups. As such they express and evoke emotion, but make no literal claim, although their appearance is such as to lead one to believe that they are grand but mysterious cosmological claims.[2]

Peirce argued that the scientific method—roughly the experimental method—was the only reliable way to fix belief. The most prominent among the philosophers who argued for an elimination of metaphysics, the logical empiricists (logical positivists), turned roughly Peircean considerations about what constitutes *reliable* belief into a criterion about what it makes *sense* to say or what would constitute *informative* discourse. They wished to establish, broadly speaking, that if a putative statement is such that if, on the one hand, no actual or even conceivable observations would establish its truth or probable truth or, on the other hand, its falsity or probable falsity (and if it is not analytic), then that putative statement is devoid of literal significance. That is, it is no statement at all, but a cognitively meaningless or unintelligible remark parading as a statement.

Such philosophers would argue we have taken the claims of the dualists, reductive materialists, and epiphenomenalists too much at face value; we have mistakenly assumed that they are genuine statements—statements with some literal meaning. But if they are such, they must be empirically testable (confirmable or infirmable) in principle, and thus not metaphysical. However, if they are metaphysical and hence in principle untestable, they are devoid of literal intelligibility. No matter which of these claims is true, there is no need to get mired in the thick muck of metaphysics. Moreover, such considerations apply to all conceptual questions, to all attempts to try to establish with respect to perplexing philosophical concepts what it makes sense to say—for example, to the central questions about determinism and indeterminism and, as we have already seen, to philosophical arguments about God, the core of which turned on questions concerning the literal intelligibility of God-talk. Repeatedly in philosophical discussions, as our arguments have illustrated, questions arise about what it makes sense to say or think, about what is intelligible, what is conceivable, what is significant, or what is or is not nonsense.

There is a crucial question behind these questions. In philosophizing we indeed analyze concepts—critical philosophy is the analytical study of concepts—but in attempting to clarify our concepts, in attempting to give them a perspicuous representation, what is our principle of clarification? We want to know when a word, symbol, or utterance is meaningful, but what requirements must words, symbols, or utterances satisfy before they can justifiably be called meaningful or intelligible? What in general is our criterion for intelligible discourse? It is to such a cluster of questions that we will now turn. They are not simply specialists' questions; as we have seen, they arise naturally and inevitably in considering the primary problems of philosophy and they are at the heart of the question about whether a metaphysical or speculative philosophy is possible.

It should be evident by now how very much I agree with William James's remark (quoted in Chapter 1) that the ultimate rationale for philosophizing is to attain a more rational conception of the frame of things than the one we normally carry about with us under our caps. But in trying to gain a more rational conception of the frame of things, questions about what it makes sense to say lie very near the center of our deliberations. Does it make sense to say that a sudden thought is a brain process, that man is nothing more than a complicated mechanism, that men are immortal, that there is an indeterministic contracausal freedom? Is it even intelligible to claim that one could have an *a priori* knowledge of the world, as rationalists think we can? And does it make sense to assert or deny the existence of a nonanthropomorphic God? Moving on to ethical theory, we can ask: Does it make sense to speak of nonnatural moral characteristics or of a *noumenal* realm of moral realities?

Any probing consideration of the primary problems of philosophy throws up these questions, and they lead us to turn upon such a cluster of philosophical questions with the higher order question: How do we determine what it makes sense to say? We are driven to this abstruse question when we ponder seriously the primary problems of philosophy and suffer from an awareness of the intractable quality of philosophical disputes and from philosophical self-questioning. We become tormented by the perplexity: What is the criterion—and do we have a single criterion and an *objective* criterion—for what it makes sense to say, for significant discourse, or for intelligibility? Can we unearth the criterion or criteria or at least litmus paper test(s) for what is intelligible? We shall be wrestling with this cluster of questions in the remaining chapters and, at the same time, with the question of whether any adequate criterion of meaning will show that metaphysics must be eliminated—that such system building should no longer be a part of any future sober philosophy. (This is by no means all that we shall be doing, but the other considerations will revolve around these questions as a central point of reference.)

III

Let us start in as commonsensical a manner as possible in our search for a criterion or at least a test for intelligibility. We are of course interested in determining when concepts, ideas, or propositions are intelligible, but we can analyze these only through analyzing words, phrases, and sentences. So to give us something we can grab on to, let us ask: when is a word not an 'empty mark' but a meaningful bit of discourse? Or, if 'meaningful word' strikes you as a pleonasm, when, to put it in a perhaps pedantically exact way, is a phonemic sequence a morpheme—an intelligible mark? And when is a string of words (alternatively, a string of phonemic sequences) a significant—that is, an intelligible—sentence? What conditions would have to be satisfied before we would say that a word or a sentence was or was not meaningful or significant?

Since a simple sentence is normally taken as expressing a complete thought—and in that way such sentences are the basic units of meaning—let us concentrate for the present on sentences rather than words. Native or fluent speakers of the language, it is at least plausible to maintain, can immediately recognize that some sentences are meaningless and some are not. Here we have examples of plainly meaningless sentences:

Nixon sleeps faster than Johnson.

Natural numbers had a dance.

Contemporary directs brass windows.

Any native speaker or fluent speaker immediately recognizes that these sentences are meaningless, although he could, of course, *give* them meaning if he chose to. As they are, however, they have no meaning. By contrast, there are sentences such as the following, which, when used to make statements, are plainly absurd, but they are not meaningless or unintelligible:

A purple Gila monster is sitting on my head.

I bought my pastrami on Mars.

I swam underwater all the way from Montreal to London.

We understand these sentences, and it is because we understand them that we know they are absurd. In this way they are quite unlike 'Nixon sleeps faster than Johnson .

The question we need to ask in as commonsensical way as possible is this: How do we distinguish between sentences like those in the first and second group? How do we distinguish between sentences we understand and those (where they are used to make statements) we believe to be true or false and, on the other hand, sentences (phonemic sequences) we do not understand and find meaningless?

That we can readily discriminate between these two groups, as in the preceding examples, shows that we know how to distinguish—in some situations anyway—between significant and meaningless sentences. That in some cases we would *not* know what to say or that there are borderline cases only shows what is evident anyway: The distinction is not a sharp one. There is an important philosophical question: Can we state a tolerably clear criterion of meaning or a test for intelligibility that will enable us to separate the black sheep (the first group of sentences) from the white (the second group)? And can we state and elucidate a criterion that in some nonarbitrary way will settle matters for us in controversial cases (including philosophical ones) where we dispute about what it makes sense to say?

Let us start with this simple criterion:

(1) A string of words is a significant or meaningful sentence only if it is at least in principle *transformable* into a grammatically sound (well-formed) sentence or set of sentences.

It looks as if this gives us at least a necessary condition for intelligibility. That is, it appears at least to be the case that no sentence can be intelligible unless this condition holds. A string of words that fails to satisfy this condition is not a sentence and is not expressive of a thought. (Examples: 'High up to the forward back', 'And the conjunction joy', 'Singularity praying events eclectic'.)

However, we must be cautious here. Consider 'I can't never feel for to do it, like'. One might be inclined (at least an American might be inclined), on hearing it just like that, to assert that it is not a grammatically well-formed sentence and to deny that one can understand it. But if we put it back in its original context in the Australian short story in which it occurred, it is perfectly intelligible:

> Mr. Treagear and his daughters were just come in for breakfast, after milking in the cold starlight dawn of an autumn morning.
> "But gurls," the old man was saying, as he held his hand to the fire, "I can't never feel for to do it, like."
> "Feel to do it! And is she to stick on there for ever, not paying a farthing of rent because you don't feel for to do it? My word! Some folk's feelings make rare pets for 'em."[3]

In its natural setting, it is seen to be perfectly intelligible. But it is also not in conflict with our preceding criterion for intelligibility, for it is *transformable* into grammatically sound English. It means either 'I can't bring myself to do it', 'I can't make myself do it', or 'I don't want to do it'.

However, even if nothing else is wrong with it, this criterion would have to be modified in certain respects to accommodate things like *Finnegans Wake*, where we have sentences, understood by some at least, which are not transformable or at least appear not to be transformable into grammatically well-formed sentences of any one natural language. However, it is not evident that such a transformation cannot be carried out even here if we use several languages and then after the initial transformations translate back into a single language; and in line with this, it is further not evident that some inessential modification of the preceding criterion to capture the use of several languages could not catch such a recalcitrant case. So it does seem at least reasonable to claim that the preceding criterion does succeed in providing us with what for the overwhelming majority of cases is a *necessary condition* for a sentence being intelligible. In other words, if the sentence in question is not *transformable* into a grammatically correct sentence or set of sentences, it is not an intelligible sentence.

Even if this is correct, however, it does not carry us very far, for it is plainly not a *sufficient* condition for intelligibility. There are sentences that meet this condition and are plainly meaningless, for example, 'The child smiled a colored tone' or 'Nixon sleeps faster than Johnson'.

Can we adumbrate a criterion or test for intelligibility that gives us a necessary *and* sufficient condition, a test that catches all and only intelligible sentences and excludes the rest? Suppose we try another criterion.

(2)   To be a significant sentence, the sentence must in principle at least be *transformable* into an ordinary idiom.

The phrase 'ordinary idiom' is vague and will arouse suspicion, but I am taking it to mean the idiom (or, when we consider natural languages other than English, the idioms) we use in communication with one another. Perhaps it remains so vague as not to be serviceable, but perhaps—since we are searching for a general criterion—it is necessary for it to be vague in this way. At any rate, it has been argued with considerable force that in clarifying a sentence that is not in this idiom, we have in the last analysis no recourse but to appeal to and utilize ordinary language in this manner.[4]

To understand a metaphysical claim such as 'The various is the Difference which is merely posited, the Difference which is no Difference', it at least surely seems that we must succeed in translating it or, at the minimum, characterizing it in an ordinary idiom if we are to understand it. Ask yourself quite honestly how else you would understand it or come to understand it.[5] Or consider a psychological generalization such as 'All anal-erotic individuals are sadomasochists'. To understand this we must be able to eliminate or at least experientially specifiy what is meant by the technical terms used in the sentence. If definitions or characterizations have not been given for these terms, then we must be able to construct our own by a careful examination of the context in which such a sentence naturally occurs. If we cannot do this, the sentence remains unintelligible.

Again this looks at best like a necessary but not a necessary and sufficient condition for intelligibility. The following sentences are in an ordinary idiom, but they remain devoid of literal meaning:

Trapezoids sip flaming music at Pete's bar.

Stones graduated from St. Johns.

Carp need interior decorating.

Jeannette ate the law of gravitation.

These are all grammatical sentences—at least if we take the conventional (the schoolmarm's) conception of grammar—and they all are in ordinary English. And they are not like 'Being and becoming are one' or 'Transcendence unfolds itself in the ineffable encompassing'. Yet, they plainly are devoid of literal meaning and in that crucial sense are unintelligible.

Pushing this same line of argument with something that *at first blush* does not appear to be unintelligible, consider an example taken from Wittgenstein: 'It is five o'clock in the afternoon on the sun'. Here is a disguised piece of nonsense. It looks like the meaningful sentence 'It is five o'clock in Heidelberg'. While someone living in New York or Timbuctoo can sensibly say 'It is five o'clock in Heidelberg' or 'It is five o'clock in San Francisco' or It is five o'clock in the afternoon in Saigon', it makes no sense at all to say 'It is five o'clock on the earth' or 'It is five o'clock on the sun'. Yet, all of these sentences, meaningful and meaningless alike, are in perfectly grammatical English. They are in an ordinary idiom and are grammatically in place (if anything is grammatically in place), but some are unintelligible at least in the sense that they do not make a literal assertion although they purport to do so.

'It is five o'clock in the afternoon on the sun' is unintelligible because nothing counts for or against its truth. It makes no sense to speak of determining the truth of this assertion, and therefore the assertion is without literal, informative content, although it purports to be a sentence used informatively. The very notion of its being a certain time (or being such-and-such o'clock) presupposes a system of time zones, and one can speak of its being a certain time only for a point or limited area within a time zone (including, of course, the entire time zone itself). Thus, one can speak of its being 5 o'clock in Aarhus but not of its being 5 o'clock on the moon. For this reason, we can see that it does not follow that a sentence is meaningful (intelligible) if it is transformable into an ordinary idiom. It may indeed be meaningless if it is not so transformable but its being so transformable or being in an ordinary idiom does not guarantee its intelligibility.

However, the remarks about 'It is five o'clock in the afternoon on the sun' do suggest another criterion, or rather two different criteria, for what it makes sense to say. These we shall discuss in the next two chapters. The first is dear to traditional empiricists such as Hume and the second to contemporary logical empiricists (logical positivists) such as Ayer, Carnap, and Schlick. The criteria may be put as follows:

(3)   A sentence in an ordinary idiom or capable at least in principle of being transformed into a grammatically well-formed sentence or set of sentences in an ordinary idiom, is meaningful if and only if the terms in the sentence either stand for sense impressions or are completely definable by terms that stand for such impressions.

(4)   A sentence in an ordinary idiom or capable at least in principle of being transformed into a grammatically well-formed sentence or set of sentences in an ordinary idiom, is meaningful if and only if a statement or proposition made by its use (its employment) is at least verifiable (confirmable or infirmable) in principle.

If either or both of these are justified, taken singly or in conjunction, then we have a rational ground for the elimination of metaphysics, where 'a metaphysical claim' is taken as a claim that there can be some *a priori* knowledge of the world or nonempirical knowledge of the world. With (3) and (4) we indeed have the heart of an empiricist philosophy. But it has been thought, and not just by metaphysicians, that this empiricist philosophy with such criteria of meaning is itself a nonempirical metaphysical dogma. Rather than eliminating metaphysics, it unwittingly invokes a set of metaphysical claims of its own. It is to these questions *and* to an examination of the adequacy of such criteria of meaning that we shall now turn.

NOTES

1. Reductive materialism strikes some philosophers in the same way that such talk of 'out-of-the-body-experiences' or a 'reconstructed spiritual body' strikes me. A colleague recently wrote me that in defending reductive materialism I was keeping very primitive company indeed, that such reductionism is naive and along with Lenin's *Materialism and Empirico-Criticism* it is of the genre of the Romantics of Swashbuckling Materialism. That there are these very different and preanalytic reactions about what is or is not plausible indeed gives a relativistic spin to the appeal to considerations of plausibility, and reflection on this cannot but give a philosopher who is also an honest man an uneasy feeling. I indeed feel uneasy, but, as I shall argue, there are good reasons for believing that the concept of plausibility and the criteria for plausibility are not utterly relative or even *essentially* contested.
2. Some classic statements of this vintage logical empiricism are collected together in A. J. Ayer (ed.), *Logical Positivism*. There, the essays by Carnap and Schlick and most particularly Carnap's "The Elimination of Metaphysics Through Logical Analysis of Language" are typical statements of such an approach. This also holds true for A. J. Ayer's own "Demonstration of the Impossibility of Metaphysics," *Mind* (1934), (reprinted in Paul Edwards and Arthur Pap (eds.), *A Modern Introduction to Philosophy*) and his little classic *Language, Truth and Logic*. Accurate brief accounts of this philosophical movement are given in John Passmore, *A Hundred Years of Philosophy*, chapter 16; in Arne Naess, *Four Modern Philosophers*, pp. 3–66; and in R. W. Ashby, "Logical Positivism," in D. J. O'Connor (ed.), *A Critical History of Western Philosophy*. For a full-length account see V. Kraft, *The Vienna Circle*.
3. H. Stone, "The Widow Dare," *Australian Short Stories*, p. 114.
4. Paul Marhenke, "The Criterion of Significance," in L. Linsky (ed.), *Semantics and the Philosophy of Language*. Much of what I argue in this chapter and the next has been influenced by Marhenke.
5. A practical utilization of this transformability criterion occurs quite naturally and unselfconsciously in the work of the German sociologist Ralf Dahrendorf. Faced with the metaphysical whopper from Hegel's *The Philosophy of Right*: "The family, as the immediate substantiality of mind, has its felt unity, love, as its condition, so that the disposition is the awareness of its individuality in this unity as the essentiality in and for itself in order not to exist as a person by itself, but as a member," Dahrendorf remarks: "If one is unimpressed by Hegel's art of linguistic camouflage and translates what he has to say into reasonable language, this [the above quotation] simply means that the family is a world of community, not of society; of love, not of right, to which the individual belongs not as a person, but as a 'member' devoid of the capacity for rational decision." Unfortunately not all metaphysical utterances are so easily transformed and demythologized. Ralf Dahrendorf, *Society and Democracy in Germany*, p. 198.

32

EMPIRICISM
AND THE VERIFICATION
PRINCIPLE: I

I

The heart of the charge of empiricists against metaphysicians is not that metaphysical statements are false but that they are devoid of literal meaning. It is claimed that metaphysics and speculative philosophy are something soberminded philosophers should eliminate, for they only stand as a pompous or mystifying encumbrance to the advancement of knowledge and to the attainment of a genuine understanding of ourselves and our world. But this empiricist claim is itself linked to a criterion of meaning which, it has been maintained, is itself an unempirical dogma reflecting the bias of much of twentieth-century culture.[1]

Before we turn to an exposition and critical examination of this criterion of meaning, we will do well to give a fuller characterization of what empiricism is taken to be.[2] Empiricism, like most such general conceptions, covers a wide variety of things. It is typically considered the philosophical doctrine that all our knowledge is based upon or derived ultimately from experience. It has been advanced as an answer to the following questions:

A. What is the origin of human knowledge?
B. What is the extent of human knowledge?
C. What kind of statements can give us a knowledge of the world?
D. What is the relationship between language and fact?

Since the *validity* of a belief is quite independent of its *origin*, we can, and should, put aside question A. But it is crucial to assess answers given by empiricists to the last three questions. Hume, who is our classical source here, has given us an answer to questions B and C when he maintained that "all the materials of thinking are derived either from our outward or inward sentiment" and that there could be no knowledge of the world not based on these sense impressions.[3] Knowledge, according to Hume, is limited to impressions gained in sense experience or ideas that consist of the recall of previous impressions in imagination or memory. Reality, he maintained, must be explained in the last analysis wholly in terms of what is in principle observable. If someone claims that he has a particular idea that does not derive from an impression or set of impressions, then his alleged idea must be bogus, for every genuine idea corresponds to an impression.

We surely should ask why this is so, and indeed if this is so. How can Hume be so confident? Hume's manner would lead us to think that he had discovered this empirically through psychological investigation. But his manner aside, if what he actually claims is correct, it cannot be right to say that we have found it out on the basis of an experiment or on the basis of experience, including even introspection. On Hume's own account we cannot know what it means to have an idea without its corresponding impression. Since we do not know what it *means* to have an idea without an impression from which it is derived, we can hardly try to see, to note, if there are any ideas *not* derived from impressions, for we do not know what to look for to ascertain that this is so. Thus, Hume's own idiom notwithstanding, there can be no intelligible talk of psychological investigation or experiment here.

Rather, appearances to the contrary, Hume is making a philosophical claim. He is setting up a *meaning criterion*. He is contending that we should assert what he asserts because a symbol or a word is only meaningful if it corresponds with pictures or items in our experience or is itself definable in terms of expressions that do this. And this provides us with an answer to question D. For language to be meaningful there must be a correspondence between language and fact, between symbol and what is symbolized. That is to say, there must be some direct relation between language and reality, and that direct relation is constituted by the fact that for words to be understandable at all they must be either directly or indirectly *ostensively* definable. In saying they are 'ostensively definable' I am saying that we come to understand their meaning by having what they refer to pointed out to us; this is done by exhibiting what in our experience the terms in question refer to. Hume is in effect maintaining that those terms that are meaningful are the ones that refer to discrete items in our experience or they are the ones definable by words that in turn stand for discrete items given in our experience.

Human thinking is inextricably linked to language using, and language in turn gets its meaning in virtue of this direct relationship between language and experience. The meaning of a symbol—any symbol you like—must be understood in terms of some correspondence between the symbol and what it symbolizes. It is this very conception of meaning which dictates this empiricist answer to the preceding questions (B) and (C). That is to say, the empiricist criterion of meaning determines the extent and limits of knowledge, and it determines for empiricists and, if correct, it should also determine for all rational men their conception of what kind of statements can give us knowledge of the world. Thus, the justifiability of empiricism turns on the justifiability of some form of an empiricist criterion of meaning. And as empiricism, viewed now as an ideology, is very pervasive among educated people in the contemporary world, we have still another reason for attempting a careful appraisal of such a criterion of meaning.

Let us start with (3), which is essentially an updated Humean criterion.

(3)   A sentence in an ordinary idiom or capable at least in principle of being transformed into a grammatically well-formed sentence or set of sentences in an ordinary idiom, is meaningful if and only if the terms in the sentence either stand for sense impressions or are completely definable by terms that stand for such impressions.

But let us ask a simple question: Why should we believe that a term in such a sentence has meaning only if it either directly or indirectly stands for a sense impression or a set of sense impressions? Is it natural to reply that we come to understand a strange term by coming to understand what it stands for, by having it ostensively defined. And until we so understand it, we do not really understand it. If we are learning a foreign language and look up a word we do not understand in a dictionary of that foreign language, we will only understand the definition if it refers to some words whose references we know by acquaintance. Ostensive definition is rock bottom in our coming to understand the meaning of terms.

The picture we have in mind is something like this. Suppose we were learning a foreign language with something like the Berlitz method, and in the first lesson the first sentence we faced was this: 'Hier ist eine Karte'. The teacher using only German in this case utters, "Hier ist eine Karte," while holding up or pointing to a map. Then pointing to the map she utters and we follow in the book, "Hier ist Ungarn" and she points to Hungary on the map; and while pointing to Sweden she says, "Und hier ist Schweden." Then complicating matters a little further she utters, again making the appropriate pointing to the map, "Schweden liegt in Nordeuropa, und Ungarn liegt in Osteuropa." In this way by ostensive definition—assuming we already understand what a map is (something which in turn can be explained ostensively)—she teaches the meaning of terms we do not understand ostensively.

Here, of course, we already know at least one other language, namely English, and are learning another similar language with equivalent and nearly equivalent terms and the like. But it illustrates the concept of what it is to learn the meaning of terms through ostensive definition. Terms stand for discrete empirically discernible realities, and to come to understand the *meaning* of a term is to come to understand the reality the term stands for. If there is no experiential something that the term stands for, the term is a meaningless empty mark. What constitutes the meaningfulness of a word is the possibility of its being ostensively defined.[4] That is to say, in order for a term to be meaningful, it must be definable by direct confrontation with what the word stands for. If this is impossible in principle, the term is meaningless. An inescapable condition for the meaningfulness of a word is that we be able to point to or at least know what it would be like to point to that to which it refers. If this is not possible in principle, the word in question is meaningless. Ostensive definition is the means of directly linking language with reality. According to such Humean empiricists, it has a temporal and logical priority over purely verbal definitions.

This empiricist criterion and its picture of how we prove that a term is meaningful is seductively simple. It appeals to 'an intuition' (a hunch) we have about how sense (meaning) is fixed and about how most fundamentally we link language with reality. But all the same, Wittgenstein and other philosophers working in his tradition have shown that, seductive as it is, it is an unrealistic picture of how language works and of what it is to establish that a term is intelligible.[5]

Consider such ubiquitous terms as 'if', 'then', 'and', 'but', 'so', 'because', and the like. They do not stand for anything and are not learned in the way 'Jones', 'pen', or 'Sweden' is learned. However, this by itself is not enough to cause anything but an inessential complicating modification of the empiricist criterion, for it can (and has) been said quite correctly that such terms are syncategormatic terms, that is, terms that have no meaning in themselves but only have meaning in linking other terms. Yet, syncategormatic terms cannot characterize or describe anything; they cannot by themselves reveal what reality is like. But the terms they link—the terms that have a meaning in their own right, the descriptive and designative terms—are meaningful only if they are directly or indirectly ostensively definable.

There are further counterexamples, however, that are more troubling and need to be faced by Humeans. What is the Humean empiricist to say about 'electrons', 'photon', or 'meson'? They surely are meaningful terms, yet they do not stand for anything observable, so according to the Humean empiricist criterion, should they not be rejected as meaningless? But this in turn would constitute a *reductio* of Humean empiricism.

It is because of this difficulty that Humeans also in effect work with a concept of ostensive definition by indirection; that is to say, there are meaningful terms definable by means of terms that are themselves quite directly definable ostensively. We cannot directly ostensively define 'golden mountain' anymore than we can 'meson', but 'golden mountain' is plainly meaningful on the empiricist model, for we can ostensively define 'golden' and 'mountain'. The fit is not so exact with the theoretical terms from physics, but something analogous can be done.

Consider how we could explain the meaning of 'electron'. We could start off with a *verbal* definition. To speak of 'an electron' is to speak of the most elementary charge of negative electricity. It is the electrical opposite of the proton. But we still remain in a circle of words far from an experiential periphery. We would naturally go on, still remaining too far from the experiential periphery for ostensive definition, and state its electrostatic units, give its mass, and point out that electrons are constituents of all atoms and that they are entirely electromagnetic. However, this characterization still remains abstract and far from something human beings might experience. In that way 'electron' is very unlike 'golden mountain' and certainly unlike such Humean paradigms as 'blue', 'lemon', 'bittersweet', 'hard', and the like. With such terms from physical science there is no clear direct link, or even the appearance of a clear direct link, between words and experience or reality. But in specifying their meaning there is a less direct but still essential link with what is experiential.

For the above abstract specification of meaning to gain any hold, so that there is an understanding of what is being said, there must be a breakthrough to what is ostensively teachable. And indeed this can be and is done. We will be told in a further specification of the meaning of 'electron'—as even some dictionaries do—that electrons have cathode rays and beta rays, and the term 'cathode ray' in turn is explained as being the rays projected from the negative pole of a vacuum tube in which an electric discharge takes place. By striking solids, cathode rays generate X-rays. In turn, X-rays are radiations of the same nature as light radiation, except that they have an extremely short wavelength. But they also have certain observable effects. They ionize the gas through which they pass. They have an action like that of photographic plates, fluorescent screens, and the like. Here at last we have something like ostensive teaching. The abstract term 'electron' does not hang in the air; in specifying its meaning we must finally rely on terms that are ostensively definable. Without that, the term would remain a mysterious, meaningless mark.

Moreover recall that (3), our updated Humean meaning criterion, does not require that all meaningful nonsyncategormatic terms be ostensively definable, but that those terms not ostensively definable must in turn be definable by terms that are themselves ostensively definable. The chain between language and experience need not always be as direct as with 'red' and 'bittersweet'. It would seem, so far as anything which has yet been established against our Humelike meaning criterion, that to meet these objections would only require a modern and inessential qualification to accommodate syncategormatic terms.

All still is not quiet on the empiricist front, however, for it is arguable that the full meaning of terms such as 'meson' and 'electron' are not so specifiable. More importantly, it is questionable whether theoretical but still scientific workaday terms such as 'gravitational potential', 'electric field', and 'neutrino' can even in a roundabout way be ostensively taught. They appear at least to be very different from 'electron'.[6]

More fundamentally still—and such esoteric matters apart—there is a more general and more damaging argument that comes from Wittgenstein against such a Humean empiricism.[7] (Wittgenstein, I should add, is probably to our century—although such historical judgments are always risky—what Hume was to his.) It shows that the Humean conception of meaning is unrealistic and incorrect not only for such esoteric terms but for the vast majority of our everyday terms. Wittgenstein (and Ryle as well) ask us to note how few words fit the model of ostensive definition of name and bearer.[8] Nouns fit it, particularly proper names such as 'Mount Washington' and 'Fred'. But it is simply not true that all or even most terms gain their meaning by a kind of christening ceremony in which we attach a name, functioning as a label, to a person, place, thing, or process. Language is not a series of labels. It is a highly systematic, interrelated affair.

This Wittgensteinian thesis needs illustration, elucidation, and justification. Completely at random I pick a sentence from the *Manchester Guardian:* 'It would be interesting to hear these conditions being argued in a court of law'. It is plainly a meaningful utterance, and none of the words in the sentence are at all suspect. But how many of these words function as do 'red', 'Fred', 'Mount Washington', or even 'color'? Note that 'it' is so context-dependent that we can hardly speak of its referent being given in sense experience so that its meaning is learned by a confrontation with the things it stands for. But perhaps by some stretch of the imagination we might come to think it stood indefinitely for this or that or something else. But 'would', 'be', 'interesting', and 'to'—the next four words—do not fit this model at all. Yet, they are perfectly intelligible, nonesoteric words we all understand, if we have any mastery of English at all. The same should be said for 'conditions', 'in', 'a', 'and', 'of'. 'These' is in about the same boat as 'it'. There is no plain referent there which could be pointed to, as with 'Mount Washington'. And 'being', 'argued', even 'court' and 'law' do not simply function as or even like labels such that we simply learn their meaning by seeing what they point to or stand for. I can utter 'Fred' and if Fred is around point to him, or utter 'Mount Washington' and if I am in the right place in Vermont point to it, but I can hardly do that with any of the words in the sentence I choose at random from the *Manchester Guardian*. Most words do not function like labels which stand for something that can be ostensively defined. Language is not composed of a collection of labels that have their meaning in isolation from each other, so that we can find out what a word means by simply finding out what it stands for or what it labels. In fact, even within a language this is only true for a few atypical words.

Wittgenstein compounds difficulties for the Humean empiricist by pointing out that the Humean model does not even work very well for typical words—for example, 'red', 'bittersweet', 'Fred', 'Mount Washington'. Words do not have a meaning in isolation. Sentences, not isolated words, convey information, express wishes, function as commands, and the like. And even these in turn gain their sense from being an intricate part of a system of language. The very conception of 'a name' or 'label' does not just sit there for man to learn simply by being made aware of its denotata (the things it stands for). There had to be a place for it in a language: a complex intersubjective activity that human beings engage in. Wittgenstein brings this out in a brilliant way when he shows that without a very considerable understanding of language, one could not even teach by ostensive definition.

> Now one can ostensively define a proper name, the name of a colour, the name of a material, a numeral, the name of a point of the compass and so on. The definition of the number two, "That is called 'two' "—pointing to two nuts—is perfectly exact.—But how can two be defined like that? The person one gives the definition to doesn't know what one wants to call "two"; he will suppose that "two" is the name given to *this* group of nuts! He *may* suppose this; but perhaps he does not. He might make the opposite mistake; when I want to assign a name to this group of nuts, he might understand it as a numeral. And he might equally well take the name of a person, of which I give an ostensive definition, as that of a colour, of a race, or even of a point of the compass. That is to say: an ostensive definition can be variously interpreted in *every* case.
>
> Perhaps you say: two can only be ostensively defined in *this* way: "This *number* is called 'two'." For the word "number" here shews what place in language, in grammar, we assign to the word. But this means that the word "number" must be explained before the ostensive definition can be understood.—The word "number" in the definition does indeed shew this place; does shew the post at which we station the word. And we can prevent misunderstandings by saying: "This *colour* is called so-and-so," "This *length* is called so-and-so," and so on. That is to say: misunderstandings are sometimes averted in this way. But is there only *one* way of taking the word "colour" or "length"?—Well, they just need defining.—Defining, then, by means of other words! And what about the last definition in this chain? (Do not say: "There isn't a 'last' definition." That is just as if you chose to say: "There isn't a last house in this road; one can always build an additional one.") . . .
>
> Suppose, however, someone were to object: "It is not true that you must already be master of a language in order to understand an ostensive definition: all you need—of course!—is to know or guess what the person giving the explanation is pointing to. That is, whether for example to the shape of the object, or to its colour, or to its number, and so on."—And what does 'point-

ing to the shape', 'pointing to the colour' consist in? Point to a piece of paper.—And now point to its shape—now to its colour—now to its number (that sounds queer).—How did you do it?—You will say that you 'meant' a different thing each time you pointed. And if I ask how that is done, you will say you concentrated your attention on the colour, the shape, etc. But I ask again: how is *that* done?[9]

How then, it is natural to ask, could we ever come to learn a language at all? I do not know how to explain that, but it is evident enough that we did not learn it in the manner the Humean model suggests, and it is evident enough that there is not the direct relationship of language to experience that that model suggests. However we came to learn language, it is not the case that we came to learn it by being given labels for something we already understood and by having new things we did not understand pointed out to us *cum* label. In fact, simply having a label for something does not teach us anything about it. Furthermore, we must not imagine, as our paradigm here, a situation in which a person already has a language and someone, who can speak that person's language and another as well, points to things and teaches him certain words in that other language. We must try to imagine the child without any language at all. In such a circumstance there is nothing like this ostensive definition or purely ostensive teaching. Indeed, there is ostensive teaching, but it is only a part of a much more complex activity.

II

Considerations of the preceding sort, plus the recognition, Hume and the classical British empiricists notwithstanding, that there are many perfectly meaningful terms for which we have no images or impressions, has lead to an abandonment on the part of most analytical philosophers of any attempt to defend an empiricist criterion of meaning. This has been hastened by the well-grounded rejection of phenomenalism. (Phenomenalism is the epistemological theory that statements about physical reality are nothing more than statements about what we do and would experience.[10]) Classically, empiricists (Hume, Mill, the early Ayer) have also been phenomenalists, and when phenomenalism was seen to be inadequate, empiricism—mistakenly, as I shall argue—was rejected along with it. Alasdair MacIntyre's remarks well sum up the overall rationale for rejecting such an empiricist criterion of meaning.

If we address ourselves to the question of what language is, we cannot escape its essentially public and social character. But on an empiricist view of language, it must be a matter of what is private and individual, rather than of what is public and shared. For on an empiricist view it is with reference to our sense-experience that our utterances are given meaning. All sense-experience is private and cannot be shared. Empiricism shuts us up in a series of private worlds and makes impossible the public communication which in fact is the central feature of our use of language.[11]

MacIntyre concludes from this that "empiricism is no longer viable." Such an essentially Wittgensteinian onslaught is well justified as an attack on phenomenalism and as an attack on the *myth of the given*—on the belief that there are to be discovered *independently of our linguistic framework* facts or events or discrete realities that are simply given and passively recorded by language. Although we do not invent facts or create them by language, it is also not the case that they are just there waiting for us to describe them. The way we apperceive the world is not independent of our conceptual—linguistic—frame of reference. Different people, so to say, cut up the pie differently.

It is not the case that a man by shunning ordinary or even extraordinary forms of speech could, by just concentrating on his 'pure experience', cut through culture and language and become aware of what the 'real facts' are. There is no way to neutralize utterly the culture-encrusted perspective of our 'natural attitudes' and in a presuppositionless way confine ourselves strictly to what is given in experience independently of the forms of language.[12] One needs some natural language with its conventions to even form an idea of labeling and classifying one's experience in some way. Language is public and is part of a culture, and there is no escaping this. We are inescapably in such a categorio-centric predicament.[13]

It is also true that it is a mistake to try to restrict the class of meaningful words to those words that stand (directly or indirectly) for things that can be sensed. Criterion (3)—our updated Humean meaning criterion—must be abandoned. It is simply not true that all meaningful words in English or French, for example, do in fact stand for sense impressions or are completely definable by means of terms that stand for sense impressions.

However, it does not follow from the fact that Humean empiricism is not viable that empiricism is not viable. The falsity or incoherence of phenomenalism does not establish the falsity or incoherence of empiricism. MacIntyre's argument will not bear the weight he puts on it. Once we delete the phenomenalism—as Carnap later did, for example—it is hardly decisive even against the general structure of argument in Ayer's *Language, Truth and Logic*, his "Elimination of Metaphysics," or Carnap's early "The Elimination of Metaphysics Through Logical Analysis of Language." The verification criterion as set out in those works and as expressed by me in (4) owes nothing to phenomenalism or to the claim that descriptive terms must in the end, if they are to be meaningful (that is, genuine descriptive terms), rest entirely on ostensive definition. There is no need for the empiricist to believe in a private language where 'descriptive meaning' is determined for each individual solely on the basis of his own private sense experience.

That and how this is so will be brought out as we examine (4).

(4)   A sentence in an ordinary idiom or capable at least in principle of being transformed into a grammatically well-formed sentence or set of sentences in an ordinary idiom, is meaningful if and only if a statement or proposition made by its use (its employment) is at least verifiable in principle.

A defender of this could be a nonphenomenalist (some are) and accept the Wittgensteinian insight that words do not generally, if ever, get their meaning simply through ostensive definition. He could adopt such a position and still consistently argue that what purports to be a statement of fact is indeed a genuine statement of fact only if it is confirmable or infirmable—testable in terms of what human beings could experience, concept-encrusted though all experience be.

We could have no reason to believe that any putative factual statement was either true or false and thus capable of doing what it purports to do—namely, convey information—if we had no idea of what experiences would count for or against its truth. If we have no idea of what it would be like for the statement to be true or false or even probably true or false, the statement is indeed an *ersatz* statement, that is, one we try to use to make a true or false claim but one without any literal significance.[14] Note that such a claim—right or wrong—does not commit a person to phenomenalism or to the myth of the given, and it allows for a *certain* relativism of conceptual categories.

What (4) and the preceding statement do is to give us to understand that scientific and commonsense factual statements are testable and thus can justifiably be said to be informative, while metaphysical statements are not so testable and thus are cognitively meaningless jargon. Metaphysical statements purport to make true or false claims, but since we can never have the slightest evidence for whether they are true or false, we do not understand what claims they make. And if indeed nothing counts for or against their truth, they in reality make no intelligible cognitive claim at all. For a statement to be a genuine factual statement, it must in the sense specified in (4) be confirmable or infirmable. And for a sentence so to function, it must have descriptive terms that apply in some situations and do not apply in others. In short, a statement made by the employment of that sentence must at least be confirmable or infirmable in principle. It is this essential claim that empiricism makes, and it is not touched by the justified rejection of the empiricist doctrine of ostensive definition or the 'Fido'-Fido criterion of meaning.[15]

There are some other criticisms, however, that are still generally thought to be definitive criticisms of even this formulation of empiricism.

But before turning in the next chapter to them and to possible empiricist counters, I want as a kind of coda to this chapter to give something more of the rationale of such vintage empiricism by exhibiting something of the argument in A. J. Ayer's classic "The Elimination of Metaphysics."[16]

III

Ayer defines 'metaphysics' as an inquiry into the nature of the reality "underlying or transcending the phenomena which the special sciences are content to study." To the charge that such a characterization of metaphysics is arbitrary or too parochial, Ayer replies that the metaphysician, unlike the plain man or the scientist, is not trying to gain his knowledge through empirical investigation, and unlike the mathematician and logician he is not content to make analytic statements. Rather, he is trying to attain a totally different kind of knowledge that is at once both synthetic and *a priori*. He is trying to attain a nonexperiential knowledge of matters of fact; he wants to attain a deeper and more fundamental knowledge of reality than anything we could attain from even the most systematic and theoretical of the sciences. He does not believe that we need to test the truth of our metaphysical claims in the way Peirce characterized. And, typically at least, he tries to seek a knowledge of some reality that transcends empirical, scientifically knowable reality.

Ayer argues that such knowledge is impossible and that metaphysics is a bogus discipline. He is not saying, as did Kant, that human beings are so limited that they can never gain any knowledge of 'supra-sensible metaphysical realities'. His point is that when we try to assert either 'There is a supra-sensible reality' or 'There is not a supra-sensible reality' that both sentences express 'pseudopropositions' and as such are devoid of cognitive meaning. (Ayer defines 'a pseudoproposition' as "a series of words that may seem to have the structure of a sentence but is in fact meaningless.") The basic thrust of his "The Elimination of Metaphysics" is to establish "that any attempt to describe the nature or even to assert the existence of something lying beyond the reach of empirical observation must consist in the enunciation of pseudo-propositions."

Ayer contends that when we ask about the meaning of a nonanalytic proposition or statement, we are trying to ascertain its truth conditions. That is to say, we are trying to discover the conditions under which it would be true and the conditions under which it would be false. If two verbally different sentences, 'Fanny is an illegitimate child' and 'Fanny is the child of an unmarried woman', have the same truth conditions, then they have the same cognitive meaning, although they may still differ in emotive meaning. (For example, 'There are black students at Uppsala' and 'There are niggers at Uppsala' differ in emotive meaning but not in cognitive meaning.) If someone maintains that there is more in the proposition 'X is a corylus' than there is in the proposition 'X is blue-eyed', then for his claim to be an intelligible one he must be able to show what this 'more' is by showing what conceivable verifiable difference there is between these two putative propositions. More generally, anything that purports to be a genuine proposition should be denied that status if no description or indication can be given of a situation that shows what it would be like to verify the proposition.

The *test* for whether a given group of words that are grammatically in place conveys a thought (expresses a genuine proposition) consists in whether it can be shown that this group of words is used to assert something that is or conceivably could be correctly labeled true or false. 'The stone is thinking about Vienna' and 'Crazy philosophers smoke icebergs' are cognitively meaningless for just this reason. But when and if we come to have some idea of how to verify them, they are no longer meaningless. (Recall how this worked in effect for our example, used in defending reductive materialism against Malcolm's criticisms: 'He talked to me last night from London' said by someone in New York before and after the invention of the telephone.)

By definition, metaphysical propositions are those that purport to make factual claims but are unverifiable even in principle. Since we cannot know what it would be like for such metaphysical claims to be either true or false, we literally cannot understand such claims. And we cannot understand them because in reality there is nothing to be understood, for they make no literal assertion since they have no truth conditions.

Ayer now faces a question that will immediately occur to anyone with the slightest historical sense. How is it that so many people, including the great classical philosophers, came to make metaphysical utterances if they are meaningless? The antimetaphysical arguments given here by Ayer are not terribly complex. Surely among metaphysicians there are many intelligent and reflective people. Could they have simply overlooked such considerations?

The reply Ayer gives us—and this is Carnap's reply as well—is that deep but thoroughly disguised emotional needs drive men to adopt metaphysical postures. Many men are not content merely to make observations, generalizations, predictions, and retrodictions and analyze concepts. They also desire a unified view of the world and wish to express their feelings about the world and man's fate. But for very understandable psychological reasons, they do not want to believe that they are merely expressing their attitudes about how things are. They want their view of the world to be rational and true and not just an emotional stance they and perhaps others as well take toward the world. For the reasons Ayer has brought forth, there can be no way for such metaphysical beliefs—such overviews—to be rationally justified. To face this squarely, given the deep human *need* to have such views of the world—to see how 'everything goes together'—is just too disquieting. Since this is so, people with these powerful metaphysical needs disguise this unpleasant reality from themselves in comforting metaphysical myths, which, of course, are not seen as myths by the people committed to them. Here language helps people along, for their utterances have the surface form of factual statements of a very general nature, but in reality these mystifying utterances are expressions of the emotions of their users.[17]

Here we have in bleak and uncompromising form a logical empiricist critique of metaphysics and a criterion of meaning. It corresponds closely to the criterion labeled as (4). In the present chapter we have seen that its Humean brother will not slay the metaphysical monster. In the next chapter we shall see whether the logical empiricist criterion (4) comes off any better.

NOTES

1. F. C. Copleston, *Contemporary Philosophy*, pp. 26–33, 42–44.
2. What I have to say about empiricism here has been influenced by and is in part a reaction against J. L. Evans, *The Foundations of Empiricism* and "On Meaning and Verification," *Mind,* vol. LXII (January, 1953), and chapter five of John Passmore's *Philosophical Reasoning*.
3. The classical references here are David Hume, *Treatise of Human Nature* and *Enquiry Concerning Human Understanding*. A. G. N. Flew has edited a useful and readily available volume, *Hume on Human Nature and the Understanding*. It contains all of the *Enquiry* and the epistemological section from the *Treatise*. Flew's essay "Hume," in D. J. O'Connor (ed.), *A Critical History of Western Philosophy*, and the article in the *Encyclopedia of Philosophy* (Paul Edwards, editor) on Hume provide sophisticated and comprehensive introductions to his thought. See also J. A. Passmore, *Hume's Intentions*. For volumes containing critical essays on Hume largely from a contemporary analytical standpoint, see D. F. Pears (ed.), *David Hume: A Symposium*; Alexander Sesonske and Noel Fleming (eds.), *Human Understanding: Studies in the Philosophy of David Hume*; and V. C. Chappell (ed.), *Hume: A Collection of Critical Essays*.
4. J. L. Evans, *The Foundations of Empiricism*, p. 11.
5. The major work here is Ludwig Wittgenstein's *Philosophical Investigations*. This profound and difficult book is not easy for someone without a considerable philosophical background to approach. In my judgment it is better to start with Wittgenstein's *The Blue Book*, although this is also rather inaccessible for anyone who lacks a certain philosophical background and orientation. The essential Wittgensteinian point we are developing about meaning here is put succinctly and elegantly by Gilbert Ryle in "The Theory of Meaning," in C. A. Mace (ed.), *British Philosophy in the Mid-Century*. (It is also reprinted in Charles E. Caton (ed.), *Philosophy and Ordinary Language*.) For reliable interpretive entrée into Wittgenstein, see Justus Hartnack, *Wittgenstein and Modern Philosophy* (elementary); George Pitcher, *The Philosophy of Wittgenstein* (somewhat more advanced); the essays by

Quinton, Malcolm, and Feyerabend in George Pitcher (ed.), *Wittgenstein: The Philosophical Investigations*, the article on Wittgenstein (written by Malcolm) in Paul Edwards (ed.), *The Encyclopedia of Philosophy*; and David Pears, "Ludwig Wittgenstein," *The New York Review of Books*, (January 16, 1969). There are other important essays in Pitcher's collection and a useful bibliography, but the ones listed above are good introductions to his thought. Reading some of this introductory material and then turning to Wittgenstein himself should make his work accessible and exciting, for his writing, unlike Hegel's or Heidegger's, is usually clear enough. The difficulty comes in seeing what he is up to and how it goes together.

6. See here the essays surrounding the topic of operational definitions in science in Arthur Danto and Sidney Morgenbesser (eds.), *The Philosophy of Science*, and Carl Hempel, *Aspects of Scientific Explanation*.

7. See the references in note 5.

8. In addition see here E. Daitz, "The Picture Theory of Meaning," *Mind*, (1953).

9. Ludwig Wittgenstein, *Philosophical Investigations*, pp. 13–14 and 16.

10. Statements and criticisms of phenomenalism are legion. Perhaps the best short account of what is at issue here is in Paul Marhenke, "Phenomenalism" in Max Black (ed.), *Philosophical Analysis*.

11. Alasdair MacIntyre, "Positivism in Perspective," *New Statesman* (April 2, 1960), p. 491.

12. It is precisely such an error—an error that is at the very heart of such an approach—that vitiates the phenomenological movement (not to be confused with phenomenalism) stemming from Edmund Husserl. The best brief statement of this position is in Edmund Husserl, *The Idea of Phenomenology*.

13. I owe this conception, as well as many of my ideas about appealing to ordinary language, to an independent, important, but neglected philosopher, Everett W. Hall. For the concept of the categorio-centric predicament, see E. W. Hall, *Categorial Analysis*, pp. 1–4, and *Philosophical Systems*, pp. 140–142.

14. It is worth noting that Father Copleston, opponent of empiricism and "the positivist mentality" that he is, seems at least to accept such a criterion. See F. C. Copleston, *Contemporary Philosophy*, pp. 58–60 and—though less clearly—on p. 46. Yet in other contexts he makes metaphysical claims that seem at least incompatible with such an empiricist criterion.

15. For crucial criticisms of this " 'Fido'-Fido" (Humean empiricist) criterion of meaning, see Evans, Ryle, and Daitz. See references in notes 2, 5, and 7.

16. A. J. Ayer, "Demonstration of the Impossibility of Metaphysics," *Mind* (1934). (It is reprinted in Paul Edwards and Arthur Pap (eds.) *A Modern Introduction to Philosophy*.) See also Ayer's "The Genesis of Metaphysics," in Margaret Macdonald (ed.), *Philosophy and Analysis*, and his "The Claims of Philosophy," in Maurice Natanson (ed.), *Philosophy and the Social Sciences*.

17. This is shown in a profound way by Axel Hägerström in his *Philosophy and Religion*, part III. I have also said something about this in my "On Speaking of God," *Theoria*, vol. XXVIII (1962), part 2, and in my "Religious Perplexity and Faith," *Crane Review*, vol. VIII, no. 1 (fall, 1963), pp. 1–17.

33

EMPIRICISM
AND THE VERIFICATION
PRINCIPLE: II

I

We have seen that there are crippling difficulties in even a contemporary version of Humean empiricism. It is not true that a word is meaningful only if it stands for an image or sense impression; it is not true that, exempting logical or topic neutral terms (for example, 'if', 'then', 'all', 'thus', 'most'), a term is meaningless or cognitively meaningless unless it is ostensively definable; and it is not true that a sentence is unintelligible—devoid of cognitive meaning or literal content—if all its topic neutral terms do not stand for sense impressions. But from this it does not follow that empiricism as articulated by Carnap, Schlick, and Ayer—their phenomenalism or one-time phenomenalism apart—is not a viable position and a good ground for eliminating metaphysics.

However, this variety of empiricism has also been subjected to extensive criticism. Indeed it is widely believed that these criticisms have been devastating to such a philosophical framework. To see what is at issue, let us come back to our formulation of the verifiability principle (4) and then to a heuristically useful simplification (4').

(4) A sentence in an ordinary idiom or capable in principle at least of being transformed into a grammatically well-formed sentence or set of sentences in an ordinary idiom, is meaningful if and only if a statement or proposition made by its use (its employment) is at least verifiable (confirmable or infirmable) in principle.

(4') A statement is meaningful (intelligible) only if it is at least verifiable in principle.

I shall initially use the shorter and less exact formulation (4') for two reasons: (1) it squares better with the terms of the actual debate and (2) it is simpler to refer to. But the problems to be discussed in the next two sections could be put in terms of (4), and in any final assessment of this core claim of logical empiricism, (4) is a more adequate statement of the verifiability criterion.

One of the most obvious objections to such a principle emerges from considering what I shall call 'the dangling-it problem'.[1] Consider this simple question: Don't we have to know what a statement or proposition *means* before we can set about verifying (confirming) whether it is true? It would seem that we would have to know or at least have some idea of what it means before we can know or have any idea of whether it is verifiable or not. But then meaning is indeed logically *prior* to verification. It is not and cannot be our litmus paper test of intelligibility, for only if we first understood it could we know whether it is indeed verifiable. Put more accurately and fully, the point against the verifiability principle is this: Where A (some person) believes p (some putative proposition) is verifiable by E, A must first know what p means in order to verify p, in order to know whether E or anything else verifies p. Since this is so, the meaning of a proposition or statement cannot be constituted by its being verifiable, for it is only possible to raise a question about whether a proposition or statement is verifiable when we already know its meaning. Thus, we must plainly give up the logical empiricist slogan that the meaning of a proposition is its method of verification. Unless we know what a proposition means we cannot possibly verify it. And with a recognition of the truth of this, we must also abandon the verifiability principle.

Even if those appealing to the verifiability criterion as a criterion of intelligibility were somehow to find a way around 'the dangling-it problem', there remain powerful arguments against taking the verifiability criterion in any form as an adequate *general* criterion of meaning. In an important article, which might be taken as another typical specimen of linguistic philosophy, G. J. Warnock argues correctly that all talk of verification must link closely with talk of truth and falsity.[2] But then he asks quite appropriately: "What are we to do with all those meaningful sentences which have no concern whatever with truth and falsity?" He goes on to observe:

Clearly there is an enormous number of such sentences. There are imperative sentences, used (mainly) to give orders; and interrogative sentences, used (mainly) to ask questions. There are sentences used as prayers; to make promises; to give verdicts; to express decisions; to pass moral judgments; or to make proposals. It is nonsensical to ask of a question, an order, a prayer, or a proposal, whether it is true or false. The judge who rules that the witness must answer the question cannot be told that what he says is untrue (and therefore it also cannot be said to be true); his ruling may be regarded as correct or improper, it may be disputed, accepted, upheld, or set aside; but it cannot be either verified or falsified. When the chairman says "I declare Mr. Jones elected," it would not be in place to question, or to affirm, the truth of what he says. It would be easy to multiply such instances as these. As soon as we think of the multifarious uses of language, it becomes glaringly obvious that there is a vast number of sentences in connection with which the question "Is it true or false?" is, in varying degrees, absurd or out of place. And to these sentences verification can have no possible application, however "weak" or "indirect". If it is nonsense and out of place to ask whether p is true or false, we cannot speak of a "method of verification" of p.

Warnock's remarks here surely are well taken. 'Pass the salt', 'What time does the train leave?', 'Please, dear', 'You must go to bed now', 'Drink to me only with thine eyes' are all perfectly intelligible, but no question about their truth or falsity can possibly arise—any fluent speaker must know that. There is no place at all here for philosophical controversy. If a person did not know that these things are so, we would not regard him as even competent in English.

Since no question about truth or falsity of these utterances can arise, and they plainly do not even purport to be true or false, no questiton can arise about their verification or verifiability, either. But they are obviously meaningful (intelligible) sentences with actual roles in our everyday language. What is now apparent, it is argued, is that in eliminating metaphysics, the logical empiricists have eliminated as well a good bit of our ordinary language—language that serves various essential human purposes without any mystification at all.

It is because questions, imperatives, commands, advice, legal injunctions, and the like serve such pervasive and indispensable purposes in human communication that we cannot reasonably take the high *a priori* road and simply assert that although those sentences are in our language, they are meaningless all the same. We understand such sentences and they surely have important uses. Moreover, if such an implicit stipulation were made and orders, rulings, questions, imperatives, and the like were declared meaningless, this, as Warnock points out, would in reality undermine the antimetaphysical thrust of the verification principle. It would "obliterate the vital distinction between, on the one hand, sentences which *pose* as being meaningful, which *purport* to make verifiable statements, and which are to be unmasked and condemned as impostors; and, on the other hand, sentences (e.g. imperatives) which do not even seem to be verifiable, true or false, and which because they make no false pretensions ought not to be condemned." And it will not do to say that only the verifiable statements have literal meaning, for clearly some questions and commands can have as literal a meaning as factual statements. They need not be at all emotive or metaphorical. So it is evident that the verifiability principle will not do as a general criterion of meaning—as a general litmus paper test—to distinguish sense from nonsense.

II

While Warnock's arguments surely show that the verifiability principle or verifiability criterion will not do as a general criterion of meaning, it does not follow from this, as Warnock is well aware, that it could not reasonably serve as a criterion of *factual* significance. That is to say, it still might be the case that the verifiability principle would give us a criterion for picking out those employments of language that make genuine factual assertions. It is plausible to argue that the actual intent of the logical empiricists was to provide us with a criterion for deciding whether a proposition or statement has factual significance.[3] So taken, we should reformulate (4') as (5') and (4) as (5).

(5')   A statement is a genuine factual statement if and only if it is at least verifiable in principle.

(5)   A sentence in an ordinary idiom or capable in principle at least of being transformed into a grammatically well-formed sentence or set of sentences in an ordinary idiom, can be used to make a genuine factual statement if and only if a statement made by its use (its employment) is at least verifiable (confirmable or infirmable) in principle.

In this section and the next I shall continue to talk about (5') for the same heuristic reason I talked about (4') rather than (4).

Does the verifiability principle in any formulation provide us with an adequate criterion of factual significance? There are many difficulties ahead. The first that we should consider is the dangling-it argument to which no verificationist reply has been made. Recall that this argument maintains that before I could think of possible ways of verifying a given proposition I must first know what it *means*. Otherwise, I would not know what I am trying to verify or what would or could verify my claim. This difficulty disappears once we give up the claim that the verifiability criterion is to serve as a general criterion of meaning. As a criterion of factual significance, it serves as a principle of demarcation, distinguishing within the corpus of meaningful sentences those declarative ones used to make genuine factual statements from those employments of language that purport to make factual claims but are in reality pseudo-factual, that is, statements that purport to be factual—true or false assertions about what there is—but actually fail to have factual significance because they have no truth conditions and thus we have no idea of what counts or could count toward establishing or disestablishing their truth.

There is no dangling-it problem here, for from within the class of admittedly intelligible uses of language, criterion (5')—and (5), of course, as well—serves as a criterion for distinguishing those employments of language that are factually assertive or that give or can give empirical information from those that are not. We properly employ (5') or (5) only when we *in some sense* already understand the utterance (we can paraphrase it and the like) we are trying to test with our criterion, but are concerned to know whether the utterance is being employed in a factually assertive way. Surely I must in some way understand what is said before I can verify a statement made by its use; but I also know that unless the statement is verifiable (confirmable or infirmable) I could not know what it would be like for it to be true or false or probable or improbable. Thus, I could not know what it would be like for it to be the case and what it would be like for it not to be the case. But if this is so, I cannot possibly know the state of affairs that the putative factual proposition allegedly characterizes. Then the statement is for me without factual content, for I have no understanding of what it asserts or denies or what conceivable experiences it allegedly describes. If the sentence is such that no one could possibly be in a better position that I am, then the antimetaphysical party (or at least its empiricist wing) maintains the sentence is devoid of factual significance.

III

Getting around the dangling-it problem is only one of the hurdles for the defender of the verifiability criterion. There is, for example, the difficulty about the status of the verifiability principle itself. Note that (5) and (5′) appear to be themselves statements or propositions. But then on empiricist principles they must either be analytic or, if they are statements of fact, they must be verifiable. If they are neither they are not genuine statements at all. But it has been frequently argued against logical empiricists that the verifiability principle is itself neither analytic nor empirical.[4] Then on the very criteria of meaning logical empiricists adopt, it must be a metaphysical statement devoid of all cognitive meaning. The logical empiricists appear at least to be hoisted by their own petard.

I shall now explain why a principle such as (5′) is said to be neither analytic nor empirical. First suppose we try to take it as analytic. If it is analytic, it must be self-contradictory to deny it. However, if we can produce paradigmatic statements in an ordinary idiom in which it is not a deviation from a linguistic regularity to say that something is factual but unverifiable even in principle, then (5′) and other standard formulations of the verifiability principle as well would have been shown to be nonanalytic. It is argued that it is easy to produce such paradigmatic statements. Surely it is not a deviation from a linguistic regularity—that is, there is nothing linguistically odd about it so that a native speaker would balk at such a sentence—to say 'The statement that God created the heavens and the earth is completely unverifiable but nonetheless it is a factual statement'.

The following two utterances are likewise plainly a part of the corpus of English, but they would be as unintelligible as is 'Johnson sleeps faster than Nixon' if (5') were analytic: 'That I dreamt of my maternal aunt is completely unverifiable, but nonetheless it is a fact that I did dream of her' and 'It is logically impossible to confirm or disconfirm that every body in the universe, including our measuring rods, is constantly expanding, the rate of expansion being exactly the same for all bodies; but such a statement is a meaningful, although absurdly false, factual statement'. Given the intelligibility of these paradigms, it is evident (5') is not analytic. That is, from examining the use of (5'), one can see that unlike 'All Protestants are Christians' it is not analytic—it is not true by definition.

Of course, we could *make* it true by definition by making suitable stipulations. But the metaphysician is free to make his stipulations too, and so such stipulations would solve nothing. What would solve something is to show that (5') is true by lexical definition—as fathers are male parents is true by definition—but our paradigms show that this is plainly not the case. (These examples also seem at least to show that (5) is not analytic.)

Why is it not the case that the verifiability criterion is an empirical generalization? If it were we would be claiming that (5') and (5) are verifiable. However, it is not treated in this way by logical empiricists, and if we do so interpret the verifiability criterion, it can again be seen to be plainly false. Note that to treat it as being itself verifiable is to treat it as being parallel to these two statements.

A. All men who are called 'bachelors' are also said to be 'unmarried men'.

B. All things that are said to be 'red' would also be said to be 'colored'.

But consider this statement:

C. All statements that are said to be 'factual statements' are also said to be 'statements that are verifiable in principle'.

This cannot be true, for the preceding paradigmatic sentences used in arguing that the verifiability criterion is not analytic also plainly disconfirm C. There are some statements that are said by some native speakers at least to be factual statements but are not said to be verifiable statements. So, as a statement concerning statements about the language, C can plainly be shown to be false. Thus, if the verifiability principle is itself taken to be an empirical claim, it is obviously a false claim.

If we say by way of reply that the crucial test is not what people *say* about their language but how they actually use it, (5) can still be seen to be a false empirical claim, if it is taken as an empirical claim, for some speakers use 'God created the heavens and the earth' in such a way that it is completely unverifiable and yet it appears at least to be factual. Without begging the question, we cannot rule it out as a disconfirming instance by denying that it is a genuinely factual statement. To simply assert that it cannot be factual because it is not verifiable is to go in a circle.

So if (5') or the verification criterion generally is taken as an empirical statement, it is a false empirical statement. Thus, it is argued, since it is neither analytic nor empirical and true, it must be either rejected as a false empirical claim, said to be cognitively meaningless (which would undermine empiricism), or said to be a metaphysical statement itself (which would also undermine empiricism by bringing into the very philosophical approach that is trying to eliminate metaphysics a metaphysical principle of its own). No matter which way they turn, logical empiricists seem to be refuted.

However, again, the logical empiricists have a standard answer to this objection. Ayer brings it out in his debate with Father Copleston.[5] The verifiability criterion, Ayer grants, is neither analytic nor empirical. In fact, it is not a descriptive statement at all and it is not—logic forbid!—a metaphysical principle. Instead, it is what Ayer calls a *persuasive* definition that functions in human discourse as a recommendation that people adopt a certain criterion of meaning.

This is highfalutin talk and needs an explanation. What is Ayer claiming here? He is maintaining that we should construe the criterion 'A statement is a meaningful factual statement if and only if it is verifiable (confirmable and infirmable) in principle' as this recommendation: 'Let us take as factually meaningful (significant) statements all those statements and only those statements that are at least verifiable (confirmable or infirmable) in principle'. This plainly is a proposal about what *to take* as having factual significance or content, just as the following is a recommendation or proposal about how to behave in class: 'Let us not all talk at once. Let us (teacher excluded) only talk after raising our hands and after being acknowledged by our instructor'. Neither recommendation can be said to be true or false, confirmable or disconfirmable, although such recommendations may be good or bad, useful or useless, arbitrary or reasonable. By so construing the verifiability criterion, Ayer has avoided the criticisms that the verifiability criterion is itself a metaphysical principle devoid of all cognitive meaning. It is not a factual statement or a putative factual statement at all, but a proposal. As such, it is a perfectly intelligible although nonfactual use of language.

There is yet another move in this particular dialectic. Faced with this defense on the part of logical empiricists, some critics have pointed out that metaphysicians and nonempiricists can make recommendations too. Why accept Ayer's recommendations? Why adopt the logical empiricist's meaning criterion for factual statements?

Ayer's reply to this should be examined. He maintains that if we are clear about what it is to understand a factual assertion, we will accept such a persuasive definition. Ayer remarks: "I understand a statement of fact if I know what to look for on the supposition that it is true. And my knowing what to look for is itself a matter of my being able to interpret the statement as referring at least to some possible experience."[6] If we adopt, instead, the metaphysician's criterion that allows as well that there are intelligible metaphysical statements underlying science and common sense that are "ultimate explanations of fact" that tell us about 'ultimate reality' (whatever that means), we must accept something that is mystifying. That is to say, we will have no criterion in virtue of which we could decide whether such metaphysical claims are true or false. But sticking to the verifiability criterion, we can fix our beliefs in an objective way. Thus, it is plainly a more useful and more reasonable criterion to adopt.

To press Ayer's rather cryptic remarks a little further: Consider examples of putative statements of fact that you are sure you understand, and then consider examples that you do not understand. Are not the ones you plainly and obviously understand actually all cases of verifiable statements? And are not the clear cases of nonsense—for example, 'It is ten o'clock on Mars' or 'Red wine talks endlessly'—examples of statements that you have no idea at all how to verify, statements you do not at all know what to look for on the supposition that they are true? And are not borderline cases—for example, 'I shall survive the death of my body'—cases of statements in which you are unsure what (if anything) would or would not count for or against their being true? However, to the extent we can conceive what it would be like to verify them—what experiences count for or against their truth—do we not understand them? Consider for yourselves, one by one, the troubling borderline cases of philosophical interest. If it is plain that they are completely unverifiable, is it not also reasonable to say that they are not factual statements? That we on careful examination should indeed say that, as I believe we should, is one of the grounds for accepting Ayer's recommendation.[7]

Part of our trouble with such metaphysical monsters as 'Being is one and not many', 'Existence precedes essence', 'The good is beyond all being' is that we do not know even how to paraphrase them or transform them into an ordinary idiom. And if we were to make some stab at a transformation into an ordinary idiom, we would have no idea whether our paraphrase was correct. But if we had some idea of what would count for or against their truth, we would precisely to that extent have some understanding of such strange utterances.

See if you can think of an utterance that you understand and that you would *unequivocally* take to be a bit of fact-stating discourse and for which you can conceive of nothing—not even anything you could con-

ceivably experience—that would count either for or against its truth. I am confident that you will fail. And if you do fail, then do we not have good grounds for adopting Ayer's criterion? Does it not clearly bring out what it is to understand a statement of fact?

IV

There have been many who have taken up this challenge and who have maintained that there are some statements that empiricists and non-empiricists would accept as factual that are not verifiable. In addition, it is claimed that in adjusting the statement of the verifiability criterion to accommodate these statements, it has been so weakened that it will no longer exclude the Teutonic camels and support the antimetaphysical party. We will now examine what is at issue here.

In this connection there is the objection made by C. I. Lewis, Stace, and Copleston, among others, that to adopt the verifiability criterion as a criterion of factual significance has the unacceptable consequence of requiring us to say that certain everyday or scientific statements we pre-analytically recognize to be factual are in actuality not factual.[8] This supposedly would be true for (5) as well as for (5'). Consider these two statements:

E.   Caesar had an affair with Cleopatra.

F.   There were dinosaurs before there were men.

We plainly understand them; to say they are meaningless or without cognitive meaning or literal content is absurd. The verificationist, it has been argued, will say they are actually equivalent to:

E'.   Old chronicles record that Caesar had an affair with Cleopatra.

F'.   There are fossil remains of dinosaurs from periods earlier than any fossil remains of man.

or to a set of sentences of the same type as E' or F'. But again this will not do, for clearly we could in logical consistency assert E' and deny E, and assert F' and deny F. The chronicles might record lies, and there might have been men roaming about even though we now have no fossil remains of them. Furthermore, E and F are statements about the past, while E' and F' and statements of that type are statements about the present. If we assert such equivalents and generalize them, we have committed ourselves to the absurdity of saying that statements about the past are really statements about the present.

There is an adequate reply to this criticism of the verifiability principle. The verificationist must indeed deny that that there is an equivalence between E and E' and F and F'. They indeed do not have the same meaning. Moreover, we must avoid the confusion of identifying the meaning of a statement, say E, with the evidence for that statement, say E'. Things like E' indirectly verify E, and although we cannot in fact directly verify E, it is not *logically* impossible directly to verify E or for that matter F. If we had been alive when Caesar and Cleopatra were alive and in the correct location, we could have directly verified E. And it is not a logical truth but an empirical truth that we were not and could not have been alive then.

Logical empiricists and other verificationists have never insisted on practical, technical verifiability as a criterion of meaning (factual significance), but only on the logical possibility of verification (confirmation and infirmation). And it is *logically* possible that we could have directly verified E and F or any statement about the past. This is why the verificationists talk about verifiability *in principle*, that is, the logical possibility of verification.

The point of this is to stress that for a proposition to make a genuine factual claim it must be logically possible to cite observations that count for or against its truth. It need not be the case that we could actually specify such evidence; rather, for the proposition to have factual significance, there must be no *conceptual ban*, as there is for imperatives or analytic statements, on looking for empirical evidence for its truth or falsity. What is ruled out is the claim that a factual proposition can be true or false even though it is *logically* impossible to specify any empirical evidence *relevant* to its truth or falsity. Such a proposition is not a factual proposition but a pseudofactual proposition.

However, there are other classes of plainly factual statements which, it has been alleged, are not even verifiable in principle. Copleston gives an example in his debate with Ayer.[9] Suppose someone asserts this:

G.   Nuclear warfare will take place, and it will blot out the entire human race.

Copleston rightly remarks that the utterance is plainly intelligible and that it makes a factual claim. Any theory that denies either contention is plainly wrong. But Copleston also claims it is not even verifiable in principle, for if the prediction were to be fulfilled there would, in terms of the very prediction, be no one to verify it. If there were anyone to verify it, it would automatically be false. We cannot possibly—and the force of 'possibly' here is logical—know it to be true.

It could be replied that some Martians, some nonhuman but humanoid observers, could verify it, or human beings could later spring up again out of the slime and verify it. However, such objections hardly get to the intent or heart of Copleston's objections. He only needs to make the statement a little more general:

H.   After tomorrow all sentient life will be destroyed everywhere forever.

But again, while H is absurd, we understood it when it was uttered. It is not like 'Procrastination drinks conservative' or 'Pencils ordered wine'. I understand it and (so Copleston would say) immediately recognize, in understanding it, that it is unverifiable even in principle. Note that the very conditions of the statement (or so it would seem) rule out the possibility of anyone verifying it.

However, both G and H are verifiable (confirmable and infirmable at least in principle), although like many statements they are not *decisively* verifiable. Carnap and Ayer, in defending verifiability, do not defend it in such a strong sense. In saying that for a statement to be a factual statement it must be verifiable, they only intend to claim that for a putative factual statement to be a genuine factual statement some kind of observation(s) must be relevant to its truth or falsehood.[10] That is, they only require that it be logically possible to conceive of some experiences that would count for or against the truth or falsity of the alleged factual proposition. But surely plenty of things count for the truth or falsity of G and H—for example, information about fallout, blast, winds and the effects of radiation and the like, and for H the astronomical improbability of the effect going throughout the whole of solar space.

The same type of considerations should be brought to bear against similar criticisms of the verifiability criterion which turn on the claim that universal statements, existential statements, and statements with mixed quantifiers are all unverifiable in one way or another. The philosophical jargon is new to you and I do not want to take time to explain it here, so let me cite examples of each kind of statement and show why they have been said to be be unverifiable.[11] Note again that each sample statement is a factual statement, and each statement is plainly intelligible.

I.   All Irishmen drink whiskey.

J.   Some human beings have natural green skin.

K.   Every substance has some solvent.

We could decisively falsify statement I but we could never decisively verify it, for we could not know whether we had examined all Irishmen or even (given that we did not specify a given time and locale to limit the class) a fair sample. Statement J, by contrast, is decisively verifiable: One such human being is enough. But it is not decisively falsifiable, for since J only says 'some', the person asserting it need not retract it no matter how long we look, for perhaps someplace somewhere, and sometime there is such a person. K, which is the most important counterexample, is neither conclusively verifiable nor conclusively falsifiable. We do not know when we have examined every substance. After all, we did not say 'every known substance in Delaware during the year 1969'. And even if we find a substance that resists being dissolved in any solvent we now have or can imagine, the defender of the truth of K need only reply that he simply asserted 'some solvent'.

However, I, J, K, like G and H, only show that there are some factual statements that are not *decisively* verifiable (confirmable or infirmable). But neither the meaning criterion for factual statements as I put it, nor as Ayer and Carnap have finally stated it, falls prey to these objections. Recall that for a statement to be factual it is only maintained that some observations be relevant to the truth or falsity of the statements in question. But for I, J, and K some observations are plainly relevant to their truth or falsity. Even K, which in principle is neither conclusively establishable nor confutable, is a statement for which some experiences are relevant to its truth. If we had a substance known for as long as substances were known and nothing dissolved it, we would have some slight reason for thinking that K was false. Certainly such observations are relevant to its truth.

Thus, the verifiability criterion stated in (5) and as Ayer has finally stated it is not refuted by such standard criticisms. However, the considerations brought out in this last paragraph point to an important fact, namely, the failure of the attempt, important in the history of logical empiricism, to state the verifiability criterion in a stronger way, such that a statement has factual significance if and only if it is itself an observation statement or it entails certain observation statements (statements referring to what is directly observable). To argue for a stronger relationship is to contend that for any statement to be a factual statement it must be such that certain statements about what is observed or observable follow from it by logical necessity. But this is plainly not true for statement K, and it can be shown not to hold for other statements as well. That is to say, without contradiction we could assert 'All human beings have some neurotic traits' no matter what we observe or could observe. There is no entailment here. Moreover, as Friedrich Waismann has powerfully and convincingly argued in his "Verifiability," no statement about a physical object (say a pen or typewriter) entails any observation statement such that to suppose the first to be true and the second false would be self-contradictory.[12] But the preceding statements of the verifiability criterion were so stated that there was no such requirement of entailment for factual significance. All that was required was that there be some empirical evidence, something observed or observable, which would be relevant to the truth or falsity of the statement in question.

V

It would not be unnatural to take this 'victory' of empiricism as a pyrrhic victory. And it is understandable why the logical empiricists struggled so valiantly to state the criterion in terms of entailment, for without it we seem at least to have so opened the floodgates that the antimetaphysical party, if it stands its grounds here, will be completely swamped. Isaiah Berlin touches the heart of the matter when he remarks that if we assert that for a statement to have factual significance it must be such that some observations be relevant to the determination of its truth or falsehood, this may well be true, but

> as it stands the suggested criterion is far too vague to be of use. Relevance is not a precise logical category, and fantastic metaphysical systems may choose to claim that observation data are 'relevant' to their truth. Such claims cannot be rebutted unless some precise meaning is assigned to the concept of relevance, which because the word is used to convey an essentially vague idea cannot be done.[13]

This weakness has led to the demand for a statement of the criterion in terms of entailment, that is: a statement has factual significance if and only if it is itself an observation statement or entails an observation statement or set of observation statements. But, as is now generally agreed, such a criterion fails even in its more refined statements.[14] So it would appear that the verifiability criterion cannot slay the metaphysical monster. Weakened as it has been, it appears to be a correct criterion, but it no longer appears to be a useful weapon for empiricist antimetaphysics.

Is there any even partial rebuttal to this argument? I neither think the dialectic of the argument should stop here nor that the empiricist has his hands tied. (Here I should warn you, and record as a sociological fact about present-day analytic philosophers, that I am in something of a minority position on this point.) I think empiricists should concede that the principle of verifiability cannot be stated in a satisfactory manner in terms of the deductive logician's concepts alone. That is to say, we cannot define the verifiability principle in terms of a principle that maintains a statement is verifiable if and only if it entails certain observation statements. Moreover, I do not know of any very successful attempt at a formal or precise statement of a criterion of relevance, and I am not at present able to give one.[15] But it also seems evident that there is no fundamental conceptual reason standing in the way of giving such a criterion of relevance. However, there are some things that can be said that may pave the way for the stating of such a criterion and will, I believe, very considerably strengthen the empiricist's position here.

We know that a statement has factual significance only if evidence can be produced that is relevant to its truth. Thus, if we have two putative factual statements, p and not-p, we know (no matter how unspecified 'relevance' remains) that there must be some evidence relevant to the truth of p that is not relevant to the truth of not-p, if these putative factual statements are indeed genuine factual statements. Otherwise we could not distinguish a statement from its denial (we could not distinguish

p from not-p) and p, as well as not-p, would indeed be devoid of significance. If p is 'Sensations are brain processes' and not-p is 'It is not the case that sensations are brain processes', it must be possible at least in principle to state certain empirically determinable states of affairs that would justify one in asserting p and certain contrasting empirically determinable states of affairs in which one will be justified in asserting not-p. If this does not obtain, it will be impossible correctly to assert of such putative factual propositions that there is evidence relevant to their truth. After all, if such a possibility is closed, it will be logically impossible to decide, even tentatively or probabilistically, what it would be like for the alleged assertion or its denial to be true. But if they are both equally compatible with anything and everything that we could even conceivably observe, then we (1) cannot (except verbally) distinguish between them and (2) no observations can be relevant to their truth or falsity.

We seem to have a necessary condition for the *relevance* of observation statements to the truth or falsity of other factual statements. This is important, for we saw with nonanthropomorphic God-talk that the assertion and the denial of 'There is a God' or 'God created the heavens and the earth' are equally compatible with any conceivable bit of empirical evidence. (Recall here the arguments for this in Chapter 21.) Thus, no evidence is relevant to their truth, and we have good grounds for maintaining that such allegedly factual propositions are devoid of factual significance. In section VI of Chapter 21, I raised the objection that I employ a criterion of factual significance that is too narrow in my argument that nonanthropomorphic God-talk is devoid of factual significance. I think, attempting now to make good on my promissory note from that earlier chapter, I have with (5) stated a version of the empiricist criterion that is neither arbitrary nor so narrow as to exclude evident factual statements, and yet sufficiently restricted to exclude in a non-*ad hoc* and non-arbitrary manner nonanthropomorphic God-talk.

It is not only the putative statements of metaphysical religiosity that come under my strictures but other genuinely metaphysical talk, or at least metaphysical talk of a certain transcendentalist genre as well. Consider these examples from Karl Jaspers' *Vernunft und Existenz.*[16]

1. Being itself is the Transcendence which shows itself to no investigative experience, not even indirectly.
2. Rather this Encompassing which I am and know as empirical existence, consciousness as such, as spirit, is not conceivable in itself but refers beyond itself.
3. Existence is the Encompassing, not in the sense of a horizon, of all horizons, but rather in the sense of a fundamental origin, the condition of selfhood without which all the vastness of Being becomes a desert.

If we have no idea of what it would be like to have or gain evidence for or against these claims, we have no idea of what they assert. Intelligibility admits of degrees, and it is not clear that these utterances are *utterly* without sense, for we understand what they assert (if indeed they assert anything) to the extent that we understand what evidence would be relevant to their truth or falsity. If we deny that any evidence does or could count for or against their truth, we then do not understand what states of affairs (facts) they allegedly assert. If we rule out by conceptual fiat the possibility that certain experienceable states of affairs are relevant to their truth and that certain states of affairs count against their truth, we in effect let it be known that they are devoid of factual significance.

Consider seriously yet critically Jaspers' high-sounding metaphysical utterances. Is it not the case that until we have some idea about how to transform them into an ordinary idiom and until we can state what would count for or against their truth, they remain nonassertive and without substantive content? That is, we do not understand what they allegedly assert. Note, as a parenthetical remark, again keeping in mind that intelligibility admits of degrees, that in this respect (1) is slightly less incoherent than (2) and (3). Statement (1) may well mean—bombast aside —something quite similar to what is meant by the following ordinary language statement, which, given an anthropomorphic reading, is itself not utterly unintelligible: 'Supernatural realities are not even observable'. (However, one cannot be at all confident that this is what Jaspers meant, and this is just one of the difficulties.) But (2) and (3) are rather more resistant to a reading—to a transformation or paraphrase into an ordinary idiom—which would make them intelligible.

Perhaps I am not being imaginative enough, but I cannot confidently give a paraphrase in an ordinary idiom, or for that matter in any idiom, which I am even remotely confident expresses what (2) or (3) says. I do not understand, even when I study the context in which they occur, what is or is not relevant to their truth or falsity, what is the difference between asserting and denying them. Thus, I do not understand them or, rather, do not understand how they could be factual assertions, could be assertions that something is the case. In order for them to have such a status there must be some at least conceivable observations relevant to their truth or falsity. If this does not obtain, then they will not be cosmological factual assertions: very general statements that are true or false statements about the world. If I am right in thinking that this inability to paraphrase (2) and (3) is not just an eccentricity with me but generally obtains, then just to that degree Jaspers' claims are devoid of factual significance.

There is a further feature that helps us at least in a negative sense to gain some perspective on what is relevant and what is not. Where we have allegedly referring expressions (expressions that are characteristically employed referentially)—for example, 'God,' 'the Encompassing,' 'Being' —which do not succeed in referring, we have no idea of what they could possibly stand for. That is, in trying to ascertain what they do refer to, we are at an utter loss, for we have no idea at all what it would be like to identify what they supposedly refer to. With reference to whatever it is that we are supposedly talking about when we use, say, 'the Encompassing', we do not understand what must transpire such that we could in theory at least identify something as existing, if there is something which the term refers to, or not existing, if there is in fact not anything of whatever it is that is being talked about. In this respect at least, 'God' and 'the Encompassing' are very different from 'brain processes', 'C-fibers', and 'pains' or even 'electron'. Moreover, they are quite different from terms that do not even purport to refer—for example, 'if', 'and', 'purport', 'moreover', 'which'—for they actually *purport* to refer but do not meet the conditions an expression must meet to be a genuine referring expression. I say this because we have no way of identifying what would count as a referent of such a term, and thus 'God' and 'the Encompassing' are bogus referring expressions. Sentences with bogus referring expressions and in the declarative mood are also sentences where we have no idea of what is relevant to their truth or falsity, and thus they are devoid of factual significance.

Such a conception of a bogus referring expression would not rule out such plainly meaningful terms as 'electron' or 'positron', for we have already seen in the last chapter for 'electron'—and similar things could be said for 'positron'—that they do make reference to empirically determinable realities. And where, as perhaps is the case with 'neutrino', no question about such a reference can arise—logically—we regard it as a purely theoretical nonreferring expression that indeed does not stand for a reality or set of realities but has another role in scientific discourse.

I have not here committed the mistake of the Humean criterion—criterion (3)—criticized in the previous chapters, for I am not arguing that all terms or even all nonsyncategormatic terms must be so characterizable to be meaningful, but only that those which are genuine referring expressions must so function. When we discover a sentence that has such bogus referring expressions, we do not and cannot know what counts for or against its truth or falsity, and thus we do not understand the putative assertion in question. That is, we do not understand it as what it purports to be, namely, an assertion.

In this section I have tried to show that, in spite of the fact that we cannot correctly define 'factual significance' in terms of statements entailing observation statements, and even with the criterion of relevance remaining vague and not sharply circumscribed, the verifiability criterion as I stated it—that is, (5)—has sufficient rigor and a discernible enough rationale to make some reasonable determinations concerning what it makes sense to assert. This, thought through, still gives the verifiability criterion some considerable force in eliminating metaphysical claims.

NOTES

1. Gilbert Ryle, "The Verification Principle," *Revue Internationale de Philosophie*, vol. 5 (1951), pp. 243–250. This objection has been used by George Mavrodes as his central criticism of my verificationist arguments about key segments of God-talk. See George Mavrodes, "God and Verification," *Canadian Journal of Theology*, vol. X (1964), pp. 187–191. But see my reply "God and Verification Again," *Canadian Journal of Theology*, vol. XI (1965), pp. 135–141.

2. G. J. Warnock, "Verification and the Use of Language," in Paul Edwards and Arthur Pap (eds.), *A Modern Introduction to Philosophy*. This is a reprint with slight revisions from *Revue Internationale de Philosophie*, vol. 5 (1951).

3. That this is the case is particularly evident in Herbert Feigl's summary statement and defense of logical empiricism in D. D. Runes (ed.), *Twentieth Century Philosophy*, and again in his more recent account of logical empiricism in his "The *Wiener Kreis* in America," in *Perspectives in American History*, vol. II, pp. 651–659.

4. E. L. Mascall, *Words and Images*, pp. 1–14, and A. C. Ewing "Meaninglessness", *Mind* (1937), reprinted in Paul Edwards and Arthur Pap (eds.), *A Modern Introduction to Philosophy*, op. cit., pp. 705–714.

5. A. J. Ayer and F. C. Copleston, "Logical Positivism—A Debate," in Paul Edwards and Arthur Pap (eds.), *A Modern Introduction to Philosophy*, ibid., pp. 726–756.

6. *Ibid.*

7. This appeal to 'what we should say when' is not simply an appeal to empirical facts about how we would talk in any sense in which it is not also about the world. In raising such a consideration we are in effect making an appeal to our fellow human beings; we are giving them to understand that we believe that if they would dwell on just what we are saying in just such a context, then they would come to see, as Stanley Cavell puts it, that "we would have spoken for all men, found the necessities common to us all." We can, of course, easily go wrong here, but this is what we are attempting to do with such a 'linguistic move'. See Stanley Cavell's important and perceptive remarks on this in "Aesthetic Problems of Modern Philosophy," in Max Black (ed.), *Philosophy in America*, pp. 96–7.

8. The most important of these critiques is C. I. Lewis's "Experience and Meaning," *Philosophical Review* (1934). It is replied to by M. Schlick in his "Meaning and Verification," *Philosophical Review* (1936). Both of these classic essays are reprinted in Herbert Feigl and Wilfred Sellars (eds.), *Readings in Philosophical Analysis*. The essay by Warnock cited in note 2 contains important criticisms of Schlick's account. For traditional criticisms of the verifiability criterion discussed here, see also W. T. Stace, "Metaphysics and Meaning" and the Copleston-Ayer debate, both reprinted in Paul Edwards and Arthur Pap (eds.), *A Modern Introduction to Philosophy*, op. cit.

9. See the Copleston-Ayer debate, op. cit., p. 746. See Copleston's further and in effect concessive remarks in his *Contemporary Philosophy*, p. 46.

10. Ayer's remark in the Copleston-Ayer debate, op. cit., p. 754.

11. These arguments are stated and carefully discussed in Carl Hempel "The

Empiricist Criterion of Meaning," in A. J. Ayer (ed.), *Logical Positivism*, pp. 108–129, and by David Rynin, "The Vindication of Logical Positivism," *Proceedings and Addresses of the American Philosophical Association*, vol. XXX (1957), and in "Cognitive Meaning and Cognitive Use," *Inquiry*, vol. 9 (summer, 1966), pp. 109–131.

12. Friedrich Waismann, *How I See Philosophy*, pp. 39–66.
13. Isaiah Berlin, "Verification," in G. H. R. Parkinson (ed.), *The Theory of Meaning*, pp. 15–34.
14. See the references in note 11, and for a brief but clear statement of the reasoning here see Alvin Plantinga, *God and Other Minds*, pp. 156–168.
15. Such an attempt has been interestingly made by David Rynin. See the second reference to him in note 11.
16. They are taken from the English translation in Walter Kaufmann (ed.), *Existentialism from Dostoevsky to Sartre*, pp. 191–192.

34

METAPHYSICS AND
THE APPEAL TO
ORDINARY LANGUAGE: I

I

I have argued that the verifiability criterion in any form will never do as a *general* criterion of what it makes sense to say. But I also argued, against the current philosophical stream, that the verifiability criterion suitably stated is a good criterion for whether a statement is a factual one. I also argued that such a criterion is a useful tool in the elimination of metaphysics. This is now generally thought *not* to be so, so you should be forewarned that my contention is a minority view. Moreover, we should keep in mind that 'metaphysics' means different things to different people, as we shall see. But, to use Ayer's way of putting it, where 'metaphysics' signifies a systematic effort to gain knowledge of the world by nonscientific or nonempirical means, or—to put it in a more technical way—where a metaphysical claim is taken to be a nonnormative *synthetic a priori* truth, my defense of the verifiability criterion would, if correct, exclude such metaphysics.

Father Copleston has talked in such a context of what he calls "a general positivist mentality" that includes many scientifically oriented philosophers who would not accept the verifiability criterion of meaning, but who would hold that all that can be known about the world can be known by means of science and that there is no higher, nonempirical, nonscientific knowledge of the world. People who have this attitude believe it is only the sciences together with commonsense *empirical* observation that give us definite knowledge about man and the world. Metaphysics, whatever else it may do, does not and cannot do this.[1]

If my arguments about the verifiability criterion have been correct, then such a general positivistic mentality is justified. It may be justified anyway, but my arguments provide a definite theoretical underpinning for it. That is to say, if my arguments are even near to their mark, a speculative metaphysics such as argued for by the Thomists or classical rationalists cannot be correct, and a speculative philosophy that "reveals the limits of science" and gives us a knowledge of 'ultimate reality' or 'the Absolute' would be impossible.

II

There are, however, many analytic philosophers—philosophers who would turn a wary and sceptical eye on speculative philosophy—who are not nearly so sanguine about the verifiability criterion as I am. Some of them even doubt that it provides an adequate criterion for fact-stating discourse. Yet, some of these philosophers themselves have remained anti-metaphysical philosophers. They simply believe, as do Ludwig Wittgenstein and John Austin (the two most distinguished of such philosophers), that such positivist or empiricist antimetaphysics is itself metaphysical. They share the logical empiricists' hostility to the pretensions of traditional metaphysics, but they distrust their methods of argument and their vast summary conclusions. Austin, for example, regarded logical empiricism, for all its down-to-earth intentions, as just another metaphysical theory, marked by "mythology and obscurity" and full of many "of the defects of its intended victims."[2]

It was their belief, and the belief of the linguistic philosophers deeply influenced by them, that we must not rely on some general criterion such as the verifiability criterion but must attack metaphysical claims piecemeal. We need to contrast the metaphysician's uses of language with ordinary uses of language. When we do this with care, when we really reflect on and come to gain a tolerably accurate view of the functions of our language in areas where we suffer from philosophical perplexity, we will find that the metaphysician has not revealed to us wondrous truths of 'the beyond' or of 'ultimate reality' or revealed to us profound human surds. Rather, although of course unwittingly, he has engaged in verbal legerdemain. Philosophy—that is, critical philosophy—is in Wittgenstein's celebrated phrase "a battle against the bewitchment of our intelligence by means of language." The rational way to break such bewilderment is to develop an awareness of the actual workings of our language. Metaphysical claims are not deep claims about the nature of 'ultimate reality', but are unwitting expressions of linguistic confusion.

I should add that Wittgenstein, whatever the final estimate of his work, is without doubt one of the profoundest philosophers of our time, if not the profoundest. He philosophized fiercely and probingly. After one has grappled with philosophical problems oneself, to read him for the first time is a revelation. Wittgenstein turned his intense analytical powers and his insight into philosophical argument to the task of breaking the spell of the deep metaphysical urges and obsessions that drive men—and drove Wittgenstein himself—into a concern with metaphysical questions. He tells us that his aim in philosophy is "to show the fly the way out of the fly-bottle." Speaking of his own conception of the task of a philosopher, he remarks, "The philosopher's treatment of a problem is like the treatment of an illness." However, do not forget that this is an analogy and that Wittgenstein was speaking of a deep conceptual illness resulting from a failure to gain a clear command of our fundamental concepts. The conceptual confusion, where it is philosophical, typically does not merely produce intellectual confusion but produces *Angst* and disquietude as well. Wittgenstein put it thus:

> The problems arising through a misinterpretation of our forms of language have the character of *depth*. They are deep disquietudes; their roots are as deep in us as the forms of our language and their significance is as great as the importance of our language.[3]

And he went on to say a page later in his *Philosophical Investigations:*

> Where does our investigation get its importance from, since it seems only to destroy everything interesting, that is, all that is great and important? (As it were all the buildings, leaving behind only bits of stone and rubble.) What we are destroying is nothing but houses of cards and we are clearing up the ground of language on which they stand.
>
> The results of philosophy are the uncovering of one or another piece of plain nonsense and of bumps that the understanding has got by running its head up against the limits of language. These bumps make us see the value of the discovery.[4]

His aim, as he put it later in *Philosophical Investigations*, is "to teach you to pass from a piece of disguised nonsense to something that is patent nonsense."[5] But while his aim was profoundly antimetaphysical, it was not nihilistic or antiintellectual. He longed to gain a perspicuous representation of those concepts that philosophically harass us. His ideal in philosophy was stern and disciplined and the clarity that was to be attained was a clarity that would bring one peace.

> . . . the clarity that we are aiming at is indeed *complete* clarity. But this simply means that the philosophical problems should *completely* disappear.
>
> The real discovery is the one that makes me capable of stopping doing philosophy when I want to.—The one that gives philosophy peace, so that it is no longer tormented by questions which bring *itself* in question.[6]

Wittgenstein's attempt to carry through a philosophical therapy is extraordinarily complex. And he warned us that in carrying through this task "there is not *a* philosophical method, though there are indeed methods, like different therapies."[7] One major strategy was to bring back the metaphysicians' extraordinary uses of language to a confrontation and comparison with the ordinary uses of language. When this is done in a certain way the metaphysical spell can be broken.

III

I can best illustrate and drive home the force of such a challenge by taking an argument from Alice Ambrose's "Metamorphoses of the Principle of Verifiability."[8] This argument is plainly and self-consciously written under the spell of Wittgenstein and, while simplifying from his complex philosophical practice, it powerfully illustrates an important strand in his philosophical therapy that makes close contact with our previous discussions. It shows how such linguistic philosophers eliminate metaphysics without making their arguments turn on the verifiability principle.[9]

Consider such typical paradoxical metaphysical assertions as:

1. Our senses can only disclose how things seem, not how they are.
2. Change is unreal, no more than mere appearance.
3. Motion is impossible.
4. Time is unreal.
5. The world is my idea. There are no material things.
6. All desires are selfish.
7. All is in flux, nothing is permanent.

All these metaphysical utterances have the surface appearance of being factual statements. But there is something odd here. Taken in a straightforward, naive way, they are all obviously and absurdly false. Moreover, the metaphysician who asserts them does not treat them as factual statements open to confirmation and disconfirmation, for he does not seek evidence for them. Rather, he engages in conceptual analysis, and in the course of that gives us ingenious arguments for accepting them. But when we follow the metaphysician's surrounding talk in justification of such claims as any of the seven paradoxical utterances supposedly express, we discover something else odd: The metaphysician, although typically unwittingly, is using certain of his key terms in a distinctively unusual way. And the shift in usage is crucial, for, as Ambrose points out, in such metaphysical arguments a given key word (for example, 'selfish', 'flux', 'appearance') is used in such a way that its antithesis is left without even a *conceivable* application. They are all terms that are ostensibly to be employed descriptively—that is, to characterize something—yet they are actually used in the *metaphysician's* context in such a way that they have no intelligible opposite. They make no nonvacuous contrast. This means that, surface appearances to the contrary, they cannot function as descriptive predicates. Note that it makes no sense at all to call something a 'small trout' without allowing anything that could at least in principle be specified to count as a 'large trout' or 'nonsmall trout'. Without such a nonvacuous contrast, 'small' cannot really characterize trout. Thus, where there is no nonvacuous contrast, no further claim is made by saying 'There is a small trout in my creel' than by saying 'There is a trout in my creel'. 'Small' ordinarily functions descriptively and as such makes a nonvacuous contrast. However, the metaphysician is just such an unwitting verbal trickster; he uses 'change', 'permanent', and 'selfish' in statements 2, 7, and 6 respectively in such a way that they make no nonvacuous contrast.

Ambrose first examines a simple case to show how this is so. Suppose we have a metaphysician who is worried about the capacity of our senses to tell us how things really are. Like Descartes, he tells us that our sense experience is inaccurate and illusory. He points out, by way of illustration, that we can never observe or see an accurate circle. Now such a claim (let us call it A) has a factual look.

A.   We can never see an accurate circle.

It looks as if it were of a type with A',

A'.   All circles drawn freehand have turned out so far to be inaccurate.

But we soon find out that A and A' are very different, for no matter what circles, drawn by the use of machines with what precision, are presented for view, the metaphysician asserting A always denies that they are really accurate. No matter what circles are presented to him, he continues to affirm A. Moreover, it soon becomes evident that the metaphysician need not even look. As anyone familiar with such metaphysical arguments is perfectly aware, our metaphysician is not interested in the slightest in empirical investigations that would confirm or disconfirm his claim. His arguments are quite *a priori*.

In his discourses, A functions very differently than A' does in ordinary discourses, where what people can actually do—in this case, draw—is plainly the key factor in assessing the truth or falsity of the nonmetaphysical claim. In such a circumstance, we can and should ask the metaphysician making such a claim what an accurate circle would look like. And if he cannot say, we should present him with examples—as central, standard, and obvious cases as we can think of—that we intend as paradigm cases and ask him (1) why these are not accurate circles which are there for us to see and (2) *if* they are not accurate circles, what would count as an accurate circle?

However, if this is done, it soon becomes evident that no imaginable or even in principle observable circle would fill the bill. Nothing that we could conceive of anyone doing—such as having very special and discerning eyes—can even in principle reveal what the metaphysician would take to be an accurate, perfectly round circle. In fact, he cannot say what would count as 'seeing an accurate perfectly round circle'. But if no seeing could (logically could) count as seeing such a circle, the phrase makes no nonvacuous contrast and as such is a bogus descriptive phrase incapable of being used in a statement to make a factual claim. Yet A is offered to us as a factual claim, as something that has been discovered by human beings to be true.

If the metaphysician's intentions are less definite and if it is impossible to tell whether the phrase makes a nonvacuous contrast or not, it remains the case that we do not understand, and he does not understand, what he is claiming when he utters, 'We can never see an accurate circle'. 'Observed accurate circle' *on his new use* is a putative description, but neither we nor he knows what it describes or what it is supposed to describe. We are lulled into thinking we do because given its ordinary use—that is, its everyday nonmetaphysical use—it does describe something observable. But on his metaphysical use it does not, for if it does not make a non-vacuous contrast (and it does not), the phrase is not being used descriptively and no factual claim can be made by A, appearances to the contrary notwithstanding.

When we come to see this and when we realize that 'circle observed to be accurate' has in such a metaphysical context no *conceivable* application, it becomes in its metaphysical employment like 'round square', a contradictory conception; and a 'circle observed to be inaccurate', like 'unmarried bachelor', becomes a pleonasm. But it also becomes evident, Ambrose argues, that language is being tinkered with by the metaphysician in a pointless and arbitrary way, for this is not the way 'accurate' and 'inaccurate' are normally employed. Their normal nonmetaphysical employment does not imply the presence of a feature that in fact is never present, or logically could not be present, in any situation in which they are normally employed. They normally are descriptive terms, and as such they both have applications that are at least possible. Thus where it makes sense to talk about something being either accurate or inaccurate, it must be logically possible to assert what conditions would obtain for something to be accurate and what conditions would have to obtain for something to be inaccurate.

If I say 'Jones measured the trout inaccurately', it must be logically possible to specify the empirical conditions in which one would be justified in asserting that he had measured it accurately. For 'accurate' to function descriptively, this condition must obtain. In such contexts there must be a nonvacuous contrast between 'accurate' and 'inaccurate'. But this does not obtain with the metaphysician's use of 'circle observed to be accurate'.

Since this is so, the metaphysician's claim, 'We can never see an accurate circle', like the claim 'It is 5 A.M. on Mars', is nonsense. *In the metaphysician's* discourse, 'observed accurate circle' is without meaning. But where A has a meaning, 'We can never see an accurate circle' is falsifiable.

It is not a valid response to this argument for the metaphysician to try to make out that A is analytic. It plainly is not analytic if we stick close to the employment of terms in English usage, for it is not self-contradictory to deny A and certainly nothing is achieved by the metaphysician *making* it analytic by stipulative redefinition. Of course, he can do that, but nothing is accomplished by such a move. He has not shown that, given the meanings the component terms have in our stream of life, A must be true. After all, this is what is at issue.

On examination it turns out that the metaphysician is either asserting something that is absurdly false; uttering outright nonsense; or, by using arbitrary stipulations to make A an analytic statement, merely unwittingly expressing a discontent with our grammar and exhibiting a new but utterly pointless notation. What he does not do is to achieve what he wants, namely, to give us a new truth about the world, show us that what we have been saying and thinking all along is false, or tell us something about the nature of reality. In making this evident, what we do is exhibit the metaphysician's unconscious shenanigans by destroying the outward similarity between a metaphysical proposition and an experiential one (in the present case, the superficial similarity between A and A'). But we also show that the metaphysical proposition is either absurdly false, nonsense, or an utterly pointless stipulation about how to talk.

Since this Wittgensteinian method of dissolving metaphysical questions is an important one and since my illustrative example of how it works may seem painfully artificial since A' is hardly a paradigm of a metaphysical statement, although the seven statements previously listed are, I shall (again following Ambrose) work with another case. This one has more intrinsic interest, for it enters into arguments about psychological egoism and hence into discussions of normative ethics. Consider statement B of the psychological egoist.

B.   All voluntary actions are selfish.

This again has a factual look. It appears to be an empirical remark concerning human motivation, but taken in a straightforward manner it is plainly false. When we think of such people as Dag Hammarskjöld, Pastor Bernard Lichtenberg, Father Kolbe, and a host of others, we realize that it is perfectly evident that not all human beings are selfish all of the time. After all, if Father Kolbe's sacrifice of himself to fight against Hitler's persecution of the Jews was not an unselfish act, pray tell what could count as an unselfish act? Moreover, we note once again a characteristic feature of metaphysical argument, namely, that metaphysicians do not bring in or even remotely consider bringing in or even search for hidden information about Father Kolbe or any other apparently unselfish or sometimes unselfish human being. There is no attempt to unsettle our paradigms of unselfish behavior by bringing in hitherto undisclosed information about the motives of the people involved which would expose their motives as selfish after all and lead us, if we are rational people, to reverse our judgment about their acting unselfishly on a given occasion.

Again the metaphysician takes the high *a priori* road. He simply points out vis-à-vis Father Kolbe or about anyone acting in a similar manner that he did what he did voluntarily and this means that there is a sense in which he *wanted* to do it. Moreover, the action and the desire so to act sprang from the self, and in that sense it is and must be a selfish act. These are indeed not the only lines of argument he might take, but they are typical; other more complicated arguments have the same *a priori* flavor.[10] Now any voluntary act becomes a selfish act in virtue of this new and stipulated meaning we have assigned to 'selfish'. But again language has gone on a holiday. B is normally an empirical claim, which happens to be false, but the metaphysician uses B such that it is analytic. To do this he has had to trifle with language, albeit unconsciously; to make his point seem at all plausible, he has had to use his key terms in an eccentric manner. There is no reason to accept that which, when unmasked, turns out to be his program of verbal legislation.

It is also apparent, given the metaphysician's use of language in defense of psychological egoism, that 'selfish' no longer modifies 'act' and that 'a selfish act' becomes what it is not in its ordinary employment, namely, a redundancy. But then 'All voluntary actions are selfish' merely means 'All voluntary actions are voluntary actions'. Again the metaphysical claim fails to make a factual claim, and if it is intelligible at all it reduces to a purely stipulative analytic statement (and a pointless stipulation at that). Psychological egoism rests on a conceptual confusion—on a failure to gain a proper view of the working of our language in such contexts. The task of the philosopher is to show this and to reduce a disguised bit of nonsense to patent nonsense.

In metaphysical case after metaphysical case, such a Wittgensteinian technique exposes disguised nonsense by pointing out, for such apparently factual claims as 'All change is apparent change' or 'All that one ever sees when one looks at a thing is a part of one's own brain', that key expressions, severed in the metaphysical utterances from their usual antitheses and finally from any logical opposite at all, only seem to have informative content. In addition, the metaphysical utterances using them do not assert a fundamental fact or even a plain old everyday fact about the world. Metaphysical utterances, such as the seven listed previously, parade as factual claims—as deep and paradoxical pronouncements about ultimate reality. (It has been said, and by an analytic philosopher, that the very "point of metaphysics is to discover the fundamental nature of reality.")[11] As such, these utterances purport to assert fundamental truths. But since their allegedly descriptive terms make no nonvacuous contrast, putative factual statements made by the use of such utterances, while still purporting to characterize the world, are in reality pseudofactual statements devoid of all informative or factual content. If to protect himself the metaphysician turns his statement into a necessary truth—that is, into an analytic statement—he is only making a pointless alteration of usage. In doing so he is in effect simply introducing a nonconventional rule of grammar.

In bringing words back from their metaphysical to their everyday use, Wittgenstein is bringing them back into the living language—stressing that to be meaningful they must have a role in such a language, which in turn is an integral part of the stream of life. Where putatively descriptive terms have no *conceivable* application, as in the metaphysician's sentences, they are merely idle and do no work.[12] The argument from nonvacuous contrast shows the senselessness of such metaphysical claims. A term functions as a genuine descriptive term only if it makes a nonvacuous contrast; more generally, a term has a meaning only if it has a use (a style of functioning) in a language; and a sentence has a meaning only if it has a use—an employment—in a language. But metaphysical terms or sentences have no role in any functioning language. They are like wheels in a machine that turn no machinery.

NOTES

1. Frederick Copleston, *Positivism and Metaphysics* (Lisbon: 1965), pp. 5–15.
2. See here G. J. Warnock, "John Langshaw Austin," *Proceeding of the British Academy,* vol. XLIX, p. 345, and Stuart Hampshire, "J. L. Austin," in Richard Rorty (ed.), *The Linguistic Turn,* p. 236.
3. Ludwig Wittgenstein, *Philosophical Investigations,* p. 47.
4. Ibid., p. 48.
5. Ibid., p. 133.
6. Ibid., p. 51.
7. Ibid.
8. Alice Ambrose, "Metamorphoses of the Principle of Verifiability," in F. C. Dommeyer (ed.), *Current Philosophical Issues.* In this connection the following further essays by Miss Ambrose should be noted: "Philosophical Doubts," *Massachusetts Review* (1960); "Linguistic Approaches to Philosophical Problems," in Richard Rorty (ed.), *The Linguistic Turn,* op. cit.; and "The Problem of Linguistic Inadequacy," in her *Essays in Analysis.*
9. Actually, although I shall not be concerned to argue it here, I do not think this is so. Wittgensteinians such as Ambrose, Malcolm, and Lazerowitz who also are of the antimetaphysical party do in effect assume the verifiability criterion as a criterion of factual significance, although it remains unargued

in their work and is actually inconsistently yoked with a rejection of that criterion as a criterion of significance. This is particularly obvious in Ambrose. In spite of a vigorous and well-taken criticism of some ways of putting the verifiability criterion, it is assumed in her article discussed in this chapter. In her "Philosophical Doubts" she says, ". . . a statement which *cannot* be falsified is not a factual assertion but one which is logically necessary, like 'Nothing is both red all over and also green'." (p. 286) and again in her "Linguistic Approaches to Philosophical Problems," pp. 148–149, she makes a similar claim. Roderick Chisholm in his criticism of Ambrose smokes out and challenges two leading assumptions in her work, namely, the claim that "if a statement is not verifiable it cannot be factual and that philosophical statements, unlike scientific statements, are not verifiable." Roderick K. Chisholm, "Comments on the 'Proposal Theory' of Philosophy," in Richard Rorty (ed.), *The Linguistic Turn*, op. cit., p. 157. I think, as my previous chapter tried to bring out, that one should assent to the claim that if a statement is not verifiable it is not factual and that this would give a deeper support to such Wittgensteinian antimetaphysical arguments. But such an *argument* is not made by the antimetaphysical Wittgensteinians.

10. I have considered some of them in my "Egoism in Ethics," *Philosophy and Phenomenological Research*, vol. XIX (June, 1959).

11. J O. Urmson, "The History of Philosophical Analysis," in Richard Rorty (ed.), *The Linguistic Turn*, op. cit., p. 296.

12. See here P. F. Strawson's review of John Passmore's *Philosophical Reasoning*, in *Philosophical Books*, vol. III, no. 2 (April, 1962), pp. 17–19.

35

METAPHYSICS
AND THE APPEAL
TO ORDINARY
LANGUAGE: II

I

The Wittgensteinian antimetaphysical argument of the last chapter has seemed to many (as it seems to me) a powerful bit of antimetaphysical weaponry. But it has raised a host of criticisms ranging from the derision heaped on it by Ernest Gellner in his *succès de scandâle, Words and Things*, to careful and searching criticisms.[1] I cannot follow all the moves and countermoves here, but we can and should tackle some of the most important ones.

It will be said that in the previous chapter I have, following Ambrose, quite uncritically used the argument from the *paradigm case*. That is to say, I have utilized an argument to the effect that to understand the meaning of a descriptive term is to understand its use in the language. And to understand *that* use is to understand that we sometimes use terms in such a way that they make nonvacuous contrasts, and we sometimes use these terms to refer to things or to situations in the world. Therefore—and here is where I allegedly sneak something in—if a given descriptive term has a use (actually is a genuinely descriptive term), this implies that we can know what it would be like for what it refers to to actually exist.

To argue in such a way is to make a paradigm-case argument. How it works will be clearer from an example. If someone asks me if in reality there are any red things, I can confidently reply that there are. Danish pillar boxes, Gyldendal's dictionaries, and American fire trucks are typical examples of red things. The word 'red' is used to refer to just such things. If they do not count as 'red things', nothing does; but, given the use of 'red', they do count as red things and there are such things, so we can conclude that in fact there really are red things. In short, the philosophical perplexity about whether something really is an X can be dissolved or rationally resolved by being shown that some particular thing—in this case one of Gyldendal's dictionaries—is a standard case (normally one of many such cases) by reference to which the descriptive expression in question has to be understood. A person could not be said to properly understand the expression unless, given the proper context, he was able to recognize such standard cases. (It is not necessary that he recognize any given one—non-Danes do not usually know about Gyldendal's dictionaries—but he must be able to recognize at least some standard examples.)

Such arguments, it has been convincingly argued, have a very limited scope.[2] Moreover, Ambrose has in effect assumed the validity of such an argument in her critique of paradoxical metaphysical claims, but Passmore has carefully argued that the paradigm-case argument does nothing to establish that such paradoxical metaphysical positions are absurd or senseless. At best, Passmore would have us believe, it serves "to remind us . . . that a philosopher's statements are not to be interpreted quite as a wholly unsophisticated person might interpret them."[3]

Such paradigm-case arguments, Passmore points out, ignore too much the context in which metaphysical statements are made; they utterly neglect the relevant philosophical controversy and the history behind them. Our motto should be: Don't ask what a metaphysician *could* mean; look and find out what he did mean in the context of what particular philosophical controversy or conceptual inquiry. Philosophers are primarily addressing themselves to the community of their fellow philosophers, and their statements should be understood against a certain background of argument and discussion.

Some distinguished philosophers—to give force to Passmore's claim by translating it into the concrete—have asserted that all statements are vague or that no empirical statements are certain. Such statements construed in a commonsense way in abstraction from their background of philosophical discussion can be shown to be absurd by the same techniques I used for 'All voluntary actions are selfish' and 'We can never see an accurate circle'. But, Passmore counters, seen in their proper philosophical contexts they are not such patent absurdities, if indeed they are absurdities at all.[4]

If 'All statements are vague' and 'No empirical statements are certain' are construed simply as the plain man would take them, it is patently obvious they are false. There are paradigm cases of nonvague and certain statements—for example, that it was colder in December 1967 on the surface of the North Pole than it was during the same month of the same year on the streets of San Antonio, Texas. That statement is an empirical statement whose truth is quite certain, and it is not vague. Yet, something has gone wrong, for surely metaphysicians—even the most paradoxical type—are not so stupid or so stubborn as to be denying such truisms. And indeed philosophers who made such paradoxical claims were not concerned to deny that 'certain' and 'clear' have a use in our language and make nonvacuous contrasts. Rather, when Ramsey, to take a distinguished example, argued that all statements are vague, he was concerned to show, against the claims of certain logicians (and thus giving his remarks a particular philosophical context), that it was impossible to formulate a statement—any statement at all—in such a way that it was *logically* impossible for anybody to misunderstand it. Ramsey's philosophical contemporaries, given their logico-analytical ideals, were looking for such a clarity. In that context his remark was perfectly sensible and no doubt true. " 'All statements are vague' is a perfectly natural response to the attempt to construct statements which are 'clear' in this very special, philosophical sense of the word."[5]

Similarly, when C. I. Lewis and Rudolf Carnap, two major contemporary analytical philosophers, claimed that no empirical statements are certain, their claim must be seen against the arguments of certain empiricists about certain observation statements and in the context of arguments against rationalism. It was an emphatic way of asserting that it is always *logically* possible for an empirical statement to be false.

The moral here about the importance of context—something Wittgenstein himself has laid heavy stress on for other purposes—is obvious. Passmore's summary of what is crucial here concerning such paradoxical metaphysical claims is worth quoting in detail.

> Only by considering how such statements are actually used in philosophical controversy can we possibly hope to understand them; we need to know the history behind them. But they are none the worse for that. The crucial point is that they are not attempts to purge the language of everyday life—to rid it of words like 'solid' and 'certain' and 'clear'; rather, they are emphatic ways of pointing out that particular philosophical criteria of solidity, certainty, clarity are never in fact satisfied. Nor do they make that point in an outrageous, willfully paradoxical way; on the contrary, they make it in the most natural manner, if the historical context of controversy is taken into account.[6]

Passmore develops another argument of considerable importance. He in effect directs a *reductio* argument against arguments of the type I employed in the last section of the preceding chapter.[7] He attempts to show that the very same arguments used to establish the absurdity of the metaphysical assertions that we can never see an accurate circle and that all voluntary actions are selfish could be used to show that the philosopher or plain man who asserts 'There are no miracles', 'There are no sacred diseases', or 'Nobody ever suffers from diabolic possession' must likewise and for the same type of reasons be saying something absurd. That is, they are either saying something plainly false or nonsensical.

This puts us in an uncomfortable position. On the one hand, we would not want to say this about these assertions concerning miracles, sacred diseases, or diabolic possession; rather, in our cultural circles Moore's vaunted plain man would say, concerning the three sentences quoted above, that the last two are used to make true statements, and many a plain man would say that of the first sentence as well. On the other hand, there at least seems to be a parity of argument here such that, if we accept the antimetaphysical arguments in the last section of the preceding chapter, we must, in order to remain consistent, accept the arguments I shall now give about miracles and sacred diseases. (Diabolic possession could easily be handled in the same way.) But if we do not regard these arguments about miracles and sacred diseases as sound or reliable ones, it would seem at least that if we have any respect for consistency, we should reject Ambrose's antimetaphysical arguments as well. It looks as though we are nicely trapped.

What is the most reasonable response to this dilemma? Passmore thinks we should reject the paradigm-case arguments I am about to give and thus reject Ambrose's antimetaphysical arguments as well. I agree with Passmore that we should reject the following paradigm-case arguments about miracles and sacred diseases, but I question whether this logically or reasonably commits us as well to rejecting the arguments (adapted from Ambrose) given in the last chapter. But that consideration must be considered after I have set out the troublemaking paradigm-case arguments for miracles and sacred diseases.

Remember the paradigm-case arguments go like this: Faced with the paradoxical metaphysical claim that there are no such things as physical objects, it can be shown that such a claim is absurd by appeals to paradigms. Chairs, lamp shades, books, pens are things we normally designate as physical objects, and there plainly are such things. Thus, if someone maintains that there are no such things as physical objects, he must be either mad, sadly misinformed, using words in a quite different way from that in which they are normally used, or all three.[8]

Now for the parallel arguments with the absurd conclusions: Faced with the claim that there are no miracles, it can be shown that such a claim is absurd by appeals to paradigms. Men sometimes inexplicably recover from almost certain death, houses that look as though they cannot possibly escape fire or earthquakes sometimes do, and people who very much need to meet and have been separated for years sometimes meet by accident thousands of miles from where they used to live. Such occurrences we conventionally call 'miracles'. And they plainly do occur. Thus, if someone maintains that there are no miracles, he must be either mad, sadly misinformed, using words in a quite different way from that in which they are normally used, or all three.

Faced with the claim—say by Hippocrates—that there are no sacred diseases, it can be shown that Hippocrates' claim is absurd by appeals to paradigms. People who suffer from epilepsy are conventionally said to suffer from 'sacred diseases'. And without doubt there are cases of epilepsy where people suffer from fits or roll on the ground in frenzy. For Hippocrates to deny that, he would have to fly in the face of the facts. Thus, if someone maintains that there are no such things as sacred diseases, he must be either mad, sadly misinformed, using words in a quite different way from that in which they are normally used, or all three.

Why are these last two arguments bad ones? Intuitively we recognize they are bad. Even if we believe in miracles or the possibility of miracles, we would not accept such an argument for miracles. My argument why they are bad will proceed somewhat indirectly by way of exploring the implications of an important distinction made by Passmore.

Passmore points out that 'miracle' and 'sacred disease' are terms that are both ostensively taught and taught by description. With such terms we are, on the one hand, given definitions and criteria for their employment and, on the other hand, taught them by paradigm exemplars. But where this obtains, Passmore argues, we have trouble with the paradigm-case argument. It is only in those cases, if indeed (as appears doubtful) there are any, where the term in question can *only* be learned *ostensively* that the paradigm-case argument could be valid.[9] However, in the arguments about 'miracles' and 'sacred diseases', there is no plausibility at all in saying that these terms could *only* be learned ostensively.

Where terms are learned *both* descriptively and ostensively, clashes can arise between the cases—the applications of the terms—and the criteria (the descriptions we have been given of what is meant by such terms). We have been taught, for example, that a miracle is a direct intervention of God into human affairs in a startling way, so that what He does is scientifically inexplicable and has great moral and religious efficacy. This spells out, at least in part, our criteria for a miracle. And here we have a situation that leads to a conflict between cases and criteria. Given such criteria (that is, given such a definition of 'miracle'), we might want to reject the whole concept of miracle because we do not believe that there is or perhaps even could be a God, or that God could intervene in the world, or that there is or perhaps even could be any matter of fact that in principle is scientifically inexplicable. And we might quite reasonably and indeed justifiably do this without denying that on some rare occasions desperately ill people whom modern science is quite unable to help do suddenly and inexplicably get well, or that on some rare occasions houses with children trapped inside are quite inexplicably saved when fire is raging around them, and the like. For people who employ the term 'miracle', these are proper applications (paradigm exemplars) of miracles. We recognize this as a plain fact about people's linguistic behavior, but given our rejection of the criteria and consequently our rejection of the intelligibility or rationality of the very concept of miracle, we will give new descriptions of these cases. Earlier in the history of our culture, people for similar reasons did this for the paradigm exemplars of 'sacred disease' and 'diabolic possession'. A natural way of asserting that this is being done is by saying 'There are no miracles' or 'There are no sacred diseases'.

Where there is a possibility of such a clash, paradigm-case arguments are suspect; where the clash is evident, they should be rejected outright. It is because there is such a clash between criteria and cases that paradigm-case arguments for miracles and sacred diseases are bad arguments. (There are further reasons as well, which will be considered later.)

Now we *seem* to have undermined our paradigm-case arguments not only about 'miracle' and 'sacred disease' but also about 'observed accurate circle' and 'selfish'. In the latter two arguments as well as the former two, the terms are not learned only through ostensive teaching but involve descriptive terms learned in both ways; typically ostensive teaching here is beefed up by descriptions and vice versa. Given this situation, we surely need to ask this: In the metaphysical cases I discussed, why is it not possible for there to be a clash between criteria and cases? And if it is possible—if it is a reasonable possibility—we could very well call into question, as we did for sacred disease and miracle, the coherence or utility of a whole mode of conceptualization, for example, characterizing behavior as selfish or unselfish. Just as we have grounds for rejecting as irrational the conceptualizing of phenomena as sacred diseases, so we could similarly reject the very category miracle or selfishness.

It is at least tempting to argue that the paradigm-case argument in these situations cannot establish what it wishes to, for it remains possible for the metaphysician reasonably to reject the criteria for the expression (concept) in question—rejecting perhaps a whole mode of talk and conceptualization—without denying that there are cases conventionally described by the *to be* rejected vocabulary and fitting the conventional manner of conceptualizing things. Given that it is a justified move with 'miracle' and 'sacred disease' to argue in this way and that it is at least a *prima facie* reasonable move with 'All statements are vague' and 'No empirical statements are certain', why could it not be justified both for the seven paradoxical metaphysical cases listed in the last chapter and for the two sample metaphysical arguments discussed there? It would seem as if the paradigm-case argument, with its implicit linguistic and conceptual conservatism, is by no means adequate to its role as Jack the Giant Killer.

II

The dialectic of the argument should not stop here. Passmore indeed shows, as others have as well and in different ways, that the paradigm-case argument should not be applied indiscriminately. Clearly, it should not be applied in those situations where there is a conflict between cases and criteria, and at most it could be a starter—although sometimes an important starter—for claims such as 'All statements are vague' and 'No empirical statements are certain'.[10]

I shall now argue that in certain circumstances the paradigm-case argument can be justifiably applied at least as a starter and that sometimes it is also quite conclusive. Whether or not it is conclusive depends on how the metaphysician argues for and takes such paradoxical metaphysical claims as the seven listed in the last section of the preceding chapter. That is, I am claiming that it remains an important weapon in the antimetaphysician's armory. Pursuant to this, I want first to show that there are relevant differences between these cases and the ones deployed in Passmore's attempted *reductio*.

. To begin this inquiry, we should first consider when we might reasonably employ paradigm-case arguments at least as starters. Consider again the simple example we used to introduce the argument several paragraphs back. One philosopher (Jytte Hansen) has maintained of such a case that it can be considered a conclusive refutation of the contra-common-sense metaphysical proposition that there are no such things as objects.[11] Such a paradoxical metaphysical claim can be shown to be absurd by appealing to paradigm exemplars of objects, for example, pencils, typewriters, trees, hunks of clay, and the like. Such things are normally classed as physical objects, and plainly there are such things. Thus, if someone maintains that there are no such things as physical objects, he must be either mad, sadly misinformed, using words in a quite different way from the way in which they are normally used, or all three. It seems fair enough to say that against the putative claim that there are no objects, Hansen's contention is well taken and perfectly decisive. (Whether any metaphysician ever maintained anything quite so absurd is not at issue here. The point is that if anyone were to argue in that way he would be mistaken, and such a paradigm-case argument can show that he is mistaken.)

That this is so is evident enough, but to be in a position to answer our lead question in the previous paragraph we must be able to explain *why* it is so. That is to say, before we can reasonably generalize, we need to understand why such a paradigm-case argument is a good one. I think Antony Flew in "Again the Paradigm" has shown us why we can say of such cases that they are good paradigm-case arguments and how they can be distinguished from the *reductio* paradigm-case arguments Passmore employs.[12] Flew first notes that we appropriately use the paradigm-case argument where we are faced with extremely paradoxical metaphysical statements such as the seven listed previously or such scientific-*sounding* statements as Eddington's paradoxical thesis that stones, steel rods, and the everyday furniture of the earth which ordinarily are described as solid are not really solid at all. When faced with such apparently bizarre assertions, we should use the paradigm-case argument.

In considering such paradoxes, paradigm-case considerations should first be employed in an elucidatory or cautionary role, namely, to function as a challenge to force people who make or support such paradoxical claims to clarify what they are claiming, to make it clear or at least clearer what they are really up to and to make it evident whether we should take their statements at face value. This is important because paradoxical metaphysical assertions such as 'There are no physical objects', 'Time is unreal', 'No one ever perceives a material thing', or 'All that one sees when one looks at a thing is a part of one's own brain' are all put forth—as Eddington's remark is put forth—as the rather startling discoveries of inquiry and as fundamental factual claims about the ultimate nature of reality. They have the ring of profound claims just there to be accepted. But if we come at them in a flat-footed literal way, it seems that they could not possibly be true, and yet we know that the metaphysicians in question think they have arguments which show that paradoxical or not they must be true. Since this is so, our first step should be to make clear whether the metaphysician's claim is to be taken at its face value and to be understood to mean just what it appears to say if the terms in his utterances are taken in an ordinary way.

This is only a first move in arguing from the paradigm case. So far we have only treated paradigm-case considerations as devices for smoking out what the paradoxical metaphysician is up to. After the ground has been cleared in this manner, it still should only be used as an *argument* if certain conditions obtain. That is, it can be a good argument only when these conditions hold.

Note that the paradigm-case argument has two steps: "The first is to bring to mind certain very familiar facts, and the second is to insist that these are paradigm exemplars of the concepts in question."[13] Now the necessary (but not sufficient) conditions that must obtain for a paradigm-case argument to be a good argument are that the alleged familar facts are indeed facts and that they are also truly paradigm exemplars of the concepts in question. In the case of the man who denies that there are any physical objects, we remind him that there are pencils, typewriters, and the like, and that these are paradigm exemplars of the concept of a physical object. In the case of the claim that there are no unselfish actions, we point out that there are people who have sacrificed their lives and fortunes for other people, and there are many rather more mundane acts as when people give others directions and instructions where they have no thought of receiving, directly or indirectly, anything in return, and that such actions are paradigmatic exemplars of what it is to act in an unselfish manner.

For a paradigm-case argument to be a good one, these two conditions must obtain. That is, where these two claims can be justified—and some-times they can—the paradoxical metaphysical claim, it has been asserted, has been shown either to be mistaken *or* not to be the claim it purports to be, but some different claim instead: a claim—or what is in effect a claim—that we should make a conceptual revision. One example is Ram-sey's assertion that all statements are vague. This is really the claim that all statements are such that it is logically possible they can be misin-terpreted.

It is in the second step of the paradigm-case argument, as Flew has characterized it, where the argument from nonvacuous contrast is em-ployed. We say of these paradigm exemplars: If these objects are not physical objects, then what would count as 'physical object'? If these acts are not unselfish, what would 'unselfish act' signify? If these objects are not solid, what criteria could 'solid object' have? If nothing it is logically possible to describe could serve as answers to these questions, it follows that terms which normally have in their ordinary use a non-vacuous contrast have been deprived of that contrast and thus are with-out descriptive content. But if this is so, then 'There are no physical objects', 'There are no unselfish acts', and 'There are no solid objects' all fail to make factual statements, for they do not even assert a con-ceivable state of affairs because their *putatively* descriptive terms are in fact not descriptive.

This last argument brings out another important limitation of the paradigm-case argument and points toward a general characterization of when it is a good argument. It shows that paradigm-case arguments are at home where we have putatively factual claims whose dispute-engender-ing terms—for example, 'physical object', 'selfish', 'solid'—are normally employed as descriptive terms. That is to say, it is properly employed where its predicates are used to distinguish between or to identify dis-crete kinds of things or activities. The terms cannot be *normative* ('good', 'lovely', and the like) or *theoretical* ('anal-erotic', 'neutrino', 'endoga-mous'). If we do not exclude theoretical terms, then, when the preceding two conditions stressed by Flew obtain, any bizarre theory that became encapsulated in ordinary language must be held to be correct. Given that we could talk about particular events or activities which undoubtedly occur utilizing the theoretical terms of this 'way-out' theory, and given that these events or activities were paradigm exemplars of the theoretical terms in that theory, then, if we allow paradigm-case arguments with statements with theoretical terms, we must grant the truth of the para-doxical assertion. But such a use of the paradigm-case argument would give an open invitation to the most diverse kinds of rubbish—for example, entelechies, phlogiston, ether, death instincts, and the like.

Indeed, sometimes what are almost universally taken to be bizarre and fanciful theories turn out, on careful examination, to be justified. But it is also true that there are superstitious and/or incoherent conceptions embedded in our forms of life. Since this is so, for a 'way-out' conception to gain acceptance or even a sympathetic hearing, it needs careful elucidation and considerable evidential support. However, use of the paradigm-case argument, where theoretical terms are involved, would in effect give direct sanction to almost any bit of fancy. A. J. Ayer has well argued in his "Common Sense and Metaphysics" that where we are raising questions about the propriety or utility of a concept and thus of the conceptual scheme in which it has its home, the existence of what is being put in question cannot be established simply by giving an example or a paradigm exemplar, "for the validity of what is presupposed in counting anything as a favorable example is just the point at issue."[14] The paradigm-case argument cannot be legitimately made where a term is a theoretical term or even a problematic term (a term expressive of a problematic concept, for example, 'miracle', 'the Absolute').

So the paradigm-case argument can be a good argument only where the terms that engender the dispute do not function normatively or theoretically, or in some way express a problematic concept. Where Flew's conditions described above obtain and where the key terms involved in the argument about the paradoxical metaphysical argument are terms which in everyday contexts function descriptively and are expressive of unproblematic concepts—for example, red or hard—the argument from the paradigm case is a good argument.

It is this limitation to descriptive uses of language and the ruling out of theoretical terms that provides the crucial difference between Passmore's cases, where using the paradigm-case argument leads to absurdity, and cases where it is an effective argument to eliminate metaphysical rubbish. The terms 'miracle', 'sacred disease', 'diabolic possession' are all expressive of theory-laden concepts. They are theoretical terms of primitive ideological systems. But 'selfish', 'accurate circle', 'see', 'red' are all plainly descriptive terms common to many conceptual systems and world-views. Indeed, theoretical terms have an empirical component—for example, to talk of diabolic possession does involve talking about things like rolling on the ground in a frenzy. But they also carry disputable commitments to particular scientific theories or ideological world-views that purely descriptive terms do not. It is indeed this that makes them problematic. Moreover, not all terms can be theoretical terms, or the very notion of 'theoretical term' would be deprived of any working force. Certainly it is a problem of considerable difficulty in the philosophy of science to distinguish these two kinds of terms. But we *must* start by recognizing that undoubtedly there is such a distinction, although it is not a sharp or clearly defined one. It is one thing to say that Hitler had paranoid traits; it is quite another to say that Hitler had only one testicle.

There are at least two different kinds of quite natural objections to this defense of the argument from the paradigm case. The first objection is that although the terms in the paradoxical metaphysical utterances I listed and in the ones I examined all have descriptive uses, I have simply begged the question in claiming that they have *unproblematic* uses. But 'senses', 'change', 'motion', 'idea', 'selfish', 'permanent', and 'observed accurate circle' are not problematical. As opposed to 'immortal', 'God', 'miracle', 'ghost', 'diabolic possession', they are not terms whose *actual meanings* are unclear to us. If you are uneasy about my reply here, it is very likely that you are confusing and in effect conflating two distinct senses of 'understanding the meaning of a term'. It is crucial to distinguish between, on the one hand, understanding a term (where this means knowing its use and being able to employ it in making statements that are either true or false and being confident that in favorable circumstances we can know whether these statements are true or false), and, on the other hand, knowing the correct *analysis* of a term. There are plenty of unproblematic terms—'hard' or 'red', for example—whose proper analysis people may be quite unclear about while understanding the terms perfectly well in the very standard and crucial sense of being able to employ them in the making of statements they know to be true— for example, 'This is not in red type'. The key terms in the seven paradoxical metaphysical utterances listed in the preceding chapter are unproblematic in this way. Indeed, the proper analysis of 'time' is up for grabs, but in normal circumstances I understand perfectly well how to determine what time it is in Frankfurt. The terms in question, when they are given their standard employments, function as descriptive terms and function in an unproblematic way.

If it is replied that I am still only engaging in counterassertion and that the metaphysician would deny that the terms in the seven metaphysical sentences are unproblematic, I shall simply say that he is mistaken and can be shown to be mistaken by an examination of the linguistic responses of fluent speakers; that is, they do not balk at the normal employment of such terms and they can ascertain the contexts in which they are used in sentences to make true statements and the contexts in which they are used to make false statements. Moreover, I have an explanation of why the metaphysician mistakenly thinks they are problematic: The metaphysician confuses being perplexed about the correct *analysis* of a term with being perplexed about how actually to employ it to make a true or false claim. Indeed, I am claiming that it is a plain matter of empirical fact that we do know the use of these terms and can confidently employ them to make statements we know to be true. If I am mistaken about these quite testable facts, then my claim is mistaken. But in such arguments we would at some point have to make such an appeal, and Passmore, for one, acknowledges that this is so. Such an appeal is relevant when he remarks that "a great deal of philosophical argument consists in recalling philosophers to such familiar facts" and that the "testing of a metaphysical theory by setting it against familiar facts is a very important method of philosophical criticism."[15]

The second objection natural to make to my line of argument is that the distinction between theoretical terms and observation terms—or theoretical terms and descriptive terms—is either a bogus distinction or a distinction that is not a sharp or clear one. There are many terms which we do not quite know whether to regard as purely descriptive or as terms that to a degree are theory-laden. Moreover, there are terms that in one historical period or in one context are used theoretically and in another historical period or another context are used descriptively. But these complications notwithstanding, the fact still remains that there are terms such as 'red', 'accurate circle', and 'selfish' which plainly are not, in most contexts at any rate, in any way theoretical or theory-laden. And there are indeed many such terms. Where *such terms* are used in paradoxical statements and where the other two conditions obtain—namely, that construing the paradoxical statement literally would lead us to deny familiar empirical facts that are paradigm exemplars of the concepts in question—then the paradigm-case argument is a reliable one, but where these conditions do not hold it is not.

Such a limitation allows the antimetaphysical arguments given in the last section of the preceding chapter to remain reliable ones. Similar points could be made about antimetaphysical arguments made about the seven metaphysical utterances listed there. Where there is any doubt that the preceding conditions clearly obtain, the paradigm-case argument could not be decisive but would have to be supplemented by other arguments. That it would often need such supplementation is indeed true, but it does not mean, *pace* Passmore, that it is not often an effective antimetaphysical argument.

We have not yet got to the bottom of the barrel. It will be pointed out that I have not met Passmore's potent argument that metaphysical claims typically have their own special contexts and that paradoxical-sounding metaphysical claims often do not have the straightforward sense that the noninitiate thinks they have, and that where they do not have such an ordinary use the paradigm-case argument is powerless against them.

However, sophisticated users of the paradigm-case argument—such as Ambrose, Flew, and Malcolm—in fact stress that point themselves.[16] The paradigm-case argument is not an argument complete in itself to meet all metaphysical argumentation. It is an important opening move which, given a certain response on the part of a metaphysician, may be a decisive move or, given a different move on his part, may push the dialectic to a stage where we need a further argument. If the metaphysician makes plain that he does not wish to deny the empirical facts or the fact that they are paradigm exemplars of the concepts expressive of the ordinary uses of the descriptive terms in question, and his claims are not incompatible with these familiar facts, it then becomes evident that he is using terms in a new and unusual fashion. We can then ask if there is any point in such a tinkering with language. It may indeed turn out that there is, if there was a point in giving up talking of diabolic possession. But by then there has occurred a metamorphosis in the metaphysical claims. They are no longer what they purport to be, namely, startling findings about the 'ultimate nature of reality'. Rather, they will be seen to be recommendations, perhaps even valuable recommendations, about *how* to conceptualize and *how* to interpret the empirical facts. When the argument has gone to that level, then we can argue in pragmatic terms about the value of alternative picture preferences. But by then the whole nature of the argument has been transformed.

Moreover, for Passmore's cases—that is, the use by Ramsey of 'All statements are vague' and by Lewis and Carnap of 'No empirical proposition is certain'—we hardly have statements made for metaphysical purposes (statements designed to be revelatory of 'ultimate reality'), but statements used in trying to advocate the adoption of a certain allegedly more perspicuous representation of the facts. Passmore does nothing to exhibit similar reasonable aims in the paradoxical metaphysical contexts the paradigm-case argument was designed to combat, for example, where we have such utterances as 'There are no material things', 'Time is unreal', or 'No one ever perceives a physical object'. The latter can perhaps be given some sense when seen in the context of empiricist arguments about perceiving only sense-data. But for the most part at any rate they remain radical paradoxes hardly analogous to the quasi-metaphysical cases Passmore discusses.

Traditional metaphysicians who make such paradoxical claims do not simply want to present a new alternative conceptual system; they wish to do fundamental ontology. That is, they wish to make new and true general assertions concerning what must fundamentally be the case about what there is in the world. Such paradigm-case arguments are effective tools in showing that what the plain man *feels* must be nonsense (that is, these paradoxical metaphysical claims) *is* nonsense. Where a careful examination of the use of the paradoxical metaphysical utterance makes it evident that it can be demythologized (as Passmore points out, 'Every entity is complex' can be demythologized or deontologized into 'Every entity can be described in a variety of ways'), we have reduced the claim either to an analytic statement or to an empirical statement for which we can give evidence. Thus, we no longer have a metaphysical claim. In either event the paradigm-case argument has been a valuable argument with a nonfallacious application in the elimination of certain distinctive obscurantist metaphysical claims.

III

Criticism of such a Wittgensteinian critique of metaphysics is not at an end. It has been repeatedly argued that such an approach shows an exaggerated respect for ordinary language. Wittgensteinians have argued that in dissolving such bizarre metaphysical puzzles as the problem of other minds or the problem of the external world, we need to contrast idling metaphysical uses of language with genuinely operative ordinary uses of language. In this way we can show that metaphysical claims are unwitting expressions of linguistic confusions, while ordinary language is "perfectly in order as it stands." Ordinary language (or at least ordinary descriptive language), such philosophers argue, is correct language; ordinary language is rock bottom and needs no defense or foundation. Philosophy can only dissolve conceptual perplexities by displaying the actual use of our living languages while remaining purely descriptive of our forms of language. Good philosophy is not a key instrument in a critique of culture but must, outside of philosophy itself, leave everything as it is.

This defense of ordinary language, as Malcolm calls it, or defense of "the language of common sense," as Ambrose calls it, has produced violent reactions from philosophers and other intelligentsia. One radical critic has maintained that such an approach to philosophy in effect makes "the true philosopher" into "the guardian of conventions" and that the "main effect of Wittgenstein's later philosophy was simply to consecrate the banalities of everyday language."[17] "Linguistic philosophy," he adds, "may be defined as a flight from the emergence of new concepts."[18] To give ordinary language such a fundamental role is to enshrine and render sacrosanct the superstitions and unargued ideologies of the ordinary man. It is argued that such a defense of the verbal status quo is also, in effect at least, a defense of the intellectual, moral, and political status quo.

Ernest Gellner, one of linguistic philosophy's most vociferous critics, has argued that such ordinary language philosophy is in effect the implicit abdication on the part of philosophy of its normative and critical functions.[19] Philosophy, he continues, has at its very center a normative or evaluative function, but such a function is lost when philosophy becomes purely descriptive, restricting itself to elucidating our various uses of language but never criticizing or assessing the rationality of the concepts these languages embody. Such an appeal to ordinary language can only be philosophically, humanly, and rationally stultifying. It undermines the central rationale of philosophic endeavor: the search for a coherent view of existence. It lulls us into the mistaken belief that there are no general issues to be settled concerning the rationality and/or intelligibility of whole conceptual areas. It makes us forget, it is natural to remark, what this book has in effect shown, that is, that there are some questions about the general viability of ethical, teleological, religious, and responsibility-making discourse that are not just or at all expressions of linguistic confusion.

There is a point in many of these remarks, and yet confusion exists as well. I do not want to be understood as defending in any wholesale manner the language of common sense, and I have not operated on the assumption that ordinary language is all right as it is and that all that critical philosophy can do or genuine philosophy can do is to perspicuously display the workings of our language.[20] However, I think such a Wittgensteinian approach can be and is effective against certain metaphysical and pseudoscientific claims, and I think that it is always or almost always an essential first move. Often it is (or at least should be) also a last move in a philosophical argument. (By 'last move' I do not envoke the "bogey of the Last Word" but simply mean that such a philosophical procedure may solve or dissolve a given philosophical problem, for example, whether inductive arguments are ever justified or whether moral judgments are universalizable.) But I do not wish, in the manner of Wittgenstein or such disciples as Malcolm or Ambrose, to attach a philosophic omnicompetence to ordinary language or use it as some final arbiter of all philosophical disputes.

In what follows, I shall try to untangle some of the contexts in which such a decisive appeal to ordinary language can be correctly made—as I think it is correctly made by Ambrose in the arguments I characterized in the previous chapter—from some of the contexts where it cannot be so used.

However, before I turn to that, I want first to state some important methodological remarks on this topic by John Austin. He ranks close to Wittgenstein in philosophic importance, and it seems to me that his remarks on this score are a needed corrective to Wittgenstein and particularly to such followers of Wittgenstein as Malcolm and Ambrose. Austin tells us that "ordinary language breaks down in extraordinary cases."[21] There are times in the face of very unusual or very complex issues or experiences where "words fail us," for our language is tailored for the rather more typical cases. Moreover, "ordinary language blinkers the already feeble imagination" and it is "infected with the jargon of extinct theories. . . ."[22] Austin stresses (and his philosophic practice brilliantly illustrates) that there is no denying the value of philosophical examinations of what we should say when and why we should say it, but he also sceptically asks about the appeal to ordinary language: "And, why should what we all ordinarily say be the only or the best or the final way of putting it? Why should it even be true?"[23]

In this context, Austin turns his irony and acute argumentative powers against what he calls the Myth of the Last Word. It is indeed true that ordinary language is a subtle and sensitive instrument of communication capable of being employed to make exact distinctions and precise claims, but it is also true that "superstition and error and fantasy of all kinds do become incorporated in ordinary language. . . ."[24] "Certainly, then," Austin concludes, "ordinary language is *not* the last word: in principle it can everywhere be supplemented and improved upon and superseded. Only remember it *is* the *first* word."[25] Austin emphasized in line with this that when we philosophize "we should know what we mean and what not" and in this endeavor careful and sophisticated attention to ordinary discourse is crucial. But he also stressed that on occasion we need "to be brutal with, to torture, to fake, and to override ordinary language. . . ."

It seems to me that the thrust of Austin's remarks here are well directed. We cannot justifiably say with the Wittgensteinians that ordinary language is all right as it is, *if* this is to be taken to mean that it is our final arbiter of sense and nonsense. It has not been shown *pace* the Wittgensteinians that all philosophical difficulties are of linguistic origin and arise not because in some particular conceptual region our languages and the concepts they enshrine are faulty, but because philosophers have mis-described them or because in thinking about them we misconstrue them.

Reflect back to our discussions of religion and to our discussions of the mind/body problem. 'God' has an established use in the language, but from this it does not at all follow that there cannot be questions about the coherence of this concept and about the rationality and appro-priateness of the whole form of life in which it functions.[26] In fact, the central thrust of my arguments, when that problem was discussed, was to show that this is so, and it has been the burden of much contempo-rary philosophical theology. Perhaps such arguments are mistaken, but this very much needs to be established. It cannot reasonably just be assumed that because God-talk is a part of ordinary language that it and the conceptions it embodies are in perfect order just as they are. Moreover, our handling of the mind/body problem indicates how ordinary language can be supplemented, for we came to see there, in talking about the mind/brain identity thesis, how deviant utterances—utterances that now have no function in the stream of ordinary mental-talk—can for all that be intelligible in certain circumstances.[27] Ordinary language is no final arbiter here. Moreover, there are still simpler and less controversial cases where this can be readily seen to be so. Consider the concepts of miracle, demonic possession, ghost, immortality, and fairy. That these concepts are or were expressed by terms securely fixed in ordinary lan-guage does not put them beyond the pale of rational appraisal and/or rejection; and it is philosophical analysis—critical philosophy, using lan-guage as its tool—that has been able to show the incoherence of such concepts. To insist that these concepts *must be in order as they are, simply because they are or were standard parts of ordinary language, is just to be caught up in an unjustified and unjustifiable philosophical dogma.*

It is also true that in examining morality or politics we cannot just assume that ordinary language is all right as it is. That certain substantive normative beliefs are enshrined in the logic of our ordinary moral discourse does not settle matters about how we are to live. In various forms of life there may be criteria for 'legitimate authority', 'good', or 'obligation' that we as rational human beings may not at all be prepared to accept, although surely in trying to gain a perspicuous display of morality and in trying to articulate a rational set of moral and political norms, we should first want to gain an understanding of the actual functioning of such concepts in human living. Here ordinary language is an important first word not to be ignored, but it is and can be no final arbiter of rationality.

When, then, should the appeal to ordinary language play a more fundamental role? I should say preeminently in two contexts: (1) when examining bizarre metaphysical claims cast up by some traditional metaphysician, phenomenologist, or existentialist and (2) when examining the claims of ideal language philosophers who think a language adequate to philosophical purposes should be a kind of calculus.[28] When someone claims that we can never know that there is an external world or whether there are other minds or that the only thing we can see is our own brains or that there are supersensible forms that are the only wholly real realities, we should, as we did, argue from ordinary usage. When faced with such paradoxical metaphysical claims—or statements like the following ones made by a contemporary scholastic philosopher: 'Man has a final end which transcends the world' and 'Man has the character of standing out from the world'—we need to get them translated into the concrete as a first step; for example, 'Do you mean that I can never know whether there are any pencils or that when a surgeon is looking at a brain he is operating on he is looking at his own brain?' (Presumably if he is operating on what he is looking at, he is operating on his own brain too!) Such a translation into the concrete usually has a salutary effect, and to find out what is going on when such metaphysical talk is engaged in, we indeed first need to discover what, if anything intelligible at all, is being said. This is best done by probing their concrete consequences and implications by translating such sentences into the concrete; for example, if time is unreal, does that mean that it is false or meaningless to assert that I put on my underwear *before* I put on my pants? Here ordinary language is indispensable.

Ordinary language is indispensable in another way as well. Such metaphysicians recognize the oddity of their claims; typically they feel or half feel themselves that there is something absurd or strained or utterly paradoxical about them, but they also feel that logic or loyalty to rational argumentation forces them to accept them, paradoxical as they are, quite against their will and quite against their sense of sound common sense. But given such a conviction—a conviction very different than the one one feels about miracles, demonic possession, God, or immortality—it is more plausible to work on the assumption that the paradoxical metaphysical statements are somehow meaningless or false and the metaphysical arguments mistaken and that we have been led astray here because we have failed to gain a proper understanding of the commonsense, scientific, or logical conceptions involved and because we have misunderstood the very logic of our language. Our working assumption should be this: Because of this failure, we are led into the obscurantist nevernever land of metaphysics where people come to believe that such everyday concepts as are captured by the English words 'seeing a physical object' or 'a world existing independently of us' are concepts incapable of exemplification. Here, if we look at the world without evasion—in fact, if we can just avoid wild fantasy—we will appeal to the superior plausibility of commonsense language *and* commonsense considerations over such dreams of a spirit seer.

Let me illustrate what I take to be a good application of the procedural principles I have been talking about. G. E. Moore, who enormously influenced both Wittgenstein and Austin and initiated such appeals to ordinary language and common sense, argued as follows against Hume's claim that we could never know that there were any material things:

> If Hume's principles are true, then, I have admitted, I do *not* know *now* that this pencil—the material object—exists. If, therefore, I am to prove I *do* know that this pencil exists, I must prove, somehow, that Hume's principles [the principles relevant to his argument about not being able to know whether physical objects exist] are not true. In what sort of way, by what sort of argument, can I prove this? It seems to me that, in fact, there really is no stronger and better argument than the following. I do know that this pencil exists; I could not know this, if Hume's principles were true; *therefore,* Hume's principles . . . are false. I think this argument really is as strong and good a one as any that could be used; and I think it really is conclusive.[29]

Moore, of course, has in mind the most favored circumstances in which a person is looking at and holding a pencil in standard light, cold sober, with others around, and the like. It seems to me that Moore is right. *Such* an appeal to common sense against *such metaphysical paradoxes* is quite decisive. In my own terms it is again the appeal to considerations of plausibility that we utilized earlier in arguing about the mind/body problem. We have two rival clashing claims: (1) an apparently tight metaphysical argument designed to show that it is logically impossible or in some way conceptually impossible ever to know that anything like a pencil exists and (2) the claim of a plain man or even of a not so plain man—sane, sober, and the like—in optimum circumstances that he knows that there is a pencil on his desk. It is more plausible to believe, I am maintaining, that somewhere there has been a slip in the metaphysical argument than to believe that the plain man in such a circumstance does not really know that there is a pencil on his desk. A man who would not recognize this would plainly lack common sense, plainly lack good judgment.[30]

Such an argument can be generalized. Moore listed a number of empirical truisms that he maintained he could be absolutely certain were true. They were such things as 'There is a body which is my body, born at such-and-such a time in the past', 'It has been for a number of years on or near the surface of the earth', 'There are a great number of material objects to which it stands in spatial and temporal relations', 'The earth has existed for many years past'. Moore maintained that any metaphysical theory that was logically incompatible with the truth of such claims could be known to be false. Again, the plausibility of believing that such truisms are true is far greater than the plausibility of any metaphysical theory no matter how tight its reasoning appears to be, if indeed we can be confident that it is incompatible with the truth of such truisms. A man lacks good judgment if he does not recognize that it is more reasonable to continue to endorse these truisms than to reject the truisms because of the metaphysical argument.

However, as later linguistic philosophers such as Ambrose, Bouwsma, Lazerowitz, Wisdom, and Malcolm have emphasized, philosophers will feel dissatisfied with such an appeal to common sense, for Moore has not gone inside the metaphysician's argument and shown the defects of his argument. These linguistic philosophers grant that if such metaphysical claims so conflict with ordinary language and common sense, then we can indeed know that the metaphysical claims are mistaken. They argue, however, that we should also carry out a linguistic analysis, such as Ambrose did about 'selfish', to show how the metaphysician was tricked into his absurd claim by a failure to grasp properly the workings of his language. As a fluent speaker he can *operate with* his language, of course, but he does not command a sufficiently clear view of it correctly to *operate upon* it, correctly to understand how it functions. But when, in the area where he is perplexed, he attains such a command of the workings of his language, the metaphysical puzzle will dissolve.

My talk of common sense will surely raise hackles. It will be said that philosophy and indeed rational inquiry exist in part at least to transcend commonsense points of view. Common sense is frequently mistaken, often grossly ethnocentric and superstitious. I, of course, agree with this, and indeed in certain contexts would want to underscore and elucidate just such an attack on the adequacy of commonsense conceptions. But how then can I in consistency appeal to common sense and ordinary language here? The answer is that I am not appealing to it in a wholesale way, but in a way where it would fit in with—that is, square with—what, in discussing the mind/body problem, I called an appeal to considerations of scientific plausibility. This, as I have argued earlier, would give us a technique for overcoming at least the grosser forms of ethnocentrism and superstition reflected in our commonsense categories and enshrined in our ordinary language. The appeal I am making here is to what Peirce called a critical commonsensism. I am not maintaining that there are any commonsense beliefs—particularly normative beliefs—distinctive of any tribe which simply must be accepted in philosophical discussion *as a rallying point—if you will, a base—of greater plausibility than any philosophical or rational argument*. Rather, I am saying that where we have certain empirical truisms—plain matters of fact—that are not culturally relative and have been confirmed massively by our experience (and on a cross-cultural basis), that it is more reasonable to accept them than it is to accept any speculative paradoxical metaphysical argument which conflicts with these beliefs, even if the reasoning for that metaphysical argument does seem airtight. We must not confuse demonstrability with certainty.

As philosophers we should not simply halt here. We should go on, employing the techniques of linguistic analysis, to do a therapeutic job on such paradoxical metaphysical arguments. We should exhibit the sources and the nature of the metaphysical conceptual confusion. But the preceding use of paradigm-case arguments, ordinary language, and common sense does give us good grounds for believing that the conceptual perplexity raised by the paradoxical metaphysical claim is a result of a failure to understand the workings of our everyday language. We bring the metaphysician's usage into confrontation with ordinary usage and show that the metaphysician has failed to grasp the working of his own language and how his own claim (as in the case of 'selfish') involves a pointless alteration of everyday usage. The metaphysician's case is quite different from that of the religious sceptic. The metaphysician does not *really* doubt that there is a pencil on his desk. He just talks about it differently in philosophical contexts, so that he can continue to say either that he does not *know* that it is on his desk—now using 'know' in an odd way—or he may want to say that he still does not know that a physical object is on his desk, because the pencil is really a bundle of sense data. But the religious sceptic really doubts whether he has a soul or whether there is a God to answer his prayers. His doubts are not merely second-order doubts (doubts about the proper *analysis* of his concepts) but first-order doubts (doubts about the reality of what he is talking about) as well. And when this condition obtains, we cannot give the kind of prominence to ordinary language and paradigm-case arguments that we did in arguing about paradoxical meta-physical statements.

IV

Suppose the metaphysician wishes to 'transcend' ordinary language or languages altogether. Here, it is natural to remark, we surely have a conflict between my claims and his, and it at least looks like I have simply assumed without argument that he is wrong. But first of all keep in mind that my argument, as stated at the end of the previous chapter, did not invoke an appeal simply to a given static bit of ordinary language. Rather, it was the claim that a term or sentence is intelligible only if it has a function in a natural language or is part of a symbolic activity, such as musical notation or mathematics or symbolic logic, which in turn is parasitical upon a natural language, or is a term or sentence which is transformable into one of these[31] But, it will be said, this only thickens the plot, for what if the metaphysician says: "I cannot transform my talk into any such system. But why say my uses of language are mis-uses or mistaken and that ordinary or scientific uses of language are correct?"

The reply should be that his claims are incorrect because there can be no merely 'private understanding' or 'private knowledge' (something that is *logically* impossible for more than one person to understand or know) or a 'private language', if by 'private language' is meant a language only one person can—logically can—possibly understand. If you will reflect on what it is to understand, know, or have a language, you will see that this is so.[32] But if a language in that sense must be public, then his talk, to be understandable to others, that is, to be a genuine lan-guage, must at least be in principle transformable into a language that is part of the public domain, or at least it must be sufficiently trans-formable into such a language that it can be taught in such a language in conjunction with ostensive techniques.

There is indeed an urge when one is engaged in metaphysical argument to try to transcend language altogether, to cut this chatter about chatter and get to how things are without linguistic fetters.[33] There have been philosophers who have said that we must see through ordinary language to "the facts, to see what real things the words refer to, and what people are actually doing with words as distinct from what they think they are doing."[34] This is indeed a very natural and very tempting and in some ways a very reasonable thing to say, but a crucial part of it is incoherent for all of that, for we do not have any criteria, independent of criteria of how words are used, for knowing what the facts are like or for knowing what the phenomena are like. Austin notwithstanding, there is no way to pry our language off the world and to look first at our languages and then look at the world and decide which of the various languages, both ordinary and contrived, most adequately represents the world. There is no language-independent way of simply coming to know the world and man's place in it. There is simply no way around this categorio-centric predicament. What is real and unreal cannot be ascertained independently of our languages, although if our languages develop concepts that claim application in the world and yet we do not know what it would be like to apply them, or if certain concepts in a language hang together poorly with other concepts in that language, or if they do not allow us to do with a given language what we want to do with it, as well as another language, we have rational grounds for modifying or rejecting certain parts of it. But there is no transcending our language altogether and gaining a pristine look at reality, for our very distinctions about what can be the case are given within languages.[35]

It is natural to react to such an approach by claiming that it is overly concerned with language. It is natural to say that in doing fundamental philosophy—in wrestling with the primary problems of philosophy—we are concerned with man-in-the-world and only in an ancillary way with language. It is tempting to complain, faced with arguments like the ones we have just been through, that by now, within contemporary analytic philosophy, a *means*—having clean tools with which to examine philosophical problems—has become the *end* and the fundamental purpose of that conceptual inquiry we call philosophy has been lost. But I must insist on a disclaimer here. For reasons I have made apparent, we indeed need to be as clear as we can about what it makes sense to say in trying to come to grips with the primary problems of philosophy, but nothing I have said or done bears out the charge that we are concerned with words or with 'meanings' (whatever that is) alone. As Austin has remarked:

> When we examine what we should say when, what words we should use in what situations, we are looking again not *merely* at words . . . but also at the realities we use the words to talk about: we are using a sharpened awareness of words to sharpen our perception of . . . the phenomena.[36]

Austin points out in that context that words of course are not "the final arbiter" of the phenomena. However, we should not take Austin's remark to suggest that there is some way of comparing words and the world to check the communication value of our words. But he does bring out that our concern in doing conceptual analysis is not purely with words or with meanings but with, if you will pardon the existentialist idiom, man-in-the-world.

What I have tried to do in the last two chapters in an elementary way—in a way that omits many considerations and skips too lightly over others—is to show how by arguing from ordinary language we can develop a powerful ground for eliminating metaphysics: a ground that superficially at least is distinct from the empiricist considerations I argued for in Chapter 33.[37]

V

Before we proceed in the subsequent chapters to examine a kind of metamorphosed metaphysics and the challenge of existentialism, we should pull together the threads of this complicated discussion so as to make it quite evident what answers I have actually proposed to the clusters of questions that have been ours in the last five chapters. I have tried to explicate and defend the empiricist claim that where metaphysical claims go beyond the bounds of sense, it must then be said that they are devoid of factual significance and that they fail to make intelligible assertions. Such metaphysical and theological 'beliefs' supposedly commit their adherents to the making of certain truth claims, but in reality they do not, for there are no such metaphysical or theological assertions that are either true or false. Such ontologizing, I have argued, is out. It is neither a reasonable nor even a coherent activity.

I have argued for such dethronement of ontology while rejecting the claim that the verifiability criterion of meaning could provide an adequate *general* criterion of meaning, although I did argue that suitably interpreted (given an interpretation such as my [5]) it is a good criterion for *factual* significance. I have thus claimed that a sentence in an ordinary idiom, or capable in principle at least of being transformed into a grammatically well-formed sentence or set of sentences in an ordinary idiom, can be used to make a genuine factual statement if and only if the statement made by its use is at least in principle confirmable or infirmable.

Such a claim may appear to conflict, but actually does not, with my explicit denial in this chapter that ordinary language is the final arbiter of sense and nonsense. I made that claim in the context of stating Austin's attack on the Myth of the Last Word, and it is quite compatible with accepting the claim that an utterance is intelligible only if it is at least in principle transformable into an ordinary idiom or, in the few situations where this is relevant, transformable into some artificial system of notation parasitical on a natural language—for example, symbolic logic, mathematics, musical notation, Morse code. There is no incompatibility here since acceptance of the transformability criterion does not commit one to the absurd position that only a given ordinary language is intelligible; accepting my criterion of meaning—to put the central consideration here in a different way—does not at all commit one to the belief that ordinary language and the conceptual status quo are all right as they are, and it does not reject conceptual innovation even in philosophy, although it does insist on (what is another thing altogether) a link between innovations and the conceptual past by laying down transform-ability in principle as a necessary, although of course not as a sufficient, condition for intelligibility. (Do not forget that even in talking about the functions of language the contexts of discovery and the contexts of confirmation are quite different.)

However, I have not in this summary section made myself sufficiently explicit on my answer to one very central problem I broached in these last five chapters: How do we ascertain what it makes sense to say? Transformability into an ordinary idiom (even with all its necessary quali-fications) is still only a *necessary* condition for intelligibility, and while verifiability conjoined with it gives—or so I argued—necessary and suf-ficent conditions for *factual* significance, it does not give necessary and sufficient conditions for significance or intelligibility period. So while I may have found a good criterion for eliminating ontologizing, I have not with it found a good general criterion for significance, so that I have at best answered only one of the central questions in these last five chapters while leaving the other (the problem about a criterion of intel-ligibility) quite unanswered.

We therefore still have this nasty question nagging us: Is there a clear or satisfactory answer to such a general question about significance? That is, have I shown what requirements a symbol (a word or sentence, for example) must satisfy in order correctly to be called meaningful or intel-ligible? The end of the last chapter states a basically Wittgensteinian criterion in terms of claiming that a term or sentence is meaningful if it has a use, has an employment or regular function, in a language. In spite of the ambiguities in the concept of use (ambiguities that we have not examined), I think this is at least the beginning of a good answer.[38] A term or utterance has a meaning of some sort if it has a use in a language such that there are rules governing its employment.[39]

However, intelligibility admits of degrees, and such a condition only guarantees a minimal intelligibility. I say 'minimal' because terms can have a fixed place in a language and still express an incoherent concept (for example, 'diabolical possession' or 'black magic') and utterances can have a fixed place in language and remain incoherent (for example, 'My soul shall persist after the death of my body' or 'To know Christ is to know the Truth'). A minimal meaning goes with use, but the question 'What does it make sense to say?' covers a number of questions that should not be conflated. The following are the most important questions philo-sophically: (1) How do we determine when a phonemic sequence has any meaning at all? (2) How do we determine when a term or terms are sufficiently intelligible to be able to be employed (given their standard use in sentences) to make assertions that are true or false? (3) How do we determine when a term or terms are sufficiently intelligible to be able to be employed (given their standard use in sentences) to make true or false *factual* assertions? (4) How do we determine whether a term or terms are sufficiently intelligible to be able to be employed (given their standard use in sentences) to make statements that can be reasonably believed? Utterances can be assessed in all these dimensions and others besides. A correct answer to the third question is very useful (some might say even essential) in arguing about whether the metaphysician's claim to have a nonexperential knowledge of what the world is like is or can be justified. But that question is plainly not the only question we could or should ask about what it makes sense to say. What we need to realize is that 'What does it make sense to say?' is naturally employed in different contexts to ask quite diverse questions. Only after we have realized that can we begin to divide and conquer.

NOTES

1. Ernest Gellner, *Words and Things*. See also his "Logical Positivism and After or The Spurious Fox," *Universities Quarterly*, vol. 2, no. 4 (August, 1957), and his "The Crisis in the Humanities and the Mainstream of Philosophy," in J. H. Plumb (ed.), *Crisis in the Humanities*. It is not true to assert, as Perry Anderson does in his "Components of the National Culture," *New Left Review*, vol. 50 (July/August, 1968), that "All critics of English philosophy owe a great debt to Gellner's classic. It is significant that it has never been answered by linguistic orthodoxy" (p. 23). Perhaps it is a classic to which we are deeply indebted intellectually. That surely is an arguable point. But it is simply not true that it has never been answered by linguistic orthodoxy—and in some detail. See here J. M. Cameron, *The Night Battle*, chapter 6, and M. Dummett, "Oxford Philosophy," *Blackfriars*, XLI (1960). For a somewhat more sympathetic but still critical treatment of Gellner, see David Pole, "Words and Mr. Gellner," *Twentieth Century*, CLXVII (1960), and J. N. Findlay, "E. Gellner: *Words and Things*," *The Indian Journal of Philosophy*, vol. III (1961). But for a reply along Wittgensteinian lines see John Gourlie, "Findlay on *Words and Things*," *The Indian Journal of Philosphy*, vol. IV (1964).

2. The key critical arguments against the employment of the paradigm-case argument occur in John Passmore, *Philosophical Reasoning*, chapter 6; Ernest Gellner, *Words and Things*, chapter 2; J. W. Watkins, "Farewell to the Paradigm-Case Argument," *Analysis*, vol. 18, no. 2 (December, 1957). There is considerable literature about the force and legitimacy of this argument in critical philosophy. The most thorough and convincing defense of the paradigm-case argument with which I am acquainted occurs in Antony Flew's "Again the Paradigm," in P. Feyerabend and G. Maxwell (eds.), *Mind, Matter and Method*. Important discussions of paradigm-case argument occur in L. D. Hoalgate, "The Paradigm-Case Argument and Possible Doubt," *Inquiry*, vol. V, no. 4 (1962); E. Sosa, "The Paradigm-Case Argument: Necessary, Causal or Normative?" *Methodos*, vol. XV (1963); Tziporah Kasachkoff, "Ontological Implications of the Paradigm-Case Argument," *Philosophical Studies* (Maynooth, Ireland), vol. XVII (1968); Jytte Hansen,

"The Paradigm-Case Argument: A Valid Ontological Argument?" *Danish Year Book in Philosophy*, vol. 2 (1965); and David Favrholdt, "The Argument From Polar Concepts," *The Danish Year Book in Philosophy*, vol. 2 (1965). Extensive bibliographies on this topic are given in the articles by Flew and Sosa cited above. Also see entry under "Paradigm-Case Argument" in Paul Edwards (ed.), *The Encyclopedia of Philosophy*. I think it is quite correct to say, as Flew does, that one will find the paradigm-case argument being employed fruitfully and in the contexts where it should be employed by Malcolm, Wisdom, Ambrose, and Lazerowitz in Paul Schilpp (ed.), *The Philosophy of G. E. Moore*. Here is where you should start in examining the argument, since here is where it is unselfconsciously (and in my judgment effectively) being put to work. You should then view the critical arguments about the argument itself against that background.

3. John Passmore, *Philosophical Reasoning*, p. 118. But see Strawson's rejoinder. P. F. Strawson, "Review of Philosophical Reasoning," *Philosophical Books*, vol. III, no. 2 (April, 1962), pp. 17–19.

4. Strawson makes the rejoinder that this is just what is wrong with them. Passmore's approach here misses the import of the spirit of G. E. Moore who, rather than being caught up in the games metaphysicians play, in effect called the metaphysicians' bluff by looking at the metaphysical enterprise with a kind of honest literalness. Moore saw and taught us to see that the emperor had on no clothes at all. No doubt there is something to be salvaged, but Moore's kind of literalness helps us see that the whole metaphysical task, if it is to go on at all, must be differently conceived. For some balanced and important remarks on this topic, see A. E. Murphy, "Moore's Defense of Common Sense," in Murphy's *Reason and the Common Good*.

5. John Passmore, *Philosophical Reasoning*, p. 112.

6. Ibid.

7. By 'a *reductio* argument' I mean an argument that shows a certain claim to be absurd by validly drawing from it absurd consequences. That is, one is shown that if one accepts the proposition in question one is logically committed to certain consequences that are absurd. Since one does not want to accept the absurd consequences (or so the argument assumes), one will reject the proposition that entails them.

8. Jytte Hansen, op. cit., p. 54

9. This was Malcolm's claim in his early and important employment of the paradigm-case argument in his "Moore and Ordinary Language," reprinted in Richard Rorty (ed.), *The Linguistic Turn*. See here Roderick Chisholm's criticism of it in "Philosophers and Ordinary Language," also reprinted in *The Linguistic Turn*, and Malcolm's reply "Philosophy for Philosophers," *Philosophical Review*, vol. LX (1951), pp. 329–340.

10. For ways in which it is an important starter, see Norman Malcolm's "The Verification Argument," in his *Knowledge and Certainty*.

11. Jytte Hansen, op. cit.

12. Antony Flew, op. cit.

13. Ibid., p. 271.

14. A. J. Ayer, "Common Sense and Metaphysics," in William Kennick and Morris Lazerowitz (eds.), *Metaphysics: Readings and Reappraisals*, p. 322.

15. John Passmore, "The Place of Argument in Metaphysics," in William Kennick and Morris Lazerowitz (eds.), *Metaphysics: Readings and Reappraisals,* p. 362.

16. See here Norman Malcolm, "Moore and Ordinary Language," in Richard Rorty (ed.), *The Linguistic Turn,* op. cit., and his important "George Edward Moore," in his *Knowledge and Certainty.* And see Alice Ambrose, "Philosophical Doubts," *Massachusetts Review* (1960), and Antony Flew, op. cit.

17. Perry Anderson, "Components of the National Culture," *New Left Review,* vol. 50 (July/August, 1968), p. 21.

18. Ibid., p. 43.

19. Ernest Gellner, "Logical Positivism and After or the Spurious Fox," *Universities Quarterly,* vol. 11, no. 4 (August, 1957), p. 359 and his "Poker Player," *New Statesman* (Nov. 28, 1969), pp. 774–776.

20. I have tried to make this clear in my "Wittgensteinian Fideism," *Philosophy* (July, 1967); "Wittgensteinian Fideism Again: A Reply to Hudson," *Philosophy* (January, 1969); and my "Language and the Concept of God," *Question II* (January, 1969).

21. John Austin, *Philosophical Papers,* p. 36. The papers by Urmson, Hampshire, Urmson and Warnock, and Cavell on Austin's method reprinted by Richard Rorty (ed.), *The Linguistic Turn,* op. cit., pp. 232–260; the short comments by Malcolm, Quine, and Hampshire, *The Journal of Philosophy,* vol. LXII, no. 19 (Oct. 7, 1965); G. J. Warnock, "John Langshaw Austin," *Proceedings of the British Academy,* Vol. XLIX; and Bernard Williams, "J. L. Austin's Philosophy," *The Oxford Magazine,* Vol. III (1962) all contain important remarks about Austin's method. For an excellent full-length study of Austin's philosophy, see Mats Furberg, *Locutionary and Illocutionary Acts: A Main Theme in J. L. Austin's Philosophy.*

22. John Austin, op. cit., pp. 36 and 130.

23. Ibid., p. 131.

24. Ibid., p. 133.

25. Ibid.

26. See the references in note 20.

27. David Cooper, "The Fallacies of Linguistic Philosophy," *The Oxford Review,* Hilary (1968).

28. I have said very little in this book about the logicizing of philosophy, for such work never really did much with what I have characterized as the primary problems of philosophy. But it was a bold philosophical program very influential in the interwar period and finding its most typical and most important exponents in the early, but not the late, work of Wittgenstein, and in the work of Russell, Carnap, and Bergmann. (Quine and Goodman are equally important but not so clearly committed to an ideal language method.) Ideal language philosophy has been devastatingly criticized by its most important former practitioner, Ludwig Wittgenstein, in his later work. Much of the point of the stress by linguistic philosophers on ordinary language needs to be understood in the context of arguments with these logicizing ideal language philosophers. For an authoritative but brief statement of the history of such arguments, see J. O. Urmson, *Philosophical Analysis.* (But for the reactions of an ideal language philosopher to this account see

Gustav Bergmann, *Meaning and Existence.*) Richard Rorty's (ed.) anthology *The Linguistic Turn*, op. cit., gives some of the crucial papers in the debate between these two different ways of doing analytic philosophy. For an expert but short and simplified account which brings out something of what is at issue, see D. F. Pears, "The Philosophy of Wittgenstein," *The New York Review of Books* (Jan. 16, 1969).

29. G. E. Moore, *Some Main Problems of Philosophy*, pp. 119–120.

30. For a rather similar argument see Norman Malcolm's essay on Moore in his *Knowledge and Certainty*.

31. For the sense in which technical terms are parasitical on ordinary language, see Charles E. Caton's introduction to his anthology *Philosophy and Ordinary Language*.

32. The classical source here is Ludwig Wittgenstein, *Philosophical Investigations*. Important brief elucidations and defenses of Wittgenstein's antiprivate language arguments occur in Rush Rhees, "Can There Be a Private Language?" reprinted in Charles E. Caton (ed.), *Philosophy and Ordinary Language;* Norman Malcolm's critical notice of *Philosophical Investigations*, reprinted in George Pitcher (ed.), *Wittgenstein;* and Peter Winch, *The Idea of a Social Science*, chapter I. For a fuller discussion of this problem see O. R. Jones (ed.), *Private Language Argument*.

33. Alice Ambrose, "The Problem of Linguistic Inadequacy," in her *Essays in Analysis*, and David Pears, "Universals," in Antony Flew (ed.), *Logic and Language* (second series) carefully examine this.

34. J. L. Mackie, *Contemporary Linguistic Philosophy—Its Strength and Its Weakness*, p. 14.

35. This is powerfully argued by Peter Winch in his *The Idea of a Social Science* and in his "Understanding a Primitive Society," reprinted in D. Z. Phillips (ed.), *Religion and Understanding*.

36. J. L. Austin, *Philosophical Papers*, p. 130. See also note 7 of Chapter 33, and Stanley Cavell, "Aesthetic Problems of Modern Philosophy," in Max Black (ed.), *Philosophy in America*, pp. 74–75 and 93–97. For a fuller account of this general problem see Stanley Cavell's *Must We Mean What We Say?*

37. But see here my remarks in note 9 of the previous chapter.

38. See here P. F. Strawson's remarks on page 10 of his introduction to the anothology he edited, *Philosophic Logic*. For a more detailed discussion of what is at issue here, see essays V, VI, VII, and VIII in G. H. R. Parkinson (ed.), *The Theory of Meaning*, and William Alston's discussion of 'use' in his *Philosophy of Language*. George Pitcher in his *The Philosophy of Wittgenstein* shows, however, how very useful this notion of use is for the purposes for which Wittgenstein employed it. It seems that given our aims here it is sufficiently clear to use as a tool in analyzing the philosophical perplexities we analyzed.

39. In an interesting paper, Gilbert H. Harman, "Three Levels of Meaning," *The Journal of Philosophy*, vol. LXV, no. 19 (Oct. 3, 1968), argues that there are different levels in the theory of meaning. Depending on what problems we are trying to clarify, we ask different questions and what is a proper answer to one question need not be—and typically is not—a proper answer to another. None of his three levels, that is, questions concerning the

meaning of thoughts, the meaning of messages, or the meaning of speech acts, exactly corresponds to what I have been concerned with here. But to the extent they do, I am concerned with questions of meaning of level one, that is, with questions about the meanings of thoughts; and it would seem that there we are giving the same answer (allowing for terminological differences), for Harman remarks: "One gives an account of the meaning of words as they are used in thinking by giving an account of their use in the evidence-inference-action game. For a speaker to understand certain words, phrases, and sentences of his language is for him to be able to use them in thinking, etc." p. 600.

36

THE RESURGENCE
OF METAPHYSICS

I

In the last four chapters I have done something to express and explain the central antimetaphysical animus of much contemporary analytic philosophy. However, it might very well be said that in what I have been saying vis-à-vis metaphysics I have been old-fashioned. After all, for the last ten years metaphysics has been 'in' again among analytic philosophers. The three major general works by analytic philosophers since Wittgenstein have been metaphysical: Peter Strawson's *Individuals* (1959), Stuart Hampshire's *Thought and Action* (1959) and W. O. Quine's *Word and Object* (1960).[1] Moreover, there have been sympathetic discussions of the very possibility of metaphysics by analytic philosophers, for example, D. F. Pears (ed.), *The Nature of Metaphysics* (1957) and W. H. Walsh, *Metaphysics* (1963).

I would like to suggest that the break with the antimetaphysical party of positivism and empiricism is more apparent than real. What is now taken as legitimate metaphysics by analytic philosophers is something very different from what the logical empiricists were attacking. While it is now generally conceded that the logical empiricist criterion of meaning is defective, there is also a very widespread agreement that the logical empiricists were right in claiming that metaphysics does not and cannot provide us with knowledge about reality which is not obtainable by scientific means.[2]

When one examines the typical claims of those who now take a tolerant attitude toward metaphysics or engage in what they call 'metaphysical analysis' or 'categorial analysis', it is evident that they have conceded to the logical empiricists the major point these empiricists wished to make about metaphysical claims. In short, there has been a metamorphosis in the very concept of metaphysics. The 'new metaphysics' is operating, as far as claims about knowledge of what is the case goes, in accordance with what Father Copleston takes to be the "general positivist mentality."[3]

What I have been claiming in the previous paragraph is well exemplified by Gilbert Ryle, a leading philosophical analyst, who remarked in the closing discussion of a symposium on the nature of metaphysics that it was "commonly expected of a metaphysician that he should assert the existence or occurrence of things unseen and give for these assertions purely philosophical or conceptual reasons."[4] But, Ryle goes on to claim, Hume and Kant have conclusively established that this is impossible. Purely conceptual considerations, purely *a priori* arguments, can never establish the existence of anything.[5] The ontological argument for the existence of God was a distinguished attempt to do this. But it failed. Such ontologizing is out.

> The reason why ontology is out is quite simple. Any assertion of the existence of something, like any assertion of the occurrence of something, can be denied without logical absurdity. So the reasons for assertions of existence or occurrence can never be purely conceptual considerations. We may indeed and often do have the best possible reasons for concluding to the existence or occurrence of something; but these reasons must themselves embody factual evidence, evidence got by experimental as distinct from merely conceptual investigations. When we want to know what there actually is or what has actually gone on in the universe, we have to quarry in the appropriate parts of the universe itself. Quarrying cannot be replaced by architect's deskwork, any more than eating can be replaced by digesting. Still less can quarrying for evidence be replaced by philosophizing. For philosophizing is the second-order business of tracing the structural stresses that develop between technical theories or the untechnical schemes of ideas of which our factual findings are the stones.[6]

Recall that Norman Malcolm tried diligently to undermine the conclusion that we cannot establish the existence of anything by purely conceptual considerations in defending a version of Anselm's ontological argument. We have seen how he failed and I should report, as a sociological fact about philosophers, that it is now generally—although not quite universally—conceded that he failed and that such endeavors are bound to fail. In other words, it seems to be quite evident that the empiricist claim is correct that no truths about what exists can be proved to be logically necessary. Such metaphysical ontologizing is out.

This is now generally accepted by both the antimetaphysical party and by those analytical philosophers sympathetic to the 'new metaphysics'. Earlier in the same symposium (*The Nature of Metaphysics*, D. F. Pears, ed.) from which I have taken the quotation from Ryle, Stuart Hampshire, whose *Thought and Action* is one of the three most distinguished examples of the 'new metaphysics', remarks quite unequivocally:

> Deductive metaphysics, system-building of the old kind, has never recovered from Kant's criticism, and I do not think that it ever will. The old idea that a

philosopher might deduce by pure reason what *must* have been the origin of things, and what *must* be the structure of the universe, at least in outline, seems to me to have been killed stone dead.[7]

A few distinguished analytical philosophers, for example, Malcolm and Plantinga (both theists, by the way), still resist such conclusions, but the vast majority side with Ryle and Hampshire. The vast majority, of course, *may* be wrong. All the same, it seems to me, for the reasons I have given in various parts of this book, that we have excellent reasons for thinking that the majority opinion is right in this instance. If this is right, then speculative philosophy or metaphysics, if it is to go on at all, must, I believe, become something very different from classical ontologizing.

II

Even among those who adopt and work in the ambience of what Copleston calls "a general positivist mentality," there are those who believe that metaphysics remains in some sense an important and worthwhile activity.[8] Metaphysicians of such a persuasion continue to ask, to put it in a popular and possibly trite manner, what we care to make of the scheme of things entire. In what terms are we to do this and how are we to seek to comprehend it? As W. H. Walsh put it, "We hanker after a unitary reading of experience, a reading which will do justice to all the phenomena and enable everything to be seen in its place. It is readings of this kind which metaphysicians presume to offer. They present considerations . . . in favor of this or that way of seeing the world and human experience as a whole."[9]

Surely there is something in this. Many people have a need to adumbrate a general world-view as a supporting background for a way of life. In fact, Hume's work, Russell's work, and Ayer's work as well, including his youthful iconoclastic manifesto for the antimetaphysical party, *Language, Truth and Logic*, are in Walsh's sense metaphysical. They give us a unitary reading of experience. Whether they are adequate or not is another question. Moreover, Ludwig Wittgenstein, the deepest of the antimetaphysicians, speaks in his most powerful book, *Philosophical Investigations*, of the need for a "perspicuous representation." Wittgenstein remarks:

> A main source of our failure to understand is that we do not *command a clear view* of the use of our words.—Our grammar is lacking in this sort of perspicuity. A perspicuous representation produces just that understanding which consists in 'seeing connexions'. . . .
> The concept of a perspicuous representation is of fundamental significance for us. It earmarks the form of account we give, the way we look at things. (Is this a 'Weltanschauung'?).[10]

Wittgenstein seems to be saying in different terminology very much the same thing Walsh says constitutes engaging in metaphysics.

It is tempting to say that this is not so, for in reality they are very different, since Wittgenstein is merely talking about language while Walsh is talking about experience and a unitary reading or picture of reality. To be concerned with that is very different from being concerned, as Wittgenstein is, with a perspicuous representation of our use of words and our forms of language.

Such an objection to my claim is confused. The difference between Walsh's enterprise and Wittgenstein's is more apparent than real. Wittgenstein was not concerned with words per se but with the uses, the functions, of words. He wrote mainly in German but taught and was discussed mainly (until very recently) in English. He was not concerned with either English or German *per se*, but with philosophical perplexities generated by our failure to understand the complex functioning of our language. His concern with language was his concern with the uses, the roles, those words played in the stream of life. And he stressed that the very forms of language were the forms of life. That is, language (or rather speech) is an activity in which people do things with words and without which they would have no view of themselves or anything else. It is not something separated from experience. To give an account of a word's meaning is to describe its role in the language and to describe this is to describe the social intercourse into which it enters. This involves, of course, our actions and our conceptions of reality. To command a clear view of these uses of words is precisely to have a unified picture of human life. This surely is at least a very large part of man's concern to attain a unitary reading of experience.

The relevant difference is not that Wittgenstein's concern is linguistic while Walsh's is experiential, but that Wittgenstein was deeply sceptical about attaining a *general* overview—a seeing of the world *as a whole*. He thought any perspicuous representation, any commanding a clear view, would be for limited domains, and that any greater drive for generality or any attempt to attain a synoptic view (such as we found J. J. C. Smart advocating with his reductive materialism and what is surely one example of what Walsh calls an interpretation of human experience as a whole) is something that is doomed to failure. Here we no longer have a clash about kinds of activity. The difference concerns the degree of generality it is reasonable to expect and what could count as a 'perspicuous representation'.

My own approach to philosophy in this book has certainly been within the ambience of what Copleston has called "a general positivist mentality." Of course, I have tried to avoid simply assuming it and dogmatically rejecting ontologizing, but I have defended reductive materialism and attacked transcendent metaphysical claims in a manner that puts me within this general positivist or, as I would prefer to call it, empiricist framework. While I would as emphatically as Ryle and Hampshire reject ontologizing, it also seems that the attempt to do metaphysics as Walsh has characterized it and as it has been practiced by Smart and Armstrong is a perfectly legitimate endeavor and is compatible with being an empiricist.

In a tentative and elementary way I have tried along with doing piecemeal conceptual analysis to do some metaphysics in the sense characterized by Walsh. I have not simply discussed the primary problems of philosophy in isolation one from the other, but I have tried to show as we went along from problem to problem and while primarily directing attention to the problems themselves, how I put together the answers I found most appropriate so that they formed a tolerably unified picture of the world. I have repeatedly stressed connections—trying to suggest here what might constitute the kernel of a *Weltanschauung*. (Recall here my synoptic remarks in Chapters 30 and 31.)

While it seems to me that such an endeavor is not only coherent but also crucial in philosophy, it also seems to me that, granting its legitimacy, it still remains too vaguely characterized. To speak of 'a unitary reading of our experience' or of 'a picture of human experience as a whole' is to indulge in metaphor—illuminating and suggestive metaphor no doubt, but still metaphor. In somewhat more literal and flat-footed terms, what constitutes the having of a metaphysical scheme? And what kind of statement is a metaphysical statement? (Or is it that there is no one kind of statement that is a metaphysical statement?) We have already ruled out what Ryle called ontologizing, that is, the attempt to gain a knowledge of the world by purely conceptual means. In that way, then, if my argument is correct, there can be no rationally intelligible metaphysical schemes. What then, in somewhat more exact terms, is a metaphysical scheme? What is it to attain metaphysical knowledge? What kind of statements are metaphysical statements? And how are they known to be true or false? Are they very general empirical statements such as I took 'Sensations are brain processes' to be, or are they analytic, or of some different category altogether, or are they of a mixed bag, or what? And how do these statements function in a metaphysical scheme, and how do we establish or disestablish a metaphysical claim? In sum, how is metaphysics disciplined by argument and rational criticism?

III

Some of the preceding battery of questions I cannot answer, at present at any rate, but I see no reason to regard any of them as unanswerable pseudoquestions, and it does seem evident to me that to pursue metaphysics (speculative philosophy) fruitfully we need answers to those questions. We should start with the first ones, namely, the attempt to more literally characterize metaphysics and a metaphysical scheme. We should winnow out from the various metaphysical practices those that are too opaque to give us a disciplined argument for adopting a particular view of the world and those that fall into the fallacy of ontologizing and thus run up against our previous antimetaphysical structures. For these purposes I shall briefly look at some metaphysical postures and attempt to discern which ones should be discarded on those grounds and which, if any, stand those tests and might afford us a more literal characterization of metaphysics as a vision or unitary picture or way of seeing the world and human experience as a whole.

Much metaphysics is in an Aristotelian mold. Such an approach regards metaphysics as the study of being. This is the most general of all studies, for it examines existence or reality as such and not simply the realities studied by the particular sciences. To engage in metaphysics is most basically to explain what it is to be. The separate sciences investigate things and their relationships. But they constantly assume, without giving an account of, the being of what they study. Metaphysics studies that which they assume. That is to say, it is the science of *being as such*. Its aim is to give us a supremely general knowledge of being, reality, or existence as such.[11]

This conception of metaphysics clearly falls prey to what I call 'ontologizing fallacies'. It requires, as Copleston admits, an 'intuition of being' to grasp what it is that we have knowledge of when we gain a knowledge of being as such. Any knowledge of being rests on some allegedly nonexperiential knowledge of being. This is evident when we come to see that statements that assert that being as such is one or is in flux or is transendent or nontranscendent are all unverifiable. Moreover, the very concept of being does not make a nonvacuous contrast with anything. Unlike 'x is hard', 'x is accurate', or 'x has mass', 'x is being' or 'x has being' has no conceivable antithesis. We cannot say what it would be like for 'x not to have being' or for 'x to be nonbeing' or for 'x to be nothing'. 'Nothing', 'not being', or 'nonbeing' cannot be used as a substantive; it does not function as a descriptive term. For uses of 'being' that are of potential philosophical value, it is not used as an attribute (characteristic) of things. 'Being' cannot characterize x no matter what value replaces the variable 'x'.

To say 'Being is such and such'—'Being is flux' or 'Being is one', for example—is equally empty because 'being', having no *conceivable* antithesis, cannot be identified. Thus we cannot know its characteristics. Since this is so there can be no knowledge either experiential or nonexperiential of being. Note that there is no way of ascertaining which of the following are true or false or even probably true or false.

Being is one.

Being is many.

Being changes.

Being is permanent.

Superficially viewed, such sentences appear to be like such genuinely fact-expressing sentences as

England is mountainous.

England is flat.

England is an island.

England is a peninsula.

But with the former list there is no way of knowing whether they are true or false or even probably true or false. We do not know what facts they are incompatible or compatible with. Whatever else metaphysics is, it is certainly correct to say, as John Passmore does, that "metaphysics is speculation controlled by rational criticism."[12] But then there must be some way in which a metaphysician's claims can be disciplined by argument. The rub here is that since such being-talk has no ascertainable truth value, while still purporting to make factual assertions of a very fundamental nature, there is no way of disciplining such metaphysical talk by reasoning. Since there is no way of deciding which of its claims are true or even probably true, it fails to satisfy a very central feature of what metaphysics is supposed to be, namely, speculation controlled by rational criticism. In short, this Aristotelian conception of metaphysics does run afoul of the traditional strictures against metaphysics and does not serve as an adequate demythologized statement of what it is to have a unitary vision or picture of the world as a whole.

Talk of metaphysics, as we find it in the writings of a British Hegelian, F. H. Bradley, is structured in terms of a fundamental distinction between appearance and reality.[13] Metaphysics, of course, gives us knowledge of or an insight into reality, while common sense and science merely concern themselves with appearances. Such a metaphysics suffers fundamentally from the same difficulties as does the Aristotelian conception. Given Bradley's metaphysical use of 'reality', it, like the Aristotelian-Thomistic use of 'being' or 'being as such', is supposedly a term with a referent, but there is no way of identifying its alleged referent. There is no way of establishing *on such a system* what is reality as distinct from appearance. Thus, such a system, no more than the Aristotelian one, will provide us with the key to the demythologized account of metaphysics.[14]

There is an utterly different conception of metaphysics that has probably found its most subtle and full statement in the work of R. J. Collingwood.[15] On such a view, metaphysics is the attempt to expose and accurately delineate the presuppositions of science and everyday life of any particular epoch. This conception of metaphysics does not commit the ontologist's fallacy and does not fall prey to our critique of metaphysics. There is no reason to believe that the statements of such a metaphysician should be logically illegitimate. But there are different kinds of difficulties in such an approach to metaphysics. These difficulties come to view when we spell out its aims. Note that it reduces metaphysics, or at least any self-conscious attempt to develop 'a new metaphysics' (a metaphysics with a Collingwoodian awareness of absolute presuppositions), to being an artful and hopefully perspicuous statement of the history of ideas of a period. But metaphysicians are typically not archaeologists of the intellect or anthropologists of general ideas. At least, that is not what they strive to be. They seek to cut new intellectual pathways, to seek a firmer rational foundation for thought. They seek to assess, and where and if necessary, to go beyond the presuppositions of an age and not simply to uncover its presuppositions. They do not wish to be merely—or even at all— historians of ideas. They seek a timeless insight, although often with a deep scepticism.

Quite independently of considerations about what metaphysicians seek, it should be pointed out against Collingwoodians that, as Strawson puts it, "there is a massive central core of human thinking which has no history—or none recorded in histories of thought. There are categories and concepts which in their most fundamental character, change not at all."[16] Perhaps Strawson's counter here is slightly exaggerated, but even if this is so, it is very unlikely that the basic categories of thought and reality are really so epoch-dependent as Collingwood would have us believe. Whether they are or not, it still remains true that metaphysicians have sought 'timeless truths'. If Collingwood is right and there are none, this would be simply another way of eliminating metaphysics. It is no doubt useful to historians of ideas to have those "archaeologists of thought" that Collingwood calls metaphysicians, but if that is all that metaphysicians can realistically do, then the metaphysician's own quest would be frustrated, and the very conception of metaphysics would undergo a radical sea change.

Such a Collingwoodian metaphysics would *not* give us a reading for 'a unitary picture or way of seeing the world and human experience as a whole', for, if he is right, we can only characterize the various presuppositions of various ages. We would have to give up as an "unrealizable metaphysical dream" such a search for a vision of the whole of human experience.

A Kantian conception of metaphysics is more likely to be closer to what we are seeking. Kant caused a Copernican turn in philosophy. In many ways he is an antimetaphysician, but he also articulated a conception of metaphysics that aims at describing the absolutely fundamental features of all possible human experience. The metaphysician should describe the necessary structure of human thought: the basic conceptual scheme of the human animal.[17]

Kant agrees with Hume and the empiricists that there is no way of stepping outside of experience, of overleaping the 'bounds of sense', to gain an Archimedean point that gives us some nonexperiential knowledge of how things must be or even how they are. But Kant argues, working from *within,* reflecting on the categories of thought and experience, we can gain, without violating empiricist principles, a completely general and final characterization of the fundamental structure of human thought and experience.

Kant recognized the almost inevitable tendency to fall into what he called "transcendental illusion" and to try to gain some formal explanation or conception of an ultimate reality that transcends all possible experience. But, like the empiricists, he stressed that when we do this we end up fighting with shadows. Long before Wittgenstein, Kant recognized how easily we are led here into verbal traps, and how we come to use language in an unintelligible way.

It is difficult to decide whether this Kantian conception of metaphysics actually commits the ontologist's fallacy. At first it appears not to do so. Kant is telling us that we cannot make knowledge claims that go beyond the limits of human experience. Yet, Kant goes on to postulate a "noumenal reality," a *Ding an sich* (a thing in itself), which somehow we can *think* but not *know.* This seems to let in the allegedly nonempirical entities or realities supposedly exorcised. Moreover, Kant thought that in such a metaphysics we are laying bare the *necessary* presuppositions of all thought and experience. But, as Hampshire points out, an empiricist would challenge that there are any such *necessities* here.[18] How can Kant prove that there are such necessities? It is either simply a brute empirical fact that human beings happen to think and experience things in a certain way, or the necessities concerning the limits of thought and experience are logical necessities. If they are logical necessities, they turn on the meaning the terms in question just happen to have. But here we do not have any synthetic *necessities* at all. The task is the crucial one of showing not only *how* but even *that* synthetic *a priori* knowledge is possible.

In Kant's contentions about the necessary structure of thought and experience, we seem to have claims that maintain we could gain some knowledge of reality that is *a priori,* and thus Kant is, after all, in making such synthetic *a priori* statements, committing the ontologist's fallacy.[19] Since this is so, the Kantian claim remains an unsafe guide in trying to give a literal account of what it is to have a metaphysical vision.

Basically in the spirit of Kant, but without his claim to necessity or talk of a *Ding an sich,* Hampshire and Strawson have engaged in what the latter has labeled 'descriptive metaphysics'. He characterizes it as the attempt "to describe the actual structure of our thought about the world."

It is contrasted with 'revisionary metaphysics', which "is concerned to produce a better structure"—to secure a unitary conceptual scheme that recommends revisions in our conceptual framework. (My arguments for reductive materialism may very well count as a bit of 'revisionary metaphysics'.) In this context it is crucial to note that such a conception of either descriptive or revisionary metaphysics does not commit the metaphysician to anything that conflicts with the empiricist's critique of metaphysics. In Ryle's terms, no ontologizing need be involved. But it is also true, as Strawson himself stresses and as Ayer points out again in discussing Strawson's work, that such metaphysical work "does not differ in kind or intention" from conceptual analysis.[20] It is simply critical philosophy done in a more systematic and synoptic way. Note that Strawson's *Individuals* or Hampshire's *Thought and Action* does not give us a new kind of knowledge—a kind of 'metaphysical knowledge' or 'philosophical knowledge' of a type we could not get in Wittgenstein's *Philosophical Investigations* or Ayer's *The Concept of a Person*. The difference between Wittgenstein and Ayer, on the one hand, and Strawson and Hampshire on the other, is, as Strawson himself puts it, only in "scope and generality."[21]

Where does this leave us in trying to get a more literal and adequate characterization of metaphysics than we found in Walsh's rather metaphorical characterization? That is, we have the useful but 'poetic' remark that in trying to comprehend the sorry scheme of things entire, in trying to get a unitary reading of all experience and a vision of how things interconnect, we are engaging in metaphysics. But we need something more literal. I think we have made this much progress: We see that at the very least we need an adequate and systematic characterization of the actual structure of our thought as it is embedded in our language. In addition, to have such a vision we would also need some awareness of the alternative ways our experience could be characterized and of what advantages, if any, there would be in having such an alternative characterization.

In doing this, it is important to get a careful elucidation of our key organizing concepts—that is, significance, thought, knowledge, truth, mind, good and bad, possible and impossible, God, man, and society. In the articulation of a metaphysical scheme, we need to understand them and to grasp the interconnections of such concepts. The evident need to gain clarity about them, if we are to articulate any responsible metaphysical scheme, ensures that critical philosophy—the analytical study of concepts—will always stand at the center of philosophy.[22] But surely it is an ideal completion of piecemeal conceptual analysis to give a perspicuous representation to them all, that is, to give a clear account of their nature and interrelations.

There is certainly need for a still greater clarity of intent here, but all the same it gives us something approximating a demythologization of talk about having a vision of the scheme of things entire or a unitary reading of experience. I see no good reason to think such a metaphysical activity is not possible and perfectly desirable. There are indeed difficulties in such an idea, but the empiricist critique or the Wittgensteinian critique of metaphysics has not established or even given us good grounds for believing that such a systematic metaphysical task is impossible to execute. That many philosophers would prefer and indeed find it better to stick to piecemeal analysis of certain troubling concepts, for example, mind/body, justice, action, truth, and the like, is understandable and indeed desirable. But the kind of metaphysical system-building I have characterized in this chapter has not been shown to be either impossible or so quixotic as to be something to be avoided.

There is a further point that has been imperfectly stressed, and it is of considerable importance. In trying to gain a synoptic and unitary reading of the whole of human experience, we should be concerned with the nature of man and moral reality as well. The work of existentialists has been *at least* of heuristic value here. They have helped, amid the increasing specialization and professionalization of philosophy, to keep us from forgetting this. Revisionary metaphysics in particular should lead to new moral insights. In saying this I am not committing the *naturalistic fallacy*. I am not trying to derive an "ought" from an "is." But I am saying that a picture of man—a picture of his powers and relations, including his relations to whatever gods there may or may not be—most surely will affect his conception of what would constitute an ideal life and a truly human society. The stress on this by existentialists (and earlier by Hegel, Feuerbach, Marx, and Dewey) has been of great value to philosophy. I shall return to this topic in the last two chapters of this book.

IV

Given the preceding conclusion, it might well be wondered why there has been so much previous attention to the attack on metaphysics. The answer I would give—and I think this is now frequently lost in the more hospitable current attitude toward metaphysics—is that generally metaphysics is not nearly so domesticated and so free from the fallacies of ontologizing as the kind of metaphysical endeavor I have just been characterizing. The kind of 'Kant-without-necessity' conception of metaphysics that I have just described, and which is at the heart of such books as Strawson's *Individuals* and Hampshire's *Thought and Action*, is not the only conception of metaphysics that has distinguished contemporary exponents.

I regard these other metaphysical approaches as vestigial elements that hopefully will disappear with some disciplined progress in philosophy.[23] (Of course, this expresses a value judgment about the fundamental rightness of my own arguments. And like everything else, it is up for argument in philosophy.) But given the present extensive existence of these other approaches, it seems to me that there is still a role for verificationist arguments and the empiricist critique of metaphysics in philosophy. I shall illustrate this by making reference to the program and claims for metaphysics set out by Father Frederick Copleston in his *Contemporary Philosophy* and his interesting series of articles "Man and Metaphysics."[24] I choose Father Copleston because, while he is such a metaphysician, it is also true that he is not 'a wild man' out of tune with contemporary analytic developments in philosophy. His work exhibits a capacity for clear and forthright statement, an understanding of and ability in conceptual analysis, and a remarkable erudition in the history of philosophy, including the history of contemporary philosophy. His claims are informed and he understands what he is revolting against. And it is true that he definitely revolts against the limitations on metaphysics argued for in this chapter and refuses to accept Ryle's claim that ontologizing is out.[25] But if what I have argued for in this book and particularly in this chapter and the preceding chapters is near to its mark, Copleston's approach to metaphysics must be fundamentally misguided.

Metaphysics, Copleston tells us, should not only, à la Kant and Strawson, be an inquiry into the fundamental conceptual structure of human thought, but an "inquiry into the fundamental conceptual structure of things." Metaphysics, he continues, will always involve the direction of the mind "towards the ultimate unconditioned and ultimate reality." This has been variously called God or the Absolute. Copleston affirms—against all the contemporary tendencies we have been discussing—that the "problem of God is *the* metaphysical problem . . ." or, as he put it in a later essay, "the chief problem of metaphysics is the problem of the Absolute."[26] He follows Aquinas here in claiming that the "whole of metaphysics is directed towards the knowledge of God as its final end." Although there have been different metaphysical systems, Copleston continues, "they have all . . . been concerned with the ultimate reality and its self-manifestation." In metaphysics we are primarily concerned not with *how* things are but with *that* things are.[27] In being concerned with ultimate reality, there is a dialectic of reason which, if we follow it relentlessly, will lead us to the problem of the reality of the transcendent unconditioned or the transcendent absolute. (Copleston argues that a nontranscendent absolute, for example, the world taken in a certain way, is a pseudoabsolute.)

This metaphysical craving of human beings grows out of their own recognition of their contingency and unstable finitude and out of the steadfast recognition "that the finite spirit has as its end a participation in the self-knowledge and self-love of the infinite Spirit."[28] This drives us into metaphysics, although Copleston stresses that "philosophizing can attain this goal only in an extremely inadequate and shadowy way."

Metaphysics, as it increasingly purifies itself from science, more adequately approximates this end. We must be very clear, Father Copleston stresses, that we do not compete with science or treat metaphysics as a kind of superscience. Purified of its role as 'a superscience' and taken as a form of life in its own right, it can be a fundamental source of insight and philosophical knowledge, although it should always make its claims in a tentative manner.

With all due respect to Father Copleston, however, it seems to me that we must flatly say that he has turned the clock back and in reality has failed to assimilate what is unassailable in what he calls "general positivist mentality." Moreover, as a historical aside, he has missed the main drift of analytical philosophy. Quine's *Word and Object*, Hampshire's *Thought and Action*, and Strawson's *Individuals* are three severely metaphysical books. They are in the post-Wittgensteinian and post-Austinian era, the most discussed and most powerful metaphysical works around.[29] Yet, neither their inspiration nor the animus of their argument has a close connection with what Father Copleston takes to be the heart of metaphysics. Furthermore, such exciting although *perhaps* less lasting metaphysical statements as J. J. C. Smart's *Philosophy and Scientific Realism* or Wilfrid Sellar's *Science, Perception and Reality* or *Science and Metaphysics* owe little, if anything, to what Copleston takes to be *the* fundamental concern of metaphysics.

Copleston might quite self-consciously wish to turn the clock back—after all, why assume that what comes later must be progress?—and he might reply that viewed from the longer standpoint of history, such Strawsonian or Quinean efforts will be of secondary interest. The mainstream of metaphysical thought, current diversions to the contrary notwithstanding, will continue to have the preoccupation he discusses. I do not know how he could know this to be so or even that it is so. Even if he is correct on this historical point, however, the central point is surely the philosophical one, namely, that to argue as he does, one must show, in the face of the Humean, Kantian, logical empiricist and Wittgensteinian critique, that such ontologizing remains a reasonable option in philosophy. Father Copleston has not been able to meet these central critiques of ontologizing.[30] If my arguments in my chapters on the philosophy of religion were in the main correct, and if what I have said about the elimination of classical metaphysics in this chapter and the previous four chapters was in the main correct, such a view of metaphysics as the one Father Copleston articulates is an impossible one. But that this conception of metaphysics should be eliminated does not at all imply that the 'Kant-without-necessity' view of metaphysics should be eliminated. However, those whose interests are almost entirely in the 'Kant-without-necessity' approach to metaphysics should not forget that the antimetaphysical party still has legitimate targets.

NOTES

1. Anthony Quinton has briefly displayed some of the background and stated some of the issues here in his "Contemporary British Philosophy," in D. J. O'Connor (ed.), *A Critical History of Western Philosophy;* in "The Philosophy of Quine," *The New York Review of Books* (1966); and in "Mortimer Adler's Machine," *The New York Review of Books* (Nov. 21, 1968).
2. Frederick Copleston, *Positivism and Metaphysics* (Lisbon: 1965), p. 9.
3. Ibid., pp. 5–7.
4. Gilbert Ryle in D. F. Pears (ed.), *The Nature of Metaphysics,* p. 144.
5. Ibid., p. 149.
6. Ibid., p. 150.
7. Stuart Hampshire in D. F. Pears (ed.), *The Nature of Metaphysics,* ibid., p. 25.
8. Paradigm cases—in a descending order of paradigmatic character—are: Friedrich Waismann, *How I See Philosophy;* John Wisdom, *Philosophy and Psycho-Analysis* and *Paradox and Discovery;* Renford Bambrough, "Principia Metaphysica," *Philosophy,* vol. XXXIX (1964), pp. 97–109; Morris Lazerowitz, *Structure of Metaphysics, Studies in Metaphilosophy,* and *Philosophy and Illusion.*
9. W. H. Walsh, "Metaphysics," reprinted in Paul Taylor and Elmer Sprague (eds.), *Knowledge and Value* (second edition).
10. Ludwig Wittgenstein, *Philosophical Investigations,* p. 49.
11. I have developed this in my "Linguistic Philosophy and Beliefs," reprinted in Jerry H. Gill (ed.), *Philosophy Today,* no. 2.
12. John Passmore, "The Place of Argument in Metaphysics," in William Kennick and Morris Lazerowitz (eds.), *Metaphysics: Reading and Reappraisals,* p. 358. In the same vein Bernard Williams remarks: ". . . it is the attempt to give a proof for his conclusion, to show by logical argument that such-and-such must be so, that chiefly distinguishes the philosophical metaphysician from the mystic, the moralist and others who express or try to express a comprehensive view of how things are or ought to be," in D. F. Pears (ed.), *The Nature of Metaphysics,* p. 39. I would want to add—because there are some very wild specimens around—that is what metaphysics should be or rather ideally is.
13. F. H. Bradley, *Appearance and Reality.* See for commentary R. A. Wollheim, *Bradley,* and W. H. Walsh, "F. H. Bradley," D. J. O'Connor (ed.), *A Critical History of Western Philosophy.*
14. R. A. Wollheim, "F. H. Bradley," in A. J. Ayer (ed.), *Revolution in Philosophy,* pp. 12–25.
15. R. G. Collingwood, *An Essay on Metaphysics* and *An Essay on Philosophical Method.*

16. P. F. Strawson, *Individuals*, p. 10.
17. The best entrée into this central part of Kant's philosophy is through I. Kant, *Prolegomena to any Future Metaphysics*. His main work here is his *Critique of Pure Reason*. G. J. Warnock's essay "Kant" in D. J. O'Connor (ed.), *A Critical History of Western Philosophy*, presents in brief space some of the central ideas of Kant on the possibility of metaphysics. See also S. Körner, *Kant*.
18. Stuart Hampshire, in D. F. Pears (ed.), *The Nature of Metaphysics*, pp. 28–38.
19. The situation is actually more complex than that. But in interpreting Kant in this straightforward way there is this standard objection.
20. A. J. Ayer, "Critical Notice of Strawson's Individuals," *The Indian Journal of Philosophy* (1960).
21. P. F. Strawson, op. cit., p. 9.
22. See Anthony Quinton's level-headed defense of this against some traditionalist objections. Anthony Quinton, "Mortimer Adler's Machine," *The New York Review of Books* (November 21, 1968).
23. On progress in philosophy see Stuart Hampshire, "The Progress of Philosophy," *Polemic*, no. 5 (1946), pp. 22–32. For an elucidation of the concept of progress and a denial that progress need be an ethnocentric concept see my "Progress," *The Lock Haven Review*, no. 7 (1965), pp. 63–72.
24. Frederick Copleston, *Contemporary Philosophy*. There are five essays under the title "Man and Metaphysics" in the following issues of *The Heythrop Journal*: vol. 1, no. 1 (January, 1960), pp. 3–17; vol. I, no. 2 (April, 1960), pp. 105–117; vol. 1, no. 3 (June, 1960), pp. 199–213; vol. I, no. 4 (October, 1960), pp. 300–313; and vol II, no. 2 (April, 1961), pp. 142–156. See also his "Philosophical Knowledge," in H. D. Lewis (ed.), *Contemporary British Philosophy*, third series, and his "The Possibility of Metaphysics," *Proceedings of the Aristotelian Society*, vol. L (1949–50), pp. 65–82.
25. Other remarks of his indicate what appears at least to be an ambivalence or an unclarity or both here. See Frederick Copleston, *Contemporary Philosophy*, pp. 41–42 and 58–60.
26. Frederick Copleston, "Man and Metaphysics, I" *Heythrop Journal*, vol. I, no. 1 (January, 1960), p. 12, and see his remark on page 227 of his *Contemporary Philosophy*.
27. Frederick Copleston, *Contemporary Philosophy*, p. 73.
28. Frederick Copleston, "Man and Metaphysics, I" *Heythrop Journal*, vol. I, no. I (January, 1960), p. 13.
29. Some of them occur in R. J. Butler (ed.), *Analytical Philosophy*, series one and two.
30. See reference in note 11.

37

EXISTENTIALISM
AND METAPHYSICS

I

I have argued for the intelligibility and feasibility of a conception of metaphysics stemming from Kant, but have not claimed that there are any synthetic *a priori* necessities of thought. I maintained that such a conception of metaphysics is quite proper and even compatible with an acceptance of a thorough logical empiricism. I also pointed out that to accept the 'Kant-without-necessity' conception of metaphysics does not in the slightest constitute a repudiation of the uncompromising stand I took with Ayer, Ryle, and Wittgenstein against traditional metaphysics or ontology. That is to say, it still seems to me that there are compelling reasons for asserting the cognitive or literal meaninglessness of the claims of a metaphysics that tries to assert the existence of "transcendent entities" or of "an ultimate transcendent reality." Moreover, there is no establishing the existence of anything nonconceptual from purely conceptual considerations. In philosophizing we indeed do and should seek a reasoned conception of a unitary reading of the frame of things, a coherent way of looking at the world and human experience. This comes to giving a characterization of the fundamental and (in fact) unchanging structures of human thought and action; to do metaphysics in this way is to give a systematic and perspicuous display of our fundamental concepts. And to do this involves giving a careful account of their connections. *If* this is to go beyond critical philosophy to speculative philosophy, then by all means we should do just that.

In my remarks about metaphysics (and generally throughout this book) I have said very little about the existentialists, and yet contemporary existentialists such as Jaspers, Heidegger, Sartre, and Tillich surely are philosophers who do metaphysics in the grand style and have been of very considerable influence in contemporary philosophical thought. Where do they fit into the picture? To answer this we need to step back for a moment and see Anglo-American philosophy and Continental philosophy in perspective and in juxtaposition.

First I should report a cluster of sociological facts. Between the philosophic worlds of such analytic philosophers as Moore, Russell, Ayer, and Wittgenstein on the one hand, and the philosophic worlds of such existentialists as Jaspers, Heidegger, Tillich, and Sartre on the other, there is a great chasm. Their philosophic style and their very manner of thought differ radically. Philosophical thought in the English-speaking countries and in Scandinavia is dominated by analytical styles of philosophizing, while philosophic thought on the Continent—Scandinavia apart—and in Latin America is largely dominated by this existentialist style of philosophizing.[1] There is, for the most part, mutual hostility or indifference between the two styles of philosophizing, and typically philosophers of one orientation are woefully ignorant of the work of philosophers of the other orientation.

Like almost everyone else, I am at least in part a child of my culture and I am not free from its orientation or what an unkind critic would call its cultural bias. While I am an admirer of much of the work of Kierkegaard, Nietzsche, the literary works of Camus, and some of Sartre, I am simply appalled at the manner of philosophizing in Sartre's metaphysical works and in the work of Heidegger, Jaspers, and Tillich. Let me cite a paradigm case: If you will read from pages 184–205 in Walter Kaufmann's anthology *Existentialism from Dostoevsky to Sartre*, you will find what I take to be one of the most muddled bits of philosophic writing that I have ever read. It is a translation of a part of Karl Jaspers' *Vernunft und Existenz*, and it will be apparent to the reader of the entire selection that Kaufmann takes from Jaspers that it is not at all a matter of selecting material out of context. Note, as you read the entire selection from Jaspers, that earlier (before page 184) in Kaufmann's anthology, when Jaspers describes how he came to enter philosophy, what his underlying philosophic interests are, and what he takes to be the contemporary significance of Kierkegaard and Nietzsche, he has some incisive or at least interesting things to say. But when, as on the pages just cited, he himself engages in what he takes to be philosophical reasoning, he comes forth with what seems to me to be a mixture of bombastic redescription, which has no discernible rational point, and talk that is simply incoherent. He sins in those passages against all the ideals of philosophic method I have tried to emphasize. This may sound like an overly harsh remark, but I invite you to put my remark to the test against the text cited or against the whole of his *Reason and Existence*.

Jaspers' influence even on the Continent has been considerably less than Heidegger's, although his student Hannah Arendt (who usually is not nearly so obscure as is Jaspers) has had a considerable influence on the American intellectual scene. But Heidegger's writings also have a turgidity and opacity that nearly equals that of Jaspers', although after considerable reading one can discern a systematic structure in Heidegger and in Tillich as well. And it should be noted that Heidegger's influence on the Continent is enormous. Moreover, in reading Heidegger the suspicion remains, even with a diligent reader from an alien tradition, that well hidden in his swollen prose may be something of substance, while with Jaspers' philosophical works—or so it seems to me—we have a bag of religious platitudes of doubtful intelligibility or coherence, the point of which is hard to discern.

II

Why then trouble with existentialism here? Why bother with these abstruse writers? There are a number of reasons of ascending importance. In talking about the possibilities and rationale for metaphysics, it is important to have an awareness of what kinds of endeavor count as 'metaphysical'. The work of the existentialists is, if nothing else, at least a culturally important exemplar of a kind of ontologizing. Moreover, and in close alignment with this, I want you to have some awareness of a totally different way of approaching philosophy from the approach that has been at the center of our attention. We must not forget that on the Continent scholars and professional philosophers take Heidegger and Sartre very seriously indeed. They feel about them the way our philosophers feel about Russell and Wittgenstein. Moreover, these existentialist metaphysicians are not cultural aberrations. They stem, as much as do Russell or Austin, from an established philosophical tradition. This tradition is very foreign to me, as it is to most analytic philosophers; and it is very uncongenial to our way of thinking. Trying to allow for that and trying to break into a different approach, with different standards of excellence, it still seems to me that in spite of its occasional insights, it is a very wrongheaded way of philosophizing. Yet, I also think it would be an unseeming and foolish arrogance—a kind of patronizing cultural hubris—to assume that all that is dross is existentialism and that all that is gold is in the analytic tradition. It would be very surprising indeed if there was nothing in the Continental tradition when such philosophers have so engaged the energies of so many reflective men. (This is by no means a conclusive argument for claiming that there is something there, for after all, shamans in certain cultures engaged the energies of reflective men.)

The most important reason for examining these philosophers is that there is a conception of philosophy and of metaphysics utilized by at least some of the existentialists that is a crucial addition to my attempt to give a morphology of metaphysical beliefs and metaphysical manners. In their conception of metaphysics and in their conception of what should be involved in philosophizing, there enters a very important dimension that is frequently neglected by analytic philosophers and traditional rationalistic metaphysicians alike.

In an essay "What Is Literature?" Sartre remarks of philosophy that it "is not a sterile discussion about abstract notions . . . it is a living effort to embrace from within the human condition in its totality." With the existentialists we have an effort to philosophize from the standpoint of the *agent*. Metaphysics, on such a view, becomes an attempt to scrutinize and then to characterize human experience in its entirety as it is felt by the individual. The crucial thing is to catch and adequately characterize life as it is experienced by living, struggling men thrust into the world. Frederick Olafson, in his attempt to domesticate Heidegger and Sartre for analytical philosophers, contends that in spite of its ontological mode, much of what the existentialists are doing can be understood as descriptive metaphysics (systematic conceptual analysis) of the concept of a *human being* in contradistinction to the concept of *thing*.[2] For them, the crucial thing is to understand what it is to be in the world, to exist in a distinctively human way.

In a similar vein, Walter Kaufmann has maintained that what is in common to all those philosophers who have been characteristically called existentialists is the conviction that "philosophy should begin neither with axioms nor with doctrines, neither with ideas nor sense impressions, but with experiences that involve the whole individual."[3] What is essential is that, free from pointless abstractions and logical schemata, we must first come to understand in depth the lived experience of human beings and then characterize it in an authentic manner.

As I shall try to show, there is something important in this, but we should surely start by noting that, Sartre to the contrary notwithstanding, it would surely be a mistake to deny to philosophy the role of discussing abstract notions. It is essential that philosophers carefully examine and elucidate such notions as truth, knowledge, good, identity, intention, and the like. Indeed, Sartre attempts this himself in his *Being and Nothingness* and elsewhere. But Sartre is surely right in maintaining that philosophy should not limit itself to this. Metaphysics, he argues, is not science, not even a peculiar alleged "first science," but an effort to understand and depict the total human condition from within.

This conception of metaphysics—and note it can readily be taken to be a kind of descriptive metaphysics of the 'Kant-without-necessity' variety —seems to me an immensely important although still teasingly obscure notion. To try to treat it as covering the whole range of metaphysical activity and as correctly setting for us what should be our endeavors within that range is surely to fall prey to the anthropomorphism reductive materialists have so rightly warned us against. But acceptance of this point about anthropomorphism does not mean that such a characterization of the human condition from within is not an important part of metaphysics and that such a characterization of man from the agent's point of view would not be essential in any adequate metaphysical vision. It is crucial in trying to philosophize in depth to see if we can come to understand exactly what is to be done here and then to do it with care and honesty.

III

In trying to carry out such a metaphysical program, existentialists examine topics of great human relevance seldom examined by analytic philosophers or traditional metaphysicians. These topics often come from the extreme experiences of life—*Grenzsituationen*—and in a *very broad sense* are ethical or related to ethics. In spite of the severe pedantry and scholasticism of many existentialist tomes—*Sein und Zeit* is long-winded and repetitious, and Jaspers' *Von der Wahrheit* is well over a thousand pages long—existentialists, far more than analytical philosophers, share a common starting point with literature. Human border situations (love, hate, guilt, death, struggle) and tragedy are at the core of literature, and they are also the starting point of much existentialist philosophizing.

Indeed, Nietzsche apart (who some wish to deny was an existentialist), there is little in their writings in the way of an articulation of a systematic ethical theory. Yet there is a persistent and probing concern with what it is to live an authentic existence as distinct from an inauthentic one. Of such ethical theorizing as I have engaged in in this book, and of traditional and analytic ethical theory generally, existentialists would say that men would be better served and moral life better grasped and perhaps even more adequately lived if we would abandon such ethical theorizing and turn our attention to the concrete realities of individual moral consciousness. Existentialists would argue that a concrete nonargumentative and nonconceptual account of moral phenomena is of greater human value than an attempt to establish formally valid ethical systems or an attempt to justify moral claims, for such a typology would lay bare the moral phenomena itself. Until this is done adequately, moral reasoning is left hanging in the air, and attempts to construct either normative ethical systems or metaethical theories are pointless.

However this may be—and for whatever it is worth, I think that it is an amalgam of truth and confusion—it is the case that in stressing the normative notion of authenticity there is among existentialists a resolute regard for what is called the rediscovery of the individual. Modern man, so the claim goes, is a deeply compartmentalized, culturally indoctrinated and often enfeebled creature living in a mass society in which he has little control over his own destiny. For the most part he has become in such a society a passive spectator (the opium of TV) rather than an active agent deciding, forging his own tablets, committing himself to projects of his own choosing. In such a society of organization men, the existentialists are trying to recall or forge a conception of authentic existence.

In line with our stress that the existentialists are centrally concerned with the concept of a human being, it is important to look at what they are doing from a slightly different angle. Peirce, you will recall, thought that the scientific method was the sole reliable one for fixing belief. By now we have seen that there are good reasons to believe that there are questions concerning religion, morality, and philosophy itself which are crucial qustions where science is not and cannot become by itself an adequate method for fixing belief. Existentialists start out from a recognition of this. They take it as something so thoroughly obvious that only someone fixated back in an old-fashioned Comtean positivism would not understand and take it for granted. Moreover, there are also questions we human beings want to ask that conceptual analysis cannot answer. There are questions that have no purely intellectualist answer. Existentialists return again and again to the theme that there are profound human questions—questions whether we make a fuss about it or not, or acknowledge it or not—we are all very concerned with, which cannot be settled by the use of the scientific method or for that matter by critical philosophy, that is, through the analytical study and systematic display of concepts.[4]

Here existentialists are very close to poets, dramatists, and novelists, for in a manner that is difficult to characterize, they attempt to come to grips with and to explore the problems essential to any attempt to decipher the meaning of life. They attempt to put us up against the wall and to make us aware of the nuances and to explore the implications of an awareness of the purposelessness of human existence. As I have remarked, dread, despair, death, failure, anguish, self-deception, love, sadism, alienation become key concepts for the existentialists. These concepts have not had much philosophical attention, and they surely should have a central role in any attempt to give a perspicuous and unitary rendering of human experience.

In the face of the professionalization of philosophy, existentialists want to link philosophy again with a way of life, with an ideology that would enable us to come to some decision concerning the sense we can make of our lives and to raise in a philosophical fashion questions about the quality of our lives. They persist in dwelling on and in probing what people usually ask only in extreme situations when their lives are collapsing around them. As William Barrett has put it, "Existentialism is a philosophy that confronts the human situation *in its totality* to ask what the basic conditions of human existence are and how man can establish his own meaning out of these conditions."[5]

IV

We must not forget that existentialism, as well as analytic philosophy, is a revolt against speculative philosophy, a revolt against rationalism. When we note Sartre's, Tillich's, Heidegger's, and Jaspers' talk about the Unconditioned Transcendent, the problem of Being, the encompassing, and the like, we are naturally inclined, if we have ever felt the steel of analytical philosophy, to say that that is the same old metaphysical stuff again. And indeed, to talk in such a way is, I believe, still to be held captive by the old pre-Kantian ontologizing conceptions or at least by a basically Hegelian outlook that never really assimilated the Kantian Copernican turn. Yet, to see the situation in this way is to see it as someone who stands outside the existentialist tradition. This is surely *not* how they see it. Heidegger talks endlessly about being, but he insists that he is doing it in a radically new way and that in his philosophy "metaphysics has been overcome."

It is indeed true that in Heidegger we have a shift in emphasis from what we find in traditional philosophies of being—for example, Aristotelian or Scholastic philosophies. Although Heidegger stresses again and again that he is concerned with Being (and thus sounds like an Aristotelian), we have in his most central and influential work, *Being and Time*, a concern with an analysis of man. Heidegger believes that to talk about being adequately, we must first talk about the being of man. This analysis reveals that we are talking about a care-ridden creature who is open to Being. What Heidegger does in reality in *Being and Time* is to describe the general structures of human existence. And while Heidegger, through an understandable distrust and detestation of 'isms', does not want to call himself an existentialist, both his matter and manner put him straight in the existentialist tradition.

Heidegger gives us a picture of man as a time-bound, care-beset, radically finite creature thrust into the world and inexorably a part of the world, but aware, in the way no other creature is, of his impending death and something of the range of human possibility. As a being acutely interested in time and his destiny, man is a being open to Being. Moreover, he is a being who projects his wishes and perplexities into fundamental human projects: ideals about how he is to live and die. He is a being with a historical and cultural consciousness, a being who makes narratives, creates pictures of his destiny, and can have a vivid awareness of his death and his place in nature. He alone of all the animals is a problem to himself. He is creature of inwardness, but at the same time he is a language-using, culture-creating being thrust into a historical world. He can never be understood apart from his history.

It has been frequently asserted that in many ways Heidegger and Sartre are held captive by the theistic set of metaphysical beliefs they have rejected. Their very problems are set by such a metaphysical religiosity. They come down heavy on man's sense of contingency and the purposeless dereliction of human life. If man, they would have us understand, is not so utterly in bad faith as to be able to avoid thoroughly rationalizing his beliefs about his condition by creating a spiritualistic fairy tale, the unfaltering recognition of his condition as that of contingency, finitude, and inevitable and final death will give him a deep and pervading sense of dread. He will see that unlike an artifact he has no essence; he is not a being made for a purpose but a brute historical reality who constantly transcends himself through his projects, which in turn—in a world where progress is an illusion—are merely arbitrary new tablets reformulating our conceptions of our destiny. What is of supreme value is to attain a sense of integrity, to learn to face ourselves honestly and to accept the implications of living *sub specie mortis* rather than to deceive ourselves into believing that we can live *sub specie aeternitatis*.

V

There are important differences concerning this sense of human destiny between atheistic and religious existentialists. Nietzsche, Sartre, Camus, and Heidegger are most certainly neither theistic existentialists nor believers, as Tillich and Jaspers are, in some Unconditioned Transcendent. Nietzsche, Sartre, and Camus are explicitly atheistic, and we find with them an unflinching acceptance of the belief that all our projects and values are arbitrary and that our lot in the world is absurd. Our life is a flight from nothingness to nothingness, a flight that the evasive disguise from themselves in various ways, including religious ways. Human dignity and integrity consists in seeing this and living unfalteringly in a consciousness of it. By contrast, religious existentialists such as Kierkegaard, Marcel, Buber, Jaspers, and Tillich finally become evasive here when faced with this unsparingly bleak picture of human destiny. To take an arbitrary leap of faith to some unknowable God or equally unknowable and rationally inarticulate conception of transcendence is a form of evasiveness.[6] One can see this cop-out plainly in Jaspers remark, "Thou and I, separated on the plane of empirical reality, are one in the transcendent." Somehow a transcendence, which he admits we cannot know or even properly understand, will provide our salvation.

Nietzsche, Sartre, and Camus, on the other hand, accept the death of God. Here, in their estimation, the philosophers of the Enlightenment were clearly right. Belief in God in the twentieth century is on the same footing as belief in elves or fairies. It is just too obvious that God is man's loneliness (as one of Sartre's characters remarks). To think anything else is impossible for a philosophically literate and nonevasive contemporary man. Such a man could only believe in God by crucifying his intellect, and then by definition he would be evasive and would be fleeing from authenticity.[7]

One would think from reading Heidegger's *Being and Time* that he believed much the same thing. But Heidegger in his "Letter on Humanism" (1947) has repudiated this atheistical interpretation. He asserts that in his analysis of God he neither affirms nor denies God. In terms of our contemporary conception of man, Heidegger maintains, we cannot even raise the problem of God, for modern man has lost his sense of the holy. Only when that concept is part of one's life can one consciously raise the problem of God intelligibly. God is dead, Heidegger contends, in the sense that we modern men have no consciousness of Him. But Heidegger takes his own philosophy to be a waiting for God, to be a waiting for a new manifestation of the Divine. In his *Hölderlinstudien*, Heidegger maintains that in an obscure yet prophetic way Hölderlin has discerned the transcendent in the "nothingness of being." And speaking for himself, Heidegger makes it plain that he takes no position at all on whether Being is necessary or temporal and finite. But he does obscurely speak in his later writings of man as the shepherd or guardian of Being. As the only being standing out from the background of nature and as a being who can raise the problem of Being, man even in these dark times remains potentially open to the mystery of Being.

Whether such talk of Being makes any literal sense is extremely questionable. It surely looks as if language has gone on a holiday and that it will not, by taking these new forms, take us to the land of Oz or reveal to us the 'truth of the human condition'. And it should also be remarked that Heidegger's talk is so obscure that it is not evident what he is maintaining or how we could determine if what he says is so. Yet, it is also evident enough that Heidegger's obscure talk here does strike a sympathetic chord in many people. Perhaps much of it can be translated out of the ontological idiom into some intelligible mixture of normative and empirical talk about the human condition. However, it remains true that in speaking as he does (and the same thing holds for Sartre, Tillich, and Jaspers), he plainly commits the fallacy of ontologizing. Without a translation out of this ontological idiom, we have much in their thought that is plainly rationally unacceptable.

We must beware, however, of throwing the baby out with the bath water, for it remains true that existentialists have importantly stressed a metaphysics of experience. Metaphysics in their hands becomes what Heidegger in the second volume of his *Nietzsche* calls "anthropomorphy —the shaping and viewing of the world in accordance with man's image."[8] Such a view, as reductive materialists have pointed out, indeed has its dangers, but it is also important that a metaphysical picture of the world also characterizes human reality from an agent's point of view and gives an authentic vision of life. Accepting such an anthropomorphy is not incompatible at a more abstract level with being a reductive materialist. Rather, the existentialist bit of descriptive metaphysics is a self-conscious attempt to characterize man's sense of himself. It *need* not and indeed *should* not, if we are to make sense of it, be viewed as an inept attempt to say what kind of entity man is. Whether the existentialists have actually succeeded or have even come close to succeeding in giving us an adequate metaphysics of experience and an authentic vision of life, if indeed they are not one and the same thing, is another matter. But in taking this as *one* fundamental task for metaphysics and indeed for philosophy, they have—particularly in our contemporary intellectual climate—given us something of genuine worth.

NOTES

1. There is also on the Continent a very widespread interest in Marxist thought and phenomenology. It is also becoming true that interest in analytic philosophy is penetrating Germany and there is an increase in America of serious study of existentialism, phenomenology, and Marxism.
2. Frederick Olafson, *Principles and Persons*.
3. Walter Kaufmann, "The Reception of Existentialism in the United States," *Midway* (summer, 1968), p. 105.
4. Note the very different attitude toward such problems exhibited in a recent remark of the logical empiricist Herbert Feigl: "Despite the many changes that have been made in the formulation of the criterion of factual meaningfullness (the verifiability criterion), its basic intent has remained the same. Essentially it amounts to eliminating from cognitive discourse questions which can neither logically nor empirically be answered. Problems which are guaranteed unsolvable are *cognitively* meaningless. But as existentialist torments indicate, questions such as 'the meaning of life', or 'why is there something rather than nothing?' may be highly significant emotionally or motivationally; cognitively, however, they are absolutely unanswerable. The proffered answers or assertions are proof against disproof. They are beyond the limits of rational discourse. To put it yet another way: we tried to establish a clear line of demarcation between genuine problems and pseudo problems." Herbert Feigl, "The *Wiener Kreis* in America," in *Perspectives in American History*, vol. II (1968), pp. 654–655. Here we have two completely different conceptual worlds: What to the existentialist is the center of his philosophical concern is to Feigl a pseudoproblem. While accepting the same criterion of factual significance that Feigl accepts, I have tried to show that rather more can be said about questions concerning the meaning of life than Feigl would allow. See my "Linguistic Philosophy and 'The Meaning of Life,'" *Cross-Currents*, vol. XIV, no. 3 (summer, 1964), and in my "Ethics Without Religion," in Paul Kurtz (ed.), *Moral Problems in Contemporary Society*.
5. He makes this remark in one of his introductions in Henry Aiken and

William Barrett (eds.), *Readings in Contemporary Philosophy*, vol. III, p. 143.

6. I have tried to establish this about Heidegger and Tillich in my "Is God So Powerful That He Doesn't Even Have to Exist?" in Sidney Hook (ed.), *Religious Experience and Truth* and in my *Quest For God*, chapters II and III.

7. I argued this in detail in discussing Kierkegaard in Chapter 20.

8. Martin Heidegger, *Nietzsche*, vol. II, p. 127.

38

PHILOSOPHY AND THE HUMAN CONDITION

I

One of the strengths of existentialism is that it does concentrate on philosophy and the human situation. One of its weaknesses is the manner in which it does this. Before saying something about how I view philosophy and the human situation, I want to give some indication why I think existentialist analyses of the condition of man are much less valuable than they are typically taken to be.

My object of criticism will be Heidegger's "The Way Back into the Ground of Metaphysics."[1] This is a good paradigm for several reasons: (1) It is in many important ways a typical existentialist document, yet it is brief enough for you easily to compare what I say about it with the text, (2) Heidegger is probably the most important of the contemporary existentialists, and he himself selected this essay to be represented in the first anthology of existentialist writings to be made in English, and (3) it exhibits both the existential link with traditional philosophy and its attempt to be revolutionary in philosophy.[2]

First I would like to say that if you are bewildered in reading Heidegger, it is his fault and not your own. If you are utterly lost in reading Mill, Moore, Ayer, Smart, or even Copleston, that is your fault and not theirs. But I do not understand much of Heidegger's essay and there are many other philosophers who also do not; and even those who claim they do understand it cannot explain what it means in any straightforward manner. Their so-called elucidations of Heidegger tend to be rehashes in the same turgid manner. The conceptually unsophisticated are very likely to be impressed by Heidegger's obscure and profound-sounding talk and think that something very deep is going on. However, I believe that for the most part it is an expression of a pseudoprofundity masking what is either a bombastic redescription of platitudes or nonsense. This may seem too harsh, but note what I have to say in the following paragraphs and then go back to Heidegger's text and make up your own mind whether I have exaggerated.

Heidegger starts by articulating a traditionalist conception of philosophy. To make evident what he wants to say, he provides us with a picture of philosophy and the sciences on analogy with a tree. Metaphysics (speculative philosophy) constitutes the roots, physics the trunk, and the branches the other sciences. Metaphysics is characterized as the study of being as beings.[3] In an attempt to "overcome metaphysics"—to go even deeper into reality—Heidegger ponders about the soil in which these roots have their hold, receive their nourishing juices and strength. "What element," Heidegger asks, "concealed in the ground, enters and lives in the roots that nourish the tree?" What is the *foundation* of metaphysics itself?

As we have just seen, Heidegger conceives of metaphysics in a basically Aristotelian manner as the science that concerns itself with beings as beings. And when we ask what beings are, "beings as such are in sight." Metaphysical thinking goes on in "the light of Being." But metaphysics, Heidegger continues, does not and cannot enable us to think about the light. Whether metaphysicians interpret beings—*Seiendes*—as mind or matter or both, or whether being is becoming or changeless, "every time beings as beings appear in the light of Being,"[4] the light is, Heidegger would have us understand, simply a given for the metaphysician. But "Being in its revelatory essence, i.e., in its truth, is not recalled."[5] But it is this very "truth of Being" that is the ground, the soil, of metaphysics, and it is this that we very much need to understand. All of us are quite aware of the many beings (*Seiendes*): the multitude of particular things that exist. We might even try to ascertain what, if anything, was common to and distinctive of all those beings. But to discover this, if indeed we could discover it at all, would not be to discover the ground of Being. It would not be to come to grasp Being as Being, as the basis of everything. Rather, our most fundamental philosophical task must be to "recall Being itself." We must strive to become open to the experience of Being. We must "make a fresh attempt to grasp by thought what precisely is said when we speak of Being."[6]

This seems to me a restatement of a very old philosophical program, but old or new, the point remains that it is not actually carried out. 'Being' for Heidegger, as for all metaphysicians who use it as a metaphysical category, is a *term of art*, a technical term. But he does not tell us what he means by it. Perhaps, as he says, it is indefinable, but nevertheless, since it is a term of art and not a term in ordinary use, in order to give us some sense of what he is talking about or even make the matter tolerably clear to himself, Heidegger needs to give some indication of what would have to happen in order for it to be either true or false or probably true or false that we are aware of Being; or he must give us some indication of what it would be like to experience or to fail to experience the "truth of Being." No such description or characterization is forthcoming.

Note that in Heidegger's talk about what must be done here, the phrase 'truth of Being' holds a rather prominent place. But this is surely a very obscure collocation of words. We understand what it is for a statement to be true. That is, a statement is true if what is asserted by it is so. The statement 'Eugene McCarthy has glasses on' is true if and only if Eugene McCarthy has glasses on. And if McCarthy is standing at a distance and someone asserts he has glasses on, you have a perfectly straightforward understanding of what it would be like to determine whether that statement is true. But it is not so easy to understand what could be meant by the phrase 'truth of Being', for it too is a Heideggerian term of art and we need to be told what it means or else it will remain simply a scarcely intelligible part of his technical jargon. Again we are not helped here. Heidegger explains 'truth of Being' by saying that to speak of truth of being is to speak of its revelatory essence. But earlier he explained 'Being in its revelatory essence' by reference to the phrase 'truth of Being'. The point is that we go around in a circle of philosophers' terms of art, none of which has any firm foundation in any form of life or form of language. To talk in this manner surely seems idle.

At this point it might be objected that I am ignoring the relevance here of Heidegger's talk, in other contexts, of truth. He deliberately uses 'truth' in a rather special way, although in a way he maintains has important roots in our culture. Moreover, he gives justificatory arguments for his departure from ordinary usage. So long as he does not deny the point of our garden-variety uses of 'truth', I see no reason to cavil at such a procedure, and it may well be that in some forms of life (and perhaps lingeringly in ours) there are such uses of 'truth' as Heidegger talks about. But what is relevant in our context is whether such talk gives sense to talk of 'truth of Being' or 'the revelatory essence of Being'.

In *Being and Time*, Heidegger tells us that 'Being-true' or 'truth' means 'Being-uncovering' or 'to be uncovered'.[7] Arne Naess, quite sensibly I believe, interprets this to mean that "an assertion is true means that it uncovers the entity, an occurrence that takes place at the entity. The assertion allows the entity to be seen in its uncoveredness."[8] Heidegger thinks that such a sense of 'truth' is not "uninhibited word-mysticism," since by going behind an overintellectualistic conception of truth stamped in by a long tradition of philosophers coming after Plato and Aristotle, it gives us a sense of "the most *primordial* phenomenon of truth"—of "taking entities out of their hiddenness (*Verborgenheit*) and letting them be seen in their unhiddenness."[9]

Man is a discourse-making animal and thus has the kind of being that makes him open to truth; true discourse is discourse that uncovers what is hidden. The search for truth in its most fundamental and primordial sense is the attempt to bring into the light what is hidden. Heidegger maintains that sheer sensory perception provides a more fundamental form of truth than assertion. To have uncovered a truth is to have come upon a discourse that leads us to see something new or to make plain or plainer what before we did not understand. A truth-unfolding discourse is a discourse that leads to such a disclosure. False discourse, by contrast, contains the notion of covering up or hiding from view. To attain truth is to put oneself in a position where something shows itself.

Yet, even if we do not boggle at any of this, we are still a long way from gaining an understanding of 'truth of Being'. Heidegger tells us that to be true is a kind of uncovering and thus truth is a *kind* of Being. In his lecture "On the Nature of Truth," Heidegger introduces the notion that freedom to disclose truth is the conscious letting be of each entity, that is, the responsiveness to it as it is itself.[10] But this posture of passivity before entities which is essential for the uncovering of truth is not one of indifference. And without man—the kind of being man has—there would be no truth in this primordial sense of 'truth'. Moreover, there is nothing beyond man that would provide the disclosure of truth; whatever enlightenment there is must come from man, for Being is present in him. We misunderstand ourselves and misunderstand the nature of truth when we seek 'the light'—the meaning of our existence—beyond ourselves.

In his "Letter on Humanism" and "Plato's Theory of Truth," published together in 1947, we get a further sense of what Heidegger is driving at. Man is a creature caught up in different forms of language that he cannot, *pace* Lewis Carroll, dispose of at will, for his very understanding of himself and of his world is given in such language forms. And we must not forget, Heidegger tells us, that "language houses Being: Man is the lodger . . . of language. Thought and poetry are guardians of the lodging. Their vigil is the fulfillment of Being as something revealed, insofar as through what they say they bring Being to expression and preserve it in language."[11] Being is man's fundamental concern and it is the concern of his most fundamental kind of nondiscursive and nonscientific thinking.

I shall grant, for the sake of this discussion, that truth (or at least the concept of truth relevant here) is or necessarily involves a disclosure of something that is hidden or obscure, and that thus to *talk* of 'the truth of Being' is to talk of 'a disclosure of Being' or 'an uncovering of Being', which is hidden by that which exists (*Seiendes*). I will even grant, again for the sake of the present argument, that through our *Angst* and through our sense of our own nothingness and the nothingness of all realities (*Seiendes*)—that is, the possibility that they will cease to be (their finitude)—we can confront Being and become aware of Being, *if indeed we ever can*. I will temporarily grant that man must learn to let himself "be addressed by Being" in order to have that disclosure of Being that is the truth of Being. He must enter into the discourses that will help produce this disclosure. But granting all this—and even adopting this very peculiar and inflated mode of speech—it remains the case that we still do not understand what it is to have Being disclosed to us. We understand the sort of *situation* in which we are supposed to be able to confront Being or in which Being will be disclosed to us if it ever is, but we still do not understand what even in this circumstance is to count as a disclosure of Being or a confrontation with Being.

We know, if Heidegger is right, that to find the truth of being is to find something which is to be found in man and which is to be given in a disclosure. But while it *may* be intelligible to say (and perhaps even be correct to say) that sensory perception gives a more fundamental form of truth than does assertion, there is no question of Being being given in sensory perception as red things or painful sensations are given in sensory perception.

Heidegger tells us in his "Letter on Humanism" that "Being is that which before all else 'is'."[12] That remark is plainly not helpful, for if we are puzzled about 'Being' we will be equally puzzled about the meaning of "that which before all else 'is'." We obviously have something that is *not* ostensively definable or teachable as is 'pain' or 'red', such that it could be something given in sense perception. If that is so, then we must have some conceptual mastery of it in the very forms of our language in order to understand what it is that would have to be disclosed to us so that we would have had such a disclosure. Without some sense of what it is that we are talking about when we use 'Being' or 'is' in such contexts, we would not be able to recognize a disclosure of Being if we had one. Only if such a term had a meaning in an ongoing form of life could we understand what is being talked about when we talk about having such a disclosure. But both 'Being' and 'is' in such a context do not have an established meaning in a form of life. Rather, they are undefined, unexplicated metaphysical terms of art.

To take it as an act of 'philosophical faith' that certain discourses will lead us to such a disclosure and thus to an understanding of 'truth of being' and of 'Being' is impossible for the same reason that a pure fideism is impossible in which we could come to believe in God even though we had no understanding of what 'God' means. (This point was argued in Chapter 21, Section V.[13]) We can only take something on faith if we understand *what* it is that we are to take on faith. For it to be possible to take something on faith, it must be possible to answer the question 'What are we taking on faith?' by asserting that we have faith in such and such. But if we have *no understanding* of 'God', 'Being', or 'a disclosure of Being', we cannot have faith in what they are thought to symbolize any more than we can have faith in Boojybus. Since we do not understand what is supposedly symbolized by these terms, we cannot trustingly accept what is denoted by the term as a reality and a guide, for, as with 'Boojybus', we are at a loss to understand what they supposedly denote. But Heidegger has not made his key terms—'Being', 'truth of Being', being 'addressed by Being'—intelligible, and thus we cannot meaningfully speak of engaging, through an act of faith or otherwise, in discourses that will reveal Being to us or the truth of Being itself. To say that we trust that if we talk in a certain way in a certain context the revelation will come makes no sense unless we have *some* idea of what would constitute a revelation in such a context.

'Being itself', 'truth of Being', 'disclosure of Being', 'revelatory essence of Being', the key cluster of terms used in his "The Way Back into the Ground of Metaphysics" and elsewhere, are all just high-sounding pompous phrases to which no determinate meaning has been attached. To use a by now familiar argument, consider

1. X is Being itself.
2. X is the truth of Being.
3. X is the revelatory essence of Being.

For whatever value replaces the variable X, Heidegger has given us no notion at all of how one could ascertain what counts or could count for or against the truth of the alleged resultant statement, and thus such statements are devoid of all factual or literal content. And he has not shown us how we might construe them as analytic statements in which the 'is' would become the 'is' of identity and the denial of these statements would be self-contradictory.

To make such a verificationist argument, a Heideggerian would no doubt immediately counter, is to confuse 'Being' *(Sein)* with particular beings *(Seiendes)*. 'Being' could not signify something determinate, for it is precisely the very Being of all beings that we are talking about. And since this is so, such verifiability arguments are utterly out of place here. But in turn it should be replied that we are trying to discern *whether* such peculiar philosophical talk is indeed intelligible. Surely if what we are talking about is intelligible and refers to what is taken to be fundamental reality or ultimate reality, it must be possible to make true or false statements using such terms. But to do that, something must count as confirming or infirming statements made by using such terms in some gramatically proper way. But, as our remarks about statements 1, 2, and 3 above indicate, these sentence forms seem not to be used, under such a program as Heidegger's, to make sentences that in turn can be employed to make true or false cosmological statements. They are utterly devoid of substantive content; they tell us nothing at all about the nature of the world or man's being in the world or about reality, yet they purport to be cosmological claims. Language, as Wittgenstein would put it, is idling here.

Suppose I say—to make the matter as simple as I know how—that 'Death is the truth of Being' or 'Love is the revelatory essence of Being' or 'Matter and energy is Being itself' or 'Being is finite' or 'Being is infinite' or 'Being is nothingness'. In no case have we been given any indication by Heidegger how to start ascertaining by any kind of argument or evidence at all which, if any, of these statements are true or false. Presumably it is somewhat better to say 'Being is nothingness', yet where is the argument or the evidence to show that being is nothingness? If it is analytic, presumably there must be some reason to believe this; if it is a cosmological factual claim, presumably there must be some evidence for it. But nothing like this is forthcoming. Since this is so, it seems fair enough to conclude that once again, as is so frequent in philosophy, language has gone on a holiday.

II

Heideggerians would reply (and perhaps others as well) that I have the whole context juxtaposed into a kind of scientific, quasiscientific or perhaps even pseudoscientific context which makes impossible a genuine coming to grips with Heidegger's thought. And Heideggerians would add for good measure (as one has) that my concluding remarks in the preceding section are the remarks of a vulgar philistine caught up in a positivistic culture with its own very limited norms of intelligibility and rationality. Criticisms such as mine are not relevant on the level of thought on which Heidegger is operating but only on the "merely technical," "merely empirical" level. To think that such considerations are relevant is to exhibit a shallow positivistic mentality. In such an atmosphere, as Heidegger puts it, language comes under the dictatorship of publicness. Where this obtains, there is a subjection to mass culture and to scienticism.

However (or so the argument runs), this is an inescapable side effect of a culture dominated by a positivistic mentality. Heidegger exhibits a thorough animosity toward science. He believes that the very influence of modern science makes for a destruction of a fully human and meaningful understanding of things.[14] He tries, particularly in his later works, to get away from anything that even remotely resembles a scientific framework.[15] To set scientific goals for fundamental thinking is an utter mistake, for it fails to understand what fundamental thinking is and it fails to come to grips with the deepest questions about the significance of life and of what it is to live as a human being. Heidegger not only exhibits an animosity toward science, he is also dismissive of moral philosophy. By now it is passé: something that only a philosopher still foolishly beguiled by the spirit of the Enlightenment could continue to take seriously. But moral philosophy, Heidegger gives us to understand, is hardly a fundamental matter in philosophy or in life. Rather, it involves the kind of ordering of life characteristic of the mentality of 'technical man'—a mass contemporary phenomenon that is to be regretted. Thus, the kind of discussions we engaged in in the sections devoted to morality would seem utterly fatuous to Heidegger.[16] He would have us believe that such endeavors will do nothing to aid us in coming to live more authentically or in coming to attain some pittance of wisdom or some understanding of how we are to live.

The directives implicit in what Heidegger takes to be such a shallow philosophical use of science and moral philosophy exhibit for him the extent to which men of contemporary sensibilities can come to live in an utterly inauthentic way, a way in which technical man, delivered up to mass-being as he is, can be brought to a dependability that is only possible through a correspondingly technical collection and ordering of his plans and actions as a whole.[17] But, of course, such a broadside on Heidegger's part is no substitute for argument. What Heidegger needs to show is that secular ethical theories such as Mill's or the one I argued for have such consequences. It is clear enough that Heidegger, like Sartre, would accept an ethical view as an objective or nonarbitrary one only if it were not simply the product of the human intellect and if it were grounded in the truth of Being. But as we saw when we examined morality, there are certain moral claims that both make sense and can be objectively justified without any such metaphysical backing. Moreover, the objections we made to grounding an ethic on Divine commands could also be made against Heidegger's claim that moral beliefs, if they are to have a ground at all, must be grounded in the truth of Being.[18]

Moreover, to simply meet a criticism such as mine with accusations of a shallow scientism or positivism will not do, for the fact remains that Heidegger is making what purport to be grand cosmological claims—he does not mean just to be expressing his feelings—and he would maintain that his claims are somehow true and penetrate more deeply into reality than do other more mundane views. But he does use terms such as 'Being itself', 'Truth of Being', and 'revelatory essence of being' without showing how or even that these terms have a sense (have a use in the language or have been given a use in the language). They do not have any function in any form of life, in any part of a working natural language, and of course they are not a part of some artificial notation such as mathematics or musical notation. But since these *terms of art* are without such a function, since they have no regulated use (a pleonasm), statements in which they occur are not sufficiently coherent to be even false. (Of course, they can be *mentioned* in coherent talk—for example 'The word "Being" is undefined in Heidegger's discourses'. But the attempt to use, and not just mention, such terms in the making of statements results in incoherent talk.)

Furthermore, lest this be thought to be simply an expression of the bias of a "positivistic mentality," note the further more restrained—and I think less to the heart of the matter but still basic—criticism of Heidegger by such a traditionalist metaphysician, opponent of 'the positivist mentality', and 'Being-philosopher' as Father Copleston.

> More important from the point of view of the student of Heidegger's philosophy is the difficulty experienced in deciphering his meaning, especially perhaps when he speaks about Being and Nothingness. In his later writings at least man appears as ex-isting or as ek-sisting as guardian of Being. But is Being to be interpreted as a general concept contained by emptying out all determinations, so that in its vacuity it seems to glide into Nothingness, or is Being to be taken in the sense of the Transcendent? Or is it a mixture of both? The answer does not appear to me to be at all clear. And the ambiguities in Heidegger's philosophy are, of course, the reason why it is always possible for him to insist that nobody has understood him. Some of his ardent disciples, indeed, go so far as to suggest that any criticism of the Master manifests an incapacity to understand him. But if they themselves understand him clearly, it is a great pity that they do not have compassion on the weakness of the rest of us and reveal the secret in unambiguous terms. Or does ambiguity belong to the essence of Heidegger's philosophy?[19]

It is indeed fairly obvious that some of Heidegger's admirers would not be bothered at all by Copleston's criticism or my severer criticisms. They would reply, as one has, that Heidegger is "struggling to communicate, and his command of his own means of communication is powerful and impressive. The difficulty comes, rather, from the obscurity of the matters with which Heidegger is grappling."[20]

However, one of the things which is at issue is whether it is really the *matter* rather than the *manner* that causes the blockage. It may be, as it has been argued, that we have a pseudoprofundity here. Moreover, to put the matter at its simplest, if Heidegger struggles to communicate, he doesn't struggle very hard. He does not even make the most elementary effort to give sense to his fundamental concepts. Yet, they are not ordinary notions that we could be expected to understand without an elucidation of what the author intends in using them. And it cannot be justly said that if we have a good understanding of the entire Western philosophical tradition, we should be able to understand him, for we have just seen that Father Copleston, one of our most acute historians of philosophy, is thoroughly perplexed by Heidegger's usage even though he is a philosopher who is himself quite willing to engage in what I would call Being-talk.

In general, it should be said in the face of the preceding defense of Heidegger (that is, it is the intrinsic obscurity of the subject matter that makes him obscure) that there are indeed matters concerning which it is exceedingly difficult to speak—say the subtle complex of feelings, thoughts, and experiences characterized by Stendhal, Proust, or Faulkner. But to describe what is obscure one need not be obscure, anymore than one needs to be thin to give slenderizing instructions. Moreover, since Heidegger's basic concepts are so unintelligible or near to being unintelligible, there is no way of knowing or having good grounds for believing that it is the *matter* rather than the *manner* that causes the difficulties. How can we be so confident, as are some epigones, that the difficulty is in the substance of what Heidegger is talking about rather than a result of his nearly unintelligible inflated idiom? It is irrational to be so confident that the difficulty lies in the very substance of what he is trying to convey, when we and they literally cannot determine what the matter is, that is, what the allegedly profound subject matter is.

To put my criticism in a minimal way and utilizing the criterion of meaning we have already defended: A necessary but not a sufficient condition for the intelligibility of any utterance is that it be transformable into an ordinary idiom (into an utterance that has a functional role in a natural language) or that it be a working part of some artificial notational system such as mathematics or musical notation that is parasitical on a natural language. Note that is how we come to understand such sentences as 'Anal-erotic individuals are sadomasochistic'. Heidegger's work abounds in such sentences as 'Being itself is indefinable but its revelatory essence can be grasped in an act of recall by someone who is open to Being.' Like 'Anal-erotic individuals are sadomasochistic', it bristles with technical terminology. If such a sentence is to be understood, it must be transformable into an ordinary idiom, or at least some key must be provided for such a transformation. But Heideggerians have not done that, and it is far from evident that it could be done. Since this is so, and since such transformability is or at least seems to be a necessary condition for intelligibility, the intelligibility of many of his key utterances is in doubt and must be established.

It is no good replying that such a criticism reveals the positivistic prejudice that whatever cannot be said clearly and distinctly is meaningless. This is not even remotely what is at issue in such an appeal to ordinary discourse. In such an appeal—that is, in an appeal to the transformability criterion—there may very well be (and indeed should be) an awareness that ordinary discourses are sometimes ambiguous and vague and, as Austin puts it, sometimes ordinary discourse needs to be overridden. But it remains ubiquitous for all of that. We may on occasion have to torture it to make evident what we mean. But it remains—and Heidegger utterly neglects this—the first word, and it remains the last word *in the sense that* where in trying to say something difficult and infrequently said, although we often stretch and struggle with the language, we still in principle at least must be able, after this is done (after the difficult insight is achieved) and in defense of the remark's intelligibility, either to paraphrase the dark saying, perhaps into a whole paragraph, in the literal and everyday language of some natural language, or to do that with supplementations by ostensive teaching of new terms expressive of novel concepts. Such an appeal to ordinary language, *pace* Gellner, does not even remotely commit one to the conceptual status quo. There is no damper placed on novelty. There is only the claim that for what is novel to be intelligible (which after all is a condition of its being genuinely novel), it must be related to the concepts that preceded it.

Moreover, since the transformability criterion provides a necessary condition and not a sufficient condition for intelligibility, the acceptance of such a criterion is compatible with the acceptance of Austin's point that ordinary language "might in certain ways be confused or incoherent and even, for certain purposes, totally inadequate."[21] But if some pretentious and obscurantist utterance such as 'Being itself dialectically transcends itself in the Encompassing Unconditioned Transcendent' cannot be transformed into some ordinary idiom, that is, made a part of a living natural discourse, then such talk is unintelligible. This is not to say that for certain purposes we might not very well mark distinctions not made in everyday speech. Surely—to take something obvious—the color discriminations we make are highly conventional and could very well be indefinitely refined. But if our discourse about them, or any discourse that supplements, supplants, or in any way clarifies some part of ordinary discourse, were not in turn transformable—admittedly also using techniques of ostensive teaching—into a set of ordinary idioms (idioms we use in communicating with each other), what is said would not be understood, would remain unintelligible. The existentialists' idiom at such key points is *not* such a natural idiom, and the only way he or we can understand what he is talking about is by transforming such talk into such an idiom. This has not been done.

Perhaps my assumption of such a criterion of significance is mistaken. Ordinary language may be simply the first word and not, even in the sense I have indicated, the last word. In fact, in another perhaps more fundamental way it seems evident that there is no such thing as 'a last word'. In principle at least we can always continue to ask questions, request clarifications and elucidations. My utilization of the transformability criterion does not mean to suggest that we commit ourselves to the ideology of the Last Word. There should be no such quest for certainty here. There are indeed, as I have already pointed out, parts of our experience that ordinary language finds itself hard put to express.[22] But a Heideggerian esoteric manner of expression has exactly the same difficulties as does plain talk here, and more as well. What is the reason (if any) to think that the resources of plain English, German, Swedish, French, or for that matter any natural language, given the complexities and flexibilities of these languages, is not sufficient to enable us to characterize these experiences? That some so-called ordinary-language philosophers have rather narrow interests is not a legitimate complaint against philosophizing from ordinary language or employing what I have called the transformability criterion.

It would be an important and legitimate criticism of such an approach from ordinary language to show that there is a range of experiences, important to the human animal, that ordinary discourse even when supplemented by ostensive teaching techniques cannot characterize or describe or enable us to understand. It would be a telling criticism of the transformability criterion to establish that there is something of a nonmathematical, nonmusical (and the like) nature which is expressible that is not expressible in ordinary discourse even by a lengthy paraphrase conjoined with ostensive teaching techniques. Such a criticism would be of fundamental importance, for if it is the case that ordinary discourse together with human observation is not both our first court of appeal and in the sense indicated our last court of appeal in a quest for criteria of intelligibility, then the transformability criterion would evidently have collapsed as an essential element in any adequate general criterion of significance. Perhaps in defending the transformability criterion I am caught up in something not unlike the Myth of the Last Word, but it is not, of course, evident to me that is so. But after all, a man who is caught up in a myth never sees it as a myth. Perhaps there is such a range of experiences and perhaps there are some things not so expressible, but neither the existentialists nor anyone else to my knowledge has given us good reasons for thinking that there are realities that might not be so expressible. Moreover, even if such a case against arguing from ordinary language were made out, existentialism would only have gone over its first critical hurdle.

III

I want to consider now some other hurdles and some other Heideggerian defenses against the onslaughts of critical philosophy. These new defenses are of an extreme nature, but they are of interest both in their own right and as further illustrations of the nature of philosophical reasoning. Heidegger has an open animus against science and logic (logic presumably is passé), and he writes in a deliberate defiance of common sense. It is evident enough, even if it turns out that they are effectively deployed, that my criticisms of him have turned on points of logical analysis and have assumed the importance in philosophy of a respect for the marshaling of evidence and supporting argument, even though I did argue in Chapters 10 and 12 that philosophy was neither simply logic nor an empirical science. However, his defenders could reply that I presuppose, in a philistine manner, the competence and relevance of common sense, science, and logic. But Heidegger does not, and thus my objections are question-begging. Philosophy for Heidegger is not a discipline that can be learned, it is not a technique of reasoning or argument that can be mastered. For him the sciences "are only servants" to philosophy, while "art and religion are its sisters."[23]

There is certainly a fundamental clash here between critical philosophy, on the one hand, and existentialism on the other. This clash, as Passmore observes, goes to even a deeper level than just a failure to share certain premises, for there is between these two approaches a radically "different idea of what philosophy consists in, of how it proceeds."[24] Passmore observes that to "many Anglo-Saxon philosophers Heidegger . . . does not fulfill the first requirement of a philosopher; his thinking, they believe, is philosophically undisciplined."[25]

By contrast, existentialists think of analytical and critical philosophy as being unimaginative and sterile: either utterly devoid of any vision of life at all or providing, as something that linguistic philosophers themselves consider to be rather ancillary to real philosophy, a very humdrum and trivial vision.[26] The analytical philosopher in turn feels that the existentialist does not really want to discuss, does not want to reason out what is at issue as far as one can go, and to try by disciplined thought to see if we can uncover exactly what problems we face and provide a solution for them or at least become keenly aware of what it would take to provide a solution, rather than simply taking one's stand—adopting a position or perhaps more accurately an attitude about the world—and trying to state that position in as persuasive a manner as possible.

In sum, the analytic philosopher believes that existentialists blur the distinction, stressed by Plato, between the philosopher and someone who is merely a sage. Existentialists ignore or make light of the hard work of argument, careful distinction, and rational defense that goes with doing philosophy. Existentialists return the compliment by maintaining that analytic philosophers are utterly lost in petty details and narrow arguments and that nothing like a penetrating vision of life could come from such an approach. To be a philosopher, they would maintain, is in its most fundamental sense to come to have a vision of life: to adopt a position about the world and man's place in it. This analytical philosophy fails to do or does in a shallow and ancillary way.

Here we have something that is very basic. I would agree with Heidegger that primary philosophy—philosophy concerned with what I have characterized as the primary problems of philosophy—does largely spring from concerns to make sense of life and from concerns growing out of religion and art. There indeed may be something in Heidegger's rather arrogant remark in a lecture that "University professors will never understand what Novalis said: 'Philosophy . . . is strictly speaking a homesickness.' "[27] The primary problems of philosophy would probably never gain a grip on a man, if he had never felt what Novalis calls homesickness (Heimweh-Trieb), that is, the kind of religious, ideological, and moral alienation where we do not feel at home anywhere, where we feel isolated, where life in the kind of world we live in seems to make no sense and yet where despairingly or confusedly we long 'to put it together', 'to make sense of it', 'to get it all together'.[28] Surely the emotional and Weltanschauung needs of philosophy are very deep and very pervasive. I doubt very much that I would have thought about philosophy for one moment if they were not there. But there also remain, when all this is taken into consideration, Plato's and Aristotle's claims about disciplined argument and reasoning concerning one's vision of things entire. In philosophy such considerations are very central and very ancient, and they link the philosopher more with the scientist and the logician than with the poet, sage, or prophet. And it is this side of philosophy that existentialists generally, and Heidegger most particularly, seem to dismiss with contempt or at least not give nearly an adequate voice.[29]

Let us put aside such broad comparisons and consider an argument: If we cast away all common sense, ignore the findings of science, put aside all sense of what constitutes an argument, all sense of the relevance of evidence, all reliance on our intelligence and on logic, we can indeed believe anything our hearts or our hates desire or dictate. We can, like the man who uses the method of tenacity, believe any nasty or childish myth we may want to believe. Moreover—to engage for the moment, in a context where it is relevant, in a deliberate ad hominem—we must not forget that while he was Rector of the University of Freiburg, it was Heidegger who fell into enthusiastic support of the Nazis. A little more respect for logic and for intelligence might have inhibited him from proclaiming to his students: "Not theorems and ideas be the rules of your being. The Fuehrer himself and alone is the present and future German reality—and its law."[30] This is indeed a dethronement of reason. If a man of education and knowledge can say that and mean it, he can say anything. Indeed, human intelligence and respect for reasoning is not everything—there is much more in life than reasoning. But if we reject the use of our intelligence, if we ignore evidence and logic and in effect adopt what Peirce called the method of tenacity or authority, we will suffer in the quite practical way that Peirce indicated we would suffer. Intelligence is not a cure for all our personal and social ills, but if we turn our backs on it we are lost. Heidegger and Jaspers as well, in spite of his praise of reason, do just that.[31] They lead us not into a profound truth concerning human existence, but into an obscurantist word-play devoid of genuine substance.

To this the existentialist might reply that the bit about Nazism indeed indicates a very severe personal failing on Heidegger's part; at best it betokens a political naiveté and at worst a deep moral and human failing, but such a personal failing hardly touches his strictly philosophical position, to say nothing of existentialism more generally. After all, Sartre has stayed consistently on the Left and Jaspers has remained courageously liberal. Moreover, my little Peircian sermon in praise of reason is quite beside the point. Given the practical affairs of life, surely intelligence has such a key role, but philosophy is fundamentally concerned with a vision of life and that takes us beyond such matters.

However, I was concerned to show what undisciplined vision can so easily come to. Moreover, if you stress philosophic vision and self-consciousness as the existentialists do, it is not so easy to excuse such personal aberrations as Heidegger's as something not relevant to his philosophy. And there is a more fundamental point to be made here. While I too have been concerned to distinguish philosophy from science, and I would agree that philosophy is not *just* an analytical study of concepts but also a vision of life, I would add that metaphysics is speculation controlled by *rational criticism* and that there is no philosophy without argument. These claims are claims of lexical definition concerning what philosophy has become and would be defended by reference to the practice of its practitioners—for example, Plato, Aristotle, Augustine, Aquinas, Scotus, Descartes, Leibnitz, Spinoza, Locke, Hume, and Kant. I admit there are borderline phenomena, such as Plotinus and the late Schelling. But they are indeed borderline cases and we do not define an activity by taking borderline cases as paradigmatic. The way I have characterized philosophy is descriptive of what it was long before the advent of analytical or linguistic philosophy. The word, I will admit, has other connotations as well that cut away from the idea of rational criticism. Heidegger is indeed at liberty to suppress these main features in the characterization of what he is doing and what he thinks philosophy *should become*. We can then say either that he is not doing philosophy or that he is doing philosophy in a manner that radically conflicts with the way in which the subject matter has been previously conceived. The verbal decision here, as far as I can see, is not terribly important, but what is important is the activity and one's decision about the kind of activity in which to engage. If in an attempt to articulate a view of the world, we simply attempt to dish out the insight surrounded by obscure talk and disdain for reasoning and rational criticism, we impoverish ourselves and dehumanize our view of the world. This is not the way to attain the authenticity existentialists so prize.

IV

I should not like to end my remarks about existentialism on such a sour note. There is something else to be said as well. It is often said by its apologists that "existentialism is opposed to schematic and abstract answers about human facts. . . ." This is indeed true of Kierkegaard and Nietzsche, and sometimes of Sartre and Camus. But what could be more abstract and schematic than the 'answers' we find in the huge metaphysical tomes of Heidegger, Tillich, and Jaspers? They are indeed remote from life and concrete moral and political experience. It is difficult to imagine anything dealing with the subject matter of man and the cosmos that could be further removed from man's existential concerns.

In Sartre, however, we get something else as well that gives substance to the point made by existentialist apologists about concreteness. While in his metaphysical writings Sartre has an obscurantist opacity that runs apace with the writings of Heidegger, Tillich, and Jaspers, in his plays and novels and in some passages of his strictly philosophical works he does something quite different, that indeed contributes to what, following him, I have characterized as a "metaphysics of experience" and an enhanced understanding of the human condition. There are indeed many things wrong with Sartre's account of ethics, but again and again in his fiction there are probing and relentless accounts of the moral experience of human beings that cut to the core of the moral life and give us something that cannot be learned from moral philosophy. In his novels and plays Sartre helps us to see that moral experience is something much more inchoate than what is or *perhaps* even can be represented as moral experience in a philosophical text.[32] Reflecting about the characters in Sartre's *The Wall, No Exit, The Childhood of a Leader, The Condemned of Altona,* and *The Devil and the Good Lord* makes us keenly aware how very much our experience is essentially like theirs. We feel to the full, in reading or seeing these works, the ambiguity and complexity of the moral life. This is also true of Camus' fictional work, and the same thing holds for the works of Tolstoy, Dostoevsky, George Eliot, and Gottfried Keller.

Vis-à-vis our very understanding of morality, something is left out in our essentially and necessarily abstract treatises in philosophical ethics that is present in such works of art. In such literary work we gain a rich display of the complexities and ambivalences of actual moral choice. This kind of understanding is better conveyed by literature than by philosophy. And to have it is critical in the making of reasonable decisions about substantive moral issues. A thorough acquaintance with such work, as well as careful reflection on it, most particularly when supplemented by a lively historical and anthropological awareness, can, when conjoined with a concrete and nonevasive reflection on one's own life, help develop a moral sensitivity and a moral awareness as nothing else can. But the rigorous reflections on justice and utility, the nature of moral judgment, and the structure of moral reasoning involved in a philosophical examination of morality can, in a different but equally crucial way, give us something essential to moral understanding. Literary or historical treatment of morality without philosophical analysis is blind in crucial respects; philosophical treatment of morals without the involvement of literature or a historical understanding is almost inevitably empty.[33]

Sartre, Camus, Nietzsche, and Kierkegaard have deepened our concrete moral understanding and have as well—particularly in the case of Nietzsche—made advances in moral philosophy proper. They have done something of considerable value in giving us a metaphysics or, if you will, a unifying picture of moral experience that is crucial in our attempt to gain some understanding of the meaning of our lives. Existentialism indeed has been very valuable here, but note that its value stems from its taking a literary or quasiliterary form rather than from its philosophical genre.

Whatever the proper genre, contemporary existentialism, as pragmatism did earlier, has served a useful purpose in thrusting at forgetful philosophers the utter centrality of questions of conduct, questions concerned with those dark, stammer-provoking perplexities about how one should live one's life. Analytic philosophers have often treated such questions as peripheral problems, if indeed as properly philosophical problems at all. Given the selection of philosophical problems in this book and my treatment of them, the distance between an analytic approach to philosophy and an existentialist approach might not have been as apparent as it would have been if I had chosen a different set of problems rather than those I regard as the primary problems of philosophy. Notice that in a *typical* and widely used anthology (Paul Edwards' and Arthur Pap's *A Modern Introduction to Philosophy*) there occur three problems largely ignored by me: "Skepticism and the Problem of Induction," "Perception and the Physical World," and "A Priori Knowledge." These problems are given detailed treatment there as they are in most analytically oriented texts and anthologies. (A recent analytical text begins with the problem of the external world and continues with the problem of perception.) Stress on such problems, which is standard fare among analytical philosophers, would have made the gap between existentialist philosophy and analytical philosophy more apparent. With my approach it is more in *the way* philosophical problems are handled than in what problems are broached. The typical analytical philosophers' preoccupation with epistemological scepticism, perception, induction, the problem of other minds, and more narrowly logical topics has made his work seem remote from life. And indeed it is, although this is not to deny that these problems provoke deep conceptual perplexities and are genuinely philosophical. But they are more peripheral to our profoundest human concerns.

I hope I have managed, while largely sticking with these (if you will) existential problems, to do something to inculcate an analytical temper of mind, to help you understand something of philosophical analysis, and indeed to actively engage in philosophical analysis yourselves in arguing with the arguments in this book. I hope I have achieved something of that and have not simply infected you with my ideology. But largely out of the same concerns existentialists feel, I have stuck with philosophical problems with which we are all concerned in one way or another. Even my discussion of meaning was ancillary to that end. And it is because we are all concerned with these problems, with these harassments, that I regard them as the primary problems of philosophy.

V

In bringing this book to an end I would like to say something about philosophy and *Weltanschauung*. As we wrestled with the problems of freedom, God, morality, and man, I made my own philosophical commitments plain enough. And no doubt you have gained some inkling of my overall normative commitments as well. What I can best do now at the very end—hoping against hope to avoid a string of secular platitudes—is to indicate to you how I put them together. You have seen something about that when I introduced the topic of metaphysics, but I wish now to return to it.

By way of a cautionary note, I should first remark that this book, given its scope, is, even more than some of my detailed studies of particular philosophical problems, a work in progress, as I think all genuine philosophy should be. I greatly admire Austin's tenacious struggle to gain definite solutions in philosophy. It seems to me that our efforts could hardly be other than that if we are serious about philosophy.[34] But once this is said, I should also say that I remain dissatisfied with my argumentation and painfully aware here how very much there is to be done. This does not mean that I do not think that my tentative answers are the best answers, for I could not give them to you as I have, in the spirit of actually defending them, if I did not think they were the best answers currently in our hands. And to say this is not hubris but a mere truism, that is, everything else being equal, the answers one seriously gives to questions are the answers one believes to be the best answers to those questions. But I hope I have not obscured for you the complexity of the arguments and the challengable nature of my claims and all philosophical claims.

These philosophical thoughts remain for me a part of 'work in progress'—a partial traveling of the human mind in the pursuit of wisdom, a set of ultimate commitments and a rational way of life.

There are analytic philosophers who believe that the real break of analytic philosophy with the older traditions in philosophy was not with its rejection of metaphysics but with its excluding the adumbration and defense of *Weltanschauung* or ideology from philosophy.[35] On the contrary, I would claim that to separate philosophy from *ideology* and *Weltanschauung* would be to destroy one of its very fundamental reasons for being. An analytical study of concepts becomes simply an interesting game—no doubt valuable for some purposes—when it is separated from questions about what unified outlooks we should take concerning man, society, and the world.[36] An ideology, I should remind you, is a systematic interconnected outlook which, while consciously incorporating certain values, aims at the alteration of man and society. On such a conception an 'irrational ideology' is not a pleonasm, and the end of ideology is not a consummation devoutly to be desired. And it is ideology in this sense that I am urging should be closely linked with philosophy (critical and speculative).[37] In trying to attain a rational view of the frame of things, a rationally justified *ideology* is one of the things with which we are most fundamentally concerned. This should be the most fundamental underlying reason for engaging in philosophy as an analytical study of concepts.

How then should I characterize my ideology? I would describe it as a form of socialist humanism with a materialistic metaphysic as its metaphysical backdrop. It is materialist because it rejects all conceptions of deity, nirvana, or spiritual or mental realities that are not characterizable in purely physical terms, including behavioral terms.[38] It is a humanism because not God or the State but the well-being and flourishing of man is the object of its ultimate loyalty. Moreover, it is a humanism because it refuses to acknowledge the moral relevance of mere tribal, racial, or national differences. Nationalism or racialism in any form, I would argue, is a sickness in the human animal. As a moral being, I will not recognize as morally relevant such differences between men.[39]

It surely is not apparent from this book why my humanism should be a socialist humanism. I have said nothing about politics here, but it is the thinking through of the application of my views on morality to society as well as my most primitive sense of humanity and social justice that leads me to a socialist humanism. But what I would say about politics and how this social ideology grows out of such a view of ethics must await another book. However, I would not want to leave the impression that my views in normative ethics logically commit one to socialism. The link is much more indirect than that.

However, something of my humanism and some of the rationale for my socialism can be glimpsed from noting the relation of my normative ethical theory to the classical utilitarianism of J. S. Mill. It is evident enough that my view is akin to his while being by no means identical to utilitarianism. Happiness, freedom, a sense of identity, an understanding of ourselves and our world seem to me ultimate rational moral aims. But we also need an independent principle of justice as fairness. The rights and needs of all human beings must, from my moral point of view, be given equal respect. We should seek not only to maximize happiness, but to maximize happiness and minimize suffering for *everyone* as much as is humanly possible. From such basic moral ideals a set of political and social ideals flow quite naturally. Freedom is an essential means to human happiness or self-development, but we must not make a fetish of human freedom at the expense of the goals of equality and justice. We should seek the greatest freedom possible compatible with a thorough equality in which the goal is an unfaltering stress on an equal distribution to all men everywhere of the goods, services, and opportunities (including the opportunities for self-development) available to mankind, and to a destruction of all positions of privilege, class, or inherited power or wealth. "Each should count for one and none should count for more than one." This is unequivocally an ideal of socialism and it is only attainable in a socialist ordering of society.

We need to order society in such a way that as many people as possible can have as much as possible of whatever it is that they on reflection and with a knowledge of their situation want that is compatible with everyone being treated in the same way. This ideal is not the ideal of a slave morality, but is a commitment to an ideal of man in society in which men, as equal brothers free from a dominating father—whether in the guise of a god, an *Ubermensch*, a ruling elite, or the State—stand on their own two feet and in dignity and freedom and with genuine self-knowledge order their own destiny severally, subject only to the limitation that this is a condition that should prevail for all.

NOTES

1. Martin Heidegger, "The Way Back into the Ground of Metaphysics," in Walter Kaufmann (ed.), *Existentialism From Dostoevsky to Sartre.* My attempt to assess this work leads me to discuss some of his other work as well.
2. In his introduction to the selection from Heidegger, Walter Kaufmann remarks that Heidegger "attaches the utmost importance" to this essay and that "he himself selected it for inclusion in the present volume," p. 206.
3. Martin Heidegger, "The Way Back into the Ground of Metaphysics," in

Walter Kaufmann (ed.), *Existentialism From Dostoevsky to Sartre*, p. 207.

4. Ibid.

5. Ibid., p. 208.

6. Ibid., p. 218.

7. Martin Heidegger, *Being and Time*, p. 262.

8. Arne Naess, *Four Modern Philosophers*, pp. 229–30.

9. Martin Heidegger, *Being and Time*, pp. 262–263, italics Heidegger's.

10. Martin Heidegger, *Vom Wesen der Wahrheit*.

11. Martin Heidegger, *Platons Lehre von der Wahrheit*, p. 53. Quoted by Arne Naess, *Four Modern Philosophers*, p. 240.

12. Quoted by Arne Naess, op. cit., p. 240.

13. I have argued that in more detail and examined certain counterarguments in my "Can Faith Validate God-Talk?" reprinted in Jery Gill (ed.), *Philosophy and Religion*.

14. Martin Heidegger, *Vorträge und Aufsätze*, p. 43. Heidegger maintains in the early parts of his *Being and Time* that the sciences as our assumed guardians of truth have gone through crises in our century and that it is his task—or rather one of his tasks—to provide a foundation for all the sciences. See also Albert Bergmann, "The Transformation of Heidegger's Thought," *Philosophy Today*, No. I, Jerry Gill (ed.).

15. See for example Martin Heidegger, *Discourse on Thinking*.

16. See the discussions in the sections on ethics and see my *Ethics Without God*.

17. Martin Heidegger, *Platons Lehre von der Wahrheit*, pp. 104–105.

18. Ibid., pp. 114–115. Also see here Arne Naess, op cit., p. 249. I have tried to show in Chapter 22, in my "Some Remarks on the Independence of Morality From Religion," in *Christian Ethics and Contemporary Philosophy*, I. T. Ramsey (ed.), and in my "God and the Good," *Theology Today*, vol. XXI (April, 1964), that ethics could not be grounded on Divine Commands. A. C. Ewing, who is a theist and a metaphysician, argues in a similar way in his "The Autonomy of Ethics," in I. T. Ramsey (ed.), *Prospect For Metaphysics*.

19. Frederick Copleston, *Contemporary Philosophy*, p. 184.

20. William Barrett in his introductory remarks in William Barrett and Henry Aiken (eds.) *Readings in Contemporary Philosophy*, vol. III, p. 153.

21. G. J. Warnock, "John Langshaw Austin," *The Proceedings of the British Academy*, vol. XLIX, p. 259.

22. That this is extremely doubtful and that complaints against ordinary language on this score by such philosophers as Whitehead and Bergson are misdirected is well argued by Alice Ambrose "The Problem of Linguistic Inadequacy," in her *Essays in Analysis*.

23. Arne Naess, op. cit., p. 174.

24. John Passmore, "The Place of Argument in Metaphysics," in William Kennick and Morris Lazerowitz (eds.) *Metaphysics: Readings and Reappraisals*, p. 359.

25. Ibid.

26. See here Quinton's line of argument and the opposition to it by Berlin and Hampshire in the discussion "Philosophy and Beliefs," *The Twentieth Century* (June, 1955). G. J. Warnock takes a similar line of argument to

Quinton's in the last chapter of his *English Philosophy since 1900*. See also Henry Aiken, "The Fate of Philosophy in the Twentieth Century," *The Kenyon Review*, vol. XXIV (1962), pp. 233–252 and D. F. Pears (ed.), *The Nature of Metaphysics*, pp. 157–165.

27. Quoted by Arne Naess, op. cit., p. 174.

28. See Isaiah Berlin's remarks about Pierre's dream on the eve of the Battle of Borodino in his *The Hedgehog and the Fox*.

29. John Passmore, "The Place of Argument in Metaphysics," in William Kennick and Morris Lazerowitz (eds.), *Metaphysics: Readings and Reappraisals*, pp. 359–360. And see also John Passmore, *A Hundred Years of Philosophy*, Chapter 19.

30. Arne Naess, op. cit., p. 182. Naess gives a balanced and, I believe, a fair account of Heidegger's relation to the Third Reich, pp. 179–186.

31. I do not mean to suggest, what would be quite contrary to the truth, that Jaspers was even remotely in sympathy with Nazism. He was not allowed to teach through most of the Hitler period and remained in Heidelberg with his Jewish wife.

32. Anthony Manser, *Sartre: A Philosophic Study*, pp. 260–265.

33. This supports and in turn is supported by my remarks about the respective roles of philosophy, literature and the social sciences in section IV of Chapter 1.

34. Stuart Hampshire's remarks about Austin here are insightful. See Stuart Hampshire, "J. L. Austin," in Richard Rorty (ed.), *The Linguistic Turn*. See also in this connection Hampshire's "Bertrand Russell," *The New York Review of Books*, vol. XI, no. 3 (August 22, 1968) and his "Philosophy and Fantasy," *The New York Review of Books*, vol. XI, no. 5 (Sept. 26, 1968).

35. See the references in note 26.

36. Ernest Gellner's remarks about the relation of ideology to philosophy are important. Ernest Gellner, "French Eighteenth Century Materialism," in D. J. O'Connor (ed.), *A Critical History of Western Philosophy*, pp. 283–284. Also see my "Norms and Politics," *The Philosophical Forum*, vol. II, no. 1 (new series) (Fall, 1970).

37. For a beautifully articulated, powerful, and convincing example of what I call 'ideological argumentation' in philosophy see Alasdair MacIntyre "Breaking the Chains of Reason," in E. P. Thompson *et al.* (eds.), *Out of Apathy*. For some significant counterargument of the same genre see J. M. Cameron, *The Night Battle*, pp. 67–75.

38. In saying this I do not mean to deny, as Peter Winch has brilliantly argued, that there are with the human sciences elements of convention and symbolic activity which make their structure and the understanding of the structure importantly different from that of the natural sciences. Acceptance of this Wittgensteinian point made by Winch about the human sciences is not incompatible with being a reductive materialist in metaphysics. See Peter Winch, *The Idea of a Social Science*.

39. The remark about nationalism should be qualified in order to obviate a possible misunderstanding. Under *certain circumstances*, nationalism can be instrumentally valuable in breaking away from imperialist domination and exploitation and in enabling a people to achieve a sense of cultural identity. Thus in the light of a pervasive American imperialism, nationalism in Latin

America and in Canada is a good thing, but only to enable a people to break free from the economic and cultural yoke of American imperialism so that, as a people with an independence and identity, they can be truly internationalist in outlook. For a truly human society and a human flourishing, independence, a cultural identity, and an active sense of the brotherhood of men are all needed. Concerning American imperialism in Canada and a search for cultural identity, see Charles Taylor, *The Pattern of Politics* (Toronto/Montreal: McClelland and Stewart Ltd., 1970).

CHAPTERS 31 THROUGH 38
SUPPLEMENTARY READINGS

Books

*Alston, William, *Philosophy of Language* (Englewood Cliffs, N.J.: Prentice-Hall, 1964.)

Austin, J. L., *Philosophical Papers* (Oxford: Clarendon Press, 1961).

*Ayer, A. J., *Language, Truth and Logic*, second edition (London: Gollancz, 1946).

*Ayer, A. J. (ed.), *Logical Positivism* (Glencoe, Ill.: Free Press, 1959).

*Ayer, A. J., et al., *The Revolution in Philosophy* (London: Macmillan, 1956).

Caton, Charles E. (ed.), *Philosophy and Ordinary Language* (Urbana, Ill.: University of Illinois Press, 1963).

Cavell, Stanley, *Must We Mean What We Say?* (New York: Scribner's, 1969).

Chappell, V. C. (ed.), *Hume* (Garden City, N.Y.: Anchor Books, 1966).

Copleston, F. C., *Contemporary Philosophy* (London: Burns and Oates, 1956).

*Cranston, Maurice, *The Quintessence of Sartrism* (Montreal: Harvest House, 1969).

*Cranston, Maurice, *Sartre* (Edinburgh and London: Oliver and Boyd, 1962).

Fann, K. T. (ed.), *Symposium on J. L. Austin* (New York: Humanities Press, 1969).

*Gellner, Ernest, *Words and Things* (London: Gollancz, 1959).

Hampshire, Stuart, *Thought and Action* (London: Chatto and Windus, 1959).

Heidegger, Martin, *Being and Time*, translated by John Macquarrie and Edward Robinson (New York: Harper & Row, 1962).

Heidegger, Martin, *Discourse on Thinking*, translated by John M. Anderson and E. Hans Freund (New York: Harper & Row, 1966).

Hume, David, *On Human Nature and the Understanding*, Antony Flew (ed.) (New York: Collier Books, 1962).

Jaspers, Karl, *Man in the Modern Age*, translated by Eden and Cedar Paul (Garden City, N.Y.: Anchor Books, 1957).

Katz, Jerrold J., *The Philosophy of Language* (New York: Harper & Row, 1966).

*Kaufmann, Walter (ed.), *Existentialism from Dostoevsky to Sartre* (New York: Meridian Books, 1956).

*Kaufmann, Walter, *From Shakespeare to Existentialism* (Garden City, N.Y.: Anchor Books, 1960).

*Kennick, W. E., and Morris Lazerowitz (eds.), *Metaphysics: Readings and Reappraisals* (Englewood Cliffs, N.J.: Prentice-Hall, 1966).

Linsky, Leonard, *Semantics and the Philosophy of Language* (Urbana, Ill.: University of Illinois Press, 1952).

Malcolm, Norman, *Knowledge and Certainty* (Englewood Cliffs, N.J.: Prentice-Hall, 1964).

Manser, Anthony, *Sartre: A Philosophic Study* (London: Athlone Press, 1966).

*Naess, Arne, *Four Modern Philosophers*, translated by Alastair Hannay (Chicago: University of Chicago Press, 1965).

*Parkinson, G. H. R. (ed.), *The Theory of Meaning* (Oxford: Oxford University Press, 1968).

Passmore, John, *A Hundred Years of Philosophy* (London: Duckworth, 1957).

*Passmore, John, *Philosophical Reasoning* (London: Duckworth, 1961).

*Pears, D. F., *Bertrand Russell and the British Tradition in Philosophy* (London: Fontana Library, 1967).

Pears, D. F. (ed.), *David Hume: A Symposium* (New York: St. Martin's, 1963).

*Pears, D. F. (ed.), *The Nature of Metaphysics* (New York: St. Martin's, 1957).

Pitcher, George (ed.), *Wittgenstein* (Garden City, N.Y.: Anchor Books, 1966).

Quine, Willard van Orman, *Ontological Relativity and Other Essays* (New York: Columbia University Press, 1969).

Quine, Willard van Orman, *Word and Object* (Cambridge Mass.: M.I.T., 1960).

Rorty, Richard (ed.), *The Linguistic Turn* (Chicago: University of Chicago Press, 1967).

Sartre, Jean-Paul, *Being and Nothingness*, translated by Hazel E. Barnes (New York: Philosophical Library, 1956).

Sartre, Jean-Paul, *The Philosophy of Jean-Paul Sartre,* Robert Cumming (ed.) (New York: Random House, 1965).

Sartre, Jean-Paul, *The Problem of Method*, translated by Hazel E. Barnes (London: Methuen, 1963).

Schilpp, Paul Arthur (ed.), *The Philosophy of G. E. Moore* (New York: Tudor Publishing Co., 1942).

Schmitt, Richard, *Martin Heidegger on Being Human* (New York: Random House, 1969).

*Schrader, George A., Jr. (ed.), *Existential Philosophers: Kierkegaard to Merleau-Ponty* (New York: McGraw-Hill, 1967).

Strawson, P. F., *Individuals* (London: Methuen, 1959).

Vendler, Zeno, *Linguistics in Philosophy* (Ithaca, N.Y.: Cornell University Press, 1967).

*Walsh, W. H., *Metaphysics* (New York: Harcourt, Brace & World, 1963).

*Warnock, Mary, *The Philosophy of Sartre* (London: Hutchinson University Library, 1965).

Williams, Bernard, and Alan Montefiore (eds.), *British Analytical Philosophy* (London: Routledge, 1966).

Winch, Peter (ed.), *Studies in the Philosophy of Wittgenstein* (New York: Humanities Press, 1969).

Wittgenstein, Ludwig, *The Blue and Brown Books* (Oxford: Basil Blackwell, 1958).

Articles and Pamphlets

*Aiken, Henry, "The Fate of Philosophy in the Twentieth Century," *The Kenyon Review*, vol. XXIV (1962).

Ambrose, Alice, "Metamorphoses of the Principle of Verifiability," *Current Philosophical Issues*, F. Dommeyer (ed.) (Springfield, Ill.: Charles C. Thomas, 1966).

*Ambrose, Alice, "Philosophical Doubts," *Massachusetts Review* (1960).

Ayer, A. J., "Novelist-Philosophers: Albert Camus," *Horizon*, vol. XIII (March, 1946).

Ayer, A. J., "Novelist-Philosophers: Jean-Paul Sartre," *Horizon*, vol. XII (1945).

*Ayer, A. J., "Philosophy and Science," *Ratio*, vol. V (December, 1963).

*Ayer, A. J., "The Claims of Philosophy," in Maurice Natanson (ed.), *Philosophy of the Social Sciences* (New York: Random House, 1963).

Ayer, A. J., "Thinking and Meaning," Inaugural Lecture (London: H. K. Lewis, 1947).

Bambrough, Renford, "Principia Metaphysica," *Philosophy*, vol. XXXIX (1964).

Cavell, Stanley, "Existentialism and Analytical Philosophy" *Daedalus*, vol. 93, no. 3 (Summer, 1964).

Cooper, David, "The Fallacies of Linguistic Philosophy," *The Oxford Review*, Hilary (1968).

Feyerabend, Paul, "Wittgenstein's *Philosophical Investigation*," *The Philosophical Review*, vol. LXIV (1953).

Findlay, J. N., "Metaphysics and Affinity," *The Monist*, vol. 47 (winter, 1963).

Flew, Antony, "Again the Paradigm," in P. Feyerabend and G. Maxwell (eds.), *Mind, Matter and Method* (Minneapolis: University of Minnesota Press, 1966).

Fodor, J. A., and J. J. Katz, "The Availability of What We Say," *Philosophical Review*, vol. LXXII (1963).

*Gellner, Ernest, "Ayer's Epistle to the Russians," *Ratio*, vol. V (December, 1963).

*Gellner, Ernest, "Poker Player," *New Statesman* (Nov. 28, 1969), pp. 744–776.

Hakin, Eleanor, "Jean-Paul Sartre: The Dialectics of Myth," *Salmagundi*, vol. I (Winter, 1966).

Hansen, Jytte, "The Paradigm-Case: A Valid Ontological Argument," *Danish Year Book in Philosophy*, vol. 2 (1965).

Henson, R. G., "Ordinary Language, Common Sense and the Time-Lag Argument," *Mind*, vol. LXXVI (January, 1967).

Henson, R. G., "What We Say," *American Philosophical Quarterly*, vol. II (1965).

Kasachkoff, Tziporah, "Ontological Implications of the Paradigm-Case Argument," *Philosophical Studies* (Maynooth, Ireland), vol. XVII (1968).

Lewis, C. I., "Experience and Meaning," *Philosophical Review* (1934).

Malcolm, Norman, "Wittgenstein's *Philosophical Investigations*," *The Philosophical Review*, vol. LXIII (1954).

*Nielsen, Kai, "Linguistic Philosophy and Beliefs," in *Philosophy Today*, no. 2, Jerry H. Gill (ed.).

Nielsen, Kai, "Wittgensteinian Fideism," *Philosophy* (July, 1967).

*Pears, D. F., "The Philosophy of Wittgenstein," *The New York Review of Books* (Jan. 16, 1969).

Quinton, Anthony, "Mortimer Adler's Machine," *The New York Review of Books* (Nov. 21, 1968).

Schlick, M., "Meaning and Verification," *Philosophical Review* (1936).

Warnock, G. J., "Verification and the Use of Language," *Revue Internationale de Philosophie* (1951).

Watkins, J. W., "Farewell to the Paradigm-Case Argument," *Analysis,* vol. 18 (December, 1967).

*Williams, Bernard, "J. L. Austin's Philosophy," *The Oxford Magazine,* N. S., vol. III (1962).

*Winch, Peter, "Contemporary British Philosophy and Its Critics," *Universities Quarterly,* vol. X (1955).

INDEX

DATE DUE
